jQuery, CSS3, AND HTML5
FOR MOBILE AND
DESKTOP DEVICES

D1530287

jQuery, CSS3, AND HTML5
FOR MOBILE AND
DESKTOP DEVICES

Oswald Campesato

MERCURY LEARNING AND INFORMATION

Dulles, Virginia
Boston, Massachusetts
New Delhi

Publisher: David Pallai
MERCURY LEARNING AND INFORMATION
22841 Quicksilver Drive
Dulles, VA 20166
info@merclearning.com
www.merclearning.com
1-800-758-3756

O. Campesato. *jQuery, CSS3, and HTML5 for Mobile and Desktop Devices.*
ISBN: 978-1-938549-03-8

Library of Congress Control Number: 2012956350

131415321   Printed in the United States of America
This book is printed on acid-free paper.

Our titles are available for adoption, license, or bulk purchase by institutions, corporations, etc.
For additional information, please contact the Customer Service Dept. at 1-800-758-3756 (toll free).

I'd like to dedicate this book to my parents—
may this bring joy and happiness into their lives.

CONTENTS

PREFACE

THE GOALS OF THIS BOOK

This book is a primer for jQuery, CSS3, and HTML5 for mobile devices and its goal is to show you how to leverage HTML5 and related technologies in order to create Web pages and mobile applications. This is a daunting task because there are many technologies that are often associated with HTML5, even though they are not formally included in the specification.

The approach of this book is to start with aspects of HTML5 (discussed in Chapter 1) that do not have significant dependencies on other technologies. After you finish reading the jQuery chapters, then you will learn about additional HTML5-related technologies from the "jQuery perspective." This strategy enables you to learn how to use jQuery plugins that provide a layer of abstraction over the associated HTML5 technology. In addition, these HTML5 technologies will be illustrated with code samples for desktop browsers and for Android-based mobile devices with browsers that support these HTML5 technologies.

There are several points to keep in mind about the code samples. First, every code sample in this book works in Google Chrome™ (version 17) and Safari® (version 5.1.2) on a Macbook®. Barring any Webkit-specific issues, these code samples will work on Webkit-based browsers on other platforms. Second, many screenshots throughout this book were taken from an Asus Prime 10" tablet with Android™ ICS (Ice Cream Sandwich) or from a Sprint® Nexus S 4G with Android ICS. Third, the HTML5 Canvas, CSS3, and SVG code samples in this book are supported on iPhone® 4/iPad® and also on Android 4.x or higher. Chapter 12 shows you how to create HTML5-based mobile applications for reproducing the screenshots in this book. Incidentally, the official name for the iPad 3 is the "New iPad," but this book uses iPad 3 in order to differentiate from the iPad 2. As this book goes to print, the iPad Mini® has already been released, and the successor to the "New iPad" might become available in the near future (so the older model will no longer be "new").

A QUICK OVERVIEW OF THIS BOOK

In Chapter 1, you will learn about new HTML5 elements (semantic tags, audio, and video), HTML5 Forms, HTML5 localStorage, HTML5 databases, and Geolocation. The theme of the main code sample in this chapter involves creating a list of words in English with their counterparts in various languages. The first version of this example uses an HTML5 Form, and a subsequent version incorporates HTML5 localStorage. We will use some simple CSS3 selectors to show you how to make HTML5 pages more vivid than their counterparts that do not use CSS selectors.

In Chapter 2, we will delve into the details of CSS3 selectors that can create more sophisticated effects. Some of the code samples in this chapter use CSS3 selectors in order to make the Web pages more visually appealing than their plain counterparts (but the code samples still work correctly even without the CSS style sheets). In some cases, it might be beneficial for you to read the relevant CSS3-related material in Chapter 2 and then re-visit the HTML5/CSS3 code samples in this chapter.

Since jQuery and jQuery Mobile comprise more than half the content of this book, the basic use of several APIs are discussed in a high-level fashion in Chapter 2; after you have read the jQuery chapters, the more detailed code samples of these APIs (used in conjunction with jQuery) will be more meaningful. This approach makes sense because you are more likely to write HTML5 pages that combine the power of jQuery with HTML5 technologies that are discussed in this book (and we also reduce the amount of similar code duplication). These jQuery-enhanced code samples are presented in Chapter 10.

Chapter 2 and Chapter 3 cover CSS3, Chapter 4 discusses CSS3 and SVG, and Chapters 5 through 9 discuss various aspects of jQuery and jQuery Mobile. Chapter 10 shows you how to use jQuery with HTML5 Drag and Drop, the File API, Geolocation, Offline Applications, Web Storage, and Web-Sockets with jQuery. Chapters 11 and 12 show you have to use jQuery with HTML5 Canvas and how to render charts and graphs. Chapter 13 shows you how to create Android applications that render HTML5 pages with Canvas-based and CSS3-based graphics effects, which will enable you to create Android mobile applications for the code samples in this book.

One more point involves the WebKit engine, which is an open source project that you can download here:

http://www.webkit.org

If you want to test the latest features of WebKit, you can download a nightly build from this Web site:

http://nightly.webkit.org/

Keep in mind that the nightly builds are not necessarily stable or complete, so make sure that you also test specific functionality in stable releases of WebKit when they become available.

If you plan to write HTML5 Web pages that are CPU intensive, then this Web site will be useful:

http://demos.hacks.mozilla.org/openweb/HWACCEL/

This Mozilla Web site performs a graphics-based test of your browser to determine its speed, measured in FPS (frames per second).

ASSUMPTIONS FOR THIS BOOK

Since this book is a primer, you will find more introductory material than advanced concepts in most of the chapters. At the same time, this book also provides you with a centralized location for a broad set of resources, including references to toolkits and libraries that are beyond the scope of this book.

As you will see, some topics in Chapter 1 are covered more lightly than others, and there are several reasons for doing so. First, this book is not an all-encompassing tome with in-depth discussion of all the aspects of jQuery, CSS3, and HTML5. Second, some aspects of HTML5 (such as WebSockets) appeal to a specialized audience, which does not fully overlap with the purpose of a primer. Third, jQuery provides a layer of abstraction over some of the more advanced HTML5 technologies, and that material is covered in a later chapter after you learn about jQuery. Given the title of this book, it makes more sense to show you "the jQuery way" of working with these technologies. Fourth, the size of this book affects its cost, and reducing duplication of material is one way to manage the selling price of this book.

In any case, whenever you want acquire more in-depth knowledge of HTML5 that is beyond the scope of this book, you can find online tutorials that delve more deeply into the facets of HTML5.

TERMINOLOGY IN THIS BOOK

Although this book makes every attempt to be consistent, there are times when terminology is not 100% correct. For example, WebKit is an engine and not a browser. Therefore, "WebKit-based browser" is correct, whereas "WebKit browser" is incorrect, but you will see both used (even though only the former is technically correct). Second, you will see "HTML Web page" and "HTML page" used interchangeably. Third, sometimes references to

HTML elements do not specify "HTML," so you will see "<p> element" and "HTML <p> element" (as well as other HTML elements) in the discussion that precedes or follows a code sample.

Some lines of code are longer than the lines of text in this book. Whenever you see a ↵ symbol in the code, the line immediately following it is a continuation that should be on the same line in your actual code. The code snippets on the companion DVD contain the code in the correct lines for use.

Please keep the preceding points in mind, and that way there won't be any confusion as you read this book.

O. Campesato
February, 2013

ACKNOWLEDGMENTS

I want to thank Andrea Campesato, his wife Gianna, and his sons Pietro, Marco, and Luca, who are always supportive. Other relatives who have influenced me include Lia Campesato and Elda and Carlo Grisostolo.

Thanks also to my lifelong friends and soulmates Laurie Dresser and Farid Sharifi, and also to Jeanine Swatton, who has been a positive influence in my daily life in Silicon Valley. Right now I cannot imagine anywhere else in the world that I would rather be, except for Japan during the winter and spring.

A special thanks to Richard Clark (technical reviewer) who spent many hours refining the content in the book. Richard Clark, M.A. (@rdclark) is an experienced software developer and instructor for Kaazing Corporation. He has taught for Apple and Hewlett-Packard, written immersive simulations, developed multiple high-performance Web applications for the Fortune 100, and published Apple iOS applications. An in-demand speaker for international conferences, he has a special interest in using mobile, connected, real-time applications to help people live, work, and play better. In his spare time, Richard does Web development for non-profits, tends a garden full of California native plants, and cooks for family and charity events.

Finally, I would be remiss if I did not thank Dave Pallai (publisher) and Rachel Leach (copyeditor), who made valuable contributions to improve the quality of this book. As always, I take responsibility for any errors or omissions that you might find in any of the chapters.

## CHAPTER 1

NEW FEATURES IN HTML5

In this chapter, you will learn about several HTML5 topics, such as HTML5-specific elements (semantic markup, audio, and video), HTML5 `Forms`, HTML5 localStorage, and HTML5 databases. Various other HTML5 technologies are intentionally deferred until Chapter 10, which follows the jQuery and jQuery Mobile chapters. Consequently, we can present jQuery (and related plugins) alongside the HTML5 technologies that are discussed in Chapter 10, and so the code samples will make more sense after you have read the jQuery material.

In this chapter, there is also a code sample that appears in several places (with different HTML5 features) which involves creating a list of words in English with their counterparts in various languages. The first version of this code sample uses an HTML5 `Form`, and a subsequent version incorporates HTML5 localStorage. We will use simple CSS3 selectors because they will make the HTML5 Web page more vivid and appealing than its counterpart that does not use CSS selectors. This involves a bit of "forward referencing" in the sense that the code sample uses some CSS3 functionality before it has been introduced to you. However, you can easily return to this code sample after you have read the information about the CSS3 functionality in a subsequent chapter. In Chapters 2, 3, and 4 we will delve into the details of CSS3 selectors that can create more sophisticated effects.

If you are new to HTML5, keep in mind that some of its features can vary considerably in terms of the complexity of their associated Application Programming Interfaces (APIs). To illustrate this point: the localStorage APIs are straightforward (as you would expect of APIs that manage name/value pairs), and they are much simpler than the HTML5 Drag And Drop APIs. Consequently, Chapter 1 attempts to provide information about several less complex (but still useful) HTML5-related technologies that you are likely to face as a Web developer, and after you have read the first nine chapters, you will be in a better position to handle various HTML5 features that are discussed in Chapter 10 and beyond.

HTML5 AND VARIOUS WORKING GROUPS

The W3C (World Wide Web Consortium), the *WHATWG* (Web Hypertext Application Technology Working Group), and the DAP (Device APIs Working Group) are organizations that provide the specifications and APIs for HTML5 and mobile devices that are covered in this book.

The W3C is an international community for various groups to work together in order to develop Web standards. The W3C is led by Web inventor Tim Berners-Lee and CEO Jeffrey Jaffe, and its homepage is here:

http://www.w3.org

Every proposal submitted to the W3C undergoes the following sequence in order to become a W3C Recommendation:

- Working Draft (WD)
- Candidate Recommendation (CR)
- Proposed Recommendation (PR)
- W3C Recommendation (REC)
- Later revisions

The HTML5-related technologies that have been submitted to the W3C are in different stages of the W3C "evaluation" process. The following link contains a diagram that provides a succinct visual display of HTML5 technologies and their status in December, 2011:

http://en.wikipedia.org/wiki/File:HTML5-APIs-and-related-technologies-by-Sergey-Mavrody.png

If you want to find the most recent status updates, the following link provides a list of HTML5 APIs and their status:

http://www.w3.org/TR/

Click on the link "JavaScript APIs" in the preceding Web site, or simply navigate to this URL, which shows you the most recent status of HTML5 APIs:

http://www.w3.org/TR/#tr_Javascript_APIs

The WHATWG focuses primarily on the development of HTML and APIs needed for Web applications. The WHATWG was founded in 2004 by employees of Apple, the Mozilla Foundation, and Opera Software. The WHATWG's main focus is the HTML standard, which also includes Web Workers, Web Storage, the Web Sockets API, and Server-Sent Events. Two links with additional information about the WHATWG:

http://www.whatwg.org/

http://wiki.whatwg.org/wiki/FAQ

HTML5 is a joint effort involving the W3C and the WHATWG. If you enjoy reading proposals, you will find links for various W3C Specifications in this chapter and in Chapter 10.

Another group is the Device APIs Working Group, whose mission is to create client-side APIs that enable the development of Web applications and Web widgets that interact with devices services such as calendar, contacts, camera, and so forth. Currently the DAP is actively working on the following specifications:

- Battery Status API
- HTML Media Capture
- Media Capture and Streams (access to `getUserMedia`)
- Network Information API
- Proximity Events
- Vibration API
- Web Intents (service discovery)

Additional information about the status of these (and other) DAP specifications is here:

http://www.w3.org/2009/dap/

HTML5 SPECIFICATIONS: W3C OR WHATWG?

According to the W3C specification:

The HTML specification published by the WHATWG is not identical to this specification. The main differences are that the WHATWG version includes features not included in this W3C version: some features have been omitted as they are considered part of future revisions of HTML, not HTML5; and other features are omitted because at the W3C they are published as separate specifications. There are also some minor differences. For an exact list of differences, please see the WHATWG specification.

In essence, the WHATWG has the master specification, which the W3C HTML Working Group takes as the foundation for the "official" specification. The W3C synchronizes its work with the WHATWG, mostly reformatting to match its publication style (including breaking it into sub-specifications).

The exact list of changes in the introduction to the WHATWG form of the specification is here:

http://www.whatwg.org/specs/web-apps/current-work/multipage/intro-duction.html#introduction

Now that you know a little bit about the groups that are in charge of various specifications, let's explore some of the facets of HTML5, which is the subject of the next section.

WHAT IS HTML5?

HTML5 currently consists of a mixture of technologies, some of which are formally included in the HTML5 specification and others that are not part of the specification. There are few people who seem to know the "definition" of HTML5, and perhaps that's why Peter Paul Koch (creator of QuirksMode.org) wryly suggested that "whatever Web technology you're working on that's cool right now...that's HTML5." As you will discover, HTML5 means different things to different people, so don't be surprised if you cannot get one consistent "definition" of HTML5 (if only the situation were so simple!).

HTML5 is the latest version of HTML that is designed with a plugin-free architecture that is backward compatible with most features of earlier versions of HTML markup. HTML5 provides a wealth of new features: new tags for audio, video, semantic markup; new input types and validation for forms; local and session storage; support for graphics-based APIs in Canvas; and Server-Sent Events and Web Sockets.

Although CSS3 is not a formal part of HTML5, many people consider it to be an important part of HTML5 Web pages. As you will see in Chapters 2 and 3, CSS3 provides support for rich visual effects, and in Chapter 4, you will learn about some of the powerful new functionality in CSS3 (such as CSS Shaders).

With regard to HTML markup, you have probably seen many Web pages with HTML markup that relies on a combination of HTML `<table>` elements and HTML `<div>` elements. Fortunately, the new HTML5 semantic tags provide more meaningful information about the purpose of each section in an HTML5 Web page, which can be discerned much more easily than Web pages written in HTML4. You will see an example of using some of these semantic tags later in this chapter.

One of the exciting aspects of HTML5 is that it's designed to run on desktop devices as well as mobile devices. In fact, HTML5-based mobile applications offer speed of development and deployment to multiple mobile devices with one code base, which is appealing to developers of mobile applications that do not require intensive computations (such as games) or access to hardware features (such as an accelerometer).

Keep in mind that mobile Web applications sometimes lack support for native application features, such as offline mode, location lookup, file system access, and camera. In addition, Web-based mobile applications do not support several Android-specific features, such as adding ringtones, performing notifications, or changing the wallpaper. However, you can transfer files using the regular Ajax API (`XmlHTTPRequest`), and File APIs are supported on Android (via JavaScript), with upcoming iOS support:

http://caniuse.com/#feat=fileapi

There is one other point to keep in mind: the specification for HTML 4.01 (the predecessor to HTML5) was introduced in 1999, so HTML5 represents the largest advance in HTML in ten years, and perhaps the inclusion of other technologies was inevitable. There is a great deal of excitement surrounding HTML5, and a major update regarding the specification is scheduled for 2014. Indeed, the enthusiasm for HTML5 may have accelerated the speed with which HTML5 will become a formal specification based on open standards.

Browser Support for HTML5

The `WebKit`-based browsers (Chrome and Safari), Mozilla Firefox, Opera, and IE10 support many HTML5 features, on desktops as well as mobile devices. In addition to the well-known browsers, there are browsers such as the Dolphin browser and the browser provided by the Tizen OS; in mid-2012, they were the top-ranked browsers in terms of support for HTML5 features.

As you know, this book focuses on WebKit-based browsers, and all code samples have been tested on a Chrome browser on a Macbook. In addition, virtually every code sample in this book can be deployed on at least one of the following devices:

- An Asus Prime tablet with Android ICS (Ice Cream Sandwich)
- A Nexus 7 with Android JB (Jelly Bean)
- An iPad 3 (and possibly an iPad 2 as well)
- A Sprint Nexus S 4G with Android ICS (or higher)

The only exceptions are the code samples (and associated screenshots) in Chapter 4 that illustrate the most recent features of CSS3 (such as CSS Shaders) that are rendered in a special Chromium build from Adobe that is installed on a Macbook. The download link for this special build is in chapter 4, and you can expect these new CSS3 features to be supported in the near future. In fact, work is already underway on CSS Blending and Compositing:
http://www.webkit.org/blog/2102/last-week-in-webkit-a-new-content-security-policy-api-and-transitioning-from-percentages-to-pixels

WHAT TECHNOLOGIES ARE INCLUDED IN HTML5?

The following list contains a combination of technologies are formally included in the HTML5 specification, as well as several other technologies that are frequently associated with HTML5:

- Canvas 2D
- CSS3
- Drag and Drop (DnD)
- File API
- Geolocation
- Microdata
- Offline Applications
- Server-Sent Events (SSE)
- SVG
- Web Intents
- Web Messaging

- Web Storage
- Web Sockets
- Web Workers

There are other technologies that are often associated with HTML5, including WebGL and XHR2 (`XmlHTTPRequest` Level 2).

Incidentally, the following link contains a diagram that provides a succinct visual display of HTML5 technologies and their status in December, 2011:

http://en.wikipedia.org/wiki/File:HTML5-APIs-and-related-technologies-by-Sergey-Mavrody.png

The preceding link classifies HTML5 technologies as follows:

- W3C Recommendation
- Candidate Recommendation
- Last Call
- Working Draft
- Non-W3C Specification
- Deprecated W3C APIs

Keep in mind that the status of some of these technologies will change, so be sure to visit the link with the details of the W3C specification for each of these technologies in order to find their most recent status. In addition, many of the HTML5 technologies in the preceding diagram are covered in Chapter 10, often with jQuery plugins that provide a layer of abstraction over HTML5 technologies.

DIFFERENCES BETWEEN HTML4 TAGS AND HTML5 TAGS

Broadly speaking, HTML5 differs from earlier versions of HTML in the following ways:

- Some HTML4.x elements are no longer supported
- Provides support for new elements
- Simplifies some existing elements
- Support for custom attributes

The HTML elements that are not recommended for new work in HTML5 include: `<acronym>`, `<applet>`, `<basefont>`, `<big>`, `<center>`, `<dir>`, `<font>`, `<frame>`, `<frameset>`, `<noframes>`, `<s>`, `<strike>`, `<tt>`, and `<u>`.

Some new tags in HTML5: `<article>`, `<aside>`, `<audio>`, `<canvas>`, `<command>`, `<datalist>`, `<details>`, `<dialog>`, `<embed>`, `<figure>`, `<footer>`, `<header>`, `<hgroup>`, `<keygen>`, `<mark>`, `<meter>`, `<nav>`, `<output>`, `<progress>`, `<rp>`, `<rt>`, `<ruby>`, `<section>`, `<source>`, `<time>`, and `<video>`.

You are probably already aware of the new HTML5 `<audio>` tag and HTML5 `<video>` tag; later in this chapter you'll see examples of how to use these tags in HTML5 web pages.

One underrated new HTML5 feature is support for custom data attributes, which always have a `data-` prefix. This support for custom data attributes provides HTML5 markup with some of the functionality that is available in XML, which is the ability to imbue HTML5 markup with application-specific logic. In fact, jQuery Mobile makes very extensive use of custom data attributes, and you will see an example later in this chapter.

USEFUL ONLINE TOOLS FOR HTML5 WEB PAGES

Before delving into the new HTML5 tags that are discussed in this chapter, you need to know about the online tools that can assist in creating well-designed HTML5 Web pages. These tools are available because of one important fact: modern browsers differ in terms of their support for HTML5 features (for desktop browsers and also for mobile browsers). Fortunately, tools such as Modernizr enable you to detect HTML5 feature support in modern browsers using simple JavaScript code.

For your convenience, the list of tools and Web sites in this section are here:

http://www.modernizr.com/
http://yepnopejs.com/
http://www.caniuse.com
http://mobilehtml5.org/
http://www.quirksmode.org/mobile/
http://html5boilerplate.com/

The following subsections contain a brief overview of these tools and how they can be helpful when you design HTML5 Web pages.

Modernizr

Modernizr is a very useful tool for HTML5-related feature detection in various browsers. Its homepage is here:

http://www.modernizr.com/

"Browser sniffing" used to be a popular technique for detecting the browser that you were using to render a particular Web page, but this technique is not as accurate (or as "clean") due to rapidly changing implementations in browsers (in other words, the logic that you use today might not work in the future). Indeed, the most popular websites that check for HTML5 support use feature detection and not browser sniffing.

At some point you will start using JavaScript in your HTML5 web pages (indeed, you probably do so already), and Modernizr provides a programmatic way to check for many HTML5 and CSS3 features in different browsers.

In order to use Modernizr, include the following code snippet in the `<head>` element of your Web pages:

```
<script src="modernizr.min.js" type="text/javascript"></script>
```

The following type of code block illustrates one way that you can use Modernizr in an HTML page:

```
if(Modernizr.canvas) {
// canvas is available
// do something here
} else {
// canvas is not available
// do something else here
}
```

Navigate to the Modernizr homepage where you can read the documentation, tutorials, and details regarding the set of feature detection.

YepNope.js

You can also use a JavaScript-loading script called `yepnope.js` (also a part of Modernizr), which is an asynchronous conditional resource loader, such as JavaScript files. Its homepage is here:

http://yepnopejs.com/

Caniuse

The following Web site ("When Can I Use…") is extremely useful because it provides information regarding support for many HTML5 features in modern browsers:

http://www.caniuse.com

Currently there are two main tabs on this Web site. The first (and default) tab is divided into a number of sections (CSS, HTML5, SVG, JS API, and Other). Each section contains a list of technical items that are hyperlinks to other Web pages that provide detailed information.

The second tab on this Web site is called "tables," and when you click on this tab you will see a tabular display of information in a set of tables. The columns in each table are modern browsers, and the rows specify features, and the cells in the tables provide the browser version numbers where the specified features are supported.

HTML5 on Mobile

The following Web sites contain information regarding support for HTML5 on mobile devices:

http://mobilehtml5.org/
http://www.quirksmode.org/mobile/

The first Web site contains a set of rows, where each row is an HTML5 feature, and the columns specify various mobile browsers. The cells contain a checkmark whenever an HTML5 feature is supported for a specific browser.

The second Web site contains a comparison of 20 WebKit-based browsers, touch-related support for browsers, and other useful information.

HTML5 BoilerPlate

HTML5 BoilerPlate is another very useful tool that provides default values for HTML5 elements. Its homepage is here:

http://html5boilerplate.com/

According to this Web site, "HTML5 Boilerplate is a professional front-end template that helps you build fast, robust, adaptable, and future-proof Web sites." This tool provides starting points for HTML, CSS, and JavaScript, and contains several useful videos. You can also integrate this tool with other tools, such as Twitter Bootstrap and 960.css, and you can replace jQuery with a different JavaScript library. It's well worth your time to visit this Web site to learn about its feature set.

DESIGNING HTML5 WEB PAGES

There are two main perspectives for designing HTML5 Web pages: graceful degradation and progressive enhancement, which use different approaches for Web page design, as discussed briefly in the following sub-sections. HTML5 BoilerPlate is a very useful tool for both approaches.

Graceful Degradation

This technique assumes that the functionality in a Web page is supported across multiple browsers, and in situations where a feature is unavailable in a specific browser, a "fallback" message is sometimes provided. You undoubtedly have seen examples of this technique whereby HTML elements include the text string "this feature is not supported" when the HTML element is not supported. For example, the code samples in this book that contain HTML5 `<canvas>` elements will always provide such a fallback message.

In generalized terms, graceful degradation prioritizes presentation, whereas progressive enhancement (discussed in the next section) places content at the center. Although this concept is hardly new (in fact, you can find links from 1998 that discuss graceful degradation), it seems to be experiencing a resurgence of interest recently.

Progressive Enhancement

This technique involves a sort of bottom-up approach: start with a core set of features that work across multiple browsers, and then gradually add new functionality. Progressive enhancement makes basic content of a particular Web page accessible to all users; users who have better browsers will have access to an enhanced version of that Web page. Toolkits such as Modernizr allow you to use progressive enhancement. One point to keep in mind is that progressive enhancement can be more challenging for web pages that make very heavy use of JavaScript for user interaction. Perform an Internet search to find articles that provide additional information about progressive enhancement.

RESPONSIVE DESIGN

Responsive Web design refers to the concept of creating Web sites in such a way that the layout and the elements "adapt" to conform to the device on which the Web site is viewed. In simplified terms, responsive Web design involves the use of media queries, flexible layouts, and flexible images and media.

Ethan Marcotte wrote an excellent article about responsive Web design:

http://www.alistapart.com/articles/responsive-web-design/

A collection of 15 articles that discuss responsive Web design is available here:

http://designwoop.com/2012/03/15-detailed-responsive-web-design-tutorials/

An Internet search will yield a number of additional articles regarding responsive Web design. You can also find numerous jQuery plugins for responsive Web design here:

http://designbeep.com/2012/03/28/38-useful-and-effective-jquery-plugins-for-responsive-web-design/

If you are unfamiliar with jQuery, then the plugins in the preceding link will make more sense after you have read the jQuery chapters in this book.

If you prefer to start with a template for responsive design instead of designing your own "from scratch," a template is available here:

http://verekia.com/initializr/responsive-template

Finally, a responsive design development kit is Skeleton, which is style-agnostic and also designed to scale well among various devices. Its homepage is here:

http://getskeleton.com/

A SIMPLE HTML5 WEB PAGE

In addition to introducing many new semantic tags, HTML5 has simplified several tags, including the `<DOCTYPE>` declaration and the attributes `lang` and `charset`. Listing 1.1 displays `Sample1.html`, which is an HTML5 Web page that illustrates the simplified syntax of HTML5.

Listing 1.1 Sample1.html

```
<!DOCTYPE html>
<html lang="en">
 <head>
  <meta charset="utf-8"/>
  <title>This is HTML5</title>
 </head>

 <body>
   <div id="outer">
   </div>
 <body>
</html>
```

Listing 1.1 contains an HTML5 `<!DOCTYPE>` element whose simple structure is very intuitive and easy to remember, especially in comparison to the
syntax for an HTML4 `<!DOCTYPE>` element (try to construct one from memory!). This markup is backward-compatible: it triggers standards mode in all
browsers that have standards mode (versus quirks mode).

In addition, the `<meta>` tag and its attributes `lang` and `charset` attributes
are simpler than their counterparts in earlier versions of HTML. Note that
HTML5 supports the new syntax as well as the earlier syntax, so your existing
HTML pages will be recognized in HTML5.

NEW HTML5 ELEMENTS

This section discusses some of the useful new elements in HTML5, which
includes semantic-related elements, the `<video>` element, and the `<audio>`
element. The new types for the `<input>` element are discussed in the section
for HTML5 `Forms` (later in this chapter). A modest knowledge of the new
HTML5 tags is required in order to follow the examples in this book, so you
can skim through this section if you do not require extensive knowledge of
HTML5 elements.

Semantic Markup HTML5 Elements

HTML5 provides new elements for "semantic markup" that were designed
to provide more meaningful structure in your HTML5 Web pages. Some of
these new tags are: `<section>`, `<article>`, `<aside>`, `<nav>`, `<header>`,
`<hgroup>`, `<canvas>`, `<video>`, `<audio>`, `<time>`, `<figure>`, `<figcap-
tion>`, and `ARIA`-related tags.

For example, the HTML5 <section> tag can be used as a "container" for a document, whereas the HTML5 <article> tag is well suited for representing the content of newspaper article or a blog post. The HTML5 <header> tag and HTML5 <footer> tag represent the header and footer of an HTML5 <section> tag. The HTML5 <aside> tag contains information that is somewhat related to the primary content of a Web page (similar in nature to a "by the way" type of comment).

The HTML5 <nav> tag supports navigation for a section of a document in a Web page. Other new tags include the HTML5 <dialog> tag for marking up conversations and the HTML5 <figure> tag for associating a caption for videos or graphics (which is useful for search engines).

The semantics of these tags are straightforward, yet there are some subtler aspects that you will learn as you gain experience with HTML5 Web pages.

Article Versus Section: How Are They Used?

The following simple example illustrates the use of the words "article" and "section." A newspaper can contain multiple sections, and each section can contain multiple articles; furthermore, an article can contain multiple sections. Thus, a section contains articles that in turn contain sections, which is a tag1-contains-tag2-contains-tag1 hierarchical scenario. Obviously this situation can make it more difficult to understand the intended usage of a <section> element and an <article> element in a lengthy and complex HTML Web page that contains many of these elements.

The contents of an HTML5 <article> element are considered ready for syndication, whereas the contents of an HTML5 <section> element that is a child element of an HTML5 <article> element is somewhat comparable to a blog post (but keep in mind that a blog post can be an article, so this analogy is only partially valid). On the other hand, an HTML5 <section> element that contains one or more HTML5 <article> elements is considered "a thematic grouping of content."

However, you might encounter HTML5 Web pages containing semantic markup elements that are used incorrectly, or you might inadvertently create such pages in your own work. You can consider the possibility of inserting one or more data- attributes to provide more context-specific information that clarifies the intended purpose of the deeply nested HTML elements (recall the days when you had to deal with HTML web pages with "div forests").

Before you use the <section> and <article> elements for content in an HTML5 Web page, think of the logical relationship of the content in order to determine the structural layout of your HTML5 Web page. If there is any possibility for confusion, it might also be helpful to include a comment section to make it easier for other people to understand the rationale for the layout of your HTML5 Web page.

Why Use Semantic Markup?

There are at least two reasons for using semantic tags in your Web pages. First, semantic tags can help you understand the structure of a Web page and the purpose of a section of markup. Second, the use of semantic tags makes it easier for you to programmatically locate and manage sets of logically similar sections of code (such as `<nav>` elements, `<aside>` elements, and so forth). These are several of the more important reasons for using semantic markup, and you can probably think of other reasons as well.

Incidentally, jQuery Mobile uses custom attributes (which always start with the string `data-`) as a way to embed data that can be accessed programmatically, and to a lesser extent, to "document" different sections of a Web page. Later in this section you will see an example of a jQuery Mobile Web page that uses custom attributes.

A Simple Web Page with Semantic Markup

Listing 1.2 displays the contents of `SemanticMarkup1.html` that illustrates how to create and manage our data using a WebSQL database.

Listing 1.2 SemanticMarkup1.html

```
<!DOCTYPE HTML>
<html>
<head>
   <meta charset="utf-8"/>
   <title>Examples of HTML5 Semantic Markup </title>
 </head>

 <body>
  <article> <!-- start article #1 -->
    <header>
      <h1>An HTML5 CSS3 Canvas Graphics Primer</h1>
    </header>

    <header>
       <aside style="font-size:larger;font-style:italic;color
:red;float:right;width:150px;">
```

```
        The book is available on Amazon as well as MercLearning.
        </aside>
    <p>This book covers the features of HTML5 Canvas graphics
and CSS3 graphics, and shows how to extend the power of CSS3 with
SVG.<p>
        <p>The material is accessible to people with basic knowledge
of HTML and JavaScript, and more advanced users will benefit from
the examples of sophisticated CSS3 2D/3D animation effects.</p>
        <p>Learn how to create HTML5 web pages that use Canvas, CSS3,
and SVG to render 2D shapes and Bezier curves, create linear and
radial gradients, apply transforms to 2D shapes and JPG files,
create animation effects, and generate 2D/3D bar charts and line
graphs.<p>

        <nav>
         <ul>
          <li><a href="http://www.amazon.ca/HTML5-Canvas-
CSS3-Graphics-Primer/dp/1936420341">Amazon Link</a></li>
          <li><a href="http://www.merclearning.com/titles/
html5_canvas_css3_graphics.html
     ">MercLearning Link</a></li>
         </ul>
        </nav>

        <details>
         <summary>More Details About the Book</summary>
    <p>The code samples in this book run on WebKit-based browsers
on desktops and tablets. A companion DVD contains all the source
code and color graphics in the book.</p>
        </details>
       </header>

        <section>
         <h3>Other Books by the Author</h3>
         <article> <!-- start article #2 -->
         <p>Previous books include: Java Graphics Programming,
Web 2.0 Fundamentals, SVG Fundamentals, and Pro Android Flash.<p>
         <footer>
           <p>Posted by: Oswald Campesato</p>
         </footer>
         <details>
         <summary>More Details</summary>
         <p>Contact me for more detailed information</p>
         </details>
         </article> <!-- end article #2 -->
```

```
      <article> <!-- start article #3 -->
   <p>SVCC (Silicon Valley Code Camp) is the biggest free code
camp in the world, and also a great way to meet like-minded people
who are interested in the latest trends in technology.</p>
          <img src="ThreeSpheres1.png" width="200"
height="100"/>
          </article> <!-- end article #3 -->
       </section>
      </article> <!-- end article #1 -->
     </body>
     </html>
```

The `<body>` tag in Listing 1.2 contains an HTML5 `<article>` tag that in turn contains two HTML5 `<header>` tags, where the second HTML5 `<header>` tag contains an HTML5 `<aside>`. The next part of Listing 1.2 contains an HTML5 `<nav>` element with three HTML `<a>` links for navigation.

Figure 1.1 displays the result of rendering the Web page `SemanticMarkup1.html` in a Chrome browser.

An HTML5 CSS3 Canvas Graphics Primer

This book covers the features of HTML5 Canvas graphics and CSS3 graphics, and shows how to extend the power of CSS3 with SVG.

The book is available on Amazon as well as MercLearning.

The material is accessible to people with basic knowledge of HTML and JavaScript, and more advanced users will benefit from the examples of sophisticated CSS3 2D/3D animation effects.

Learn how to create HTML5 pages that use Canvas, CSS3, and SVG to render 2D shapes and Bezier curves, create linear and radial gradients, apply transforms to 2D shapes and JPG files, create animation effects, and generate 2D/3D bar charts and line graphs.

- Amazon Link
- MercLearning Link

▶ More Details About the Book

Other Books by the Author

Previous books include: Java Graphics Programming, Web 2.0 Fundamentals, SVG Fundamentals, and Pro Android Flash.

Posted by: Oswald Campesato

▶ More Details

SVCC (Silicon Valley Code Camp) is the biggest free code camp in the world, and also a great way to meet like-minded people who are interested in the latest trends in technology.

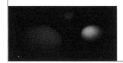

FIGURE 1.1 An HTML5 Web page with semantic markup in a Chrome browser.

The HTML5 <hgroup> Element

The HTML5 <hgroup> element enables you to "group" together a set of heading-related tags inside an HTML5 <header> element. The HTML5 <hgroup> element must contain at least two of the <h1> through <h6> elements (and nothing else). The purpose of this element is similar to that of a nested outline: it is for grouping a title with one or more subtitles.

> **NOTE** *The HTML5 <hgroup> element can only contain <h1> through <h6> elements, whereas an HTML5 <header> element can contain <h1> through <h6> as well as other HTML elements. If you do not need an <hgroup> subtitle or other <header> content, simply use the <h1> through <h6> elements.*

The indentation of the tags inside the HTML5 <hgroup> element is displayed in a "local" hierarchical fashion that is distinct from the normal hierarchical display of heading tags.

The following simple code fragment shows you how to use an HTML5 <hgroup> element inside an HTML5 <header> element:

```
<header>
 <hgroup>
  <h1>Title of post One</h1>
  <h2>subtitle of the post One</h2>
 </hgroup>
 <p>posted 12-10-2012</p>
</header>
```

Although the HTML5 <hgroup> element can be useful, it is not a high-priority item in this chapter, so we will not provide a complete code sample, but you can easily copy and paste the preceding code block into an HTML5 Web page and see the results when you launch the Web page in a browser.

Custom Attributes in HTML5

HTML5 supports custom attributes, which effectively enables you to write HTML5 Web pages in which you can store custom data that is private to the Web page or application.

Listing 1.3 displays the contents of the Web page CustomAtributes1. html that illustrates some of the custom attributes that are available in jQuery Mobile.

Listing 1.3 CustomAttributes1.html

```
<!doctype html>
<html lang="en">
  <head>
   <meta charset="utf-8"/>
   <title>Hello World from jQuery Mobile</title>
  </head>

  <body>
    <div id="page1" data-role="page">
      <header data-role="header" data-position="fixed">
        <h1>jQuery Mobile</h1>
      </header>

      <div class="content" data-role="content">
        <h3>Content Area</h3>
      </div>

      <footer data-role="footer" data-position="fixed">
        <h3>Fixed Footer</h3>
      </footer>
    </div>
  </body>
</html>
```

Listing 1.3 displays the structure of an HTML5 Web page for jQuery Mobile, but it is incomplete because it does not contain references to any jQuery JavaScript files or CSS stylesheets. The purpose of Listing 1.3 is to shows you the layout of a simple jQuery Mobile page, which in this case consists of one so-called "page view," along with some of the custom data attributes that are common in jQuery Mobile. We will delve into jQuery Mobile Web pages in greater detail in Chapters 8 and 9.

The HTML5 <audio> Element

The HTML5 <audio> tag is very simple to use, and its syntax looks like this:

```
<audio src="Sample1.mp3" controls autoplay loop>
  HTML5 audio tag not supported
</audio>
```

The HTML5 `<audio>` tag supports several attributes, including `autoplay` (play the audio as soon as it's ready), `controls` (displays the `play`, `pause`, and `volume` controls), `loop` (replays the audio), `preload` (loads the audio so it's ready to run on page load), and `src` (specifies the location of the audio file).

A minimalistic example of how to use the `<audio>` tag in an HTML5 Web page is illustrated in Listing 1.4, which displays the contents of `HTML5Audio1.html`.

Listing 1.4 HTML5Audio1.html

```
<!doctype html>
<html>
<head>
    <meta charset="utf-8"/>
    <title>HTML5 Audio</title>
</head>

<body>
    <h1>Audio Recording in Japanese</h1>

    <!-- Display control buttons -->
    <audio src="Japanese1.mp3" controls autoplay loop>
        HTML5 audio tag not supported  </audio>
</body>
</html>
```

Listing 1.4 is very straightforward: boilerplate code and one HTML5 `<audio>` element that specifies the `mp3` audio file `Japanese1.mp3`, along with audio controls that enable users to replay the audio clip.

Different browsers support different audio file formats; fortunately, the HTML5 `<audio>` tag supports a `<source>` element, which in turn provides an `src` attribute that enables you to specify different file formats, as shown here:

```
<audio controls="true">
    <source src="s.mp3" type="audio/mp3">
    <source src="s.ogg" type="audio/ogg">
    <source src="s.aac" type="audio/mp4">
    HTML5 audio not supported
</audio>
```

The preceding HTML5 `<audio>` tag specifies a file in multiple formats, and when you launch a Web page with this tag, your browser will start from the first `<source>` element in order to find a format that it recognizes and then play the audio file that is specified in the `src` attribute.

You can also programmatically control the `<audio>` tag using JavaScript code. Listing 1.5 displays the contents of an HTML5 Web page with an `<audio>` tag and some error-handling JavaScript code.

Listing 1.5 HTML5Audio2.html

```
<!DOCTYPE HTML>
    <html lang="en">
     <head>
      <meta charset="utf-8"/>
      <title>HTML5 Audio With Error Detection</title>
      <script>
       function ReportError(e) {
        switch (e.target.error.code) {
          case e.target.error.MEDIA_ERR_ABORTED:
            alert("User aborted the playback.");
            break;
          case e.target.error.MEDIA_ERR_NETWORK:
            alert("Network error.");
            break;
          case e.target.error.MEDIA_ERR_DECODE:
            alert("The File is Corrupted.");
            break;
          case e.target.error.MEDIA_ERR_SRC_NOT_SUPPORTED:
            alert("Unsupported Format or File not Found.");
            break;
          default:
            alert("An Unknown Error Occurred.");
            break;
         }
       }
      </script>
     </head>

     <body>
      <h1>HTML 5 Audio</h1>
```

```
    <audio controls onerror="ReportError(event)" src="Japanese1.
mp3">
      </audio>
    </body>
  </html>
```

Listing 1.5 contains the JavaScript function `ReportError()` that is invoked when an error occurs while playing the audio file in this `<audio>` element:

```
    <audio controls onerror="ReportError(event)" src= "Japanese1.
mp3">
```

The `ReportError()` function contains a `switch` statement that displays an alert when any of the following errors occurs:

```
MEDIA_ERR_ABORTED
MEDIA_ERR_NETWORK
MEDIA_ERR_DECODE
MEDIA_ERR_SRC_NOT_SUPPORTED
```

Some interesting audio demos in Google Chrome are here:

http://chromium.googlecode.com/svn/trunk/samples/audio/index.html

If you want to learn more about HTML5 `audio` features, you can read the W3C `audio` specification here:

https://dvcs.w3.org/hg/audio/raw-file/tip/webaudio/specification.html

The HTML5 <video> Element

The HTML5 `<video>` tag can be as minimal as the HTML5 `<audio>` tag, and its syntax looks like this:

```
<video>
  <source type="video/mp4" src="filename">
</video>
```

As you might have surmised, you can also include multiple `<source>` elements in the HTML5 `<video>` element, as shown here:

```
<video poster="MyVideo.gif" controls>
  <source src='MyVideo.mp4'
        type=›video/mp4; codecs=»avc1.4D401E, mp4a.40.2»›>
  <source src='MyVideo.ogv'
        type=›video/ogg; codecs=»theora, vorbis»›>
  <source src='MyVideo.webm'
        type=›video/webm; codecs=»vp8.0, vorbis»›>
```

```
<p>Your browser does not support the video element</p>
</video>
```
The current HTML5 specification does not specify any video formats whose support is required, but the following video formats are commonly supported in modern browsers:

- MP4 (MPEG4 files with H.264 video codec and AAC audio codec).

- Ogg files (with Theodora video codec and Vorbis audio codec) are commonly supported in modern browsers. On mobile devices, the iPhone simulator supports MP4, Android hardware support h.264, and the Android simulator supports Ogg Vorbis.

- WebM or VP8, which is a royalty-free open audio-video compression format with the .WebM extension (currently has a low adoption rate).

On the mobile side of things, both iOS and Android only support MP4 video.

Listing 1.6 displays the contents of `HTML5Video1.html` that illustrates how to play a video file in an HTML5 Web page.

Listing 1.6 HTML5Video1.html

```
<!DOCTYPE HTML>
<html>
<head>
  <meta charset="utf-8"/>
  <title>Working With HTML5 Video</title>
</head>

<body>
  <video width="800" height="500"
         controls poster="Laurie2.jpeg" id="video1">
    <source src="Rectangle1.mov" type="video/mp4">
    <source src="Rectangle1.ogg" type="video/ogg">
  </video>
</body>
</html>
```

Listing 1.6 contains some boilerplate code, along with an HTML5 <video> element whose attributes are similar to the HTML5 <audio> element. Note that the HTML5 <video> element in Listing 1.6 specifies two <source> elements whose src attribute references the same video file, but in two different formats. Browsers handle an HTML5 <video> element in a similar fashion as an HTML5 <audio> element: when you launch an HTML5 Web

page with an HTML5 <video> element in a browser, your browser will play
the first video whose format is recognized by the browser.

NOTE *You need to provide a video file for Listing 1.6 in order to see the
video functionality.*

In a previous section, you saw how to use JavaScript to bind to audio elements, and you can do the same thing with video elements (and also include
a custom progress bar).

Listing 1.7 displays the contents of HTML5Video2.html that illustrates how
to play a video file in an HTML5 Web page that contains error-handling code
in JavaScript.

Listing 1.7 HTML5Video2.html

```
<!DOCTYPE HTML>
<html lang="en">
<head>
   <meta charset="utf-8"/>
   <title></title>

 <style>
   /* selectors for playing and paused */
   .paused  { }
   .playing { }
 </style>

 <script>
  function init() {
    var video = document.getElementById("video1");
    var toggle = document.getElementById("toggle1");

    toggle.onclick = function() {
      if (video.paused) {
        video.play();
        toggle.className="playing"
      } else {
        video.pause();
        toggle.className="paused"
      }
    }
 }
 </script>
</head>

    <body onload="init()">
```

```
<figure>
  <video src="media/video1.webm" controls autoplay
          id="video1" width="400" height="300"
          data-description="Sample Video">
    This browser does not support the video tag </video>
  <legend>Sample Video</legend>
</figure>

<div id="toggle1"> </div>
</body>
</html>
```

Listing 1.7 contains a JavaScript `init()` method that is executed when the Web page is loaded into a browser. This method contains JavaScript code that handles the play and pause events for the video element, as shown here:

```
var video = document.getElementById("video1");
var toggle = document.getElementById("toggle1");

toggle.onclick = function() {
    if (video.paused) {
      video.play();
      toggle.className="playing"
    } else {
      video.pause();
      toggle.className="paused"
    }
}
```

Listing 1.7 also contains boilerplate code and an HTML5 `<video>` element that specifies a video file and also video controls that users can use to control the video, as shown here:

```
<video src="media/video1.webm" controls autoplay
        id="video1" width="400" height="300"
        data-description="Sample Video">
  This browser does not support the video tag
</video>
```

As you can see, the CSS selectors playing and paused are currently empty; their contents would contain properties that perform your styling effects.

NOTE *You need to provide a video file for Listing 1.7 in order to see the video functionality.*

A useful link with information about the status of HTML5 video and a link to an interesting Web site for HTML5 video support are here:

http://www.longtailvideo.com/html5/
http://videojs.com/

The HTML `<video>` element also supports the `canPlayType()` method that enables you to determine programmatically how likely your browser can play different video types. This method returns "probably," "maybe," or an empty string.

Listing 1.8 displays the contents of `HTML5Video3.html` that illustrates how to check browser support for different video types.

Listing 1.8 HTML5Video3.html

```
<!DOCTYPE HTML>
<html lang="en">
<head>
   <meta charset="utf-8"/>
   <title>Detecting Video Support</title>

 <script>
  var videoTypes = ['video/ogg; codecs="theora, vorbis"',
                    'video/ogg',
                    'video/mp4',
                    'video/ogv',
                    'video/webm'
                   ];

   function init() {
     var video = document.getElementById("video1");
     var canPlay, videoType;

     for(var v=0; v<videoTypes.length; v++) {
        videoType = videoTypes[v];
        canPlay = video.canPlayType(videoType);

console.log("Type: "+videoType+" Can Play: "+canPlay);
     }
 }
 </script>
</head>
```

```
<body onload="init()">
 <figure>
   <video src="media/HelloWorld.ogg" controls autoplay
          id="video1" width="400" height="300"
          data-description="Sample Video">
     This browser does not support the video tag </video>
   <legend>Sample Video</legend>
 </figure>
</body>
</html>
```

Listing 1.8 contains a JavaScript array `videoTypes` that specifies information about various video formats, and the first entry is the most detailed information. The JavaScript function `init()` is invoked when the Web page is loaded into a browser, and it contains a loop that iterates through the array of video formats and checks which ones are supported by your browser.

If you launch a Chrome browser (version 19 or higher) on a Macbook, you will see the following output in the console:

```
Type: video/ogg; codecs="theora, vorbis" Can Play: probably
Type: video/ogg Can Play: maybe
Type: video/mp4 Can Play: maybe
Type: video/ogv Can Play:
Type: video/webm Can Play: maybe
```

Notice that the first line specifies the codecs. The browser has determined that it can probably play the given video type, whereas the second line is "maybe" because the codecs are not specified.

Popcorn.js: HTML5 Media Framework

`Popcorn.js` is part of the Mozilla Popcorn project. It is a JavaScript-based HTML5 media framework for creating time-based interactive media. The `Popcorn.js` homepage and the download link are here:

http://popcornjs.org

http://popcornjs.org/download

`Popcorn.js` consists of a core JavaScript library (available as a separate download) and plugins. You can also create a customized download of `Popcorn.js`, along with minified and debug versions. Navigate to the homepage for additional information, as well as documentation and a video with a demonstration of `Popcorn.js`.

HTML5 <video> and Web Camera Support

You can use the HTML5 <video> tag for real-time camera support. This functionality is already available in Opera (see the link below). As this book goes to print, this functionality has appeared in the Chrome "nightly" builds, which is accessible via the getUserMedia() API.

For other useful information regarding HTML5 video, visit this Web site:

http://html5video.org/

Listing 1.9 displays the contents of WebCamera1.html. It illustrates how to activate a camera in a browser (currently this works only in Opera).

Listing 1.9 WebCamera1.html

```
<!DOCTYPE HTML>
<html>
<head>
  <meta charset="utf-8"/>
  <title>HTML5 Web Camera</title>
</head>

<body>
<h1>Web camera display demo</h1>
<video autoplay></video>
<script>
 var video = document.getElementsByTagName('video')[0],
     heading = document.getElementsByTagName('h1')[0];

if(navigator.getUserMedia) {
  navigator.getUserMedia('video', successCallback, errorCallback);
  function successCallback( stream ) {
    video.src = stream;
  }
  function errorCallback( error ) {
    heading.textContent =
        "An error occurred: [CODE " + error.code + "]";
  }
} else {
  heading.textContent =
      "Native web camera streaming is not supported in this brows-
er";
}
</script>
</body>
</html>
```

Listing 1.9 checks for the presence of `navigator.getUserMedia`, and if it does exist, then an invocation of the `getUserMedia()` method searches for the HTML5 `<video>` tag and provides both success and failure JavaScript callback functions, as shown here:

```
navigator.getUserMedia('video', successCallback, errorCallback);
```

An Opera build that provides web camera support for Linux, Mac, Windows, and Android is available for download here:

http://dev.opera.com/articles/view/labs-more-fun-using-the-web-with-getusermedia-and-native-pages/

The next section discusses HTML5 forms. You will see the first version of `Form1.html` that allows users to keep track of a set of words and their translations in multiple languages.

HTML5 FORMS

The HTML5 `Form` element supports new elements, and the input-related elements can display suitable "prompts" for the type of input data that is expected. Some of these new element types can display the appropriate keyboard input for various input types when they are part of an HTML5 Web page that is rendered on a mobile device. For example, an e-mail input type and a URL input type display different keyboards that simplify the process of entering the appropriately formatted information. Note that there are no voice-enabled input tags.

New Input Types

The new HTML5 `Form` input types include: `color`, `date`, `email`, `month`, `datetime`, `datetime-local`, `number`, `range`, `search`, `tel`, `time`, `url`, and `week`. The new input types are named after the functionality that they provide: an e-mail type is for e-mail addresses, a number type is for numbers, a search type is for search fields, and so forth. The HTML5 `Form` in Listing 1.9 that is shown later in this chapter shows you how to use some of these new input types (and new attributes as well).

An excellent Web site with information regarding the HTML5 `Form` element is here:

http://www.wufoo.com/html5/

The HTML5 Web page in this section enables users to enter new words in the input fields that are part of a `Form` element. This version addresses some of the UI aspects of the HTML5 `Form`, including some simple CSS3 selectors that we will use to style various HTML5 elements in this HTML5 Web page. The second iteration of this `Form`-based example shows you how to use localStorage in order to persist the contents of your dictionary. The third iteration illustrates how we can use `IndexedDB` (instead of localStorage) to store the contents of our dictionary in a database in an HTML5-compliant browser. In addition to creating new entries, we will be able to delete or update existing entries, and search for specific words in our dictionary.

New Attributes

This section briefly discusses some of the useful new attributes that are available for HTML5 `<input>` elements.

The `autocomplete` attribute: specify a value of `on` when you want to save the value that is entered in a field (the other value is `off`).

The `autofocus` attribute: specify this attribute for an element that will receive the focus after a Web page is loaded into a browser.

The `novalidate` attribute: specify this attribute for `<form>` elements that do not require validation.

The `placeholder` attribute specifies a string that is displayed in an input field:

```
<input type="text" size="20" placeholder="Full name">
```
The `required` attribute makes the associated field mandatory:

```
<input type="text" name="name"
        required placeholder="Name"/>
```
The `pattern` attribute supports a regular expression that is used to validate the data that is entered in the associated field. For example, the expression `\d{3}` (which is available in many programming languages) specifies a pattern of three digits, each of which is between `0` and `9`.

The `form` attribute associates an element with a form, and the value that you provide must match the `id` attribute of the `Form` element.

The `list` attribute associates the element with a `<datalist>` element to display a list (such as a menu) of possible values for the element, and the value provided must be the `id` attribute of the `<datalist>` element.

A Simple HTML5 Form Example

Listing 1.10 displays the contents of `HTML5Form1.html,` which illustrates how to specify several of the new HTML5 input types and attributes.

Listing 1.10 HTML5Form1.html

```
<!DOCTYPE HTML>
<html lang="en">
<head>
 <meta charset="utf-8"/>
  <title>HTML5 Form Input Fields</title>
</head>

<body>
      <form action="" method="post">
       <label for="name">Name:</label>
       <input type="text" name="name"
             required placeholder="Name"/>

       <label for="email">Email:</label>
       <input type="email" name="email"
             required placeholder="email@foo.com"/>

       <label for="message">Message:</label>
       <textarea name="message" required</textarea>

       <label for="number">Number:</label>
       <input type="number" name="number"
             min="0" max="50" step="1"
             required placeholder="Maximum 50">

       <label for="range">Range:</label>
       <input type="range" name="range" min="0" max="10" step="2"/>

       <label for="website">Website:</label>
       <input type="url" name="website" required
             placeholder="http://www.acme.com"/>

       <input type="submit" value="Send Message"/>
      </form>
</body>
</html>
```

Listing 1.10 contains an HTML Form element with several HTML `<input>` elements, four of which specify the `required` attribute, which means that those `<input>` elements require users to enter a value. These same `<in-`

put> elements specify a `placeholder` attribute, along with a text string for this attribute; this text string is displayed when the Web page is rendered. In essence, the placeholder attribute acts as a "hint" for the type of string or pattern that users need to provide for the `<input>` element.

In Listing 1.10, the first `<input>` element displays the placeholder string `Name`, and no validation is performed other than ensuring that this field is non-empty:

```
<input type="text" name="name" required placeholder="Name"/>
```

However, the second `<input>` element displays the placeholder string `email@foo.com`. Validation is performed, which means that users must provide an e-mail string that has the correct format:

```
<input type="email" name="email" required
        placeholder="email@foo.com"/>
```

Figure 1.2 displays the result of rendering the HTML5 Web page `HTML-5Form1.html` in landscape mode on an Android ICS tablet.

FIGURE 1.2 An HTML5 Form on an Android ICS tablet.

Listing 1.11 displays the contents of `MultiLingualForm1.html`, which illustrates how to enter a word in English and its counterpart in Japanese (Romanji), Italian, Spanish, and French.

Listing 1.11 `MultiLingualForm1.html`

```
<!DOCTYPE HTML>
<html lang="en">
```

```
<head>
 <meta charset="utf-8"/>
  <title>Our Multi-Lingual Dictionary</title>
</head>

<style>
label {
  width: 30%;
  float: left;
  text-align: right;
  margin-right: 0.5em;
  display: block
}

input[type="text"] {
  width: 60%;
  background: #FFCCCC;
}
</style>

<body>
  <h1>Our Multi-Lingual Dictionary</h1>
  <form action="" id="dictionary" method="post">
   <fieldset>
      <label for="english">English:</label>
      <input type="text" size="30" name="english" id="english"/>
      <label for="japanese">Japanese:</label>
      <input type="text" size="30" name="japanese" id="japanese"/>
      <label for="spanish">Spanish:</label>
      <input type="text" size="30" name="spanish" id="spanish"/>
      <label for="french">French:</label>
      <input type="text" size="30" name="french" id="french"/>
      <label for="italian">Italian:</label>
      <input type="text" size="30" name="italian" id="italian"/>
      <input type="submit" name="Save"/>
   </fieldset>
  </form>
</body>
</html>
```

Listing 1.11 is a basic HTML5 Form containing a set of `<div>` elements, each of which contains an `<input>` element (with a corresponding `<label>` element) of type text that enable users to enter words in English, Japanese, Spanish, French, and Italian. Note that no validation is performed, which means that users can enter misspelled words and words for the wrong language. There is one `<input>` element of type `submit` that enables users to submit the form, but currently nothing is actually done with the users' words.

Figure 1.3 displays the result of rendering `MultiLingualForm1.html` in landscape mode on a Sprint Nexus S 4G smartphone with Android ICS.

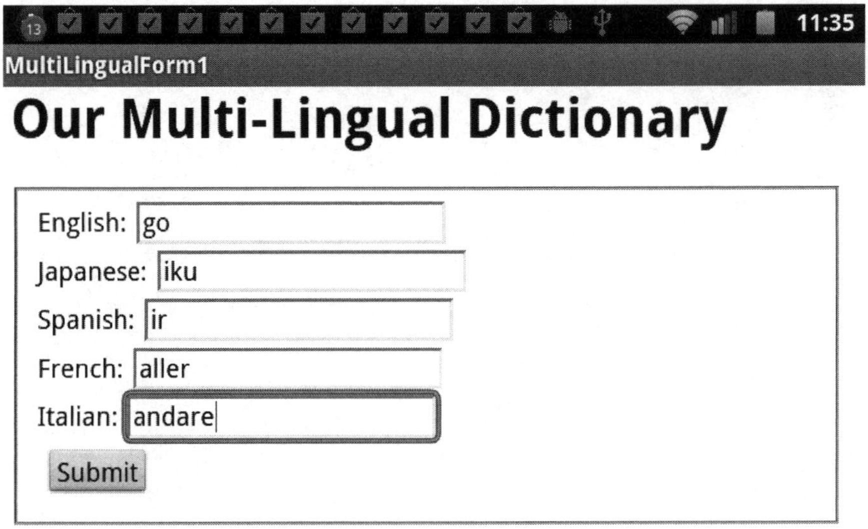

FIGURE 1.3 An HTML5 Form on a Sprint Nexus S 4G with Android ICS.

As you can see, the form in Figure 1.3 is functional, but it's also bland and uninspiring for users. Fortunately, we can use simple CSS3 selectors to style this web page in order to make it much more interesting, as shown in the next section.

The HTML5 FormData Object

The HTML5 `FormData` object can be programmatically instantiated and populated with data, and then submitted via XHR2 (`XmlHTTPRequest` Level 2), as shown here:

```
var formData = new FormData();

formData.append("username", "Dave");
formData.append("accountId", 54321);
// other data values appended here

var myXHR = new XMLHttpRequest();
```

```
myXHR.open("POST", "http://www.acme.com/FormSubmission.php");
myXHR.send(formData);
```

In Chapter 10, you will see a more detailed example of how to use HTML5 `FormData` and XHR2.

Now that you know how to create an HTML5 `Form` that handles data input, you're ready for the next code sample, which demonstrates how to create an HTML5 `Form` that manages that input data using HTML5 online localStorage.

USING HTML5 WEB STORAGE

The essence of HTML5 Web Storage is that it provides a very simple way to store key/value pairs, along with a set of APIs for managing your data. In addition to storing simple key/value pairs, you can create a value string consisting of a JSON expression that contains a set of name/value pairs. You can serialize the JSON data before storing it in Web Storage, and then deserialize that JSON data whenever you retrieve it from Web Storage.

Although there is no query language for localStorage, you can determine the number of keys in localStorage through `localstorage.length`, and you can use regular expressions to select the appropriate keys as you iterate through the items in localStorage. As a simple example, the following code block iterates through the keys in localStorage and checks for the values that start with the string `Emp`:

```
var itemCount = localStorage.length, i=0, key="", value="";

while ( ++i < itemCount ) {
      // retrieve the value of the current key
      key = localStorage.key( i );

      // retrieve the value associated with the current key
      value = localStorage.getItem( key );

      if(value.substr(0,3) == "Emp") {
         // do something with this element
      }
}
```

In addition to storing strings in Web Storage, you can also store JSON data, as shown here:

http://www.codeproject.com/Articles/361428/HTML5-Web-Storage

The advantage of HTML5 Web Storage (both local and session) is the simplicity of the APIs. The disadvantages of HTML5 Web Storage include:

1. An initial platform-specific limit for data.
2. No transactional support.
3. No query language for accessing structured data.

Each browser has its own mechanism for increasing the amount of available storage after the initial limit is exceeded.

HTML5 Web Storage versus IndexedDB

The first advantage of `IndexedDB` over HTML5 Web Storage is its capacity: `IndexedDB` has a larger limit (50MB quota in Firefox 4+), and when that limit is exceeded, Firefox prompts the user for permission to increase the maximum size. The manner in which the quota is increased depends on the browser (for desktops and mobile devices), so you need to look into the details for each browser if you are writing a cross-browser application.

The choice between Web Storage and `IndexedDB` depends on the complexity of your data and the requirements for your application.

Later in this chapter, you will see an example of using `IndexedDB`. Its advantages and disadvantages are the opposite of the first two advantages of HTML5 Web Storage that are listed in a previous section.

HTML5 Web Storage versus Cookies

An HTTP cookie is a set of key/value pairs that is used to communicate with a web server. Cookies are included in an HTTP request header, provided that the cookie data is still valid and the requested domain and path also match the original cookie domain and path. Although cookies are convenient, they do have some drawbacks, such as their size and count (typically 4K bytes and 300 cookies), performance, and security.

localStorage and sessionStorage are intended to provide support for storing a larger amount of data (megabytes instead of kilobytes), storing data beyond a current session, and also support for transactions that occur in multiple browser windows simultaneously, all of which makes HTML5 Web Storage a more powerful technology than cookies.

HTML5 Web Storage and Security

The APIs are subject to the "same origin" policy, in the same way that security is defined for the XMLHTTPRequest object. Consequently, do not use localStorage on a shared domain, because every Web page on that domain can access your stored data. By default, your locally stored data is not shared among subdomains.

More information about the "same origin" policy is here:

https://developer.mozilla.org/en/Same_origin_policy_for_JavaScript

Now that you have a basic understanding of localStorage, the next section contains a code sample that illustrates how to store text strings (consisting of concatenated words) in localStorage.

AN EXAMPLE OF HTML5 LOCALSTORAGE

The example in this section uses localStorage so that we can persist the data in the multilingual dictionary. If you decide to replace localStorage with session storage, the data will be available only for the current browser session (hence the name "session storage").

Listing 1.12 displays the contents of MultiLingualForm2.html, which illustrates how to create and manage our data in localStorage.

Listing 1.12 MultiLingualForm2.html

```
<html lang="en">
<head>
 <meta charset="utf-8"/>
 <title>Our Multi-Lingual Dictionary</title>
 <link rel="stylesheet" media="screen" href="MultiLingualForm2.
css"/>

<script>
 function displayItem() {
    var dictionary  = document.forms["dictionary"];
    var english     = dictionary.english.value;
    var storageItem = localStorage.getItem(english);

    var splitItem   = item.split(":");
    var english     = splitItem[0];
    var japanese    = splitItem[1];
    var spanish     = splitItem[2];
```

```
   var french      = splitItem[3];
   var italian     = splitItem[4];

   dictionary.english.value  = english;
   dictionary.japanese.value = japanese;
   dictionary.spanish.value  = spanish;
   dictionary.french.value   = french;
   dictionary.italian.value  = italian;
}

function addWord() {
   var dictionary = document.forms["dictionary"];

   var english   = dictionary.english.value;
   var japanese  = dictionary.japanese.value;
   var spanish   = dictionary.spanish.value;
   var french    = dictionary.french.value;
   var italian   = dictionary.italian.value;
   var incomplete = 0;

   var concatenated =  english + ":" + japanese + ":" +
                       spanish + ":" + french + ":" +
                       italian;

   if(english == ""||japanese == ""||spanish == ""||
      french == ""||italian == "")
   {
      ++incomplete;
console.log("Skipping incomplete/empty row!");
      return;
   }

   try {
      localStorage.setItem(english, concatenated);
      alert("added new word: "+ concatenated);
      clearFields();

      // append new words to dropdown list
      option = new Option( english );
      wordList.options[wordList.length] = option;
   } catch (e) {
      if (e == QUOTA_EXCEEDED_ERR) {
         alert("Local Storage Quota exceeded");
         // you can clear local storage here:
         //clearLocalStorage();
      }
```

```
    }
  }

  function clearFields() {
     var dictionary = document.forms["dictionary"];

     dictionary.english.value  = "";
     dictionary.japanese.value = "";
     dictionary.spanish.value  = "";
     dictionary.french.value   = "";
     dictionary.italian.value  = "";
  }

  function clearLocalStorage() {
    localStorage.clear();
    populateDropDownList();
  }

  // remove the options from the list
  function removeItemsFromDropDownList() {
    while ( wordList.options.length ) wordList.options[0] = null;
  }

  function createTestData() {
    removeItemsFromDropDownList();
    clearLocalStorage();

    localStorage.setItem("eat", "eat:taberu:comer:manger:mangiare")
;
    localStorage.setItem("go",  "go:iku:andar:aller:andare");
    localStorage.setItem("buy", "buy:kau:comprar:acheter:comprare")
;
  }

  function populateDropDownList() {
    // the length property contains the item count in the storage
    var i = -1, key, itemCount, items = {};

    createTestData();
    itemCount = localStorage.length;

// option = new Option( "eat:taberu:comer:manger:mangiare" );
// wordList.options[wordList.length] = option;

    while ( ++i < itemCount ) {
       // retrieve the value of the current key
```

```
      key = localStorage.key( i );

      // retrieve the value of the current item
      items[key] = localStorage.getItem( key );

      option = new Option( key );

      // Append to existing options
      wordList.options[wordList.length] = option;
   }

   // Ensure option 0 is selected
   wordList.selectedIndex = 0;
 }
</script>
</head>

<body onLoad="populateDropDownList()">
  <h1>Our Multi-Lingual Dictionary</h1>
  <form id="dictionary" onsubmit="return false;">
  <form>
   <fieldset>
    <div>
      <button id="add" onClick="addWord()">Add New Words</button>
    </div>
    <div>
      <label for="english">English:</label>
      <input type="text" name="english" id="english"/>
    </div>

    <div>
      <label for="japanese">Japanese:</label>
      <input type="text" name="japanese" id="japanese"/>
    </div>

    <div>
      <label for="spanish">Spanish:</label>
      <input type="text" name="spanish" id="spanish"/>
    </div>

    <div>
      <label for="french">French:</label>
      <input type="text" name="french" id="french"/>
    </div>

    <div>
```

```
        <label for="italian">Italian:</label>
        <input type="text" name="italian" id="italian"/>
    </div>

    <div>
        <button id="clear1" onClick="clearFields()">Clear Input
Fields</button>
        <button id="clear2" onClick="clearLocalStorage()">Clear Lo-
cal Storage</button>
    </div>
    <label for="none">The List of Words in Our Dictionary:</label>
    <br/>
    <div>
    <select id="wordList" onchange="update()">
      <option value=""></option>
    </select>
    </div>
    </fieldset>
  </form>
</body>
</html>
```

Listing 1.12 contains the JavaScript functions for handling associated functionality. Whenever a new row is added, the JavaScript function `addWord()` performs a concatenation of the words in that row, with a semi-colon (":") as the delimiter between words, as shown here:

```
var concatenated = english + ":" + japanese + ":" +
                   spanish + ":" + french + ":" +
                   italian;
```

Next, the concatenated string is stored as part of a "dictionary" in localStorage in a `try/catch` block with the following line of code:

```
localStorage.setItem(english, concatenated);
```

Keep in mind that the preceding code snippet is equivalent to this snippet:

```
localStorage["eat"] = "eat:taberu:comer:manger:mangiare";
```

Conversely, when the words are retrieved from the dictionary, the JavaScript function `displayItem()` will "split" each concatenated string into the words that are stored in the concatenated string, and then the individual words are displayed in the corresponding language field.

The JavaScript function `displayItem()` displays a word in each input field for each of the specified languages. The JavaScript functions `clearFields()`

and `clearLocalStorage()` remove the data from the input fields and from the dictionary in localStorage.

Note that each time the HTML page is loaded, the `populateDropDown-List()` function is invoked, which creates some test data (via the JavaScript function `createTestData()`) and then populates the drop-down list with the words that are in the dictionary in localStorage, as shown here:

```
localStorage.setItem("eat", "eat:taberu:comer:
                      manger:mangiare");
localStorage.setItem("go", "go:iku:andar:aller:andare");
localStorage.setItem("buy", "buy:kau:comprar:acheter:
                      comprare");
```

Finally, the JavaScript function `removeItemsFromDropDownList()` removes the data from the drop-down list with this line of code:

```
while ( wordList.options.length ) wordList.options[0] = null;
```

Listing 1.13 MultiLingualForm2.css

```css
fieldset {
   float: left;
   border: 2; width: 50%;
   background: #F88;}

div label {
   float: left;
   border: 0; width: 20%;
   background: #FF0;
   -webkit-border-radius: 6px;
   -webkit-box-shadow: 0 0 4px #222222;
}

label {
   float: left;
   border: 0; width: 60%;
   background: #0AD;
   -webkit-border-radius: 6px;
   -webkit-box-shadow: 0 0 4px #222222;
}

input {
   border: 0; width: 40%;
   border: 2px solid white;
   background: #F44;
```

```
    -webkit-border-radius: 6px;
    -webkit-box-shadow: 0 0 4px #333333;
}

button, select {
    font-size: 16px;
    border: 1px solid white;
    background: #CCC;
    -webkit-border-radius: 6px;
    -webkit-box-shadow: 0 0 4px #222222;
    width: 60%;
    padding: 6px;
}
```

Listing 1.13 displays CSS3 selectors for four HTML elements: `fieldset`, `label`, `input`, and the `submit` button. The selectors specify attributes such as the border, width, padding, and rounded corners for the corresponding HTML elements. For example, the CSS3 selector for the HTML `<label>` element specifies yellow (`#FF0`) for the `background` and a `border-radius` of six pixels, as shown here:

```
    background: #FF0;
    -webkit-border-radius: 6px;
```

Similar comments apply to the other CSS selectors in Listing 1.12, whose content is similar to the CSS selector for the `<label>` element.

Figure 1.4 displays the rendered HTML5 Web page `MultiLingualForm2.html`. This page is much more vivid than Figure 1.3, which does not contain any CSS3 selectors.

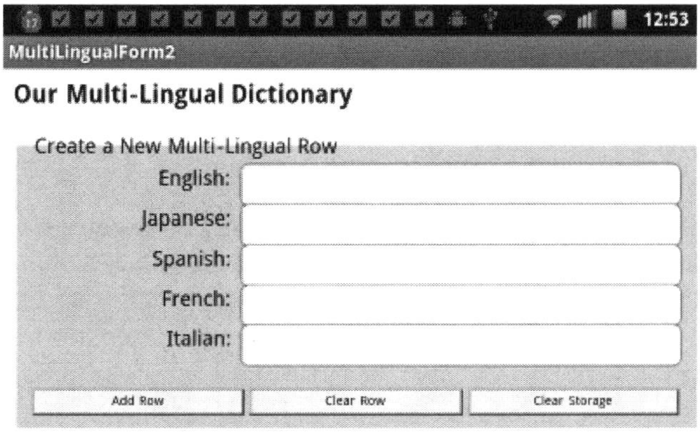

FIGURE 1.4 An HTML5 Form with CSS3 on a Sprint Nexus S 4G with Android ICS.

The example in the next section also uses an HTML5 `Form` that handles data input, but this time the data will be stored in an HTML5 database instead of online localStorage.

LocalStorage and iOS 5.1

Unfortunately, iOS 5.1 treats localStorage as "transient" data, which means that on iOS 5.1 devices, data in localStorage can be disposed when storage space is low:

http://www.infoworld.com/d/mobile-technology/new-ipad-complicates-life-html5-developers-190266

By the time this book goes to print, this issue will probably be resolved.

Storing Images in localStorage

In addition to storing simple text strings in HTML5 localStorage, you can also store images and files. You can find some useful information and code samples here:

https://hacks.mozilla.org/2012/02/saving-images-and-files-in-localstorage/

You can get the complete code for the preceding article from Github:

https://github.com/robnyman/robnyman.github.com/tree/master/html5demos/localstorage

Note that it's better to store images in `IndexedDB` because of size limitations for localStorage.

HTML5 WEB DATABASES

In addition to using Web Storage for storing data, there are two databases that provide more robust functionality. The database that is actively being developed is `IndexedDB`, which has not been fully implemented in all modern browsers as this book goes to print.

Another database is `WebSQL`, but development on this database was discontinued in November 2010. However, if you have a Web application that uses `WebSQL`, the following article provides useful information to help you migrate to `IndexedDB`:

http://www.html5rocks.com/en/tutorials/webdatabase/websql-indexeddb/

There are various open source projects available that provide database features for Web applications. For example, html5sql is a JavaScript module that focuses on sequential processing of SQL statements in a transaction:

http://html5sql.com/

With html5sql you can process SQL as a single-statement string, as an array of strings or objects, or from a separate file that contains SQL statements.

Another open source project is the JavaScript database TaffyDB. Its homepage is here:

http://taffydb.com/

This open source project includes features such as update and insert, along with cross-browser support, and the ability to extend the database with your own functions. In addition, TaffyDB is compatible with multiple toolkits, such as jQuery, YUI, and Dojo.

The next section introduces you to IndexedDB and shows you how to store text strings in an IndexedDB database.

USING AN HTML5 INDEXEDDB DATABASE

In this section, we will use an IndexedDB database to store the data in our multilingual dictionary. IndexedDB supports SQLITE syntax, which may be familiar to you.

Listing 1.14 displays selected portions of the contents of the HTML5 Web page MultiLingualForm2DB1.html, which illustrates how to create and manage our data using an IndexedDB database. Note that Listing 1.14 is available in its entirety on the DVD.

Listing 1.14 MultiLingualForm2DB1.html

```
<html lang="en">
<head>
 <meta charset="utf-8"/>
 <title>Our Multi-Lingual Dictionary with IndexedDB</title>
 // code omitted for brevity

<script>
/* some database-related initialization here */
var dbName = "MultiLingual1";
var multilingual = {};
```

```
var indexedDB = window.indexedDB || window.webkitIndexedDB ||
                window.mozIndexedDB || window.moz_indexedDB;

console.log("indexedDB: "+indexedDB);

if ('webkitIndexedDB' in window) {
  window.IDBTransaction = window.webkitIDBTransaction;
  window.IDBKeyRange = window.webkitIDBKeyRange;
  console.log("initializing transaction and range");
}

multilingual.indexedDB = {};
multilingual.indexedDB.db = null;

multilingual.indexedDB.onerror = function(e) {
  console.log(e);
};
```

The preceding code block created an IndexedDB database called MultiLingual1, and also checks for the existence of indexedDB using various browser-specific prefixes, after which the code defines the onerror() JavaScript function.

```
multilingual.indexedDB.open = function() {
//console.log("dbName in open: "+dbName);
  var request = indexedDB.open(dbName, 1);

  request.onsuccess = function(e) {
//console.log("top of onsuccess function");
    var v = "1.0";
    multilingual.indexedDB.db = e.target.result;
    var db = multilingual.indexedDB.db;

    // We can only create Object stores in a setVersion
      transaction;
    if (v != db.version) {
      var setVrequest = db.setVersion(v);

      // onsuccess is the only place we can create Object Stores
        setVrequest.onerror = multilingual.indexedDB.onerror;

      setVrequest.onsuccess = function(e) {
        if(db.objectStoreNames.contains(dbName)) {
          db.deleteObjectStore(dbName);
        }
```

```
        var store = db.createObjectStore(dbName,
                                {keyPath: "timeStamp"});

        multilingual.indexedDB.getAllWords();
      };
    }
    else {
      multilingual.indexedDB.getAllWords();
    }
  };

  request.onerror = multilingual.indexedDB.onerror;
}
```

The preceding code block defines the `open()` JavaScript function that opens our database `MultiLingual1` that will contain our multilingual information. Version checking is also performed so that we have the flexibility of creating different versions of our database.

```
function addWord() {
  // code omitted for brevity
    var concatenated =  english + ":" + japanese + ":" +
                        spanish + ":" + french + ":" +
                        italian;
  // more code omitted for brevity

  // add new words to our database
  multilingual.indexedDB.addWord(concatenated);
}
```

The preceding block of code contains almost the same code as the corresponding function in Listing 1.12, with the exception of the line of code in bold, which shows you how straightforward it is to add a new row to our `IndexedDB` multilingual dictionary.

```
multilingual.indexedDB.deleteWord = function(id) {
  var db = multilingual.indexedDB.db;
  var dbNameArray = new Array();
  dbNameArray.push(dbName);

  var trans = db.transaction(dbNameArray, IDBTransaction.READ_
WRITE);
  var store = trans.objectStore(dbName);

  var request = store.delete(id);
```

```
request.onsuccess = function(e) {
  multilingual.indexedDB.getAllWords();
};

request.onerror = function(e) {
  console.log("Error Adding: ", e);
};
};
```

The preceding block of code shows you how to delete a row in a transaction-oriented manner from an `IndexedDB` database, where the `id` represents the row that we want to delete from the database.

Note that only the storage functionality has changed in Listing 1.14, and that when you launch this Web page, it will look identical to Figure 1.4.

STORING TWITTER TWEETS IN A WEB DATABASE

Remy Sharp created an open source project that uses Web database APIs to store Twitter tweets. You can fork his code project here:

http://html5demos.com/database

Instead of displaying the code for Remy's project, this section will provide some screenshots in Google Chrome, which in turn can be helpful when you are debugging JavaScript code in your applications.

Navigate to the preceding Web page and right-click on the screen, and after a few moments you will see the Chrome console. Now select `Resources > html5demos > tweets` and after dragging the horizontal panel separator up slightly, you will see something similar to Figure 1.5.

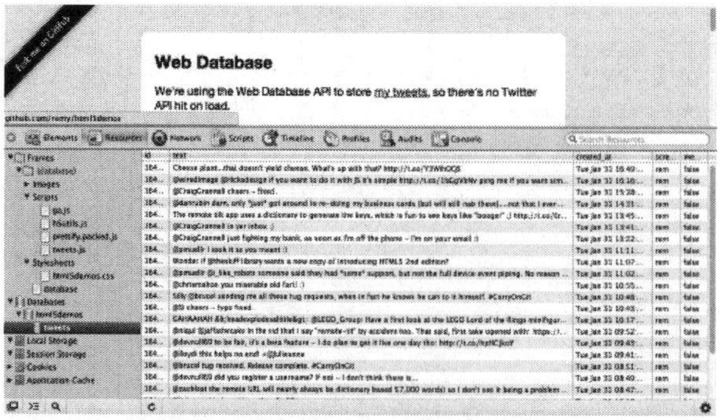

FIGURE 1.5 Remy Sharp's Twitter database.

Now select `Resources` > `html5demos` and to the right of the ">" prompt in the middle of the screen, type the following SQL command:

```
select * from tweets;
```

After a few moments you will see a set of data rendered in the console (with the exception of any new tweets that have been added to localStorage). The nice thing about this functionality is that you can invoke whatever SQL commands that you need in order to view different aspects of the data in the database.

You can also view the contents of the JavaScript file `tweet.js` in the Chrome console by navigating via the path that is shown in Figure 1.6.

FIGURE 1.6 Remy Sharp's tweet.js source code.

WEB DATABASE AND MOBILE DEVICES

You can try to use the same techniques for mobile applications that you use for web applications, but you will encounter similar constraints in both environments. Although you can use native code to access a database, the solution will be specific to each type of device. The choice that you make depends on the requirements of your application.

One cross-platform solution is to use CouchDB Mobile, which is the mobile version of CouchDB. Another mobile-based alternative is Touch-DB, which is a lightweight database engine that is compatible with Apache CouchDB. The creator of TouchDB makes the analogy that "if CouchDB is MySQL, then TouchDB is SQLite." An Android port and an iOS port of TouchDB are available here:

https://github.com/couchbaselabs/TouchDB-Android
https://github.com/couchbaselabs/TouchDB-iOS

PERFORMANCE, DEBUGGING, AND TESTING TOOLS

Several excellent performance and debugging tools are available, and this section briefly mentions several of these tools:

- Blaze (mobile Web sites)
- Chrome Speed Tracer
- Page Speed
- WEINRE
- YSlow

Before we discuss these tools, remember that the code samples in this book are for WebKit-based browsers, and in case you haven't already done so, you ought to familiarize yourself with the Web Inspector, which is built into Chrome and Safari. Whenever you navigate to a Web page, right-click on that Web page and you can view details about the Web page that you have launched.

For example, Figure 1.7 shows you what you will see if you launch the HTML5 Web page HTML5Video1.html (displayed in Listing 1.6) in a Chrome browser, right-click on the page, and then click on "Resources."

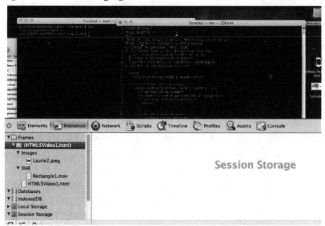

FIGURE 1.7 An example of Chrome's Web Inspector.

The Web Inspector is a very useful tool, and it's well worth your time to familiar yourself with its features. A Wiki page with useful information about Web Inspector is here:

http://trac.webkit.org/wiki/WebInspector

Blaze

Blaze provides test results for the performance of a mobile Web site, which includes overall load time as well as load times for individual pages. Blaze supports multiple mobile devices, including iPhone, iPad 2 (but not iPad 3), and devices with Android 2.2/2.3/3.0 (but no support yet for Android ICS).

Navigate to the following URL and follow the instructions:

http://www.blaze.io/mobile/

Chrome Speed Tracer

Chrome Speed Tracer is an open source project that assists you in identifying performance bottlenecks in your Web applications. Its homepage is here:

https://developers.google.com/web-toolkit/speedtracer/

Speed Tracer performs low-level instrumentation, and after performing an analysis, the results are displayed in a visually oriented fashion. Speed Tracer is currently available as a Chrome extension and works on its supported platforms (Windows and Linux).

PageSpeed

PageSpeed is actually a "family" of tools for optimizing the performance of Web pages. Its homepage is here:

https://developers.google.com/speed/pagespeed

The PageSpeed available tools are:

- PageSpeed browser extensions
- PageSpeed Insight
- The `mod_pagespeed` Apache module
- PageSpeed Service

The PageSpeed browser extensions are available for Chrome and Firefox, help you improve the performance of your Web pages.

PageSpeed Insights is a Web-based tool that analyzes pages in any browser, without downloading an extension. The `mod_pagespeed` Apache module automatically rewrites pages and resources to improve their performance. Finally, PageSpeed Service is an online service that speeds up loading of your Web pages.

You can also use Google PageSpeed to test load time on desktop browsers, and there is also a Web version of Google PageSpeed for analyzing mobile performance. Google PageSpeed ranks a page between 1 and 100, and also provides suggestions for improving the performance of a mobile Web site:

http://pagespeed.googlelabs.com/

WEINRE

WEINRE (pronounced "winery") is an excellent debugging tool that uses the same UI display as Chrome's Web Inspector. Its homepage is here:

http://phonegap.github.com/weinre/

WEINRE supports remote debugging, which means that you can see Web pages on mobile devices. You can find YouTube videos, documentation, and discussion groups regarding WEINRE here:

http://www.youtube.com/results?search_query=weinre
http://callback.github.com/callback-weinre
http://groups.google.com/group/weinre

Firebug for Firefox

Firebug is a debugging tool that is an add-on for Firefox. You can install Firebug here:

https://addons.mozilla.org/en-US/firefox/addon/firebug/

There are also simulation tools available, such as the one by Remy Sharp that allows you to simulate motion events on mobile devices. Its homepage is here:

http://remote-tilt.com/

You can use this tool by including one line of JavaScript in your Web pages, after which a pop-up window will appear that enables you to simulate various motion events.

Unfortunately, additional discussion about these tools is beyond the primary scope of this book, but it's definitely worth learning at least one of them, which will provide you with knowledge that you can use for debugging purposes outside of the code samples this book.

jsconsole

jsconsole is a JavaScript and CoffeeScript Web console that is useful for debugging purposes. This tool (created by Remy Sharp) is available for download here:

https://github.com/remy/jsconsole

You can see examples of the functionality of jsconsole on this Web site:

http://jsconsole.com/

Socketbug

Socketbug is a tool created by Peter Schmalfeldt that helps you debug mobile applications. Its homepage is here:

http://socketbug.com/

Socketbug supports iOS Safari, Android Webkit, and Palm WebOS, and you can use any modern browser as your debug console.

Adobe Shadow

Adobe Shadow is a mobile debugging tool by Adobe. Its homepage is here:

http://labs.adobe.com/technologies/shadow/

Adobe Shadow provides a way to test your Web sites on multiple devices simultaneously, which is also appealing if you are interested in responsive design. Adobe Shadow uses WEINRE in order to perform remote DOM inspection on devices, and it currently supports Mac (OS X 10.6 and 10.7) and Windows 7. A four-minute video about Adobe Shadow is here:

http://tv.adobe.com/watch/adobe-technology-sneaks-2012/adobe-shadow

Another useful debugging tool is WebKit Remote Debugging, which has been available since 2011, and is also shipping in iOS and Android. Details are available here:

http://www.webkit.org/blog/1875/announcing-remote-debugging-proto-col-v1-0/

ADDITIONAL USEFUL LINKS

A more recent Web site is HTML5 Please, which consists of contributions from well-known industry people:

http://html5please.com

The preceding Web site provides an input field where you can specify HTML5 and CSS3 features to determine if they are ready for use, and also see how to use them.

The W3C provides a free online validation service for HTML web pages, including HTML5 Web pages:

http://validator.w3.org/#validate_by_uri+with_options

The preceding Web site enables you to validate a URL, a file, or direct input of code.

The following Web site provides "boilerplate" templates for HTML5 e-mail input fields (and also templates for CSS and jQuery):

http://favbulous.com/post/848/6-useful-web-development-boilerplates

The following two links are for the HTML5 draft specification and the HTML5 Draft Recommendation (May 2009).

http://www.w3.org/TR/html5/
http://www.whatwg.org/specs/web-apps/current-work/

There is also a "Web developer edition" of the HTML5 specification that is streamlined for readability (without vendor-oriented details) that you can read here:

http://developers.whatwg.org

SUMMARY

This chapter provided an overview of several HTML5-related techniques for managing and persisting user-provided data using HTML5 `Forms`. In this chapter, you learned how to perform the following:

- Create HTML5 Web pages
- Use new semantic markup
- Use the HTML5 `<audio>` and `<video>` elements
- Create HTML5 Web pages with Web `Forms`
- Use simple CSS3 to enhance HTML5 Web pages
- Save data in a persistent manner to localStorage
- Save data in a persistent manner to an online database

The next three chapters discuss CSS3-based features (along with examples of combining CSS3 with SVG), and delve into some of the more sophisticated features of CSS3 that can help you create HTML5 Web pages with vivid and interesting visual effects.

INTRODUCTION TO CSS3

This chapter is the first of two chapters devoted entirely to CSS3. A significant amount of CSS3-related content is discussed and usually illustrated in a code sample or in a code block. In some cases concepts are presented without code samples due to space limitations; however, those concepts are included because it's important for you to be aware of them. Although many CSS3 topics are omitted, you will acquire a working knowledge of various aspects of CSS3.

By necessity, this chapter assumes that you have a moderate understanding of CSS, which means that you know how to set properties in CSS selectors. If you are unfamiliar with CSS selectors, there are many introductory articles available through an Internet search. If you are convinced that CSS operates under confusing and seemingly arcane rules, then it's probably worth your while to read an online article about CSS box rules, after which you will have a better understanding of the underlying logic of CSS.

The first part of this chapter contains code samples that illustrate how to create shadow effects, how to render rectangles with rounded corners, and how to use linear and radial gradients. The second part covers CSS3 transforms (`scale`, `rotate`, `skew`, and `translate`), along with code samples that illustrate how to apply transforms to HTML elements and to JPG files.

The third part of this chapter briefly discusses CSS3 Media Queries, which enable you to detect some characteristics of a device, and therefore render an HTML5 Web page based on those properties. You'll see some examples of using CSS3 Media Queries, such as changing the layout of a Web page based on the orientation of a mobile device. The last portion of this chapter discusses CSS3 Web Fonts, and you will see an example of how to use Web Fonts in an HTML5 Web page.

When you have completed this chapter you will know how to use the CSS3 transform methods `translate()`, `rotate()`, `skew()`, and `scale()`. This will prepare you for the material in Chapter 3, which contains code samples with additional new CSS3 features (such as 2D/3D animation), as well as an overview of some CSS frameworks.

You can launch the code samples in this chapter in a WebKit-based browser on a desktop or a laptop; you can also view them on mobile devices, provided that you launch them in a browser that supports the CSS3 features that are used in the code samples. For your convenience, many of the code samples in this chapter are accompanied by screenshots of the code samples on a Sprint Nexus S 4G and an Asus Prime Android ICS 10" tablet (both on Android ICS), which enables you to compare those screenshots with the corresponding images that are rendered on WebKit-based browsers on desktops and laptops. In Chapter 13, you will learn the process of creating Android applications that can launch HTML5 Web pages. Don't forget that the Android apk files are available on the accompanying DVD, and you can launch them on an Android that supports Android ICS (or higher).

CSS3 SUPPORT AND BROWSER-SPECIFIC PREFIXES FOR CSS3 PROPERTIES

Before we delve into the details of CSS3, there are two important details that you need to know about defining CSS3-based selectors for HTML pages. First, you need to know the CSS3 features that are available in different browsers. One of the best Web sites for determining browser support for CSS3 features is here:

http://caniuse.com/

The preceding link contains tabular information regarding CSS3 support in IE, Firefox, Safari, Chrome, and Opera.

Another highly useful tool that checks for CSS3 feature support is Enhance.js, which tests browsers to determine whether or not they can support a set of essential CSS and JavaScript properties, and then delivers features to those browsers that satisfy the test. You can download Enhance.js here:

http://filamentgroup.com/lab/introducing_enhancejs_smarter_safer_apply_progressive_enhancement/

The second detail that you need to know is that many CSS3 properties currently require browser-specific prefixes in order for them to work correctly. The prefixes -ie-, -moz-, and -o- are for Internet Explorer, Firefox, and Opera, respectively. As an illustration, the following code block shows examples of these prefixes:

```
-ie-webkit-border-radius: 8px;
-moz-webkit-border-radius: 8px;
-o-webkit-border-radius: 8px;
border-radius: 8px;
```

In your CSS selectors, specify the attributes with browser-specific prefixes before the "generic" attribute, which serves as a default choice in the event that the browser-specific attributes are not selected. The CSS3 code samples in this book contain WebKit-specific prefixes, which helps us keep the CSS stylesheets manageable in terms of size. If you need CSS stylesheets that work on multiple browsers (for current versions as well as older versions), there are essentially two options available. One option involves manually adding the CSS3 code with all the required browser-specific prefixes, which can be tedious to maintain and also error-prone. Another option is to use CSS toolkits or frameworks (discussed in the next chapter) that can programmatically generate the CSS3 code that contains all browser-specific prefixes.

In 2012, Opera announced its plans to also support the -webkit- prefix for CSS3 properties in addition to the -o- prefix, which is discussed extensively in a blog post by Bruce Lawson (a well-known Opera evangelist):

http://dev.opera.com/articles/view/opera-mobile-emulator-experimental-webkit-prefix-support/

Finally, an extensive list of browser-prefixed CSS properties is here:

http://peter.sh/experiments/vendor-prefixed-css-property-overview/

A QUICK OVERVIEW OF CSS3 FEATURES

CSS3 adopts a modularized approach for extending existing CSS2 functionality as well as supporting new functionality. As such, CSS3 can be logically divided into the following categories:

- Backgrounds/borders
- Color
- Media queries
- Multi-column layout
- Selectors

With CSS3 you can create boxes with rounded corners and shadow effects, create rich graphics effects using linear and radial gradients, detect portrait and landscape mode, detect the type of mobile device using media query selectors, and produce multi-column text rendering and formatting.

In addition, CSS3 enables you to define sophisticated node selection rules in selectors using pseudo-classes, first or last child (`first-child`, `last-child`, `first-of-type`, and `last-of-type`), and also pattern-matching tests for attributes of elements. Several sections in this chapter contain examples of how to create such selection rules.

CSS3 PSEUDO-CLASSES, ATTRIBUTE SELECTION, AND RELATIONAL SYMBOLS

This brief section contains examples of some pseudo-classes, followed by snippets that show you how to select elements based on the relative position of text strings in various attributes of those elements. Although this section focuses on the `nth-child()` pseudo-class, you will become familiar with various other CSS3 pseudo-classes. In the event that you need to use those pseudo-classes, a link is provided at the end of this section which contains more information and examples that illustrate how to use them.

CSS3 supports an extensive and rich set of pseudo-classes, including `nth-child()`, along with some of its semantically related "variants," such as `nth-of-type()`, `nth-first-of-type()`, `nth-last-of-type()`, and `nth-last-child()`.

CSS3 also supports Boolean selectors (which are also pseudo-classes) such as `empty`, `enabled`, `disabled`, and `checked`, which are very useful for Form-related HTML elements. One other pseudo-class is `not()`, which returns a set of elements that do not match the selection criteria.

CSS3 uses the meta-characters ^, $, and * (followed by the = symbol) in order to match an initial, terminal, or arbitrary position for a text string. If you are familiar with the Unix utilities `grep` and `sed`, as well as the `vi` text editor, then these meta-characters are very familiar to you.

CSS3 Pseudo-Classes

The CSS3 `nth-child()` is a very powerful and useful pseudo-class, and it has the following form:

```
nth-child(insert-a-keyword-or-linear-expression-here)
```

The following list provides various examples of using the `nth-child()` pseudo-class in order to match various subsets of child elements of an HTML `<div>` element (which can be substituted by other HTML elements as well):

```
div:nth-child(1): matches the first child element
div:nth-child(2):matches the second child element
div:nth-child(even):matches the even child elements
div:nth-child(odd): matches the odd child elements
```

The interesting and powerful aspect of the `nth-child()` pseudo-class is its support for linear expressions of the form `an+b`, where `a` is a positive integer and `b` is a non-negative integer, as shown here (using an HTML5 `<div>` element):

```
div:nth-child(3n):matches every third child, starting from
                                              position 0
div:nth-child(3n+1):matches every third child, starting from
                                              position 1
div:nth-child(3n+2):matches every third child, starting from
                                              position 2
div:nth-child(3n+3): the same as div:nth-child(3n)
```

As you can see in the last example above, if the value of the constant `b` equals the value of the constant `a`, the resulting expression "wraps around." Consequently, the expression `nth-child(an)` and `nth-child(an+a)` are equivalent. Hence, you can focus on the "offsets" that are between `0` and `a-1` inclusive (if it helps, this behavior is the same as modular arithmetic).

CSS3 Attribute Selection

You can specify CSS3 selectors that match HTML elements (as well as HTML elements based on the value of an attribute of an HTML element) using various regular expressions. For example, the following selector selects `img` elements whose `src` attribute starts with the text string `Laurie`, and then sets the `width` attribute and the `height` attribute of the selected `img` elements to `100px`:

```
img[src^="Laurie"] {
   width: 100px; height: 100px;
}
```

The preceding CSS3 selector is useful when you want to set different dimensions to images based on the name of the images (`Laurie`, `Shelly`, `Steve`, and so forth).

The following HTML `<img>` elements do not match the preceding selector:

```
<img src="3Laurie" width="200" height="200"/>
<img src="3Laurrie" width="200" height="200"/>
```

The following selector selects HTML `img` elements whose `src` attribute ends with the text string `jpeg`, and then sets the `width` attribute and the `height` attribute of the selected `img` elements to `150px`:

```
img[src$="jpeg"] {
  width: 150px; height: 150px;
}
```

The preceding CSS3 selector is useful when you want to set different dimensions to images based on the type of the images (`jpg`, `png`, `jpeg`, and so forth).

The following selector selects HTML `img` elements whose `src` attribute contains any occurrence of the text string `baby`, and then sets the `width` attribute and the `height` attribute of the selected HTML `img` elements to `200px`:

```
img[src*="baby"] {
  width: 200px; height: 200px;
}
```

The preceding CSS3 selector is useful when you want to set different dimensions to images based on the "classification" of the images (`mybaby`, `yourbaby`, `babygirl`, `babyboy`, and so forth).

If you want to learn more about patterns (and their descriptions) that you can use in CSS3 selectors, an extensive list is available here:

http://www.w3.org/TR/css3-selectors

CSS3 Relational Symbols

In addition to support for pseudo-classes, CSS3 also introduces the symbols >, +, and ~ in order to specify the type of relationship between elements that will be selected as part of the "result set," as shown here:

`div > p`: matches `<p>` elements that are a child of a `<div>` element.

`div + p`: matches one `<p>` element that follows a `<div>` element, both of which have the same parent element.

`div ~ p`: matches all the `<p>` elements that 1.) are on the same level, 2.) follow a `<div>` element, and 3.) have the same parent element.

These relational symbols are very useful when you need to process lists of elements, typically in conjunction with user-based selections, in HTML5

Web pages that contain HTML `Form` elements. Furthermore, you can use the same relational symbols in HTML5 Web pages that contain jQuery and jQuery Mobile code.

This concludes the first part of this chapter. The next section delves into CSS3 graphics-oriented effects, such as rounded corners and shadow effects.

CSS3 SHADOW EFFECTS AND ROUNDED CORNERS

CSS3 shadow effects are useful for creating vivid visual effects with simple selectors. You can use shadow effects for text as well as rectangular regions. CSS3 also enables you to easily render rectangles with rounded corners, so you do not need JPG files in order to create this effect.

Specifying Colors with RGB and HSL

Before we delve into the interesting features of CSS3, you need to know how to represent colors. One method is to use `(R,G,B)` triples, which represent the `Red`, `Green`, and `Blue` components of a color. For instance, the triples `(255,0,0)`, `(255,255,0)`, and `(0,0,255)` represent the colors `Red`, `Yellow`, and `Blue`. Other ways of specifying the color include: the hexadecimal triples `(FF, 0, 0)` and `(FF, 0, 0)`; the decimal triple `(100%,0,0)`; or the string `#F00`.

You can also use `(R,G,B,A)`, where the fourth component specifies the opacity, which is a decimal number between `0` (invisible) to `1` (opaque) inclusive.

However, there is also the `HSL` (`Hue`, `Saturation`, and `Luminosity`) representation of colors, where the first component is an angle between `0` and `360` (0 degrees is north), and the other two components are percentages between `0` and `100`. For instance, `(0,100%,50%)`, `(120, 100%, 50%)`, and `(240, 100%, 50%)` represent the colors `Red`, `Green`, and `Blue`, respectively.

The code samples in this book use `(R,G,B)` and `(R,G,B,A)` for representing colors, but you can perform an Internet search to obtain more information regarding `HSL`.

CSS3 and Text Shadow Effects

A shadow effect for text can make a Web page look more vivid and appealing, and many websites look better with shadow effects that are not overpowering for users (unless you specifically need to do so).

Listing 2.1 displays the contents of the HTML5 page `TextShadow1.html` that illustrate how to render text with a shadow effect, and Listing 2.2 displays the contents of the CSS stylesheet `TextShadow1.css` that is referenced in Listing 2.1.

Listing 2.1 TextShadow1.html

```
<!DOCTYPE html>
<html lang="en">
<head>
  <meta charset="utf-8"/>
  <title>CSS Text Shadow Example</title>
  <link href="TextShadow1.css" rel="stylesheet" type="text/css">
</head>

<body>
  <div id="text1">
    Line One Shadow Effect
  </div>
  <div id="text2">
    Line Two Shadow Effect
  </div>
  <div id="text3">
    Line Three Vivid Effect
  </div>

<div id="text4">
    <span id="dd">13</span>
    <span id="mm">August</span>
    <span id="yy">2012</span>
  </div>

  <div id="text5">
    <span id="dd">13</span>
    <span id="mm">August</span>
    <span id="yy">2012</span>
  </div>

  <div id="text6">
    <span id="dd">13</span>
    <span id="mm">August</span>
    <span id="yy">2012</span>
  </div>
</body>
</html>
```

The code in Listing 2.1 is straightforward: there is a reference to the CSS stylesheet `TextShadow1.css` that contains two CSS selectors. One selector specifies how to render the HTML `<div>` element whose `id` attribute has value `text1`, and the other selector matches the HTML `<div>` element whose `id` attribute is `text2`. Although the CSS3 `rotate()` function is included in this example, we'll defer a more detailed discussion of this function until later in this chapter.

Listing 2.2 TextShadow1.css

```
#text1 {
  font-size: 24pt;
  text-shadow: 2px 4px 5px #00f;
}

#text2 {
  font-size: 32pt;
  text-shadow: 0px 1px 6px #000,
               4px 5px 6px #f00;
}

#text3 {
  font-size: 40pt;
  text-shadow: 0px 1px 6px  #fff,
               2px 4px 4px  #0ff,
               4px 5px 6px  #00f,
               0px 0px 10px #444,
               0px 0px 20px #844,
               0px 0px 30px #a44,
               0px 0px 40px #f44;
}

#text4 {
  position: absolute;
  top: 200px;
  right: 200px;
  font-size: 48pt;
  text-shadow: 0px 1px 6px  #fff,
               2px 4px 4px  #0ff,
               4px 5px 6px  #00f,
               0px 0px 10px #000,
               0px 0px 20px #448,
               0px 0px 30px #a4a,
               0px 0px 40px #fff;
  -webkit-transform: rotate(-90deg);
}
```

```
#text5 {
  position: absolute;
  left: 0px;
  font-size: 48pt;
  text-shadow: 2px 4px 5px #00f;
  -webkit-transform: rotate(-10deg);
}

#text6 {
  float: left;
  font-size: 48pt;
  text-shadow: 2px 4px 5px #f00;
  -webkit-transform: rotate(-170deg);
}

/* 'transform' is explained later */
#text1:hover, #text2:hover, #text3:hover,
#text4:hover, #text5:hover, #text6:hover {
-webkit-transform : scale(2) rotate(-45deg);
-transform : scale(2) rotate(-45deg);
}
```

The first selector in Listing 2.2 specifies a `font-size` of `24` and a `text-shadow` that renders text with a blue background (represented by the hexadecimal value `#00f`). The attribute `text-shadow` specifies (from left to right) the x-coordinate, the y-coordinate, the blur radius, and the color of the shadow. The second selector specifies a font-size of `32` and a red shadow background (`#f00`). The third selector creates a richer visual effect by specifying multiple components in the `text-shadow` property, which were chosen by experimenting with effects that are possible with different values in the various components.

The final CSS3 selector creates an animation effect whenever users hover over any of the six text strings. The details of the animation will be deferred until later in this chapter.

Figure 2.1 displays the result of matching the selectors in the CSS stylesheet `TextShadow1.css` with the HTML `<div>` elements in the HTML page `TextShadow1.html`. The landscape-mode screenshot is taken from an Android application (based on the code in Listing 2.1 and Listing 2.2) running on a Nexus S 4G (Android ICS) smartphone.

FIGURE 2.1 CSS3 text shadow effects.

CSS3 and Box Shadow Effects

You can also apply a shadow effect to a box that encloses a text string, which can be effective in terms of drawing attention to specific parts of a Web page. However, the same caveat regarding over-use applies to box shadows.

Listing 2.3 displays the contents of the HTML page BoxShadow1.html that renders a box shadow effect, and Listing 2.4 displays the contents of Box-Shadow1.css that contains the associated CSS3 selectors.

Listing 2.3 BoxShadow1.html

```
<!DOCTYPE html>
<html lang="en">
<head>
  <meta charset="utf-8"/>
  <title>CSS Box Shadow Example</title>
  <link href="BoxShadow1.css" rel="stylesheet" type="text/css">
</head>

<body>
  <div id="box1"> Line One with a Box Effect </div>
  <div id="box2"> Line Two with a Box Effect </div>
  <div id="box3"> Line Three with a Box Effect </div>
</body>
</html>
```

The code in Listing 2.3 references the CSS stylesheet BoxShadow1.css (instead of TextShadow1.css) that contains three CSS selectors. These selectors specify how to render the HTML <div> elements whose id attribute has value box1, box2, and box3, respectively (and these three HTML <div> elements are defined in BoxShadow1.html).

Listing 2.4 BoxShadow1.css

```
#box1 {
  position:relative;top:10px;
  width: 50%;
  height: 30px;
  font-size: 20px;
  -moz-box-shadow: 10px 10px 5px #800;
  -webkit-box-shadow: 10px 10px 5px #800;
  box-shadow: 10px 10px 5px #800;
}

#box2 {
  position:relative;top:20px;
  width: 80%;
  height: 50px;
  font-size: 36px;
  padding: 10px;
  -moz-box-shadow: 14px 14px 8px #008;
  -webkit-box-shadow: 14px 14px 8px #008;
  box-shadow: 14px 14px 8px #008;
}

#box3 {
```

```
position:relative;top:30px;
width: 80%;
height: 60px;
font-size: 52px;
padding: 10px;
-moz-box-shadow: 14px 14px 8px #008;
-webkit-box-shadow: 14px 14px 8px #008;
box-shadow: 14px 14px 8px #008;
}
```

The first selector in Listing 2.4 specifies the attributes `width`, `height`, and `font-size`, which control the dimensions of the associated HTML `<div>` element and also the enclosed text string. The next three attributes consist of a Mozilla-specific `box-shadow` attribute, followed by a `WebKit`-specific `box-shadow` property, and finally the "generic" `box-shadow` attribute.

Figure 2.2 displays a landscape-mode screenshot that is taken from a Nexus S 4G with Android ICS (based on the code in Listing 2.3 and Listing 2.4).

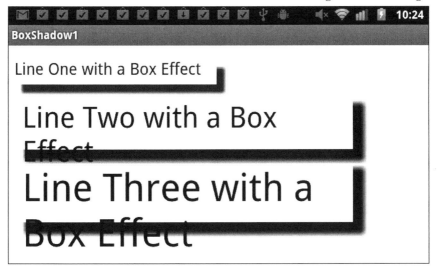

FIGURE 2.2 CSS3 box shadow effect on a Sprint Nexus S 4G with Android ICS.

CSS3 and Rounded Corners

Web developers have waited a long time for rounded corners in CSS, and CSS3 makes it very easy to render boxes with rounded corners.

Listing 2.5 displays the contents of the HTML page `RoundedCorners1.html` that renders text strings in boxes with rounded corners, and Listing 2.6 displays the CSS file `RoundedCorners1.css`.

Listing 2.5 RoundedCorners1.html

```html
<!DOCTYPE html>
<html lang="en">
<head>
  <meta charset="utf-8"/>
  <title>CSS Text Shadow Example</title>
  <link href="RoundedCorners1.css" rel="stylesheet" type="text/
css">
</head>

<body>
  <div id="outer">
    <a href="#" class="anchor">Text Inside a Rounded Rectangle</a>
  </div>

  <div id="text1">
    Line One of Text with a Shadow Effect
  </div>

  <div id="text2">
    Line Two of Text with a Shadow Effect
  </div>
</body>
</html>
```

Listing 2.5 contains a reference to the CSS stylesheet RoundedCorners1. css that contains three CSS selectors that match the elements whose id attribute has values anchor, text1, and text2, respectively. The CSS selectors defined in RoundedCorners1.css create visual effects, and as you will see, the hover pseudo-selector enables you to create animation effects.

Listing 2.6 RoundedCorners1.css

```css
a.anchor:hover {
background: #00F;
}

a.anchor {
background: #FF0;
font-size: 24px;
font-weight: bold;
padding: 4px 4px;
color: rgba(255,0,0,0.8);
text-shadow: 0 1px 1px rgba(0,0,0,0.4);
-webkit-transition: all 2.0s ease;
-transition: all 2.0s ease;
```

```
-webkit-border-radius: 8px;
border-radius: 8px;
}

#text1 {
 font-size: 24pt;
 text-shadow: 2px 4px 5px #00f;
}

#text2 {
 font-size: 32pt;
 text-shadow: 4px 5px 6px #f00;
}

#round1 {
 -moz-border-radius-bottomleft: 20px;
 -moz-border-radius-bottomright: 20px;
 -moz-border-radius-topleft: 20px;
 -moz-border-radius-topright: 20px;
 -moz-box-shadow: 2px 2px 10px #ccc;
 -webkit-border-bottom-left-radius: 20px;
 -webkit-border-bottom-right-radius: 20px;
 -webkit-border-top-left-radius: 20px;
 -webkit-border-top-right-radius: 20px;
 -webkit-box-shadow: 2px 2px 10px #ccc;
 background-color: #f00;
 margin: 25px auto 0;
 padding: 25px 10px;
 text-align: center;
 width: 260px;
}
```

Listing 2.6 contains the selector a.anchor:hover that changes the text color from yellow (#FF0) to blue (#00F) during a two-second interval whenever users hover over any anchor element with their mouse.

The selector a.anchor contains various attributes that specify the dimensions of the box that encloses the text in the <a> element, along with two new pairs of attributes. The first pair specifies the transition attribute (and a WebKit-specific prefix), which we will discuss later in this chapter. The second pair specifies the border-radius attribute (and the WebKit-specific attribute) whose value is 8px, which determines the radius (in pixels) of the rounded corners of the box that encloses the text in the <a> element. The last two selectors are identical to the selectors in Listing 2.1.

Figure 2.3 displays the result of matching the selectors that are defined in the CSS stylesheet RoundedCorners1.css with elements in the HTML page

`RoundedCorners1.html` in a landscape-mode screenshot taken from an Asus Prime tablet with Android ICS.

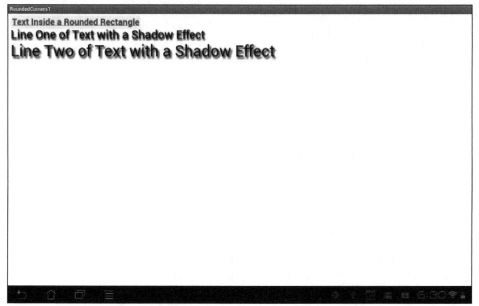

FIGURE 2.3 CSS3 rounded corners effect on an Asus Prime tablet with Android ICS.

CSS3 GRADIENTS

CSS3 supports linear gradients and radial gradients, which enable you to create gradient effects that are as visually rich as gradients in other technologies such as SVG. The code samples in this section illustrate how to define linear gradients and radial gradients in CSS3 and then match them to HTML elements.

Linear Gradients

CSS3 linear gradients require you to specify one or more "color stops," each of which specifies a start color, an end color, and a rendering pattern. `WebKit`-based browsers support the following syntax to define a linear gradient:

- A start point

- An end point
- A start color using `from()`
- Zero or more stop-colors
- An end color using `to()`

A start point can be specified as an `(x,y)` pair of numbers or percentages. For example, the pair `(100,25%)` specifies the point that is `100` pixels to the right of the origin and `25%` of the way down from the top of the pattern. Recall that the origin is located in the upper-left corner of the screen.

Listing 2.7 displays the contents of `LinearGradient1.html` and Listing 2.8 displays the contents of `LinearGradient1.css`, which illustrate how to use linear gradients with text strings that are enclosed in `<p>` elements and an `<h3>` element.

Listing 2.7 LinearGradient1.html

```
<!doctype html>
<html lang="en">
<head>
  <meta charset="utf-8"/>
  <title>CSS Linear Gradient Example</title>
  <link href="LinearGradient1.css" rel="stylesheet" type="text/
css">
</head>

<body>
  <div id="outer">
    <p id="line1">line 1 with a linear gradient</p>
    <p id="line2">line 2 with a linear gradient</p>
    <p id="line3">line 3 with a linear gradient</p>
    <p id="line4">line 4 with a linear gradient</p>
    <p id="outline">line 5 with Shadow Outline</p>
    <h3><a href="#">A Line of Gradient Text</a></h3>
  </div>
</body>
</html>
```

Listing 2.7 is a simple Web page containing four `<p>` elements and one `<h3>` element. Listing 2.7 also references the CSS stylesheet `LinearGradient1.css` that contains CSS selectors that match the four `<p>` elements and the `<h3>` element in Listing 2.7.

Listing 2.8 LinearGradient1.css

```
#line1 {
```

```
width: 50%;
font-size: 32px;
background-image: -webkit-gradient(linear, 0% 0%, 0% 100%,
                                   from(#fff), to(#f00));
background-image: -gradient(linear, 0% 0%, 0% 100%,
                            from(#fff), to(#f00));
-webkit-border-radius: 4px;
border-radius: 4px;
}

#line2 {
width: 50%;
font-size: 32px;
background-image: -webkit-gradient(linear, 100% 0%, 0% 100%,
                                   from(#fff), to(#ff0));
background-image: -gradient(linear, 100% 0%, 0% 100%,
                            from(#fff), to(#ff0));
-webkit-border-radius: 4px;
border-radius: 4px;
}

#line3 {
width: 50%;
font-size: 32px;
background-image: -webkit-gradient(linear, 0% 0%, 0% 100%,
                                   from(#f00), to(#00f));
background-image: -gradient(linear, 0% 0%, 0% 100%,
                            from(#f00), to(#00f));
-webkit-border-radius: 4px;
border-radius: 4px;
}

#line4 {
width: 50%;
font-size: 32px;
background-image: -webkit-gradient(linear, 100% 0%, 0% 100%,
                                   from(#f00), to(#00f));
background-image: -gradient(linear, 100% 0%, 0% 100%,
                            from(#f00), to(#00f));
-webkit-border-radius: 4px;
border-radius: 4px;
}

#outline {
font-size: 2.0em;
font-weight: bold;
```

```
color: #fff;
text-shadow: 1px 1px 1px rgba(0,0,0,0.5);
}

h3 {
width: 50%;
position: relative;
margin-top: 0;
font-size: 32px;
font-family: helvetica, ariel;
}

h3 a {
position: relative;
color: red;
text-decoration: none;
-webkit-mask-image:  -webkit-gradient(linear, left top, left bot-
tom,
                          from(rgba(0,0,0,1)),
                          color-stop(50%, rgba(0,0,0,0.5)),
                          to(rgba(0,0,0,0))));
}

h3:after {
content:"This is a Line of Gradient Text";
color: blue;
}
```

The first selector in Listing 2.8 specifies a `font-size` of 32 for text, a `border-radius` of 4 (which renders rounded corners), and a linear gradient that varies from white to blue, as shown here:

```
#line1 {
width: 50%;
font-size: 32px;
background-image: -webkit-gradient(linear, 0% 0%, 0% 100%,
                          from(#fff), to(#f00));
background-image: -gradient(linear, 0% 0%, 0% 100%,
                          from(#fff), to(#f00));
-webkit-border-radius: 4px;
border-radius: 4px;
}
```

As you can see, the first selector contains two attributes with a `-webkit-` prefix and two standard attributes without this prefix. Since the next three selectors in Listing 2.8 are similar to the first selector, we will not discuss their content.

The next CSS selector creates a text outline with a nice shadow effect by rendering the text in white with a thin black shadow, as shown here:

```
color: #fff;
text-shadow: 1px 1px 1px rgba(0,0,0,0.5);
```

The final portion of Listing 2.8 contains three selectors that affect the rendering of the <h3> element and its embedded <a> element: the h3 selector specifies the width and font size; the h3 selector specifies a linear gradient; and the h3:after selector specifies the text string to display. Other attributes are specified, but these are the main attributes for these selectors.

Figure 2.4 displays the result of matching the selectors in the CSS stylesheet LinearGradient1.css to the HTML page LinearGradient1.html in a landscape-mode screenshot taken from an Android application running on an Asus Prime tablet with Android ICS.

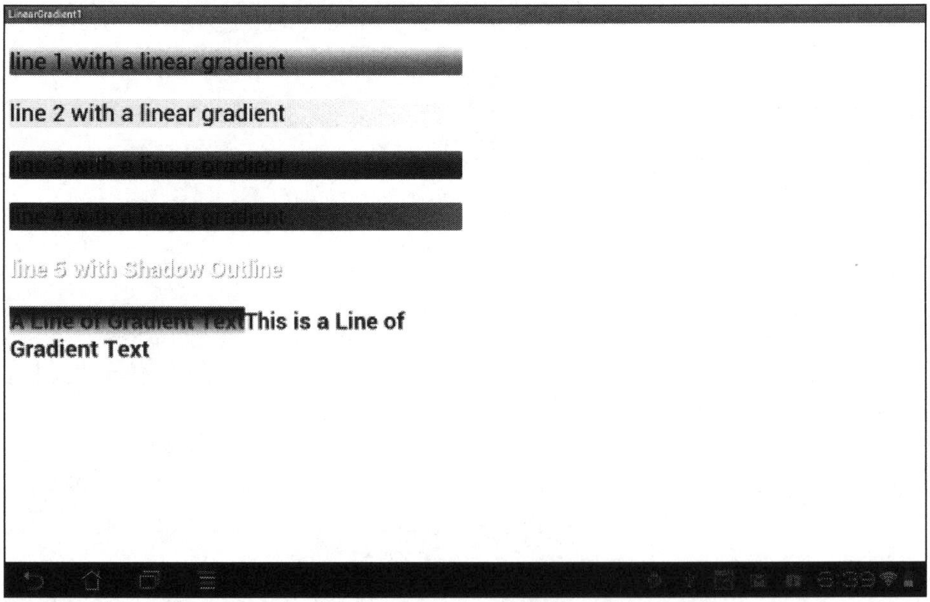

FIGURE 2.4 CSS3 linear gradient effect on an Asus Prime tablet with Android ICS.

Radial Gradients

CSS3 radial gradients are more complex than CSS3 linear gradients, but you can use them to create more complex gradient effects. WebKit-based browsers support the following syntax to define a radial gradient:

- A start point

- A start radius
- An end point
- An end radius
- A start color using `from()`
- Zero or more stop-colors
- An end color using `to()`

Notice that the syntax for a radial gradient is similar to the syntax for a linear gradient, except that you also specify a start radius and an end radius.

Listing 2.9 displays the contents of `RadialGradient1.html` and Listing 2.10 displays the contents of `RadialGradient1.css`, which illustrate how to render various circles with radial gradients.

Listing 2.9 RadialGradient1.html

```
<!doctype html>
<html lang="en">
<head>
  <meta charset="utf-8"/>
  <title>CSS Radial Gradient Example</title>
  <link href="RadialGradient9.css" rel="stylesheet" type="text/
css">
</head>

<body>
 <div id="outer">
  <div id="radial3">Text3</div>
  <div id="radial2">Text2</div>
  <div id="radial4">Text4</div>
  <div id="radial1">Text1</div>
 </div>
</body>
</html>
```

Listing 2.9 contains five HTML `<div>` elements whose `id` attribute has value `outer`, `radial1`, `radial2`, `radial3`, and `radial4`, respectively. Listing 2.9 also references the CSS stylesheet `RadialGradient1.css` that contains five CSS selectors that match the five HTML `<div>` elements.

Listing 2.10 RadialGradient1.css

```
#outer {
position: relative; top: 10px; left: 0px;
}

#radial1 {
```

```
font-size: 24px;
width:  300px;
height: 300px;
position: absolute; top: 300px; left: 300px;

background: -webkit-gradient(
   radial, 500 40%, 0, 301 25%, 360, from(red),
   color-stop(0.05, orange), color-stop(0.4, yellow),
   color-stop(0.6, green), color-stop(0.8, blue),
   to(#fff)
 );
}


#radial2 {
font-size: 24px;
width:  500px;
height: 500px;
position: absolute; top: 100px; left: 100px;

background: -webkit-gradient(
   radial, 500 40%, 0, 301 25%, 360, from(red),
   color-stop(0.05, orange), color-stop(0.4, yellow),
   color-stop(0.6, green), color-stop(0.8, blue),
   to(#fff)
 );
}


#radial3 {
font-size: 24px;
width:  600px;
height: 600px;
position: absolute; top: 0px; left: 0px;

background: -webkit-gradient(
   radial, 500 40%, 0, 301 25%, 360, from(red),
   color-stop(0.05, orange), color-stop(0.4, yellow),
   color-stop(0.6, green), color-stop(0.8, blue),
   to(#fff)
 );
-webkit-box-shadow:  0px 0px 8px #000;
}


#radial4 {
font-size: 24px;
width:  400px;
height: 400px;
```

```
position: absolute; top: 200px; left: 200px;

background: -webkit-gradient(
  radial, 500 40%, 0, 301 25%, 360, from(red),
  color-stop(0.05, orange), color-stop(0.4, yellow),
  color-stop(0.6, green), color-stop(0.8, blue),
  to(#fff)
 );
}
```

The first part of the `#radial1` selector in Listing 2.10 contains the attributes `width` and `height` that specify the dimensions of a rendered rectangle, and also a `position` attribute that is similar to the `position` attribute in the `#outer` selector.

The `#radial1` also contains a `background` attribute that defines a radial gradient using the `-webkit-` prefix, as shown here:

```
background: -webkit-gradient(
  radial, 100 25%, 20, 100 25%, 40, from(blue), to(#fff)
 );
```

The preceding radial gradient specifies the following:

- A start point of (`100, 25%`)
- A start radius of 20
- An end point of (`100, 25%`)
- An end radius of 40
- A start color of blue
- An end color of white (`#fff`)

Notice that the start point and end point are the same, which renders a set of concentric circles that vary from blue to white.

The other four selectors in Listing 2.10 have the same syntax as the first selector, but the rendered radial gradients are significantly different. You can create these (and other) effects by specifying different start points and end points, and by specifying a start radius that is larger than the end radius.

The `#radial4` selector creates a "ringed effect" by means of two `stop-color` attributes, as shown here:

```
color-stop(0.2, orange), color-stop(0.4, yellow),
color-stop(0.6, green), color-stop(0.8, blue),
```

You can add additional color-stop attributes to create more complex radial gradients.

Figure 2.5 displays the result of matching the selectors in the CSS stylesheet `RadialGradient1.css` to the HTML page `RadialGradient1.ht-`

`mlin` a landscape-mode screenshot taken from an Android application running on an Asus Prime tablet with Android ICS.

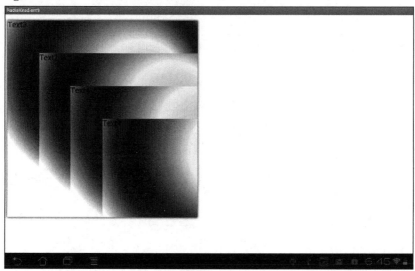

FIGURE 2.5 CSS3 radial gradient effect on an Asus Prime tablet with Android ICS.

Online Tools For Creating CSS3 Gradients

Now that you know how to create gradient definitions manually, you may also be happy to know that there are various online tools that can create gradients for you. The tools that are available at the following websites support the creation of visually appealing CSS3 gradient effects:

http://css3please.com
http://www.westciv.com/tools/gradients
*http://gradients.glrza*d.com

Since these tools provide different sets of options, experiment with each Web site to evaluate which of these tools are best suited for your specific needs. If these tools lack the functionality that you need, perform an Internet search for additional Web sites that create CSS3-based effects.

CSS3 2D TRANSFORMS

In addition to transitions, CSS3 supports four transforms that you can apply to 2D shapes and also to JPG files. The four CSS3 transforms are `scale`, rotate, skew, and translate. The following sections contain code samples that illustrate how to apply each of these CSS3 transforms to a set of JPG files. The animation effects occur when users hover over any of the JPG files; moreover, you can create "partial" animation effects by moving your mouse quickly between adjacent JPG files.

Zoom In/Out Effects with Scale Transforms

The CSS3 transform attribute allows you to specify the scale() function in order to create zoom in/out effects, and the syntax for the scale() method looks like this:

```
scale(someValue);
```

You can replace someValue with any non-zero number. When someValue is between 0 and 1, you will reduce the size of the 2D shape or JPG file, which creates a "zoom out" effect; values greater than 1 for someValue will increase the size of the 2D shape or JPG file, which creates a "zoom in" effect; and a value of 1 does not perform any changes.

Listing 2.11 displays the contents of Scale1.html and Listing 2.12 displays the contents of Scale1.css, which illustrate how to scale JPG files to create a "hover box" image gallery.

Listing 2.11 Scale1.html

```
<!DOCTYPE html>
<html lang="en">
<head>
  <meta charset="utf-8"/>
  <title>CSS Scale Transform Example</title>
  <link href="Scale1.css" rel="stylesheet" type="text/css">
</head>

<body>
  <header>
   <h1>Hover Over any of the Images:</h1>
  </header>

  <div id="outer">
    <img src="Laurie1.jpeg" class="scaled" width="150"
height="150"/>
   <img src="Laurie2.jpeg" class="scaled" width="150" height="150"/>
   <img src="Laurie1.jpeg" class="scaled" width="150" height="150"/>
   <img src="Laurie2.jpeg" class="scaled" width="150" height="150"/>
  </div>
```

```
</body>
</html>
```

Listing 2.11 references the CSS stylesheet `Scale1.css` (which contains selectors for creating scaled effects) and four HTML `<img>` elements that references the JPG files `Lauriel.jpeg` and `Laurie2.jpeg`. The remainder of Listing 2.12 is straightforward, with simple boilerplate text and HTML elements.

Listing 2.12 `Scale1.css`

```css
#outer {
float: left;
position: relative; top: 50px; left: 50px;
}

img {
-webkit-transition: -webkit-transform 1.0s ease;
-transition: transform 1.0s ease;
}

img.scaled {
  -webkit-box-shadow: 10px 10px 5px #800;
  box-shadow: 10px 10px 5px #800;
}

img.scaled:hover {
-webkit-transform : scale(2);
-transform : scale(2);
}
```

The `img` selector in Listing 2.12 contains specifies a `transition` property that applies a `transform` effect that occurs during a one-second interval using the `ease` function, as shown here:

```css
-transition: transform 1.0s ease;
```

Next, the selector `img.scaled` specifies a `box-shadow` property that creates a reddish shadow effect (which you saw earlier in this chapter), as shown here:

```css
img.scaled {
  -webkit-box-shadow: 10px 10px 5px #800;
  box-shadow: 10px 10px 5px #800;
}
```

Finally, the selector `img.scaled:hover` specifies a `transform` attribute that uses the `scale()` function in order to double the size of the associated

JPG file whenever users hover over any of the `<img>` elements with their mouse, as shown here:

```
-transform : scale(2);
```

Since the `img` selector specifies a one-second interval using an `ease` function, the scaling effect will last for one second. Experiment with different values for the CSS3 `scale()` function and also different value for the time interval to create the animation effects that suit your needs.

Another point to remember is that you can scale both horizontally and vertically:

```
img {
-webkit-transition: -webkit-transform 1.0s ease;
-transition: transform 1.0s ease;
}

img.mystyle:hover {
-webkit-transform : scaleX(1.5) scaleY(0.5);
-transform : scaleX(1.5) scaleY(0.5);
}
```

Figure 2.6 displays the result of matching the selectors in the CSS stylesheet `Scale1.css` to the HTML page `Scale1.html`. The landscape-mode screenshot is taken from an Android application (based on the code in Listing 2.11 and Listing 2.12) running on a Nexus S 4G smartphone with Android ICS.

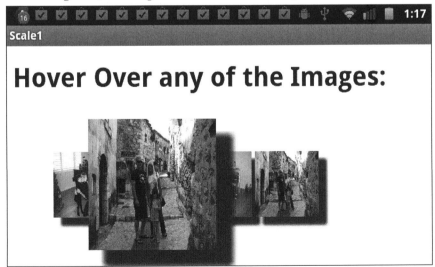

FIGURE 2.6 CSS3-based scaling effect on JPG files.

Rotate Transforms

The CSS3 `transform` attribute allows you to specify the `rotate()` function in order to create scaling effects, and its syntax looks like this:

```
rotate(someValue);
```

You can replace `someValue` with any number. When `someValue` is positive, the rotation is clockwise; when `someValue` is negative, the rotation is counterclockwise; and when `someValue` is zero, there is no rotation effect. In all cases, the initial position for the rotation effect is the positive horizontal axis.

Listing 2.13 displays the contents of `Rotate1.html` and Listing 2.14 displays the contents of `Rotate1.css`, which illustrate how to rotate JPG files in opposite directions.

Listing 2.13 Rotate1.html

```
<!DOCTYPE html>
<html lang="en">
<head>
  <meta charset="utf-8"/>
  <title>CSS Rotate Transform Example</title>
  <link href="Rotate1.css" rel="stylesheet" type="text/css">
</head>

<body>
  <header>
   <h1>Hover Over any of the Images:</h1>
  </header>

  <div id="outer">
   <img src="Laurie1.jpeg" class="imageL" width="150" height="150"/>
   <img src="Laurie2.jpeg" class="imageR" width="150" height="150"/>
   <img src="Laurie1.jpeg" class="imageL" width="150" height="150"/>
   <img src="Laurie2.jpeg" class="imageR" width="150" height="150"/>
  </div>
</body>
</html>
```

Listing 2.13 references the CSS stylesheet `Rotate1.css` (which contains selectors for creating rotation effects) and an HTML `<img>` element that references the JPG files `Laurie1.jpeg` and `Laurie2.jpeg`. The remainder of Listing 2.13 consists of simple boilerplate text and HTML elements.

Listing 2.14 Rotate1.css

```
#outer {
float: left;
```

```
position: relative; top: 100px; left: 150px;
}

img {
-webkit-transition: -webkit-transform 1.0s ease;
-transition: transform 1.0s ease;
}

img.imageL {
  -webkit-box-shadow: 14px 14px 8px #800;
  box-shadow: 14px 14px 8px #800;
}

img.imageR {
  -webkit-box-shadow: 14px 14px 8px #008;
  box-shadow: 14px 14px 8px #008;
}

img.imageL:hover {
-webkit-transform : scale(2) rotate(-45deg);
-transform : scale(2) rotate(-45deg);
}

img.imageR:hover {
-webkit-transform : scale(2) rotate(360deg);
-transform : scale(2) rotate(360deg);
}
```

Listing 2.14 contains the `img` selector that specifies a `transition` attribute that creates an animation effect during a one-second interval using the `ease` timing function, as shown here:

```
-transition: transform 1.0s ease;
```

Next, the selectors `img.imageL` and `img.imageR` contain a property that renders a reddish and bluish background shadow, respectively.

The selector `img.imageL:hover` specifies a `transform` attribute that performs a counterclockwise scaling effect (doubling the original size) and a rotation effect (45 degrees counterclockwise) whenever users hover over the `<img>` element with their mouse, as shown here:

```
-transform : scale(2) rotate(-45deg);
```

The selector `img.imageR:hover` is similar, except that it performs a clockwise rotation of 360 degrees.

Figure 2.7 displays the result of matching the selectors in the CSS stylesheet `Rotate1.css` to the elements in the HTML page `Rotate1.html`. The landscape-mode screenshot is taken from an Android application (based on the code in Listing 2.13 and Listing 2.14) running on a Nexus S 4G smart-phone with Android ICS.

FIGURE 2.7 CSS3-based rotation effects on JPG files.

Skew Transforms

The CSS3 transform attribute allows you to specify the `skew()` function in order to create skewing effects, and its syntax looks like this:
```
skew(xAngle, yAngle);
```
You can replace `xAngle` and `yAngle` with any number. When `xAngle` and `yAngle` are positive, the skew effect is clockwise; when `xAngle` and `yAngle` are negative, the skew effect is counterclockwise; and when `xAngle` and `yAngle` are zero, there is no skew effect. In all cases, the initial position for the skew effect is the positive horizontal axis.

Listing 2.15 displays the contents of `skew1.html` and Listing 2.16 displays the contents of `skew1.css`, which illustrate how to skew a JPG file.

Listing 2.15 Skew1.html

```html
<!DOCTYPE html>
<html lang="en">
<head>
  <meta charset="utf-8"/>
  <title>CSS Skew Transform Example</title>
  <link href="Skew1.css" rel="stylesheet" type="text/css">
```

```
</head>

<body>
  <header>
   <h1>Hover Over any of the Images:</h1>
  </header>

  <div id="outer">
    <img src="Laurie1.jpeg" class="skewed1" width="150"
            height="150"/>
    <img src="Laurie2.jpeg" class="skewed2" width="150"
            height="150"/>
    <img src="Laurie1.jpeg" class="skewed3" width="150"
            height="150"/>
    <img src="Laurie2.jpeg" class="skewed4" width="150"
            height="150"/>
  </div>
</body>
</html>
```

Listing 2.15 references the CSS stylesheet Skew1.css (which contains selectors for creating skew effects) and an `<img>` element that references the JPG files Laurie1.jpeg and Laurie2.jpeg. The remainder of Listing 2.15 consists of simple boilerplate text and HTML elements.

Listing 2.16 Skew1.css

```
#outer {
float: left;
position: relative; top: 100px; left: 100px;
}

img {
-webkit-transition: -webkit-transform 1.0s ease;
-transition: transform 1.0s ease;
}

img.skewed1 {
  -webkit-box-shadow: 14px 14px 8px #800;
  box-shadow: 14px 14px 8px #800;
}

img.skewed2 {
  -webkit-box-shadow: 14px 14px 8px #880;
  box-shadow: 14px 14px 8px #880;
}
```

```
img.skewed3 {
  -webkit-box-shadow: 14px 14px 8px #080;
  box-shadow: 14px 14px 8px #080;
}

img.skewed4 {
  -webkit-box-shadow: 14px 14px 8px #008;
  box-shadow: 14px 14px 8px #008;
}

img.skewed1:hover {
-webkit-transform : scale(2) skew(-10deg, -30deg);
-transform : scale(2) skew(-10deg, -30deg);
}

img.skewed2:hover {
-webkit-transform : scale(2) skew(10deg, 30deg);
-transform : scale(2) skew(10deg, 30deg);
}

img.skewed3:hover {
-webkit-transform : scale(0.4) skew(-10deg, -30deg);
-transform : scale(0.4) skew(-10deg, -30deg);
}

img.skewed4:hover {
-webkit-transform : scale(0.5, 1.5) skew(10deg, -30deg);
-transform : scale(0.5, 1.5) skew(10deg, -30deg);
opacity:0.5;
}
```

Listing 2.16 contains the img selector and specifies a transition attribute that creates an animation effect during a one-second interval using the ease timing function, as shown here:

```
-transition: transform 1.0s ease;
```

The four selectors img.skewed1, img.skewed2, img.skewed3, and img.skewed4 create background shadow effects with darker shades of red, yellow, green, and blue, respectively (all of which you have seen in earlier code samples).

The selector img.skewed1:hover specifies a transform attribute that performs a skew effect whenever users hover over the first <img> element with their mouse, as shown here:

```
-transform : scale(2) skew(-10deg, -30deg);
```

The other three CSS3 selectors also use a combination of the CSS functions skew() and scale() to create distinct visual effects. Notice that the fourth hover selector also sets the opacity property to 0.5, which takes place in parallel with the other effects in this selector.

Figure 2.8 displays the result of matching the selectors in the CSS stylesheet Skew1.css to the elements in the HTML page Skew1.html. The landscape-mode screenshot is taken from an Android application (based on the code in Listing 2.15 and Listing 2.16) running on a Nexus S 4G smartphone with Android ICS.

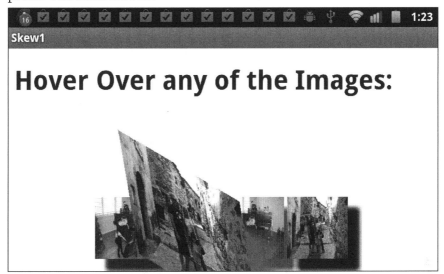

FIGURE 2.8 CSS3-based skew effects on JPG files.

Translate Transforms

The CSS3 transform attribute allows you to specify the translate() function in order to create an effect that involves a horizontal and/or vertical "shift" of an element, and its syntax looks like this:

```
translate(xDirection, yDirection);
```

The translation is in relation to the origin, which is the upper-left corner of the screen. Thus, positive values for xDirection and yDirection produce a shift toward the right and a shift downward, respectively, whereas negative values for xDirection and yDirection produce a shift toward the left and a shift upward; zero values for xDirection and yDirection do not cause any translation effect.

Listing 2.17 displays the contents of Translate1.html and Listing 2.18 displays the contents of Translate1.css, which illustrate how to apply a translation effect to a JPG file.

Listing 2.17 `Translate1.html`

```
<!DOCTYPE html>
<html lang="en">
<head>
  <meta charset="utf-8"/>
  <title>CSS Translate Transform Example</title>
  <link href="Translate1.css" rel="stylesheet" type="text/css">
</head>

<body>
  <header>
   <h1>Hover Over any of the Images:</h1>
  </header>

  <div id="outer">
    <img src="Laurie1.jpeg" class="trans1" width="150"
height="150"/>
    <img src="Laurie2.jpeg" class="trans2" width="150"
height="150"/>
    <img src="Laurie1.jpeg" class="trans3" width="150"
height="150"/>
    <img src="Laurie2.jpeg" class="trans4" width="150"
height="150"/>
  </div>
</body>
</html>
```

Listing 2.17 references the CSS stylesheet `Translate1.css` (which contains selectors for creating translation effects) and an `<img>` element that references the JPG files `Laurie1.jpeg` and `Laurie2.jpeg`. The remainder of Listing 2.17 consists of straightforward boilerplate text and HTML elements.

Listing 2.18 `Translate1.css`

```
#outer {
float: left;
position: relative; top: 100px; left: 100px;
}

img {
-webkit-transition: -webkit-transform 1.0s ease;
-transition: transform 1.0s ease;
}

img.trans1 {
  -webkit-box-shadow: 14px 14px 8px #800;
  box-shadow: 14px 14px 8px #800;
```

```
}

img.trans2 {
  -webkit-box-shadow: 14px 14px 8px #880;
  box-shadow: 14px 14px 8px #880;
}

img.trans3 {
  -webkit-box-shadow: 14px 14px 8px #080;
  box-shadow: 14px 14px 8px #080;
}

img.trans4 {
  -webkit-box-shadow: 14px 14px 8px #008;
  box-shadow: 14px 14px 8px #008;
}

img.trans1:hover {
-webkit-transform : scale(2) translate(100px, 50px);
-transform : scale(2) translate(100px, 50px);
}

img.trans2:hover {
-webkit-transform : scale(0.5) translate(-50px, -50px);
-transform : scale(0.5) translate(-50px, -50px);
}

img.trans3:hover {
-webkit-transform : scale(0.5,1.5) translate(0px, 0px);
-transform : scale(0.5,1.5) translate(0px, 0px);
}

img.trans4:hover {
-webkit-transform : scale(2) translate(50px, -50px);
-transform : scale(2) translate(100px, 50px);
}
```

Listing 2.17 contains the `img` selector and specifies a transform effect during a one-second interval using the `ease` timing function, as shown here:
```
-transition: transform 1.0s ease;
```
The four selectors `img.trans1`, `img.trans2`, `img.trans3`, and `img.trans4` create background shadow effects with darker shades of red, yellow, green, and blue, respectively, just as you saw in the previous section.

The selector `img.trans1:hover` specifies a `transform` attribute that performs a scale effect and a translation effect whenever users hover over the first `<img>` element with their mouse, as shown here:

```
-webkit-transform : scale(2) translate(100px, 50px);
transform : scale(2) translate(100px, 50px);
```

The other three selectors contain similar code involving a combination of a translate and a scaling effect, each of which creates a distinct visual effect.

Figure 2.9 displays the result of matching the selectors defined in the CSS3 stylesheet `Translate1.css` to the elements in the HTML page `Translate1.html`. The landscape-mode screenshot is taken from an Android application (based on the code in Listing 2.17 and Listing 2.18) running on a Nexus S 4G smartphone with Android ICS.

FIGURE 2.9 JPG files with CSS3 scale and translate effects.

CSS3 MEDIA QUERIES

This section contains an assortment of CSS3 Media Queries, which are very useful logical expressions that enable you detect mobile applications on devices with differing physical attributes and orientations. For example, with CSS3 Media Queries you can change the dimensions and layout of your applications so that they render appropriately on smartphones as well as tablets.

Specifically, you can use CSS3 Media Queries in order to determine the following characteristics of a device:

- Browser window width and height
- Device width and height

- Orientation (landscape or portrait)
- Aspect ratio
- Device aspect ratio
- Resolution

CSS3 Media Queries are Boolean expressions that contain one or more "simple terms" (connected with `and` or `or`) that evaluate to `true` or `false`. Thus, CSS3 Media Queries represent conditional logic that evaluates to either `true` or `false`.

As an example, the following link element loads the CSS stylesheet `mystuff.css` only if the device is a screen and the maximum width of the device is `480px`:

```
<link rel="stylesheet" type="text/css"
    media="screen and (max-device-width: 480px)" href="mystuff.css"/>
```

The preceding link contains a media attribute that specifies two components: a `media` type of `screen` and a query that specifies a `max-device-width` whose value is `480px`. The supported values for media in CSS3 Media Queries are `braille`, `embossed`, `handheld`, `print`, `projection`, `screen`, `speech`, `tty`, and `tv`.

The next CSS3 Media Query checks the media type, the maximum device width, and the resolution of a device:

```
@media screen and (max-device-width: 480px) and (resolution:
160dpi) {
  #innerDiv {
    float: none;
  }
}
```

If the CSS3 Media Query in the preceding code snippet evaluates to `true`, then the nested CSS selector will match the HTML element whose `id` attribute has the value `innerDiv`, and its `float` property will be set to `none` on any device whose maximum screen width is `480px`. As you can see, it's possible to create compact CSS3 Media Queries that contain non-trivial logic, which is obviously very useful because CSS3 does not have any `if/then/else` construct that is available in other programming languages.

The next CSS3 Media Query tests the media type, the minimum device width, and the resolution of a device:

```
@media screen and (min-device-width: 481px) and (resolution:
```

```
160dpi) {
  #innerDiv {
    float: left;
  }
}
```

In the preceding CSS3 selector, the HTML element whose `id` attribute has the value `innerDiv` will have a `float` property whose value is left on any device whose minimum screen width is `481px`.

The next CSS3 Media Query sets the width of `div` elements to `100px` if the screen width is between `321` and `480`:

```
@media screen and (min-width: 321px) and (max-width: 480px) {
   div { width: 100px; }
}
```

In the following example, `myphone.css` would apply to devices that the browser considers "handheld" or devices with screens <= 320px wide.
```
<link rel="stylesheet" media="handheld, only screen and (max-de-
vice-width: 320px)" href="myphone.css">
```

NOTE *The use of the "only" keyword in Media Queries causes non CSS3-compli-ant browsers to ignore the rule. As another example, the following* `<link>` *loads a CSS stylesheet for screen sizes between* `641px` *and* `800px`:

```
<link rel="stylesheet" media="only screen and (min-width: 641px)
and (max-width: 800px)" href="wide.css">
```

Media Queries can be included in inline `<style>` tags, as shown in this query, which is for all media types in `portrait` mode:

```
<style>   @media only all and (orientation: portrait) { ... } </
style>
```

Now that you have a basic understanding of the sorts of things that you can do with CSS3 Media Queries, you can follow the code in the next section, which contains an HTML5 Web page and a CSS3 stylesheet that illustrate how to handle a change of orientation of a mobile device.

Detecting Orientation with CSS3 Media Queries

Listing 2.19 and 2.20 display the contents of the stylesheet `CSS3MediaQuery1.css` and the HTML5 Web page `CSS3MediaQuery1.html` that illustrate how to change the size of two images when users rotate their mobile device.

Listing 2.19 CSS3MediaQuery1.css

```
@media all and (orientation: portrait) {
```

```
 #img1, #img2 {
    float: left;
    width:120px;height:300px;
    }
}

@media all and (orientation: landscape) {
   #img1, #img2 {
    float: left;
    width:200px;height:200px;
    }
}
```

The code in Listing 2.19 is straightforward: the first selector specifies values for the `float`, `width`, and `height` properties of two JPG files when your mobile device is in portrait mode; the second selector specifies different values for the `width` and `height` properties of the two JPG files when your device is in landscape mode.

Listing 2.20 CSS3MediaQuery1.html

```
<!DOCTYPE html>
<html lang="en">
<head>
  <meta charset="utf-8"/>
  <title>CSS3 Media Query </title>
  <link href="CSS3MediaQuery1.css" rel="stylesheet" type="text/
css">
</head>

<body>
  <header>
   <h2>Rotate Your Device:</h2>
  </header>

  <div id="outer">
    <div id="one">
      <img id="img1" src="Laurie1.jpeg"/>
    <div>
    <div id="two">
      <img id="img2" src="Laurie1.jpeg"/>
    <div>
  </div>
</body>
</html>
```

Listing 2.20 references the CSS stylesheet `CSS3MediaQuery1.css` in Listing 2.19 in order to apply CSS selectors to the JPG files in the `<body>` element. Next, the HTML `<body>` element contains two HTML `<div>` elements whose `id` attributes have the values `img1` and `img2` that are referenced in the corresponding CSS selectors.

Figure 2.10 displays the result of rendering the HTML page `CSS3Media-Query.html` in landscape mode on a Sprint Nexus S 4G smartphone with Android ICS.

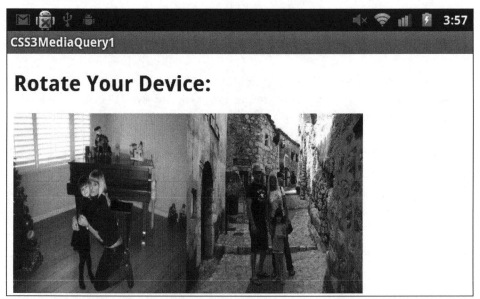

FIGURE 2.10 CSS3 Media Query on a Sprint Nexus S 4G smartphone with Android ICS.

Detecting Orientation with Simple JavaScript

Earlier in this chapter, you saw how to use CSS3 Media Queries in order to detect an orientation change of a mobile device. However, keep in mind that it's also possible to do the same thing with simple JavaScript code, so you are not "forced" to use CSS3 Media Queries.

Listing 2.21 displays the contents of the Web page `CSS3OrientationJS1.html` that illustrates how to use standard JavaScript in order to change the size of two images when users rotate their mobile device.

Listing 2.21 CSS3OrientationJS1.html

```
<!DOCTYPE html>
<html lang="en">
<head>
  <meta charset="utf-8"/>
```

```
<title>CSS3 and Orientation with JS</title>

<style>
 #img1, #img2 {
    float: left;
    width:120px;height:300px;
 }
</style>

<script>
  function init() {
    // Event listener to determine device orientation
    window.onresize = function() { updateOrientation(); }
  }

  function updateOrientation() {
    var orientation = window.orientation;

    switch(orientation) {
      case 0: /* portrait mode */
        document.getElementById("img1").style.width  = "120px";
        document.getElementById("img1").style.height = "300px";
        document.getElementById("img2").style.width  = "120px";
        document.getElementById("img2").style.height = "300px";
         break;

      case 90: /* landscape (screen turned to the left) */
        document.getElementById("img1").style.width  = "200px";
        document.getElementById("img1").style.height = "200px";
        document.getElementById("img2").style.width  = "200px";
        document.getElementById("img2").style.height = "200px";
         break;

      case -90: /* landscape (screen turned to the right) */
        document.getElementById("img1").style.width  = "200px";
        document.getElementById("img1").style.height = "200px";
        document.getElementById("img2").style.width  = "200px";
        document.getElementById("img2").style.height = "200px";
         break;
    }
  }
</script>
</head>

<body onload="init()">
  <header>
```

```
    <h2>Rotate Your Device:</h2>
  </header>

  <div id="outer">
    <div id="one">
      <img id="img1" src="Laurie1.jpeg"/>
    </div>
    <div id="two">
      <img id="img2" src="Laurie1.jpeg"/>
    </div>
  </div>
</body>
</html>
```

As you can see, there is much more code in Listing 2.21 compared to List-ing 2.20. In essence, the code uses the value of the variable `window.orienta-tion` in order to detect four different orientations of your mobile device, and in each of those four cases, the dimensions of the JPG files are updated with the following type of code:

```
document.getElementById("img1").style.width = "120px";
document.getElementById("img1").style.height = "300px";
```

Although this is a very simple example, hopefully this code gives you an appreciation for the capabilities of CSS3 Media Queries.

WORKING WITH WEB FONTS

Web fonts were introduced in CSS2, and now you can combine them with CSS3 selectors. In case you have not worked with them, you declare each form of the font family using the `@font-face` selector and then reference each font by means of the `font-family` property. Please make sure that you check the license terms for each font that you plan to use in your Web pages.

Listing 2.22 and Listing 2.23 display the contents of `WebFonts1.html` and `WebFonts1.css` that illustrate how to use CSS3 Web Fonts in an HTML5 Web page.

Listing 2.22 WebFonts1.html

```
<!DOCTYPE html>
<html lang="en">
  <head>
    <meta charset="utf-8"/>
    <title>CSS Transition Example</title>
    <link href="WebFonts1.css" rel="stylesheet" type="text/css">
  </head>
```

```
<body>
  <h1>H1 Heading: a WebFont and Shadow</h1>
  <h2>H2 Heading: a WebFont, Spacing, and Shadow</h2>
  <h3>H3 Heading: Does not Use a WebFont or Effects</h3>
</body>
</html>
```

Listing 2.22 references the CSS stylesheet `WebFonts1.css` (shown in Listing 2.23), followed by some boilerplate HTML that is styled according to the Web Font in the CSS stylesheet.

Listing 2.23 WebFonts1.css

```
@font-face {
  font-family: "Kimberley";
  src: url(http://www.princexml.com/fonts/larabie/kimberle.ttf)
format("truetype");
}

h1 {
  font-family: "Kimberley", sans-serif;
  text-shadow: 2px 4px 5px #00f;
}

@import url(http://www.princexml.com/fonts/larabie/index.css) all;

h2 { font-family: Goodfish, serif;
  letter-spacing: 0.1em;
  text-shadow: 0px 1px 6px #000,
               4px 5px 6px #f00;
}
```

Listing 2.23 starts with a `@font-face` definition that specifies the value of the `font-family`, along with the URL where the font is located.

Next, the `h1` selector specifies the font for the HTML `<h1>` element in Listing 2.22, as well as an `h2` selector that specifies a font and also a text shadow effect to style the HTML `<h2>` element.

In between these two selectors there is an `@import` rule that contains definitions for many other fonts, including the `Goodfish` font that is specified in the `h2` selector. The definitions in the imported stylesheet have lower priority than definitions that have already been defined in Listing 2.23.

Online Resources for Fonts

Several online resources are available for fonts. If you plan to work with custom fonts, consider using "Font Dragr," which is an online tool for testing custom fonts:

http://www.css3.info/css3-resource-preview-custom-web-fonts-with-font-dragr/

An excellent resource for a wide assortment of free fonts is here:

http://www.fontsquirrel.com/

Font Squirrel provides prepackaged font face "kits" that contain TrueType Fonts (TTF), EOT fonts, WOFF fonts, SVG fonts, and Cufon fonts. Moreover, you can upload your own fonts and use Font Squirrel's font face generator in order to generate your own font face kit.

CSS3 AND PRESENTATION TOOLS

There are various open source presentation tools based on CSS3 transforms and transitions (and some JavaScript) that enable you to create nice presentations.

One tool is `Deck.js`, which uses CSS3 as well as jQuery, and its homepage is here:

http://imakewebthings.github.com/deck.js/

A "slide" in `Deck.js` consists of HTML whose structure is shown in Listing 2.24.

Listing 2.24 A Sample Slide

```html
<body class="deck-container on-slide-1">
  <section class="slide deck-previous">
    <h1>A Simple Presentation</h1>
  </section>

  <section class="slide deck-current">
    <h1>Slide Header</h1>
    <p>The main points:</p>
    <ul>
     <li>Item #1</li>
     <li>Item #2</li>
     <li>Item #3</li>
    </ul>
  </section>

  <section class="slide deck-next">
    <h1>Slide Two</h1>
```

```
      <blockquote cite="http://some.website.com">
        <p>Quod erat demonstratum </p>
        <p><cite>Unknown</cite></p>
      </blockquote>
    </section>
  </body>
```

`Deck.js` contains a module for keeping track of the states of the deck and its slides, and it uses CSS in order to render each state.

Another presentation tool is `impress.js`, which uses CSS3 and JavaScript (but not jQuery). You can download the source code on its homepage:

https://github.com/bartaz/impress.js

`Impress.js` uses CSS3 3D transforms for presenting elements in 3D, along with CSS transitions for handling transitions between presentation steps. Keep in mind that if your browser does not have hardware acceleration, you might experience noticeable delays between transitions. `Impress. js` also requires browser support for some other HTML5 functionality, including `classList` and `dataset`. Consult the documentation on the Web site for additional details.

There will undoubtedly be many other presentation tools available in the near future, and you can perform an Internet search to find other tools and compare their supported features. If you feel inspired, perhaps you can contribute enhancements to their projects, or perhaps create your own presentation tool!

SUMMARY

This chapter showed you how to create graphics effects, shadow effects, and how to use CSS3 transforms in CSS3. You learned how to create animation effects that you can apply to HTML elements. You saw how to define CSS3 selectors to do the following:

- Render rounded rectangles
- Create shadow effects for text and 2D shapes
- Create linear and radial gradients
- Use the methods `translate()`, `rotate()`, `skew()`, and `scale()`
- Create CSS3-based animation effects

Now that you have a basic understanding of some CSS3 graphics-oriented functionality, you are ready for the next chapter, which shows you how to use `keyframes` in order to create CSS3 2D and 3D animation effects.

CSS3 2D/3D ANIMATION AND CSS FRAMEWORKS

This chapter continues the discussion of CSS3 that was introduced in Chapter 2, starting with an example of applying CSS3 transforms to a CSS3-based cube, followed by examples of CSS3 transitions for creating simple animation effects (such as glow effects and bouncing effects) and also examples of creating 3D effects. This part of the chapter also contains code samples that show you how to define CSS3 selectors that perform more sophisticated effects with text, such as rendering multi-column text.

The second part of this chapter shows you how to define CSS3 selectors to create 3D effects and 3D animation effects. Specifically, you will learn how to use CSS3 `keyframes` and the CSS3 functions `scale3d()`, `rotate3d()`, and `translate3d()` that enable you to create 3D animation effects.

The final portion of this chapter introduces you to CSS-based frameworks (such as Sass, Compass, and CSS Scaffold) that can help you develop code more quickly and also simplify the task of code maintenance. Although you can create CSS stylesheets manually, keep in mind that CSS frameworks provide powerful functionality that is not available in pure CSS3.

Although the HTML pages in the three CSS3-oriented chapters of this book use CSS3 without JavaScript, keep in mind that you can also combine CSS3 with JavaScript in order to create visual effects that are easier than using CSS3 alone. In fact, Chapter 6 contains an example of combining jQuery with CSS3 in order to create rich graphics effects.

Recall that you can use CSS3 `Media Queries` (discussed in Chapter 2) for rendering HMTL5 Web pages differently on different mobile devices. This chapter also includes an example of using JavaScript to detect orientation changes in your mobile device. Thus, you can use a combination of JavaScript, CSS3, and other technologies in your HTML5 Web pages, and the decision depends on your software and hardware constraints (such as no JavaScript, or support for smartphones and tablets) and as well as the required functionality for your HTML5 Web pages.

There are several advantages to using CSS3 in your HTML5 Web pages. First, you will learn how to create your own visual effects using CSS3 3D. Second, toolkits such as jQuery Mobile rely heavily on CSS3 for rendering content and for creating animation effects (including page transitions). Hence, the knowledge that you gain from the CSS3-related chapters in this book will give you a foundation that will help you understand how jQuery Mobile performs its "magic," and perhaps even also make it easier for you to read the jQuery Mobile source code.

Third, it's easier to create very impressive CSS3-based graphics and animation effects (especially in 3D) than creating the same effects in other languages (including SVG). Fourth, your code is likelier to be more compact if you use CSS3 instead of relying on JavaScript and JPG files for graphics and animation, which is a particularly important point for mobile devices. Note that hardware acceleration is mandatory for many CSS3 3D effects, and the good news is that an increasing number of mobile devices support hardware acceleration for CSS3 (there is also such support for HTML5 Canvas).

Remember that the screenshots in Chapter 2 were taken on an Asus Prime Android ICS 10" tablet, a Sprint Nexus S 4G mobile phone with Android ICS, and an iPad 3; the same is true for the screenshots in this chapter. Once again, you can compare the screenshots in this chapter with the result of rendering the code samples on WebKit-based laptop and desktop browsers.

A CSS3-BASED CUBE

This section shows you how to create a cube using CSS3, which involves rendering the front face (a rectangle), the top face (a parallelogram), and the right face (also a parallelogram).

We will use the following CSS3 transforms and effects in this section:

1. The CSS3 skew() function to create the left and right faces.
2. The CSS3 scale() and rotate() functions to create the top face.
3. Linear and radial gradients for shading effects.

The example in this section contains a lot of CSS3 code, and it's probably helpful for you to launch the Web page in a browser as you study the code.

Listing 3.1 displays the contents of 3DCube1.html and Listing 3.2 displays the contents of 3DCube1.css, which illustrate how to simulate a cube in CSS3.

Listing 3.1 3DCube1.html

```
<!DOCTYPE html>
<html lang="en">
<head>
 <meta charset="utf-8"/>
<title>CSS 3D Cube Example</title>
   <link href="3DCSS1.css" rel="stylesheet" type="text/css">
</head>

<body>
<header>
 <h1>Hover Over the Cube Faces:</h1>
</header>

   <div id="outer">
    <div id="top">Text1</div>
    <div id="left">Text2</div>
    <div id="right">Text3</div>
   </div>
  </body>
  </html>
```

Listing 3.1 is a straightforward HTML page that references the CSS stylesheet 3DCSS1.css, which contains the CSS3 selectors for styling the HTML <div> elements in this Web page.

Listing 3.2 3DCube1.css

```
/* animation effects */
#right:hover {
-webkit-transition: -webkit-transform 3.0s ease;
-transition: transform 3.0s ease;

-webkit-transform : scale(1.2) skew(-10deg, -30deg) rotate(-
45deg);
-transform : scale(1.2) skew(-10deg, -30deg) rotate(-45deg);
}

#left:hover {
-webkit-transition: -webkit-transform 2.0s ease;
-transition: transform 2.0s ease;
```

```
-webkit-transform : scale(0.8) skew(-10deg, -30deg) rotate(-45deg);
-transform : scale(0.8) skew(-10deg, -30deg) rotate(-45deg);
}

#top:hover {
-webkit-transition: -webkit-transform 2.0s ease;
-transition: transform 2.0s ease;

-webkit-transform : scale(0.5) skew(-20deg, -30deg) rotate(45deg);
-transform : scale(0.5) skew(-20deg, -30deg) rotate(45deg);
}

/* size and position */
#right, #left, #top {
position:relative;  padding: 0px;  width: 200px;  height: 200px;
}
#left {
  font-size: 48px;
  left: 20px;

  background-image:
    -webkit-radial-gradient(red 4px, transparent 28px),
    -webkit-repeating-radial-gradient(red 0px,  yellow 4px, green
                                                            8px,
                              red 12px, transparent 26px,
                              blue 20px, red 24px,
                              transparent 28px, blue 12px),
    -webkit-repeating-radial-gradient(red 0px,  yellow 4px, green
                                                            8px,
                              red 12px, transparent 26px,
                              blue 20px, red 24px,
                              transparent 28px, blue 12px);

  background-size: 100px 40px, 40px 100px;
  background-position: 0 0;

  -webkit-transform: skew(0deg, 30deg);
}

#right {
  font-size: 48px;
  width:  170px;
  top: -192px;
  left: 220px;

  background-image:
```

```
      -webkit-radial-gradient(red 4px, transparent 48px),
      -webkit-repeating-linear-gradient(0deg, red 5px,   green 4px,
                                  yellow 8px, blue 12px,
                                  transparent 16px, red 20px,
                                  blue 24px, transparent 28px,
                                  transparent 32px),
      -webkit-radial-gradient(blue 8px, transparent 68px);

  background-size: 120px 120px, 24px 24px;
  background-position: 0 0;

  -webkit-transform: skew(0deg, -30deg);
}

#top {
  font-size: 48px;
  top: 50px;
  left: 105px;

  background-image:
    -webkit-radial-gradient(white 2px, transparent 8px),
    -webkit-repeating-linear-gradient(45deg, white 2px,   yellow
8px,
                                  green 4px, red 12px,
                                  transparent 26px, blue 20px,
                                  red 24px, transparent 28px,
                                  blue 12px),
    -webkit-repeating-linear-gradient(-45deg, white 2px,   yellow
8px,
                                  green 4px, red 12px,
                                  transparent 26px, blue 20px,
                                  red 24px, transparent 28px,
                                  blue 12px);

  background-size: 100px 30px, 30px 100px;
  background-position: 0 0;

  -webkit-transform: rotate(60deg) skew(0deg, -30deg); scale(1,
1.16);
}
```

The first three selectors in Listing 3.2 define the animation effects whenever users hover on the top, left, or right faces of the cube. In particular, the `#right:hover` selector performs an animation effect during a three-second interval whenever users hover over the right face of the cube, as shown here:

```
#right:hover {
-webkit-transition: -webkit-transform 3.0s ease;
```

```
-transition: transform 3.0s ease;

-webkit-transform : scale(1.2) skew(-10deg, -30deg) rotate(-
45deg);
-transform : scale(1.2) skew(-10deg, -30deg) rotate(-45deg);
}
```

The transition attribute is already familiar to you, and notice that the transform attribute specifies the CSS3 transform functions `scale()`, `skew()`, and `rotate()`, all of which you have seen already in this chapter. These three functions are invoked simultaneously, which means that you will see a scaling, skewing, and rotating effect happening at the same time instead of sequentially.

The last three selectors in Listing 3.2 define the properties of each face of the cube. For example, the `#left` selector specifies the font size for some text and also positional attributes for the left face of the cube. The most complex portion of the `#left` selector is the value of the `background-image` attribute, which consists of a `WebKit`-specific combination of a radial gradient, a repeating radial gradient, and another radial gradient. Notice that the left face is a rectangle that is transformed into a parallelogram using this line of code:

```
-webkit-transform: skew(0deg, -30deg);
```

The `#top` selector and `#right` selector contain code that is comparable to the `#left` selector, and you can experiment with their values in order to create other pleasing visual effects.

Figure 3.1 displays the result of matching the CSS selectors in `3DCube1.css` to the `<div>` elements in the HTML page `3DCube1.html` in a landscape-mode screenshot taken from an Android application running on an Asus Prime Android ICS 10" tablet.

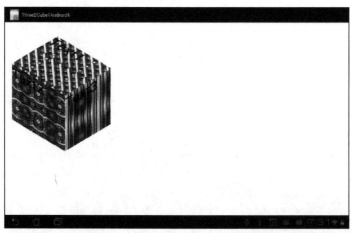

FIGURE 3.1 A CSS3-based cube on an Asus Prime Android ICS 10" tablet.

CSS3 TRANSITIONS

CSS3 transitions involve changes to CSS values in a smooth fashion. They are initiated by user gestures, such as mouse clicks, focus, or "hover" effects. Transitions are very useful because you can use them to create animation effects on CSS properties for a specific length of time using a so-called "easing functions," which produce animation effects at different rates of change. For example, some easing functions vary at a constant rate during an animation effect, whereas others create non-linear effects (slow-fast-slow, fast-slow-fast, and so forth). Easing functions are powerful and useful because they enable you to create realistic effects, such as watching a baseball moving toward you through the air (this is an example of fast-slow-fast animation).

WebKit originally developed CSS3 transitions, and they are also available in Safari, Chrome (3.2 or higher), Opera (10.5 or higher), and Firefox (4.0 or higher) by using browser-specific prefixes, which you will see later in this section. Keep in mind that there are toolkits (such as jQuery and Prototype) that support similar transitions effects as their CSS3-based counterparts.

The basic syntax for creating a CSS transition is a "triple" that specifies:

- A CSS property
- A duration (in seconds)
- A transition timing function

Here is an example of a WebKit-based transition:
```
-webkit-transition-property: background;
-webkit-transition-duration: 0.5s;
-webkit-transition-timing-function: ease;
```
Fortunately, you can also combine these transitions in one line, as shown here:
```
-webkit-transition: background 0.5s ease;
```
Here is an example of a CSS3 selector that includes these transitions:
```
a.foo {
padding: 3px 6px;
background: #f00;
-webkit-transition: background 0.5s ease;
}

a.foo:focus, a.foo:hover {
background: #00f;
}
```

Transitions currently require browser-specific prefixes in order for them to work correctly in all browsers. Here is an example of specifying a property using browser-specific prefixes for Internet Explorer, Firefox, and Opera:

```
-ie-webkit-transition: background 0.5s ease;
-moz-webkit-transition: background 0.5s ease;
-o-webkit-transition: background 0.5s ease;
```

Currently you can specify one of the following transition timing functions (using browser-specific prefixes):

- Ease
- Ease-in
- Ease-out
- Ease-in-out
- Cubic-bezier

If none of these transition functions is sufficient for your needs, you can create custom functions using this online tool:

www.matthewlein.com/ceaser

A Web site that displays a comparison of transition timing functions is here:

http://www.roblaplaca.com/examples/bezierBuilder/

You can specify many properties with `-webkit-transition-property`. An extensive list of properties is here:

https://developer.mozilla.org/en/CSS/CSS_transitions

SIMPLE CSS3 ANIMATION EFFECTS

The CSS3-based code samples that you have seen so far involved primarily static visual effects (but you did see how to use the hover pseudo-selector to create an animation effect). The CSS3 code samples in this section illustrate how to create "glowing" effects and "bouncing" effects for form-based elements.

Animation Effects with CSS3 keyframes

The CSS3 `@keyframes` rule contains a set of selectors that are identified via a number that represents a percentage between `0` and `100`. You also specify the duration of an animation effect on an element; the duration of each portion of the `keyframe` is calculated as a percentage of the duration of the effect.

For example, the following CSS3 `@keyframes` rule uses the `-webkit-` prefix, and it defines what happens during the first half of the animation as well as the second half of the animation:

```
@-webkit-keyframes glow {
  0% {
    -webkit-box-shadow: 0 0 24px rgba(255, 255, 255, 0.5);
  }
  50% {
    -webkit-box-shadow: 0 0 24px rgba(255, 0, 0, 0.9);
  }
  100% {
    -webkit-box-shadow: 0 0 24px rgba(255, 255, 255, 0.5);
  }
}
```

Thus, if the animation effect lasts for 10 seconds, then the first two animation effects last for 5 seconds, followed by the visual effect that is created when the animation effect has completed.

The preceding code block is a simple yet illustrative example that shows you how to use CSS3 `@keyframes` rules, and you will learn about the details of the preceding animation effect in the next section.

Glowing Effects

The example in this section uses `keyframes` and the `hover` pseudo-selector in order to create an animation effect whenever users hover with their mouse on a specific element in an HTML page.

Listing 3.3 displays the contents of `Transition1.html` and Listing 3.4 displays the contents of `Transition1.css`, which contains CSS3 selectors that create a "glowing" effect on an input field.

Listing 3.3 `Transition1.html`

```
<!DOCTYPE html>
<html lang="en">
<head>
  <meta charset="utf-8"/>
```

```
<title>CSS Animation Example</title>
<link href="Transition1.css" rel="stylesheet" type="text/css">
</head>

<body>
  <div id="outer">
    <input id="input" type="text" value="This is an input line"</
input>
  </div>
</body>
</html>
```

Listing 3.3 is a simple HTML page that contains a reference to the CSS stylesheet `Transition1.css` and one HTML `<div>` element that contains an `<input>` field element. As you will see, an animation effect is created when users hover over the `<input>` element with their mouse.

Listing 3.4 Transition1.css

```
#outer {
position: relative; top: 20px; left: 20px;
}

@-webkit-keyframes glow {
  0% {
    -webkit-box-shadow: 0 0 24px rgba(255, 255, 255, 0.5);
  }
  50% {
    -webkit-box-shadow: 0 0 24px rgba(255, 0, 0, 0.9);
  }
  100% {
    -webkit-box-shadow: 0 0 24px rgba(255, 255, 255, 0.5);
  }
}

#input {
font-size: 24px;
-webkit-border-radius: 4px;
border-radius: 4px;
}

#input:hover {
 -webkit-animation: glow 2.0s 3 ease;
}
```

Listing 3.4 contains a CSS3 `@keyframes` rule called `glow` that specifies three shadow effects. The first shadow effect (which occurs at time `0` of the animation effect) renders a white color with an opacity of 0.5. The second shadow effect (at the midway point of the animation effect) renders a red color with an opacity of 0.9. The third shadow effect (which occurs at the end of the animation effect) is the same as the first animation effect.

The #input selector matches the input field in Transition1.html which produces a rounded rectangle. The selector #input:hover selector uses the glow @keyframes rule in order to create an animation effect for a two-second interval, repeated three times, using an ease function, as shown here:

```
-webkit-animation: glow 2.0s 3 ease;
```

Figure 3.2 displays the result of launching the HTML page Transition1.html on a Sprint Nexus S 4G with Android ICS. Keep in mind that on desktop browsers you can trigger the animation effect simply by hovering on the input field, whereas on mobile devices you need to tap the input field in order to trigger the animation effect, which will also cause the keyboard to be displayed.

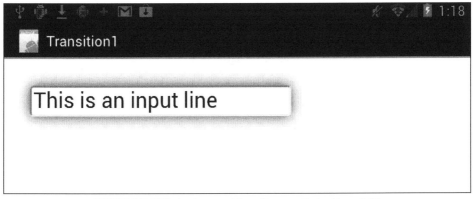

FIGURE 3.2 CSS3 glowing transition effect on a Sprint Nexus S 4G.

Image Fading and Rotating Effects with CSS3

The previous example showed you how to create a glowing animation effect. This section shows you how to create a fading effect with JPG images.

Listing 3.5 displays the contents of FadingImages1.html and Listing 3.6 displays the contents of FadeRotateImages1.css, which illustrate how to create a "fading" effect on a JPG file and a glowing effect on another JPG file.

Listing 3.5 FadeRotateImages1.html

```
<!DOCTYPE html>
<html lang="en">
```

```
<head>
  <meta charset="utf-8"/>
  <title>CSS3 Fade and Rotate Images</title>
  <link href="FadingImages1.css" rel="stylesheet" type="text/css">
</head>

<body>
  <div id="outer">
    <img class="lower" width="200" height="200" src="Ellen1.jpg"/>
    <img class="upper" width="200" height="200" src="Ellen2.jpg"/>
  </div>

  <div id="third">
    <img width="200" height="200" src="Laurie1.jpg"/>
  </div>
</body>
```

Listing 3.5 contains a reference to the CSS stylesheet FadingImages1.css that contains CSS selectors for creating a fading effect and a glowing effect. The first HTML <div> element in Listing 3.5 contains two <img> elements; when users hover over the rendered JPG file, it will "fade" and reveal another JPG file. The second HTML <div> element contains one <img> element, and when users hover over this JPG, a CSS3 selector will rotate the referenced JPG file about the vertical axis.

Listing 3.6 FadingImages1.css

```
#outer {
 position: absolute; top: 20px; left: 20px;
 margin: 0 auto;
}

#outer img {
 position:absolute; left:0;
 -webkit-transition: opacity 1s ease-in-out;
 transition: opacity 1s ease-in-out;
}

#outer img.upper:hover {
  opacity:0;
}

#third img {
position: absolute; top: 20px; left: 250px;
}

#third img:hover {
 -webkit-animation: rotatey 2.0s 3 ease;
```

```
}

@-webkit-keyframes rotatey {
  0% {
    -webkit-transform: rotateY(45deg);
  }
  50% {
    -webkit-transform: rotateY(90deg);
  }
  100% {
    -webkit-transform: rotateY(0);
  }
}
```

We will skip the details of the code in Listing 3.6 that is already familiar to you. The key point for creating the fading effect is to set the opacity value to 0 when users hover over the left-most image. The one line of code in the CSS selector is shown here:

```
#outer img.upper:hover {
  opacity:0;
}
```

As you can see, this code sample shows you that it's possible to create attractive visual effects without complicated code or logic.

Next, Listing 3.6 defines a CSS3 selector that creates a rotation effect about the vertical axis by invoking the CSS3 function `rotateY()` in the `keyframes` labeled `rotatey`. Note that you can create a rotation effect about the other two axes by replacing `rotateY()` with the CSS3 function `rotateX()` or the CSS3 function `rotateZ()`. You can even use these three functions in the same `keyframes` in order to create 3D effects. CSS3 3D effects are discussed in more detail later in this chapter.

Figure 3.3 displays the result of launching `FadeRotateImages1.html` on a Sprint Nexus S 4G with ICS, after tapping on the left image (which is initially the same as the right-side image) that is rendered using a fading effect. Note that on desktop browsers users can hover over either image, and that doing so on the right-side image creates a rotating effect.

FIGURE 3.3 CSS3 fade and rotate JPG effects on a Sprint Nexus S 4G.

Bouncing Effects

The previous example showed you how to create a fading animation effect, and this section shows you how to create a "bouncing" animation effect.

Listing 3.7 displays the contents of Bounce2.html and Listing 3.8 displays the contents of Bounce2.css, which illustrate how to create a "bouncing" effect on an input field.

Listing 3.7 Bounce2.html

```
<!DOCTYPE html>
<html lang="en">
<head>
  <meta charset="utf-8"/>
  <title>CSS Animation Example</title>
  <link href="Bounce2.css" rel="stylesheet" type="text/css">
</head>

<body>
  <div id="outer">
    <input id="input" type="text" value="An input line"/ >
  </div>
</body>
</html>
```

Listing 3.7 is another straightforward HTML page that contains a reference to the CSS stylesheet Bounce2.css and one HTML <div> element that contains an `<input>` field element. The CSS stylesheet creates a bouncing animation effect when users hover over the `<input>` element with their mouse.

Listing 3.8 Bounce2.css

```css
#outer {
position: relative; top: 50px; left: 100px;
}

@-webkit-keyframes bounce {
  0% {
    left: 50px;
    top: 100px;
    background-color: #ff0000;
  }
  25% {
    left: 100px;
    top: 150px;
    background-color: #ffff00;
  }
  50% {
    left: 50px;
    top: 200px;
    background-color: #00ff00;
  }
  75% {
    left: 0px;
    top: 150px;
    background-color: #0000ff;
  }
  100% {
    left: 50px;
    top: 100px;
    background-color: #ff0000;
  }
}

#input {
font-size: 24px;
-webkit-border-radius: 4px;
border-radius: 4px;
}

#outer:hover {
 -webkit-animation: bounce 2.0s 4 ease;
}
```

Listing 3.8 contains a @keyframes rule labeled bounce that specifies five time intervals: the 0%, 25%, 50%, 75%, and 100% points of the duration of the animation effect. Each time interval specifies values for the attributes left, top, and background-color of the <input> field. Despite the simplicity of this @keyframes rule, it creates a pleasing animation effect.

The #input selector matches the input field in Bounce2.html and that results in a rounded rectangle. The selector #input:hover selector uses the bounce keyframes in order to create an animation effect for a two-second interval, repeated four times, using an ease function, as shown here:

```
-webkit-animation: bounce 2.0s 4 ease;
```

Figure 3.4 displays a snapshot of the animation effect in the HTML Web page Bounce2.html on a Sprint Nexus S 4G with Android ICS.

FIGURE 3.4 CSS3 bouncing animation effect on a Sprint Nexus S 4G.

CSS3 EFFECTS FOR TEXT

You have seen examples of rendering text strings as part of several code samples in the previous chapter (and in TextShadow1.html in particular). In this section, we discuss a very nice new feature of CSS3 that enables you to render text in multiple columns.

Rendering Multi-Column Text

CSS3 supports multi-column text, which can create a very nice visual effect when a Web page contains significant amounts of text.

Listing 3.9 displays the contents of MultiColumns1.html and Listing 3.10 displays the contents of MultiColumns1.css, which illustrate how to render multi-column text.

Listing 3.9 MultiColumns1.html

```
<!doctype html>
```

```
<html lang="en">
<head>
  <meta charset="utf-8"/>
  <title>CSS Multi Columns Example</title>
  <link href="MultiColumns.css"  rel="stylesheet"  type="text/
             css">
</head>

<body>
  <header>
   <h1>Hover Over the Multi-Column Text:</h1>
  </header>

  <div id="outer">
   <p id="line1">.</p>
   <article>
     <div id="columns">
       <p> CSS enables you to define selectors that specify the
style or the manner in which you want to render elements in an
HTML page. CSS helps you modularize your HTML content and since
you can place your CSS definitions in a separate file. You can
also re-use the same CSS definitions in multiple HTML files.
       </p>
       <p> Moreover, CSS also enables you to simplify the up-
dates that you need to make to elements in HTML pages. For ex-
ample, suppose that multiple HTML table elements use a CSS rule
that specifies the color red. If you later need to change the
color to blue, you can effect such a change simply by making one
change (i.e., changing red to blue) in one CSS rule.
       </p>
       <p> Without a CSS rule, you would be forced to manu-
ally update the color attribute in every HTML table element that
is affected, which is error-prone, time-consuming, and extremely
inefficient.
       <p>
     </div>
   </article>
   <p id="line1">.</p>
  </div>
</body>
</html>
```

The HTML5 page in Listing 3.9 contains semantic tags (which are discussed in Chapter 1) that render the text in several HTML <p> elements. As you can see, this HTML5 page is straightforward, and the multi-column effects are defined in the CSS stylesheet MultiColumns1.css that is displayed in Listing 3.10.

Listing 3.10 MultiColumn1.css

```css
/* animation effects */
#columns:hover {
-webkit-transition: -webkit-transform 3.0s ease;
-transition: transform 3.0s ease;

-webkit-transform : scale(0.5) skew(-20deg, -30deg)
   rotate(45deg);
-transform : scale(0.5) skew(-20deg, -30deg) rotate(45deg);
}

#line1:hover {
-webkit-transition: -webkit-transform 3.0s ease;
-transition: transform 3.0s ease;

-webkit-transform : scale(0.5) skew(-20deg, -30deg)
   rotate(45deg);
-transform : scale(0.5) skew(-20deg, -30deg) rotate(45deg);
background-image: -webkit-gradient(linear, 0% 0%, 0% 100%,
                                from(#fff), to(#00f));
background-image: -gradient(linear, 0% 0%, 0% 100%,
                             from(#fff), to(#00f));
-webkit-border-radius: 8px;border-radius: 8px;}

#columns {
-webkit-column-count : 3;
-webkit-column-gap : 80px;
-webkit-column-rule : 1px solid rgb(255,255,255);
column-count : 3;
column-gap : 80px;
column-rule : 1px solid rgb(255,255,255);
}

#line1 {
color: red;
font-size: 24px;
background-image: -webkit-gradient(linear, 0% 0%, 0% 100%,
                                from(#fff), to(#f00));
background-image: -gradient(linear, 0% 0%, 0% 100%,
                             from(#fff), to(#f00));
-webkit-border-radius: 4px;border-radius: 4px;
}
```

The first two selectors in Listing 3.10 create an animation effect whenever users hover over the <div> elements whose id attribute is columns or line1.

Both selectors create an animation effect during a three-second interval using the CSS3 functions `scale()`, `skew()`, and `rotate()`, as shown here:

```
-webkit-transition: -webkit-transform 3.0s ease;
-transition: transform 3.0s ease;
-webkit-transform : scale(0.5) skew(-20deg, -30deg)
rotate(45deg);
```

The second selector also defines a linear gradient background effect.

The `#columns` selector in Listing 3.10 contains three layout-related attributes. The `column-count` attribute is `3`, so the text in displayed in three columns; the `column-gap` attribute is `80px`, so there is a space of `80` pixels between adjacent columns; the `column-rule` attribute specifies a white background.

The `#line1` selector specifies a linear gradient that creates a nice visual effect above and below the multi-column text.

Figure 3.5 displays the result of matching the CSS selectors in `MultiColumns.css` with the text in the HTML page `MultiColumns.html` in a landscape-mode screenshot taken from an iOS application running on an iPad 3.

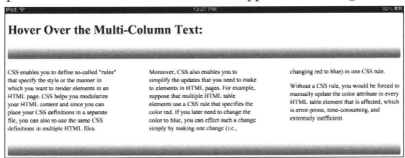

FIGURE 3.5 Multi-column text in landscape mode on an iPad 3.

3D EFFECTS IN CSS3

CSS3 provides support for creating 3D effects, but currently these 3D effects are only supported in `WebKit`–based browsers (Chrome and Safari) on Windows Vista and MacBook. Support will probably be available soon in other browsers such as Opera.

Listing 3.11 displays the contents of `Threed2.html` that creates 3D effects with CSS3 selectors.

Listing 3.11 Threed2.html

```
<!DOCTYPE html>
<html lang="en">
<head>
  <meta charset="utf-8"/>
  <title>CSS 3D Effects Example</title>
  <link href="Threed2.css" rel="stylesheet" type="text/css">
</head>

<body>
  <h2>Hover Over the Rectangles:</h2>
  <div id="outer">
    <div id="radial1">Text1</div>
    <div id="radial2">Text2</div>
  </div>
</body>
</html>
```

Listing 3.11 is a simple Web page that references the CSS stylesheet
Threed2.css in the HTML <head> element. The top-level <div> element
whose id attribute is outer contains two more HTML <div> elements that
are rendered with radial gradient shading. The CSS selectors in Listing 3.12
result in animation effects on the elements that they match in the HTML
elements in Listing 3.11.

Listing 3.12 Threed2.css

```
#outer {
  position: relative; top: 10px; left: 0px;
}

#radial1 {
opacity: 0.8;
font-size: 24px;
width:  200px;
height: 200px;
position: absolute; top: 0px; left: 0px;

background: -webkit-gradient(
  radial, 300 40%, 0, 301 25%, 360, from(blue),
  color-stop(0.05, orange), color-stop(0.4, yellow),
  color-stop(0.6, green), color-stop(0.8, red),
  to(#fff)
 );
}
```

```
#radial2 {
opacity: 0.6;
font-size: 24px;
width:   200px;
height: 200px;
position: absolute; top: 200px; left: 200px;

background: -webkit-gradient(
   radial, 300 40%, 0, 301 25%, 360, from(red),
   color-stop(0.05, orange), color-stop(0.4, yellow),
   color-stop(0.6, green), color-stop(0.8, blue),
   to(#fff)
 );
}


#radial1:hover {
  -webkit-transform: rotate3d(20,30,40, 50deg)
translate3d(50px,50px,50px) skew(-15deg,0);
  transform: rotate3d(20,30,40, 50deg) translate3d(50px,50px,50px)
skew(-15deg,0);
}


#radial2:hover {
  -webkit-transform: rotate3d(1,0,0, 60deg) scale3d(1.5, 0.5,
0.75);
  transform: rotate3d(1,0,0, 60deg) scale3d(1.5, 0.5, 0.75);
}
```

The #outer selector in Listing 3.12 contains simple position properties, followed by the definitions for the #radial1 and #radial2 selectors, both of which specify radial gradient patterns that are similar to those that you have seen in the section that discusses CSS3 radial gradients.

The #radial1:hover selector contains the -webkit-transform property that specifies the rotate3d() function that takes a vector (20,30,40), as well as an angle of rotation of 50 degrees. The relative values of these numbers will determine the rotation. For example, you can replace the vector (20,30,40) with the vector (2,3,4), or (200,300,400), or any other multiple of the specified vector, and the rotation effect will be the same. The second part of the -webkit-transform property of this selector also contains the translate3d() function (that is analogous to the 2D translate() function), which specifies the destination point in pixels, and in this case the destination point is (50px,50px,50px). The third and final part of the -webkit-transform property of this selector specifies the CSS3 2D function skew(-15deg,0) because there is no 3D counterpart for this function.

The #radial2:hover selector also contains the -webkit-transform property that specifies the rotate3d() function that takes a vector (1,0,0), as well as an angle of rotation of 50 degrees. In this case the rotation will be about the x axis because (1,0,0) specifies the positive x axis. You can rotate about the y axis or the z axis by specifying the vectors (0,1,0) or (0,0,1), respectively.

The second part of the -webkit-transform property of this selector also contains the function scale3d(), which is the CSS3 3D counterpart of the CSS3 2D function scale(). The values specified in this function are (1.5,0.5,0.75), which creates a scaling effect of 1.5, 0.5, and 0.75 along the x, y, and z axes, respectively.

This simple example illustrates how to use the three 3D transform functions that are available, and you can experiment with this code to create some interesting visual effects of your own.

Figure 3.6 displays the result of matching the selectors in the stylesheet ThreeD2.css with the elements in the HTML page ThreeD2.html.

FIGURE 3.6 CSS3 3D effect.

CSS3 3D ANIMATION EFFECTS

As you know by now, CSS3 provides keyframes that enable you to create different animation effects at various points during an animation sequence. The example in this section uses CSS3 keyframes and various combinations of the CSS3 functions scale3d(), rotate3d(), and translate3d() in order to create an animation effect that lasts for four minutes.

Listing 3.13 displays the contents of `Anim240Flicker3DLGrad4.html` which is a very simple HTML page that contains four HTML `<div>` elements.

Listing 3.13 `Anim240Flicker3DLGrad4.html`

```
<!DOCTYPE html>
<html lang="en">
<head>
  <meta charset="utf-8"/>
  <title>CSS3 Animation Example</title>
  <link href="Anim240Flicker3DLGrad4.css" rel="stylesheet"
type="text/css">
</head>

<body>
 <div id="outer">
  <div id="linear1">Text1</div>
  <div id="linear2">Text2</div>
  <div id="linear3">Text3</div>
  <div id="linear4">Text4</div>
 </div>
</body>
</html>
```

Listing 3.13 is a very simple HTML5 page with corresponding CSS selectors (shown in Listing 3.14). As usual, the real complexity occurs in the CSS selectors that contain the code for creating the animation effects.

As you will see, some of the CSS selectors in Listing 3.14 contain the CSS3 `matrix()` function, which requires a knowledge of matrices to fully understand the effects that you can create with the CSS3 `matrix()` function. If you are interested in learning about matrices (which is beyond the scope of this book), you can read this introduction to matrices (in the context of CSS3):

http://www.eleqtriq.com/2010/05/css-3d-matrix-transformations/

Since `Anim240Flicker3DLGrad4.css` is such a lengthy code sample, only a portion of the code is displayed in Listing 3.14. However, the complete code is available on the DVD for this book.

Listing 3.14 `Anim240Flicker3DLGrad4.css`

```
@-webkit-keyframes upperLeft {
    0% {
        -webkit-transform: matrix(1.5, 0.5,  0.0, 1.5, 0, 0)
                           matrix(1.0, 0.0,  1.0, 1.0, 0, 0);
    }
    10% {
```

```
                    -webkit-transform: translate3d(50px,50px,50px)
                                       rotate3d(50,50,50,-90deg)
                                       skew(-15deg,0) scale3d(1.25, 1.25, 1.25);
}
// similar code omitted
90% {
    -webkit-transform: matrix(2.0, 0.5,  1.0, 2.0, 0, 0)
                       matrix(1.5, 0.0,  0.5, 2.5, 0, 0);

}
95% {
    -webkit-transform: translate3d(-50px,-50px,-50px)
                       rotate3d(-50,-50,-50, 120deg)
                       skew(135deg,0) scale3d(0.3, 0.4, 0.5);

}
96% {
    -webkit-transform: matrix(0.2, 0.3, -0.5, 0.5, 100, 200)
                       matrix(0.4, 0.5,  0.5, 0.2, 200, 50);

}
97% {
    -webkit-transform: translate3d(50px,-50px,50px)
                       rotate3d(-50,50,-50, 120deg)
                       skew(315deg,0) scale3d(0.5, 0.4, 0.3);

}
98% {
    -webkit-transform: matrix(0.4, 0.5,  0.5, 0.3, 200, 50)
                       matrix(0.3, 0.5, -0.5, 0.4, 50, 150);

}
99% {
    -webkit-transform: translate3d(150px,50px,50px)
                       rotate3d(60,80,100, 240deg)
                       skew(315deg,0) scale3d(1.0, 0.7, 0.3);

}
100% {
    -webkit-transform: matrix(1.0, 0.0,  0.0, 1.0, 0, 0)
                       matrix(1.0, 0.5,  1.0, 1.5, 0, 0);

}
}
// code omitted for brevity
#linear1 {
font-size: 96px;
text-stroke: 8px blue;
text-shadow: 8px 8px 8px #FF0000;
width:   400px;
height: 250px;

position: relative; top: 0px; left: 0px;
```

```
background-image: -webkit-gradient(linear, 100% 50%, 0% 100%,
                                    from(#f00),
                                    color-stop(0.2, orange),
                                    color-stop(0.4, yellow),
                                    color-stop(0.6, blue),
                                    color-stop(0.8, green),
                                    to(#00f));
// similar code omitted
-webkit-border-radius: 4px;
border-radius: 4px;
-webkit-box-shadow:  30px 30px 30px #000;
-webkit-animation-name: lowerLeft;
-webkit-animation-duration: 240s;
}
```

Listing 3.14 contains a WebKit-specific keyframes definition called up-perLeft that starts with the following line:

```
@-webkit-keyframes upperLeft {
       // percentage-based definitions go here
}
```

The #linear selector contains properties that you have seen already, along with a property that references the keyframes identified by lower-Left, and a property that specifies a duration of 240 seconds, as shown here:

```
#linear1 {
  // code omitted for brevity
  -webkit-animation-name: lowerLeft;
  -webkit-animation-duration: 240s;
}
```

Now that you know how to reference a keyframes definition in a CSS3 selector, let's look at the details of the definition of lowerLeft, which contains 19 elements that specify various animation effects. Each element of lower-Left occurs during a specific stage during the animation. For example, the eighth element in lowerLeft specifies the value 50%, which means that it will occur at the halfway point of the animation effect. Since the #linear selector contains a -webkit-animation-duration property whose value is 240s (shown in bold in Listing 3.14), this means that the animation will last for four minutes, starting from the point in time when the HTML5 page is launched.

The eighth element of lowerLeft specifies a translation, rotation, skew, and scale effect (all of which are in three dimensions), an example of which is shown here:

```
50% {
    -webkit-transform: translate3d(250px,250px,250px)
                       rotate3d(250px,250px,250px,-120deg)
                       skew(-65deg,0) scale3d(0.5, 0.5, 0.5);
}
```

The animation effect occurs in a sequential fashion, starting with the translation, and finishing with the scale effect, which is also the case for the other elements in `lowerLeft`.

Figure 3.7 displays the initial view of matching the CSS3 selectors defined in the CSS3 stylesheet `Anim240Flicker3DLGrad4.css` with the HTML elements in the HTML page `Anim240Flicker3DLGrad4.html` in a landscape-mode screenshot taken from an iOS application running on an iPad 3.

FIGURE 3.7 CSS3 3D animation effects on an iPad 3.

CSS3 ANIMATION AND CSS SPRITES

CSS sprites reduce the number of HTTP requests (which reduces response time for Web pages) and also reduce the total file size. The idea is simple: download a single image (which is called a sprite) that contains all the smaller images on a Web site, and then reference the smaller images by their location in the sprite.

This process requires two steps: 1.) create the sprite, and 2.) for each image in the sprite, calculate its location in the sprite and then update CSS selectors accordingly. Although you can perform these two steps manually, a much simpler alternative that will save you a lot of time and effort is an excellent tool called SpriteMe whose homepage is here:

http://spriteme.org/

This Web site contains a demonstration that shows you how to install the tool in your bookmarks toolbar and how to easily create a sprite in a matter of minutes. In addition, you can download the generated sprite and the CSS selectors that contain the location of each image that is included in the sprite. After you have created a sprite, you can use the techniques that you learned earlier in this chapter in order to apply 2D and 3D animation effects on your sprite.

Another useful Web site that contains a collection of techniques and tutorials involving CSS sprites is here:

http://namburivk.blogspot.in/2012/05/building-faster-websites-with-css. html?goback=%2Egde_2071438_member_120537762

SLIDING PANELS WITH CSS3 ANIMATION

Menu-oriented mobile applications often involve touch-enabled "pages" that use a sliding effect to display detail-related pages, which in turn typically have a "back" button to navigate (also via a sliding effect) back to the main menu.

At this point, you have the knowledge to create this type of mobile application, which involves HTML, simple JavaScript (for handling touch-related events), CSS selectors, and simple CSS3 animation for the sliding effects.

The code in this section will give you an understanding of the technical details required for creating sliding effects, and insight into the effort involved in writing a more sophisticated menu-oriented mobile application. Keep in mind that the only CSS3 functionality in the CSS stylesheet involves the sliding animation effect.

Listing 3.15 displays the contents of `SlidingPanels.html` and Listing 3.16 displays the contents of `SlidingPanels.css`, which illustrate how to use CSS3 animation to create a sliding effect when users click or tap on menu items in a list.

Listing 3.15 SlidingPanels.html

```
<!DOCTYPE html>
<html>
<head>
  <meta charset="utf-8"/>
  <title>Sliding Panels without jQuery</title>
  <meta name="viewport"
        content="width=device-width; initial-scale=1.0; minimum-
scale=1.0; maximum-scale=1.0;">
  <link rel="stylesheet" href="SlidingPanels.css">
</head>

<body>
  <section id="outer">
    <dl id="panelContainer" style="width: 2000px; ">
      <!-- the "left" panel displays the menu items -->
      <dd id="leftPanel" style="width: 1000px; ">
        <header class="pageHeader">
          <span>Sliding Panels without jQuery</span>
        </header>

        <article class="content" id="mainPage">
<p>This is the main content of this web page, and to view the con-
tents of a details page, simply click or tap on any of the menu
items below. The clicked menu item will slide (toward the left)
out of view, and then you will see the details page. When you
click on the icon in the upper-right corner of any of the details
pages, the currently displayed details page will slide toward the
right and the original menu items are displayed again. The speed
of the sliding effect is specified by the value of the JavaS-
cript variable 'speed' in this HTML web page. Notice the different
rounded corner effects in the top and bottom menu items: this is
created by specifying a 'px' value for the top and by specifying a
'%' value for the bottom.
</p>
        </article>

        <!-- display the list of menu items -->
        <nav>
          <dl>
            <dd onclick="clickedMenuItem(event)">
                About <img src="BlueBall1.png">
            </dd>
            <dd onclick="clickedMenuItem(event)">
                Work Areas <img src="BlueBall1.png">
            </dd>
```

```
            <dd onclick="clickedMenuItem(event)">
                Recent Blog Posts <img src="BlueBall1.png">
            </dd>
            <dd onclick="clickedMenuItem(event)">
                Recent Blog Comments <img src="BlueBall1.png">
            </dd>
            <dd onclick="clickedMenuItem(event)">
                Contact <img src="BlueBall1.png">
            </dd>
        </dl>
      </nav>
    </dd>

    <!-- the "right" panel is the details panel -->
    <dd id="rightPanel" style="width: 1000px; ">
      <header class="pageHeader">
        <span id="headerText">Details Page</span>
        <img src="BlueBall1.png" id="backButton">
      </header>

      <article class="content" id="detailsPage">
        <p>This is the contents of the right panel.</p>
      </article>
    </dd>
  </dl>
</section>

<script>
    var panelContainer, leftPanel, rightPanel, panelCount = 2;
    var backButton, clickedMenuText = "", detailsText, speed =
300;

    window.addEventListener('load', init, false);

    function init() {
        //hide the browser address bar in iPhone/Android
        setTimeout(function() { window.scrollTo(0, 1); }, 10);

        panelContainer = document.getElementById("panelContainer");
        panelContainer.style.width =
                            (panelCount*window.innerWidth)+ "px";

        leftPanel = document.getElementById("leftPanel");
        leftPanel.style.width = window.innerWidth + "px";

        rightPanel = document.getElementById("rightPanel");
```

```
                rightPanel.style.width = window.innerWidth + "px";

                backButton = document.getElementById("backButton");
                backButton.addEventListener("click",
                                            backButtonClicked, false);
        }

        function clickedMenuItem(event) {
            // slide left panel to the left...
            panelContainer.style.webkitTransform =
                    "translate3d(-" + window.innerWidth + "px, 0, 0)";

            panelContainer.style.webkitTransitionDuration = speed +
                                                                "ms";
            clickedMenuText =
                    event.currentTarget.firstChild.nodeValue.trim();
            headerText.innerText = clickedMenuText +" Menu Item";

            detailsText = document.getElementById("detailsPage");
            detailsPage.innerText =
                    headerText.innerText +": "+ detailsPage.innerText;
        }

        function backButtonClicked() {
            // slide right panel to the right...
            panelContainer.style.webkitTransform = "translate3d(0, 0,
                                                                0)";
            panelContainer.style.webkitTransitionDuration = speed +
                                                                "ms";
        }
        </script>
    </body>
</html>
```

Listing 3.15 contains the HTML5 elements `<section>`, `<article>`, and `<nav>` that provide semantic markup, and they are familiar to you from Chapter 1.

The initial or main page contains the `<nav>` element that consists of five menu items; whenever users click on one of these items, the main page slides toward the left and the contents of the details page are displayed. When users click on the icon in the upper-right corner of the details page, the details page slides toward the right and the contents of the main page are displayed again.

The JavaScript code contains the following code snippet, which executes the JavaScript function `init()` after the Web page is loaded into a browser:

```
window.addEventListener('load', init, false);
```

The JavaScript `init()` function initializes the JavaScript variables `left-Panel`, `rightPanel`, and `backButton` that are referenced whenever users click on menu items in the main page and on the back button in the details page.

The JavaScript `menuItemClicked()` function contains the code for sliding the main page to the left in order to display the contents of the details page, whereas the JavaScript function `backButtonClicked()` handles the opposite transition.

After reading this code sample, you will probably be more inclined to use mobile toolkits (such as jQuery Mobile) that can handle many of the tedious details of writing cross-browser mobile applications.

Listing 3.16 SlidingPanels.css

```
* { margin:0; padding:0;}

html { background-color:#FCC; }

p { color: #00f; }

/* layout details for "outer" div */
#outer {
    width:100%;
    height:auto;
    overflow:hidden;
}

#outer dl {
    -webkit-transition:-webkit-transform ease;
}

#outer dl dd {
    float:left;
}

.pageHeader {
    width:100%;
    line-height:40px;
    padding-top:4px;
    color: #FFF;
    display: block;
    overflow:hidden;
    text-align: center;
    background-color:#4444FF;
}
```

```
#backButton {
    position:relative;
    top:5px;
    width:50px;
    float:right;
    margin-right:5px;
}

/* layout details for article */
article.content {
    width:90%;
    margin:10px 10px auto 10px;
}

/* panel-related selectors */
#leftPanel nav {
    width:95%;
    margin:3%;
    height:auto;
    overflow:hidden;
    margin-bottom:40px;
}

#leftPanel nav dl {
    width:100%;
    height:100%;
    overflow:hidden;
}

#leftPanel nav dl dd {
    width:90%;
    background-color:#FFF;
    border:1px solid #AAAAAA;
    padding-left:10px;
    padding-top:10px;
    padding-bottom:10px;
    padding-right:10px;
    color: #333333;
    display: block;
    font-size: 14px;
    font-weight: bold;
    margin-bottom: -2px;
}

#leftPanel nav dl dd img {
    float:right;
```

```
    height:20px;
}

/* rounded corners for the first menu item */
#leftPanel nav dl dd:first-of-type {
    -webkit-border-top-left-radius: 15px;
    -webkit-border-top-right-radius: 15px;
}

/* rounded corners for the last menu item */
#leftPanel nav dl dd:last-of-type {
    -webkit-border-bottom-left-radius: 30%;
    -webkit-border-bottom-right-radius: 30%;
}
```

Listing 3.16 contains various selectors that contain standard CSS properties, most of which are familiar to you, so the discussion of that code is omitted. There are two points that you need to notice because of the way that they affect the layout of the HTML Wb page. First, the HTML Web page occupies the full screen because the first line in Listing 3.16 sets the `margin` and `padding` attributes of *every* element in Listing 3.16 to 0:

```
* { margin:0; padding:0;}
```

Second, the rounding effect is noticeably different for the first and bottom menu items due to the use of the values `15px` and `30%`, respectively.

Figure 3.8 displays the result of launching `SlidingPanels1.html` on an iOS application running on an iPad 3.

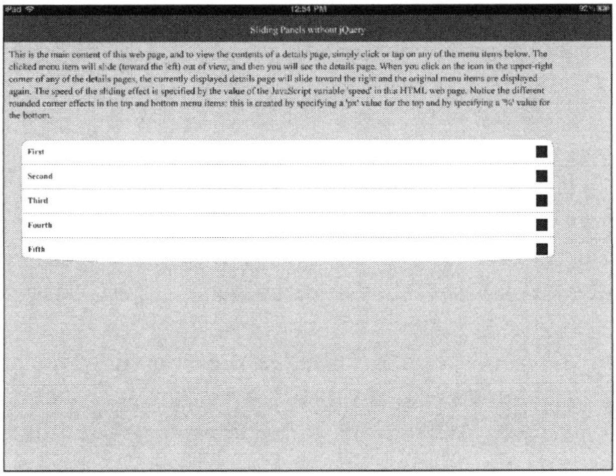

FIGURE 3.8 Sliding panels on an iPad 3.

CSS FRAMEWORKS

CSS3 provides powerful functionality, but you need to include browser-specific code in your selectors if you want your code to work in multiple browsers. Maintenance can be a tedious and error-prone process, especially when you have many CSS stylesheets, and enhancing the functionality in your CSS stylesheets can become a non-trivial task.

There are limitations to CSS, such as lack of support for variables or for "mixins" (discussed later in this section) which are similar to macros or functions in other programming languages.

Fortunately, there are numerous CSS frameworks (such as Twitter Boilerplate, HTML5 Boilerplate, LESS, Blueprint, and many others) available that extend the features of CSS in a manner that simplifies maintenance of your CSS stylesheets. This section contains a condensed overview of several well-known CSS frameworks, along with some code samples that illustrate how to use some of their features. After you have finished this section, you will have a rudimentary understanding of the functionality that CSS frameworks provide in terms of creating and maintaining CSS stylesheets.

A deeper understanding of the relative strengths of these CSS frameworks obviously requires that you perform a more detailed analysis, which you can do by reading the corresponding documentation and also by reading various articles (that are available through an Internet search), some of which discuss other people's experiences with these and other CSS frameworks.

As you can surmise, CSS stylesheets can become very lengthy, even without the inclusion of browser-specific prefixes. For instance, you will find CSS stylesheets containing more than 600 lines in this CSS3 project:

http://code.google.com/p/css3-graphics

Consequently, the task of maintaining and enhancing CSS stylesheets can be both tedious and error-prone.

Fortunately, there are many CSS frameworks (an Internet search will return links for dozens of frameworks) that can help you simplify the task of maintaining your CSS stylesheets, including Compass/Sass, Blueprint, and LESS.

Note that you need to have Ruby installed on your machine in order to use the Blueprint validator and the LESS framework. Second, you need to have Node.js installed if you want to use the server-side functionality that is supported by the LESS framework.

The Compass/Sass Framework

Compass is a framework that enables you to create CSS stylesheets using Sass instead of pure CSS. Its homepage is here:

http://compass-style.org/

The link for the Sass language (which you will use with Compass) is here:

http://sass-lang.com/

Sass supports the following features:

- `@import`
- Arguments
- Arithmetic operations and functions
- Mixins
- Nesting
- Parent referencing
- Variables

If you want to use the Sass-based code samples, you need to install Ruby if you have a Windows machine or a Linux machine (search the Internet for instructions), and if you're using OS X, you already have Ruby installed.

After installing Ruby, install Sass by invoking the following command:

- `gem install sass`

The next several subsections contain simple code samples that illustrate some of the features of the Sass framework.

Sass Variables

Sass supports the use of variables, which are useful for modifying CSS stylesheets quickly and easily. Listing 3.15 displays the contents of `Sass1.scss` and Listing 3.16 displays the generated CSS stylesheet `Sass1.css`. The content of both files is straightforward and self-explanatory, so we will not provide further details.

Listing 3.17 `Sass1.scss`

```
$theColor1: #ff0000;
$theColor2: #0000ff;
$theWidth: 400;
$theHeight: 300;
```

```
#linear1 {
width: $theWidth;
height: $theHeight;
color: $theColor1;
}

a {
color: $theColor1;
&:hover: { background: $theColor2; }
}
```

Listing 3.18 Sass1.css

```
#linear1 {
width: 400;
height: 300;
color: #ff0000;
}
a {
color: #ff0000;
a:hover: { background: #0000ff; }
}
```

Sass Mixins

Sass mixins enable you to re-use styles in multiple CSS selectors, and they are defined using the `@mixin` directive. As an example of Sass mixins, Listing 3.19 displays the contents of `Sass2.scss` and Listing 3.20 displays the generated CSS stylesheet `Sass2.scss`.

Listing 3.19 Sass2.scss

```
@mixin rounded-top {
   $side: top;
   $radius: 10px;

   border-#{$side}-radius: $radius;
   -moz-border-radius-#{$side}: $radius;
   -webkit-border-#{$side}-radius: $radius;
}

#navbar li { @include rounded-top; }
#footer { @include rounded-top; }
```

Notice that the two selectors at the bottom of Listing 3.19 reference the `rounded-top` mixin via an `@include` statement, which will have the effect of replacing this statement with the contents of `rounded-top` after replacing the specified variables with their values whenever they are referenced.

Listing 3.20 Sass2.css

```
#navbar li {
   border-top-radius: 10px;
   -moz-border-radius-top: 10px;
   -webkit-border-top-radius: 10px;
}

#footer {
   border-top-radius: 10px;
   -moz-border-radius-top: 10px;
   -webkit-border-top-radius: 10px;
}
```

Listing 3.20 displays the contents of the CSS selectors that are generated from the Sass file in Listing 3.19 after performing the specified substitutions.

The preceding example illustrates how easy it is to use variables and mixins with Sass. For more information, navigate to the Sass reference guide (which provides an extensive list of features and code snippets) and the following Sass tutorial:

http://sass-lang.com/docs/yardoc/file.SASS_REFERENCE.html
http://sass-lang.com/tutorial.html

The Blueprint Framework

The Blueprint CSS framework provides an extensive set of features, and its homepage is here:

http://www.blueprintcss.org

Blueprint supports the following features:

- A CSS reset stylesheet
- Form styles
- Print styles
- Plugins for buttons, tabs, and sprites
- Editors, templates, and tools

You need to include the following three CSS stylesheets in your HTML5 pages in order to use Blueprint: `screen.css`, `print.css`, and `ie.css`. For example, you can include these three stylesheets with the following HTML fragment:

```
<link rel="stylesheet" href="css/blueprint/screen.css"
      type="text/css" media="screen, projection">
<link rel="stylesheet" href="css/blueprint/print.css"
      type="text/css" media="print">
<!-[if lt IE 8]>
  <link rel="stylesheet" href="css/blueprint/ie.css"
        type="text/css" media="screen, projection">
<![endif]-->
```

Notice that the third stylesheet listed above uses conditional logic to determine whether or not to include the stylesheet (only for Internet Explorer whose version is less than 8).

One of the important features of Blueprint is its support for grids. Consult the online documentation to learn about Blueprint grid and its other features.

The LESS Framework

The LESS CSS framework runs on both the client-side (IE 6+, Webkit, and Firefox) and server-side (with `Node.js`). Its homepage is here:

http://lesscss.org/

LESS supports the following features:

- Functions
- Mixins
- Operations
- Variables

You can put LESS code in a text file (typically with an extension of `.less`) and then compile that file into CSS code from the command line as follows:

```
lessc mylessfile.less > mycssfile.css
```

The following subsections show you how to use variables and mixins in the LESS framework.

LESS Variables

The following example illustrates how to use variables in LESS code:

```
@color: #FF0000;
```

```
#header {
  color: @color;
}
p {
  color: @color;
}
```

The preceding code block defines the variable `@color` and references this variable in two selectors. The content of the generated CSS code is shown here:

```
#header {
  color: #FF0000;
}
p {
  color: #FF0000;
}
```

As you can see, the variable `@color` is replaced by its value `#FF0000` in both CSS selectors (which is obviously the expected behavior).

LESS mixins

The following example illustrates how to use a mixin in LESS:

```
#rounded-corners (@radius:4px) {
  border-radius: @radius;
  -webkit-border-radius: @radius;
  -moz-border-radius: @radius;
}
#header {
  #rounded-corners;
}
#footer {
  #rounded-corners(10px);
}
```

The preceding code block contains the `#rounded-corners` mixin that defines the variable `radius` whose default value is `4px`, along with three attributes that are assigned the value of the variable `radius`. The generated CSS code is shown here:

```
#header {
  border-radius: 4px;
  -webkit-border-radius: 4px;
  -moz-border-radius: 4px;
}
#footer {
```

```
  border-radius: 10px;
  -webkit-border-radius: 10px;
  -moz-border-radius: 10px;
}
```

Notice that the attribute `border-radius` in the `#header` selector has the value 4px, which is the default value for the `radius` variable in the `rounded-corners` mixin, whereas `border-radius` in the `#footer` selector has the value 10px.

You can also use operators and functions in LESS to create sophisticated mixins, which are illustrated in the online documentation for LESS.

Using LESS in Client-Side and Server-Side Code

This is a straightforward process that involves the inclusion of a LESS CSS stylesheet and the LESS JavaScript file. Include the following link to a LESS stylesheet as follows:

```
<link rel="stylesheet/less" type="text/css" href="styles/less"/>
```

Download the JavaScript file `less.js` from the LESS homepage and then include the following line of code that references the LESS JavaScript file as follows:

```
<script src="less.js"/>
```

A detailed discussion of `Node.js` is beyond the scope of this book, and if you do not plan to use the server-side functionality of LESS, you can omit this section without loss of continuity. On the other hand, if you do intend to use `Node.js`, download the distribution onto your machine from the `Node.js` homepage:

http://nodejs.org

After you have installed `Node.js` and `npm` (the `Node` package manager), install LESS with the following command:

```
npm install less
```

The latest version of LESS can be installed with the following command:

```
npm install less@latest
```

This concludes our brief discussion of CSS frameworks, and despite the simplicity of the code samples, you can see the power of the functionality that these frameworks provide for writing and maintaining CSS stylesheets.

CSS3 PERFORMANCE

Although this topic is covered briefly here, CSS3 performance is obviously important. Many of the CSS3 stylesheets in this book contain selectors with 2D/3D animation effects, and hardware acceleration will significantly improve performance. In fact, some tablet devices do not provide good hardware acceleration, and stylesheets with many 2D or 3D animation effects are almost impossible on those devices.

Fortunately, there is a technique for triggering hardware acceleration for CSS3 selectors (using `translateZ(0)` or `translate3d(0,0,0)`) for devices with a GPU, and also debugging techniques for `WebKit` (Safari and Chrome). The following 30-minute video by Paul Irish (a Developer Advocate at Google) discusses these and other techniques:

http://paulirish.com/2011/dom-html5-css3-performance/

An article that provides information for writing more efficient CSS selectors is here:

http://www.pubnub.com/blog/css3-performance-optimizations

Information regarding "best practices" for writing CSS3 selectors is provided here:

http://webdesignerwall.com/trends/css3-examples-and-best-practices
http://www.impressivewebs.com/css3-best-practices/

Perform an Internet search to find other online videos and tutorials regarding CSS3 performance and "best practices" for CSS3 as well as HTML5 Canvas.

USEFUL LINKS

The following alphabetical list of links is short yet useful. Each link contains very good information (and you can always perform your own Internet search as well).

A nice set of "sketch-like" visual effects that use CSS3 is here:

http://andrew-hoyer.com/index.html

Compatibility tables for support of HTML5, CSS3, SVG, and more in desktop and mobile browsers is here:

http://caniuse.com

A Web site for generating CSS3 code using various CSS3 features is here:

http://CSS3generator.com

A Web site that enables you to perform live editing of the contents of various CSS3 selectors and then see the results is here:

http://CSS3please.com

A toolkit that handles the details of browser-specific extensions for CSS3 properties so that you can write prefix-less CSS3 selectors is here:

http://ecsstender.org

A Web site that enables you to create gradients online and view the associated CSS3 code is here:

http://gradients.glrzad.com

Another Web site with information regarding browser support for HTML5 and CSS3 features is here:

http://html5readiness.com

An extensive collection of articles regarding HTML5 is available here:

http://www.html5rocks.com/en/

A JavaScript utility that emulates CSS3 pseudo-classes and attribute selectors in IE6-8:

http://selectivizr.com

A Web site devoted to all things pertaining to CSS3 is here:

http://www.CSS3.info

An excellent source for browser compatibility information on the Internet (maintained by Peter-Paul Koc):

http://www.quirksmode.org

A very good online tool that allows you to experiment with many CSS3 features and also display the associated CSS3 code:

http://www.westciv.com/tools/3Dtransforms/index.html

These links provide a wealth of information and useful techniques, so there's a very good chance that you can find the information that you need to create the visual effects that you want for your Web site.

A comparison of 15 cross-browser testing tools (most are free, and some are commercial) with a tabular comparison of features is here:

http://www.smashingmagazine.com/2011/08/07/a-dozen-cross-browser-testing-tools/

SUMMARY

This chapter showed you how to create graphics effects, including shadow effects, and how to use CSS3 transforms in CSS3 to define CSS3 selectors. You learned how to create 2D/3D animation effects that you can apply to HTML elements. You saw how to define CSS3 selectors to do the following:

- Create simple animation effects
- Display multi-column text
- Create 2D/3D effects with CSS3 selectors
- Use CSS frameworks to create CSS stylesheets
- Use variables and mixins to generate stylesheets

The next chapter gives you an introduction to CSS Shaders, along with various code samples. Then you will learn how to combine CSS3 selectors with SVG.

CSS3 AND SVG

In the previous chapter, you learned how to create CSS3-based gradients and 2D/3D animation effects. The first part of this chapter discusses some of the upcoming CSS3 features, with code samples that illustrate CSS Exclusions, CSS Regions, and CSS Shaders. As this book goes to print, the only way to view this code samples in `WebKit` is in a "special build" of Chromium from Adobe. After Adobe merges its code into the main trunk of `WebKit`, it's possible that some of the code samples in this chapter will not work with the latest "general availability" build of `WebKit` containing the code from Adobe. However, if you download and install the currently available Adobe version of `WebKit` (a link is provided later in this chapter), then the code samples will render correctly with this special build of Chromium.

The second part of this chapter shows you how to combine CSS3 with SVG (Scalable Vector Graphics), which is an XML-based technology for rendering 2D shapes. I will provide some guidelines for situations where it's better to use SVG versus CSS3 (or when to use them together). SVG supports linear gradients, radial gradients, filter effects, transforms (`translate`, `scale`, `skew`, and `rotate`), and animation effects using an XML-based syntax. Although SVG does not support 3D effects, SVG provides functionality that is unavailable in CSS3, such as support for arbitrary polygons, elliptic arcs, quadratic and cubic Bezier curves, and filters. Another nice SVG feature is the ability to define event handlers on SVG elements.

Fortunately, you can reference SVG documents in CSS selectors via the CSS `url()` function, and the third part of this chapter contains examples of combining CSS3 and SVG in HTML Web pages. As you will see, the combination of CSS3 and SVG gives you a powerful mechanism for leveraging the functionality of SVG in CSS3 selectors. In fact, you can even use SVG with some of the new features of CSS3 that you will see in this chapter.

The SVG Appendix on the DVD provides an overview of SVG that is more than sufficient to understand the code samples in this chapter. After reading this chapter you can learn more about SVG by performing an Internet search and then choosing from many online tutorials that provide SVG code samples. Many of the SVG-based samples (lines, circles, ellipses, Bezier curves, and so forth) in SVG in the Appendix have HTML5 Canvas counterparts that are discussed in Chapter 11.

The final part of this chapter provides a very short overview of some of the CSS-related IDEs, such as Sencha Animator and Adobe Edge, and also the open source toolkit AliceJS for CSS3.

Keep in mind that the CSS3 examples in this book are for WebKit-based browsers, but you can insert the CSS3 code for other browsers by using browser-specific prefixes (which were discussed briefly in Chapter 1). Unless otherwise specified, the code samples in the portion of this chapter that covers new CSS features are rendered in a Chrome browser on a Macbook.

NEW CSS3 FEATURES

Several new CSS features are under development, and most (possibly all) of them will be available in WebKit-based browsers. In many cases, the W3C specification for each of the new CSS features is a "work-in-progress," so it's possible that they will be modified by the time you read this book. Check a Web site such as *www.caniuse.com* for information about the latest feature support in your browser of choice.

Fortunately, Adobe has provided a downloadable "special build" of Chromium that you can use in order to render the code samples that illustrate some of the new features of CSS3.

If you want to launch the code samples in this chapter, you need to use Adobe's version of Chromium, which is downloadable here:

https://github.com/adobe/webkit/downloads

In fact, many of the code samples are derived from the code that is included in the download file containing Adobe's version of Chromium.

Among the new and experimental features that you will find in this special build of Chromium are:

1. CSS Compositing
2. CSS Exclusions

3. CSS Regions
4. CSS Shaders

Please keep in mind that the CSS Shaders code samples in this chapter involve concepts whose full coverage is beyond the scope of this book, and many details are "glossed over" in the explanations that follow the code listings. However, you can still familiarize yourself with the functionality of the code, and also how the different code blocks fit together. You can also experiment with the code samples and view the effect of your code changes (always using Adobe's build of Chromium). This process will help you gain a better understanding of the upcoming features in CSS3, and also decide which features that you want to explore in greater depth. In addition, the screenshots that are included in the sections with code samples will enable you to decide whether or not that functionality is useful for your own HTML Web pages.

With the preceding points in mind, here is a list of some of the new CSS3 features:

- CSS Canvas Backgrounds (`WebKit` and FF)
- CSS Device Adaptation (IE10)
- CSS Exclusions (IE10)
- CSS Filters (IE10 and `WebKit`)
- CSS Flexbox (IE10)
- CSS Grid (IE10 and `WebKit`)
- CSS Regions (IE10 and `WebKit`)
- CSS Shaders (`WebKit`)
- CSS Templates (IE10)

Most of these features are discussed briefly in their corresponding sections later in this chapter. The sections that discuss CSS Exclusions, CSS Regions, and CSS Shaders contain code samples and screenshots that illustrate how to create graphics effects with these CSS3 features.

CSS CANVAS BACKGROUNDS

Canvas backgrounds is not a new feature, but it is included in this chapter because its functionality was recently included as an official CSS feature. Canvas backgrounds enable you to specify an image rendered via the

HTML5 Canvas APIs as the background image for the background property as follows:

```
.myelement {
  background: -webkit-canvas(mycanvas);
}
```

Listing 4.1 displays the contents of CSSCanvasBackground2.html that illustrates how to specify an HTML5 <canvas> element as the value of the background property in a CSS selector.

Listing 4.1 CSSCanvasBackground2.html

```
<!DOCTYPE HTML>
<html>
 <head>
  <meta charset="utf-8"/>
  <title>CSS Canvas Background</title>
 <style>
  div {
     background: -webkit-canvas(multisquares);
     width:600px; height:400px;
     border:4px solid black
  }
 </style>

 <script>
   function draw(width, height) {
    var ctx = document.getCSSCanvasContext("2d",
                 "multisquares", width, height);

    ctx.fillStyle = "rgb(192,0,0)";
    ctx.fillRect (10, 10, 50, 50);

    ctx.fillStyle = "rgba(0, 0, 192, 0.5)";
    ctx.fillRect (35, 35, 50, 50);
   }
  </script>
 </head>

 <body onload="draw(200, 200)">
   <div></div>
 </body>
</html>
```

Listing 4.1 invokes the drawGraphics() JavaScript function when the Web page is loaded into a browser. In this example, the drawGraphics() method contains code for rendering a red rectangle and a blue rectangle, but obviously you can render many other shapes as well.

Notice that the `getCSSCanvasContext()` method specifies the name `mul-tisquares`, which is referenced in the value that is assigned to the `back-ground` property, as shown here:

```
background: -webkit-canvas(multisquares);
```

The interesting point about Listing 4.1 is that the JavaScript `draw()` function defines a pattern that consists of a pair of overlapping squares, and that pattern is rendered multiple times in a "cookie cutter" fashion.

The `<div>` element specifies a width and height of `600` and `400`, respectively, and the JavaScript `draw()` method is invoked with the values `200` and `200`, which renders a grid-like layout of two rows and three columns containing the basic pattern. If you change the dimensions of the `<div>` element to `1000` and `800`, you will see a grid-like layout consisting of four rows and five columns of the basic pattern.

Launch the HTML Web page in Listing 4.1 and you will see the effect that is created (the screenshot for Listing 4.1 is omitted but it is available on the DVD).

CSS DEVICE ADAPTATION

CSS Device Adaptation enables you to use CSS in order to specify the size, zoom factor, and orientation of the `viewport` meta element in your HTML5 Web pages. As a simple example, the following selector specifies the `width` property and the `zoom` property:

```
@viewport {
  width: device-width;
  zoom: 0.5;
}
```

You can also embed `@viewport` inside `@media` (using conditional logic that is already familiar to you, as shown in the following example):

```
@media screen and (min-width: 200px) {

  @viewport {
    width: 100px;
  }
}

@media screen and (max-width: 200px) {
  @viewport {
    width: 300px;
```

```
    }
}
```

The permissible values for the `viewport` meta element are listed here:

- `width`
- `height`
- `initial-scale`
- `minimum-scale`
- `maximum-scale`
- `user-scalable`
- `target-densityDpi`

More information about CSS Device Adaptation is available in the W3C specification (which is a work-in-progress):

http://www.w3.org/TR/css-device-adapt/

CSS EXCLUSIONS

CSS Exclusions gives you the ability to specify an arbitrary region that is excluded from the flow of text, which means that text will flow around the region. The opposite case, where text flows inside a region, is supported by CSS Regions (discussed later in this chapter). The interesting fact is that you can CSS Exclusions on any CSS block-level element, which effectively extends the notion of content wrapping that was previously limited to floats.

CSS Exclusions specify a shape that acts as a "boundary" for text, in the sense that text will be rendered either inside (an "inclusion") or outside (an "exclusion") the region. CSS Shapes can be applied to any element, and this controls the geometric shapes used for wrapping text either outside or inside an element. For example, a circle shape on a float causes text to wrap around the circle shape instead of the bounding box of the float.

Listing 4.2 displays a portion of the contents of `CSSExclusions1.html` that illustrates how to create exclusion effects with text in an HTML5 Web page. The complete code listing is available on the DVD.

Listing 4.2 CSSExclusions1.html

```
<!--
Copyright 2011 Adobe Systems, incorporated
```

```
-->
<!DOCTYPE HTML>
<html>
<head>
   <meta charset="UTF-8">
   <title>CSS Regions - Simple Template Demo</title>
   <style type="text/css">

<!-- code omitted for brevity -->

.exclusion {
   position:absolute;
   height:300px;
   width:300px;

   /* flow text around this element */
   -webkit-wrap-shape-mode: around;

   /* display the shape outline */
   /* -webkit-render-wrap-shape: auto; */
}

.circle{
  /* shape the element as a circle */
  -webkit-wrap-shape: polygon(0px, 150px 3px, 120px 12px, 92px
26px, 66px 44px, 44px 66px, 26px 92px, 12px 120px, 3px 150px, 0px
180px, 3px 208px, 12px 234px, 26px 256px, 44px 274px, 66px 288px,
92px 297px, 120px 300px, 150px 297px, 180px 288px, 208px 274px,
234px 256px, 256px 234px, 274px 208px, 288px 180px, 297px 150px,
300px 120px, 297px 92px, 288px 66px, 274px 44px, 256px 26px, 234px
12px, 208px 3px, 180px 0px, 150px 0px, 150px);
}

.heart{
  /* shape the element as a heart */
  -webkit-wrap-shape: polygon(150px, 32px 142px, 23px 132px, 15px
122px, 9px 112px, 4px 100px, 1px 89px, 0px 77px, 0px 64px, 2px
53px, 6px 42px, 11px 32px, 18px 23px, 25px 16px, 34px 10px, 44px
5px, 55px 2px, 67px 0px, 80px 0px, 92px 2px, 103px 6px, 114px
```

```
11px, 125px 17px, 135px 25px, 144px 35px, 151px 73px, 180px 89px,
194px 103px, 208px 116px, 226px 128px, 246px 139px, 270px 150px,
300px 161px, 270px 172px, 246px 184px, 226px 197px, 208px 211px,
194px 227px, 180px 265px, 151px 275px, 144px 283px, 135px 289px,
125px 294px, 114px 298px, 103px 300px, 92px 300px, 80px 298px,
67px 295px, 55px 290px, 44px 284px, 34px 277px, 25px 268px, 18px
258px, 11px 247px, 6px 236px, 2px 223px, 0px 211px, 0px 200px, 1px
188px, 4px 178px, 9px 168px, 15px 158px, 23px 150px, 32px 150px,
32px);
}


<!-- code omitted for brevity -->
     <div id="container">
          <p>Lo&shy;rem ip&shy;sum do&shy;lor sit
amet, con&shy;sec&shy;te&shy;tur ad&shy;ipisc&shy;ing
elit. Vi&shy;va&shy;mus ac nul&shy;la ac nunc
ves&shy;ti&shy;b&shy;u&shy;lum sod&shy;ales sed eget
pu&shy;rus. In&shy;te&shy;ger tris&shy;tique neque at urna
eleif&shy;end por&shy;ta. Mau&shy;ris a sa&shy;pi&shy;en augue,
ve&shy;hic&shy;u&shy;la rutrum augue. Sus&shy;pend&shy;isse
pre&shy;tium pulvi&shy;nar tris&shy;tique. Nul&shy;la
el&shy;e&shy;men&shy;tum blan&shy;dit mas&shy;sa,
pel&shy;len&shy;tesque el&shy;e&shy;men&shy;tum orci
tem&shy;pus sed. Cur&shy;a&shy;bi&shy;tur eget est neque, nec
pel&shy;len&shy;tesque enim. Sed blan&shy;dit do&shy;lor et neque
tin&shy;ci&shy;dunt rutrum. Lo&shy;rem ip&shy;sum do&shy;lor
sit amet, con&shy;sec&shy;te&shy;tur ad&shy;ipisc&shy;ing
elit. Nul&shy;lam tin&shy;ci&shy;dunt do&shy;lor vel neque
eleif&shy;end frin&shy;g&shy;il&shy;la. Prae&shy;sent et
orci nec jus&shy;to vulpu&shy;tate ul&shy;tri&shy;c&shy;ies
ac in leo. In nec ip&shy;sum enim. Donec sus&shy;cip&shy;it
plac&shy;er&shy;at ad&shy;ipisc&shy;ing. Nul&shy;la a nunc mi.
Sed ve&shy;hic&shy;u&shy;la sus&shy;cip&shy;it mag&shy;na sed
con&shy;val&shy;lis. Donec ul&shy;trices con&shy;se&shy;quat
tor&shy;tor, at fer&shy;men&shy;tum augue mal&shy;esua&shy;da in.
Ut cur&shy;sus, odio non port&shy;ti&shy;tor var&shy;i&shy;us,
dui neque luc&shy;tus la&shy;cus, in rhon&shy;cus dui
odio eges&shy;tas libe&shy;ro. Mae&shy;ce&shy;nas
po&shy;s&shy;u&shy;ere con&shy;sec&shy;te&shy;tur lec&shy;tus,
vi&shy;tae con&shy;sec&shy;te&shy;tur lig&shy;u&shy;la
con&shy;sec&shy;te&shy;tur eu.</p>


<!-- code omitted for brevity -->
   </div>
</body>
</html>
```

The first point to observe in Listing 4.2 is that CSS Exclusions in `WebKit`-based browsers supports the property `-webkit-wrap-shape-mode` that takes the value `around` when you want text to flow around a specified shape:

```
-webkit-wrap-shape-mode: around;
```

The second point is that you specify a shape with the `-webkit-wrap-shape` property, which you can assign to a polygon using the `polygon()` function, as shown here:

```
-webkit-wrap-shape: polygon(150px, 32px 142px, . . . );
```

Notice that the `circle` selector and the `heart` selector both use the `polygon()` function to render the corresponding shapes.

Figure 4.1 displays the result of rendering `CSS3Exclusions1.html` in a Chrome browser on a Macbook.

FIGURE 4.1 CSS3 Exclusions in a Chrome browser on a Macbook.

You can get additional information from the CSS Exclusions specification (which is work-in-progress):

http://dev.w3.org/csswg/css3-exclusions/

CSS Filters

A filter effect is something that you create when you apply a graphical operation on an element in an HTML Web page. Filters can take zero or more input images, and possibly some input parameters. The output image is either displayed in an HTML Web page, or it can be used as the input for yet another filter effect, or provided as a CSS image value.

You have already seen how to use SVG filters in SVG documents, and they do not have direct counterparts in CSS. However, WebKit-based browsers will support the following CSS filters (which are shown with sample values):

```
-webkit-filter: blur(3px);
-webkit-filter: grayscale(100%);
-webkit-filter: hue-rotate(80deg);
-webkit-filter: opacity(0.8);
-webkit-filter: sepia(80%);
-webkit-filter: saturate(2);
-webkit-filter: brightness(0.5);
-webkit-filter: contrast(0.6 );
-webkit-filter: hue-rotate(120deg);
-webkit-filter: invert(0.4);
```

You can apply these CSS filters to JPG files, as shown in the following selector, which styles all the <img> elements with a CSS blur filter:

```
img {
    -webkit-filter: blur(3px);
}
```

You can get a complete list of filters and other information from the W3C Editor Draft (which is a work-in-progress):

https://dvcs.w3.org/hg/FXTF/raw-file/tip/filters/index.html

Two other Web sites that contain useful information about filters are here:

http://www.ssi-developer.net/css/visual-filters.shtml
https://html5-demos.appspot.com/static/css/filters/index.html

Incidentally, CSS TextWrapper is an online tool that generates CSS code that "wraps" text inside. Its homepage is here:

http://www.csstextwrap.com/

CSS Flexbox (Flexible Box)

CSS Flexbox is a CSS layout model in which the children of a flexbox can not only be laid out in any direction, but they can also adjust their sizes, either expanding to fill unused space or shrinking to avoid overflowing the parent. You can also nest flexboxes in order to create various layouts in two dimensions:

http://ie.microsoft.com/testdrive/Graphics/hands-on-css3/hands-on_flex.htm

As an example, consider the following `<style>` code block that specifies an HTML `<div>` element of width `300px` that contains four `<button>` elements, each of which has width `80px`:

```
<style>
 #div1 {
  display: flexbox;
  flex-flow: row wrap;
  width: 300px;
 }

 button {
  flex:80px 1;
 }
<style>

<div id="div1">
  <button id="button1">Elephant</button>
  <button id="button2">Tiger</button>
  <button id="button3">Antelope</button>
  <button id="button4">Wildebeest</button>
</div>
```

Since the HTML `<div>` element is not wide enough to accommodate the four buttons on a single row, the first three buttons are rendered in the first row and the fourth button is rendered as the lone element in the second row. In addition, the three buttons in the first row expand from `80px` to `100px`, and the fourth button expands from `80px` to `300px`.

This "expanding" behavior and the creation of a second row for the fourth button occur because the `flex-flow` property is set to "`row wrap`," which allows for a multi-line flexbox.

You can get additional information from the CSS Flexbox specification (which is a work-in-progress):

http://www.w3.org/TR/css3-flexbox/

CSS Grid

CSS Grid enables you to control the layout of elements of an HTML web page in a grid-like fashion. The CSS Grid involves a display mode of `grid` and the use of a new unit of measure called `fr` ("fraction") for the unit length. You also specify the number of rows and columns using `pxs`, `ems`, or `auto` as the unit of measure.

For example, the following selector specifies four columns and three rows:

```
#mydiv {
    display: grid;
    grid-columns: 2fr 1fr 1fr 2fr;
    grid-rows: 50px auto 50px;
}
```

In the preceding selector, the first and last columns occupy two-sixths of the width of the grid, whereas the middle pair of columns each occupy one-sixth of the grid width. The top and bottom rows both have a height of 50px, and the middle row occupies the remaining space.

CSS Grid supports sophisticated layout definitions whose layout is far from obvious. For example, the following selector specifies four columns and three rows:

```
body {
    grid-columns: * * (0.5in * *) [2];
    grid-rows: 20% *;
    columns:3; column-gap:0.5in;
}
```

The preceding CSS selector contains the following information:

- An explicit grid is specified.
- The parenthetical expression is a repeating pattern.
- The integer in square brackets is the number of repetitions.
- The asterisk syntax represents a proportional length, which means that each "*"is assigned equal space allocation.

You can get additional information from the CSS Grid specification (which is a work-in-progress):

http://www.w3.org/TR/css3-grid/

CSS Regions

CSS Regions enable you to specify how text is displayed when users resize their browser. For example, you can specify the "from" and "to" region for text, which creates the impression that text is "flowing" from one region to another.

The key idea is to specify the source and destination of text using the Web-Kit-specific CSS properties `-webkit-flow-from` and `-webkit-flow-into`, respectively, which is illustrated in the code sample in this section.

Adobe and Microsoft co-authored CSS3 Regions and CSS3 Exclusions (now part of the CSS3 specification), and this functionality is supported in Internet Explorer 10 and some versions of Chrome.

Listing 4.3 and Listing 4.4 display the contents of `CSS3FlowRegions1.css` and `CSS3FlowRegions1.html`, which illustrate how to use CSS3 Flow Regions with text in an HTML5 Web page.

Listing 4.3 CSS3FlowRegions1.css

```css
@-webkit-keyframes resize {
    from { width: 100%; }
    to { width: 50%; }
}

html, body { margin: 0; padding: 0; }

.container {
    background-color: #EBEBEB;
    margin: 0 auto;
    max-width: 800px;
    padding: 20px 0;
    width: 100%;
}

.container:hover {
  -webkit-animation: resize 3s alternate infinite;
}

#content {
    -webkit-flow: 'foo';
    -webkit-flow-into: foo;
    color: #666;
    font: normal 16px/1.25 'Helvetica Neue', sans-serif;
}

div[class^='content'] {
```

```
    background-color: white;
    border: 1px solid red;
    -webkit-box-sizing: border-box;
    content: -webkit-from-flow('foo');
    -webkit-flow-from: foo;
    margin: 20px 5%;
    height: 82px;
    overflow: hidden;
    padding: 10px;
    width: 90%;
}

div.content-2 {
    margin-left: 50%;
    width: 45%;
}

div.content-3 {
    margin-right: 40%;
    width: 55%;
}
```

Listing 4.3 contains selectors whose properties are familiar to you (so we will skip the discussion about these properties). Notice that the content selector specifies a -webkit-flow property whose value is foo, and a webkit-flow-into property whose value is foo, as shown here:

```
#content {
    -webkit-flow: 'foo';
    -webkit-flow-into: foo;
    color: #666;
    font: normal 16px/1.25 'Helvetica Neue', sans-serif;
}
```

Text flows into the HTML <div> element whose id attribute has value content, and when users resize the Web page, text will flow into the HTML <div> elements that contain a class whose name starts with the string content, as shown here:

```
div[class^='content'] {
    // properties omitted
    content: -webkit-from-flow('foo');
    -webkit-flow-from: foo;
    // properties omitted
}
```

Listing 4.4 CSS3FlowRegions1.html

```
<!DOCTYPE html>
<html lang="en">
<head>
  <meta charset="utf-8"/>
  <title>CSS3 Flow Regions</title>
  <link href="CSS3FlowRegions1.css" rel="stylesheet" type="text/
css">
</head>

<body>
 <div class="container">
    <p id="content">Once upon a time, a mouse, a bird, and a sau-
sage entered into partnership and set up house together. For a
long time all went well; they lived in great comfort, and pros-
pered so far as to be able to add considerably to their stores.
The bird's duty was to fly daily into the wood and bring in fuel;
the mouse fetched the water, and the sausage saw to the cooking.</p>
    <div class="content-1"></div>
    <div class="content-2"></div>
    <div class="content-3"></div>
 </div>
</body>
</html>
```

Listing 4.4 contains simple HTML markup, along with an HTML <p> element whose id attribute has the value content. There are also three HTML <div> elements whose class attribute contains a class with a name that starts with the string content. Thus, when users resize the Web page, the text will flow from the HTML <p> element into these three HTML <div> elements.

Figure 4.2 displays the result of matching the selectors in CSS3FlowRegions1.css with the elements in the HTML page CSS3FlowRegions1.html taken from a Google Chrome browser on a Macbook.

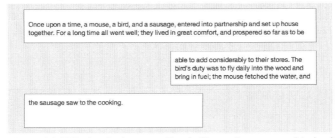

FIGURE 4.2 CSS3 Flow Regions on a Google Chrome browser on a Macbook.

You can get additional information from the CSS Regions Module specification (which is a work-in-progress):

http://dev.w3.org/csswg/css3-regions/

CSS Shaders

CSS Shaders provides functionality that is conceptually very similar to some concepts in WebGL, which enables you to create much more sophisticated visual effects by referencing shader-based functionality in CSS3 selectors. WebGL and CSS Shaders have a pipeline-based architecture where the output of one stage can be used as the input for the next stage in the pipeline. The declaration type of a variable (such as `uniform`, `varying`, or `attribute`) in a vertex shader specifies whether the value of a variable is available for every stage or for only a single stage in the pipeline.

The implementation details of the shader-based effects are in a separate file containing code that runs on the GPU, and that code is written in a C-like language called GL Shader Language (GLSL). You can use multiple vertex shaders in code samples that use CSS Shaders. For example, Listing 4.8 creates an animation effect that involves a single vertex shader called `3DCube1S-VAnimation1.vs`, but you can easily modify Listing 4.8 to specify different vertex shaders at different points in time during the animation effect.

CSS Shaders and WebGL use vertex shaders and fragment shaders in order to render graphics effects. A vertex shader is GLSL code that applies transforms to a "model" (which consists of a set of 3D points) and then calculates the 2D representation of the 3D points. A fragment shader is GLSL code that calculates the color for each 2D pixel that is rendered on the screen. Vertex shaders are the same in CSS Shaders and in WebGL; however, fragment shaders in CSS Shaders are significantly different from fragment shaders in WebGL.

The first example in this section is the Web page `3DCube1CSSShaders1.html` that references two files: the CSS3 stylesheet `3DCube1CSSShaders1.css` whose contents are identical to the contents of `3DCube1.css` (so we will not reproduce its contents in this section), and also the file `SimpleVertexParamsFlag.vs`, which contains code for a vertex shader.

The next three subsections contain code samples that show you how to create some very interesting visual effects using CSS Shaders.

Simple Vertex CSS Shaders

The basic idea involves specifying a CSS3 selector with the `filter` property that references a file containing code with C-like syntax (GLSL) that performs the calculations for the specific CSS Shader.

The code samples in this section comprise an HTML5 Web page and a vertex shader file whose filename has the suffix ".vs" for vertex shader or ".fs" for fragment shader (fragment shaders are not used in the samples in this section), and sometimes a CSS stylesheet as well (with code that you have seen in other code samples). Note that you have the option of placing the CSS selector with the `filter` property in the HTML5 web page or in a CSS stylesheet.

Listing 4.5 displays the contents of `3DCube1CSSShaders1.html`, which is an HTML Web page that references a CSS Shader. Listing 4.6 displays the contents of `SimpleVertexParamsFlag.vs`, which is an example of how you can specify a vertex shader.

Listing 4.5 3DCube1CSSShaders1.html

```
<!--
Copyright 2012 Adobe Systems, Incorporated
This work is licensed under a Creative Commons Attribution-
Noncommercial-Share Alike 3.0 Unported License http://creative-
commons.org/licenses/by-nc-sa/3.0/ .
Permissions beyond the scope of this license, pertaining to
the examples of code included within this work are available at
Adobe http://www.adobe.com/communities/guidelines/ccplus/commer-
cialcode_plus_permission.html .
-->
<!DOCTYPE html>
<html lang="en">
<head>
  <meta charset="utf-8"/>
  <title>CSS 3D Cube Example</title>
      <link   href="3DCube1CSSShaders1.css"   rel="stylesheet"
type="text/css">

  <style type="text/css">
     #top, #left, #right {
        -webkit-filter: custom(url(SimpleVertexParamsFlag.vs),
                     20 20, phase 270.0,
                  amplitude 180.0, txf rotateX(50deg));
     }
  </style>
</head>
```

```
<body>
  <header>
   <h1>Hover Over the Cube Faces:</h1>
  </header>

 <div id="outer">
  <div id="top">Text1</div>
  <div id="left">Text2</div>
  <div id="right">Text3</div>
 </div>
</body>
</html>
```

The new code in Listing 4.5 (which is shown in bold) contains a CSS selector that specifies a `filter` property whose value references the custom vertex shader called `SimpleVertexParamsFlag.vs`. In addition, several comma-separated pairs of values are specified, which matches the name of a corresponding variable in the vertex shader file. In this example, the variables are two floating point variables called `phase` and `amplitude`, and a matrix called `txf`.

Listing 4.6 `SimpleVertexParamsFlag.vs`

```
/*
Copyright 2012 Adobe Systems, Incorporated
This work is licensed under a Creative Commons Attribution-
Noncommercial-Share Alike 3.0 Unported License http://creative-
commons.org/licenses/by-nc-sa/3.0/ .

Permissions beyond the scope of this license, pertaining to
the examples of code included within this work are available at
Adobe http://www.adobe.com/communities/guidelines/ccplus/commer-
cialcode_plus_permission.html .
*/

precision mediump float;

attribute vec4 a_position;
attribute vec2 a_texCoord;

uniform mat4 u_projectionMatrix;

// These uniform values are passed in using CSS.
uniform mat4 txf;
uniform float phase;
uniform float amplitude;

varying vec2 v_texCoord;
```

```
const float PI = 3.1415;
const float degToRad = PI / 180.0;

void main()
{
    v_texCoord = a_texCoord;
    vec4 pos = a_position;

    float phi = degToRad * phase;
    pos.z = (amplitude / 1000.0) * cos(pos.x * PI * 2.0 + phi);
    gl_Position = u_projectionMatrix * txf * pos;
}
```

Listing 4.5 contains three variables that are referenced (in the section in bold) in Listing 4.6, and their counterparts in Listing 4.6 are shown here:

```
uniform mat4 txf;
uniform float phase;
uniform float amplitude;
```

If you look at the selector in Listing 4.5, you can see that phase and amplitude specify floating point numbers whereas txf specifies a transformation, which is represented by the matrix type called mat4.

Listing 4.6 calculates the new position of each transformed point by setting its z value that is based on a calculation that uses its x value as part of a cosine expression, as shown here:

```
pos.z = (amplitude / 1000.0) * cos(pos.x * PI * 2.0 + phi);
```

Recall that the cosine function is essentially a shifted sine function (its exact offset depends on its frequency), so the coordinates of the transformed points will appear to have a sine-like distortion.

Listing 4.6 also references two important built-in variables whose values are always available in the pipeline. One variable is u_projectionMatrix, which is a projection matrix (of type mat4) that is used during the calculation of the 2D representation of 3D points. The other variable is gl_Position, which contains the 2D coordinates of the projected points.

Figure 4.3 displays the result of rendering 3DCube1CSSShaders1.html in a landscape-mode screenshot taken from a Google Chrome browser on a Macbook.

FIGURE 4.3 CSS Shaders on a Google Chrome browser on a Macbook.

You can easily modify the code in Listing 4.6 to create variations of the distortion effects in Figure 4.3. For example, substitute the code in bold in Listing 4.6 with the following code block:

```
<style type="text/css">
    #top, #left, #right {
        -webkit-filter: custom(url(SimpleVertexParamsFlag.vs),
                               20 20, phase 270.0,
                        amplitude 180.0, txf rotateX(50deg));
    }
</style>
```

Figure 4.4 displays the result of rendering the modified version of the HTML page `3DCube1CSSShaders1.html`, which is screenshot taken from a Google Chrome browser on a Macbook.

FIGURE 4.4 CSS Shaders on a Google Chrome browser on a Macbook.

You can get additional information from the CSS Shaders specification (which is a work-in-progress):

https://dvcs.w3.org/hg/FXTF/raw-file/tip/custom/index.html

Animation Effects with CSS Shaders

CSS Shaders can also be referenced in CSS `keyframes`, which means that they can be used during animation effects.

Listing 4.7 displays the contents of `3DCube1SVAnimation1.html`, which is an HTML Web page that references a CSS Shader. Listing 4.8 displays the relevant portion of the CSS stylesheet `3DCube1SVAnimation1.css`.

The file `3DCube1SVAnimation1.vs` is not displayed because its contents are the same as Listing 4.6.

Listing 4.7 `3DCube1SVAnimation1.html`

```
<!--
Copyright 2012 Adobe Systems, Incorporated
This work is licensed under a Creative Commons Attribution-
Noncommercial-Share Alike 3.0 Unported License http://creative-
commons.org/licenses/by-nc-sa/3.0/ .
Permissions beyond the scope of this license, pertaining to
the examples of code included within this work are available at
Adobe http://www.adobe.com/communities/guidelines/ccplus/commer-
cialcode_plus_permission.html .
-->

<!DOCTYPE html>
<html lang="en">
<head>
  <meta charset="utf-8"/>
  <title>CSS 3D Cube with CSS Shaders Animation Example</title>
  <link href="3DCube1SVAnimation1.css" rel="stylesheet">
</head>

<body>
 <div id="outer">
  <div id="top">Text1</div>
  <div id="left">Text2</div>
  <div id="right">Text3</div>
 </div>

  <p class="license">Unless otherwise noted, code and content
is licensed under a <a href="http://creativecommons.org/public-
```

```
domain/zero/1.0/">Public Domain License</a>.</p>
    </body>
  </body>
  </html>
```

Listing 4.7 contains a reference to the CSS stylesheet in Listing 4.8 below, but otherwise its contents are the same as the HTML Web page 3DCube1. html.

Listing 4.8 3DCube1SVAnimation1.css

```
@-webkit-keyframes wave {
  0%, 100% {
        -webkit-filter: custom(url(3DCube1SVAnimation1.vs),
                              20 20, phase 270.0,
                              amplitude 40, txf rotateX(30deg));
  }

  50% {
        -webkit-filter: custom(url(3DCube1SVAnimation1.vs),
                              20 20, phase -90.0,
                              amplitude 180, txf rotateX(75deg));
  }
}

#outer {
  -webkit-filter: custom(url(3DCube1SVAnimation1.vs),
                        20 20, phase 270.0,
                        amplitude 40, txf rotateX(30deg));

  -webkit-animation-name: wave;
  -webkit-animation-duration: 10s;
}
```

Every selector in Listing 4.8 contains the WebKit-based filter property that references the custom code in the vertex shader 3DCube1SVAnimation1. vs.

Figure 4.5 displays the result of launching 3DCube1SVAnimation1.html and 3DCube1CSSShaders1.html in a screenshot taken from a Google Chrome browser on a Macbook.

FIGURE 4.5 CSS Shaders on a Google Chrome browser on a Macbook.

Experiment with the CSS Shaders code to create interesting variations in the graphics images. For example, try replacing this code snippet:

```
pos.z = (amplitude / 1000.0) * cos(pos.x * PI * 2.0 + phi);
```

...with the following line of code:

```
pos.z = (amplitude / 1000.0) * sin(pos.x * PI * 2.0 + phi)
                             / cos(pos.x * PI * 2.0 + phi);
```

The preceding code snippet computes the `tangent` of an angle instead of the `cosine` of an angle. The new graphics image is displayed in Figure 4.5, which is a screenshot taken from a Google Chrome browser on a Macbook.

CSS Shaders and Detached Tiles

CSS Shaders enables you to subdivide an image in an HTML5 Web page into a set of multiple subtiles, where the image can be a JPG file or an SVG document.

Listing 4.9 displays the contents of `DetachedTiles.html`, which is an HTML Web page that references a CSS stylesheet. Listing 4.10 displays the contents of the CSS stylesheet `DetachedTiles.css`, which in turn references the vertex shader `DetachedTiles.vs` in Listing 4.11.

Listing 4.9 DetachedTiles.html

```
<!--
Copyright 2012 Adobe Systems, Incorporated
```

```
<!DOCTYPE html>
<html>
 <head>
  <title>CSS Shaders - Vertex shader - using detached tiles</title>
  <link rel="stylesheet" href="DetachedTiles.css" media="all"/>
  <script src="http://adobe.github.com/web-platform-assets/js/BrowserDetector.js">
  </script>
 </head>

 <body>
   <h3>Hover on the Image to see the detached tiles (change along Z axis).</h3>

    <div id="content" class="shader">
      <div id="multi-col">
        <img id="png-img" src="Lauriel.jpeg" />
      </div>
    </div>

    <p class="license">Unless otherwise noted, code and content is licensed under a <a href="http://creativecommons.org/public-domain/zero/1.0/">Public Domain License</a>.</p>
 </body>
</html>
```

Listing 4.9 is a simple Web page that contains boilerplate HTML markup and a pair of nested HTML `<div>` elements (with corresponding selectors in the CSS stylesheet), along with an HTML `<img>` element that specifies a JPEG file that is rendered when users click on the Web page to open the curtains.

Listing 4.10 DetachedTiles.css

```
.shader{
    -webkit-filter: custom(url(DetachedTiles.vs),
```

```
                         20 20 border-box detached, amount 0.5,
                             t 0.0, transform rotateX(0deg));

    -webkit-filter-margin: 40%;
    -webkit-transition: -webkit-filter linear 1s;
}

.shader:hover {
    -webkit-filter: custom(url(DetachedTiles.vs),
                           20 20 border-box detached, amount 0.5,
                               t 1.0, transform rotateX(25deg)
                               rotateZ(-80deg));

}
```

Both selectors in Listing 4.10 contain the WebKit-specific property filter that references the vertex shader DetachedTiles.vs (shown in Listing 4.11) whose code performs the animation effect when users hover inside the Web page.

In addition, the WebKit-specific filter property specifies values for amount, t, and transform, which are used in the calculations in DetachedTiles.vs.

Listing 4.11 DetachedTiles.vs

```
/*
Copyright 2012 Adobe Systems, Incorporated
This work is licensed under a Creative Commons Attribution-
Noncommercial-Share Alike 3.0 Unported License http://creative-
commons.org/licenses/by-nc-sa/3.0/ .
Permissions beyond the scope of this license, pertaining to
the examples of code included within this work are available at
Adobe http://www.adobe.com/communities/guidelines/ccplus/commer-
cialcode_plus_permission.html.
*/

precision mediump float;

attribute vec4 a_position;
attribute vec2 a_texCoord;
attribute vec3 a_triangleCoord;

uniform mat4 u_projectionMatrix;

// These uniform values are passed in using CSS
uniform mat4 transform;
uniform float amount;
```

```
uniform float t;

mat4 perspectiveMatrix(float p)
{
    float perspective = - 1.0 / p;
    return mat4(
        1.0, 0.0, 0.0, 0.0,
        0.0, 1.0, 0.0, 0.0,
        0.0, 0.0, 1.0, perspective,
        0.0, 0.0, 0.0, 1.0);
}

// Random function based on the tile coordinate.
// This will return the same value for all the vertices in the
// same tile (i.e. two triangles).
float random(vec2 scale)
{
    // Use the fragment position as a different seed per-pixel.
        return    fract(sin(dot(vec2(a_triangleCoord.x,    a_
triangleCoord.y), scale)) * 4000.0);
}

void main()
{
    float r = random(vec2(10.0, 80.0));

    vec4 pos = a_position;

    float dz = -amount * t * r;
    vec3 tc = a_triangleCoord;

    if (mod(tc.x + tc.y, 2.0) == 0.0) {
        dz = amount * t * r;
    }

    pos.z += dz;

    gl_Position = u_projectionMatrix *
                  perspectiveMatrix(0.9) *
                  transform * pos;
}
```

Listing 4.11 contains code that is not difficult in terms of its complexity, but the underlying concepts are beyond the scope of this book. However, you can easily use this code to create the same effect for your own JPG files. If you use SVG in your HTML5 Web pages, there is additional good news: you can also create this animation effect with SVG (which might surprise you!).

Figure 4.6 displays the result of launching `DetachedTiles.html` in a Google Chrome browser on a Macbook, which uses the file `Laurie1.jpeg` to create the graphics image.

Hover on the Image to see the detached tiles (change along Z axis).

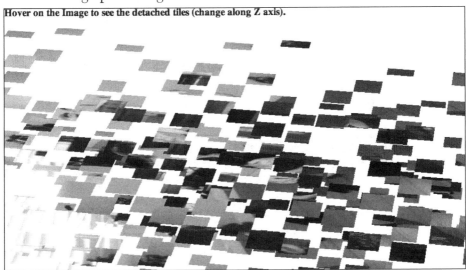

FIGURE 4.6 CSS3 Detached Files on a Google Chrome browser on a Macbook.

CSS Shaders and Curtain Effects

One of the most pleasing visual effects that you can create with CSS Shaders is a curtain animation effect that will remind you of the way that curtains open on a theatre stage. You can easily create this effect in CSS3, which means that you can craft some interesting HTML Web pages with this type of functionality.

Figure 4.7 displays the result of launching the HTML page `Curtain.html` in a landscape-mode screenshot taken from a Google Chrome browser on a Macbook.

Curtain CSS Shader: Click Inside to Toggle Open/Closed

FIGURE 4.7 Curtain effect on a Google Chrome browser on a Macbook.

When users click in the Web page the curtains will open, and then close again when users click in the Web page a second time. Figure 4.8 shows you the contents of the Web page when the curtains are open. If users click on the Web page again, then the curtains will close and return to their original state.

FIGURE 4.8 Open Curtain Effect on a Google Chrome browser on a Macbook.

This concludes our discussion of some new CSS3 features. If you are interested in CSS Shaders, additional CSS3 code samples that are combined with various CSS Shaders are here:

http://code.google.com/p/css-shader-graphics

The next portion of this chapter delves into SVG (an XML-based technology for rendering 2D shapes) that you can reference in CSS selectors.

CSS3 AND SVG

CSS3 selectors can reference SVG documents using the CSS3 url() function, which means that you can incorporate SVG-based graphics effects (including animation) in your HTML pages. As a simple example, Listing 4.12 shows you how to reference an SVG document in a CSS3 selector.

Listing 4.12 Blue3DCircle1.css

```
#circle1 {
opacity: 0.5; color: red;
width: 250px; height: 250px;
position: absolute; top: 0px; left: 0px;
font-size: 24px;
-webkit-border-radius: 4px;
-moz-border-radius: 4px;
border-radius: 4px;
-webkit-background: url(Blue3DCircle1.svg) top right;
-moz-background: url(Blue3DCircle1.svg) top right;
background: url(Blue3DCircle1.svg) top right;
}
```

Listing 4.12 contains various property/value pairs, and the portion containing the CSS url() function is shown here:

```
-webkit-background: url(Blue3DCircle1.svg) top right;
-moz-background: url(Blue3DCircle1.svg) top right;
background: url(Blue3DCircle1.svg) top right;
```

This name/value pair specifies the SVG document Blue3DCircle1.svg as the background for an HTML <div> element in an HTML5 page whose id attribute is circle1. Note that the use of an attribute with a -moz- prefix means that this code will work in WebKit-based browsers (such as Safari and Chrome) and also in the Firefox browser.

Listing 4.13 displays the contents of `Blue3DCircle1.html` that references the CSS stylesheet in Listing 4.12 (which in turn contains a reference to the SVG document `Blue3DCircle1.svg`).

Listing 4.13 `Blue3DCircle1.html`

```html
<!DOCTYPE html>
<html lang="en">
<head>
  <meta charset="utf-8"/>
  <title>SVG and CSS3 Example</title>
  <link href="Blue3DCircle1.css" rel="stylesheet" type="text/css">
</head>

<body>
  <div id="outer">
   <div id="circle1"></div>
   <article>
     <div id="columns">
      <p>
Line one in the first paragraph. Line two in the first paragraph.
Line three in the first paragraph. Line four in the first para-
graph. Line five in the first paragraph. Line six in the first
paragraph. Line seven in the first paragraph. Line eight in the
first paragraph. Line nine in the first paragraph. Line ten in the
first paragraph. Line eleven in the first paragraph. Line twelve
in the first paragraph. Line thirteen in the first paragraph. Line
fourteen in the first paragraph.
      </p>
      <p>
Line one in the second paragraph. Line two in the second para-
graph. Line three in the second paragraph. Line four in the second
paragraph. Line five in the second paragraph. Line six in the sec-
ond paragraph. Line seven in the second paragraph. Line eight in
the second paragraph. Line nine in the second paragraph. Line ten
in the second paragraph. Line eleven in the second paragraph. Line
twelve in the second paragraph. Line thirteen in the second para-
graph. Line fourteen in the second paragraph.
      </p>
     </div>
   </article>
  </div>
</body>
</html>
```

Listing 4.13 contains straightforward HTML5 markup consisting of several HTML `<p>` elements and an HTML5 `<article>` element. Notice that Listing 4.13 contains an HTML `<div>` element whose `id` attribute has value `circle1`, which has a corresponding CSS selector in Listing 4.12 that references the SVG document whose code renders an opaque circle.

Figure 4.9 displays the result of rendering the HTML page `Blue3DCircle1.html` in a Chrome browser on a Macbook.

FIGURE 4.9 SVG 3D effect and text in a Chrome browser on a Macbook.

CSS3 and SVG Bar Charts

Now that you know how to reference SVG documents in CSS3 selectors, let's look at an example of referencing an SVG-based bar chart in a CSS3 selector. Listing 4.14 displays the contents of the HTML5 page `CSS3SVG-BarChart1.html`; Listing 4.15 displays the contents of the CSS3 stylesheet `CSS3SVGBarChart1.css` (whose selectors are applied to the contents of Listing 4.12); and Listing 4.14 displays the contents of the SVG document `CSS3-VGBarChart1.svg` (referenced in a selector in Listing 4.13) that contains the SVG code for rendering a bar chart.

Listing 4.14 CSS3SVGBarChart1.html

```
<!doctype html>
<html en>
 <head>
  <meta charset="utf-8"/>
  <title>CSS Multi Column Text and SVG Bar Chart</title>
  <link href="CSS3SVGBarChart1.css" rel="stylesheet" type="text/
                                                            css">
```

```
</head>

<body>
<div id="outer">
  <article>
   <p id="line1">.</p>
    <div id="columns">
       <p>
CSS enables you to define so-called "selectors" that specify the
style or the manner in which you want to render elements in an
HTML page. CSS helps you modularize your HTML content and since
you can place your CSS definitions in a separate file, you can
also re-use the same CSS definitions in multiple HTML files.</p>
       <p>
Moreover, CSS also enables you to simplify the updates that you
need to make to elements in HTML pages. For example, suppose that
multiple HTML table elements use a CSS rule that specifies the
color red. If you later need to change the color to blue, you can
effect such a change simply by making one change (i.e., changing
red to blue) in one CSS rule.</p>
       <p>
Without a CSS rule, you would be forced to manually update the
color attribute in every HTML table element that is affected,
which is error-prone, time-consuming, and extremely inefficient.</
p>
       <p>
 As you can see, it's very easy to reference an SVG document in
CSS selectors, and in this example, an SVG-based bar chart is ren-
dered on the left-side of the screen.</p>
       </div>

       <p id="line1">.</p>
    </article>
   </div>
   <div id="chart1">
   </div>
</body>
</html>
```

In Chapter 2, you saw an example of rendering multi-column text, and
the contents of Listing 4.14 is essentially the same as that example. However,
there is an additional HTML <div> element (whose id attribute has value
chart1) that is used for rendering an SVG bar chart via a CSS selector in
Listing 4.15.

Listing 4.15 CSS3SVGBarChart1.css

```
#columns {
-webkit-column-count : 4;
-webkit-column-gap : 40px;
-webkit-column-rule : 1px solid rgb(255,255,255);
column-count : 3;
column-gap : 40px;
column-rule : 1px solid rgb(255,255,255);
}

#line1 {
color: red;
font-size: 24px;
background-image: -webkit-gradient(linear, 0% 0%, 0% 100%,
from(#fff), to(#f00));
background-image: -gradient(linear, 0% 0%, 0% 100%, from(#fff),
to(#f00));
-webkit-border-radius: 4px;
border-radius: 4px;
}

#chart1 {
opacity: 0.5;
color: red;
width: 800px;
height: 50%;
position: absolute; top: 20px; left: 20px;
font-size: 24px;
-webkit-border-radius: 4px;
-moz-border-radius: 4px;
border-radius: 4px;
border-radius: 4px;
-webkit-background: url(CSS3SVGBarChart1.svg) top right;
-moz-background: url(CSS3SVGBarChart1.svg) top right;
background: url(CSS3SVGBarChart1.svg) top right;
}
```

The #chart selector contains various attribute, along with a reference to an SVG document (that renders an actual bar chart), as shown here:

```
-webkit-background: url(CSS3SVGBarChart1.svg) top right;
-moz-background: url(CSS3SVGBarChart1.svg) top right;
background: url(CSS3SVGBarChart1.svg) top right;
```

Now that you've seen the contents of the HTML5 page and the selectors in the CSS stylesheet, let's take a look at the SVG document that renders the bar chart.

Listing 4.16 CSS3SVGBarChart1.svg

```
<?xml version="1.0" encoding="iso-8859-1"?>
<!DOCTYPE svg PUBLIC "-//W3C//DTD SVG 20001102//EN"
 "http://www.w3.org/TR/2000/CR-SVG-20001102/DTD/svg-20001102.dtd">

<svg xmlns="http://www.w3.org/2000/svg"
     xmlns:xlink="http://www.w3.org/1999/xlink"
     width="100%" height="100%">
  <defs>
    <linearGradient id="pattern1">
      <stop offset="0%"    stop-color="yellow"/>
      <stop offset="40%"   stop-color="red"/>
      <stop offset="80%"   stop-color="blue"/>
    </linearGradient>

    <radialGradient id="pattern2">
      <stop offset="0%"    stop-color="yellow"/>
      <stop offset="40%"   stop-color="red"/>
      <stop offset="80%"   stop-color="blue"/>
    </radialGradient>

    <radialGradient id="pattern3">
      <stop offset="0%"    stop-color="red"/>
      <stop offset="30%"   stop-color="yellow"/>
      <stop offset="60%"   stop-color="white"/>
      <stop offset="90%"   stop-color="blue"/>
    </radialGradient>
  </defs>

<g id="chart1" transform="translate(0,0) scale(1,1)">
   <rect width="30" height="235" x="15"  y="15"  fill="black"/>
   <rect width="30" height="240" x="10"  y="10"
         fill="url(#pattern1)"/>

   <rect width="30" height="145" x="45"  y="105" fill="black"/>
   <rect width="30" height="150" x="40"  y="100"
         fill="url(#pattern2)"/>

   <rect width="30" height="195" x="75"  y="55"  fill="black"/>
   <rect width="30" height="200" x="70"  y="50"
         fill="url(#pattern1)"/>

   <rect width="30" height="185" x="105" y="65"  fill="black"/>
   <rect width="30" height="190" x="100" y="60"
         fill="url(#pattern3)"/>
```

```
      <rect width="30" height="145" x="135" y="105" fill="black"/>
      <rect width="30" height="150" x="130" y="100"
            fill="url(#pattern1)"/>

      <rect width="30" height="225" x="165" y="25"  fill="black"/>
      <rect width="30" height="230" x="160" y="20"
            fill="url(#pattern2)"/>

      <rect width="30" height="145" x="195" y="105" fill="black"/>
      <rect width="30" height="150" x="190" y="100"
            fill="url(#pattern1)"/>

      <rect width="30" height="175" x="225" y="75"  fill="black"/>
      <rect width="30" height="180" x="220" y="70"
            fill="url(#pattern3)"/>
  </g>

  <g id="chart2" transform="translate(250,125) scale(1,0.5)"
                  width="100%" height="100%">
    <use xlink:href="#chart1"/>
  </g>
</svg>
```

Listing 4.16 contains an SVG <defs> element in which three gradients are defined (one linear gradient and two radial gradients) whose id attribute has values pattern1, pattern2, and pattern3, respectively. These gradients are referenced by their id in the SVG <g> element that renders a set of rectangular bars for a bar chart. The second SVG <g> element (whose id attribute has value chart2) performs a transform involving the SVG translate() and scale() functions, and then renders the actual bar chart, as shown in this code:

```
<g id="chart2" transform="translate(250,125) scale(1,0.5)"
                width="100%" height="100%">
  <use xlink:href="#chart1"/>
</g>
```

Figure 4.10 displays the result of matching the selectors in CSS3SVGBarChart1.css with the elements in the HTML page CSS3SVGBarChart1.html, in a landscape-mode screenshot taken from an Android application running on an Asus Prime Android ICS 10" tablet.

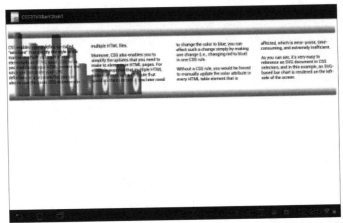

FIGURE 4.10 CSS3 and SVG bar chart on an Asus Prime Android ICS 10" tablet.

RENDERING 3D SURFACES IN SVG

Although SVG does not provide 3D support, you can create 3D effects based on a combination of JavaScript and SVG. In fact, you can find an extensive set of SVG code samples illustrating 3D effects here:

http://code.google.com/p/svg-filter-graphics

Figure 4.11 displays the result of rendering `TroughPattern3S2.svg` (which is part of the preceding open source project) in a Chrome browser on a Macbook. Note that SVG filters are not supported on Android ICS.

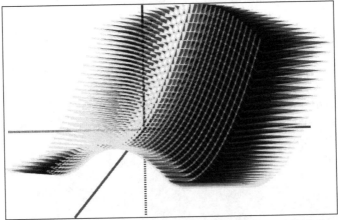

FIGURE 4.11 SVG 3D "Trough" shape in a Chrome browser on a Macbook.

If you are interested in creating 3D effects with SVG, you get more information (including details about matrix manipulation) and code samples here:

http://msdn.microsoft.com/en-us/library/hh535759(v=vs.85).aspx

If you are interested in other toolkits that use SVG, you can find information about D3 and Raphael, along with various code samples, in the Appendices on the DVD.

SIMILARITIES AND DIFFERENCES BETWEEN SVG AND CSS3

This section briefly summarizes the features that are common to SVG and CSS3 and also the features that are unique to each technology. Chapters 2 through 4 and Appendix A contain code samples that illustrate many of the features that are summarized in this section. Incidentally, Chapter 11 summarizes the similarities and differences between SVG and HTML5 Canvas, which will give you a good understanding of the relationship among these three important technologies.

SVG and CSS3 both provide support for the following:

- Linear and radial gradients
- 2D graphics and animation effects
- The ability to create shapes such as rectangles, circles, and ellipses
- WAI ARIA

SVG provides support for the following features that are not available in CSS3:

- Bezier curves
- Hierarchical object definitions
- Custom glyphs
- Rendering text along an arbitrary path
- Defining event listeners on SVG objects
- Programmatic creation of 2D shapes using JavaScript
- "Accessibility" to XML-based technologies and tools

CSS3 provides support for the following features that are not available in SVG:

- 3D graphics and animation effects
- Multi-column rendering of text
- WebGL-oriented functionality (e.g., CSS Shaders)

Note that SVG Filters and CSS Filters will become one and the same at some point in the not-too-distant future.

In general, SVG is better suited than CSS3 for large data sets that will be used for data visualization, and you can reference the SVG document (which might render some type of chart) in a CSS3 selector using the CSS3 `url()` function. You have already seen such an example in Chapter 3, where the SVG document contains the layout for a bar chart. In general, there might be additional processing involved where data is retrieved or aggregated from one or more sources (such as databases and Web services), and then manipulated using some programming language (such as XSLT, Java, or JavaScript) in order to programmatically create an SVG document or perhaps create SVG elements programmatically in a browser session.

CSS3 TOOLKITS AND IDES

Currently there are two excellent CSS3 IDEs available: Sencha Animator and Adobe Edge, both of which are simplify the creation and generation of CSS3-based selectors for web pages. Neither IDE requires you to write any code, so they are accessible to web designers as well as Web developers. However, if you want a toolkit that provides more programmatic access to CSS3, you can use AliceJS, which is an open source toolkit.

Currently these tools are available as free downloads, so you can experiment with these products (and other IDEs that become available) to determine which one suits your needs.

Sencha Animator

Sencha Animator is a desktop application for developing CSS3 animations for `WebKit` browsers and mobile devices, and its homepage (with a download link) is here:

http://www.sencha.com/products/animator

Sencha Animator enables you to create various 2D shapes, with support for transitions, 2D/3D transforms, animation effects, and property panels for modifying the properties of shapes. In addition, Sencha Animator allows you to define custom CSS effects, and supported devices include iPhone, iPad, iPod Touch, BlackBerry Torch, Android, and Google Chrome.

Sencha Animator and Adobe Edge (discussed in the next section) offer some similar functionality, but they do differ significantly in terms of their supported features.

You can get more detailed information in this blog post:

http://www.sencha.com/blog/rocking-the-boat-of-flash-with-css3-animations/

Several videos about Sencha Animator are available, and they can give you an overview of how to use the features of Sencha Animator:

http://vimeo.com/16219355

http://notes.sencha.com/post/1416864756/sencha-animator-introduction-video-19-47

After performing the download and installation, launch Sencha Animator and create a new project to experiment with the various features. There is an export feature that enables you to export the contents of your project as an HTML5 page.

For example, after creating a Sencha Animator project with a circle, rectangle (with simple animation), line segment, and text, and then exporting this project, the generated HTML page `index.html` contains all the necessary CSS3 code and HTML markup.

The best way to learn about Sencha Animator is to install the tool and explore its capabilities.

Adobe Edge

Adobe Edge is a tool that enables you to create animated and interactive content using HTML5, CSS3, and JavaScript, and its homepage is here:

http://labs.adobe.com/technologies/edge/

Adobe Edge is an interesting Adobe tool that was made available in August 2011 as a beta product. Adobe Edge enables you to create sophisticated graphics and animation effects (based on a custom framework that resembles CSS3 and JavaScript) that does not require coding experience. Experienced designers who are accustomed to Adobe's product suite will be very comfortable with Adobe Edge.

Adobe Edge enables users to rapidly develop sophisticated and professional-looking visual effects. Some of the advantages of Adobe Edge include:

- Import GIF, JPG, PNG, or SVG files
- Choreograph animation with the timeline editor
- Animate position, size, color, shape, and rotation at the property level
- Copy/paste transitions and also invert them
- Support for more than 25 built-in easing effects

More Adobe Edge features are here:

http://labs.adobe.com/technologies/edge/?tabID=details#tabTop

Adobe Edge release notes:

http://download.macromedia.com/pub/labs/edge/edge_p1_releasenotes.pdf

http://news.cnet.com/8301-30685_3-20085619-264/adobe-dives-into-html-with-new-edge-software/

AliceJS

AliceJS is an acronym for A Lightweight Independent CSS Engine, and its supports CSS3-based graphics and animation effects. The AliceJS homepage is here:

http://blackberry.github.com/Alice/

AliceJS is a self-contained JavaScript toolkit that sets up animations through CSS manipulations. AliceJS consists of a set of modularized JavaScript files, each of which performs one effect. No images or CSS dependencies are needed. AliceJS does not perform an event handling, but you can use AliceJS to animate jQuery UI components.

SUMMARY

This chapter started with examples of combining SVG with CSS3, followed by an overview of some of the exciting new features of CSS3. In particular you learned about the following topics:

- CSS Exclusions with code samples

- CSS Flexbox overview
- CSS Regions with code samples
- CSS Shaders with code samples
- How to reference SVG documents in CSS3 selectors

CSS3 and SVG support additional features for creating sophisticated effects, and you can perform an Internet search to find links that discuss those features.

The next chapter gives you an introduction to jQuery, and you will see HTML5 web pages that use jQuery which are rendered on an Asus Prime tablet and a Sprint Nexus S 4G smartphone (both running Android ICS) and an iPad 3.

FUNDAMENTALS OF JQUERY

This chapter introduces you to jQuery and provides examples of using jQuery APIs to manipulate elements in HTML5 Web pages. jQuery is an extremely popular open source JavaScript-based toolkit that provides a layer of abstraction over JavaScript in order to facilitate the creation of HTML Web pages that run in multiple browsers. You can download the compressed production version for production Web sites, or the uncompressed development version (which is a larger yet readable file because it contains comments and whitespaces) of jQuery from the jQuery Web site:

http://jquery.org

The first part of this chapter provides an introduction to jQuery, along with examples of how to use jQuery in HTML5 Web pages. This section contains many code snippets that illustrate the syntax of useful jQuery commands; however, later chapters contain detailed code samples that show you how to use many of these jQuery commands in a more contextually relevant fashion.

The second part of this chapter contains examples of how to create animation effects in jQuery, such as toggling the visibility of HTML `<div>` elements and updating the values of CSS3 properties. You will also see how to use jQuery to set properties in CSS3 selectors to create 2D and 3D graphics effects, including animation.

Please keep in mind that the jQuery chapters are primarily intended to help you achieve a working knowledge of jQuery and jQuery Mobile. This knowledge will help you learn how to create HTML5 Web pages that contain a combination of jQuery, CSS3, and other HTML5-related technologies. In addition, it's also possible that some jQuery functions that could be useful to you are covered in this book. Hence, it might be worth your while to read the jQuery documentation, which provides many useful code blocks and live samples.

Third, the code samples in this chapter contain jQuery methods that are sometimes "out of sequence" (in the sense that they use jQuery methods that are discussed later in the chapter). This is normal behavior when you try to solve meaningful tasks. For instance, the code sample that shows you how to use the jQuery `.remove()` method also invokes the jQuery `.filter()` method, which enables you to remove only a subset of elements that meet a specific criterion. This type of code makes sense, because you need to know how to remove selected elements of a specific type in an HTML Web page.

Fourth, the names of HTML Web pages in this book that contain jQuery often start with the letters "JQ," and the HTML Web pages that contain jQuery Mobile start with the letters "JQM."

Finally, since we can only cover a subset of jQuery functionality, it is important for you to experiment with the jQuery code samples in order to become proficient in jQuery.

WHAT IS JQUERY?

jQuery is an open source JavaScript toolkit that enables you to write cross-browser and cross-platform JavaScript code for managing elements in an HTML Web page, which includes finding, creating, updating, and deleting not only elements, but also element attributes. This also includes the ability to add or remove style-related attributes of elements.

Some of the important and useful features of jQuery (in no particular order) include its support for:

- Cross-browser code
- Third-party jQuery plugins
- Theme-able widgets
- Event handling
- Ajax support
- Simpler DOM traversal

jQuery is an extensible toolkit, and currently there are thousands of jQuery plugins available in multiple categories. Sorting through the available plugins takes some effort, but it is well worth the time to do so, especially when you find a plugin that saves you from writing and maintaining your own code to implement specific functionality. Plugins often have an associated demo page and also a rating by other users, which can greatly simplify the selection process.

The jQuery project is also divided into four parts:

- jQuery Core: we will use this code in this book
- jQuery UI: animation, advanced effects, and theme-able widgets
- QUnit: a unit testing toolkit
- Sizzle: a JavaScript-based CSS selector engine

In this book, we will focus on the jQuery Core functionality and also include some of the jQuery UI functionality for creating animation effects. Navigate to the jQuery homepage to get additional information about the other two components of jQuery.

Referencing jQuery Files in HTML5 Web Pages

There are at least four ways to reference the jQuery JavaScript files in your HTML Web pages:

- Download jQuery files and use a local reference in your HTML5 Web pages
- Download jQuery files and use a "generic" reference
- Reference jQuery files via http
- Use a CDN (Content Distribution Network)

The first approach requires that you get the latest jQuery code whenever you need a more recent version of jQuery. You also need to modify the version number in your HTML5 Web pages.

The second approach involves making a copy of the downloaded jQuery code using a name such as `jquery-latest.js`. Whenever you download a newer version of jQuery, you don't need to modify the version of jQuery in your HTML5 Web pages, but you still need to remember the version of jQuery that is referenced in your HTML5 Web pages.

The third approach eliminates the need for downloading files, but you still need to modify the version number in your HTML5 Web pages whenever you need to reference a newer version of jQuery. Note that many of the jQuery examples in this book use the third or fourth approach instead of downloading the files locally.

HTML WEB PAGES WITHOUT JQUERY

Before delving into jQuery code samples, let's briefly look at some non-jQuery JavaScript methods that are available:

```
getElementById()
getElementsByTagName()
getElementsByClassName()
querySelector()
querySelectorAll()
```

The first three methods are intuitively named, and there are corresponding methods in jQuery. The `querySelectorAll` method supports pseudo-selectors, which enables you to select sets of elements that are based on simple or complex selection criteria. For example, the following line of code binds the `showAlert2` JavaScript function to the first HTML `<p>` element of the HTML `<div>` element whose `id` has value `outer`, which means that the JavaScript function `showAlert2` is executed whenever users click on this `<p>` element:

```
document.querySelector("#outer p:first-child").onclick = show-
Alert2;
```

The code sample in this section is a simple example of how to attach event listeners to HTML elements using JavaScript.

Listing 5.1 displays the contents of `QuerySelectors1.html` that illustrates how to attach click handlers to elements in an HTML Web page.

Listing 5.1 QuerySelectors1.html

```
<!DOCTYPE html>
<html lang="en">
 <head>
  <meta charset="utf-8"/>
  <title>JavaScript Query Selector</title>

  <script>
    function clickElements() {
       var divList = document.querySelectorAll("#outer div");
       for(var v=0; v<divList.length; v++) {
          divList[v].onclick=showAlert;
       }

       document.querySelector("#outer").onclick = showAlert2;
    }
```

```
   function showAlert() {
     var id = this.id;
     alert("You clicked inner <div> "+id);
   }

   function showAlert2() {
     var id = this.id;
     alert("You clicked outer <div> "+id);
   }

   window.onload = clickElements;
  </script>
 </head>

 <body>
   <div id="outer">Outer DIV
     <div id="inner1">Inner DIV1 </div>
     <div id="inner2">Inner DIV2 </div>
     <div id="inner3">Inner DIV3 </div>
   </div>
 </body>
</html>
```

Listing 5.1 contains the JavaScript function `clickElements()` that iterates through the list of HTML `<div>` elements that are child elements of the HTML `<div>` element whose `id` attribute has value `outer`, and then adds a click event listener called `showAlert()` to each of those HTML `<div>` elements. Notice that this function also adds the click event listener `showAlert2()` to the parent HTML `<div>` element.

When users launch this Web page, the function `clickElements()` is executed because of this code snippet:

```
window.onload = clickElements;
```

The final portion of Listing 5.1 contains an HTML `<body>` element with HTML `<div>` elements that are processed by the `clickElements()` function.

Obviously Listing 5.1 contains simple code that is easy to read and understand, but creating (as well as debugging, maintaining, and enhancing) HTML Web pages becomes more complicated when you need to write JavaScript code for multiple versions of multiple browsers. Imagine yourself in a position where you need to develop and maintain a non-trivial Web application that supports Internet Explorer 6 (and above) in addition to Firefox and `WebKit`-based browsers. Such an application can become tedious and difficult in terms of maintenance and making enhancements.

Consequently, the JavaScript methods that are listed at the beginning of this section are insufficient if you need to manipulate more complex selections of elements, which is one reason for using a JavaScript toolkit. One solution is to use jQuery (and jQuery Mobile for mobile Web pages) in order to quickly and easily create cross-browser Web pages. The advantage of jQuery is that you can avoid dealing with the tedious details of JavaScript and focus on implementing the functionality of your HTML Web pages.

USING JQUERY TO FIND ELEMENTS IN WEB PAGES

The code in the previous section showed you how to add event listeners to elements in an HTML Web page. Now let's look at how you can use jQuery to manage elements in a Web page in a cross-browser manner.

A key point to remember is that the "$" prefix is the jQuery function, which is a shorthand form of `jQuery()`, which means that the following two lines of code are the same:

```
var pElements1 = $("p");
var pElements2 = jQuery("p");
```

A third option is the use of `window.jQuery`, but this is less common than using `jQuery` or simply the "$" dollar sign.

Another point to remember is that a jQuery search actually returns a "result set," which is the set of elements that match the selection criteria. Each time a set of elements is returned, that set of elements can be passed to a second jQuery search, which in turn will return a set of elements matching the selection criteria of the second jQuery search. In fact, this process is called method chaining, and you "chain" together as many function invocations as you wish. Method chaining enables you to write very compact yet powerful code, as you will see in some examples in this chapter. As a preview, the following code snippet from Listing 5.10 illustrates the use of jQuery method chaining:

```
$("ul li#item4").next().next().css({'font-size':24,
                          'background-color':'blue'});
```

As a simple example of how to use jQuery to select a set of elements in an HTML Web page, the following code snippet returns the set of <p> elements (if any) in an HTML Web page and assigns that set of elements to the JavaScript variable `pElements`:

```
var pElements = $("p");
```

The following code samples illustrate these and other jQuery concepts.

A "Hello World" Web Page with jQuery

The example in this section finds a single HTML <p> element and then changes its text. Later you will also see the modified code that enables you to manipulate an HTML Web page containing multiple HTML <p> elements.

Listing 5.2 displays the contents of HelloWorld1.html that illustrates how to add jQuery functionality to an HTML5 Web page that contains a single HTML <p> element.

NOTE *Listing 5.2 contains* console.log() *that is available in* WebKit-*based browsers, but might not be available without some type of plugin or extension for other browsers.*

Listing 5.2 HelloWorld1.html

```
<!DOCTYPE html>
<html lang="en">
 <head>
  <meta charset="utf-8"/>
  <title>Hello World</title>

  <script src="http://code.jquery.com/jquery-1.7.1.min.js">
  </script>
 </head>

 <body>
 <p id="Steve">Hello World From a Paragraph</p>

  <script>
   $(document).ready(function(){
     // get the text in the <p> element
     var pText = $("p").text();
     console.log (pId+" says "+pText);

     // update the text in the <p> element
     $("p").text("Goodbye World From a Paragraph");
     pText = $("p").text();
     console.log(pId+" says "+pText);
   });
  </script>
 </body>
</html>
```

Listing 5.1 references a required jQuery file with this code snippet:

```
<script src="http://code.jquery.com/jquery-1.7.1.min.js">
</script>
```

Notice that the first HTML `<script>` element in the HTML `<body>` element starts with this line:

```
$(document).ready(function(){
    // do something here
});
```

The preceding construct ensures that the DOM has been loaded into memory, so it's safe to access and manipulate DOM elements.

You can use the `$` sign to represent jQuery, and you can get the value of an attribute of an HTML element (such as a `<p>` element) using the jQuery `attr()` function. For example, you can get the value of the `id` attribute of an HTML `<p>` element as follows:

```
var pId   = $("p").attr('id');
```

You can get the text string in an HTML `<p>` element using the jQuery `text()` function, as shown here:

```
// get the text in the <p> element
var pText = $("p").text();
console.log (pId+' says '+pText);
```

Finally, you can update the text in an HTML `<p>` element using the jQuery `text()` function, as shown here:

```
// update the text in the <p> element
$("p").text("Goodbye World From a Paragraph");
```

Launch the file in Listing 5.2 and open the Inspector that is available in your `WebKit`-based browser. Next, select "Inspect Element," and click the ">>" symbol at the bottom of the Web page to see the output from the two `console.log()` statements in Listing 5.2.

You can use Chrome Web Inspector to view the contents of variables, which can be very helpful for debugging purposes. You can experiment with the features of Chrome Web Inspector, and also read online tutorials about this excellent tool.

jQuery Qualifiers versus jQuery Methods

In simple terms, a jQuery method is code (preceded with a dot "."), whereas a qualifier (preceded with a colon ":") is interpreted in a selector. A jQuery qualifier involves some type of logic, whereas a jQuery method retrieves the value of a property or assigns values to properties.

For example, the following code snippet uses a jQuery qualifier to retrieve the text value of the first HTML <p> element in a Web page:

```
var pText = $("p:eq(0)").text();
```

Contrast the preceding code snippet with the following line of code, which retrieves the text value of all the HTML <p> elements in a Web page:

```
var pText = $("p").text();
```

In Listing 5.2 you saw how to manipulate a single HTML <p> element. You can modify the first occurrence of an HTML <p> element by modifying Listing 5.2 as shown here:

```
<body>
  <p style="color:red" id="Steve">Hello From a Paragraph</p>
  <p style="color:blue" id="Steve2">Hello2 From a Paragraph</
p>

  <script>
   $(document).ready(function(){
      // $("p") is a collection of <p> elements
      var pId   = $("p:eq(0)").attr('id');

      // get the text in the <p> element
      var pText = $("p:eq(0)").text();
      console.log(pId+' says '+pText);

      // update the text in the <p> element
    $("p:eq(0)").text("Goodbye From a Paragraph");
      pText = $("p:eq(0)").text();
      console.log(pId+' says '+pText);
   });
  </script>
 </body>
```

The text that is highlighted in bold is modified code, which manipulates only the first HTML <p> element using the jQuery :eq() qualifier. jQuery provides a rich set of qualifiers and functions for selecting subsets of elements. In addition, you can combine jQuery functions via "method chaining" (discussed later) that enables you to write very compact yet sophisticated jQuery code for manipulating elements in HTML Web pages.

Using Web Storage with jQuery

In Chapter 1, you learned about HTML5 localStorage, and you already know enough about jQuery to understand how to read strings entered by users and then how to store those string in a browser's localStorage. Although it's better not to store sensitive information such as passwords in localStorage, this example illustrates how you can store contextual information that will be available for retrieval in different browser sessions.

Listing 5.3 displays the contents of JQLoginLS.html that illustrates how to create a login page that uses jQuery and localStorage.

Listing 5.3 JQLoginLS.html

```
<!DOCTYPE html>
<html lang="en">
 <head>
  <meta charset="utf-8"/>
  <title>jQuery and Local Storage</title>

  <script src="http://code.jquery.com/jquery-1.7.1.min.js">
  </script>
 </head>

 <body>
 <p>Please register with a user name an email address: </p>

 <form id="LoginForm" action="">
  <fieldset>
   <legend>Enter a Username and EMail Address</legend>
    <label for="username">Username:</label>
    <input type="text" id="username" width="50"/>
    <label for="email">EMail:</label>
    <input type="text" id="email" width="50"/>
    <input type="button" id="register" value="Register"/>
  </fieldset>
  </div>
 </form>

 <script>
```

```
$(document).ready(function(){
  $("#register").click(function() {
    var username = $("#username").val();
    var password = $("#password").val();
    var userExists = localStorage.getItem("username");

    if(userExists && username == userExists) {
      alert("Error: "+userExists+" already exists");
    } else {
      alert("Saving "+username+"/"+email+" to local
                                     storage");
      console.log("Saving "+username+"/"+email+" to local
                                     storage");
      localStorage.setItem("username", username);
      localStorage.setItem("email", email);
    }
  });
});
</script>
</body>
</html>
```

Listing 5.3 references the required jQuery file and then contains the code for a simple HTML Form that captures a username and password.

The jQuery code for accessing and storing a username and password in localStorage is inside the click event handler for the HTML button, as shown here:

```
var username = $("#username").val();
var password = $("#password").val();
var userExists = localStorage.getItem("username");

if(userExists && username == userExists) {
  alert("Error: "+userExists+" already exists");
} else {
  alert("Saving "+username+" to local storage");
  localStorage.setItem("username", username);
  localStorage.setItem("password", password);
}
```

The preceding code block also performs some simple validation, and the value of the text fields is retrieved in jQuery using the val() function, as shown here:

```
var username = $("#username").val();
var password = $("#password").val();
```

Since the rest of the code is already familiar to you, this concludes the discussion of the code in Listing 5.2.

Figure 5.1 displays the result of rendering the page JQLoginLS.html in a landscape-mode screenshot taken from a Chrome browser on a Macbook.

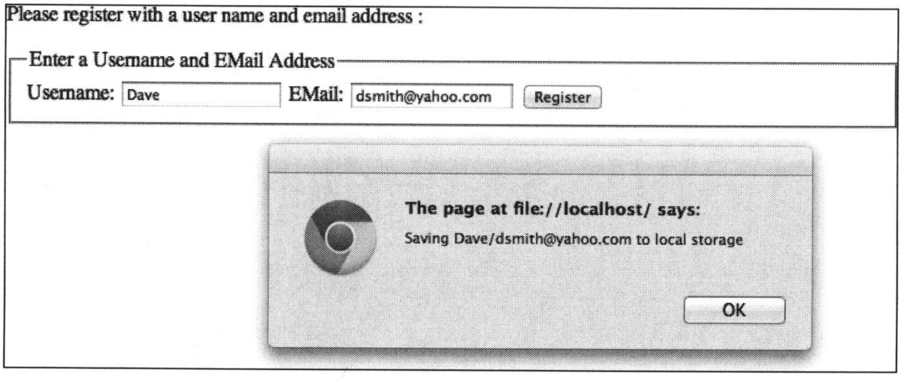

FIGURE 5.1 Saving user data in localStorage in a Chrome browser on a Macbook.

QUERYING AND MODIFYING THE DOM WITH JQUERY

Earlier in this chapter you saw how to use the jQuery eq() selector to find the first HTML <p> element in a set of <p> elements. This section shows you how to use various jQuery modifiers that make it very easy to find and update elements in an HTML5 Web page. The code samples are short because they illustrate only one or two qualifiers, but you can obviously combine them to perform very sophisticated DOM traversals and context-sensitive modifications to DOM elements.

Some of the qualifiers that are discussed in the code samples in this section include :first, :last, :even, and :odd. A partial list of selectors includes :eq(), :lt(), :gt(), :has(), :contains(), and :eq().

Find and Modify Elements With :first and :last Qualifiers

The example in this section shows you how to use the jQuery :first and :last qualifiers to manipulate the text in HTML elements.

Listing 5.4 displays the contents of JQModifyElements1.html that illustrates how to switch the contents of two <p> elements.

Listing 5.4 JQModifyElements1.html

```
<!DOCTYPE html>
```

```
<html lang="en">
<head>
  <meta charset="utf-8"/>
  <title>jQuery and Modifying Elements</title>

  <script src="http://code.jquery.com/jquery-1.7.1.min.js">
  </script>
</head>

<body>
  <p style="color:red" id="Steve">Hello From Paragraph One</p>
  <p style="color:blue" id="Dave">Goodbye From Paragraph
                                                    Two</p>

  <script>
    $(document).ready(function(){
      // get information in first paragraph:
      var pId1   = $("p:first").attr('id');
      var pText1 = $("p:first").text();

      // get information in last paragraph:
      var pId2   = $("p:last").attr('id');
      var pText2 = $("p:last").text();

      $("p:first").html(pText2);
      $("p:last").html(pText1);
    //$("p:first").text(pText2);
    //$("p:last").text(pText1);
    });
  </script>
</body>
</html>
```

Listing 5.4 references the required jQuery file, adds two HTML <p> elements, and then extracts the value of the id attribute and the text in the first <p> element as shown here:

```
// get information in first paragraph:
var pId1   = $("p:first").attr('id');
var pText1 = $("p:first").text();
```

The next block of code performs the same thing with the second <p> element, and then the text of the two <p> elements is switched with the following two lines of code:

```
$("p:first").html(pText2);
$("p:last").html(pText1);
```

Despite the simplicity of the jQuery code, this illustrates the ease with which you can manipulate HTML elements in an HTML Web page by means of the available jQuery functions.

Incidentally, you can get and set the value of an HTML <input> field (whose id attribute has value myInput) with the following two lines of code:

```
$("#myInput").val()
$("#myInput").text("new input value");
```

Figure 5.2 displays the result of rendering the page JQModifyElements1. html in a landscape-mode screenshot taken from an Asus Prime tablet with Android ICS.

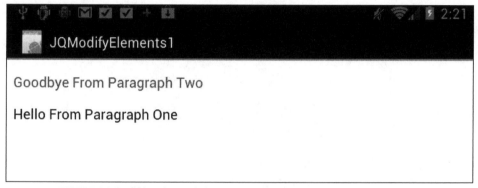

FIGURE 5.2 Modifying element in jQuery on an Asus Prime tablet with Android ICS.

The next section shows you how to use jQuery methods that can set collection of elements with the jQuery qualifiers :even() and :odd().

Finding Elements with :even and :odd Qualifiers

The example in this section shows you more sophisticated operations, such as setting the color of all the even-numbered or odd-numbered HTML <p> elements in a single line of code.

Listing 5.5 displays the contents of JQFindByEvenOrOdd1.html that illustrates how to select and update elements by their relative position (such as first, last, even, or odd) in an HTML Web page.

Listing 5.5 JQFindByEvenOrOdd1.html

```
<!DOCTYPE html>
<html lang="en">
<head>
  <meta charset="utf-8"/>
  <title>Using jQuery find with even or odd</title>
```

```
<script src="http://code.jquery.com/jquery-1.7.1.min.js">
</script>

<style>
   #div1 {
      position: relative;
      width:   400px;
      height: 200px;
      background: #aaa;
   }
</style>
</head>

<body>
   <div id="div1">
      <p style="color:red"      id="Steve">Hello From Paragraph
One</p>
      <p style="color:blue"     id="Dave">Goodbye From Paragraph
Two</p>
      <p style="color:yellow" id="Jane">Jane Says Hello</p>
      <p style="color:green"   id="Michelle">Michelle Says Good-
bye</p>
      <p style="color:black"   id="Jim">Jim Just Woke Up</p>
   </div>

   <script>
    $(document).ready(function(){
      // get information in first paragraph:
      var pId1   = $("p:first").attr('id');
      var pText1 = $("p:first").text();

      // get information in last paragraph:
      var pId2   = $("p:last").attr('id');
      var pText2 = $("p:last").text();

      $("p:first").html(pText2);
      $("p:last").html(pText1);

      $("p:even").css({color:'white'});
      $("p:odd").css({color:'red'});
      $("p:last").css({color:'blue'});
    });
   </script>
  </body>
</html>
```

Listing 5.5 references the required jQuery file, adds several HTML <p> elements, and switches the contents of the first and last <p> elements in the same manner as Listing 5.4. In addition, Listing 5.5 sets the even-numbered <p> elements to white, the odd-numbered <p> elements to red, and the last <p> element to blue, as shown here:

```
$("p:even").css({color:'white'});
$("p:odd").css({color:'red'});
$("p:last").css({color:'blue'});
```

Finding Elements with :eq, :lt, and :gt Qualifiers

There are many jQuery functions available to perform sophisticated manipulations of HTML elements with relative ease. This section contains some useful code snippets that illustrate some of the other jQuery functions that are available.

For example, the jQuery qualifiers :eq(), :lt(), and :gt() match elements whose position is equal to, less than, or greater than, respectively, in a list of items. Recall that lists in jQuery start from index 0.

An example of finding the <p> element with index 3:

```
$('p:eq(3)').text('index equals three');
```

An example of finding the <p> element with index greater than 3:

```
$('p:gt(3)').text('index is greater than three');
```

An example of finding the <p> element with index less than 3:

```
$('p:lt(3)').text('index is less than three');
```

The preceding code snippets show you some of the things that are possible with jQuery functions. There are jQuery functions that perform conditional tests on HTML elements.

For example, jQuery provides custom selectors, such as :has(), :contains(), and :eq(). You can use these selectors to select elements, as in the following example:

```
$("div:contains('foo')"))
```

You can use these selectors to filter other selectors, as shown here:

```
$("div").contains('foo')
```

In addition, you can search for elements based on the value of their id attribute or by a specific `class` attribute, as shown in the next section.

Finding HTML Elements by class or id

jQuery uses same syntax as CSS selectors: the "#" symbol refers to an `id` attribute and a "." symbol refers to a `class` attribute. For example, if you want to find an HTML `<div>` element whose `id` attribute is `abc`, then jQuery uses the string `#abc` when searching for that `<div>` element. If you want to find an HTML `<p>` element whose `id` attribute is `abc`, then jQuery uses the string `.abc` when searching for that `<p>` element.

Listing 5.6 displays the contents of `JQFindByClassOrId1.html` that illustrates how to select and update elements by `id` or `class` in an HTML Web page.

Listing 5.6 `JQFindByClassOrId1.html`

```
<!DOCTYPE html>
<html lang="en">
<head>
  <meta charset="utf-8"/>
  <title>Using jQuery find with class or id</title>

  <script src="http://code.jquery.com/jquery-1.7.1.min.js">
  </script>

  <style>
    #div1 {
      position: relative;
      width:  400px;
      height: 200px;
      background: #aaa;
    }

    .class1 {
      background: #f00;
    }

    .class2 {
      background: #fff;
    }
  </style>
</head>

<body>
  <div id="div1">
```

```
        <p style="color:red"      id="Steve">Hello From Paragraph
One</p>
        <p style="color:blue"     id="Dave">Goodbye From Paragraph
Two</p>
        <p style="color:yellow" id="Jane">Jane Says Hello</p>
        <p style="color:green"    class="Michelle">Michelle Says
Goodbye</p>
        <p style="color:black"  class="Jim">Jim Just Woke Up</p>
      </div>

      <script>
       $(document).ready(function(){
         // get information in first paragraph:
         var pId1   = $("p:first").attr('id');
         var pText1 = $("p:first").text();

         // get information in last paragraph:
         var pId2   = $("p:last").attr('id');
         var pText2 = $("p:last").text();

         // update the first and last paragraphs
         $("p:first").html(pText2);
         $("p:last").html(pText1);

         // update the paragraph with class "Michelle"
         $("p.Michelle").css({'font-size':20, color:'blue'});

         // update the paragraph with class "Jim"
         $("p.Jim").css({'font-size':24, color:'red'});

         // add the CSS class css-class1
         $('div').addClass('class1');
         // remove the CSS class css-class1
         $('div').removeClass('class2');
       });
      </script>
     </body>
    </html>
```

The first portion of Listing 5.6 is similar to Listing 5.4, along with new code that shows you how to use the jQuery css() function in order to update the CSS properties of HTML elements.

For example, you can set the font-size property, which is in quotes because of the hyphen, as shown here:

```
// update the paragraph with class "Michelle"
```

```
$("p.Michelle").css({'font-size':20, color:'blue'});
```

You can add a CSS class to an HTML element using the `addClass()` method, as shown here:

```
// add the CSS class css-class1
$('div').addClass('class1');
```

Finally, you can remove a CSS class from an HTML element using the `removeClass()` method, as shown here:

```
// remove the CSS class css-class1
$('div').removeClass('class2');
```

Incidentally, you can specify more complex criteria when you perform method chaining, as in the following example (can you guess what it does?):

```
$("ul li#item4").prev().css({'font-size':24,
                                'background-color':'blue'});
```

The preceding code snippet will be discussed in a code sample later in this chapter.

Finding and Setting Element Attributes

You've seen how to use various jQuery functions to manipulate elements, and also how to find the value of an attribute. This section contains examples of updating the attributes of elements.

The following snippet gets the value of the `src` attribute of an element:

```
var $source = $("img").attr("src");
```

The next code snippet shows how to set the value of one attribute:

```
$("img").attr("src", "/images/MyHouse.jpg");
```

The following code snippet shows how to set multiple attributes in one command (displayed over multiple lines for convenience):

```
$("img").attr({
      src: "/images/MyHouse.jpg",
      title: "House",
      alt: "House"
});
```

Notice that the syntax of the jQuery `attr()` method is very similar to the jQuery `css()` method, so when you understand one function, you will understand the other one as well.

HTML5 supports custom attributes, provided that the attribute name starts with the string `data-` followed by an attribute name. Although you might not need to use custom attributes right now, jQuery Mobile relies heavily on custom attributes, so this functionality is extremely useful.

You can retrieve the values of custom attributes using the jQuery `.data()` method. For example, suppose your HTML Web page contains this snippet:

```
<div data-role="page" data-value="99" data-status="new"></div>
```

You can retrieve the values of these custom attributes as follows:

```
$("div").data("role") returns the value page
$("div").data("value") returns the value 99
$("div").data("status") returns the value true
```

You will see more examples of manipulating custom data attributes in jQuery Mobile code samples, and if you're really ambitious, you can find more examples in the jQuery Mobile source code.

Finding Form Elements and Their Attributes

jQuery enables you to select HTML `Form` elements based on various criteria using an intuitive syntax. For example, you can find elements (checkboxes, input fields, and so forth) that are in various states (checked, unchecked, hidden, visible) using the selectors that are listed here:

`:checkbox` (elements with type attribute checkbox)
`:checked` (checked radio buttons and checkboxes)
`:input` (button, input, select, and textarea)
`:radio` (elements with type attribute "radio")
`:text` (elements with type attribute "text")
`:hidden` (selects hidden elements)
`:visible` (selects visible elements)

You can find the size of the result set that is returned by a query using this syntax:

```
var textCount = $(":text").length;
```

You can select elements based on the values of their attributes by using the following selectors:

`[attribute]` selects elements with the specified attribute
`[attribute=somevalue]` selects elements whose attribute equals somevalue

`[attribute!=somevalue]` selects elements whose attribute does not equal `somevalue`

If you have written JavaScript code that deals with HTML `Form` elements, then you can easily see how useful these selectors will be for writing the jQuery counterparts to your JavaScript code.

Using nth-child() for Finding Elements

You know how to use `:even` and `:odd` in CSS in order to specify elements in the even and odd position in a set of elements; if you like this functionality, then you will really like the jQuery `nth-child()` operator, which enables you to specify arithmetic expressions, as well as `:even`, `:odd`, and specific positional values.

Listing 5.7 displays the contents of `JQFindByCSS3StyleExpressions1.html` that illustrates how to select and update elements in an HTML Web page using the jQuery selector `nth-child()`.

Listing 5.7 JQFindByCSS3StyleExpressions1.html

```
<!DOCTYPE html>
<html lang="en">
<head>
  <meta charset="utf-8"/>
  <title>Using the jQuery find Method</title>

  <script src="http://code.jquery.com/jquery-1.7.1.min.js">
  </script>

  <style>
    #div1 {
      position: relative;
      width:   400px;
      height: 350px;
      background: #aaa;
    }
    ul li {
      font-size: 18px;
      color: blue;
    }
  </style>
</head>

<body>
  <div id="div1">
    <ul>
```

```
          <li>List Item 1</li>
          <li>List Item 2</li>
          <li>List Item 3</li>
          <li>List Item 4</li>
          <li>List Item 5</li>
          <li>List Item 6</li>
          <li>List Item 7</li>
          <li>List Item 8</li>
          <li>List Item 9</li>
       </ul>
     </div>

     <script>
      $(document).ready(function(){
        // get information in first paragraph:
        var pId1   = $("ul li:first").attr('id');
        var pText1 = $("ul li:first").text();

        // get information in last paragraph:
        var pId2   = $("ul li:last").attr('id');
        var pText2 = $("ul li:last").text();

        $("ul li:first").html(pText2);
        $("ul li:last").html(pText1);

        $("ul li:nth-child(even)").css({color:"#f00",
                                        "font-size":8});
        $("ul li:nth-child(3n+1)").css({"font-size":24});
      $("ul li:nth-child(1)").css({color:"#ff0","font-size":18});
      });
     </script>
    </body>
  </html>
```

Listing 5.6 contains an unordered list of elements, along with the following code to switch the text of the first and last list elements. This code is similar to the code in Listing 5.4 that switches the text of the first and last <p> elements:

```
// get information in first paragraph:
var pId1   = $("ul li:first").attr('id');
var pText1 = $("ul li:first").text();

// get information in last paragraph:
var pId2   = $("ul li:last").attr('id');
var pText2 = $("ul li:last").text();
```

```
$("ul li:first").html(pText2);
$("ul li:last").html(pText1);
```

The interesting code in Listing 5.6 uses the jQuery `css()` function to update CSS properties of the even elements, as shown here:

```
$("ul li:nth-child(even)").css({color:"#f00","font-size":8});
```

The next code snippet updates every third list element, starting from the second list element:

```
$("ul li:nth-child(3n+1)").css({"font-size":24});
```

The last line of code in Listing 5.6 updates the second list element:

```
$("ul li:nth-child(1)").css({color:"#ff0","font-size":18});
```

Other useful and related jQuery selectors are `:first-child()`, `:last-child()`, and `parent()`, which you can use in order to find the first child, last child, and the parent, respectively.

Figure 5.3 displays `JQFindByCSS3StyleExpressions.html` rendered in a landscape-mode screenshot taken from an Asus Prime tablet with Android ICS.

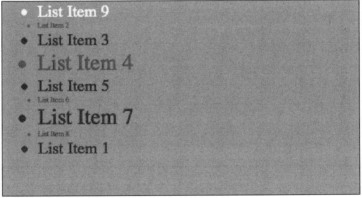

FIGURE 5.3 Finding elements in jQuery on an iPad 3.

Using jQuery to Remove Elements

As you can probably guess, jQuery enables you to remove elements in addition to finding and modifying elements in an HTML Web page.

Listing 5.8 displays the contents of `JQRemovingElements1.html` that illustrates how to select and remove elements by `id` or `class` in an HTML Web page.

Listing 5.8 JQRemovingElements1.html

```
<!DOCTYPE html>
<html lang="en">
<head>
  <meta charset="utf-8"/>
  <title>Removing Elements with jQuery</title>

  <script src="http://code.jquery.com/jquery-1.7.1.min.js">
  </script>

  <style>
    #div1 {
      position: relative;
      width:  400px;
      height: 200px;
      background: #aaa;
    }
  </style>
</head>

<body>
  <div id="div1">
    <p style="color:red"    id="Steve">Hello From Paragraph
                                                One</p>
    <p style="color:blue"   id="Dave">Goodbye From Paragraph
                                                Two</p>
    <p style="color:yellow" id="Jane">Jane Says Hello</p>
    <p style="color:green"  id="Michelle">Michelle Says Good
                                                bye</p>
    <p style="color:black"  id="Jim">Jim Just Woke Up</p>
    <p style="color:red"    id="Tracy">Tracy Went To Sleep</p>
  </div>

  <script>
   $(document).ready(function(){
     $("p:even").css({color:'white'});
     $("p:odd").css({color:'red'});
     $("p:first").css({color:'yellow'});
     $("p:last").css({color:'blue'});

     // remove the <p> element Dave
     $("#Dave").remove();

     // remove the <p> element Michelle
     $("div1").remove("#Michelle");
```

Fundamentals of jQuery • **211**

```
    // remove <p> elements containing "Goodbye"
    $("p").filter(":contains('Goodbye')").remove();
  });
 </script>
 </body>
</html>
```

Listing 5.8 contains three lines of code for removing elements, the first of which is shown here (the second is similar):

```
// remove the <p> element Dave
$("#Dave").remove();
```

Although the preceding code snippet performs just as you would expect, an example that illustrates the real power of jQuery is shown in the following code snippet, which uses the jQuery `filter()` method to find and then remove all the HTML <p> elements that contain the string `Goodbye`:

```
$("p").filter(":contains('Goodbye')").remove();
```

Compare the simple and intuitive nature of the preceding single line of jQuery code with the corresponding JavaScript code that is required to perform the same functionality.

Figure 5.4 displays the result of rendering `RemovingElements1.html` in a portrait-mode screenshot taken from an iOS application running on an iPad 3.

FIGURE 5.4 Removing Elements via jQuery on an iPad 3.

Creating DOM Elements

jQuery provides the `clone()` method and the `append()` method for creating new DOM elements. The `clone()` method creates a true copy of an element, and if you specify true, then `clone(true)` will also propagate the event handlers of the source element. On the other hand, the `append()` method operates on the specified element. Listing 5.9 displays the contents of JQCre-

`atingElements1.html` that illustrates how to use both of these jQuery methods in order to create new elements in an HTML Web page.

Listing 5.9 JQCreatingElements1.html

```
<!DOCTYPE html>
<html lang="en">
<head>
  <meta charset="utf-8"/>
  <title>Creating Elements with jQuery</title>

  <script src="http://code.jquery.com/jquery-1.7.1.min.js">
  </script>

  <style>
    div {
      position: relative;
      width:  400px;
      background: #aaa;
    }
  </style>
</head>

<body>
  <div id="div1">
      <p style="color:red"      id="Steve">Hello From Paragraph
One</p>
  </div>
  <div id="div2">
      <p style="color:red"      id="Dave">Dave Says Goodbye From
Two</p>
  </div>
  <div id="div3">
    <p style="color:yellow" id="Jane">Jane Says Hello</p>
  </div>
  <div id="div4">
      <p style="color:green"   id="Michelle">Michelle Says Good-
bye</p>
  </div>
  <div id="div5">
    <p style="color:black"   id="Jim">Jim Just Woke Up</p>
  </div>
  <div id="div6">
    <p style="color:red"      id="Tracy">Tracy Went To Sleep</p>
  </div>

  <script>
   $(document).ready(function(){
```

```
   // append a clone of the #Dave element to "#div2":
   $("#Dave").clone().css({color:"#000"}).appendTo("#div2");

   // append another clone of the #Dave element to "#div2":
   $("#Dave").clone().css({color:"#00f"}).appendTo("#div2");

   // move the red #Dave to the end of "#div4":
   $("#Dave").appendTo("#div4");

   // prepend #Dave to all the 'div' elements:
  //$("#Dave").clone().prependTo("div");
   });
  </script>
 </body>
</html>
```

Listing 5.9 introduces the jQuery `clone()` method, an example of which is shown here:

```
// append a clone of the #Dave element to "#div2":
$("#Dave").clone().css({color:"#000"}).appendTo("#div2");
```

The purpose of the preceding code snippet is clear, and you can even read it from left to right to grasp its purpose: clone the element whose id is Dave, set its color to black, and append this cloned element to the element whose id is div2.

The only other new functionality in Listing 5.9 is the jQuery `prependTo()` function, which inserts an element before (instead of after) a specified element, as shown here:

```
    // prepend #Dave to all the 'div' elements:
   //$("#Dave").clone().prependTo("div");
```

There are other jQuery methods for inserting DOM elements, some of which are described in the next section.

Figure 5.5 displays the result of rendering JQCreatingElements1.html in a landscape-mode screenshot taken from an iOS application running on an iPad 3.

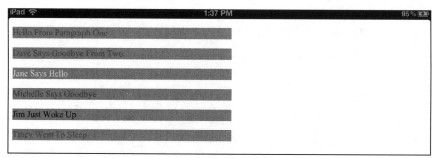

FIGURE 5.5 Creating elements with jQuery on an iPad 3.

Other jQuery Methods for Inserting DOM Elements

jQuery provides one set of methods that are used when the source element already exists in an HTML Web page. Another set of methods are used when you are dynamically creating a new element.

For example, if `myDiv1` and `myImg1` are two elements in an HTML Web page, then you can create a clone of `myDiv1` and insert it into the DOM immediately after the `myImg1` using the jQuery `append()` method, as shown here:

```
$("myDiv1").clone().append("#myImg1");
```

On the other hand, the following code snippet creates a new `<div>` element dynamically, so you must use the jQuery `appendTo()` method, as shown here:

```
$("myDiv1").clone().appendTo("#myImg1");
```

Moving elements in an HTML Web page:

```
$("#myDiv2").insertBefore("#myDiv1");
$("#myDiv3").insertAfter("#myDiv1");
```

Another convenient use for the jQuery `appendTo()` method is for inserting CSS stylesheets based on conditional logic, as shown here:

```
if ($('body').width() > 900) {

  $('<link rel="stylesheet" href="wide.css"/>')

    .appendTo('head');

} else {

    $('link[href=wide.css]').remove();

  }
```

The preceding code block inserts the CSS stylesheet `wide.css` if the width of the HTML<body> element is greater than `900`; otherwise, this stylesheet is removed. You can use this type of code in lieu of CSS Media Queries, but be careful that you don't inadvertently "scatter" this type of logic in your HTML Web pages, which could make them more difficult to debug or enhance with new functionality.

jQuery supports the following methods for creating new DOM elements and inserting them in different locations relative to an existing DOM element:

```
append()
insert()
prepend()
appendTo()
appendAfter()
insertBefore()
insertAfter()
```

The jQuery methods `append()`, `insert()`, and `prepend()` are used when the source element already exists in an HTML Web page; the other methods are used when you are dynamically creating a new element.

Useful jQuery Code Blocks

This section contains a set of code snippets that enable you to perform conditional logic and then execute your custom code. The code samples in this section are straightforward, and the comments explain their purpose.

Check if jQuery is loaded:

```
if (typeof jQuery == 'undefined') {
    // jQuery is not loaded
}
```

Check if an element exists:

```
if ( $('#myElement').length > 0 ) {
    // the element exists
}
```

Check for empty elements:

```
$('*').each(function() {
    if ($(this).text() == "") {
        //do something here
    }
```

```
});
```

Returns true or false based on content of a <div> element:

```
var emptyTest = $('#myDiv').is(':empty');
```

Determine if a checkbox is checked (returns true/false):

```
$('#checkBox').attr('checked');
```

Find all checked checkboxes:

```
$('input[type=checkbox]:checked');
```

Disable/enable inputs for a button element:

```
$("#submit-button").attr("disabled", true);
```

Remove an attribute from a button element:

```
$("#submit-button").removeAttr("disabled");
```

Another important class of jQuery functions involves functions that enable you to navigate around the DOM, and some of these methods are discussed in the next section.

JQUERY ELEMENT NAVIGATION METHODS

At this point you know how to use jQuery to find, update, delete, and create elements in an HTML Web page. However, sometimes you need to process an element whose position is relative to another element. For example, suppose you have an unordered list of elements, and whenever users click on an element, you interchange its position with the element immediately following (or preceding) the clicked element. Fortunately, jQuery provides such functionality with intuitively named methods, as discussed in the next section.

The next()/prev()/closest()/parent() Methods

The jQuery next() method selects the next immediate sibling of the current "context" element, whereas the jQuery prev() method selects the immediate preceding sibling. The jQuery parent() method selects the parent of the current element, and the jQuery closest() method selects the closest element matching the specified type.

Listing 5.10 displays the contents of JQNextPrevClosestParent1.html that illustrates how to use these methods in order to manipulate elements in an HTML Web page.

Listing 5.10 JQNextPrevClosestParent1.html

```
<!DOCTYPE html>
<html lang="en">
<head>
  <meta charset="utf-8"/>
  <title>jQuery and next, previous, closest parent</title>

  <script src="http://code.jquery.com/jquery-1.7.1.min.js">
  </script>

  <style>
    #div1 {
      position: relative;
      width:   400px;
      height: 250px;
      background: #aaa;
    }
    ul li {
      font-size: 18px;
      color: white;
    }
  </style>
</head>

<body>
 <div id="div1">
   <ul>
     <li id="item1">List Item 1</li>
     <li id="item2">List Item 2</li>
     <li id="item3">List Item 3</li>
     <li id="item4">List Item 4</li>
     <li id="item5">List Item 5</li>
     <li id="item6">List Item 6</li>
     <li id="item7">List Item 7</li>
     <li id="item8">List Item 8</li>
     <li id="item9">List Item 9</li>
   </ul>
 </div>

 <script>
  $(document).ready(function(){
```

```
$("ul li#item1").next().css({color:'#fff',
                            'background-color':'red'});
$("ul li#item4").prev().css({'font-size':24,
                            'background-color':'blue'});
$("ul li#item4").next().next().css({'font-size':24,
                            'background-color':'blue'});
      $("ul   li#item6").closest("div").css({"background-
color":"#aa4"});
    $("ul li#item7").parent().parent().css({'width':500});
  });
</script>
</body>
</html>
```

Listing 5.10 references the required jQuery file, followed by an HTML <ul> element that contains 10 list items, each of which contains an id attribute.

Listing 5.10 also contains some interesting jQuery code that relies on method chaining to find and update HTML elements. For example, the following code snippet in Listing 5.10 uses the jQuery css() function to update properties of the HTML <li> element that follows the <li> element (by invoking the jQuery next() function) whose id attribute has value item1:

```
$("ul li#item1").next().css({color:'#fff',
                            'background-color':'red'});
```

The following code snippet uses the jQuery css() function to update properties of the HTML <li> element that follows the <li> element (by invoking the jQuery next() function) whose id attribute has value item1:

```
$("ul li#item4").next().next().css({'font-size':24,
                            'background-color':'blue'});
```

Based on what you have seen thus far, you can readily surmise the result of invoking next().next() as well as parent().parent() in two other lines of code in Listing 5.10.

The only line of code that we have not discussed finds the closest parent HTML <div> element that contains the HTML <li> element whose id attribute has value item6, and then sets its background color to aa4:

```
$("ul li#item6").closest("div").css({"background-
                            color":"#aa4"});
```

Once again, jQuery enables you to specify complex selection criteria using method chaining that would be much more tedious to write using plain JavaScript.

Figure 5.6 displays the result of rendering `JQNextPrevClosestParent1.
html` in a landscape-mode screenshot taken from an iOS application running
on an iPad 3.

FIGURE 5.6 Finding siblings in jQuery on an iPad 3.

Other jQuery Navigational Selection Methods

In addition to the relative navigation methods that were discussed in the
previous section, jQuery supports relative selection methods. For example,
the jQuery `.siblings()` method selects all the siblings of the current element, and the `.children()` method selects all the child elements of the current element.

The jQuery code in this section is both concise and clear, and comprises
only one-fourth of the contents of the Web page. An interesting exercise is
performing the same functionality using only JavaScript (without the benefit
of any toolkits) and then comparing the size of the code with the code in Listing 5.11, as well as the readability of the JavaScript code and the amount of
time that you needed to write it.

Listing 5.11 displays the contents of `JQSiblingsChildren1.html` that
illustrates how to use the jQuery methods `.siblings()`, `.children()`,
`.each()`, and `data()` in order to perform various manipulations of elements
in an HTML Web page.

Listing 5.11 JQSiblingsChildren1.html

```html
<!DOCTYPE html>
<html lang="en">
<head>
  <meta charset="utf-8"/>
  <title>Siblings and Children with jQuery</title>

  <style>
  ul { float:left; font-size:14px; }
  li { color:blue; font-size:16px; }
  p  { color:red;  font-size:16px; }
  </style>

  <script src="http://code.jquery.com/jquery-1.7.1.min.js">
  </script>
</head>

<body>
  <ul>
    <li id="top1">List 1 One</li>
    <li>List 1 Two</li>
    <li List 1 Three</li>
    <li>List 1 Four</li>
  </ul>

  <ul>
    <li>List 2 One</li>
    <li>List 2 Two</li>
    <li id="middle2">List 2 Three</li>
    <li>List 2 Four</li>
    <li>List 2 Five</li>
  </ul>

  <ul>
    <li>List 3 One</li>
    <li>List 3 Two</li>
    <li List 3 Four</li>
    <li>List 3 Five</li>
    <li id="bottom3">List 3 Five</li>
  </ul>

  <script>
    $(document).ready(function(){
      $("#top1").siblings()
                .css("color", "red");
```

```
$("#middle2").parent().css("font-size", 32);

$("#bottom3").siblings().each(function() {
    if (this.style.color != "blue") {
        this.style.color = "red";
    } else {
        this.style.color = "yellow";
    }
  });
 });
 </script>
</body>
</html>
```

Listing 5.11 defines three HTML `<ul>` elements, each of which has a list element with an `id` attribute whose value is `top1`, `middle2`, and `bottom3`, respectively.

The first jQuery block of code finds the siblings of the element whose `id` attribute is `top1` and then sets those elements to `red`, as shown here:

```
$("#top1").siblings().css("color", "red");
```

The second jQuery code snippet finds the parent of the element whose `id` attribute is `middle1` and then sets its `font-size` to 32:

```
$("#middle2").parent().css("font-size", 32);
```

The final jQuery code block is the most complex, and it finds the siblings of the element whose `id` attribute is `bottom3` and sets their `color` property to `red` if they are not currently `blue`, otherwise the code sets their color to `yellow`:

```
$("#bottom3").siblings().each(function() {
    if (this.style.color != "blue") {
        this.style.color = "red";
    } else {
        this.style.color = "yellow";
    }
 });
```

Launch the code in Listing 5.11 to verify that the jQuery code performs the updates that are described here.

CACHING RESULTS OF JQUERY INVOCATIONS

For HTML5 Web pages with non-trivial functionality that also perform many DOM-based searches, you can improve performance by caching the results of traversing a DOM structure via jQuery.

For example, if your HTML Web page has many <li> elements, you can write more efficient code by retrieving the list of all the HTML <ul> elements in an HTML Web page, storing that list in a variable, and then invoking operations on the variable instead of traversing the DOM multiple times, as shown here:

```
$("button").click(function() {
    // store the list of <ul> elements in a variable
    var ulList = $("ul");

    // remove the first <li> element
    ulList.find("li:first-element").remove();

    // change the text of the last <li> element
    ulList.find("li:last-element").text("last li");
})
```

The preceding code block is a simple one, but for an HTML page with hundreds of similar HTML elements, this coding technique can definitely improve your performance. When in doubt, compare the speed differences when you write your HTML Web pages without using this caching technique.

WHAT ABOUT THIS, $this, and $(this)?

The previous section contains a code samples with the this keyword, and it's actually common to find this keyword in HTML Web pages. Unfortunately, it can be a source of confusion, so this section provides a brief description to help you understand its purpose and how to use the this keyword.

The this keyword in JavaScript is determined as follows:

- If a method of an object callingObject caused the current block of code to be executed, then this is the object callingObject, unless.
- The function reference is passed to an event handler.

One of the really nice things about jQuery is that it simplifies the rather tricky rules regarding the this keyword.

For example, if you associate a click event on a button and users click on that button, then in jQuery the keyword `this` refers to the clicked button (as opposed to other buttons on the Web page that have not been clicked yet). However, we must "jQueryify" the keyword `this` by "wrapping" it in parentheses (with an initial "$" sign) in order to have access to jQuery methods, as shown here:

```
$("button").click(function() {
    $(this).css('background-color', "red");
    $(this).text("I am a red clicked button");
})
```

Keep in mind that you must use `$(this)` in order to invoke jQuery functions, and that jQuery adds jQuery-specific functions to the `$(this)` object.

Recall that in an earlier section you learned how to cache the results of a jQuery DOM traversal in a variable. Although you do not gain a performance improvement, you can also cache the reference to the `this` keyword, as shown here:

```
$("button").click(function() {
    var $this = $(this);
    $this.css('background-color', "red");
    $this.text("I am a red clicked button");
})
```

HANDLING CLICK EVENTS IN JQUERY

jQuery provides support for various types of events and user gestures that you can "bind" to custom code (written by you) that is executed whenever those events or gestures take place. The events that you can detect and bind in jQuery Mobile include `click`, `tap`, `taphold`, `swipe`, `swipeleft`, and `swipeeright` (more details about these events are discussed later).

The `click()` function enables you to handle click events, and one example of the syntax is here:

```
$("#button1").click(function() {
    // do something

    }
```

There are several techniques for handling events (more details are provided later in this chapter), and the recommended technique for doing so is shown here:

```
$("#button1").on("click"), function() {
    // do something

}
```

In a similar fashion, you can use the two preceding code snippets to define event handlers for the other jQuery events shown above as well as the mouse events that are listed in an upcoming section.

The `dblclick()` function enables you to handle double click events. An example of the syntax is here:

```
$("#button2").dblclick(function() {
  // do something
    }
```

The `focus()` function provides focus on selected elements. For example, this code displays a cursor when you click on an input field whose `id` attribute equals `firstInput`:

```
$("#firstInput").focus(function() {
  // do something
});
```

Listing 5.12 displays the contents of `JQClickDivs1.html` that illustrates how to detect click events and then update the contents of both `<div>` elements in this HTML5 Web page.

Listing 5.12 JQClickDivs1.html

```
<!DOCTYPE html>
<html lang="en">
<head>
  <meta charset="utf-8"/>
  <title>Detecting Click Events with jQuery</title>

  <script src="jquery-1.7.1.js"></script>

  <style>
   div {
     position: relative;
     width: 200px;
     height : 100px;
     background-color: red;
     color: white;
     margin: 2px;
```

```
    }
  </style>
</head>

<body>
  <div id="div1">The first div element </div>
  <div id="div2">The second div element </div>

  <script>
   var click1=0, click2=0, total=0;

   $(document).ready(function() {
      $("#div1").click(function() {
        ++click1;
        ++total;
        $(this).text("Clicked: "+click1+" total: "+total);
        $("#div2").text("Clicked: "+click2+" total: "+total);
      });

      $("#div2").click(function() {
        ++click2;
        ++total;
        $(this).text("Clicked: "+click2+" total: "+total);
        $("#div1").text("Clicked: "+click1+" total: "+total);
      });
    });
  </script>
 </body>
</html>
```

Listing 5.12 references the required jQuery file, followed by some CSS styling definitions, along with two HTML <div> elements:

```
<div id="div1">The first div element </div>
<div id="div2">The second div element </div>
```

The code for adding a click event listener to the first HTML <div> element is shown here (with similar jQuery code for the second HTML <div> element):

```
$("#div1").click(function() {
    ++click1;
    ++total;
    $(this).text("Clicked: "+click1+" total: "+total);
    $("#div2").text("Clicked: "+click2+" total: "+total);
});
```

Whenever users click on the preceding HTML `<div>` element, its click count and the total click count are incremented, and the text of both HTML `<div>` elements are updated with the click count for the individual `<div>` elements as well as the sum of the click counts for both `<div>` elements.

Although the example in Listing 5.12 is simplistic, it does illustrate how to keep track of events in different HTML elements in an HTML Web page. A more realistic example could involve an HTML Web page with an HTML `Form` that has inter-dependencies between elements in the form.

Figure 5.7 displays the result of rendering the HTML page `JQClickDivs1.html` in a landscape-mode screenshot taken from an iOS application running on an Asus Prime tablet with Android ICS.

FIGURE 5.7 Counting click events on an Asus Prime tablet with Android ICS.

JQUERY APIS FOR TRAVERSING ELEMENTS

jQuery supports the jQuery `.find()` method, which is a very powerful jQuery API that enables you to perform sophisticated DOM traversals and manipulate the result sets.

For example, you can set multiple CSS properties, such as the `background` and `width` attributes. In this section, you will see additional examples of the jQuery `css()` function.

Listing 5.13 displays the contents of `JQFindAndUpdate1.html` that illustrates how to find various sets of `<li>` elements and then update one or more of their CSS properties.

Listing 5.13 `JQFindAndUpdate1.html`

```
<!DOCTYPE html>
<html lang="en">
<head>
  <meta charset="utf-8"/>
  <title>Using the jQuery find Method with Lists</title>

  <script src="http://code.jquery.com/jquery-1.7.1.min.js">
  </script>

  <style>
    li { width: 50%; padding: 1px; }
  </style>
</head>

<body>
   <ul class="level-1">
     <li class="item-i">I
       <ul class="level-2">
         <li class="item-a">A</li>
       </ul>
     </li>

     <li class="item-ii">II
       <ul class="level-2">
         <li class="item-a">A</li>
         <li class="item-b">B
           <ul class="level-3">
             <li class="item-1">1</li>
             <li class="item-2">2</li>
           </ul>
         </li>
         <li class="item-c">C</li>
       </ul>
     </li>

     <li class="item-iii">III
       <ul class="level-2">
         <li class="item-1">1</li>
         <li class="item-2">2</li>
       </ul>
     </li>
```

```
        <li class="item-iv">IV
          <ul class="level-2">
            <li class="item-1">3</li>
            <li class="item-2">4</li>
          </li>
        </li>
      </ul>

    <script>
     $(document).ready(function(){
       // 'li' descendants of item II are now green:
     $('li.item-i').find('li').css('background-color', 'green');

       // 'li' descendants of item II are now red:
      $('li.item-ii').find('li').css('background-color', 'red');

       // the first 'li' of list B under item II is now black:
       var item1 = $('li.item-1')[0];
       $('li.item-ii').find(item1).css('background-color',
                                                    'black');

       // the 'li' descendants of item III are now yellow:
       var $allListItems = $('li');
       $('li.item-iii').find($allListItems).css({
               'background-color': 'yellow', 'width': '100px' });

       // 'li' descendants of item IV are now blue:
       $('li.item-iv').find('li').css({'background-color':
                                 'blue', 'width': '100px' });
     });
    </script>
  </body>
</html>
```

Listing 5.13 contains the usual initialization, followed by an HTML `<ul>` element with nested sublists. The section of jQuery code contains a comment that explains the purpose of each jQuery code snippet. As you can see, each code snippet starts from a specific element, selects a subset of the child elements using the jQuery `find()` method, and then updates various CSS properties using the jQuery `css()` method.

Launch the code in Listing 5.13 and compare the results with what you expected (are they the same?). As a final example, think of what this code snippet will do and then insert this code in Listing 5.13 to confirm your guess:

```
$('*').find('li').css('background-color', 'red');
```

You can find more information about the jQuery `.find()` method here:

http://api.jquery.com/find/

Another useful link with an extensive list of DOM traversal examples is here:

http://api.jquery.com/category/traversing/

Figure 5.8 displays the result of rendering `JQFindAndUpdate1.html` in a landscape-mode screenshot taken from an Asus Prime tablet with Android ICS.

FIGURE 5.8 Find and update elements on an Asus Prime tablet with Android ICS.

CHAINING JQUERY FUNCTIONS

You have already seen examples of chaining jQuery commands, and this section shows you how to execute more sophisticated chained commands. Specifically, the code sample in this section shows you how to use the `.end()` method, which enables you to "reset" the context list whenever you need to do so in a sequence of chained commands:

http://blog.pengoworks.com/index.cfm/2007/10/26/jQuery-Understanding-the-chain

By comparison, you might have used chained commands in Java (especially with JAXB) such as the following:

```
myList().getFirstElem().getCustomer().setFirstName("Dave");
```

However, jQuery chaining can involve more sophisticated operations because you can change the reference to the current result set before applying a new operation.

Listing 5.14 displays the contents of JQChaining1.html that illustrates how to invoke chained commands in jQuery.

Listing 5.14 JQChaining1.html

```
<!DOCTYPE html>
<html lang="en">
 <head>
  <meta charset="utf-8"/>
  <title>Chaining jQuery Methods</title>

  <script src="http://code.jquery.com/jquery-1.7.1.min.js">
  </script>

  <style>
    #outer {
      width:300px;
      height:300px;
      background:red;
    }
    #first {
      width:400px;
      height:150px;
      background:green;
    }
    #second {
      width:400px;
      height:200px;
      background:yellow;
    }
  </style>
 </head>

 <body>
  <div id="outer">
```

```
<ul>
  <li class="item-iii">III
    <ul class="level-2">
      <li class="item-1">1</li>
      <li class="item-2">2</li>
    </ul>
  </li>
</ul>
</div>

<script>
  $(document).ready(function(){
    // create the first div
    var $first = $("<div id='first'>first</div>")
    // append it to a new second div
    .appendTo("<div id='second'>second</div>")
    // next change the jQuery chain to the "second" div
    .parent()
    // append the second div to the 'outer' div
    .appendTo("#outer")
    // finally, go back to the last destructive command,
    // giving us back a pointer to the "first" div
    .end();
  });
</script>
</body>
</html>
```

Listing 5.14 contains a reference to a required jQuery file, some CSS styling, an HTML <ul> element, and a block of jQuery code that looks like this when you remove the comments:

```
var $first = $("<div id='first'>first</div>")
               .appendTo("<div id='second'>second</div>")
               .parent()
               .appendTo("#outer")
               .end();
```

Although jQuery enables you to construct expressions of almost arbitrary complexity, such expressions are also much more prone to error. By way of comparison (and it's only an analogy), if you have written complex regular expressions, you probably remember the time required to come up with the expression that does exactly what you need.

HTML5 GEOLOCATION WITH JQUERY

Chapter 10 provides a more detailed discussion of HTML5 Geolocation, which you can read if you are unfamiliar with the Geolocation APIs. The example in this section illustrates how you can use jQuery to render a user's current location. As you will see, the jQuery code in Listing 5.14 is a very short block of code (shown in bold) at the end of the HTML Web page, which illustrates the point that there are situations when you can write HTML Web pages containing mostly "regular" JavaScript code.

Listing 5.15 displays the contents of JQGeoLocation1.html that illustrates how to determine a user's location and then render that location in a Google Map.

Listing 5.15 JQGeoLocation1.html

```
<!DOCTYPE html>
<html lang="en">
<head>
  <meta charset="utf-8"/>
  <title>Geolocation</title>

<style>
#div1 {
font-size: 16px;
height: 200px;
width:   400px;
}
</style>

<script src="http://ajax.googleapis.com/ajax/libs/jquery/
                            1.5.0/jquery.min.js">
</script>

<!-- Google maps API -->
<script src="http://maps.google.com/maps/api/js?sensor=false">
</script>

<script>
function findUserLocation() {
  // this method specifies the 'success' and 'fail' JS
                                          functions
  navigator.geolocation.getCurrentPosition(successCallback,
                                          errorCallback);

}
```

```
function successCallback(position) {
  var latitude  = position.coords.latitude;
  var longitude = position.coords.longitude;
  var latlong   = new google.maps.LatLng(latitude, longitude);

  var myOptions = {
      zoom: 14,
      center: latlong,
      mapTypeId: google.maps.MapTypeId.ROADMAP
  };

  // use Google Maps to display the current location
  var map = new google.maps.Map(document.getElementById("div1"),
                                               myOptions);
  map.setCenter(latlong);

  var marker = new google.maps.Marker({
      position: initialLocation,
      map: map,
      title: "I Am Here!"
  });
}

function errorCallback(error) {
  if(error.code = error.PERMISSION_DENIED) {
    console.log("Error: you must enable geolocation access");
  } else if(error.code = error.PERMISSION_UNAVAILABLE) {
    console.log("Error: geolocation unavailable");
  } else if(error.code = error.TIMEOUT) {
    console.log("Error: timeout occurred");
  }

//console.log(error);
}

function positionDetails(position) {
 var positionStr =
   "latitude:"+ pos.coords.latitude +"<br>"+
   "longitude:"+ pos.coords.longitude +"<br>"+
   "accuracy:"+ pos.coords.accuracy +"<br>"+
   "altitude:"+ pos.coords.altitude +"<br>"+
   "altitudeAccuracy:"+ pos.coords.altitudeAccuracy +"<br>"+
   "heading:"+ pos.coords.heading +"<br>"+
   "speed:"+ pos.coords.speed +"";

   // without jQuery:
```

```
      document.getElementById("position").innerHTML = position
                                                           Str;
      // with jQuery:
      // $("#position").html(positionStr);
      console.log(positionStr);
  }
</script>
</head>

<body>
  <div id="div1">
    <p>Click the button to display your location:</p>
    <form id="geoLocationForm">
      <input type="button" id="geobutton" value="Find My
                                       Current Location">
    </form>
  </div>

<script>
  $(document).ready(function() {
    $('#geobutton').click(findUserLocation);
  });
</script>
</html>
```

Listing 5.15 starts with some CSS styling, a reference to a required jQuery file, and also a reference to the Google Maps JavaScript file.

Next, the JavaScript function `findUserLocation()` invokes the method `getCurrentPosition()` of the `geolocation` object (which is exposed via the `navigator` object) to get a user's current position, as shown here:

```
// this method specifies the 'success' and 'fail' JS functions
navigator.geolocation.getCurrentPosition(successCallback,
                                           errorCallback);
```

Notice that the preceding code snippet specifies the JavaScript `success-Callback()` function and the JavaScript `errorCallback()` function that are invoked when the function `getCurrentPosition()` succeeds or fails, respectively.

The `successCallback()` function is supplied with a position parameter that we can use to determine three positional values of a user's current location, as shown here:

```
function successCallback(position) {
  var latitude  = position.coords.latitude;
```

```
var longitude = position.coords.longitude;
var latlong   = new google.maps.LatLng(latitude, longitude);
// other code omitted
```

The JavaScript variable `myOptions` specifies attributes, such as the type of map that we want to display, as shown here:

```
var myOptions = {
      zoom: 14,
      center: latlong,
      mapTypeId: google.maps.MapTypeId.ROADMAP
};
```

The JavaScript map variable uses the `myOptions` variable to create a map and render the map in the HTML `<div>` element whose `id` attribute has value `div1`, as shown here:

```
// use Google Maps to display the current location
var map = new google.maps.Map(document.getElementById("div1"),
                              myOptions);
map.setCenter(latlong);
```

The error function is also important, because it can provide information regarding the cause of the error that occurred, as shown here:

```
function errorCallback(error) {
  if(error.code = error.PERMISSION_DENIED) {
     console.log("Error: you must enable geolocation access");
  } else if(error.code = error.PERMISSION_UNAVAILABLE) {
     console.log("Error: geolocation unavailable");
  } else if(error.code = error.TIMEOUT) {
     console.log("Error: timeout occurred");
  }

//console.log(error);
}
```

Listing 5.15 also contains a JavaScript function `positionDetails()` that contains additional details that you can also include in the JavaScript callback function that handles the successful invocation of the `getCurrentPosition()` JavaScript function.

Finally, Listing 5.15 contains an HTML `Form` element with a button whose `id` attribute has the value `geobutton`, followed by a very short jQuery code block (shown in bold) that invokes the JavaScript function `getCurrentPosition()` whenever users click on that button, as shown here:

```
$('#geobutton').click(findUserLocation);
```

As you can see, the code in Listing 5.15 is straightforward, and it gives you a basic understanding of how to write HTML Web pages containing geolocation-related details. The next section contains the final example in this chapter, and you will learn how to obtain and display accelerometer-related details for a mobile device.

Figure 5.9 displays the result of rendering JQGeoLocation1.html in a Chrome browser on a Macbook.

FIGURE 5.9 Getting geolocation in a Chrome browser on a Macbook.

ACCELEROMETER VALUES WITH JQUERY

The example in this section illustrates how you can use jQuery to obtain accelerometer values for a mobile device.

Listing 5.16 displays the contents of JQAccelerometer1.html that illustrates how to display the accelerometer values of a mobile device whenever the device undergoes acceleration in any direction. Listing 5.16 displays the contents of the CSS stylesheet JQAccelerometer1.css whose selectors are used to match elements in the HTML Web page.

Listing 5.16 JQAccelerometer1.html

```
<!DOCTYPE html>
<html lang="en">
<head>
 <meta charset="utf-8"/>
 <title>jQuery and Accelerometer</title>
 <script
  src="http://ajax.googleapis.com/ajax/libs/jquery/1.6.4/jque-
```

```
ry.min.js">
  </script>

<script>
    var colorX = "", colorY = "", colorZ = "";
    var intx = 0, inty = 0, intz = 0;
    var colors = ['#f00', '#ff0', '#00f'];

    $('document').ready(function(){
      $(window).bind("devicemotion", function(e){
        var accelEvent = e.originalEvent,
            acceler = accelEvent.accelerationIncludingGravity,
            x = acceler.x, y = acceler.y, z = acceler.z;

        if(x < 0)        { intx = 0; }
        else if(x < 1) { intx = 1; }
        else             { intx = 2; }

        if(y < 0)        { inty = 0; }
        else if(y < 1) { inty = 1; }
        else             { inty = 2; }

        if(z < 0)        { intz = 0; }
        else if(z < 1) { intz = 1; }
        else             { intz = 2; }

        colorX = colors[intx];
        colorY = colors[inty];
        colorZ = colors[intz];

        $("#valueX").css("backgroundColor", colorX);
        $("#valueY").css("backgroundColor", colorY);
        $("#valueZ").css("backgroundColor", colorZ);

        $("#valueX").html("<p>Acceleration x: <b>" + x +
                                        "</b></p>");
        $("#valueY").html("<p>Acceleration y: <b>" + x +
                                        "</b></p>");
        $("#valueZ").html("<p>Acceleration z: <b>" + x +
                                        "</b></p>");
      });
    });
  </script>
  </head>

  <body>
```

```
<h2>Accelerometer Values</h2>
<div id="outer">
  <div id="valueX"></div>
  <div id="valueY"></div>
  <div id="valueZ"></div>
</div>
</body>
</html>
```

The code in Listing 5.16 obtains accelerometer values for three directions (all perpendicular to each other) for a mobile device, and then computes integer values to be used as indexes into an array of color values. After determining the color associated with each direction, the associated rectangular `<div>` element is updated with the corresponding color.

After binding the `window` object to the `devicemotion` event, we can use the event object (in this case it's called `e`) to obtain a JavaScript reference to the acceleration object (which is called `acceler`) and then extract current values for the three different axes, as shown here:

```
$('document').ready(function(){
    $(window).bind("devicemotion", function(e){
        var accelEvent = e.originalEvent,
            acceler = accelEvent.accelerationIncludingGravity,
            x = acceler.x, y = acceler.y, z = acceler.z;
```

For simplicity, the array of colors contains only three colors, and the following code computes a number between 0 and 2 in order to determine the color for the x direction:

```
if(x < 0)        { intx = 0; }
else if(x < 1) { intx = 1; }
else             { intx = 2; }
```

The color for the x direction is calculated like this:

```
colorX = colors[intx];
```

The background color of the HTML `<div>` element that is associated with the x direction is updated with the following code:

```
$("#valueX").css("backgroundColor", colorX);
```

Finally, the current value of the acceleration in the x direction is displayed using the following code snippet:

```
$("#valueX").html("<p>Acceleration x: <b>" + x + "</b></p>");
```

The corresponding values for the y direction and the z direction are computed in a similar fashion.

Listing 5.17 JQAccelerometer1.css

```
#outer {
position: relative; top: 10px; left: 0px;
}

p { font-size: 24px; }

#valueX {
width:   480px;
height: 100px;
position: absolute; top: 0px; left: 0px;
background-color: white;
}

#valueY {
width:   480px;
height: 100px;
position: absolute; top: 100px; left: 0px;
background-color: white;
}

#valueZ {
width:   480px;
height: 100px;
position: absolute; top: 200px; left: 0px;
background-color: white;
}
```

Listing 5.17 is very straightforward: it contains three selectors that specify the initial properties of three HTML <div> elements that are in Listing 5.16, and this code ought to look very familiar to you.

Figure 5.10 displays the result of rendering the HTML Web page in Listing 5.16 in a landscape-mode screenshot taken from an Android application running on an Asus Prime tablet with Android ICS.

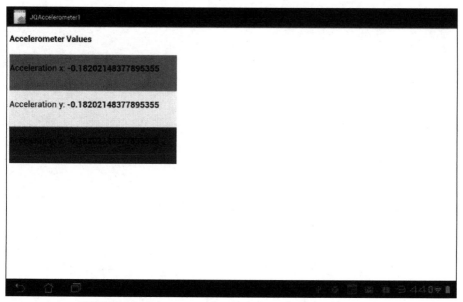

FIGURE 5.10 Accelerometer on an Asus Prime tablet with Android ICS.

USING JQUERY PLUGINS

In the overview of jQuery, you learned that jQuery supports plugins, and that there are literally hundreds (possibly even thousands) available. This topic is out of scope for this book, but please do avail yourself of the plethora of jQuery plugins, because they can save you a lot of work. Two links that provide an assortment of jQuery plugins are here:

http://www.devarticles.com/c/a/JavaScript/More-of-the-Top-jQuery-Plugins-for-Animation/

http://www.devarticles.com/c/a/JavaScript/The-Top-jQuery-Slider-Plugins/

You can also perform an Internet search to find more recent jQuery plugins and then select the plugins that suit your needs. If you do not find anything that is tailored to your requirements, you can find online tutorials that show you how to create your own jQuery plugins.

SUMMARY

This chapter introduced you to jQuery, along with code samples that illustrated how to use jQuery functions to create simple animation effects. You saw code samples that showed how to do the following:

- Create a simple jQuery-based HTML5 Web page
- Find and modify elements with :first and :last qualifiers
- Find elements with :even and :odd qualifiers
- Find elements with :eq, :lt, and :gt qualifiers
- Find HTML elements
- Find elements by class or id
- Find/set element attributes
- Find form elements and their attributes
- CSS3-style expressions for finding elements
- Remove DOM elements
- Create DOM elements
- Handle events in jQuery
- Use the click() function
- Detect keyboard events
- Handle mouse events
- jQuery APIs for traversing elements
- Chaining jQuery functions

The next chapter shows you how to use jQuery in order to create HTML5 Web pages that create animation effects and also provide interactivity for users.

ANIMATION EFFECTS WITH JQUERY AND CSS3

This chapter shows you how to create HTML5 Web pages that create animation effects and provide interactivity for users. You'll see an assortment of jQuery functions that create various animation effects that you can easily incorporate in your HTML5 Web pages. This eclectic chapter is intended to provide you with many animation effects, along with an assortment of code samples and code fragments that you can incorporate into your other HTML5 Web pages.

The first part of this chapter shows you how to use jQuery in order to manipulate the attributes of an element by setting the values of properties in CSS3 selectors, along with examples of creating animation effects using `animate` and `effect`. You'll see code examples that create slide-based and fade-related (`fadeIn`, `fadeOut`, `fadeTo`) animation effects. This section also illustrates how to create 2D animation effects using jQuery together with CSS3 `keyframes`.

The second part of this chapter illustrates how to create a "follow the mouse" HTML5 Web page that uses CSS3 for the visual effect and jQuery for updating the location of the gradient-filled rectangle.

The third part of this chapter contains examples of dynamically creating HTML `<div>` elements with CSS3-based gradient colors whose visual effects are comparable with those using SVG graphics or Canvas-based graphics. Remember that the CSS3 examples in the chapters of this book are specifically for `WebKit`-based browsers, but you can modify the code samples to include vendor-specific prefixes so that the code samples will run in other browsers. The last example in this chapter illustrates how to render SVG with jQuery using a jQuery plugin.

Note that this chapter covers jQuery animation effects and Chapter 8 contains some corresponding animation effects using jQuery Mobile. Both chapters contain CSS3-based animation effects as well. Due to space constraints, this chapter covers only a portion of the animation-related functionality that is available in jQuery. You can learn more about jQuery animation by reading the online jQuery documentation or by performing an Internet search for additional tutorials and articles.

WORKING WITH CSS3 SELECTORS IN JQUERY

This section contains code samples that illustrate how to use jQuery to programmatically create HTML elements and to style them with CSS3 to create various effects, such as rounded corners, gradients, and shadow effects. You can certainly create these effects by manually creating the required CSS3 selectors and the HTML elements, and you can leverage the power of jQuery to create even more sophisticated visual effects.

HTML <div> Elements and the jQuery css() Function

The jQuery `css()` function enables you to set the values of attributes in HTML <div> elements that you create using `$('div')`. You can do so by specifying key/value pairs in a manner that is similar to the property/value pairs in a CSS selector, and then you can use the jQuery `append()` method to append those new elements to existing elements.

Listing 6.1 displays the contents of `JQCssDivElements1.html` that illustrates how to dynamically create an HTML <div> element.

Listing 6.1 JQCssDivElements1.html

```
<!DOCTYPE html>
<html lang="en">
  <head>
   <meta charset="utf-8"/>
   <title>Creating div elements with jQuery</title>
   <script src="http://code.jquery.com/jquery-1.7.1.min.js"></
script>
  </head>

  <body>
    <div id="outer"> </div>

    <script>
```

```
var basePointX = 50, basePointY = 50;
var rectWidth   = 60, rectHeight = 60;
var currentX    = 0, currentY = 0;
var rowCount    = 5, colCount = 8;
var fillColor   = "";

var fillColors = ["rgb(255, 0, 0)",
                   "rgb(0, 255, 0)",
                   "rgb(255, 255, 0)",
                   "rgb(0, 0, 255)"];

$(document).ready(function() {
   for(var r=0; r<rowCount; r++) {
      for(var c=0; c<colCount; c++) {
         currentX  = basePointX+c*rectWidth;
         currentY  = basePointY+r*rectHeight;
        fillColor = fillColors[(r+c) % fillColors.length];

         // create a rectangle at the current position
         newNode = $('<div>').css({'position':'absolute',
                                    'width':rectWidth+'px',
                                    'height':rectHeight+'px',
                                    left: currentX+'px',
                                    top: currentY+'px',
                                    'backgroundColor':
fillColor
                                   });

         $("#outer").append(newNode);
      }
   }
});
</script>
</body>
</html>
```

Listing 6.1 renders a grid-like display of HTML <div> elements using the jQuery css() function, as shown here:

```
newNode = $('<div>').css({'position':'absolute',
                           'width':rectWidth+'px',
                           'height':rectHeight+'px',
                           left: currentX+'px',
                           top: currentY+'px',
                           'backgroundColor': fillColor
                          });
```

Each newly created element is appended to the container <div> element with this code snippet:

```
$("#outer").append(newNode);
```

Keep in mind that this code renders the correct effect because the position property is set to absolute for each dynamically constructed <div> element. Experiment with different values for the position property to see the effects that are created.

Figure 6.1 displays the result of rendering JQCssDivElements1.html on an Asus Prime tablet with Android ICS.

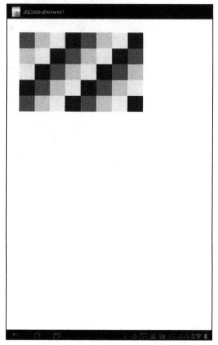

FIGURE 6.1 A rectangular grid in jQuery on an Asus Prime tablet with Android ICS.

Creating Rounded Corners with jQuery

The previous example uses the jQuery css() function to create a rectangular array of HTML <div> elements, and in this section you'll see an example of creating rounded corners by specifying randomly generated values for the CSS3 border-radius property via the css() function.

Listing 6.2 displays the contents of JQRoundedCorners1.html that illustrates how to render a rectangular grid of dynamically created HTML <div> elements with rounded corners.

Listing 6.2 RoundedCorners1.html

```
<!DOCTYPE html>
<html lang="en">
  <head>
   <meta charset="utf-8"/>
   <title>Creating div elements with jQuery</title>
   <script src="http://code.jquery.com/jquery-1.7.1.min.js">
                                                   </script>
  </head>

  <body>
    <div id="outer"> </div>

    <script>
      var basePointX = 20, basePointY = 20;
      var rectWidth  = 60, rectHeight = 60;
      var currentX   = 0, currentY = 0;
      var rowCount   = 5, colCount = 8;
      var index = 0, fillColor  = "";
      var radius = 0, radiusValues = [0, 10, 20, 30, 40, 50];

      var fillColors = ["rgb(255, 0, 0)",
                        "rgb(0, 255, 0)",
                        "rgb(255, 255, 0)",
                        "rgb(0, 0, 255)"];

      $(document).ready(function() {
         for(var r=0; r<rowCount; r++) {
            for(var c=0; c<colCount; c++) {
               currentX  = basePointX+c*rectWidth;
               currentY  = basePointY+r*rectHeight;
              fillColor = fillColors[(r+c) % fillColors.length];
               index     = Math.floor(
                       Math.random()*radiusValues.length+1);
               radius    = radiusValues[index];

               // create a rectangle at the current position
             newNode = $('<div>').css({'position':'absolute',
                                  'width':rectWidth+'px',
                                 'height':rectHeight+'px',
                                  left: currentX+'px',
                                  top: currentY+'px',
                                  'backgroundColor':
fillColor,
                                  'borderRadius': ra-
dius+'%'
                                 });
```

```
                 $("#outer").append(newNode);
              }
           }
        });
     </script>
   </body>
</html>
```

The key point of Listing 6.2 (which is very similar to Listing 6.1) is to set the value of the CSS3 `border-radius` property to an integer between 0 and 50. In jQuery, you need to use so-called "camel case" notation for hyphenated CSS properties; thus, you must use `borderRadius` in the jQuery `css()` function.

When the value of `border-radius` is `0`, there is no rounding effect, so the `<div>` element looks like a rectangle. When the value of `border-radius` is `50`, the `<div>` element is rendered as a circle if the `width` and `height` properties are equal; otherwise, the `<div>` element is rendered as an ellipse.

Incidentally, there are jQuery plugins that create rounded corner effects, and you can perform an Internet search to find what is currently available. You can review their functionality to see if 1.) any of them contain functionality that you need and 2.) they support features that are easier to user than writing the code manually yourself.

Figure 6.2 displays the result of rendering `JQRoundedCorners1.html` in a Chrome browser on a Macbook.

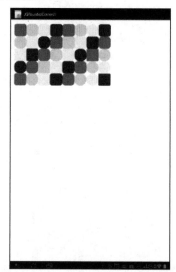

FIGURE 6.2 Rounded corners in jQuery on an Asus Prime tablet with Android ICS.

Gradients and Shadow Effects with jQuery

The first two examples in this chapter gave you a basic understanding of how to create rounded corners using the jQuery css() function. This section contains an example of programmatically adding CSS3 gradients and creating shadow effects.

The main purpose of this code sample is to illustrate how to use various CSS properties with a simple equation in order to create an interesting visual effect.

Listing 6.3 displays JQArchTripleShadowSkewEllipsesGrad3.html that illustrates how to create an HTML5 Web page with <div> elements (which follow the path of an Archimedean spiral) that have linear gradients, radial gradients, and shadow effects.

The CSS stylesheet JQArchTripleShadowSkewEllipsesGrad3.html is displayed in Listing 6.4.

Listing 6.3 JQArchTripleShadowSkewEllipsesGrad3.html

```
<!DOCTYPE html>
<html lang="en">
  <head>
   <meta charset="utf-8"/>
   <title>Archimedean Ellipses With Gradients and Shadows
                                               </title>

   <link rel="stylesheet"
         href="ArchTripleShadowSkewEllipsesGrad3.css"/>
   <script src="http://code.jquery.com/jquery-1.7.1.min.js">
                                               </script>
  </head>

  <body>
   <div id="outer"> </div>

   <script>
     var fillColor   = "rgb(255, 0, 0)";
     var basePointX = 400, basePointY = 160;
     var majorAxis = 40, minorAxis = 80;
     var currentX  = 0, currentY = 0;
     var deltaAngle = 3, maxAngle = 720;
     var Constant = 0.25, newNode, addClass;
     var rVal = 0, gVal = 0, bVal = 0;
     var stripCount = 10, currStrip = 0;
     var stripWidth = Math.floor(maxAngle/stripCount);
```

```
$(document).ready(function() {
  for(var angle=0; angle<maxAngle; angle++) {
    radius   = Constant*angle;
    offsetX  = radius*Math.cos(angle*Math.PI/180);
    offsetY  = radius*Math.sin(angle*Math.PI/180);
    currentX = basePointX+offsetX;
    currentY = basePointY-offsetY;

    rVal = 0; gVal = 0; bVal = 0;
    currStrip = Math.floor(angle/stripWidth);

    if(currStrip % 3 == 0) {
      rVal = Math.floor(255*(angle%stripWidth)/strip
                                                Width);
    } if(currStrip % 3 == 1) {
      rVal = Math.floor(255*(angle%stripWidth)/strip
                                                Width);
      gVal = Math.floor(255*(angle%stripWidth)/strip
                                                Width);
    }
    else {
      bVal = Math.floor(255*(angle%stripWidth)/strip
                                                Width);
    }

    fillColor  = "rgb("+rVal+","+gVal+","+bVal+")";

    // create an ellipse at the current position
    if(angle % 20 == 0) {
      newNode = $('<div>').css({
                            'position':'absolute',
                      'width':(0.75*majorAxis)+'px',
                      'height':(2.5*minorAxis)+'px',
                            left: currentX+'px',
                            top: currentY+'px',
                               'backgroundColor':
                                          fillColor,
                         'borderRadius': '20%'
                            }).
                         toggleClass("skew1");
    } else {
      newNode = $('<div>').css({
                      'position':'absolute',
                      'width':majorAxis+'px',
                      'height':minorAxis+'px',
                      left: currentX+'px',
```

```
                              top: currentY+'px',
                         'backgroundSize': '240px 240px,
                                            80px 80px',
                         'backgroundColor': fillColor,
                         'borderRadius': '40%'
                         }).
                    toggleClass("radial13");
        }

        $("#outer").append(newNode);

        // create an ellipse at the current position
        newNode = $('<div>').css({'position':'absolute',
                                 'width':majorAxis+'px',
                                 'height':minorAxis+'px',
                        left: (currentX+majorAxis)+'px',
                             top: currentY+'px',
                             'backgroundColor': fill
                                               Color,
                             'borderRadius': '50%'
                             }).
                        toggleClass("skew2");

        $("#outer").append(newNode);

        // create an ellipse at the current position
        newNode = $('<div>').css({
                            'position':'absolute',
                            'width':majorAxis+'px',
                            'height':minorAxis+'px',
                   left: (currentX+majorAxis/2)+'px',
                   top: (currentY-minorAxis/2)+'px',
                            'backgroundColor': fillColor,
                            'borderRadius': '50%'
                            }).
                        toggleClass("skew1");

        $("#outer").append(newNode);
        }
    });
    </script>
    </body>
</html>
```

Listing 6.3 contains code that is familiar to you. Each programmatically created `<div>` element is appended to the `<div>` element (which is initially

empty) whose id value is `outer`. Note that you can make this code more robust by checking for the existence of this element and then either displaying
an appropriate message if the element does not exist, or programmatically
creating such an element and then appending it to the DOM.

In addition, Listing 6.3 uses conditional logic for specifying a set of CSS3
properties for each `<div>` element. In this example, the code uses the following code block:

```
if(angle % 20 == 0) {
  // create a <div> element and use method
  // chaining to invoke toggleClass()
} else {
  // create another <div> element and also use
  // method chaining to invoke toggleClass()
}
```

Note that you learned about jQuery method chaining in Chapter 5; later in
this chapter, you will learn about the jQuery `toggleClass()` method.

Listing 6.4 JQArchTripleShadowSkewEllipsesGrad3.css

```
#outer {
  position: absolute;
  width: 90%; height: 90%;
  border: solid 2px #000;
}


.radial13 {
background-color:white;
background-image:
  -webkit-radial-gradient(red 4px, transparent 48px),
  -webkit-repeating-linear-gradient(25deg, yellow 2px,
                                           green 4px,
                                  yellow 8px, blue 12px,
                     transparent 16px, blue 20px, red 24px,
                     transparent 28px, transparent 32px),
  -webkit-repeating-linear-gradient(-25deg, yellow 2px,
                                           green 4px,
                                  yellow 8px, blue 12px,
                     transparent 16px, blue 20px, red 24px,
                     transparent 28px, transparent 32px),
  -webkit-radial-gradient(blue 8px, transparent 68px);
  -webkit-transform : skew(60deg, -20deg) scale(2, 1);

background-size: 240px 240px, 380px 380px;
-webkit-box-shadow:  1px 1px 1px #000;
```

```
}

.skew1 {
 -webkit-transform : skew(60deg, -10deg) scale(0.75, 1.75)
                                             rotate(-60deg);
 -transform : skew(60deg, -10deg) scale(0.75, 1.75) rotate
                                             (-60deg);
-webkit-box-shadow: 3px 1px 1px #00f;
 box-shadow: 2px 1px 1px #00f;
}

.skew2 {
 -webkit-transform : skew(-80deg, 60deg) scale(1.5, 0.5)
                                             rotate(50deg);
 -transform : skew(-80deg, 60deg) scale(1.5, 0.5) rotate(50deg);
-webkit-box-shadow: 3px 3px 3px #000;
 box-shadow: 3px 3px 3px #000;
}
```

Listing 6.4 contains CSS3 selectors that are referenced in the code in List-ing 6.3. As you can see, the `skew1` CSS3 selector specifies a radial gradient that also uses the CSS3 property `repeating-radial-gradient`, followed by a `webkit-transform` property that specifies a skew, rotation, and a scale effect.

Similar comments apply to the CSS3 selectors `skew2` and `radial13`, and you can refer to Chapter 2 if you need to refresh your memory about CSS3 radial gradients.

Figure 6.3 displays `JQArchTripleShadowSkewEllipsesGrad3.html` on an Asus Prime tablet with Android ICS.

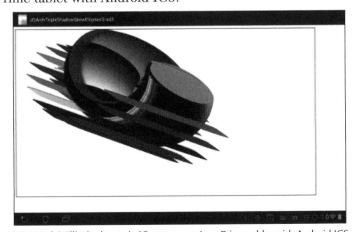

FIGURE 6.3 Elliptic shapes in jQuery on an Asus Prime tablet with Android ICS.

BASIC ANIMATION EFFECTS IN JQUERY

This section contains code fragments rather than complete code listings, and these code fragments illustrate how to create animation effects in jQuery using the functions `hide()` and `show()`, and also how to set the animation speed. You'll also learn how to use the jQuery `toggle()` function to toggle CSS properties.

Keep in mind that this section covers only a portion of the rich set of functionality that is available with jQuery functions that create animation effects. Be sure to read the jQuery online documentation to learn about many other features that are supported.

The jQuery `hide()` and `show()` functions enable you to change the visibility of elements in an HTML page. For example, the following code block hides the second button when users click the first button; when users double click on the first button, the second button becomes visible:

```
$("#myButton1").click(function() {
  $(#myButton2").hide();
});
$("#myButton1").dblclick(function() {
  $(#myButton2").show();
});
```

The jQuery `toggle` function can handle two or more occurrences of the same event on an element. For example, the following code fragment handles one, two, or three click events on an element with the specified `id` value:

```
$("#myDiv1").toggle(
    function() {
      $("myText").text("First click");
    },
    function() {
      $("#myText").text("Second click");
    },
    function() {
      $("#myText").text("Third click");
    }
});
```

Two other useful jQuery methods are `removeClass()` and `addClass()`, which remove or add CSS classes, respectively. An example is here:

```
$("#myDiv1").toggle(
    function() {
      $("myText").addClass("shiny");
    },
    function() {
      $("#myText").addClass("dark");
    }
});
```

The jQuery `addClass()` method adds a CSS class, whereas the `toggle-Class()` method "toggles" the CSS class; i.e., the class is added if it's not present, but it's removed if it is already included.

Other related jQuery methods include `fadeClass()`, which uses a fading effect, and `slideClass()`, which creates a sliding effect.

Using Callback Functions

Many jQuery functions (including `hide()`, `show()`, `toggle()`, and slide-related functions) enable you to specify a callback function that is executed after the specified action is completed. For example, you can define the following code block:

```
$("#myButton1").click(function() {
  $(#myButton2").hide('slow',
    function callback() {
      // do something else
    });
});
```

When users click on an element whose `id` is `myButton1`, the preceding code block slowly hides the element whose `id` is `myButton2`, and after the animation is completed, the code in the `callback` function is executed.

This book contains `WebKit`-based code samples, but if you decide to use the preceding code block with IE, keep in mind that there is a bug involving the use of named functions in callbacks in IE. The following article provides useful information regarding named functions:

http://kangax.github.com/nfe

JQUERY FADE AND SLIDE ANIMATION EFFECTS

The jQuery fade-related and slide-related effects are easy to create, and if you define them appropriately, they can create very nice visual effects in your Web pages.

The following example combines the jQuery `.fadeIn()` and `.fadeOut()` functions and also shows you how to chain these functions so that you can create multiple animation effects.

The fadeIn(), fadeOut(), and fadeToggle() Functions

The three jQuery methods `.fadeIn()`, `.fadeOut()`, and `.fadeToggle()` can specify three parameters. Their syntax is shown here:

```
jQuery(list-of-elements).fadeIn(speed);
jQuery(list-of-elements).fadeOut(speed);
jquery(list-of-elements).fadeTo(speed);
```

The following code block illustrates how to use these three jQuery functions:

```
$("#something").click(function() {
    $(this).fadeIn('slow');
});
$("#something").click(function() {
    $(this).fadeOut('slow');
});
$("#something").click(function() {
    $(this).fadeTo('slow', .65);
});
```

Listing 6.5 displays the contents of `FadeInOut.html` that illustrates how to perform simple and chained fading effects in jQuery.

Listing 6.5 FadeInOut.html

```
<!DOCTYPE html>
<html lang="en">
  <head>
    <meta charset="utf-8"/>
    <title>jQuery Fade-Related Effects</title>

<script
    src="http://code.jquery.com/jquery-1.7.1.min.js">
</script>
    </head>
```

```
<body>
  <div>
    <div> <p>Hello World from jQuery (hover on me)</p> </div>
    <div> <p>Goodbye World from jQuery (hover on me)</p>
                                                    </div>
    <div>
      <input type="button" id="button1" value="Hide Me"/>
    </div>
  </div>

  <script>
    $(document).ready(function(){
     var para = $("div > p");

       para.each(function(){
          var p = $(this);
          p.append('<span style="color:red;font-size:18px"'+
                   '>This Text Will Fade on Hover</span>');
       });

       para.hover(function() {
          // you can use 'slow' or 'fast'
         //$(this).find("span").fadeIn("slow");
          $(this).find("span").fadeIn(3000).fadeOut("fast")
                              .fadeIn("slow");
       }, function() {
         //$(this).find("span").hide();
          $(this).find("span").fadeOut(2000).fadeIn("slow")
                              .fadeOut("fast").fadeIn(2000)
                              .fadeOut("slow");
       });

       $("#button1").click(function() {
          $(this).fadeOut(500, function() {
         //$(this).remove();
          });
       });
    });
  </script>
</body>
</html>
```

Listing 6.5 starts with two HTML <p> elements and an HTML <button> element, followed by jQuery code for applying fade-related effects to the HTML <p> elements. The first point to notice is the JavaScript variable para that stores a reference to the HTML <p> elements that are direct child elements of HTML <div> elements, as shown here:

```
$(document).ready(function(){
  var para = $("div > p");
  // code omitted
}
```

The next code block dynamically adds an HTML <span> element to the HTML <p> elements that are referenced in the para variable:

```
para.each(function(){
  var p = $(this);
  p.append('<span style="color:red;font-size:18px"'+
           '>This Text Will Fade on Hover</span>');
});
```

When users hover over any of the HTML <p> elements, the jQuery code creates multiple fade-related effects for the HTML <p> elements using jQuery method chaining, an example of which is here:

```
$(this).find("span").fadeOut(2000).fadeIn("slow")
                    .fadeOut("fast").fadeIn(2000)
                    .fadeOut("slow");
```

You can use jQuery methods to apply effects to elements other than the element that has the current focus. For example, if you want to hide a sibling element during a hover event, you can do something like this:

```
$(this).next().fade();
```

The next section shows you how to use jQuery slide-related functions in order to create slide-related animation effects.

jQuery Slide-Related Functions

The jQuery slideUp(), slideDown(), and slideToggle() methods can specify three parameters. They have the following syntax:

```
jQuery(elements).slideUp([milliseconds],
                         [easing-function],
                         [callback-function]);

jQuery(elements).slideDown([milliseconds],
                           [easing-function],
                           [callback-function]);

jQuery(elements).slideToggle([milliseconds],
                             [easing-function],
                             [callback-function]);
```

The value of `milliseconds` specifies the duration of the animation effect and the `callback-function` is an optional JavaScript function that is executed after the animation is completed.

Listing 6.6 displays the contents of `JQSlideUpDown.html` that illustrates how to perform simple and chained sliding effects in jQuery.

Listing 6.6 `JQSlideUpDown.html`

```html
<!DOCTYPE html>
<html lang="en">
  <head>
    <meta charset="utf-8"/>
    <title>jQuery Slide-Related Effects</title>

<script
    src="http://code.jquery.com/jquery-1.7.1.min.js">
</script>
  </head>

  <body>
    <div>
      <div> <p>Hello World from jQuery (hover on me)</p> </div>
      <div> <p>Goodbye World from jQuery (hover on me)</p> </div>
        <div>
          <input type="button" id="button1"
                 value="Click to Slide Me Up and Hide Me"/>
        </div>
    </div>

    <script>
      $(document).ready(function(){
        var para = $("div > p");

        para.each(function(){
            var p = $(this);
            p.append('<span style="color:red;font-size:18px">'+
                    'This Text Will Slide on Hover</span>');
        });

        para.hover(function() {
            // you can use 'slow' or 'fast'
            //$(this).find("span").slideDown("slow");
            $(this).find("span").slideDown(3000).slideUp("fast")
                                .slideDown("slow");
```

```
            }, function() {
            //$(this).find("span").hide();
              $(this).find("span").slideUp(2000).slideDown("slow")
                                   .slideUp("fast").slideDown(2000)
                                   .slideUp("slow");
            });

            $("#button1").click(function() {
               $(this).slideUp(2000, function() {
               //$(this).remove();
               });
            });
         });
      </script>
   </body>
</html>
```

Listing 6.6 is similar to Listing 6.5, except that slide-related jQuery methods are used instead of fade-related jQuery methods. Therefore, the description of this code sample is analogous to the description of Listing 6.5.

One point to keep in mind is that sliding effects do not always work as expected (some jerkiness may occur) for elements that have CSS `padding` or `margin` properties or a `width` property that is not set to a fixed width. Experiment with these scenarios to see if the resultant behavior is what you expect, or is acceptable for your Web pages.

Incidentally, you can also combine slide and fade functions in your own function definition, as shown here:

http://stackoverflow.com/questions/5207301/looking-for-jquery-easing-functions-without-using-a-plugin

```
$.fn.slideFadeToggle   = function(speed, easing, callback) {
   return this.animate(
      {opacity: 'toggle', height: 'toggle'}, speed, easing, call-
back);
   };
```

You can use the preceding custom function as follows:

```
$("#something").click(function() {
   $(this).slideFadeToggle();
});
```

Easing Functions in jQuery

jQuery supports a set of so-called "easing" functions that provide different types of animation effects. In general terms, an easing function uses some type of equation as the path for an animation effect. For example, you can use a linear equation to create animation with constant speed, and you can use a quadratic equation (a polynomial of degree two) to create animation effects with acceleration or for quadratic Bezier curves, as well as cubic equations for cubic Bezier curves.

jQuery also provides easing functions for animation whose speed is more complex (slow, fast, slow) at different positions of an easing function. Before you search for jQuery plugins, it's well worth your time to explore the existing jQuery easing functions, some of which are listed here:

http://clintmckoy.com/post/9423631421/jquery-easing-functions-list

- `linear`
- `swing`
- `jswing`
- `easeInQuad`
- `easeOutQuad`
- `easeInOutQuad`
- `easeInCubic`
- `easeOutCubic`
- `easeInOutCubic`
- `easeInQuart`
- `easeOutQuart`
- `easeInOutQuart`
- `easeInQuint`
- `easeOutQuint`
- `easeInOutQuint`
- `easeInSine`
- `easeOutSine`
- `easeInOutSine`
- `easeInExpo`
- `easeOutExpo`
- `easeInOutExpo`
- `easeInCirc`
- `easeOutCirc`
- `easeInOutCirc`
- `easeInElastic`
- `easeOutElastic`

- easeInOutElastic
- easeInBack
- easeOutBack
- easeInOutBack
- easeInBounce
- easeOutBounce
- easeInOutBounce

You can find numerous links that provide an extensive set of demonstration of jQuery easing functions, such as the two shown here:

http://jqueryui.com/demos/effect/easing.html
http://james.padolsey.com/demos/jquery/easing/

If you're curious about the jQuery code for the jQuery easing functions, the following code block contains two definitions:

```
$.extend($.easing,
{
    def: 'easeOutQuad',
    swing: function (x, t, b, c, d) {
        //alert($.easing.default);
        return $.easing[$.easing.def](x, t, b, c, d);
    },
    easeInQuad: function (x, t, b, c, d) {
        return c*(t/=d)*t + b;
    },
    // code omitted for brevity
}
```

There are many jQuery plugins available for custom animation-related easing functions, or you can create your own jQuery plugin if you cannot find one that fits your needs.

THE JQUERY .ANIMATE() METHOD

The jQuery `animate()` method can take four parameters, and they look like this:

```
jQuery(elements).animate([properties],
                         [milliseconds],
                         [easing-function],
                         [complete-function]);
```

The `properties` parameter contains the list of properties to animate, and the `milliseconds` parameter specifies the duration of the animation effect. The `easing-function` parameter specifies one of the easing functions discussed in the previous section, and the `complete-function` specifies the JavaScript callback function to execute when the animation effect has completed.

Listing 6.7 displays the contents of `JQAnimate1.html` that illustrates how to use the jQuery `animate()` function in order to create animation effects on two PNG files.

Listing 6.7 `JQAnimate1.html`

```
<!DOCTYPE html>
<html lang="en">
  <head>
   <meta charset="utf-8"/>
   <title>jQuery Animate Function</title>

<script
   src="http://code.jquery.com/jquery-1.7.1.min.js">
</script>
   </head>

   <body>
     <div id="outer">
       <div>
         <img id="text1" width="200" height="200" src="text1.
                                                     png">
         <img id="text2" width="200" height="200" src="text2.
                                                     png">
       </div>
       <div>
        <input type="button" id="button1" value="Animate
                                                 Left"/>
        <input type="button" id="button2" value="Animate
                                                 Right"/>
       </div>
     </div>

     <script>
       $(document).ready(function(){
         $('#button1').click(function() {
           $('#text1').animate({
             opacity: 0.25,
             left: '+=50',
             height: '+=100'
```

```
        }, 5000, function() {
          // Animation complete (do something else)
        });
      });

      $('#button2').click(function() {
        $('#text1').animate({
          opacity: 0.25,
          left: '+=50',
          height: 'toggle'
        }, 5000, function() {
          // Animation complete (do something else)
        });
      });
    });
  </script>
  </body>
</html>
```

Listing 6.7 contains two PNG images, along with jQuery click handlers for two HTML <button> elements.

Whenever users click on the left button, the jQuery code decreases the PNG opacity from 1.0 to 0.25, shifts the image file 50 units to the right, and increases its height by 100 units during a five-second interval, as shown here:

```
$('#text1').animate({
   opacity: 0.25,
   left: '+=50',
   height: '+=100'
 }, 5000, function() {
   // Animation complete (do something else)
});
```

Whenever users click on the second button, the jQuery code performs similar animation effects on the right-side image file. Launch the code in Listing 6.7 and click the buttons to see the animation effects.

If you create an HTML Web page with many animation effects, another interesting property is jQuery.fx.off, which deactivates all the jQuery animation effects in a Web page. This functionality can be very convenient if you need to do so because of response time on a device.

You can see a variation of the animation effects in Listing 6.7 in the HTML Web page JQAnimate2.html, which is available on the DVD.

Listing 6.8 displays the contents of JQAnimate3.html that illustrates how to use the jQuery animate() function in order to create sequential and parallel animation effects on <div> elements in an HTML5 Web page.

Listing 6.8 JQAnimate3.html

```
<!DOCTYPE html>
<html lang="en">
  <head>
    <meta charset="utf-8"/>
    <title>jQuery Animate Function</title>

<script
    src="http://code.jquery.com/jquery-1.7.1.min.js">
</script>

    <style>
      #div1 {
       position:relative;
       left:50px;
       width:200px;
       height:100px;
       background-color:#f00;
       border:2px solid yellow;
       }

      #div2 {
       position:relative;
       left:50px;
       width:200px;
       height:100px;
       background-color:#00f;
       border:2px solid red;
       }
     </style>
    </head>

    <body>
      <div id="outer">
        <div id="div1"> </div>
          <input type="button" id="button1" value="Click me to
Animate"/>
          <div>
          <div id="div2"> </div>
            <input type="button" id="button2" value="Click me to
Animate"/>
          </div>
        </div>

      <script>
        $(document).ready(function(){
```

```
$('#button1').click(function() {
  $("#div1").animate({
    width: "80%",
    opacity: 0.6,
    marginLeft: "1.0in",
    fontSize: "4em",
    borderWidth: "12px"
    }, 2000 );
  });

  $('#button2').click(function() {
    $("#div2").animate({"left": "+=100px"}, "slow")
              .animate({"width": "+=150px"}, "slow")
              .animate({"height": "+=50px"}, "slow");
    });
  });
</script>

</body>
</html>
```

Listing 6.8 contains code that is similar to Listing 6.7 that illustrates animation effects for two HTML `<div>` elements. In addition, Listing 6.8 creates an interesting sequential animation effect by using method chaining with the jQuery `animation()` method, which is invoked when users click on the second HTML `<div>` element:

```
$("#div2").animate({"left": "+=100px"}, "slow")
          .animate({"width": "+=150px"}, "slow")
          .animate({"height": "+=50px"}, "slow");
});
```

As you can see, the preceding code block simply changes the value of the `left` property of the second HTML `<div>` element in each of the three jQuery `animation()` invocations.

You can use the jQuery `animate()` function to create other interesting visual effects by changing different CSS properties of HTML elements. For example, the following code creates a "wobbling" effect with list items that are part of an HTML `<ul>` element:

```
$('#mylist li').hover(function() {
  $(this).animate({paddingLeft: '+=15px'}, 200);
}, function() {
  $(this).animate({paddingLeft: '-=15px'}, 200);
  });
```

You can also create `linear` and `swing` animation effects, as shown here:

```
$('p:first').toggle(function() {
  $(this).animate({'height':'+=150px'}, 1000, 'linear');
}, function() {
  $(this).animate({'height':'-=150px'}, 1000, 'swing');
});
```

Custom CSS Animation Using the .animate() Function

You can use jQuery to animate many CSS properties, including `border-width`, `bottom`, `font-size`, `height`, `margin`, `opacity`, `padding`, `right`, `top`, `width`, and `word-spacing`. In addition, you can specify the duration with `slow`, `fast`, or an integer value that represents milliseconds.

The following code animates the `width` and `height` attributes of an HTML `<div>` element so that their final values will be `500` and `300`, respectively:

```
$("#myDiv").click(function() {
  $(this).animate({
    width:'500px', height: '300px'
  });
});
```

In the preceding jQuery code snippet, the `width` will increase to `500px` if its initial value is less than `500px`; otherwise, it will decrease the `width` to `500px` (similar comments apply to the `height` attribute).

The jQuery Queue and Animation Effects

The jQuery queue is the list of animations that are waiting to be executed on an element in an HTML Web page. Since the jQuery queue is a First-In-First-Out (FIFO), animations are executed in the order in which they are appended to this list, and new animations are added to the end of the list.

jQuery enables you to control the animation queue by means of the jQuery actions `dequeue`, `queue`, and `stop`, as well as the `queue` option.

For example, the following code block uses the jQuery `animate()` function to change CSS properties of the first `<p>` element in an HTML Web page, as well as values for `duration`, `easing`, and `complete`, and also setting the `queue` to `false`, which means that the animation effects will begin immediately:

```
$('p:first').animate( {
  height: '+=150px',
```

```
  backgroundColor: 'red'
},
{
  duration: 'fast',
  easing: 'swing',
  complete: function() {console.log('Finished.');},
  queue: false
}
);
```

Other useful functionality includes the `clearQueue` parameter, which removes all animations in the queue when `clearQueue` is set to `true`, and the `gotoEnd` parameter, which skips the animation and goes to the final state of a particular animation effect. Check the jQuery documentation for additional details regarding the jQuery queue.

CREATING A SLIDESHOW WITH IMAGES

Listing 6.9 displays the contents of `JQSlideShow1.html` that illustrates how to create a slideshow with JPG images using jQuery.

Listing 6.9 JQSlideShow1.html

```
<!DOCTYPE html>
  <head>
   <meta charset="utf-8"/>
   <title>jQuery Slide-Related Effects</title>

   <script src="http://code.jquery.com/jquery-1.7.1.min.js">
   </script>
  </head>

  <body>
    <div id="photos">
      <img class="show" src="Laurie1.jpeg" width="250"
                                            height="250"/>
      <img            src="Laurie2.jpeg" width="250"
                                            height="250"/>
      <img            src="Laurie3.jpeg" width="250"
                                            height="250"/>
    </div>

    <script>
      var i = 0, curr, next, shortPause = 3000;
      $(document).ready(function(){
```

```
            slideShow();
        });

        function slideShow() {
          $("img").hide();

          var curr = $("#photos .show");
          curr.fadeIn("slow")
              .removeClass("show");

          next = curr.next().length ? curr.next() :
                    curr.parent().children(':first');
          next.addClass("show");

          setTimeout(slideShow, shortPause);
        }
    </script>
  </body>
</html>
```

The code in Listing 6.9 references a required jQuery file, and then defines three HTML `<img>` elements, where only the first one specifies the "show" CSS class, which serves as a placeholder to identify the current HTML `<img>` element that we want to display during the slideshow. The animation effect starts by invoking the JavaScript function `slideShow()`, which initially hides all the HTML `<img>` elements:

```
$("img").hide();
```

Next the code finds the current HTML `<img>` element, slowly displays this element, and then removes the `show` class, as shown here:

```
var curr = $("#photos .show");
curr.fadeIn("slow")
    .removeClass("show");
```

The next section of code in Listing 6.9 determines the next HTML `<img>` element (which wraps around to the first image in the list when we reach the right-most image) and adds the `show` attribute, as shown here:

```
next = curr.next().length ? curr.next() :
              curr.parent().children(':first');
next.addClass("show");
```

Finally, the code in Listing 6.9 invokes the JavaScript `setTimeout()` function with a delay of `shortPause` (which has value `3000` milliseconds) and then invokes the JavaScript function `slideShow()`, as shown here:

```
setTimeout(slideShow, shortPause);
```

Add more images to Listing 6.9 and experiment with the code (such as adding a `start` and `stop` button) in order to create other slideshow effects.

CSS3-BASED ANIMATION EFFECTS

This section illustrates a variety of animation effects that you can create with CSS3, where the code samples use CSS3 `@keyframes` rules and 2D/3D transforms.

Animation Effects with CSS3 Keyframes and 2D Transforms

Listing 6.10 displays the contents of `JQButtonAnimation1.html` that illustrates how to create button-related animation effects that are triggered by the `hover` pseudo-class.

Listing 6.10 JQButtonAnimation1.html

```
<!DOCTYPE html>
<html lang="en">
  <head>
   <meta charset="utf-8"/>
   <title>jQuery Button Animation Effect</title>

<script src="http://code.jquery.com/jquery-1.7.1.min.js">
                                                    </script>

    <style>
      @-webkit-keyframes AnimButton {
        0% {
           font-size: 18px;
           background-color: #0f0;
          -webkit-transform: translate(0px,0px) rotate(-60deg)
                             skew(-15deg,0);
        }
        25% {
           font-size: 24px;
           background-color: #0ff0
           -webkit-transform: translate(100px,100px)
                             rotate(-180deg) skew(-15deg,0);
        }
        50% {
           font-size: 32x;
```

```
            -webkit-transform: translate(50px,50px)
                            rotate(-120deg)skew(-25deg,0);
         background-color: #00f;
      }
      75% {
         font-size: 24px;
         background-color: #0ff;
         -webkit-transform: translate(100px,100px) rotate(-
                                                    180deg)
                         skew(-15deg,0);
      }
      100% {
         font-size: 18px;
         -webkit-transform: translate(0px,0px)
                            rotate(0)  skew(0,0);
         background-color: #f00;
      }
   }

   #button1 {
    font-size: 12px;
    background-color: #f00;
   }

   #button1:hover {
    font-size: 36px;
    background-color: #00f;
   -webkit-animation-name: AnimButton;
   -webkit-animation-duration: 4s;
   }

   #button2 {
    font-size: 12px;
    background-color: #00f;
   }

   #button2:hover {
    font-size: 24px;
    background-color: #00f;
   -webkit-animation-name: AnimButton;
   -webkit-animation-duration: 2s;
   }
 </style>
</head>

<body>
```

```
<div>
    <input type="button" id="button1"
           value="Click Me or Hover Over Me"/>
</div>
<div>
    <input type="button" id="button2"
           value="Click Me or Hover Over Me"/>
  </div>
</div>

<script>
  $(document).ready(function(){
    $("#button1").click(function() {
       $(this).fadeOut(500, function() {
       //$(this).remove();
       });
    });

    $("#button2").click(function() {
       $(this).fadeOut(500, function() {
       //$(this).remove();
       });
    });
  });
</script>

</body>
</html>
```

Listing 6.10 contains an HTML `<style>` element with a CSS3 `keyframes` definition (which you could also move to a separate CSS stylesheet), followed by two HTML `<input>` elements of type `button`, both of which have click event handlers defined in the `<script>` element in Listing 6.10.

Whenever users click on either button, CSS3 `keyframes` are applied to the button, which creates animation effects using combinations of the functions `translate()`, `rotate()`, and `skew()` for the time periods (either 2 seconds or 4 seconds) specified in the associated selectors. In addition, the click handlers create a fading effect that lasts for 500 milliseconds.

When you launch the HTML Web page `JQButtonAnimation1.html` in a browser, you will see the animation effect whenever you hover over either of the buttons.

2D Transforms with CSS3 and jQuery

The code sample in this section shows you how to apply CSS transforms directly to elements (based on user-initiated events) using the jQuery `css()` function.

Listing 6.11 displays the contents of `JQTransforms2D1.css` that contains CSS3 selectors that are applied to the HTML5 Web page `JQTransforms2D1.html` shown in Listing 6.11.

Listing 6.11 JQTransforms2D1.css

```
#outer {
  position: absolute;
  left: 50px;
  top: 150px;
}

#inner1 {
  float: left;
  background-color:#F00;
  width: 200px;
  height:150px;
}

#inner2 {
  float: left;
  background-color:#FF0;
  width: 200px;
  height:150px;
}

#inner3 {
  float: left;
  background-color:#00F;
  width: 200px;
  height:150px;
}
```

Listing 6.11 is very straightforward: several properties, such as the `width` and `height`, are specified for three HTML `<div>` elements that are defined in Listing 6.12.

Listing 6.12 JQTransforms2D1.html

```
<!DOCTYPE html>
<html lang="en">
<head>
<title>jQuery Transform Effects</title>
```

```
<meta charset="utf-8"/>
<link href="Transforms1.css"
            rel="stylesheet" type="text/css">
<script src="http://code.jquery.com/jquery-1.7.1.min.js">
</script>
</head>

    <body>
<h1>Click Inside Any of the Rectangles:</h1>

      <div id="outer">
        <div id="inner1"></div>
        <div id="inner2"></div>
        <div id="inner3"></div>
        </div>
      </div>

      <script>
       $(document).ready(function() {
          $("#inner1").click(function() {
            $("div").css({height: '300px',
              'webkit-transform': 'scale(0.5, 0.5)
                                    skew(-10deg, 20deg)'
            });
          });

          $("#inner2").click(function() {
            $("div").css({height: '200px',
                          width: '250px',
              'webkit-transform': 'scale(0.5, 0.8) rotate(-45deg)'
            });
          });

          $("#inner3").click(function() {
            $("div").css({height: '100px',
                          width: '250px',
              'webkit-transform': 'skew(-10deg, 10deg)
                                    rotate(-45deg)'
            });
          });
        });
      </script>

    </body>
  </html>
```

Listing 6.12 defines event handlers for the click event for three HTML `<div>` elements, all of which invoke the jQuery `css()` function in order to update properties of the `<div>` element that received a click event.

For example, the first HTML `<div>` element is updated as follows whenever users click on this element:

```
$("div").css({height: '300px',
    'webkit-transform': 'scale(0.5, 0.5) skew(-10deg, 20deg)'
});
```

As you can see, the height property is set to `300px`, and transforms are applied to the `<div>` elements when users click on them.

Keep in mind that you can move the CSS3 code that is referenced in the click handlers in Listing 6.12 to a separate CSS stylesheet, which makes it easier to maintain the CSS3 code in a single file. You can also reference the same CSS stylesheet in multiple HTML Web pages.

In addition to CSS3 2D animation effects, you can obviously create CSS3 3D animation effects. Experiment with the code in Listing 6.12 by adding some of the 3D effects that are available in Chapter 2, or from the following open source project:

http://code.google.com/p/css3-graphics

Figure 6.4 displays `JQTransforms2D1.html`on in a Chrome browser on a Macbook.

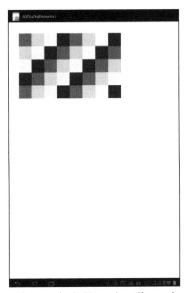

FIGURE 6.4 Transformed rectangles in jQuery in a Chrome browser on a Macbook.

The remainder of this chapter contains examples that are different from the previous code samples. Listing 6.13 and Listing 6.14 involve mouse-related functionality and how to handle mouse events programmatically. Listing 6.14 shows you a very rudimentary game-oriented code sample that combines JavaScript, jQuery, and CSS3 more extensively than earlier examples.

A FOLLOW THE MOUSE EXAMPLE WITH JQUERY

The code sample in this section extends the functionality introduced in the previous section by showing you how to programmatically create HTML `<div>` elements and append them to the DOM.

Listing 6.13 displays the contents of `JQSketchFollowMouse1.html` that illustrates how to render a `<div>` element under the current location of a user's mouse using jQuery and CSS3 in an HTML5 Web page.

Listing 6.13 JQSketchFollowMouse1.html

```
<!DOCTYPE html>
<html lang="en">
<head>
    <meta charset="utf-8"/>
    <title>jQuery Follow the Mouse Example</title>
    <script
        src="http://code.jquery.com/jquery-1.7.1.min.js">
    </script>
</head>

<body>
    <script>
        $(document).ready(function() {
            var rectWidth   = 20;
            var rectHeight  = 20;
            var moveCount   = 0;
            var insertNode  = true;
            var currColor   = "";
            var rectColors  = new Array('#ff0000', '#ffff00',
                                        '#00ff00', '#0000ff');
            var newNode;

            $(document).mousemove(function(e) {
                ++moveCount;

                // are users are moving their mouse?
```

```
        if(insertNode == true) {
            // create a rectangle at the current position
    newNode = $('<div id=newNode>').css({'position':'absolute',
                                'background-color':'#ff0000',
                                    'width':rectWidth+'px',
                                    'height':rectHeight+'px',
                                    top: e.pageY,
                                    left: e.pageX
                                });

        //append the rectangle to body
        $(document.body).append(newNode);
        insertNode = false;
    } else {
        currColor = rectColors[moveCount % rectColors.length];

        $('div').each(function() {
            $(this).css({top: e.pageY,
                        left: e.pageX,
                        'background-color': currColor
            });
        });
    }
    });
    });
    </script>
    </body>
</html>
```

Listing 6.13 initializes some JavaScript variables and then uses the jQuery css() method to dynamically create an HTML <div> element whose upper-left vertex has the same coordinates of the point where a mousemove event occurs, thereby creating a "follow the mouse" effect:

```
// create a rectangle at the current position
newNode = $('<div id=newNode>').css({'position':'absolute',
                            'background-color':'#ff0000',
                                'width':rectWidth+'px',
                                'height':rectHeight+'px',
                                top: e.pageY,
                                left: e.pageX
                            });

//append the rectangle to body
$(document.body).append(newNode);
```

The key point to note is that the event object (called e in this code sample) gives us access to the coordinates of the current move position via the attributes e.pageX and e.pageY, which we can use to set the CSS properties left and top, respectively.

YOUR FIRST SKETCHING PROGRAM

Listing 6.14 displays the contents of JQSketchSolid1.html that illustrates how to create a rudimentary sketching program with jQuery and CSS3 in an HTML5 Web page. Subsequent code samples will illustrate how to create more sophisticated effects, such as adding gradients and creating animation.

Listing 6.14 JQSketchSolid1.html

```
<!DOCTYPE html>
<html lang="en">
<head>
   <meta charset="utf-8"/>
   <title>jQuery Follow the Mouse Example</title>

  <script
     src="http://code.jquery.com/jquery-1.7.1.min.js">
  </script>
</head>

<body>
  <script>
   $(document).ready(function() {
     var draw = false;

     //mousedown means draw:
     $(document).mousedown(function() { draw=true; });

     //mouseup means no draw:
     $(document).mouseup(function() { draw=false; });

     $(document).mousemove(function(e) {
        // are users are moving their mouse?
        if(draw==true) {
           // create a rectangle at the current position
           pointer = $('<span>').css({'position':'absolute',
                                   'background-color':'#ff0000',
```

```
                                  'width':'4px',
                                  'height':'4px',
                          top: e.pageY ,      //offsets
                          left: e.pageX       //offsets
                              });

            //append the rectangle to body
            $(document.body).append(pointer);
         }
       });
     });
   </script>
 </body>
</html>
```

Listing 6.14 is similar to Listing 6.13, except that now we create and append a new HTML `<div>` element to the DOM whenever users move their mouse, which creates a sketching effect. You can also add other CSS3 effects, such as gradients and animation, and perhaps enable users to select different "pen" colors (and sizes and shapes) in order to create richer visual effects.

Figure 6.5 displays `JQSketchSolid1.html`in a Chrome browser on a Macbook.

FIGURE 6.5 Sketching with jQuery in a Chrome browser on a Macbook.

If you enjoy creating this type of visual effect, the accompanying DVD contains the Web pages `JQSketchGradient2.html` and `JQSketchAnima-tion1.html` that enhance the code in Listing 6.14 by adding gradients and animation effects.

OTHER ANIMATION EFFECTS WITH JQUERY

The jQuery plugin `rotate3di` for 3D animation enables you to animate HTML content, along with other visual effects. Its homepage is here:

http://www.zachstronaut.com/projects/rotate3di/

You can also combine jQuery with SVG instead of dynamically creating `<div>` elements that are styled with CSS3 selectors. The accompanying DVD contains the HTML5 Web page for `JQArchDoubleEllipse1Rotate1.html`, which illustrates how to combine jQuery with SVG. However, this code is similar to earlier code samples, so its contents are omitted from this chapter.

RENDERING A SET OF BOUNCING BALLS WITH JQUERY AND CSS3

The example in this section shows you how to render a set of bouncing balls in jQuery Mobile. As the "balls" bounce around inside a rectangle, their width, height, and color are updated, and their shape changes from a rectangle to a circle. Although this code sample is primarily for fun, you can experiment with the code to create other interesting effects by modifying additional CSS properties dynamically.

Listing 6.15 displays the contents of `JQBouncingBalls1.html` that illustrates how to render a set of vertically bouncing balls in a jQuery HTML5 Web page.

Listing 6.15 JQBouncingBalls1.html

```
<!DOCTYPE html>
<html lang="en">
<head>
  <meta charset="utf-8"/>
  <title>JQuery Bouncing Balls</title>

  <style>
    #outer {
      width: 400px; height: 300px;
      margin:0px; padding:0;
      border: 3px solid blue;
    }

    #circle0 { left:  50px; top: 250px; }
```

```
      #circle1 { left: 100px; top: 200px; }
      #circle2 { left: 150px; top: 150px; }
      #circle3 { left: 200px; top: 100px; }
      #circle4 { left: 250px; top:  80px; }
      #circle5 { left: 250px; top:  80px; }
      #circle6 { left: 250px; top:  80px; }
      #circle7 { left: 250px; top:  80px; }
      #circle8 { left: 250px; top:  80px; }
      #circle9 { left: 250px; top:  80px; }

      div[id^="circle"] {
        position:absolute;
        width:  40px; height: 40px;
        margin:0px; padding:0;
        -webkit-border-radius: 50%;
      }
    </style>
  </head>

<body onload="startAnimation()">
  <div id="outer">
    <div id="circle0"> </div>
    <div id="circle1"> </div>
    <div id="circle2"> </div>
    <div id="circle3"> </div>
    <div id="circle4"> </div>
    <div id="circle5"> </div>
    <div id="circle6"> </div>
    <div id="circle7"> </div>
    <div id="circle8"> </div>
    <div id="circle9"> </div>
  </div>

  <script src="http://code.jquery.com/jquery-1.7.1.min.js">
  </script>

  <script>
  //var xPosPts    = [50, 100, 150, 200, 250, 80, 30, 180,
                                                  130, 250];
     var xPosPts    = [0, 50, 100, 150, 200, 250, 300, 350,
                                                  400, 450];
     var yPosPts    = [250, 200, 150, 100, 50, 80, 30, 180,
                                                  130, 250];

  //var dirXPts    = [1, -1, 1, -1, 1, 1, -1, 1, -1, 1];
     var dirXPts    = [0,  0, 0,  0, 0, 0,  0, 0,  0, 0];
```

```
      var dirYPts      = [-1, 1, 1, -1, 1, -1, 1, 1, -1, 1];

      var deltaXPts   = [5, 10, 15, 20, 25, 15, 10, 25, 10, 20];
      var deltaYPts   = [25, 20, 15, 10, 5, 15, 10, 25, 10, 20];

var leftX = 20, rightX = 380, topY = 60, bottomY = 250;
      var loopCount = 0, maxCount = 500, shortPause = 80;
      var currWidth = 0, currHeight = 0, tapCount = 0;
      var index = 0, radius = 10, color="", theTimeout;

      var ballColors = ['#f00','#ff0','#0f0','#00f','#f0f'];

      function updatePosition() {
         for(var i=0; i<xPosPts.length; i++) {
           xPosPts[i] += dirXPts[i]*deltaXPts[i];
           yPosPts[i] += dirYPts[i]*deltaYPts[i];

           if(xPosPts[i] < leftX) {
              xPosPts[i] = leftX;
              dirXPts[i] *= -1;
           }

           if(xPosPts[i] >= rightX) {
              xPosPts[i] = rightX;
              dirXPts[i] *= -1;
           }

           if(yPosPts[i] <= topY) {
              yPosPts[i] = topY;
              dirYPts[i] *= -1;
           }

           if(yPosPts[i] >= bottomY) {
              yPosPts[i] = bottomY;
              dirYPts[i] *= -1;
           }
         }

         displayBalls();

         // bounce again?
         if(++loopCount < maxCount) {
            if(theTimeout != null) {
              theTimeout = setTimeout("updatePosition()",
                                      shortPause);
            }
```

```
      }
    }

  function displayBalls() {
   //index = loopCount % 40;
     index = Math.floor(loopCount/40);

     if(index % 2 == 0) {
       currWidth  = (5+loopCount%40)+'px';
       currHeight = (5+loopCount%40)+'px';
     } else {
       currWidth  = (45-(loopCount%40))+'px';
       currHeight = (45-(loopCount%40))+'px';
     }

     for(var i=0; i<xPosPts.length; i++) {
     //color = ballColors[i % ballColors.length];
     color = ballColors[(i+loopCount) % ballColors.length];

       var theCircle = $("#circle"+i);
       // update the attributes of the ball...
       $(theCircle).css('left',        xPosPts[i]+'px');
       $(theCircle).css('top',         yPosPts[i]+'px');
       $(theCircle).css('width',       currWidth);
       $(theCircle).css('height',      currHeight);
       $(theCircle).css('background',  color);
      $(theCircle).css('borderRadius', (loopCount%50)+"%");
       }
    }

  function startAnimation() {
     event.preventDefault();
     theTimeout = setTimeout("updatePosition()",
                        shortPause);

     updatePosition();
    }
  </script>
 </body>
</html>
```

Listing 6.15 is longer than many of the other code samples that you've seen in this chapter, but it can be divided into logical units. The first portion contains an HTML <style> element that defines a set of HTML <div> elements, followed by a code block that sets various properties for those elements, as shown here:

```
div[id^="circle"]
    position:absolute;
    width:   40px; height: 40px;
    margin:0px; padding:0;
    -webkit-border-radius: 50%;
}
```

The next block of code initializes some JavaScript variables, including two arrays that contain the values for the upper-left vertex of the <div> elements, as shown here:

```
//var xPosPts    = [50, 100, 150, 200, 250, 80, 30, 180,
                                              130, 250];
    var xPosPts    = [0, 50, 100, 150, 200, 250, 300, 350,
                                              400, 450];
    var yPosPts    = [250, 200, 150, 100, 50, 80, 30, 180,
                                              130, 250];

//var dirXPts    = [1, -1, 1, -1, 1, 1, -1, 1, -1, 1];
    var dirXPts    = [0,  0, 0,  0, 0, 0,  0, 0,  0, 0];
    var dirYPts    = [-1, 1, 1, -1, 1, -1, 1, 1, -1, 1];
```

Next, the JavaScript function updatePosition() updates the location of the HTML <div> elements by iterating through a loop that calculates the new positions. Whenever the new positions exceed the boundaries of the bounding rectangle, the code reverses the direction of the movement of the HTML <div> elements, as shown here:

```
function updatePosition() {
    for(var i=0; i<currentXPts.length; i++) {
        xPosPts[i] += dirXPts[i]*deltaXPts[i];
        yPosPts[i] += dirYPts[i]*deltaYPts[i];

        if(xPosPts[i] < leftX) {
            xPosPts[i] = leftX;
            dirXPts[i] *= -1;
        }
        // code omitted for brevity
    }
}
```

In the preceding code block, the code updates the position of the upper-left vertex of each HTML <div> element, and if the <div> element moves to the left of the left boundary of the outer bounding rectangle, its direction is reversed and its left-most value (which represents the horizontal direction) is re-set to the left border, as shown here:

```
if(xPosPts[i] < leftX) {
    xPosPts[i] = leftX;
    dirXPts[i] *= -1;
}
```

Similar conditional logic is used to ensure that each <div> element does not move to the right of the bounding rectangle; in addition, two other code blocks ensure that the <div> elements do not move past the upper and lower horizontal boundaries of the bounding rectangle.

The next portion of the updatePosition() function renders the bouncing balls in their newly computed locations, and also checks whether or not to continue the animation effects, as shown here:

```
displayBalls();

// bounce again?
if(++loopCount < maxCount) {
        theTimeout = setTimeout("updatePosition()",
                                shortPause);
}
```

The JavaScript function displayBalls() contains some conditional logic for updating the value of the border-radius property, followed by a loop that iterates through the set of HTML <div> elements to render them at their new locations.

The final portion of this HTML Web page contains some jQuery code that stops the animation whenever the tap count is odd, and restarts the animation when the tap count is even.

You can also specify user gestures to initiate the animation effects. For example, if you want to start the animation effect when users touch the screen, use the following code block:

```
$("#outer").bind("vmousedown",function(e, ui){
    e.preventDefault();
    updatePosition();
});
```

If you want to see the balls bouncing around the four sides of the enclosing rectangle, simply reverse the order of the active code in the following code snippet:

```
//var dirXPts    = [1, -1, 1, -1, 1, 1, -1, 1, -1, 1];
  var dirXPts    = [0,  0, 0,  0, 0, 0,  0, 0,  0, 0];
```

Figure 6.6 displays the result of rendering the HTML5 Web page in Listing 6.16 on an Asus Prime tablet with Android ICS.

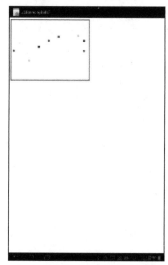

FIGURE 6.6 Bouncing balls on an Asus Prime tablet with Android ICS.

HANDLING OTHER EVENTS WITH JQUERY

You have seen code samples that illustrate how to use jQuery to handle various events. jQuery provides extensive support for mouse-related events and also support for keyboard events, as described in the next two sections.

Handling Mouse Events

jQuery supports the following common mouse events that are probably familiar to you: `mousedown`, `mouseenter`, `mouseleave`, `mousemove`, `mouseout`, `mouseover`, and `mouseup`. You can detect each of these mouse events in jQuery using the following jQuery code constructs:

```
$("#myInput").mousedown(function() {
```

```
   // do something
});
$("#myInput").mouseenter(function() {
   // do something
});
$("#myInput").mouseleave(function() {
   // do something
});
$("#myInput").mousemove(function() {
   // do something
});
$("#myInput").mouseout(function() {
   // do something
});
$("#myInput").mouseover(function() {
   // do something
});
$("#myInput").mouseup(function() {
   // do something
});
```

You can include any of the preceding code snippets that you need in your HTML Web pages and then add the processing logic to provide the intended functionality.

Handling Events in jQuery 1.7 and Beyond

In jQuery 1.7 and beyond, the preferred method for defining an event handler uses the following construct:

```
$("some-element").on(some-event)
```

However, versions of jQuery prior to version 1.7 provide several techniques to bind events to elements, and three of these techniques have been deprecated. Since version 1.7 was introduced recently, you will probably be exposed to HTML Web pages containing earlier versions of jQuery for quite some time. Consequently, you need to be aware of those other coding techniques so that you will be able to read the jQuery code in HTML Web pages that use earlier versions of jQuery.

For the purpose of illustration, suppose that you need to bind a "click" event to an HTML <div> element whose id attribute is div1.

The preferred method for defining an event handler with this code block (which you saw earlier in this chapter) is shown here:

```
$("#div1").on("click"), function() {
```

```
    // do something
}
```

However, HTML Web pages using older versions of jQuery also use an event handler defined like this:

```
$("#div1").click(function() {
    // do something
}
```

A third method for defining an event handler is to use the bind() method, which has been deprecated in version 1.7:

```
$("#button1").bind("click"), function() {

    // do something

}
```

A fourth method for defining an event handler is to use the live() method, which has also been deprecated in version 1.7:

```
$("#div1").live("click"), function() {
    // do something
}
```

The bind() method and the live() method attach a handler to an event to any element that matches the current selector. In addition, the live() method attaches the same handler to elements created later, which match the current selector.

A fifth method for defining an event handler is to use the delegate() method, which has also been deprecated in version 1.7:

```
$("#div1").delegate("click"), function() {
    // do something
}
```

In the preceding code blocks, an event handler was defined in order to handle a click event, but similar comments apply to other user-initiated events, such as swipeleft and swiperight. If you want to learn more about other changes in jQuery 1.7, you can find a summary of the changes (with links) here:

http://api.jquery.com/category/version/1.7/

You can also get detailed information regarding new functionality and changes in jQuery 1.7 on this Web page:

http://blog.jquery.com/2011/11/03/jquery-1-7-released/

Handling Keyboard Events

You can also detect `keypress`, `keyup`, and `keydown` events in jQuery. For example, this code displays an alert when users click on the uppercase "Z" key:

```
$("#myInput").keypress(function(e) {
  if (e.which == 90) alert ('Z was typed.')
});
```

You can check for other key events, keeping in mind that uppercase A is decimal 65 (hexadecimal 41), lowercase a is decimal 97 (hexadecimal 61), and lowercase z is decimal 122 (hexadecimal 7A).

You can also add many other effects, including the animation effects that are available in previous code samples in this chapter.

SUMMARY

This chapter introduced you to jQuery graphics and animation effects, along with code samples that illustrated how to use jQuery functions to create simple animation effects. In particular you learned how to do the following:

- Basic animation effects in jQuery
- The effect action in jQuery
- Scrolling effects in jQuery
- Working with CSS3 selectors in jQuery
- Setting properties with the `css()` function
- Toggling CSS properties
- Creating rounded corners
- Creating shadow effects
- Setting linear and radial gradients
- Working with images
- The `hide()` and `show()` functions
- Using callback functions
- The `fadeIn()`, `fadeOut()`, and `fadeTo()` methods
- Setting the speed
- Toggling `hide()` and `show()`

- jQuery fade and slide animation effects
- The `fadeIn()` and `fadeOut()` functions
- jQuery `slideUp()` and `slideDown()` functions
- Easing functions in jQuery
- Custom CSS animation using `animate()`
- Creating a slideshow with images
- CSS3-based animation effects
- Simple sliding effects with CSS3
- Updating multiple attributes with CSS3
- Sliding effects with CSS
- Animation effects with CSS3 `keyFrames` and 2D transforms
- 2D transforms with CSS3 and jQuery
- 3D transforms with CSS3 and jQuery
- A follow the mouse example with jQuery
- Your first sketching program

The next chapter introduces you to various jQuery UI controls, along with code samples that show how to render some jQuery UI controls in HTML5 Web pages.

jQUERY UI CONTROLS

This chapter introduces you to various jQuery UI Controls, along with code samples that show how to render some jQuery UI controls in HTML5 Web pages. The rationale for using these UI controls is simple: they require much less effort than writing your own custom UI controls, and you don't need to maintain the code for these controls. You will see examples of using jQuery to render accordions, buttons, combo boxes, date pickers, progress bars, sliders, and tabs. In addition, you will learn how to programmatically handle user-initiated events involving jQuery UI controls. There are more UI controls available that you can learn about by consulting the jQuery homepage.

The jQuery UI controls in this chapter are presented alphabetically, so feel free to skip around to read about the UI controls that are of interest to you. Although information about these UI controls is available in the jQuery documentation, this is a primer book, so it's more appropriate to include a list of UI controls in one convenient location instead of telling you to "go read the documentation." After you have read this chapter, you will also be in a better position to understand the lengthy code sample at the end of the chapter that illustrates an HTML5 Web page with various jQuery UI controls in a manner that reflects a somewhat realistic scenario.

This chapter also contains code samples for handling user click events that trigger updates in other (sometimes graphical) elements that are defined elsewhere in the same HTML5 Web page. This approach makes it easy to understand how to implement event-related functionality. Hopefully you will be able to adapt the code samples in this chapter to your specific needs.

One point to keep in mind is that the HTML Web pages in this chapter contain both HTML markup as well as jQuery code. For longer Web pages it makes more sense to put jQuery code in a separate file (just as we have done with CSS stylesheets). However, almost every Web page in this chapter is short (between 1 and 1.5 pages), so it's a choice based on convenience to keep the code in a single file.

A second point involves how to write your own jQuery plugins, which is beyond the scope of this book. You can find online tutorials that show you how to write jQuery plugins if you cannot find any existing jQuery plugins that meet your needs.

ACCORDION EFFECTS

http://jqueryui.com/demos/accordion/

jQuery UI supports an accordion widget, which contains one or more "folders" whose contents are shown only when users click on a particular folder.

Listing 7.1 displays the contents of the HTML5 Web page JQUIAccordion1.html that illustrates how to render an accordion widget.

Listing 7.1 JQUIAccordion1.html

```
<!DOCTYPE html>
<html lang="en">
 <head>
        <meta charset="utf-8"/>
        <title>jQuery Accordion</title>

  <link href="JQUIAccordion1.css" rel="stylesheet"
        type="text/css">
        <link type="text/css"
              href="css/themename/jquery-ui-
    1.8.14.custom.css"/>
        <script src="http://code.jquery.com/jquery-1.7.1.min.js">
                                            </script>
        <script src="js/jquery-ui-1.8.14.custom.min.js"></script>
        <link href="JQUIAccordion1.css" rel="stylesheet"
              type="text/css">
</head>

      <body>
      <script>
        $(function() {
          $("#accordion").accordion();
        });
      </script>
```

```
<div id="accordion">
    <h3><a href="#">Section 1</a></h3>
    <div>
        <p> This is the first section of the accordion. </p>
    </div>

    <h3><a href="#">Section 2</a></h3>
    <div>
        <p> This is the second section of the accordion. </p>
        <ul>
            <li>List item one</li>
            <li>List item two</li>
            <li>List item three</li>
        </ul>
    </div>

    <h3><a href="#">Section 3</a></h3>
    <div>
        <p> This is the section of the third accordion. </p>
    </div>
    <h3><a href="#">Section 4</a></h3>
    <div>
        <p> This is the section of the fourth accordion. </p>
        <div id="outer">
            <div id="inner1"></div>
            <div id="inner2"></div>
            <div id="inner3"></div>
        </div>
    </div>
  </div>
 </body>
</html>
```

Listing 7.1 is straightforward: after the usual file references, there is an HTML <script> element that references a HTML <div> element (whose id attribute has value accordion). You might be surprised to learn that jQuery code renders the contents of this HTML <div> element as an accordion with one line of code, as shown here:

```
<script>
  $(function() {
    $("#accordion").accordion();
  });
</script>
```

In fact, the code in the preceding `<script>` element is the typical manner in which jQuery renders the contents of an HTML `<div>` element as a jQuery widget:

```
$("#theDivID").widgetType();
```

In this example, the `widgetType` function is the jQuery `accordion()` function. You can create different accordion effects by overriding some of the default CSS definitions for a jQuery accordion. For example, insert the following section of code before the first section of the accordion in Listing 7.1 and see how this changes the effect of selecting each section in the accordion:

```
<h3 class="ui-accordion-header ui-helper-reset ui-state-active
ui-corner-top">
    <span class="ui-icon ui-icon-triangle-1-s"/>
    <a href="#">Section 1</a>
</h3>
```

Listing 7.2 JQUIAccordion1.css

```
#inner1 {
   float: left;
   background-color:#F00;
   width: 200px;
   height:200px;
}

#inner2 {
   float: left;
   background-color:#FF0;
   width: 200px;
   height:200px;
}

#inner3 {
   float: left;
   background-color:#00F;
   width: 200px;
   height:200px;
}
```

The three selectors in Listing 7.2 match corresponding their corresponding HTML `<div>` elements in Listing 7.1, which renders three rectangular shapes with red, yellow, and blue. This effect is visible when users click on the lowest folder (labeled "Section 4") in the accordion. In a sense, an accordion can be viewed as a set of vertical tabs, where the content of each tab contains whatever HTML content that you want to render, including graphics-like effects.

Launch the HTML5 Web page in Listing 7.1 and click on each "folder" in the rendered accordion, which will reveal the contents of the currently selected folder and also hide the contents of the other folders of this accordion.

Figure 7.1 displays the result of rendering JQUIAccordion1.html in Listing 7.1 in a landscape-mode screenshot taken from an Android application running on a Nexus S 4G with Android ICS.

FIGURE 7.1 A jQuery accordion on a Nexus S 4G with Android ICS.

BUTTONS

Buttons are obviously important in Web pages, especially for submitting form-based data, and jQuery provides significant support for button-related functionality. You can define CSS3 selectors to apply whatever styling effects that you need to HTML buttons, including gradients and shadow effects.

Listing 7.3 displays the contents of the HTML5 Web page JQUIButtons1. html that illustrates how to render buttons in an HTML Web page. The CSS stylesheet JQUIButtons1.css is omitted because its contents are the same as Listing 7.2.

Listing 7.3 JQUIButtons1.html

```html
<!DOCTYPE html>
<html lang="en">
 <head>
   <meta charset="utf-8"/>
   <title>jQuery Buttons</title>

  <link href="JQUIButtons1.css" rel="stylesheet"
        type="text/css">
  <link type="text/css" rel="stylesheet"
        href="css/themename/jquery-ui-1.8.14.custom.css"/>
 <script
     src="http://code.jquery.com/jquery-1.7.1.min.js">
</script>
<script
     src="http://code.jquery.com/jquery-ui-
              1.8.14.custom.min.js">
</script>
   <script src="js/jquery-ui-1.8.14.custom.min.js"></script>

    <script>
       var divColors = new Array('#000', '#F0F', '#F00',
                                 '#0F0', '#00F', '#0FF');
       var clickCount = 0;
       var color1 = "";
    </script>
   </head>

   <body>
    <div id="outer">
     <div class="buttons">
       <button>A regular button</button>
       <input type="submit" value="A submit button">
       <a href="#">An anchor button</a>
     </div>

     <div id="inner1"></div>
     <div id="inner2"></div>
     <div id="inner3"></div>
    </div>

    <script>
       $(function() {
          $( "input:submit, a, button", ".buttons" ).button();
```

```
      });
   </script>

   <script>
    $(document).ready(function() {
       $("button").click(function() {
         ++clickCount;
         color1 = divColors[(clickCount) % divColors.length];
         $("#inner1").css({background: color1});
       });

       $("input").click(function() {
         ++clickCount;
         color1 = divColors[(clickCount) % divColors.length];
         $("#inner2").css({background: color1});
       });

       $("a").click(function() {
         ++clickCount;
         color1 = divColors[(clickCount) % divColors.length];
         $("#inner3").css({background: color1});
       });
    });
   </script>

  </body>
  </html>
```

Listing 7.3 contains an HTML `<script>` element that applies the jQuery `button()` method to three HTML elements and converts them into jQuery buttons with one line of code, as shown in this code snippet:

```
$("input:submit, a, button", ".buttons").button();
```

Notice that the class `.buttons` (which is used to style an HTML `<div>` element that contains the HTML buttons and anchors) is also specified in the preceding code snippet. This extra class is redundant in this code snippet, but it does show you the flexibility of specifying a set of HTML elements that you want to convert into jQuery buttons.

The next block of code renders three HTML `<div>` elements with colors that are specified in their corresponding selectors and that are defined in the associated CSS stylesheet.

Launch the HTML Web page in Listing 7.3, and when you click on the top row of buttons (which includes the anchor link), the rectangles will change color. For example, the buttons change color whenever users click on them because of the following code:

```
$("button").click(function() {
    ++clickCount;
    color1 = divColors[(clickCount) % divColors.length];
    $("#inner1").css({background: color1});
});
```

In the preceding event handler, the colors are selected from a JavaScript array called divColors that contains a set of colors.

Figure 7.2 displays the result of rendering JQUIButtons1.html in Listing 7.3 in a landscape-mode screenshot taken from an iPad 3.

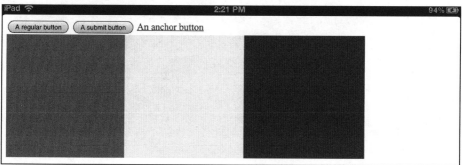

FIGURE 7.2 Buttons on an iPad 3.

CHECK BOXES AND RADIO BUTTONS

jQuery enables you to add event handlers to HTML checkboxes and radio buttons so that you can determine which ones users have selected.

Listing 7.4 displays the contents of JQUICheckBoxRadio1.html that illustrates how to render a checkbox and a set of radio buttons in an HTML Web page. The CSS stylesheet JQUICheckBoxRadio11.css is omitted because its contents are the same as Listing 7.2.

Listing 7.4 JQUICheckBoxRadio1.html

```
<!DOCTYPE html>
<html lang="en">
<head>
  <meta charset="utf-8"/>
  <title>jQuery Checkbox and Radio ButtonsEffect</title>
```

```
<link href="JQCheckBoxRadio1.css" rel="stylesheet"
      type="text/css">
<link type="text/css"
      href="css/themename/jquery-ui-1.8.14.custom.css"/>
<script src="http://code.jquery.com/jquery-1.7.1.min.js">
                                                      </script>

    <style>
    #CheckBoxRadioInfo, #CheckBoxRadioInfo2 {
        font-size: 20px;
        top: 10px;
        width: 50%;
        height: 50px;
    }
    </style>
</head>

<body>
  <div id="outer">
    <div>
     <fieldset id="CheckBoxRadioInfo">
     <label for="checkbox1"><strong>Check Something:</strong></
                                                          label>
      <input type="checkbox" name="checkbox1" id="checkbox1"></
                                                           input>

      <input type="radio" name="radio"
             value="radio1" checked="checked"></input>
      <input type="radio" name="radio" value="radio2"></input>
      <input type="radio" name="radio" value="radio3"></input>
     </fieldset>
    </div>

    <div>
     <fieldset id="CheckBoxRadioInfo2">
      <label for="input1"><strong>You Clicked On:</strong></
                                                          label>
      <input type="input" name="input1" id="input1"></input>
     </fieldset>
    </div>
    </div>
   </div>

   <script>
    $(document).ready(function() {
      $("input[name='checkbox1']").click(function() {
```

```
        $("#input1").val("checkbox1");
      });

      $("input[name='radio']").click(function() {
        $("#input1").val($(this).val());
      });
    });
  </script>
 </body>
</html>
```

Listing 7.4 contains two HTML `<div>` elements that contain an HTML `<fieldset>` element, which specifies an HTML checkbox followed by HTML radio buttons.

You can find the state of the checkbox whose `name` attribute has the value `checkbox1` with this event handler:

```
$("input[name='checkbox1']").click(function() {
  $("#input1").val("checkbox1");
});
```

Similarly, you can determine which radio button is checked with this code:

```
$("input[name='radio']").click(function() {
  $("#input1").val($(this).val());
});
```

In addition, you can also check which radio button is selected with the following code snippet:

```
var value = $("input[@name= fieldname] :checked" ).val();
```

In the preceding snippet, you need to replace the word "fieldname" with the corresponding name in the form field.

```
$('input:radio[ name="postage" ]').change( function(){
  if ($(this).is( ':checked' ) && $(this).val( ) == 'Yes') {
  // append goes here
  }
});
```

Figure 7.3 displays the result of rendering `JQUICheckBoxRadio1.html` in Listing 7.4 in a Chrome browser on a Macbook.

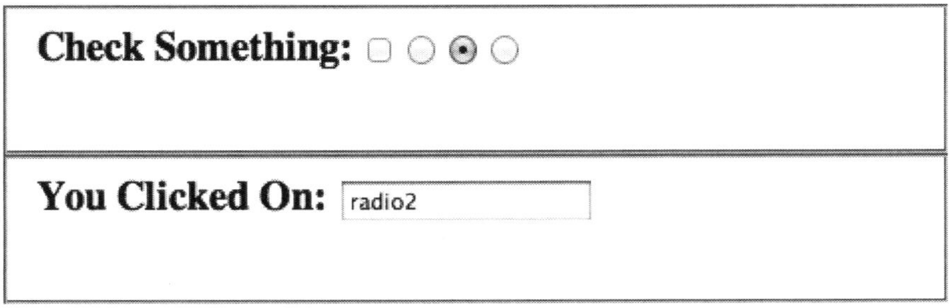

Check Something: ☐ ○ ◉ ○

You Clicked On: radio2

FIGURE 7.3 Checkboxes/button in a Chrome browser on a Macbook.

COMBO BOXES

jQuery provides support for HTML combo boxes, to which you can attach event handlers to detect events that are associated with those HTML elements.

Listing 7.5 displays the contents of `JQUIComboBox1.html` that illustrates how to render a combo box in an HTML Web page, and to execute a block of code whenever users select a different value in the combo box.

Listing 7.5 JQUIComboBox1.html

```
<!DOCTYPE html>
<html lang="en">
<head>
  <meta charset="utf-8"/>
  <title>jQuery ComboBox</title>

  <link type="text/css"
        href="css/themename/jquery-ui-1.8.14.custom.css"/>
  <script src="js/jquery-1.5.1.min.js"></script>
  <script src="js/jquery-ui-1.8.14.custom.min.js"></script>

  <style>
   #ComboBoxInfo {
      position: relative;
      font-size: 20px;
      top: 10px;
      width: 50%;
      height: 50px;
   }
  </style>
</head>
```

```
<body>
  <div id="outer">
   <div>
    <fieldset id="ComboBoxInfo">
     <label for="ComboBox"><strong>My ComboBox:</strong></la-
bel>
      <select id="ComboBox" >
        <option value="1">Value 1</option>
        <option value="2">Value 2</option>
        <option value="3">Value 3</option>
        <optgroup label="Group1">
          <option value="4">Value 4</option>
          <option value="5">Value 5</option>
          <option value="6">Value 6</option>
        </optgroup>
      </select>

      <label for="selected1"><strong>You selected:</strong></
label>
      <input id="selected1" type="text" value="">
     </fieldset>
    </div>
   </div>

   <script>
    $(document).ready(function() {
      $("#ComboBox").change(function() {
        // display the selected value
        $("#selected1").val(
          $("#ComboBox option:selected").text());
      });
    });
   </script>
  </body>
</html>
```

Listing 7.5 is straightforward: the first section references the required
jQuery files; this is followed by an HTML `<style>` element, and then the
definition of the items in a combo box.

Whenever users change the selected item in the combo box, this block of
code is executed:

```
$("#ComboBox").change(function() {
  // display the selected value
  $("#selected1").val(
```

```
        $("#ComboBox option:selected").text());
    });
```

Figure 7.4 displays the result of rendering `JQUIComboBox1.html` in Listing 7.5 in a Chrome browser on a Macbook.

My ComboBox: [Value 4 ‡] **You selected:** [Value 4]

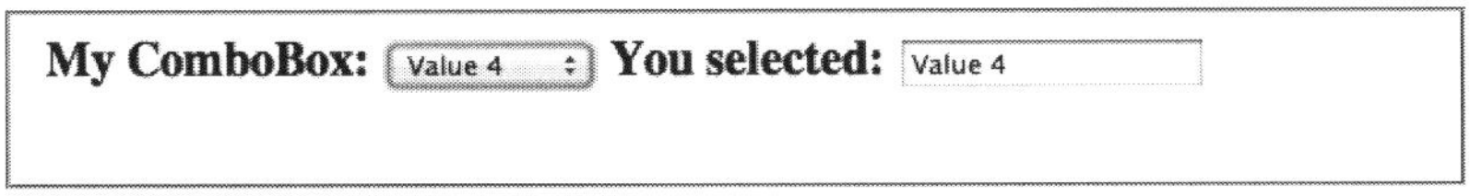

FIGURE 7.4 Combo box in a Chrome browser on a Macbook.

DATE PICKERS

jQuery supports a "date picker" functionality that enables you to set the past, current, and future dates, as well as the ability to modify those dates in a contextually relevant manner.

Listing 7.6 displays the contents of the HTML5 Web page `JQUIDatePicker1.html` that illustrates how to render a jQuery date picker widget in an HTML Web page. The CSS stylesheet `JQUIDatePicker1.css` is omitted because its contents are the same as Listing 7.2.

Listing 7.6 JQUIDatePicker1.html

```
<!DOCTYPE html>
<html lang="en">
<head>
  <meta charset="utf-8"/>
  <title>jQuery Date Picker</title>

  <link type="text/css"
          href="css/themename/jquery-ui-1.8.14.custom.css"/>
  <script src="http://code.jquery.com/jquery-1.7.1.min.js">
  </script>
  <script src="js/jquery-ui-1.8.14.custom.min.js"></script>

  <style>
   #input1, #input2, #input3 {
     width: 150px;
     height: 50px;
     float: left;
   }
  </style>
</head>
```

```
<body>
  <div id="outer">
    <div id="input1">
      Last Week:
      <input type="text" name="date" id="date1"/>
    </div>

    <div id="input2">
      Today's Date:
      <input type="text" name="date" id="date2"/>
    </div>

    <div id="input3">
      A Future Date:
      <input type="text" name="date" id="date3"/>
    </div>
  </div>

  <script>
    $(document).ready(function() {
      $("#date1").datepicker();
      $("#date2").datepicker();
      $("#date3").datepicker();

      // set date to last week
      var defaultDate1 = $("#date1").datepicker("option",
                                          "defaultDate" );
      $("#date1").datepicker( "option", "defaultDate", -7 );

      // set date to today
      var defaultDate2 = $("#date1").datepicker("option",
                                          "defaultDate");
      $("#date2").datepicker("option", "defaultDate", +0 );

      // set date to the future
      var futureDate = "07/07/2017";
      $("#date3").datepicker("setDate",futureDate);
    });
  </script>
</body>
</html>
```

Listing 7.6 references the usual jQuery files, followed by a `<style>` element that applies styling to the three HTML `<div>` elements. Next, the HTML `<body>` element specifies the contains of the three HTML `<div>` elements, followed by a block of code that converts three HTML `<input>` fields into jQuery `date` objects, as shown here:

```
$("#date1").datepicker();
$("#date2").datepicker();
$("#date3").datepicker();
```

You can specify a future date and when you want to change that future date; jQuery will display the previous and next months that are relative to that date, as shown here:

```
// set date to the future
var futureDate = "07/07/2017";
$("#date3").datepicker("setDate",futureDate);
```

Figure 7.5 displays the result of rendering `JQUIDatePicker1.html` in Listing 7.6 in a Chrome browser on a Macbook.

Last Week:	Today's Date:	A Future Date:
		07/07/2017

PrevNext
June 2012

Su	Mo	Tu	We	Th	Fr	Sa
					1	2
3	4	5	6	7	8	9
10	11	12	13	14	15	16
17	18	19	20	21	22	23
24	25	26	27	28	29	30

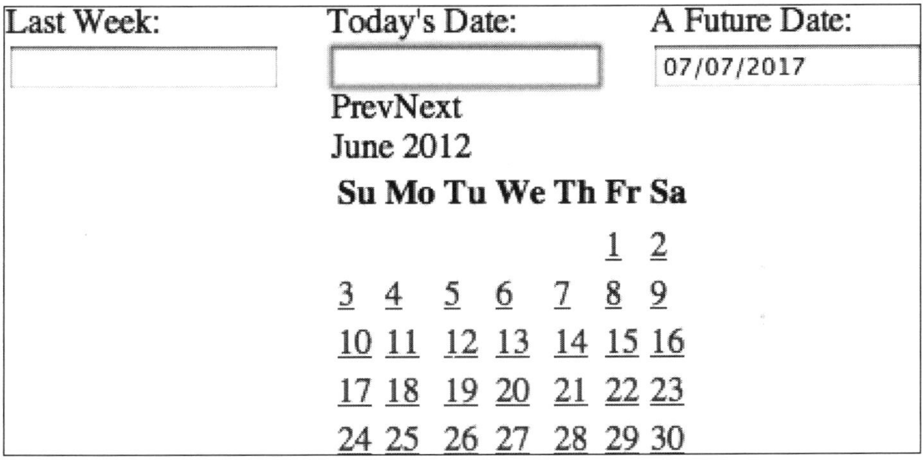

FIGURE 7.5 A date picker in a Chrome browser on a Macbook.

PROGRESS BARS

You can create and update progress bars very easily using jQuery. Listing 7.7 displays the contents of `JQUIProgressBar1.html` that illustrates how to render a progress bar in an HTML Web page.

Listing 7.7 JQUIProgressBar1.html

```
<!DOCTYPE html>
<html lang="en">
<head>
```

```
    <meta charset="utf-8"/>
    <title>jQuery Progress Bar</title>
<link rel="stylesheet" type="text/css"
 href="http://ajax.googleapis.com/ajax/libs/jqueryui/1.8/
 themes/base/jquery-ui.css"/>
    <script src="http://ajax.googleapis.com/ajax/libs/
                      jquery/1.5/jquery.min.js">
    </script>
    <script
     src="http://ajax.googleapis.com/ajax/libs/jqueryui/
              /1.8 jquery-ui.min.js">
    </script>
    <style>
      #progressBarDiv1 {
        width: 30%;
      }
    </style>
  </head>

  <body>
   <div id="outer">
     <div id="progressBar1">
       Progress Bar:
       <div id="progressBarDiv1"> </div>
     </div>

     <div id="value1">
       Progress Bar Value:
       <input id="text1" type="text" value="0"/>
     </div>

     <div id="newValue">
       Set New Value:
       <input id="newVal" type="text" value="0"/>
     </div>

   <script>
    $(document).ready(function() {
        $("#progressBarDiv1").progressbar({ value: 40 });
      $("#text1").val( $("#progressBarDiv1").progressbar("value")
);

        $("#newValue").bind("change", function() {
          var newVal = $("#newVal").val();
          $("#progressBarDiv1").progressbar("option", "value",
                                       parseInt(newVal));
```

```
          });
      });
    </script>
</body>
</html>
```

Listing 7.7 references the usual jQuery files, followed by an HTML <div> element (whose id value is outer) that contains the HTML code for a progress bar, the current value of the progress bar (which is initialized to 40), and an input field that allows users to change the value of the status bar.

The creation, display, and update of the value of the progress bar is handled in the following code block:

```
$(document).ready(function() {
    $("#progressBarDiv1").progressbar({ value: 40 });

    $("#text1").val( $("#progressBarDiv1").progressbar
                                                  ("value") );

    $("#newValue").bind("change", function() {
        var newVal = $("#newVal").val();

        $("#progressBarDiv1").progressbar("option", "value",
                                          parseInt(newVal));
    });
});
```

As you can see, the preceding code block binds a change event to the second HTML <input> field, and when users enter a new value, the progress bar is updated with that value.

Figure 7.6 displays the result of rendering JQUIProgressBar1.html in Listing 7.7 in a Chrome browser on a Macbook.

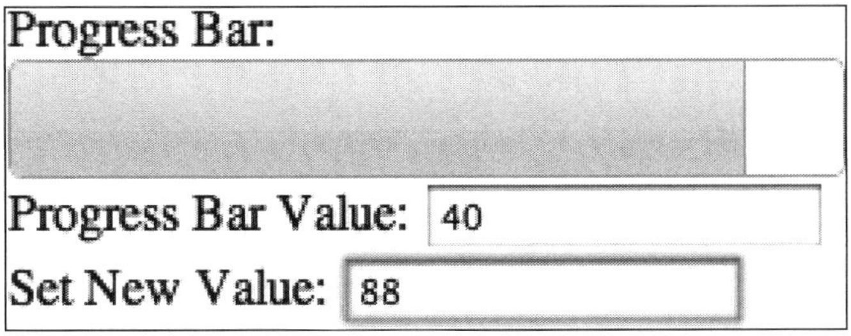

FIGURE 7.6 Progress bar in a Chrome browser on a Macbook.

SCROLL PANES WITH THE JQUERY JSCROLLPANE PLUGIN

Currently jQuery does not provide scroll pane widgets, but you have other options available. One option is to use HTML5 progress bars, which are simple to use and provide some "reasonable" functionality. If HTML5 progress bars are insufficient for your needs, you use a jQuery plugin that supports scroll pane widgets, such as the jScrollPane plugin, whose homepage is here:

http://jscrollpane.kelvinluck.com/

The jScrollPane plugin provides the `jScrollPane-<version>.min.js` JavaScript file as well as a CSS stylesheet (`jScrollPane.css`) that you can override with your own customizations.

This plugin provides over 20 demos that show you how to create scroll bars (horizontal, vertical, or both), the use of arrow buttons, its `scrollTo` and `scrollBy` methods, how to style scrollbars in an `IFRAME`, and various other effects.

Navigate to the homepage of the jScrollPane plugin where you will find links for these demos, along with examples and the download link for this jQuery plugin.

SLIDERS

The jQuery UI slider widget supports various options, methods, and events, some of which are illustrated in the code sample in this section.

Listing 7.8 displays the contents of `JQUISlider1.html` that illustrates how to render horizontal and vertical sliders in an HTML Web page.

Listing 7.8 JQUISlider1.html

```
<!DOCTYPE html>
<html lang="en">
 <head>
  <meta charset="utf-8"/>
  <title>jQuery Slider</title>

  <link href="http://ajax.googleapis.com/ajax/libs/
                  jqueryui/1.8/themes/base/jquery-ui.css"
       rel="stylesheet" type="text/css"/>
  <script src="http://ajax.googleapis.com/ajax/libs/
                  jquery/1.5/jquery.min.js"></script>
  <script src="http://ajax.googleapis.com/ajax/libs/
```

```
                    jqueryui/1.8/jquery-ui.min.js"></script>

  <style>
    #slider1 {
            width: 50%; padding: 5px; background-color: #fcc;
    }
#sliderDiv2 {
  height: 120px; width: 50px; padding: 1px; background-color:
                                                    #ccf;
}
  </style>
  </head>

  <body>
   <div id="outer">
     <div id="slider1">
       Horizontal Slider:
       <br>
       <div id="sliderDiv1"></div>
     </div>

     <div id="value1">
       <br>
       Horizontal Slider Value:
       <input id="text1" type="text" value="0"/>
     </div>

     <div id="slider2">
       <br>
       Vertical Slider:
       <br>
       <div id="sliderDiv2"></div>
     </div>

     <div id="value2">
       <br>
       Vertical Slider Value:
       <input id="text2" type="text" value="0"/>
     </div>
   </div>

   <script>
    $(document).ready(function() {
      $("#sliderDiv1").slider({
          orientation: 'horizontal',
          min: 0,
```

```
            max: 200,
            step: 10,
            value: 100
     });

  $("#sliderDiv1").bind("slidechange", function(event, ui) {
    var slider1Val = $("#sliderDiv1").slider(
                                     "option", "value");
    $("#text1").val(slider1Val);
  });

  $("#sliderDiv2").slider({
      orientation: 'vertical',
      min: 0,
      max: 200,
      value: 100
  });

  $("#sliderDiv2").bind("slidechange", function(event, ui) {
    var slider2Val = $("#sliderDiv2").slider
                                    ("option", "value");
    $("#text2").val(slider2Val);

    if( slider2Val > 100) {
      $("#sliderDiv2").slider({
          orientation: 'horizontal'});
    } else {
      $("#sliderDiv2").slider({
          orientation: 'vertical'});
    }
  });
 });
 </script>
</body>
</html>
```

Listing 7.8 references the usual jQuery files, defines some CSS-based styling for a horizontal slider, and then creates a horizontal slider, a vertical slider, and two HTML <input> fields. Whenever users change the value of either jQuery slider, the associated text field is updated with the current value of the jQuery slider.

jQuery sliders can be dynamically changed from a vertical slider to a horizontal slider (or vice versa). In this code sample, the vertical slider becomes to a horizontal slider whenever the value of the slider exceeds 100, as shown in this code fragment:

```
$("#sliderDiv2").bind("slidechange", function(event, ui) {
  var slider2Val = $("#sliderDiv2").slider("option", "value");
  $("#text2").val(slider2Val);

  if( slider2Val > 100) {
    $("#sliderDiv2").slider({
        orientation: 'horizontal'});
  } else {
    $("#sliderDiv2").slider({
        orientation: 'vertical'});
  }
});
```

The preceding code fragment also sets (or resets) the vertical slider to a vertical slider its value does not exceed 100. Additional information regarding other options, methods, and events for jQuery UI sliders is here:

http://jqueryui.com/demos/slider/

Keep in mind that sometimes combining CSS3 effects with sliders can produce unintended visual effects.

For example, add the following code snippet to the HTML `<style>` element in Listing 7.8 and watch what happens when you move the vertical jQuery slider:

```
#sliderDiv2 {
  height: 120px; width: 50px; padding: 1px; background-color:
#ccf;

}
```

Figure 7.7 displays the result of rendering JQUISlider1.html in Listing 7.8 in a Chrome browser on a Macbook.

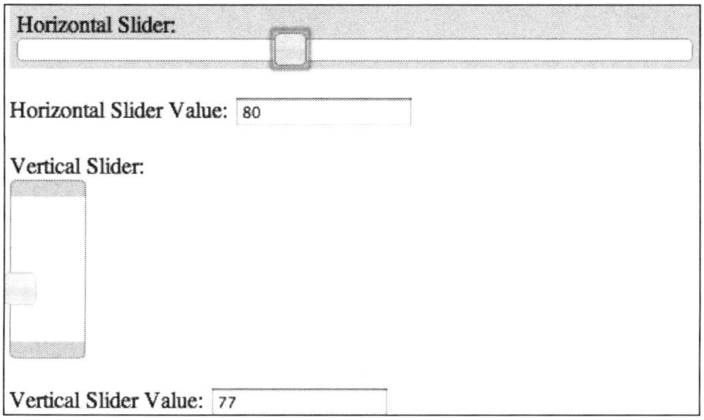

FIGURE 7.7 Slider in a Chrome browser on a Macbook.

One simple use of jQuery sliders is to use them to control the speed of animation effects (which can also be done with a spinner).

Listing 7.9 displays the contents of JQUIAnimSlider1.html that illustrates how to use a slider widget to control an animation effect. The CSS stylesheet JQUIAnimSlider1.css is not displayed because this CSS stylesheet is the same as Listing 7.2:

http://awardwinningfjords.com/2011/04/13/adjustable-animations-with-sliders.html

Listing 7.9 JQUIAnimSlider1.html

```
<!DOCTYPE html>
<html lang="en">
<head>
  <meta charset="utf-8"/>
  <title>jQuery Slider Animation Effect</title>

  <link href="AnimSlider1.css" rel="stylesheet" type="text/
                                                       css">

  <link href="http://ajax.googleapis.com/ajax/libs/
                  jqueryui/1.8/themes/base/jquery-ui.css"
       rel="stylesheet" type="text/css"/>
  <script src="http://ajax.googleapis.com/ajax/libs/
                       jquery/1.5/jquery.min.js"></script>
    <script  src="http://ajax.googleapis.com/ajax/libs/jque-
ryui/1.8/jquery-ui.min.js"></script>
  </head>

  <body>
    <div id="outer">
      <header>
       <h2>Select a Duration and Easing Function and Click on a
Rectangle</h2>
      </header>

      <div id="input1">
        <!-- Integers between 0-5000 (default is 500) -->
        Duration:
        <span id="speedSpan">500</span>
        <br>
        <input id="speed" class="range" type="range"
              min="0" max="5000" step="1" value="500">
        <br>
```

```
      Easing:
      <select class="easing">
       <option></option>
       <option>swing</option>
       <option>easeInOut</option>
      </select>
    </div>

    <div id="inner1"></div>
    <div id="inner2"></div>
    <div id="inner3"></div>
  </div>

  <script>
   $(document).ready(function() {
      $("#speed").change(function() {
         var newVal = $("#speed").val();
         $("#speedSpan").html(newVal);
      });

      $("#inner1").click(function() {
        $("#inner1").animate(
          { left: 480, width: 100, height: 100 },
          { duration: $("input[type=range]").val() }
        );
      });

      $("#inner2").click(function() {
        $("#inner1").css({background: 'blue'});
        $("#inner2").css({background: 'red'});
        $("#inner3").css({translate: [100, 200]});
      });

      $("#inner3").click(function() {
        $("#inner1").css({background: 'red'});
        $("#inner2").css({background: 'yellow'});
        $("#inner3").css({background: 'blue'});
      });
    });
  </script>
 </body>
</html>
```

After referencing the required jQuery files, Listing 7.9 has an HTML <body> element that in turn contains an HTML <div> element (whose id attribute has value outer). This HTML5 <div> element acts as a container for several elements: an HTML <header> element (to display instructions), an HTML <input> element (to display the animation speed in milliseconds), and three HTML <div> elements that are rendered as rectangles with different colors.

Whenever users change the value of the horizontal jQuery slider, the value of the animation speed is displayed with the following code block that binds to the change event:

```
$("#speed").change(function() {
    var newVal = $("#speed").val();
    $("#speedSpan").html(newVal);
});
```

When users click on the left-most rectangle, an animation effect is created using the following code:

```
$("#inner1").click(function() {
    $("#inner1").animate(
        { left: 480, width: 100, height: 100 },
        { duration: $("input[type=range]").val() }
    );
});
```

Notice how the preceding code block uses the jQuery animate() method, in conjunction with the user-selected value for the animation speed, in order to create an animation effect.

For best viewing of the animation effect in this code sample, launch Listing 7.10 in a Chrome browser.

TABS

The jQuery tab widget supports various options, methods, and events, some of which are illustrated in the code sample in this section.

Listing 7.10 displays the contents of JQUITabs.html that illustrates how to render tab in an HTML Web page.

Listing 7.10 JQUITabs.html

```
<!DOCTYPE html>
<html>
  <head>
    <meta charset="utf-8"/>
    <title>jQuery Tabs</title>
```

```
<link href="JQUITabs.css" rel="stylesheet"
      type="text/css">
<script src="http://ajax.googleapis.com/ajax/libs/
                          jquery/1.7.1/jquery.min.js">
</script>

<style>
  .tabs a {
    padding:5px 10px;
    background:#f88;
    color:#fff;
    text-decoration:none;
  }

  .tabs li {
    list-style:none;
    display:inline;
  }
</style>

<script>
  $(document).ready(function(){
    $('ul.tabs').each(function(){
      // keep track of the currently active tab
      var $active, $content, $links = $(this).find('a');

      // first link is the initial active tab
      $active = $links.first().addClass('active');
      $content = $($active.attr('href'));

      // hide the other tabs
      $links.not(':first').each(function () {
        $($(this).attr('href')).hide();
      });

      // bind the click event handler
      $(this).on('click', 'a', function(e){
        // Make the old tab inactive.
        $active.removeClass('active');
        $content.hide();

      // Update the variables with the new link and content
        $active = $(this);
        $content = $($(this).attr('href'));

        // Make the tab active
```

```
                    $active.addClass('active');
                    $content.show();

                    // prevent the anchor's default click action
                    e.preventDefault();
                });
            });
        });
    </script>
    </head>

    <body>
      <ul class='tabs'>
        <li><a href='#tab1'>Tab 1</a></li>
        <li><a href='#tab2'>Tab 2</a></li>
        <li><a href='#tab3'>Tab 3</a></li>
        <li><a href='#tab4'>Tab 4</a></li>
      </ul>

        <div id="tab1">
            <p>Some text in the first tab. Some text in the first
tab. Some text in the first tab.</p>
        </div>

        <div id="tab2">
            <p>Some text in the second tab. Some text in the second
tab. Some text in the second tab.</p>
        </div>

        <div id="tab3">
            <p>Some text in the third tab. Some text in the third
tab. Some text in the third tab.</p>
        </div>

        <div id="tab4">
          <div id="outer">
            <div id="inner1"></div>
            <div id="inner2"></div>
            <div id="inner3"></div>
          </div>
        </div>
      </body>
    </html>
```

Listing 7.10 references the required jQuery files, followed by an HTML
<style> element that adds some styling effects to the tabs (which are HTML

<div> elements) that are specified later in the document. In particular, note the following code snippet for the child <a> elements of the <div> with the "tabs" class:

```
text-decoration:none;
```

...as well as the following code snippet for the child <li> elements of the <div> element with the "tabs" class:

```
list-style:none;
```

These code snippets enable us render the tabs in a horizontal row without a "bullet" point, so they appear to be actual tabs.

The following code block keeps track of the currently active tab and makes it visible, while also making the content of all the other tabs invisible:

```
var $active, $content, $links = $(this).find('a');

// first link is the initial active tab
$active = $links.first().addClass('active');
$content = $($active.attr('href'));

// hide the other tabs
$links.not(':first').each(function () {
    $($(this).attr('href')).hide();
});
```

Figure 7.9 displays the result of rendering JQUITabs.html in Listing 7.10 (and clicking on the fourth tab) in a Chrome browser on a Macbook.

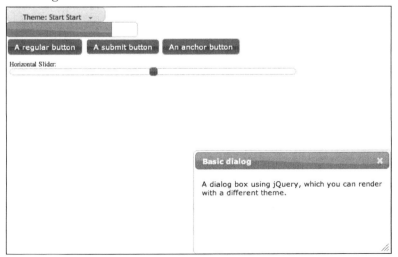

FIGURE 7.9 Tabs in a Chrome browser on a Macbook.

THEMING JQUERY UI

jQuery UI provides very nice support for switching between different themes, which consist of different look-and-feel effects that are applied to widgets and text. You can find very good information about jQuery themes on these Web sites:

http://jqueryui.com/docs/Theming
http://jqueryui.com/docs/Theming/API
http://jqueryui.com/docs/Theming#Using_ThemeRoller_and_Themes

Listing 7.11 displays the contents of JQUIThemes1.html that illustrates how to dynamically apply different themes to an HTML Web page with a set of widgets:

http://midnightprogrammer.net/post/Change-Page-Themes-Dynamically-Using-JQuery-Theme-Roller.aspx

Listing 7.11 JQUIThemes1.html

```
<!DOCTYPE html>
<html>
<head>
  <meta charset="utf-8"/>
  <title>jQuery Themes</title>

  <link type="text/css" rel="stylesheet" href="http://jqueryui.
com/themes/base/ui.all.css"/>
  <link rel="stylesheet"
     href="http://ajax.googleapis.com/ajax/libs/jqueryui/1.8.2/
themes/base/jquery-ui.css"
        type="text/css" media="all"/>
  <link rel="stylesheet" href="http://static.jquery.com/ui/css/
demo-docs-theme/ui.theme.css"
        type="text/css" media="all"/>
  <script src="http://jqueryui.com/js/jquery.js"></script>
  <script       src="http://ajax.googleapis.com/ajax/libs/jque-
ry/1.4.2/jquery.min.js">
  </script>
  <script       src="http://ajax.googleapis.com/ajax/libs/jque-
ryui/1.8.2/jquery-ui.min.js">
  </script>

  <script>
     $(document).ready(function () {
        // the set theme roller
```

```
        $('#MyThemeRoller').themeswitcher();

        // style the buttons
        $( "input:submit, a, button" ).button();

        // create a slider
        $("#sliderDiv1").slider({
            orientation: 'horizontal',
            min: 0,
            max: 200,
            step: 10,
            value: 100
        });
    });

    // display a Dialog
    $(function () {
        $("#MyDialog").dialog();
    });

    // display a progress bar
    $(function () {
        $("#MyProgressbar").progressbar({
            value: 80
        });
    });
  </script>

  <style>
    #slider1 { width: 50%; padding: 5px; }
  </style>
</head>

<body style="font-size:60%;">
    <script src="http://jqueryui.com/themeroller/themeswitcher-
tool/">
    </script>

    <div id="MyThemeRoller"></div>

    <div id="MyProgressbar" style="width:200px;"> </div>

    <div id="MyDialog" title="Basic dialog">
        <p> A dialog box using jQuery, which you can render with a
different theme.</p>
    </div>
```

```
<div class="buttons">
  <button>A regular button</button>
  <input type="submit" value="A submit button">
  <a href="#">An anchor button</a>
</div>

<div id="slider1">
  Horizontal Slider:
  <br>
  <div id="sliderDiv1"></div>
</div>
</body>
</html>
```

The primary purpose of Listing 7.11 is to illustrate how easily you can switch jQuery themes; except for the jQuery dialog box, all other other elements in Listing 7.12 have been discussed in previous code samples.

As you can see in the first part of Listing 7.11, the theming-related functionality involves more files than previous code samples: first there are references to two CSS files for jQuery theming; these are followed by references to the core jQuery file and to a pair of jQuery theme-related JavaScript files.

Figure 7.10 displays the result of rendering `JQUIThemes1.html` in Listing 7.11 in a Chrome browser on a Macbook.

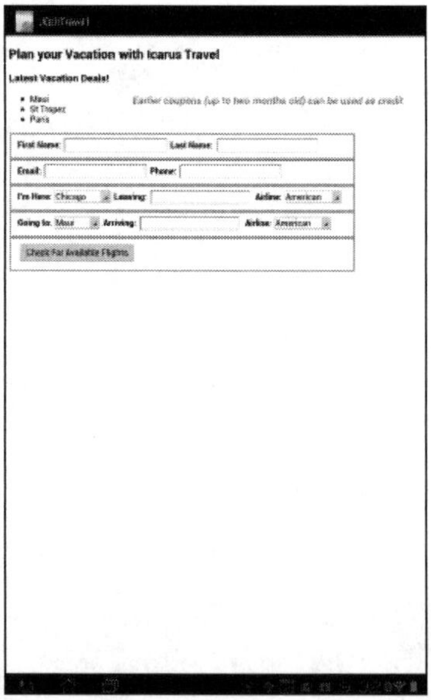

FIGURE 7.10 jQuery theme switching in a Chrome browser on a Macbook.

You might have already guessed that jQuery UI provides support for custom themes. You can find useful information here:

http://jqueryui.com/docs/Theming/CustomThemes

This is a more advanced topic that is outside the scope of this book, but it's definitely worth reading the plethora of information on this Web site if you need to create custom themes for your Web pages.

THE JQUERY UI EFFECT FUNCTION

The following example is purely for fun, and you might even find a good use for the jQuery `effect()` function, which enables you to create some nice visual effects.

Listing 7.12 displays the contents of `JQUIEffects1.html` that illustrates how to horizontally shake and then "explode" an HTML `<div>` element and its HTML `<p>` child elements.

Listing 7.12 JQUIEffects1.html

```
<!DOCTYPE html>
  <head>
   <meta charset="utf-8"/>
   <title>jQuery Effect Function</title>

<link rel="stylesheet"
    href="http://ajax.googleapis.com/ajax/libs/jqueryui/1.8.2/
themes/base/jquery-ui.css"
        type="text/css" media="all"/>

<link rel="stylesheet" href="http://static.jquery.com/ui/css/
demo-docs-theme/ui.theme.css"
        type="text/css" media="all"/>

<script src="http://jqueryui.com/js/jquery.js"></script>
<script        src="http://ajax.googleapis.com/ajax/libs/jque-
ry/1.4.2/jquery.min.js">
</script>
<script src="http://ajax.googleapis.com/ajax/libs/jque-
ryui/1.8.2/jquery-ui.min.js">
</script>

   <style>
     #outer {
```

```
          width: 300px;
          height: 150px;
          border: 1px solid black;
      }
   </style>
  </head>

  <body>
    <div id="outer">
      <div> <p id="p1">Hello World from jQuery</p> </div>
      <div> <p id="p2">Click Inside the Rectangle</p> </div>
      <div> <p id="p3">Goodbye World from jQuery</p> </div>
    </div>

    <script>
      $(document).ready(function(){
        $("#outer").click(function() {
          $("#outer").effect('shake', {times:3}, 300)
               .effect('highlight', {}, 3000)
               .hide('explode', {}, 1000);
        });
      });
    </script>
  </body>
</html>
```

Listing 7.12 contains mainly boilerplate markup, along with a "container" HTML <div> element (whose id attribute has value outer) that has three child HTML <div> elements.

The interesting part of Listing 7.12 is the <script> element that defines a click handler for the container HTML <div> element by means of method chaining that uses the jQuery effect() method, as shown here:

```
$("#outer").effect('shake', {times:3}, 300)
         .effect('highlight', {}, 3000)
         .hide('explode', {}, 1000);
```

When users click on this element, it will first shake horizontally three times (each time for 300 milliseconds), then change the color to a highlight effect, and after three seconds, it will create an "exploding" effect that lasts for one second.

Since it's not possible to capture a realistic snapshot of the "exploding" effect in Listing 7.12, launch the HTML Web page in Listing 7.12 in a WebKit-based browser and you will see an example of the interesting visual effects that are possible with the jQuery effect() method. As an exercise, try to create the same effect using JavaScript and/or CSS3 without the use of a toolkit such as jQuery. Even if you do not plan to use this functionality, you can probably appreciate some of the "bells and whistles" that are available in jQuery.

A SAMPLE WEB PAGE WITH VARIOUS UI COMPONENTS

The example in this section illustrates how to use some of the UI components that you saw earlier in this chapter. The validation details have been omitted in order to illustrate how to manipulate the UI components in a code sample of reasonable length, using techniques that you can use in your own Web pages.

Listing 7.13 displays the contents of `JQUITravel1.html` that illustrates how to programmatically determine user-selected values and how to handle user-initiated events involving UI components.

Listing 7.13 `JQUITravel1.html`

```
<!DOCTYPE html>
<html lang="en">
<head>
  <meta charset="utf-8"/>
  <title>Using jQuery Widgets</title>

    <link href="JQUIButtons1.css" rel="stylesheet" type="text/
css">
        <link   href="http://ajax.googleapis.com/ajax/libs/jque-
ryui/1.8/themes/base/jquery-ui.css"
          rel="stylesheet" type="text/css"/>
        <script  src="http://ajax.googleapis.com/ajax/libs/jque-
ry/1.5/jquery.min.js"></script>
        <script  src="http://ajax.googleapis.com/ajax/libs/jque-
ryui/1.8/jquery-ui.min.js"></script>

    <script>
      var startCity = "", destCity = "",
          flightItem = "", submitButton = "";

      var flightTimes = new Array('11-09-2011 5AM',
                                  '11-09-2011 3PM',
                                  '11-09-2011 6PM');

      var flightCount = flightTimes.length;
      var flightDest = new Array(flightCount);
```

```
    </script>
  </head>

<body>
 <article>
   <header>
     <h1>Plan your Vacation with Icarus Travel</h1>
     <p><time pubdate datetime="2011-10-30T14:14-14:00">
                                            </time></p>
   </header>

   <header>
     <h3>Latest Vacation Deals!</h3>
      <aside style="font-size:larger;font-style:italic;color
                          :red;float:right;width:550px;">
        Earlier coupons (up to two months old) can be used as
                                                    credit.
      </aside>
     <p></p>
     <nav>
       <ul>
         <li><a href="Maui092011.html">Maui</a></li>
         <li><a href="SaintTropez092011.html">St Tropez</a>
                                                    </li>
         <li><a href="Paris092011.html">Paris</a></li>
       </ul>
     </nav>
   </header>
 </article> <!-- end article #1 -->

<div id="outer">
  <form action="">
    <fieldset id="nameinfo">
      <label for="firstName"><strong>First Name:</strong>
                                            </label>
      <input type="text" name="firstName" id="firstName"
                                            value="" />

      <label for="lastName"><strong>Last Name:</strong>
                                            </label>
      <input type="text" name="lastName" id="lastName"
                                            value="" />
    </fieldset>

    <fieldset id="contactinfo">
      <label for="email"><strong>Email:</strong></label>
      <input type="text" name="email" id="email" value="" />
```

```
   <label for="phone"><strong>Phone:</strong></label>
  <input type="text" name="phone" id="phone" value="" />
</fieldset>

<fieldset id="FromAndDate">
  <label for="startFrom"><strong>I'm Here:</strong>
                                    </label>
   <select id="startFrom">
     <option>Chicago</option>
     <option>New York</option>
     <option>Minneapolis</option>
   </select>

   <label for="departureDate"><strong>Leaving:</strong>
                                    </label>
   <input type="date" name="departureDate"
          id="departureDate" value="" />

   <label for="goingPreferredAirline"><strong>Airline:
                                    </strong>
   </label>
   <select id="goingPreferredAirline">
     <option>American</option>
     <option>JapaneseAir</option>
     <option>Ana Air</option>
   </select>
</fieldset>

<fieldset id="departureDate">
  <label for="destination"><strong>Going to:</strong>
                                    </label>
  <select id="destination">
     <option>Maui</option>
     <option>Bahamas</option>
     <option>Paris</option>
     </select>

   <label for="arrivalDate"><strong>Arriving:</strong>
                                    </label>
   <input type="date" name="arrivalDate"
          id="arrivalDate" value="" />

   <label for="returningPreferredAirline">
          <strong>Airline:</strong></label>
   <select id="returningPreferredAirline">
     <option>American</option>
     <option>JapaneseAir</option>
```

```
            <option>Ana Air</option>
          </select>
      </fieldset>

      <fieldset id="checkAvailableFlights">
        <input id="availableFlights" type="submit"
               value="Check For Available Flights">
      </fieldset>

      <div id="availableFlightsList">
      </div>
    </form>
  </div> <!-- outer -->

  <script>
    var search = function() {
      $("#availableFlights").parent().remove();
      startCity = $("#startFrom").val();
      destCity  = $("#destination").val();

      for(var i=0; i<flightCount; i++) {
        flightItem    = flightTimes[i]+" from "+
                        startCity+" to "+destCity;
        submitButton =
        "<input id=\"reserve\" type=\"submit\" value=\"Reserve
Me!\">";
        flightDetails = flightItem+submitButton;

        $("#availableFlightsList").append(
                    "<li>"+flightItem+submitButton+"</li>");
      }
    };

    $(document).ready(function() {
      // user changed the 'start city'...
      $("#startFrom").change(search);

      // user changed the 'destination city'...
      $("#destination").change(search);

      // user wants to see the available flights...
      $("#searchNow").change(search);
    });
  </script>
 </body>
</html>
```

Listing 7.13 is an example of a fictitious travel agency that displays options for selecting travel destinations. After some initial boilerplate markup, Listing 7.13 contains JavaScript variables such as `startCity` and `destCity` for tracking the endpoints of a flight, and the JavaScript variable `flightTimes` that contains a hard-coded list of flight times.

The next portion of Listing 7.13 contains an HTML `Form` element with several HTML drop-down lists, followed by a JavaScript code block that defines a JavaScript variable that handles search functionality whenever users change a selection in an of the drop-down lists, as shown here:

```
var search = function() {
      $("#availableFlights").parent().remove();
      startCity = $("#startFrom").val();
      destCity  = $("#destination").val();

      for(var i=0; i<flightCount; i++) {
        flightItem   = flightTimes[i]+" from "+
                           startCity+" to "+destCity;
        submitButton =
        "<input id=\"reserve\" type=\"submit\" value=\
                                           "Reserve Me!\">";
        flightDetails = flightItem+submitButton;

        $("#availableFlightsList").append(
                  "<li>"+flightItem+submitButton+"</li>");
      }
};
```

The final portion of Listing 7.13 binds a "change" event whenever users change a selection in any of the three drop-down lists, which then executes the code in the JavaScript variable search so that the result of users' selections are displayed in the Web page.

Figure 7.11 displays the result of rendering `JQUITravel1.html` in Listing 7.13 in a Chrome browser on a Macbook.

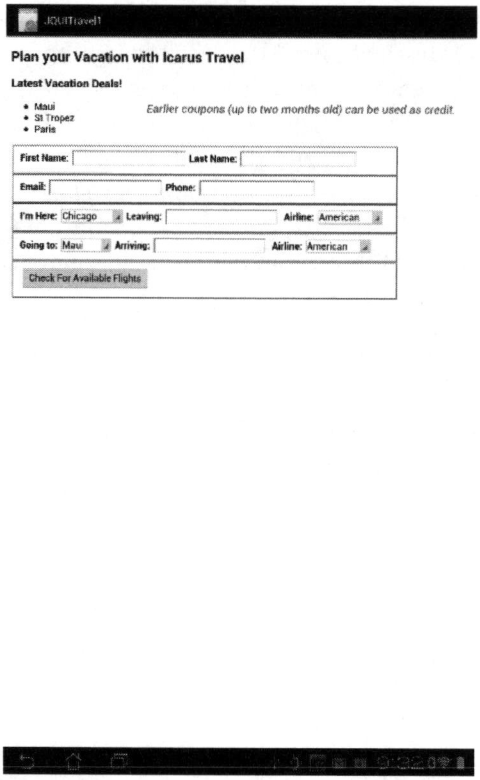

FIGURE 7.11 jQuery widgets in a Chrome browser on a Macbook.

This concludes our discussion of jQuery UI controls and jQuery theme-related functionality. The next section provides some information about upcoming versions of jQuery, and some important changes regarding browser support.

FUTURE VERSIONS OF JQUERY

As this book goes to print, jQuery 1.8 (beta) is now available. jQuery 1.9 will support older versions (6, 7, and 8) of IE when it's released in 2013, and the jQuery team will continue supporting version 1.9 after jQuery 2.0 is released. However, jQuery 2.0 will drop support for IE 6, 7, and 8.

According to projections, jQuery 2.1 is unlikely to arrive before 2014. The goal of the jQuery team is to keep versions 1.x and 2.x of jQuery synchronized, and to add functionality via plugins.

Some of the new jQuery 1.8 are:

- The ability to build a custom version of jQuery that excludes one or more modules

- Prefix generation for non-prefixed property names based on the current browser

- The Sizzle CSS selector engine

- XSS protection with the new method `$.parseHTML`

The modules you can currently exclude are `ajax`, `css`, `dimensions`, `effects`, and `offset`. As a simple example of prefix generation, if your HTML Web page contains the following jQuery snippet on Chrome:

```
$("#myscroll").css("marquee-direction", "backwards")
```

...then jQuery will set the CSS to the following:

```
-webkit-marquee-direction: backwards
```

The preceding information, along with a detailed list of other improvements in jQuery 1.8, is available here:

http://blog.jquery.com/2012/06/28/jquery-core-version-1-9-and-beyond/
http://blog.jquery.com/2012/07/01/jquery-1-9-and-2-0-tldr-edition/

USEFUL LINKS

The jQuery UI Web site provides extensive documentation and details regarding jQuery UI components, and its homepage is here:

http://jqueryui.com/

Another useful jQuery UI link is a Web site that provides demos of jQuery UI components:

http://jqueryui.com/demos/

You can use the jFormer jQuery plugin with HTML5 `Forms`:

https://www.jformer.com/

A collection of jQuery plugins for playing audio and video files is here:

http://superdit.com/2011/04/27/12-jquery-plugins-for-playing-audio-video-files/

The jQuery plugin jTweetsAnywhere for displaying tweets is here:

http://thomasbillenstein.com/jTweetsAnywhere/

SUMMARY

This chapter introduced you to jQuery UI controls, along with code samples that illustrated how to create HTML5 Web pages with jQuery UI controls. You learned how to use the following jQuery UI controls:

- Accordion effects
- Buttons
- Check boxes and radio buttons
- Combo boxes
- Date pickers
- Dialog boxes
- Progress bars
- Scroll panes
- Sliders
- Tabs
- Theming jQuery UI
- ThemeRoller and themes

The next chapter contains an introduction to jQuery Mobile that shows you how to create HTML5-based applications using jQuery Mobile.

INTRODUCTION TO JQUERY MOBILE

This chapter contains an introduction to jQuery Mobile that shows you how to create HTML5-based applications using jQuery Mobile. Web pages for desktop browsers are rendered differently on mobile devices, which is immediately apparent whenever you see the tiny font size of the rendered text on a mobile device. Fortunately, jQuery Mobile is highly "page aware" and provides many useful before-and-after page-related events that you can override with customizations that are tailored to your needs.

In fact, jQuery Mobile is designed around the notion of (mostly) single-page applications with multiple "page views" (discussed later in this chapter), whereas jQuery was designed when multi-page sites and applications were predominant. Thus, jQuery Mobile has a view-oriented model, whereas jQuery has a Web page-oriented model. This important distinction will help you understand the rationale for the features that are available in jQuery Mobile.

If you want to write Web pages that display correctly on different devices, then at a minimum you need to take into account the dimensions (width and height) of those devices. Other considerations include (but are not limited to) DPI (dots per inch), which varies between mobile devices, and whether or not you want to allow users to pinch or zoom into the Web page. One of the strengths of jQuery Mobile, along with its rich feature set and support for many mobile platforms, is that device differences are handled automatically for you.

The first part of this chapter provides an overview of some features of jQuery Mobile, as well as some important differences from jQuery. You will see how jQuery Mobile programmatically enhances your Web pages with extra functionality that reduces the coding effort on your part in order to create mobile-enabled Web pages, and also ensures that your web pages will render correctly on different mobile devices. In addition, you will learn about page-related events that are exposed by jQuery Mobile (there are many of them), and some of the default behavior that you can override programmatically.

The second part of this chapter discusses multi-page views in jQuery Mobile, and various ways for positioning headers and footers. The third part of this chapter discusses buttons in jQuery Mobile, which is an extensive topic with lots of rich functionality, and you will see complete code samples and useful code snippets.

The fourth part of this chapter contains code samples that illustrate how to work with various widgets, including list views, navigation bars, and menus in jQuery Mobile. The intent of these code samples is to show you not just how to use these widgets, but also how to incorporate CSS3-based graphics effects in the code samples. Some of these effects, such as shadow and gradients (which you learned how to do in Chapter 3), show you how to create a richer visual effect that goes beyond the "out of the box" functionality of jQuery Mobile. The final portion of this chapter contains code samples that show you how to use Ajax and Geolocation in HTML Web pages with jQuery Mobile.

As you read the material in this chapter, please keep in mind the following points. First, the code samples with HTML widgets are discussed from the standpoint of how to use them in jQuery Mobile pages. The implicit assumption is that you have a rudimentary understanding of HTML, so details regarding HTML widgets are omitted. Second, the information in this chapter will prepare you for the code samples in Chapter 9, where you will learn how to create animation effects in jQuery Mobile applications.

Third, when you have finished reading this chapter you will understand many of the main differences between jQuery and jQuery Mobile, and you will also understand how to use various HTML widgets in jQuery Mobile applications.

OVERVIEW OF JQUERY MOBILE

jQuery Mobile is essentially a collection of jQuery plugins and widgets that enable you to write mobile Web applications that run on multiple platforms. You already know that jQuery focuses on desktop web applications; by contrast, jQuery Mobile (which includes a CSS stylesheet and a JavaScript library) is intended for mobile devices. However, jQuery Mobile does rely on the "base" jQuery library that you must reference prior to including the jQuery Mobile library in a Web page. In addition, jQuery Mobile uses features of HTML5 and CSS3 (such as transitions and animation), and small icons for navigation.

jQuery Mobile relies on custom attributes with a `data-` prefix, and a simple jQuery Mobile page has the following structure:

- An optional `<div>` element with a `data-role="header"` attribute
- A mandatory `<div>` element with a `data-role="content"` attribute
- An optional `<div>` element with a `data-role="footer"` attribute

During initialization, jQuery Mobile pre-processes a Web page and inserts additional markup, CSS classes, and event handlers. You will see an example of how jQuery Mobile modifies a Web page in the "Hello World" code sample later in this chapter.

There are several important details that you need to be aware of when writing jQuery Mobile Web pages. First, jQuery Mobile provides the following page-related events that you can invoke programmatically during the life-cycle of a jQuery Mobile page: `pageInit()`, `pageCreate()`, `pageShow()`, and `pageHide()`. Second, jQuery Mobile supports custom events for handling user gestures such as `swipe`, `tap`, `tap-and-hold`, and orientation changes of a device. Third, jQuery Mobile uses themes to customize the look and feel of mobile applications, along with progressive enhancement (discussed briefly in Chapter 1) to enable your mobile application to run on a diverse set of web-enabled devices.

Another key point to keep in mind is that jQuery uses this construct:

```
$(document).ready() {
  // do something here
}
```

On the other hand, jQuery Mobile uses this construct:

```
$(selector).live('pageinit', (function(event){
  // do something here
}));
```

Notice the different focus: jQuery sends an event when a Web page has been loaded, whereas jQuery Mobile sends an event when a page (or page view) has been initialized.

Key Features and Components in jQuery Mobile

If you have read the previous chapters that cover jQuery, you have already acquired substantial knowledge of jQuery features. This knowledge is useful for another reason: jQuery Mobile uses jQuery as its foundation, and the jQuery library must always precede the jQuery Mobile library in your HTML5 Web pages.

jQuery Mobile provides many useful features that will simplify the process of creating mobile applications. Some of the jQuery Mobile features are listed here:

- Compatible with major mobile platforms (Android, iOS, and others)
- Uses HTML5 markup
- Adopts progressive enhancement approach
- Provides a compact toolkit (about 12K compressed)
- Supports plugins and themes
- Supports touch and mouse-based user gestures
- Supports WAI-ARIA

In addition, jQuery Mobile supports the following components (and others that are not listed here):

- Buttons
- Form elements
- List views
- Pages and dialogs
- Toolbars

The jQuery code samples in this book use a simple naming convention: the names of HTML5 Web pages that contain jQuery code start with "JQ," while the names of HTML5 Web pages that contain jQuery Mobile start with the letters "JQM." Keep in mind that this naming convention is only for this book.

A MINIMAL JQUERY MOBILE WEB PAGE

Listing 8.1 displays the contents of JQMHelloWorld1.html that illustrates how to display the message "Hello World" in an HTML5 Web page that is rendered on a desktop browser, tablet, or smartphone.

Listing 8.1 JQMHelloWorld1.html

```
<!DOCTYPE html>
<html lang="en">
  <head>
   <meta charset=utf-8"/>
   <title>Hello World from jQuery Mobile</title>

   <link rel="stylesheet"
      href="http://code.jquery.com/mobile/1.1.0/jquery.mobile-
1.1.0.min.css"/>
   <script src="http://code.jquery.com/jquery-1.7.1.min.js"></
script>
      <script  src="http://code.jquery.com/mobile/1.1.0/jquery.
mobile-1.1.0.min.js">
   </script>
  </head>

  <body>
    <div  data-role="page">
      <div data-role="header">
        <h2>This is the Header</h2>
      </div>
      <div data-role="content">
        <p>Hello World from a Simple jQuery Mobile Page</p>
      </div>
      <div data-role="footer">
        <h2>This is the Footer</h2>
      </div>
    </div>
  </body>
</html>
```

Listing 8.1 is straightforward: it consists of a single page view (an HTML `<div>` element with a `data-role="page"` attribute) that contains three `<div>` elements: a header section, the content section, and the footer section, respectively.

Figure 8.1 displays the result of rendering the HTML web page in Listing 8.1 in a landscape-mode screenshot taken from an Asus Prime tablet with Android ICS.

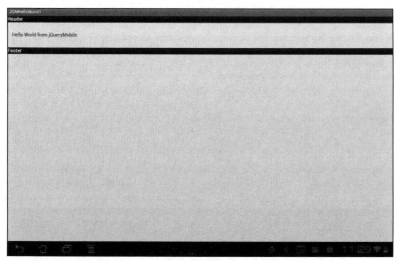

FIGURE 8.1 "Hello World" on an Asus Prime tablet with Android ICS (landscape mode).

Compare Figure 8.1 with Figure 8.2, which shows the sample jQuery Mobile application running on a Sprint Nexus S 4G smartphone with Android ICS in landscape mode, using the same Android `apk` binary that was used for capturing Figure 8.1. Notice how the header and footer extend automatically to the width of the screen in both screenshots.

Figure 8.2 displays the result of rendering the HTML Web page in Listing 8.1 in landscape mode on a Sprint Nexus S 4G smartphone with Android ICS.

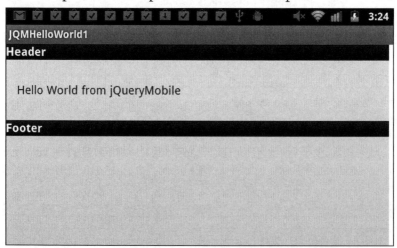

FIGURE 8.2 "Hello World" on a Sprint Nexus S 4G with Android ICS (landscape mode).

Now launch Listing 8.1 in a `WebKit`-based browser, and compare what you see in Figure 8.1 and Figure 8.2.

Earlier you learned that jQuery Mobile enhances a mobile Web page with additional tags and CSS classes. Listing 8.2 displays `JQMHelloWorld1En-hanced.html`, which is how jQuery Mobile enhances the HTML Web page `HelloWorld1.html`.

Listing 8.2 JQMHelloWorld1Enhanced.html

```
<!DOCTYPE html>
<html lang="en" class="ui-mobile landscape min-width-320px
min-width-480px min-width-768px max-width-1024px">
  <head>
   <meta name="viewport" content="width=device-width, minimum-
scale=1, maximum-scale=1">
   <base href="file:///Users/ocampesato/jqm/">
   <title>Hello World from jQuery Mobile</title>
   <link rel="stylesheet" href="jQuery.mobile-1.1.0.min.css">

   <script src="jQuery-1.7.1.js">
   </script>
   <script src="jQuery.mobile-1.1.0.min.js">
   </script>
  </head>

  <body class="ui-mobile-viewport">
    <div data-role="page" class="ui-page ui-body-c ui-page-ac-
tive">
        <div data-role="header" class="ui-bar-a ui-header"
role="banner">Header</div>
      <div data-role="content" class="ui-content" role="main">
        <p>Hello World from jQuery Mobile</p>
      </div>
        <div data-role="footer" class="ui-bar-a ui-footer"
role="contentinfo">Footer</div>
    </div>

    <div class="ui-loader ui-body-a ui-corner-all" style="top:
295.5px; ">
      <span class="ui-icon ui-icon-loading spin"></span>
      <h1>loading</h1>
    </div>
  </body>
</html>
```

As you can see in Listing 8.2, jQuery Mobile "injects" various CSS classes (that are part of jQuery Mobile) into the HTML5 Web page in Listing 8.1. In general, you will not need to be concerned with these details; however, you can delve into the jQuery Mobile source code if you need a deeper understanding of these details.

MORE DIFFERENCES BETWEEN JQUERY AND JQUERY MOBILE

jQuery is a toolkit for creating HTML Web pages on desktop browser, whereas jQuery Mobile provides support for additional functionality that is relevant for mobile devices:

- Support for multiple page views
- Custom attributes with a `data-` prefix for page views and transitions
- Page transitions (`pagebeforehide`, `pagebeforeshow`, and so forth)
- The `jqmData()` custom selector
- The `mobileInit` event

jQuery Mobile Page Views

As you saw in a previous code sample, each page view in a jQuery Mobile application is defined by an HTML `<div>` element with a `data-role="page"` attribute, along with an optional header element, a mandatory content element, and an optional footer element.

Navigation between page views is straightforward: simply add a link to the `<div>` element with the `data-role="content"` attribute in the jQuery Mobile application, as shown here:

```
<div data-role="content">
  <p>A second page view<a href="#home">Home</a></p>
</div>
```

The transition between page views occurs when users tap on a link, and jQuery Mobile automatically handles the necessary details of the transition. A complete example of a jQuery Mobile Web page with multiple page views (and how to navigate between the page views) is provided later in this chapter.

jQuery Mobile Custom Attributes

The `data-` prefix for custom attributes is part of the HTML5 specification (section 3.2.3.8), and jQuery Mobile makes extensive use of custom attributes with a `data-` prefix, whereas custom attributes are not used in jQuery. In fact, jQuery Mobile uses this custom attribute for specifying behavior, functionality, and layout. Two custom attributes that you will encounter frequently are `data-role` and `data-transition`.

The `data-role` attribute is used to identify different parts of a "page view" (which is essentially one screen), and some of its supported values are `page`, `header`, `content`, and `footer`. The `data-role` attribute is also used to enhance HTML elements. For example, if you specify the attribute `data-role="listview"` as part of the HTML `<ul>` tag of an unordered list, then jQuery Mobile will make the necessary enhancements (such as inserting markup, adding CSS classes, and exposing listeners) so that you can treat the unordered list as though it were a widget.

As another example, you can create a navigation bar by adding the attribute `data-role="navbar"` to the block-level HTML5 `<nav>` element. The text strings in the associated list items (which are enclosed in the HTML5 `<nav>` element) are displayed as tab elements in the navigation bar.

The `data-transition` attribute specifies transition effects when changing page views or displaying dialogs. Since these transitions are based on CSS3, these transitions work only in browsers that support CSS3 (such as `WebKit`-based browsers). The allowable values for the `data-transition` attribute are `fade`, `flip`, `pop`, `slide`, `slidedown`, and `slideup`.

Some of the other custom jQuery Mobile attributes are `data-backbtn`, `data-divider`, `data-direction`, `data-icon`, `data-inline`, `data-position`, `data-rel`, and `data-url`.

JQUERY MOBILE PAGE TRANSITIONS

jQuery Mobile provides page transitions, as well as the `event` and `ui` objects, that you can reference in custom code blocks that you bind to any page transition. Keep in mind that a "page" can be a separate HTML Web page as well as an HTML `<div>` element inside the currently loaded HTML Web page.

Here is the sequence of page events that occurs during a page initialization:

```
pagebeforecreate: fires first
pagecreate: fires when DOM is populated
```

```
pageinit: after initialization is completed
pagebeforeshow: fires on 'to' page before transition
pageshow: fires on 'to' page after transition
```

Whenever users tap a link that navigates to a page that is loaded for the first time, the following sequence of events occurs:

```
pagebeforehide: fires on the 'from' page before transition
pagebeforeshow: fires on the 'to' page before transition
pagehide: fires on the 'from' page after transition
pageshow: fires on the 'to' page after transition
```

Whenever a new page is loaded using Ajax, the following sequence of events occurs:

```
pagebeforeload: before the AJAX call is made
pageload: after the AJAX call is completed
pageloadfailed: fired if an AJAX call has failed
```

During page transitions, `ui.nextPage` is assigned the target page of the transition, or an empty jQuery object if there is no next page. Similarly, `ui.prevPage` is assigned the current page prior to the transition, or an empty jQuery object if there is no previous page.

jQuery Mobile uses Ajax-based asynchronous method invocations for its internal functionality, so it distinguishes page load events from page show and hide events. Page load events occur when a file is loaded into the browser in a synchronous manner, and the `jQuery(document).ready()` method is available, along with other initialization events. Note that in some cases you can explicitly specify synchronous instead of asynchronous method invocation, but this feature is not discussed in this chapter (check the online jQuery Mobile documentation if you want more details).

As you will see later in this chapter, a single HTML Web page may contain multiple jQuery Mobile page views, and users can navigate among those page views multiple times. These transitions do not fire page load events; jQuery Mobile provides a set of events that happen every time a page transition occurs.

Since the page hide and show events are triggered every time a page transition happens, make sure that you do not bind the event handlers more than once by first checking if the event handler is not already bound (otherwise do nothing), or by clearing the binding prior to rebinding to a given event.

Listing 8.3 displays the contents of `JQMPageEvents1.html` that illustrates the sequence in which page events are executed.

Listing 8.3 JQMPageEvents1.html

```
<!DOCTYPE html>
<html lang="en">
<head>
 <meta charset="utf-8">
 <title>JQuery Mobile Page Events`</title>

 <link rel="stylesheet"
      href="http://code.jquery.com/mobile/1.1.0/jquery.mobile-
1.1.0.min.css"/>
  <script
     src="http://code.jquery.com/jquery-1.7.1.min.js">
  </script>
  <script
     src="http://code.jquery.com/mobile/1.1.0
                /jquery.mobile-1.1.0.min.js">
  </script>
</head>

<body>
 <div data-role="page" id="page1">
   <div data-role="header">
     <h3>JQuery Mobile Page Events</h3>
   </div>
   <div data-role="content" id="content">
   </div>
   <div data-role="footer"><h3>Footer</h3></div>
 </div>

 <script>
   $("#page1").live('pagebeforecreate', (function(event){
      console.log("pagebeforecreate event");
      })
   );

   $("#page1").live('pagecreate', (function(event){
      console.log("pagecreate event");
      })
   );

   $("#page1").live('pageinit', (function(event){
      console.log("pageinit event");
      })
   );

   $("#page1").live('pagebeforehide', (function(event){
      console.log("pagebeforehideevent");
```

```
      })
   );

   $("#page1").live('pagebeforeshow', (function(event){
      console.log("pagebeforeshow event");
      })
   );

   $("#page1").live('pagehide', (function(event){
      console.log("pagehide event");
      })
   );

   $("#page1").live('pageshow', (function(event){
      console.log("pageshow event");
      })
   );
  </script>
</body>
</html>
```

Listing 8.3 is a simple HTML5 Web page with HTML markup and jQuery Mobile code for a single page view. The main block of code uses the jQuery `live()` method to bind various page-related events, which displays a message in the console whenever the page event occurs.

Figure 8.3 displays the result of rendering the HTML Web page in Listing 8.3 in a Chrome browser on a Macbook. The Chrome Inspector at the bottom of Figure 8.3 shows you the sequence of page-related events that are fired in jQuery Mobile.

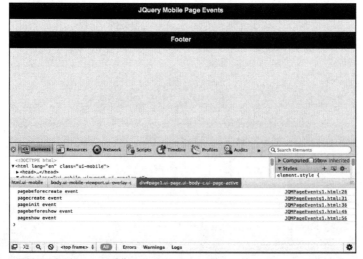

FIGURE 8.3 jQuery Mobile page events on a Chrome browser on a Macbook.

JQUERY MOBILE AND CSS-RELATED PAGE INITIALIZATION

In addition to exposing page-related events, jQuery Mobile performs additional processing on an HTML Web page before the Web page is rendered in a browser. First jQuery Mobile triggers the `beforecreate` event and then adds the `ui-page` class to all page elements, and also adds the `ui-nojs` class to all page elements which have `data-role="none"` or `data-role="nojs"` applied to them.

Next, jQuery Mobile searches for child elements with a data- attribute and adds theming classes, an appropriate ARIA role, and (if necessary) also adds a back button to the header for any pages beyond the first page.

Finally, jQuery Mobile enhances buttons, control groups, and form controls, and makes any necessary adjustments to toolbars.

Thus, jQuery Mobile performs a significant amount of work on your behalf, which means that you are unencumbered with these tedious and low-level details so that you can concentrate on the functionality of your mobile applications.

There is even more good news: jQuery Mobile automatically handles page transitions and back buttons as users navigate through the various pages of your mobile application, and also handle external pages by performing an asynchronous fetch (using Ajax) and then integrating that external page into the current document (and an error message is displayed if the external page was not found). The external page is incorporated into the first element with a `data-role="page"` attribute into the current document (and all other content of that page is ignored).

Note that jQuery Mobile displays an error message if it cannot find the Web page or if the Web page does not contain an element with a `data-role="page"` attribute. Make sure that the `id` values in the external Web page are distinct from the `id` values of the current Web page.

By the way, you can override the default page loading in two ways: specifying a target attribute on a link (such as `_blank`) or by specifying a `rel="external"` attribute on the link.

The mobileinit Event

jQuery Mobile triggers the `mobileinit` event on the document object immediately upon execution, so you can bind to it and override any default configuration.

For instance, suppose you need to prevent jQuery Mobile from applying styling rules to specific types of HTML elements throughout a mobile application. The following code block prevents jQuery Mobile from applying its styling rules (on a global level) to HTML `<input>` and `<textarea>` elements:

```
$(document).bind('mobileinit',function () {
    $.mobile.page.prototype.options.keepNative = "input, textarea";
});
```

Note that the `data-role="none"` attribute serves the same purpose as the previous code block, except that it is only applied to the specific element that includes this attribute.

JQUERY MOBILE OPTIONS AND CUSTOMIZATION

jQuery Mobile provides options and methods for various objects, including `.mobile`, `.mobile.path`, and `.mobile.history`. There are many options that you can configure for your mobile application, and we'll cover just a few of them in this section. One method that is obviously useful is the jQuery Mobile `pageLoading()` method that shows and hides the jQuery Mobile loading dialog. You call this method with a Boolean value of `true` to hide the dialog, and call this method without a parameter to show the dialog, as shown here:

```
// Show the page loading dialog
$.mobile.pageLoading();


// Hide the loading dialog
$.mobile.pageLoading(true);
```

You can also customize the "loading message" and the type of transition effect, as shown here:

```
$.mobile.loadingMessage = "wait a few moments ";
$.mobile.defaultPageTransition = "pop";
```

Another way of doing the same thing as the previous two lines is shown here:

```
$.extent($.mobile, {
    "loadingMessage" = "wait a few moments",
```

```
      "defaultPageTransition" = "pop"
});
```

In fact, you can configure jQuery Mobile with your own initialization as follows: 1.) create a script that loads before jQuery Mobile is loaded, and 2.) bind an event handler to the `mobileinit` event.

If you want more information about jQuery Mobile custom initialization, options, and methods, read the jQuery documentation for an in-depth explanation of how you can use them.

PAGE NAVIGATION AND CHANGING PAGES

As users navigate around your mobile Web application, jQuery Mobile also updates the `location.hash` object, with the unique URL of each page view (which is defined by an element with a `data-role="page"` attribute). jQuery Mobile automatically stores the URL for each page in the `data-url` attribute that jQuery Mobile assigns to the "container" element of a page.

jQuery Mobile also provides a set of methods that enable you to programmatically handle page changes and scrolling. One of these methods is `changePage()`, whose syntax looks like this:

```
changePage(to, transition, back, changeHash);
```

The `to` parameter is a string that specifies an element id or a filename (along with many other options), and it is a reference to the target page. The `transition` parameter is the name of the transition effect that is created when the application goes to the target page. The `back` parameter is a Boolean value that specifies whether or not a transition is in reverse. Finally, the `changeHash` parameter is a Boolean that specifies whether or not to update the `location.hash` object.

The `changePage()` method enables you to create more sophisticated page transition effects. For example, the following code snippet goes to page `#first` when users click on the `.back-btn`, with a "flip" effect in reverse without updating the location hash:

```
$(".back-btn").bind("click", function() {
  changePage("#first", "flip", true, false);
    });
```

jQuery Mobile also provides the `silentScroll()` method with a single integer value that specifies the y-position of the destination. When this method is invoked, the scroll event listeners are not triggered. As an example, the following code snippet scrolls down to position 200:

```
$.mobile.silentScroll(200);
```

The jqmData() Custom Selector

In a previous chapter, you learned about the jQuery `data()` method. jQuery Mobile provides a corresponding method called `jqmData()`, which is a custom selector specifically for selecting custom `data-` attributes.

For example, in jQuery you can select all the elements in a Web page that contain a `data-role` attribute whose value is `page` using this code snippet:

```
$("[data-role='page']")
```

You can select the same set of elements using `jqmData()` as shown here:

```
$(":jqmData(role='page')")
```

Select all elements with any custom `data-` attribute within those selected pages: `$(":jqmData(role='page')").jqmData(role)`

Note that the `jqmData()` selector automatically handles namespacing for you by specifying a value for the string `namespace-` (which is empty by default), thereby avoiding tagname collisions.

MULTIPLE PAGE VIEWS IN ONE HTML5 WEB PAGE

jQuery Mobile enables you to conveniently define multiple page views in a single HTML5 Web page, along with a simple mechanism for users to navigate among the different page views in the HTML5 Web page. The use of a single HTML5 Web page is recommended because this approach is more efficient than creating a mobile application with multiple HTML5 Web pages. Although the initial download for the HTML5 Web page might be longer, there are no additional Internet accesses required when users navigate to different parts of the Web page.

Listing 8.4 displays the contents of `JQMMultiPageViews1.html` that illustrates how to navigate between multiple internal page views in a single HTML5 Web page.

Listing 8.4 JQMMultiPageViews1.html

```
<!DOCTYPE html>
<html>
```

```
<head>
  <meta charset=utf-8"/>
  <title>jQuery Mobile: Multiple Page Views</title>

  <link rel="stylesheet"
     href="http://code.jquery.com/mobile/1.1.0/jquery.mobile-
1.1.0.min.css"/>
    <script
      src="http://code.jquery.com/jquery-1.7.1.min.js">
    </script>
    <script src="http://code.jquery.com/mobile/1.1.0
                      /jquery.mobile-1.1.0.min.js">
    </script>
  </head>

  <body>
   <div data-role="page" id="home">
     <div data-role="header"> <h1>Home Page Header</h1> </div>
     <div data-role="content">
       <p>This is the content of the main page</p>
       <p><a href="#about">Click here to get more information</
a></p>
     </div>
     <div data-role="footer"> <h1>Home Page Footer</h1> </div>
   </div>

   <div data-role="page" id="about">
      <div data-role="header"> <h1>About This Page Header</h1>
</div>
     <div data-role="content">
       <p>A second page view (that's all for now)</p>
       <a href="#home"> Click Here or the 'Back' Button to go
Home</a>
     </div>
      <div data-role="footer"> <h1>About This Page Footer</h1>
</div>
   </div>
  </body>
  </html>
```

Listing 8.4 contains two page views, as specified by the HTML <div> elements whose id attribute has value home and about (shown in bold in Listing 8.4). When users navigate to the second page view, this code snippet returns to the first page view:

```
<a href="#home"> Click Here or the 'Back' Button to go Home</a>
```

The page views or screens in a jQuery Mobile application are top-level sibling elements, each of which contains the attribute `data-role="page"` (so pages cannot be nested).

The jQuery Mobile framework automatically generates a back button and a home button on every page view, but you can suppress the back button by specifying the attribute `data-backbtn="false"` attribute, as shown here:

```
<div data-role="header" data-backbtn="false">
  <h1>Page Header</h1>
</div>
```

Figure 8.4 displays the result of rendering the HTML Web page in Listing 8.4 in a landscape-mode screenshot taken from a Sprint Nexus S 4G with Android ICS.

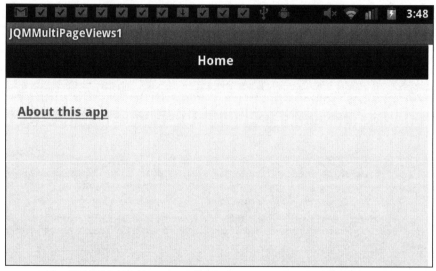

FIGURE 8.4 Multi-page app on a Sprint Nexus S 4G with Android ICS.

When you click on the link on the Web page, the application navigates to the second screen, whose code definition is also included in Listing 8.4.

Figure 8.5 displays the result of rendering the HTML Web page in Listing 8.4 in a landscape-mode screenshot taken from a Sprint Nexus S 4G with Android ICS.

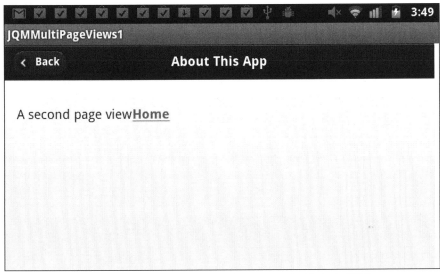

FIGURE 8.5 Multi-page app on a Sprint Nexus S 4G with Android ICS.

POSITIONING THE HEADER AND FOOTER IN PAGE VIEWS

jQuery Mobile can dynamically position the header and footer toolbars in three ways:

Standard: The toolbars are presented according to the document flow, scrolling into and out of the viewport as the user scrolls through data. This is the default.

Fixed: The header and footer will appear at the top and bottom of the viewport and remain there as the user scrolls. Tapping on the screen will cause them to return to their regular position in the document flow.

Fullscreen: The header and footer will appear within the viewport and stay present as the user scrolls, regardless of where the user is in the content. Tapping on the screen will hide them. Essentially, the header and footer are removed from the document flow and are always dynamically positioned at the top and bottom of the viewport.

Include the `data-position="fixed"` attribute in the `<header>` or `<footer>` tags to create a fixed header and footer, as illustrated in Listing 8.5 that displays the contents of `JQMFixed1.html`.

Listing 8.5 JQMFixed1.html

```
<!DOCTYPE html>
<html lang="en">
 <head>
   <meta charset="utf-8"/>
   <title>Fixed Header and Footer in jQueryMobile</title>

       <link rel="stylesheet"
          href="http://code.jquery.com/mobile/1.1.0/jquery.mobile-
   1.1.0.min.css"/>
       <script
           src="http://code.jquery.com/jquery-1.7.1.min.js">
       </script>
       <script src="http://code.jquery.com/mobile/1.1.0
                        /jquery.mobile-1.1.0.min.js">
       </script>
 </head>

 <body>
   <div id="page1" data-role="page">
     <header data-role="header" data-position="fixed">
       <h1>jQuery Mobile</h1>
     </header>
     <div class="content" data-role="content">
       <h3>Content area.</h3>
     </div>
     <footer data-role="footer" data-position="fixed">
       <h3>Fixed Footer</h3>
     </footer>
   </div>
 </body>
</html>
```

Listing 8.5 contains HTML markup and a single page view that also specifies the attribute data-position="fixed" for the header and footer elements.

You can also create a fullscreen header or footer by including the attribute data-fullscreen="true" in the element that contains the data-role="page" attribute, along with the attribute data-position="fixed" to the header and footer elements, as shown here:

```
<section id="page1" data-role="page" data-fullscreen="true">
  <header data-role="header" data-position="fixed">
    <h1>jQuery Mobile</h1>
  </header>
  <div class="content" data-role="content">
    <h3>Content area</h3>
  </div>
  <footer data-role="footer" data-position="fixed">
    <h3>Mercury Learning</h3> </footer>
  </div>
</section>
<p><a href="#about" data-transition="flip">About this app</a></p>
```

Figure 8.6 displays the result of rendering the HTML5 Web page in Listing 8.5 in a Chrome browser on a Macbook.

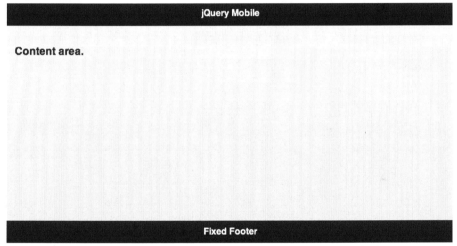

FIGURE 8.6 Fixed headers/footers in a Chrome browser on a Macbook.

Launch the HTML5 Web page in Listing 8.5 in a Chrome browser, and as you resize your browser horizontally or vertically, notice how the header and footer "bar" remain anchored to the top and the bottom of the screen, respectively.

Now that you understand the structure of an HTML5 Web page in jQuery Mobile, let's see how to add jQuery Mobile buttons to an HTML5 Web page.

WORKING WITH BUTTONS IN JQUERY MOBILE

jQuery Mobile provides a set of button markup options that enable you to style links as buttons, and also built-in support for automatically handling various types of HTML `<input>` elements as though they were buttons. In addition, jQuery Mobile supports inline buttons, grouped buttons (both vertical and horizontal), and an assortment of theming effects for buttons.

jQuery Mobile creates stylized buttons by applying `data-role="button"` to HTML `<input>` buttons, `<button>` tags, and anchor links. Buttons are as wide as their containing element; however, if you specify the attribute `data-inline="true"`, then buttons are rendered only as wide as their content.

In some of the earlier versions (prior to 1.7) of jQuery Mobile, you could prevent jQuery Mobile from applying its styling to a button by placing your custom markup inside an HTML `<div>` element that is located inside the HTML5 `<header>` element. However, this functionality is no longer available in version 1.7 (and beyond), so keep this in mind in case you encounter this functionality in Web pages that use older versions of jQuery Mobile.

You can also create a reverse transition without going back in history by using the attribute `data-direction="reverse"` instead of `data-rel="back"`, as shown here:

```
<div data-role="header">
  <a href="index.html" data-direction="reverse">Reverse
                                          Transition</a>
  <h1>Left and Right Buttons </h1>
  <!-- This appears on the right -->
  <a href="info.html" data-icon="plus">Add</a>
</div>
```

Buttons can be moved to the left or right, as shown here:

```
<div data-role="header">
<a href="index.html" class="ui-btn-right">Right</a>
 <h1>Page title</h1>
<a href="info.html" class="ui-btn-left">Left</a>
</div>
```

Navigation Buttons as Anchor Links

In jQuery Mobile the recommended practice is to define navigation buttons as anchor links and to define form submission buttons as button elements.

An anchor link that contains the attribute `data-role="button"` is styled as a button, as shown here:

```
<a href="external.html" data-role="button">Link-based button</a>
```

A jQuery Mobile button element or input element whose type is `submit`, `reset`, `button`, or `image` does not require the attribute `data-role="button"` because jQuery Mobile automatically treats these elements as a link-based button.

Although the original form-based button is not displayed, it is included in the HTML markup, and when a click event occurs on a link button, a corresponding click event occurs on the original form button.

Groups of Buttons and Column Grids

jQuery Mobile enables you to render a set of buttons (or checkboxes or radio buttons) as a block by defining a container HTML `<div>` element that specifies the attribute `data-role="controlgroup"`, and then include one or more button elements. The default rendering of the included buttons is horizontal (a row), and you can render the buttons as a vertical group by specifying the attribute `data-type="vertical"`.

jQuery Mobile renders the buttons, removes margins (and drop shadows) between buttons, and also "rounds" the first and last buttons in order to create a group-like effect. The following code block shows you how to specify a horizontal group of buttons:

```
<div data-role="controlgroup">
  <a href="index1.html" data-role="button">One</a>
  <a href="index2.html" data-role="button">Two</a>
  <a href="index3.html" data-role="button">Three</a>
</div>
```

One point to keep in mind: the buttons will "wrap" to additional rows if the number of buttons exceeds the screen width. Listing 8.5 shows you how to render a horizontal group and a vertical group of buttons.

The jQuery Mobile framework enables you to render CSS-based columns through a block style class convention called `ui-grid`. You can render two-column, three-column, four-column, and five-column layouts by using the class value `ui-grid-a`, `ui-grid-b`, `ui-grid-c`, and `ui-grid-d`, respectively. The following code block illustrates how to render a two-column layout:

```
<div class="ui-grid-a">
  <div class="ui-block-a">Block 1 and text inside will wrap</div>
  <div class="ui-block-b">Block 2 and text inside will wrap</div>
</div>
```

Notice the difference in the following code block that displays a three-column layout:

```
<div class="ui-grid-b">
  <div class="ui-block-a">Block 1 and text inside will wrap</div>
  <div class="ui-block-b">Block 2 and text inside will wrap</div>
  <div class="ui-block-c">Block 3 and text inside will wrap</div>
</div>
```

You can find more details and code samples here:

http://jquerymobile.com/demos/1.0b1/#/demos/1.0/docs/content/content-grids.html

Rendering Buttons with Themes

jQuery Mobile has an extensive theming system, labeled "a" through "e," for controlling the manner in which buttons are styled. When a link is added to a container, jQuery Mobile will assign it a theme "swatch" letter that matches the theme of its parent. For example, a button placed inside a content container with a theme of "a" (black in the default theme) is automatically assigned the button theme of "a" (charcoal in the default theme).

An example of a button theme is shown here:

```
<div data-role="footer" class="ui-bar">
 <a href="left.html" data-icon="arrow-l"
    data-role="button" data-theme="a">Left</a>
</div>
```

Listing 8.6 displays the contents of JQMButtons1.html, which illustrates how to render buttons horizontally and vertically, how to apply different themes, and how to specify custom CSS selectors.

Listing 8.6 JQMButtons1.html

```
<!DOCTYPE html>
<html lang="en">
  <head>
  <meta charset="utf-8"/>
   <title>Multiple Buttons and Themes in jQuery Mobile</title>
   <link rel="stylesheet" href="CSS3Background1.css"/>
    <link rel="stylesheet"
    href="http://code.jquery.com/mobile/1.1.0/jquery.mobile-
                                          1.1.0.min.css"/>
   <script
      src="http://code.jquery.com/jquery-1.7.1.min.js">
   </script>
   <script src="http://code.jquery.com/mobile/1.1.0
                   /jquery.mobile-1.1.0.min.js">
```

```
  </script>
</head>

<body>
  <div id="page1" data-role="page">
    <div data-role="header">
      <!-- This button appears on the left -->
      <a href="abc.html" data-icon="arrow-l"
         data theme="b">Index</a>

      <h1>Rendering Buttons in jQuery Mobile</h1>

      <!-- This button appears on the right -->
      <a href="def.html" data-icon="plus" data-theme="e">Add</a>
    </div>

    <div class="content" data-role="content">
      <div data-role="controlgroup" data-type="horizontal">
        <a href="index1.html" data-role="button">One</a>
        <a href="index2.html" data-role="button">Two</a>
        <a href="index3.html" data-role="button">Three</a>
        <a href="index4.html" data-role="button">Four</a>
        <a href="index5.html" data-role="button">Five</a>
      </div>

        <a href="index6.html" class="shadow"
           data-role="button">Vertical1</a>
        <a href="index7.html" class="shadow"
           data-role="button">Vertical2</a>
        <a href="index8.html" class="shadow"
           data-role="button">Vertical3</a>

      <div data-role="controlgroup">
        <a href="index6.html" data-role="button">Vertical1</a>
        <a href="index7.html" data-role="button">Vertical2</a>
        <a href="index8.html" data-role="button">Vertical3</a>
      </div>

      <div>
        <a href="index9.html" data-role="button"  id="cancel"
           data-inline="true">Cancel</a>
        <a href="index10.html" data-role="button" id="submit"
           data-inline="true" data-theme="b">Save</a>
      </div>
    </div>
  </div>

    <!-- Display four directional array keys -->
```

```
    <div data-role="footer" class="ui-bar">
     <a href="left.html" data-icon="arrow-l"
        data-role="button" data-theme="a">Left</a>
     <a href="up.html" data-icon="arrow-u"
        data-role="button" data-theme="b">Up</a>
     <a href="down.html" data-icon="arrow-d"
        data-role="button" data-theme="c">Down</a>
     <a href="right.html" data-icon="arrow-r"
        data-role="button"data-theme="e">Right</a>
    </div>

  </div>
 </body>
</html>
```

Listing 8.6 contains HTML markup and references to jQuery files, followed by a single page view that renders an assortment of buttons (they have a `data-role="button"` attribute), some of which are in a horizontal group, and others are in a vertical group.

Notice that the vertical buttons are rendered with a reddish-tinged background shadow, which creates a richer visual effect, simply by specifying a value of `shadow` for the `class` attribute, as shown in bold in this code block:

```
<a href="index6.html" class="shadow" data-
                                role="button">Vertical1</a>
<a href="index7.html" class="shadow" data-
                                role="button">Vertical2</a>
<a href="index8.html" class="shadow" data-

                                role="button">Vertical3</a>
```

In addition, the "cancel" and "submit" buttons specify `class="shadow"`, and they are rendered with a psychedelic effect, which you obviously don't want to render in most cases. Nevertheless, you see how easily you can style buttons with custom CSS3-based visual effects, and the definition of the `shadow` selector is shown in Listing 8.7.

The bottom row of four HTML `<a>` elements in Listing 8.5 renders four directional arrows because they have a `data-icon` attribute that is set to `arrow-l`, `arrow-u`, `arrow-d`, and `arrow-r`, respectively. In addition, these four HTML `<a>` elements specify different values for the attribute data-theme, and they are rendered according to the visual display for each of these predefined jQuery Mobile themes.

Note that the HTML `<a>` elements in Listing 8.6 reference HTML Web pages that are not defined for this mobile application, so when users click on these links, they will see an error message.

Listing 8.7 CSS3Background1.css

```
#cancel, #submit, .shadow {
 background-color:white;
 background-image:
  -webkit-radial-gradient(red 4px, transparent 18px),
  -webkit-repeating-radial-gradient(red 2px,  green 4px,
                                    yellow 8px, blue 12px,
                                    transparent 28px,
                                    green 20px, red 24px,
                                    transparent 28px,
                                    transparent 32px),
  -webkit-repeating-radial-gradient(red 2px,  green 4px,
                                    yellow 8px, blue 12px,
                                    transparent 28px,
                                    green 20px, red 24px,
                                    transparent 28px,
                                    transparent 32px);

 background-size: 50px 60px, 70px 80px;
 background-position: 0 0;
 -webkit-box-shadow:  30px 30px 30px #400;
}
```

Listing 8.7 contains definitions that are familiar to you from Chapter 4, and you can refer to the relevant sections in that chapter if you need to refresh your memory.

Figure 8.7 displays the result of rendering the HTML Web page in Listing 8.6 on a Sprint Nexus S 4G with Android ICS.

FIGURE 8.7 Buttons on a Sprint Nexus S 4G with Android ICS.

As you can see, there are many styling-related options available in jQuery mobile, so a summary of the discussion about jQuery Mobile buttons might be helpful:

- An anchor link with the attribute `data-role="button"` rendered as a button
- Any input element with the type button, submit, reset, or image is assigned a class of `ui-btn-hidden` and a link-based button is displayed
- Add a `data-icon` attribute to create a button with an icon
- Add a `data-iconpos` attribute to change the position of the icon
- Specify `data-inline="true"` to render a button only as wide as its text
- `data-role="controlgroup"` (`data-type="horizontal"`) groups buttons vertically (horizontally) in a `<div>` element
- `data-theme="e"` attribute is the fifth of five jQuery themes ("a" through "e")

JQUERY MOBILE ICONS

jQuery Mobile provides a default set of button icons that are frequently used in mobile applications as well as support for custom icons. As you saw in Listing 8.5 in the previous section, you add a built-in icon to a button by including a `data-icon` attribute on the anchor that specifies the icon in question, an example of which is shown here:

```
<a href="index.html" data-role="button"
                           data-icon="delete">Delete</a>
```

You also saw in Listing 8.5 that jQuery Mobile supports icon sets for left arrow, right arrow, up arrow, and down arrow, which are identified with corresponding names (e.g., `data-icon="arrow-d"` is for down arrow). Other supported icon sets include `alert`, `back`, `check`, `delete`, `down`, `forward`, `gear`, `grid`, `home`, `info`, `minus`, `plus`, `refresh`, `search`, and `star`, and their corresponding `data-icon` value is the same as the icon name (e.g., `data-icon="alert"` for the alert icon).

The default position for built-in icons in a button is to the left of button text; in addition, jQuery Mobile supports the following options: left (`iconpos="left"`), right (`iconpos="right"`), top (`iconpos="top"`), bottom (`iconpos="bottom"`), and notext (`iconpos="notext"`).

The following code snippet illustrates how to place the data icon to the right of the text:

```
<a href="abc.html" data-role="button" data-icon="home"
                        data-iconpos=»right»>Home</a>
```

If you want to use custom icons, specify a `data-icon` value whose name is unique, and jQuery Mobile will generate a class name that is a concatenation of `ui-con` with the unique name that you specified. For example, if you specify `abc` as the unique name, then jQuery Mobile generates the class `ui-icon-abc`. You can then write a CSS rule that targets the `ui-icon-abc` class to specify the icon background source.

jQuery Mobile includes a single white icon sprite in order to minimize download size, along with a semi-transparent black circle behind the icon to ensure that it contrasts well with any background color.

FORMS AND FORM ELEMENTS IN JQUERY MOBILE

Forms in jQuery Mobile conform to the same guidelines as plain HTML, and form submission occurs using via POST or GET. jQuery Mobile renders elements to fit the width of mobile device screens. If the screen is wider than `480px`, then labels and associated elements are displayed adjacent to each other; otherwise, elements are rendered under their associated label. Note that you can prevent jQuery Mobile from enhancing elements by specifying `data-role="none"`, as shown here:

```
<input id="myinput1" data-role="none" value=""/>
```

The example in this section contains a `<form>` element with the following elements: checkboxes, drop-down lists, radio buttons, sliders, text input, and text area.

jQuery Mobile automatically enhances checkboxes and radio buttons into button-like elements in the user interface. You can group them together into control groups adding the attribute `data-role="controlgroup"` in a containing element. Control groups are vertical stacks of buttons that stretch to the width of their containing element, but you can also create a horizontal control group via `data-type="horizontal"`.

Listing 8.8 displays the contents of `JQMForm1.html` that illustrates how to render various types of HTML widgets. The code sample in this section is intended to show you how to create some interesting visual effects, but make sure that you read the note just before Listing 8.9.

Listing 8.8 JQMForm1.html

```
<!DOCTYPE html>
<html lang="en">
  <head>
   <meta charset=utf-8"/>
   <title>jQueryMobile Form Example</title>

   <link rel="stylesheet" href="CSS3Background2.css"/>

   <link rel="stylesheet"
    href="http://code.jquery.com/mobile/1.1.0/jquery.mobile-
                                      1.1.0.min.css"/>
   <script
       src="http://code.jquery.com/jquery-1.7.1.min.js">
   </script>
   <script src="http://code.jquery.com/mobile/1.1.0
                    /jquery.mobile-1.1.0.min.js">
```

```
 </script>
</head>

<body>
 <div data-role="content">
   <form action="#" method="get">
     <div data-role="fieldcontain">
        <label for="name">Text Input:</label>
        <input id="textinput" type="text"
               name="name" id="name" value="" />
     </div>

     <div data-role="fieldcontain">
       <label for="textarea">Textarea:</label>
       <textarea id="textarea" cols="40" rows="3"
                 name="textarea" id="textarea"></textarea>
     </div>

     <div data-role="fieldcontain">
        <label for="searchinput">Search Input:</label>
        <input id="searchinput" type="search"
               name="password" value="" />
     </div>

     <div data-role="fieldcontain">
       <label for="flip1">Flip switch:</label>
       <select name="flip1" id="flip1" data-role="slider">
         <option value="off">Off</option>
         <option value="on">On</option>
       </select>
     </div>

     <div data-role="fieldcontain">
       <label for="slider">Slider:</label>
       <input type="range" name="slider" id="slider" value="50"
              min="0" max="100" data-highlight="true" />
     </div>


     <div data-role="fieldcontain">
      <fieldset id="control1" data-role="controlgroup"
                data-type="horizontal">
       <legend>Drink type:</legend>
       <label for="checkbox-1">Beer</label>
       <input type="checkbox" name="checkbox-1"
              id="checkbox-1" class="custom"/>
```

```
      <label for="checkbox-2"><em>Wine</em></label>
      <input type="checkbox" name="checkbox-2"
             id="checkbox-2" class="custom"/>

      <label for="checkbox-3">Champagne</label>
      <input type="checkbox" name="checkbox-3"
             id="checkbox-3" class="custom"/>
    </fieldset>
  </div>

  <!-- radio buttons -->
  <div data-role="fieldcontain">
      <fieldset data-role="controlgroup" data-
type="horizontal">
        <legend>Disposition:</legend>
        <input type="radio" name="radio-choice-b"
               id="radio-choice-c" value="on"
checked="checked"/>
        <label for="radio-choice-c">Sunny</label>
        <input type="radio" name="radio-choice-b"
               id="radio-choice-d" value="off"/>
        <label for="radio-choice-d">Noirish</label>
        <input type="radio" name="radio-choice-b"
               id="radio-choice-e" value="other"/>
        <label for="radio-choice-e">Introspective</label>
      </fieldset>
  </div>

  <!-- drop-down list -->
  <div data-role="fieldcontain">
    <label for="select-choice" class="select">Your type:</la-
bel>
    <select name="select-choice" id="select-choice">
      <option value="MP">Morning Person</option>
      <option value="NP">Night Person</option>
      <option value="NP">Neither</option>
    </select>
  </div>

  <div class="ui-body ui-body-b">
    <fieldset class="ui-grid-a">
     <div class="ui-block-a"><button type="submit"
          data-theme="d">Cancel</button></div>
     <div class="ui-block-b"><button type="submit"
          data-theme="a">Submit</button></div>
    </fieldset>
  </div>
```

```
      </form>
    </div>
  </body>
</html>
```

Listing 8.8 contains a single HTML `<div>` element that contains various widgets, such as a text input field, a textarea, a slider, multiple checkboxes, radio buttons, a drop-down list, and two buttons.

The text-related fields and the slider-related widgets have styling applied to them via the selectors in the CSS stylesheet `CSS3Background2.css`, whose contents are displayed in Listing 8.8.

> **NOTE** *The rounded corners and drop shadows for the text input fields might lead users to think that they are buttons instead of input fields, so keep this point in mind whenever you create these types of visual effects.*

Listing 8.9 CSS3Background2.css

```
#textinput, #textarea {
 background-image:
  -webkit-radial-gradient(red 8px);
  -webkit-box-shadow:  10px 10px 20px #400;
}

#flip1, #slider {
 background-image:
  -webkit-radial-gradient(red 8px);
  -webkit-box-shadow:  10px 10px 20px #004;
}
```

The first selector in Listing 8.8 matches the text input fields in Listing 8.7, and the second selector matches the slider and the "flip" element. The first selector renders a shadow effect with a reddish tinge, whereas the second selector renders a shadow with a bluish tinge. One thing that you will notice is that you can apply custom styling to input fields and buttons, but other types of widgets don't necessarily "pick up" your custom effects, so you need to test your selectors against other types of jQuery widgets (such as drop-down lists and combo boxes) that are included in your HTML Web pages.

jQuery Mobile also handles input fields and text areas; input fields can apply a `type` attribute and use several of the new values defined in HTML5 to help the user by displaying the correct kind of keyboard to use. For example, an input with a `type="number"` will show the numeric keyboard in most mobile devices, and so forth. Text areas will increase in height as the user types in input, which avoids the creation of scrollbars. jQuery Mobile uses the text input plug-in to handle text areas and input fields, as shown here:

```
$("#page").live('pageinit', (function(event){
  // Disable an input $("#myinput").textinput('disable');
  // Enable an input $("#myotherinput").textinput("enable");
})
```

Figure 8.8 displays the result of rendering the HTML Web page in Listing 8.8 in a screenshot taken in a Chrome browser on a Macbook.

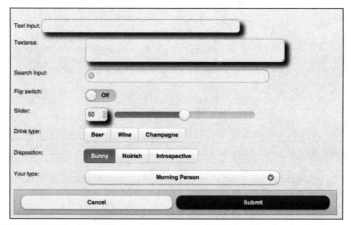

FIGURE 8.8 Checkboxes and radio buttons in a Chrome browser on a Macbook.

LIST VIEWS IN JQUERY MOBILE

jQuery Mobile supports list views (which are very common in mobile applications), and several variations, including list view buttons, nested list views, and list view split buttons.

Simple List Views with Buttons

jQuery Mobile can enhance ordered lists and unordered lists by applying the attribute `data-role="listview"` to a list. List view elements that are embedded inside anchor tags respond to user gestures, as shown in Listing 8.10, which displays the contents of the jQuery Mobile Web page `JQMSimpleListView1.html`.

Listing 8.10 JQMSimpleListView1.html

```
<!DOCTYPE html>
<html lang="en">
  <head>
    <meta charset=utf-8"/>
    <title>Simple List Views in jQuery Mobile</title>

    <link rel="stylesheet"
      href="http://code.jquery.com/mobile/1.1.0/jquery.mobile-
                                          1.1.0.min.css"/>
    <script
        src="http://code.jquery.com/jquery-1.7.1.min.js">
    </script>
    <script src="http://code.jquery.com/mobile/1.1.0
                      /jquery.mobile-1.1.0.min.js">
    </script>
  </head>

  <body>
    <div data-role="page">
      <div data-role="header"> <h2>This is the Header</h2> </div>
      <div data-role="content">
        <h3>Simple Unordered List Example</h3>
        <ul data-role="listview">
          <li><a href="#">Unordered Item 1</a></li>
          <li><a href="#">Unordered Item 2</a></li>
          <li><a href="#">Unordered Item 3</a></li>
        </ul>
        <h3>Simple Ordered List Example</h3>
        <ol data-role="listview">
          <li><a href="#">Ordered Item 1</a></li>
          <li><a href="#">Ordered Item 2</a></li>
          <li><a href="#">Ordered Item 3</a></li>
        </ol>
      </div>
      <div data-role="footer"> <h2>This is the Footer</h2> </div>
    </div>
  </body>
</html>
```

Whenever users tap on any list item in Listing 8.10, you can detect that event and execute custom code (if any) that you have bound to that event. In this example, the href attribute has value #, so the page is reloaded when users tap or click on the list items.

Figure 8.9 displays the result of rendering the HTML Web page in Listing 8.10 in landscape mode on an Asus Prime tablet with Android ICS.

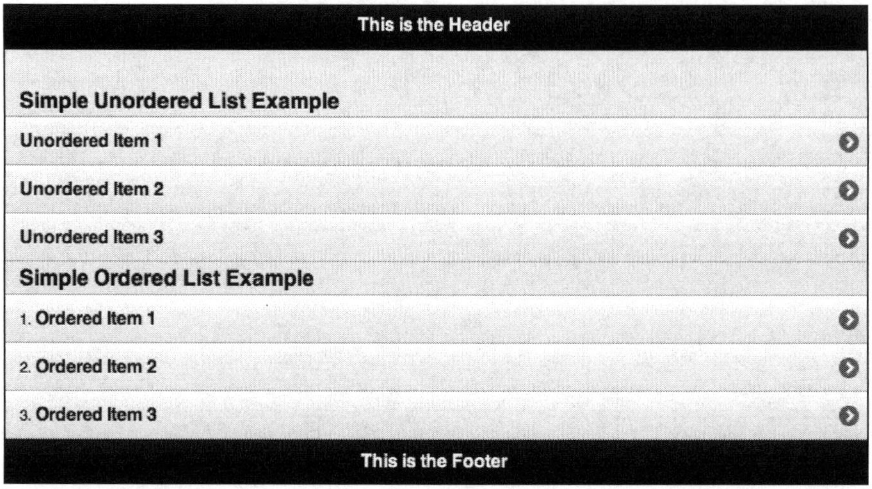

FIGURE 8.9 List view on an Asus Prime tablet with Android ICS.

Nested List Views

jQuery Mobile can create interactive views with nested lists, and users can "drill down" by tapping on list items. The first view displays the items in the top-level list, and tapping on one of those items will display the sublist for that item (and so forth). In addition, jQuery Mobile automatically provides a back button and also takes care of the URL mapping and transitions between pages.

Listing 8.11 displays the contents of JQMNestedListViews1.html, which is a jQuery Mobile Web page that illustrates how to render nested lists and how to navigate between pages when users click on list items.

Listing 8.11 JQMNestedListViews1.html

```
<!DOCTYPE html>
<html lang="en">
  <head>
   <meta charset="utf-8"/>
   <title>Nested List Views jQuery Mobile</title>

   <link rel="stylesheet"
    href="http://code.jquery.com/mobile/1.1.0/jquery.mobile-
1.1.0.min.css"/>
   <script
       src="http://code.jquery.com/jquery-1.7.1.min.js">
   </script>
   <script src="http://code.jquery.com/mobile/1.1.0
                   /jquery.mobile-1.1.0.min.js">
```

```
    </script>
  </head>

  <body>
    <div data-role="page">
      <div data-role="header"> <h2>This is the Header</h2> </div>

      <div data-role="content">
        <h3>Nested List Example (States &gt; Cities)</h3>
        <ul data-role="listview">
          <li>US States
            <ul>
              <li>California
                <ul>
                  <li>Mountain View</li>
                  <li>San Francisco</li>
                  <li>Los Angeles</li>
                </ul>
              </li>
              <li>Illinois
                <ul>
                  <li>Chicago</li>
                  <li>Champagne</li>
                  <li>Golconda</li>
                </ul>
              </li>
              <li>Florida
                <ul>
                  <li>Miami</li>
                  <li>St Pete</li>
                  <li>Miami</li>
                </ul>
              </li>
            </ul>
          </li>
        </ul>
      </div>


      <div data-role="footer"> <h2>This is the Footer</h2> </div>
    </div>
  </body>
</html>
```

Listing 8.11 is a simple HTML Web page that contains HTML markup and a content-related HTML `<div>` element that contains the text for the nested lists. The top-level list contains one item labeled "US States," and when users click on this item, three states are displayed: California, Illinois, and Florida. When users click on any of these three states, they will see a list of three cities that are located in those states.

You can also use a list divider to separate items. Its syntax looks like this:

```
<li data-role="list-divider">F</li>
```

Split buttons are useful and common in mobile applications because they provide two functions in a single list item. jQuery Mobile can render a list of buttons that are split into two regions: the left-side region is relatively wide, and the right-side region occupies the remaining space. jQuery Mobile provides a straightforward way to create a split button: simply add two anchor tags to each list item. For example, you could include a link for making reservations (in this case, using PHP code that is not shown) for a restaurant in a particular city, as shown here:

```
<li>
  <a href="Berghoff.html">Chicago</a>
  <a href="reservations.php?restaurant=123">Make Reservations</a>
</li>
```

Figure 8.10 displays the result of rendering the HTML Web page in Listing 8.11 in a landscape-mode screenshot taken from a Sprint Nexus S 4G with Android ICS.

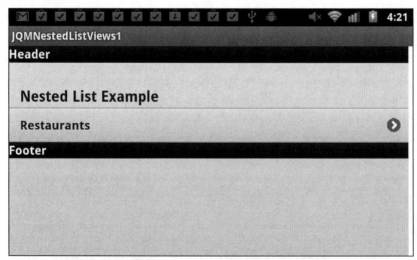

FIGURE 8.10 A nested list view on a Sprint Nexus S 4G with Android ICS.

The next step is to click on one of the links in Listing 8.11, and you will see another page with a list of US states.

Figure 8.11 displays the result of "clicking through" the HTML Web page in Listing 8.11 in landscape mode on a Sprint Nexus S 4G with Android ICS.

FIGURE 8.11 A nested list view on a Sprint Nexus S 4G with Android ICS.

Click on a US state in Listing 8.10, and you will see another page with a list of cities in that state.

Figure 8.12 displays the result of rendering the HTML Web page in Listing 8.11 in landscape mode on a Sprint Nexus S 4G with Android ICS.

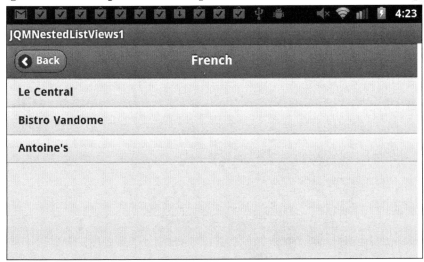

FIGURE 8.12 A nested list view on a Sprint Nexus S 4G with Android ICS.

NAVIGATION BARS

Navigation bars in mobile applications often consist of a set of buttons that enable users to navigate through the page views. jQuery Mobile allows you to include navigation bars in the header, footer, or content areas of a page view (and also provide the appropriate formatting for the navigation bars).

To designate a navigation bar, apply the `data-role="navigation"` to a block level element like the HTML5 `<nav>` element. Anchor tags contained within a designated navigation element will be formatted as a button group, and jQuery Mobile will handle changing the active and inactive states of the buttons automatically, as shown in Listing 8.12.

Listing 8.12 JQMNavigationBar1.html

```
<!DOCTYPE html>
<html lang="en">
  <head>
   <meta charset=utf-8"/>
   <title>jQuery Mobile Navigation Bar</title>

   <link rel="stylesheet" href="CSS3Background3.css"/>

   <link rel="stylesheet"
    href="http://code.jquery.com/mobile/1.1.0/jquery.mobile-
1.1.0.min.css"/>
   <script
       src="http://code.jquery.com/jquery-1.7.1.min.js">
   </script>
   <script src="http://code.jquery.com/mobile/1.1.0
                    /jquery.mobile-1.1.0.min.js">
   </script>
  </head>

  <body>
    <div data-role="page">
      <div data-role="header">
        <div data-role="navbar">
          <a href="#" class="ui-btn-active">HBar1</a>
          <a href="#">HBar2</a>
          <a href="#">HBar3</a>
          <a href="#">HBar4</a>
          <a href="#">HBar5</a>
          <a href="#">HBar6</a>
        </div>
      </div>
```

```
      <div data-role="content">
        <div data-role="navbar">
         <ul>
          <li><a href="#" class="ui-btn-active">Content1</a></li>
          <li><a href="#">Content2</a></li>
          <li><a href="#">Content3</a></li>
          <li><a href="#">Content4</a></li>
          <li><a href="#">Content5</a></li>
          <li><a href="#">Content6</a></li>
         </ul>
        </div>

        <div data-role="navbar">
          <a href="#" class="ui-btn-active">CBar11</a>
          <a href="#">CBar22</a>
          <a href="#">CBar33</a>
          <a href="#">CBar44</a>
          <a href="#">CBar55</a>
        </div>
      </div>

      <div data-role="footer">
        <div data-role="navbar">
          <a href="#" class="ui-btn-active">FBar1</a>
          <a href="#">FBar2</a>
          <a href="#">FBar3</a>
          <a href="#">FBar4</a>
          <a href="#">FBar5</a>
          <a href="#">FBar6</a>
        </div>
      </div>
    </div>
  </body>
</html>
```

Listing 8.12 contains HTML markup and jQuery code for a single page view, along with four HTML <div> elements that contain the attribute data-role="navbar" that designated navigation bars.

The first navigation bar is displayed in the HTML <div> element with the data-role="header" attribute; the second and third are displayed in the HTML <div> element with the data-role="content" attribute; and the fourth is displayed in the HTML <div> element with the data-role="footer" attribute.

The custom CSS stylesheet CSS3Background3.css (displayed in Listing

8.13) contents a selector that styles the HTML <a> elements in Listing 8.12 with a shadow effect, which makes some of the content stand out more vividly (with somewhat of a 3D effect) than the effect without the CSS selector.

Note that jQuery Mobile will fit up to five items in a formatted navigation bar; if additional elements are specified, jQuery Mobile stacks them into two columns.

Listing 8.13 CSS3Background3.css

```
a {
 background-image:
  -webkit-radial-gradient(red 12px);
  -webkit-box-shadow:  20px 20px 40px #880;
}
```

Listing 8.13 contains a single selector that styles the HTML <a> elements with a yellow-tinged shadow effect, as you can see in Figure 8.13, which renders the HTML Web page in Listing 8.12 on a Sprint Nexus S 4G with Android ICS.

FIGURE 8.13 Navigation bar on a Sprint Nexus S 4G with Android ICS.

SELECT MENUS IN JQUERY MOBILE

jQuery Mobile enables you to show and hide a list of menu options, and you can also use transitions to create animation effects as the menu list is displayed or hidden from view. Listing 8.14 displays the contents of JQMMenu1. html that illustrates how to create a sliding menu in an HTML5 Web page.

Listing 8.14 JQMMenu1.html

```
<!DOCTYPE html>
<html lang="en">
  <head>
   <meta charset="utf-8"/>
   <title>Sliding Menus in jQuery Mobile</title>

   <link rel="stylesheet" href="CSS3Background4.css"/>

   <link rel="stylesheet"
    href="http://code.jquery.com/mobile/1.1.0/jquery.mobile-
1.1.0.min.css"/>
   <script
       src="http://code.jquery.com/jquery-1.7.1.min.js">
   </script>
   <script src="http://code.jquery.com/mobile/1.1.0
                    /jquery.mobile-1.1.0.min.js">
   </script>
  </head>

  <body>
    <div id="page1" data-role="page">
      <header data-role="header">
        <h1>JQuery Mobile Sliding Menu Example (header)</h1>
      </header>

      <p class="show-menu">Show/Hide Menu</p>
      <div data-role="content" class="sliding-menu slide out">
        <label for="select-choice-1"
               class="select">Choose a Menu Item:</label>
        <select name="select-choice-1" id="select-choice-1">
           <option value="item1">First menu item</option>
           <option value="item2">Second menu item</option>
           <option value="item3">Third menu item</option>
        </select>
      </div>

      <footer data-role="footer">
```

```
        <h1>JQuery Mobile Sliding Menu Example (footer)</h1>
      </footer>
    </div>

    <script>
      $("#page1").live('pageinit', (function(event){
        $(".show-menu").click(function() {
          $(".sliding-menu").toggleClass("reverse out in");
        })
      }))
    </script>
  </body>
</html>
```

Listing 8.14 contains HTML markup, a reference to a CSS3 stylesheet (in Listing 8.15), and the jQuery Mobile code for a single page view. The list of menu items is contained inside an HTML `<div>` element that has the multiple values assigned to the `class` attribute, as shown here:

```
<div class="sliding-menu slide out">
```

The list of menu items is hidden when the Web page is initially rendered. When users can click on the HTML `<p>` element that contains the text string "Show/Hide Menu," the following code is executed, which uses the jQuery `toggleClass()` method and a sliding effect to display the menu items:

```
$(".show-menu").click(function() {
    $(".sliding-menu").toggleClass("reverse out in");
})
```

Listing 8.15 CSS3Background4.css

```
div {
 background-image:
  -webkit-radial-gradient(red 12px);
  -webkit-box-shadow:  20px 20px 40px #400;
}
```

Listing 8.14 contains a single selector that styles the HTML `<div>` elements with a red-tinged shadow effect. Figure 8.13 displays the result of rendering the HTML Web page in Listing 8.14 in landscape mode on a Sprint Nexus S 4G with Android ICS.

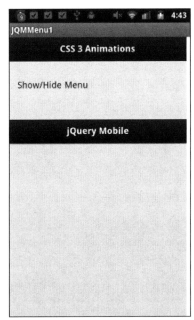

FIGURE 8.14 Menu bar on a Sprint Nexus S 4G with Android ICS.

jQuery Mobile and Ajax

jQuery Mobile uses Ajax for form submission, and will attempt to integrate the server response into the DOM of the application, providing transitions as expected. If you wish to prevent jQuery Mobile from using Ajax to handle a form, apply the attribute `data-ajax="false"` to the form tag.

Listing 8.16 displays the contents of `JQMAjax1.html` that illustrates how to handle Ajax invocations in a jQuery Mobile application.

Listing 8.16 JQMAjax1.html

```
<!DOCTYPE html>
<html lang="en">
<head>
   <meta charset="utf-8"/>
   <title>jQuery Mobile and AJAX</title>

   <link rel="stylesheet"
    href="http://code.jquery.com/mobile/1.1.0/jquery.mobile-
1.1.0.min.css"/>
   <script
       src="http://code.jquery.com/jquery-1.7.1.min.js">
   </script>
```

```
  <script src="http://code.jquery.com/mobile/1.1.0/jquery.mobile-
1.1.0.min.js">
  </script>
</head>

<body>
  <script>
    var xmlData = "", count = 0;

    $("#page1").live('pageinit', (function(event){
      $.ajax({
        url: 'http://localhost:9000/sample.xml',
        dataType: 'xml',
        success: function(data) {
                    $(data)
                      .find('svg')
                      .children()
                      .each(function() {
                        var node = $(this);
                        var x      = node.attr('x');
                        var y      = node.attr('y');
                        var width  = node.attr('width');
                        var height = node.attr('height');
                        var stroke = node.attr('stroke');
                        var fill   = node.attr('fill');

                        // other processing here...
                        ++count;

                        console.log("element: "+node);
                      });
                    console.log("element count: "+count);
        },
        error: function() {
          alert('no data found');
        }
      })
    })
    );
  </script>

  <div id="page1" data-role="page">
    <div data-role="header">Header</div>
    <div data-role="content">
      <p>Hello World from jQuery Mobile</p>
    </div>
```

```
      <div data-role="footer">Footer</div>
    </div>
  </body>
</html>
```

Listing 8.16 contains HTML markup and a jQuery Mobile Ajax invocation that is executed after this Web page is loaded into a browser, after which the code processes all the child elements of the `<svg>` element in the XML document `sample.xml` (displayed in Listing 8.17), as shown here:

```
var node = $(this);
var x      = node.attr('x');
var y      = node.attr('y');
var width  = node.attr('width');
var height = node.attr('height');
var stroke = node.attr('stroke');
var fill   = node.attr('fill');
```

For the purpose of illustration, this code makes the assumption that the XML document `sample.xml` in Listing 8.17 contains XML elements that have the attributes specified in the preceding code block.

Listing 8.17 sample.xml

```
<?xml version='1.0' encoding='iso-8859-1'?>
<svg xmlns="http://www.w3.org/2000/svg"
     xmlns:xlink="http://www.w3.org/1999/xlink"
     width="100%" height="100%">
  <rect x="50"  y="10" width="100" height="200"
        stroke="blue" fill="red"/>
  <rect x="200" y="10" width="100" height="200"
        stroke="blue" fill="green"/>
  <rect x="350" y="10" width="100" height="200"
        stroke="blue" fill="blue"/>
</svg>
```

Place the files in Listing 8.16 and 8.17 in the same directory, and launch a web server that serves requests on port 9000. Launch the HTML Web page in Listing 8.16 in a Chrome browser on a laptop or desktop, open Chrome Inspector, and inspect the contents of the Chrome console. You will see something similar to the contents of Figure 8.15, which displays the contents of the Chrome Inspector in a Chrome browser on a Macbook.

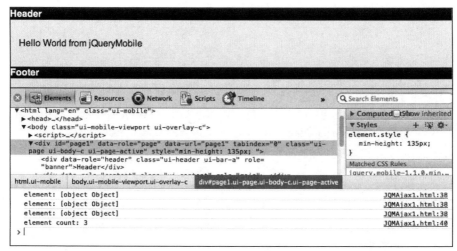

FIGURE 8.15 A jQuery Mobile Ajax invocation on a Chrome browser on a Macbook.

JQUERY MOBILE AND GEOLOCATION

In Chapter 5, you learned how to obtain geolocation information for users. In this section you will see how to use jQuery Mobile in order to obtain geolocation information.

Listing 8.18 displays the contents of JQMGeoLocation1.html that illustrates how to obtain geolocation information in an HTML5 Web page.

Listing 8.18 JQMGeoLocation1.html

```
<!DOCTYPE html>
<html lang="en">
<head>
  <meta charset="utf-8">
  <title>JQueryMobile Geolocation</title>

  <link rel="stylesheet"
    href="http://code.jquery.com/mobile/1.1.0/jquery.mobile-
1.1.0.min.css"/>
  <script
      src="http://code.jquery.com/jquery-1.7.1.min.js">
  </script>
  <script src="http://code.jquery.com/mobile/1.1.0
                    /jquery.mobile-1.1.0.min.js">
  </script>
```

```
    <!-- google maps API -->
    <script src="http://maps.google.com/maps/api/js?sensor=false">
    </script>

    <style>
#theMap, #theCoords {
font-size: 16px;
height: 200px;
width:  400px;
}
    </style>

<script>
    function findUserLocation() {
        // specify the 'success' and 'fail' JavaScript functions
        navigator.geolocation.getCurrentPosition(successCallback,
                                                 errorCallback);
    }

function successCallback(position) {
  var latitude  = position.coords.latitude;
  var longitude = position.coords.longitude;
  var latlong   = new google.maps.LatLng(latitude, longitude);

  var myOptions = {
      zoom: 14,
      center: latlong,
      mapTypeId: google.maps.MapTypeId.ROADMAP
  };

  // use Google Maps to display the current location
  var map = new google.maps.Map(document.getElementById("theMap"),
myOptions);
  map.setCenter(latlong);

/*
    var marker = new google.maps.Marker({
      position: initialLocation,
      map: map,
      title: "I Am Here!"
  });
*/

  // display position details in the console
  positionDetails(position);
```

```
}

function errorCallback(error) {
  if(error.code = error.PERMISSION_DENIED) {
     console.log("Error: you must enable geolocation access");
  } else if(error.code = error.PERMISSION_UNAVAILABLE) {
     console.log("Error: geolocation unavailable");
  } else if(error.code = error.TIMEOUT) {
     console.log("Error: timeout occurred");
  }

//console.log(error);
}

function positionDetails(pos) {
 var positionStr =
    "Latitude:"+ pos.coords.latitude +"<br>"+
    "Longitude:"+ pos.coords.longitude +"<br>"+
    "Accuracy:"+ pos.coords.accuracy +"<br>"+

    "Altitude:"+ pos.coords.altitude +"<br>"+
    "AltitudeAccuracy:"+ pos.coords.altitudeAccuracy +"<br>"+
    "Heading:"+ pos.coords.heading +"<br>"+
    "Speed:"+ pos.coords.speed +"";

    $("#theCoords").html(positionStr);
    console.log(positionStr);
}
</script>
</head>

 <body>
    <div data-role="page" id="page1">
      <div data-role="header"><h3>JQuery Mobile Geolocation</div>
      <div data-role="content" id="content">
        <div id="theMap"> </div>

        <form id="geoLocationForm">
          <input type="button" id="geobutton"
                  value="Click to Find My Current Location">
        </form>
        <div id="theCoords"> </div>
      </div>
      <div data-role="footer"><h3>Footer</h3></div>
    </div>
```

```
  <script>
    $("#page1").live('pageinit', (function(event){
       $("#geobutton").bind("vmousedown",function(event, ui){
          findUserLocation();
       });
    })
   );
  </script>
 </body>
</html>
```

Listing 8.18 contains code that is very similar to the code sample that you saw in Chapter 5. The only difference is that the code in Listing 8.18 has been adapted to jQuery Mobile, whereas the code in Chapter 5 uses jQuery. As such, you can read the explanation that is provided immediately after the related code sample in Chapter 5.

If you are interested in mobile maps, there are many such examples available, including the details on this Web site:

http://jquery-ui-map.googlecode.com/svn/trunk/demos/jquery-google-maps-mobile.html

SUMMARY

In this chapter, you learned about various features of jQuery Mobile, along with code samples that showed you examples of how to handle events, create Web pages with multiple page views, and how to create forms with HTML widgets. You also saw how to use CSS3 shadow and gradient effects (which you learned in Chapter 3) to style buttons in jQuery Mobile Web pages. You learned how to do the following in HTML Web pages that use jQuery Mobile:

- Render buttons
- Display simple and nested lists
- Render sliding menus
- Use jQuery Mobile with Ajax
- Use jQuery Mobile with Geolocation

Now that you understand how to create mobile applications with jQuery Mobile, the next chapter shows you how to create animation effects in jQuery Mobile.

USER GESTURES AND ANIMATION EFFECTS IN JQUERY MOBILE

This chapter contains a number of code samples that demonstrate how to handle user gestures and also how to create animation effects in jQuery Mobile. Fortunately, jQuery Mobile "emits" events for user gestures, such as `orientationchange`, `scrollstart`, `scrollstop`, `swipe`, `swipeleft`, `swiperight`, `tap`, and `taphold`. The first part of this chapter shows you how to handle some of these user gestures. In addition, there are various jQuery plugins that are specifically for handling user gestures (two are mentioned in this chapter) that you can use instead of writing your own code. You will also see code samples that show you how to create slide-related and fade-related animation effects in jQuery. The final portion of this section briefly discusses jQuery Mobile virtual mouse events, which can simplify your code when you want to handle mouse-related events as well as touch-related events in an HTML Web page.

The second part of this chapter shows you how to create CSS3 2D/3D animation effects with jQuery Mobile. You will see how to programmatically create HTML `<div>` elements in order to create sketch-like effects in Web pages. The final portion of this chapter contains a code sample that shows you how to use jQuery Mobile to create a 3D cube effect; another code sample on the DVD creates a "bouncing balls" effect using jQuery Mobile and CSS3. The final code sample in this chapter illustrates how to access accelerometer values for a mobile device and display the real-time values in a jQuery Mobile Web page.

Recall that in Chapter 2 you learned how to create CSS3 2D and 3D animation effects, and in Chapter 5 you learned how to combine those effects with jQuery in HTML5 Web pages. In this chapter, you will see how to create some of the corresponding effects using jQuery Mobile.

HANDLING USER GESTURES AND EVENTS IN JQUERY MOBILE

jQuery Mobile emits an assortment of events for user gestures, such as `orientationchange`, `scrollstart`, `scrollstop`, `swipe`, `swipeleft`, `swiperight`, `tap`, and `taphold`.

If you need to handle many user gestures, consider the option of using a jQuery plugin instead of writing your own code. There are various plugins available, and the next section briefly discusses two of them.

When you want to detect user gestures on a HTML Web page, you can write custom jQuery code using the jQuery `bind()` method (which you have seen in various code samples in earlier chapters) to handle those gestures. Keep in mind that the jQuery `bind()` method is deprecated in version 1.7 and beyond, but you are likely to encounter this method in existing code that uses versions of jQuery. This book contains a section that discusses methods that are deprecated in jQuery 1.7 and beyond, as well as the recommended jQuery method for handling events.

As you probably know, a `tap` event occurs whenever users tap on an element, whereas a `taphold` event occurs when users touch an element and maintain contact for one second. You can bind to a `tap` event and a `taphold` event in jQuery Mobile with the following code snippets:

```
$("body").bind("tap", function () {
  console.log("Tap Event on the body Element");
  return false;
});
```

```
$("body").bind("taphold", function () {
  console.log("Tap Hold Event on the body Element");
  return false;
});
```

The `return false` statement inside a jQuery event handler is effectively the same as invoking `e.preventDefault()` (which prevents the default event from occurring) and also `e.stopPropagation()` (which *does* prevent the event from "bubbling up") on the jQuery `Event` object that is passed as a parameter to the JavaScript function (which is not supplied in this example). Keep in mind that the `return false` statement in non-jQuery event handlers does *not* prevent "bubbling up" behavior on the event that occurred.

A `swipe` event occurs when there is a horizontal drag at the rate of `30px` (or greater) during a one-second interval. The `swipeleft` and `swiperight` events occur when the swipe event is toward the left or toward the right, respectively.

Listing 9.1 displays the contents of `JQMSwipeEvents1.html` that illustrates how to handle `tap` events as well as `swipeleft` and `swiperight` events in jQuery Mobile.

Listing 9.1 JQMSwipeTapEvents1.html

```
<!DOCTYPE html>
<html lang="en">
  <head>
   <meta charset=utf-8"/>
   <title>Swipe and Tap Events in jQuery Mobile</title>

   <link rel="stylesheet"
   href="http://code.jquery.com/mobile/1.1.0/jquery.mobile-
1.1.0.min.css"/>
    <script
        src="http://code.jquery.com/jquery-1.7.1.min.js">
    </script>
    <script src="http://code.jquery.com/mobile/1.1.0
                     /jquery.mobile-1.1.0.min.js">
    </script>
  </head>

  <body>
    <div data-role="page" id="page1">
      <div data-role="header"> <h3>Header</h3> </div>
      <div data-role="content">
       <img id="laurie1" src="Laurie1.jpeg" width="150"
height="150" >
       <img id="laurie2" src="Laurie1.jpeg" width="150"
height="150" >
       <img id="laurie3" src="Laurie1.jpeg" width="150"
height="150" >
       <div id="result1">Left Image:</div>
       <div id="result2">Middle Image:</div>
```

```
    <div id="result3">Right Image:</div>
    </div>
    <div data-role="footer"> <h3>Footer</h3> </div>
  </div>

  <script>
    <!-- jQuery event handling code starts here -->
    $("#page1").live('pageinit', (function(event){
      // handler for tap hold event
      $("#laurie1").bind("taphold",function(event, ui){
        console.log("Left image: tap hold event");
        $("#result1").html("Left image: tap hold event");
      })

      // handler for swipe left event
      $("#laurie2").bind("swipeleft",function(event, ui){
        console.log("Middle image: swipe left event");
        $("#result2").html("Middle image: swipe left event");
      })

      // handler for swipe right event
      $("#laurie3").bind("swiperight",function(event, ui){
        console.log("Right image: swipe right event");
        $("#result3").html("Right image: swipe right event");
      })
    })
    );
  </script>
 </body>
</html>
```

Listing 9.1 displays a horizontal row of three images, and under those three images there are three text strings that act as "labels" for user gestures that are associated with the left, middle, and right image, respectively. Listing 9.1 also contains `console.log()` messages that are displayed in Chrome Inspector whenever users tap or swipe one of the rendered images.

Incidentally, the code in Listing 9.1 was deployed as an Android application from inside Eclipse, and after the DDMS (Dalvik Debug Monitor Server) perspective, you might see the following type of message in the Eclipse console if you swipe your finger too quickly:

"Miss a drag as we are waiting for Webcore's response for touch down."

Figure 9.1 displays the result of rendering JQMSwipeEvents1.html in List-ing 9.1 in a landscape-mode screenshot taken from an Android application running on an Asus Prime tablet with Android ICS.

FIGURE 9.1 Swipe and tap events on an Asus Prime tablet with Android ICS.

Two jQuery Plugins for Detecting User Gestures

The jGestures jQuery plugin handles a vast set of user gestures, including pinch, rotate, swipe-related and tap-related user gestures. This jQuery plugin is available for download here:

https://jgestures.codeplex.com/

The syntax for handling user gestures uses the jQuery bind method. For example, you can bind a swipe gesture with the jGestures plugin with the fol-lowing code snippet:

```
jQuery('#swipe').bind('swipeone',eventHandler);
```

Another jQuery Mobile plugin that handles various user gestures is here:

https://github.com/eightmedia/hammer.js

This JavaScript toolkit has a good collection of samples that illustrate how to handle user gestures. You can view them online here:

http://eightmedia.github.com/hammer.js/demo/
http://eightmedia.github.com/hammer.js/slideshow/
http://eightmedia.github.com/hammer.js/scroll/

http://eightmedia.github.com/hammer.js/drag/
http://eightmedia.github.com/hammer.js/draw/
http://eightmedia.github.com/hammer.js/zoom/

Since there are many jQuery Mobile plugins available for handling user gestures, it's a good idea to perform an Internet search to find many of those plugins, after which you can assess them to determine which ones best fit your needs.

Scroll Events in jQuery Mobile

jQuery Mobile supports the following custom events: `orientationchange` (triggered by changing the orientation of a device, either vertically or horizontally), `scrollstart` (triggered when a scroll begins), and `scrollstop` (triggered when a scroll ends). You can bind to these events like you would with other jQuery events, using `live()` **or** `bind()`, whose usage prior to version 1.7 of jQuery is discussed in Chapter 6. In addition, when your jQuery Mobile code binds to the `orientationchange` event, the callback function can specify a second argument that contains an `orientation` property equal to either `portrait` or `landscape`.

Listing 9.2 displays the contents of `JQMScrollEvents1.html` that illustrates how to handle scrolling events in jQuery Mobile.

Listing 9.2 JQMScrollEvents1.html

```
<!DOCTYPE html>
<html lang="en">
  <head>
   <meta charset=utf-8"/>
   <title>Scroll Events in jQuery Mobile</title>

   <link rel="stylesheet"
   href="http://code.jquery.com/mobile/1.1.0/jquery.mobile-
1.1.0.min.css"/>
    <script
        src="http://code.jquery.com/jquery-1.7.1.min.js">
    </script>
    <script src="http://code.jquery.com/mobile/1.1.0
                    /jquery.mobile-1.1.0min.js">
    </script>
  </head>

  <body>
    <div data-role="page" id="page1">
```

```
    <div data-role="header"> <h3>Header</h3> </div>
    <div data-role="content">
     <img id="laurie1" src="Laurie1.jpeg" width="400"
height="400" >
     <img id="laurie2" src="Laurie2.jpeg" width="400"
                                        height="400" >
     <img id="laurie3" src="Laurie3.jpeg" width="400"
                                        height="400" >
     <img id="laurie4" src="Laurie1.jpeg" width="400"
                                        height="400" >
     <img id="laurie5" src="Laurie2.jpeg" width="400"
                                        height="400" >
     <img id="laurie6" src="Laurie3.jpeg" width="400"
                                        height="400" >
     <div id="events"></div>
    </div>
    <div data-role="footer"> <h3>Footer</h3> </div>
  </div>

  <script>
    $("#page1").live('pageinit', (function(event,ui){
      var eventsElement = $('#events');
      $(window).bind('scrollstart', function () {
        console.log('Scroll start');
        $('.ui-body-c').css('background', 'green');
        eventsElement.append('<li><a href="">Start Scroll</a></
li>');
        eventsElement.listview('refresh');
      });

      $(window).bind('scrollstop', function () {
        console.log('Scroll stop');
        $('.ui-body-c').css('background', 'red');
        eventsElement.append('<li><a href="">Stop Scroll</a></
li>');
        eventsElement.listview('refresh');
      });

      $(window).bind('orientationchange', function () {
        console.log('Orientationchange change');
        $('.ui-body-c').css('background', 'red');
        eventsElement.append('<li><a href="">Orientation</a></
li>');
        eventsElement.listview('refresh');
      });
    })
  );
```

```
    </script>
  </body>
</html>
```

Listing 9.2 renders six images whose display (three rows of two images, or one row of six images, and so forth) depends on the dimensions of your current browser session. In addition, there is a `<div>` element whose `id` value is `events`; this `<div>` element is where messages are appended whenever a bound event occurs.

The messages in Listing 9.2 simply report scroll stop and start events, as well as orientation changes of a mobile device, but you can provide more fine-grained messages in other locations of the Web page. For example, the following code block detects landscape versus portrait mode for a mobile device, and then updates the `<header>` element or the `<footer>` element with a suitable text string:

```
$(document).on("orientationchange", function(event) {
  if(event.orientation == "landscape") {
    $("header h1").text("JQM landscape");
    $("footer h1").text("JQM landscape");
  } else {
    $("header h1").text("JQM portrait");
    $("footer h1").text("JQM portrait");
  }
});
```

Figure 9.2 displays the result of rendering `JQMScrollEvents1.html` in Listing 9.2 in a landscape-mode screenshot taken from an Asus Prime tablet with Android ICS.

FIGURE 9.2 Scroll events on an Asus Prime tablet with Android ICS.

Portrait Mode Versus Landscape Mode

In addition to detecting orientation of a mobile device, you will probably need to change the CSS class that is used to style elements in a Web page when there is a change of orientation.

Listing 9.3 displays the contents of JQMOrientation1.html that illustrates how easily you can change the CSS classes associated with HTML elements based on the orientation of a mobile device.

Listing 9.3 JQMOrientation1.html

```html
<!DOCTYPE html>
<html lang="en">
  <head>
   <meta charset="utf-8"/>
   <title>jQuery Mobile Orientation</title>

   <link rel="stylesheet"
   href="http://code.jquery.com/mobile/1.1.0/jquery.mobile-
1.1.0.min.css"/>
    <script
        src="http://code.jquery.com/jquery-1.7.1.min.js">
    </script>
    <script src="http://code.jquery.com/mobile/1.1.0
                      /jquery.mobile-1.1.0.min.js">
    </script>

    <style>
     .portrait { background-color: red; width: 320px; }
     .landscape{ background-color: blue; width: 480px; }
    </style>
  </head>

  <body>
    <div  data-role="page" id="page1">
      <div data-role="header"><h3>Orientation</h3></div>
      <div data-role="content" class="portrait" id="content">
       <p>Hello from jQuery Mobile</p>
      </div>
      <div data-role="footer"><h3>Footer</h3></div>
    </div>

  <script>
   $("#page1").live('pageinit', (function(event,ui){
      $(window).bind ('orientationchange', function (e) {
       console.log("new orientation: "+e.orientation);
```

```
    $("#content").removeClass('portrait landscape')
            .addClass (e.orientation ? 'landscape' :
                                            'portrait');
    });
  })
 );
</script>
</body>
</html>
```

In Listing 9.2, you saw how to detect orientation changes for a mobile device, and Listing 9.3 shows you how to remove CSS classes and add the correct CSS class based on the orientation of the mobile device, as shown in this code snippet:

```
$(window).bind ('orientationchange', function (e) {
    $("#content").removeClass('portrait landscape')
            .addClass (e.orientation ? 'landscape' : 'por-
trait');
    });
```

Notice that the `orientationchange` event is bound to the window object. In the current example, the background color is set to `red` and the `width` is set to `320px` in `portrait` mode, whereas the background color is set to `blue` and the `width` is set to `480px` in landscape mode.

One other thing to keep in mind is that `window.orientation` has the value `0` for `portrait` mode and either `-90` or `90` for `landscape` mode.

Another approach is to use the following type of code in your HTML Web page:

```
@media all and (orientation: portrait) { body {background-
color: red} }
```

```
<link rel="stylesheet"
      media="all and (orientation: landscape)" href="landscape.
css"/>
```

Figure 9.3 displays the result of rendering `JQMOrientation1.html` in Listing 9.3 in a landscape-mode screenshot taken from an Asus Prime tablet with Android ICS.

FIGURE 9.3 Detecting orientation on an Asus Prime tablet with Android ICS.

ANIMATION EFFECTS USING JQUERY MOBILE

There are various jQuery-based animation effects that you can create with jQuery Mobile, which includes fading effects, sliding effects, and also custom animation effects. The methods for creating animation effects (available in both jQuery and jQuery Mobile) include: `animation()`, `clearQueue()`, `delay()`, `dequeue()`, `fadeIn()`, `fadeOut()`, `fadeTo()`, `fadeToggle()`, `hide()`, `queue()`, `show()`, `slideDown()`, `slideToggle()`, `slideUp()`, `stop()`, and `toggle()`.

This section contains code samples that illustrate how to create some of these animation effects in jQuery Mobile.

Fade-Related Methods

The jQuery `.fadeIn()` and `.fadeOut()` methods provide an easy way to create simple animation effects.

Listing 9.4 displays the contents of `JQMFadeInOut1.html` that illustrates how to use the jQuery `.fadeIn()` and `.fadeOut()` methods in a jQuery Mobile page.

Listing 9.4 JQMFadeInOut1.html

```
<!DOCTYPE html>
<html lang="en">
 <head>
   <meta charset=utf-8"/>
   <title>jQuery Mobile FadeIn</title>

  <link rel="stylesheet"
  href="http://code.jquery.com/mobile/1.1.0/jquery.mobile-
1.1.0.min.css"/>
   <script
       src="http://code.jquery.com/jquery-1.7.1.min.js">
   </script>
   <script src="http://code.jquery.com/mobile/1.1.0
                     /jquery.mobile-1.1.0.min.js">
   </script>
  </head>

  <body>
    <div data-role="page" id="page1">
      <div id="header" data-role="header">
        <h3>Click Header To Show Text</h3>
      </div>
      <div id="context" data-role="content">
        <img id="laurie1" src="Laurie1.jpeg" width="200"
height="200" >
        <img id="laurie2" src="Laurie2.jpeg" width="200"
height="200" >
        <img id="laurie3" src="Laurie3.jpeg" width="200"
height="200" >
        <p>Hello World from jQuery Mobile</p>
        <p>Goodbye World from jQuery Mobile</p>
        <p>Click on this text to toggle this paragraph.</p>
      </div>
      <div data-role="footer"><h3>Footer</h3></div>
    </div>

    <script>
      $("#page1").live('pageinit', (function(event,ui){
      var imgs = $("img");
```

```
      // fade out when users click on the first <img>
      $("img:first").click(function () {
        $("img:first").fadeOut("slow");
      });

      // display first <img> when users click on the last <img>
      $("img:last").click(function () {
        $("img:first").fadeIn("slow");
      });

      // fade when users click on the first <p>
      $("p:first").click(function () {
        $("p:first").fadeOut("slow");
      });

      // display first <p> when users click on the last <p>
      $("p:last").click(function () {
        $("p:first").fadeIn("slow");
      });
    })
  );
  </script>
 </body>
</html>
```

Listing 9.4 contains the jQuery Mobile code for a single page view that responds to click events by storing a reference to the images with this code snippet:

```
var imgs = $("img");
```

If you have an HTML page with many `<img>` elements, the use of a variable such as `imgs` can sometimes be more efficient because jQuery performs a DOM traversal only once. In this code sample, we don't use the `imgs` variable because have just three `<img>` elements, so there is no noticeable performance penalty involved in performing a search each time we reference an `<img>` element; however, it's important for you to be aware of this coding technique.

The click event on the first image causes the image to slowly fade, as shown here:

```
      // fade out when users click on the first <img>
      $("img:first").click(function () {
```

```
    $("img:first").fadeOut("slow");
});
```

The first image is slowly displayed again whenever users click on the right-most image:

```
// display first <img> when users click on the last <img>
$("img:last").click(function () {
    $("img:first").fadeIn("slow");
});
```

You can use similar code blocks to capture events on other HTML elements. In this example, we could have also captured all the <p> elements with this snippet:

```
var para = $("p");
```

However, in Listing 9.4 we reference the first and last HTML <p> elements using $("p:first") and $("p:last"), and we then perform similar fade effects.

Figure 9.4 displays the result of rendering JQMFadeInOut1.html in Listing 9.4 in landscape mode in a Chrome browser on a Macbook.

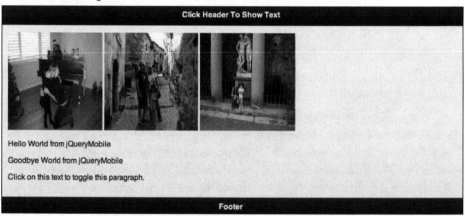

FIGURE 9.4 Fade effects on a Chrome browser on a Macbook.

Slide-Related jQuery Methods

As you can surmise, the jQuery .slideUp() and .slideDown() methods provide slide-related functionality for jQuery Mobile.

Listing 9.5 displays the contents of JQMSlideUpDown1.html that illustrates how to use the jQuery `.slideUp()` and `.slideDown()` methods in a jQuery Mobile Web page.

Listing 9.5 JQMSlideUpDown1.html

```
<!DOCTYPE html>
<html lang="en">
<head>
   <meta charset=utf-8"/>
   <title>jQuery Mobile Slide Up and Slide Down</title>

  <link rel="stylesheet"
  href="http://code.jquery.com/mobile/1.1.0/jquery.mobile-
1.1.0.min.css"/>
   <script
       src="http://code.jquery.com/jquery-1.7.1.min.js">
   </script>
   <script
       src="http://code.jquery.com/mobile/1.1.0
                    /jquery.mobile-1.1.0.min.js">
   </script>

  <style>
    #first, #second, #third, #fourth {
      background:#ff0000; margin:2px; width:100px;
      height:50px; float:left;
    }
    p {
      font-size:24px;
      color:blue;
    }
  </style>
</head>

<body>
   <div data-role="page" id="page1">
     <div data-role="header"><h3>Header</p3></div>
     <div data-role="content">
       <p>Click me or one of the Rectangles:</p>
       <div name="first" id="first">First</div>
       <div id="second">Second</div>
       <div id="third">Third</div>
       <div id="fourth">Fourth</div>
     </div>
     <div data-role="footer"><h3>Footer</p3></div>
   </div>
```

```
<script>
  $("#page1").live('pageinit', (function(event,ui) {
    $("#page1").click(function() {
      if ($("div:first").is(":hidden")) {
       $("div").show("slow");
      } else {
       $("div[name='first']").slideUp(2000);
      }

      $("div[name='first']").css({background:'#00f'})
              .show(2000).hide(2000).slideDown(2000);
    })
   })
  )
 </script>
</body>
</html>
```

Listing 9.5 contains a `<style>` element that uses CSS to apply some styling to four rectangles, followed by a code block that handles a click event anywhere in the page view:

```
$("#page1").click(function() {
  // handle a click event on the page
}
```

The heart of the jQuery Mobile code in Listing 9.5 consists of one line of code that uses method chaining to create a multi-part animation effect that 1.) changes the background color to red, 2.) performs a "show" and "hide" animation effect for two seconds, followed 3.) by a "slide" effect that occurs during two seconds, whenever users click on a rectangle, as shown here:

```
$("div[name='first']").css({background:'#00f'})
        .show(2000).hide(2000).slideDown(2000);
```

Figure 9.5 displays the result of rendering `JQMSlideUpDown1.html` in Listing 9.5 in landscape mode on an Asus Prime tablet with Android ICS.

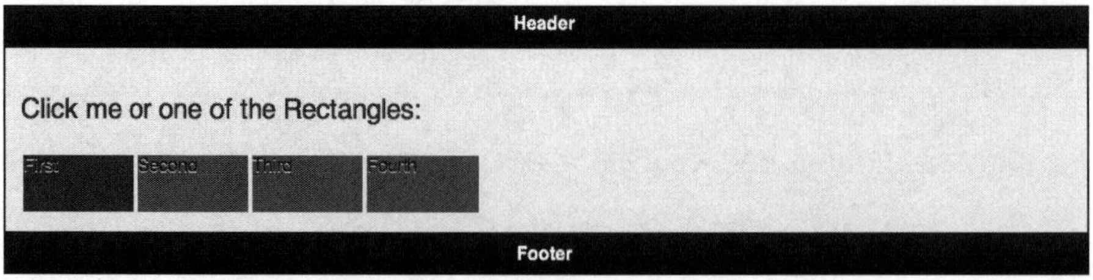

FIGURE 9.5 Fade effects on an Asus Prime tablet with Android ICS.

JQUERY MOBILE AND TRANSITION EFFECTS

jQuery Mobile uses `WebKit`-based CSS3 transforms for animating the page transitions, and `WebKit`-based browsers currently provide the best support for CSS3 transforms (but other browsers are improving their level of support). Since `WebKit`–based browsers use hardware acceleration, CSS animation effects appear smooth on mobile devices as well as laptops and desktops.

You specify a transition by applying the `data-transition` property, whose seven supported values are:

- `Fade`: simply fade the page or dialog in over the previous content
- `Flip`: an animated page flip, rotating the current view out with the other view on the reverse side
- `Pop`: the page springs into view from the center of the screen
- `Slide`: slide in from the left or right, pushing previous content out of the way
- `Slidedown`: slide down from the top, over the top of the current content
- `Slideup`: slide up to the top, revealing the next content below

jQuery Mobile also provides the `animationComplete` event, which you can be useful after adding or removing a class that applies a CSS transition.

Listing 9.6 displays the contents of `JQMTransition1.html` that illustrates how to use `slidedown` and `flip` transitions in a jQuery Mobile page.

Listing 9.6 JQMTransition1.html

```
<!DOCTYPE html>
<html lang="en">
<head>
  <meta charset=utf-8"/>
  <title>jQuery Mobile Transitions</title>

  <link rel="stylesheet"
  href="http://code.jquery.com/mobile/1.1.0/jquery.mobile-
1.1.0.min.css"/>
  <script
    src="http://code.jquery.com/jquery-1.7.1.min.js">
  </script>
  <script
    src="http://code.jquery.com/mobile/1.1.0
              /jquery.mobile-1.1.0.min.js">
  </script>
```

```
</head>

<body>
  <div data-role="page" id="first">
    <div data-role="header">
      <h2>This is the first page header</h2>
    </div>

    <div data-role="content">
     <p>
      <a href="#second" data-transition="slidedown">Go to Page
Two</a>
      </p>
    </div>

    <div data-role="footer">
      <h2>This is the first page footer</h2>
    </div>
  </div>

  <div data-role="page" id="second">
    <div data-role="header">
      <h2>This is the second page header</h2>
    </div>

    <div data-role="content">
      <p>You saw a slidedown effect
       <a href="#first" data-transition="flip"
                        data-direction="reverse">
         Go to Page #1 via 'flip' and reverse</a>
      </p>
    </div>

    <div data-role="footer">
      <h2>This is the second page footer</h2>
    </div>
  </div>
 </body>
</html>
```

Listing 9.4 contains the code for a jQuery Mobile Web page, and when you click on the link in the first page view, you will see a slide effect created by the following code snippet in the content HTML <div> of the first page view (whose id attribute has value first):

```
<a href="#second" data-transition="slidedown">Go to Page Two</a>
```

The second page view displays the following text and hyperlink:

`You saw a slidedown effect` Go to Page #1 via 'flip' and reverse

When you click on the preceding link, you will see a flip effect that is created with the following code snippet in the `content` HTML `<div>` of the second page view (whose `id` attribute has value `second`):

```
<a href="#first" data-transition="flip"
            data-direction="reverse">
```

Note that jQuery Mobile will attempt to use the reverse transition when using the automatic back button or when hiding a dialog. This simple example illustrates some page transition effects that you can create when you navigate between page view, and you can experiment with a number of different transition effects to find the effects that are suitable for your requirements.

Figure 9.6 displays the result of rendering `JQMTransition1.html` in Listing 9.6 in landscape mode in a Chrome browser on a Macbook.

FIGURE 9.6 Transition effects on a Chrome browser on a Macbook.

JQUERY MOBILE AND ANIMATION EFFECTS WITH CSS3

Recall that jQuery Mobile uses `WebKit`-based CSS3 transforms for animating the page transitions, so they only work in `WebKit`-based browsers, or browsers (such as Opera) that support the −webkit- prefix for CSS3 properties. Since WebKit browsers use hardware acceleration, CSS animation effects appear smooth on mobile devices as well as laptops and desktops.

Listing 9.7 displays the contents of JQMJPG1.html that illustrates how to use slideDown() and slideUp() in conjunction with JPG files in a jQuery Mobile page.

Listing 9.7 JQMRenderJPG1.html

```
<!DOCTYPE html>
<html lang="en">
<head>
  <meta charset=utf-8"/>
  <title>jQuery Mobile Transitions</title>

  <link rel="stylesheet"
  href="http://code.jquery.com/mobile/1.1.0/jquery.mobile-
1.1.0.min.css"/>
  <script
      src="http://code.jquery.com/jquery-1.7.1.min.js">
  </script>
  <script src="http://code.jquery.com/mobile/1.1.0
                    /jquery.mobile-1.1.0.min.js">
  </script>
 </head>

  <body>
    <div data-role="page" id="page1">
      <div data-role="header">
        <h3>Header</h3>
      </div>

      <div data-role="content">
        <img id="laurie1" src="Laurie1.jpeg" width="200"
height="200" >
        <img id="laurie2" src="Laurie2.jpeg" width="200"
height="200" >
        <p>
          <a id="button1" href="#" data-role="button">
            Click Me To Display The Right Image</a>
          <a id="button2" href="#" data-role="button">
            Click Me To Shrink The Right Image</a>
        </p>
      </div>
      <div data-role="footer">
        <h3>Footer</h3>
      </div>
```

```
    </div>

    <script>
      $("#page1").live('pageinit', (function(event,ui) {
        $("#laurie2").hover(function() {
          $(this).slideUp(800);
        });

        $("#laurie2").hover(function() {
          $(this).css({'position':'relative',
                       'width':'200px',
                       'height':'200px'
                       });
        });

        $("#button1").click(function() {
          $("#laurie2").slideDown(800);
        });

        $("#button2").click(function() {
          $("#laurie2").css({'position':'relative',
                             'width':'100px',
                             'height':'100px'
                             });
        });
      })
    )
    </script>
  });
 </body>
</html>
```

Listing 9.7 renders two images and also contains two buttons that bind to click events, and the visual effects depend on the sequence in which the buttons are clicked. When users click on the second button ("Click Me To Shrink The Right Image"), the right-most image is reduced from its initial dimensions of 200x200 to dimensions of 100x100 using this code block:

```
$("#button2").click(function() {
  $("#laurie2").css({'position':'relative',
                     'width':'100px',
                     'height':'100px'
                 });
});
```

As you can see, the preceding code block uses the jQuery css() function to modify the width and height of the right-most image, which means there is no transition effect.

Next, if users hover over the right-most image (which is now reduced in size), the image will shrink (and disappear) with a transitional effect because of the following code block:

```
$("#laurie2").hover(function() {
    $(this).slideUp(800);
});
```

Now if users click on the first button ("Click Me To Display The Right Image"), the second image will reappear (again using a transitional effect) with its original dimensions because of the following code:

```
$("#button1").click(function() {
    $("#laurie2").slideDown(800);
});
```

This code samples illustrates how easy it is to write jQuery code for creating some pleasing animation effects with images. Moreover, you can combine the jQuery animation effects with the jQuery `css()` function. For example, you can use the `css()` function to render an image with a background radial gradient effect when users click on the image, or update any other CSS properties of the image (or element) in question.

Thus, you can combine your knowledge of jQuery animation, CSS, and CSS3 graphics and animation to create interesting effects by means of simple and compact jQuery code.

Figure 9.7 displays the result of rendering `JQMJPG1.html` in Listing 9.7 in landscape mode on a Chrome browser on a Macbook.

FIGURE 9.7 Resizing JPGs with animation effects on an Chrome browser on a Macbook.

JQUERY MOBILE VIRTUAL MOUSE EVENTS

jQuery Mobile provides a set of "virtual" mouse events for handling mouse and touch events. These events are useful because each one handles a mouse event as well as its corresponding touch-based event, which can reduce the amount of code that you need to write in your Web pages. In addition, the use of virtual mouse events can support both the desktop metaphor as well as the mobile metaphor in the same Web page.

The name of a virtual mouse event in jQuery Mobile starts with the letter "v" (for "virtual") followed by the common or standard name for a mouse event. For example, the `vmousedown` virtual event "delivers" the `mousedown` event and also the `touchstart` event. The list of virtual mouse events (and their corresponding touch-related and mouse-related events) is shown here:

`vclick` (touchend or mouse click events)
`vmousecancel` (touch or mouse mousecancel events)
`vmousedown` (touchstart or mousedown events)
`vmousemove` (touchmove or mousemove events)
`vmouseover` (touch or mouseover events)
`vmouseup` (touchend or mouseup events)

Note that on touch-enabled devices, the `vclick` event is dispatched after the `vmouseup` event; however, `vmouseup` is dispatched before `vmousedown`, and `vmousedown` is dispatched before `vclick`, as you would expect. Furthermore, the `event` object contains the properties `pageX`, `pageY`, `screenX`, `screenY`, `clientX`, and `clientY`, which contain coordinate information, as you will see in a subsequent code sample.

JQUERY MOBILE AND PAGE-TURNING EFFECTS

You can create page-turning effects in jQuery Mobile applications in various ways, and in this section you will see how to use the jQuery plugin `Turn.js` whose homepage is here:

http://www.turnjs.com

This code sample contains many examples of handling jQuery Mobile virtual events as well as user gestures and key events. Although space precludes us from discussing every detail of this code sample, it's well worth your time to read the code in detail to learn some useful techniques.

Listing 9.8 displays the contents of `JQMPageTurn1.html` that illustrates how to use `Turn.js` in order to simulate page-turning effects in a jQuery Mobile application.

Listing 9.8 JQMPageTurn1.html

```html
<!DOCTYPE html>
<html lang="en">
  <head>
   <meta charset="utf-8"/>
   <title>jQuery Mobile Page Turn</title>
  <link rel="stylesheet"
  href="http://code.jquery.com/mobile/1.1.0/jquery.mobile-
1.1.0.min.css"/>
   <script
       src="http://code.jquery.com/jquery-1.7.1.min.js">
   </script>
   <script src="http://code.jquery.com/mobile/1.1.0
                     /jquery.mobile-1.1.0.min.js">
   </script>

   <script src="jquery.easing.1.3.js"></script>
   <script src="turn.min.js"> </script>

   <style>
    #magazine {
      width:800px;
      height:300px;
      border-style: solid;
      border-width: 4px;
      border-color: black;
    }

    #magazine .turn-page{
      width:400px;
      height:300px;
      background-color:#fcc;
    }
   </style>
  </head>

  <body>
    <div data-role="page" id="page1">
      <div data-role="header"><h2>Header1</h2></div>
      <div data-role="content" id="content">
        <div turn-effect="flipboard">
          <p>Create page-turning effects in HTML5 web pages with
```

```
Turn.js:</p>
        <p>http://www.turnjs.com</p>
        </p>
    </div>

    <div id="magazine" class="pages shadow turn-page">
        <div> This is content for Page 1
          <p>
          Using HTML5 Web Storage
          Storing Images in HTML5 LocalStorage
          HTML5 Web Databases
          Using An HTML5 IndexedDB Database
          </p>
        </div>

        <div> This is content for Page 2
          <p>
          Using HTML5 Web Storage
          Storing Images in HTML5 LocalStorage
          HTML5 Web Databases
          Using An HTML5 IndexedDB Database
          </p>
        </div>

        <div> This is content for Page 3
          <p>
          CHAPTER 1 HTML5 Features
          A High-Level Perspective Of HTML5
          What is HTML5?
          Useful Online Tools for HTML5 Web Pages
          Modernizr
          </p>
        </div>

        <div> This is content for Page 4
          <p>
            This is a great plugin!
          </p>
        </div>
      </div>
    </div>
    <div data-role="footer"><h2>Footer1</h2></div>
  </div>

  <script>
    $("#page1").live('pageinit', (function(event,ui) {
```

```
  $('#magazine').turn();
 })
)

$('#page1').bind('vmousedown', function(event) {
    $('#magazine').turn('next');
})

$('#page2').bind('vmousedown', function(event) {
    $('#magazine').turn('next');
})

$('#page3').bind('vmousedown', function(event) {
    $('#magazine').turn('next');
})

$('#page4').bind('vmousedown', function(event) {
    $('#magazine').turn({page:1});
});

<!--
  The following lengthy code block uses method chaining in
  order to bind touchstart, touchmove, and touchend events
-->
$('#page1').bind('touchstart', function(e) {
  var t = e.originalEvent.touches;
  if (t[0]) touchStart = {x: t[0].pageX, y: t[0].pageY};

  touchEnd = null;
}).bind('touchmove', function(e) {
  var t = e.originalEvent.touches, pos = $('#magazine').off-
set();

  if (t[0].pageX>pos.left && t[0].pageY>pos.top &&
      t[0].pageX<pos.left+$('#magazine').width() &&
      t[0].pageY<pos.top+$('#magazine').height()) {

    if (t.length==1)
    e.preventDefault();
    if (t[0]) touchEnd = {x: t[0].pageX, y: t[0].pageY};
  }
}).bind('touchend', function(e) {
  if (window.touchStart && window.touchEnd) {
    var that = $('#magazine'),
      w = that.width()/2,
      d = {x: touchEnd.x-touchStart.x,
```

```
                    y: touchEnd.y-touchStart.y},
            pos = {x: touchStart.x-that.offset().left,
                    y: touchStart.y-that.offset().top};

        if (Math.abs(d.y)<100)
          if (d.x>100 && pos.x<w)
            $('#magazine').turn('previous');
          else if (d.x<100 && pos.x>w)
            $('#magazine').turn('next');
      }
    });
  </script>

  <script>
    $(window).bind('keydown', function(e){
        if (e.keyCode==37) {
            $('#magazine').turn('previous');
        } else if (e.keyCode==39) {
            $('#magazine').turn('next');
        }
    }).bind('hashchange', function() {
        var page = checkHash();
        $('#magazine').turn('page', page);
    });
  </script>
</body>
</html>
```

Listing 9.8 contains jQuery Mobile code that simulates a page turning effect using two JavaScript libraries:

```
<script src="jquery.easing.1.3.js"></script>
<script src="turn.min.js"> </script>
```

The "pages" are rendered in multiple HTML `<div>` elements that are children of an outer "container-like" HTML `<div>` element whose id attribute has value magazine.

```
<div id="magazine" class="pages shadow turn-page">
  <div> This is content for Page 1
    <p>
    Using HTML5 Web Storage
    Storing Images in HTML5 LocalStorage
    HTML5 Web Databases
    Using An HTML5 IndexedDB Database
```

```
        </p>
      </div>
      // other <div> elements omitted
    </div>
```

Note that the container `<div>` element contains a `class` attribute that specifies three CSS classes called `pages`, `shadow`, and `turn-page` that are specific to `Turn.js`.

The page-turning effect is performed when a click or mouse-down event with this type of code:

```
$('#page1').bind('vmousedown', function(event) {
    $('#magazine').turn('next');
})
```

You can also control the direction (forward or backward) of the page that is rendered. For example, when users click on the final page (which is `page4`), the following code block displays the first page in the magazine:

```
$('#page4').bind('vmousedown', function(event) {
    $('#magazine').turn({page:1});
});
```

In addition to the functionality in Listing 9.7, `Turn.js` supports method chaining for turning multiple pages. For example, you can turn two pages forward with this code snippet:

```
$('selector').turn('next').turn('next');
```

Turn to the next page and then the previous page (no change):

```
$('selector').turn('next').turn('previous');
```

Turn to the next page without using a page flip effect:

```
$('selector').turn('next').turn('stop');
```

Explore the `Turn.js` documentation, where you will find even more useful functionality in this toolkit.

Figure 9.8 displays the result of rendering `JQMPageTurn1.html` in Listing 9.8 in landscape mode on an Asus Prime tablet with Android ICS.

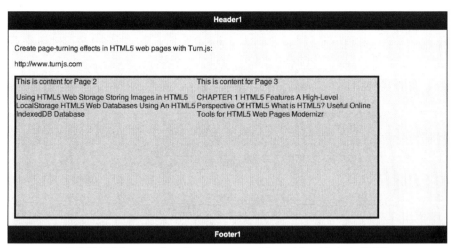

FIGURE 9.8 Page-turning effects on an Asus Prime tablet with Android ICS.

CSS3 2D/3D ANIMATION EFFECTS WITH JQUERY MOBILE

Listing 9.9 displays the contents of `JQM2DAnimationRGrad4Reflect1.html` and Listing 9.10 displays a portion of `JQM2DAnimationRGrad4Reflect1.css` that illustrates how to create CSS3 2D animation effects in jQuery Mobile.

Listing 9.9 `JQM2DAnimationRGrad4Reflect1.html`

```
<!DOCTYPE html>
<html lang="en">
<head>
  <meta charset="utf-8"/>
  <title>CSS3 2D Animation Radial Gradient Example</title>

  <link rel="stylesheet" href="JQM2DAnimationRGrad4Reflect1.css"
        type="text/css">

  <link rel="stylesheet"
   href="http://code.jquery.com/mobile/1.1.0/jquery.mobile-
1.1.0.min.css"/>
    <script
       src="http://code.jquery.com/jquery-1.7.1.min.js">
    </script>
      <script src="http://code.jquery.com/mobile/1.1.0
                      /jquery.mobile-1.1.0.min.js">
    </script>
```

```
</head>

<body>
  <div  data-role="page">
    <div data-role="header"><h3>Header</h3></div>
    <div data-role="content">
      <div id="outer">
        <div id="radial3">Text3</div>
        <div id="radial2">Text2</div>
        <div id="radial4">Text4</div>
        <div id="radial1">Text1</div>
      </div>
    </div>
    <div data-role="footer"><h3>Footer</h3></div>
  </div>
</body>
</html>
```

Listing 9.9 is straightforward: the jQuery Mobile code contains four HTML `<div>` elements that have corresponding CSS3 selectors in the associated CSS stylesheet. The four CSS3 selectors define radial gradients (defined in Listing 9.10), which are very similar to CSS3 code samples in Chapter 2 (read the appropriate section if you need to refresh your memory).

Listing 9.10 JQM2DAnimationRGrad4Reflect1.css

```
#outer {
position: relative; top: 10px; left: 0px;
width:   600px;
height:  400px;
}

/* define animation effects */
@-webkit-keyframes upperLeft {
    0% {
        -webkit-transform: matrix(1.0, 0.5, -0.5, 1.0, 0, 0);
    }
    50% {
        -webkit-transform: matrix(1.0, 0.5,  0.0, 1.0, 0, 0);
    }
    75% {
        -webkit-transform: matrix(1.0, 0.0,  0.5, 1.0, 0, 0);
    }
    100% {
        -webkit-transform: matrix(1.0, 0.0,  0.0, 1.0, 0, 0);
    }
```

```
}
// three other similar keyframes omitted for brevity
#radial1 {
font-size: 24px;
width:   600px;
height: 100px;
position: absolute; top: 400px; left: 0px;

background: -webkit-gradient(
  radial, 400 25%, 20, 100 25%, 40, from(red),
  color-stop(0.05, orange), color-stop(0.4, yellow),
  color-stop(0.6, red), color-stop(0.9, blue),
  to(#fff)
 );
-webkit-box-reflect: right 15px;
-box-reflect: right 15px;
-webkit-animation-name: upperLeft;
-webkit-animation-duration: 10s;
}
// three other similar selectors omitted for brevity
```

Listing 9.10 displays the definition of a CSS3 `keyframes` called `upper-Left`, and also the contents of the CSS3 selector `#radial1` that is used to style to the corresponding HTML `<div>` element in Listing 9.9. Only a portion of the code is shown in Listing 9.10 to avoid code duplication, but the entire code listing is available on the accompanying DVD.

The key point to notice is that even though the visual effects in this code sample are not new, this code demonstrates you how easily you can combine jQuery Mobile code with CSS3 2D/3D graphics and animation effects.

Figure 9.9 renders `JQM2DAnimationRGrad4Reflect1.html` in Listing 9.9 in landscape mode on an iPad 3.

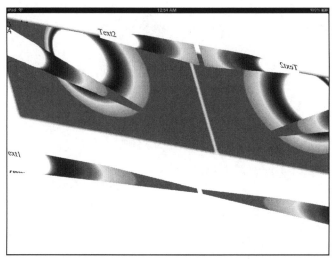

FIGURE 9.9 CSS3 2D effects on an iPad 3.

The JQM3DAnimRotate3DLGrad2SkewOpacityRep4Reflect1.html HTML5 Web page creates CSS3 3D animation effects. Its contents are not displayed here because the code is similar to Listing 9.12, but you can find the entire code listing on the accompanying DVD.

Figure 9.10 displays JQM3DAnimRotate3DLGrad2SkewOpacityRep4Reflect1.html in landscape mode on an Asus Prime tablet with Android ICS.

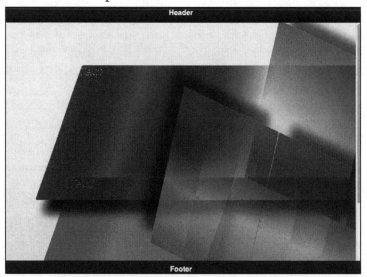

FIGURE 9.10 CSS3 3D effects on an Asus Prime tablet with Android ICS.

CSS3 3D ANIMATION WITH TAP EVENTS

The HTML5 Web page JQMCSS3AnimTap.html shows you how to detect user tap events and then create CSS3 3D animation effects. The complete code is available on the accompanying DVD, and its contents are not shown here because most of it is already familiar to you.

However, Figure 9.11 displays JQMCSS3AnimTap.html in landscape mode on an Asus Prime tablet with Android ICS.

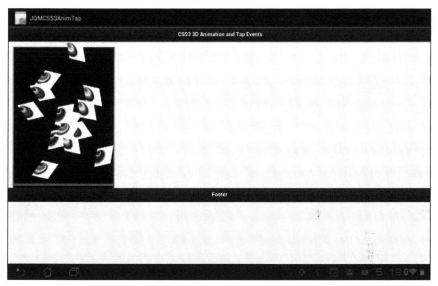

FIGURE 9.11 CSS3 3D tap animation on an Asus Prime tablet with Android ICS.

JQUERY MOBILE AND DYNAMIC ANIMATION EFFECTS

Earlier in this chapter you learned about jQuery Mobile virtual mouse events, and in this section you will see an example of how to create DOM elements and to associate them with animation-related CSS3 selectors.

Listing 9.11 displays the contents of JQMSketchSolidDynamicDOM1.html that illustrates how to capture user gestures to dynamically create and append new HTML <div> elements into the HTML <div> element whose id attribute has value content in order to create a "sketching" program.

Listing 9.11 JQMSketchSolidDynamicDOM1.html

```
<!DOCTYPE html>
<html lang="en">
<head>
  <meta charset=utf-8"/>
  <title>jQuery Mobile Sketching Example</title>

  <link rel="stylesheet"
    href="http://code.jquery.com/mobile/1.1.0/jquery.mobile-
1.1.0.min.css"/>
  <script
      src="http://code.jquery.com/jquery-1.7.1.min.js">
  </script>
  <script src="http://code.jquery.com/mobile/1.1.0
                      /jquery.mobile-1.1.0.min.js">
  </script>
  <style>

  #content {
      width: 100%;
      height: 300px;
  }
  </style>
</head>

<body>
  <div data-role="page" id="page1">
    <div data-role="header"> <h3>Header</h3> </div>
    <div data-role="content" id="content"> </div>
    <div data-role="footer"> <h3>Footer</h3> </div>
  </div>

  <script>
   $("#page1").live('pageinit', (function(event,ui){
      var insertNode = false;
      var newNode;

      // mouse-down means insertNode:
      $("#content").bind('vmousedown', function() {
        console.log("start");
        insertNode = true;
      });

      // mouse-up means no insertNode:
      $("#content").bind('vmouseup', function() {
        console.log("stop");
```

```
        insertNode = false;
    });

    $("#content").bind('vmousemove', function(e) {
        // are users are moving their mouse?
        if(insertNode == true) {
            console.log("move");

            // create a rectangle at the current position
            newNode = $('<div>').css({'position':'absolute',
                                      'background-
color':'#ff0000',

                                      'width':'8px',
                                      'height':'8px',
                                      top: e.pageY,
                                      left: e.pageX
                                     });

            //append the rectangle to the content <div>
            $("#content").append(newNode);
        }
    });
    })
    );
  </script>
 </body>
</html>
```

Listing 9.11 contains jQuery Mobile code that binds to the vmousedown, vmouseup, and vmousemove virtual events. The code uses the first two virtual mouse events to determine if a vmousemove event is accompanied with a vmousedown event; if the latter is true, then a new HTML <div> element is programmatically created at the current location of a user's mouse and then inserted into the DOM, as shown here:

```
// create a rectangle at the current position
newNode = $('<div>').css({'position':'absolute',
                          'background-color':'#ff0000',
                          'width':'8px',
                          'height':'8px',
                          top: e.pageY,
                          left: e.pageX
                         });
```

```
//append the rectangle to the content <div>
$("#content").append(newNode);
```

Listing 9.11 is yet another example of combining coding techniques that you learned earlier in this chapter in order to create a new visual effect (i.e., freestyle sketching on the screen).

Figure 9.12 displays JQMSketchSolidDynamicDOM1.html in landscape mode in a Chrome browser on a Macbook.

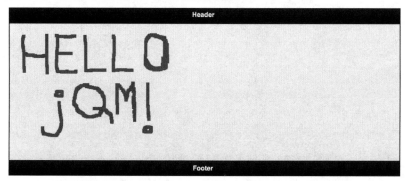

FIGURE 9.12 Sketching effects on a Chrome browser on a Macbook.

JQUERY MOBILE AND 3D CUBE ANIMATION EFFECTS

In earlier chapters, you learned how to create an HMTL5 Web page using CSS3 to create a 3D cube whose faces move when users hover with their mouse over any of the three faces of the cube. This section shows you how to convert that code into a jQuery Mobile Web page.

Listing 9.12 displays the contents of JQM3DCube1.html that illustrates how to render a 3D cube with CSS3. Since the CSS stylesheet is the same as the corresponding code samples in earlier chapters, its contents are not shown in this section, but the source code is available on the accompanying DVD.

Listing 9.12 JQM3DCube1.html

```
<!DOCTYPE html>
<html lang="en">
 <head>
  <title>CSS3 3D Cube Example</title>
  <meta charset="utf-8"/>
  <link href="JQM3DCube1.css" rel="stylesheet" type="text/css">

  <link rel="stylesheet"
```

```
   href="http://code.jquery.com/mobile/1.1.0/jquery.mobile-
                                           1.1.0.min.css"/>
   <script
       src="http://code.jquery.com/jquery-1.7.1.min.js">
   </script>
   <script src="http://code.jquery.com/mobile/1.1.0
                     /jquery.mobile-1.1.0.min.js">
   </script>
  </head>
 </head>

  <body>
    <div data-role="page" id="page1">
      <div data-role="header">
        <h3>Tap on the Cube Faces:</h3>
      </div>
      <div data-role="content">
        <div id="outer">
         <div id="top">Text1</div>
         <div id="left">Text2</div>
         <div id="right">Text3</div>
        </div>
      </div>
      <div data-role="footer"> <h3>Footer</h3> </div>
    </div>

    <script>
      $("#page1").live('pageinit', (function(event,ui){ }));
    </script>
  </body>
</html>
```

Listing 9.12 contains jQuery Mobile code that contains the definition for three HTML <div> elements that serve as placeholders for the left, top, and right faces of the cube, and a tiny jQuery Mobile code snippet, as shown here:

```
<script>
  $("#page1").live('pageinit', (function(event,ui){ }));
</script>
```

All the real "action" in this code sample takes place in the CSS3 stylesheet JQM3DCube1.css, a portion of which is shown in Listing 9.13.

Listing 9.13 JQM3DCube1.css

```
/* animation effects */
#right:hover {
```

```
-webkit-transition: -webkit-transform 3.0s ease;
-transition: transform 3.0s ease;

-webkit-transform : scale(1.2) skew(-10deg, -30deg)
rotate(-45deg);
-transform : scale(1.2) skew(-10deg, -30deg) rotate(-45deg);
}

#left:hover {
-webkit-transition: -webkit-transform 2.0s ease;
-transition: transform 2.0s ease;

-webkit-transform : scale(0.8) skew(-10deg, -30deg)
rotate(-45deg);
-transform : scale(0.8) skew(-10deg, -30deg) rotate(-45deg);
}

#top:hover {
-webkit-transition: -webkit-transform 2.0s ease;
-transition: transform 2.0s ease;

-webkit-transform : scale(0.5) skew(-20deg, -30deg) rotate(45deg);
-transform : scale(0.5) skew(-20deg, -30deg) rotate(45deg);
}
// details omitted for brevity
```

The CSS3 selectors in Listing 9.13 are taken from a code sample in Chapter 2 that also illustrates how to render a cube using CSS3 selectors. In this example, the CSS3 selectors apply various 3D animation effects whenever users tap or hover over one of the faces of the 3D cube.

Figure 9.13 displays JQM3DCube1.html in Listing 9.12 in landscape mode on an Asus Prime tablet with Android ICS.

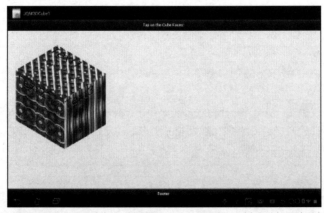

FIGURE 9.13 jQuery Mobile and CSS3 on an Asus Prime tablet with Android ICS.

JQUERY MOBILE BOUNCING BALLS

In Chapter 6, you learned how to render a set of "bouncing balls" using jQuery, and you can create the same effect using jQuery Mobile. The DVD contains several other code samples with similar techniques using jQuery Mobile, and you can use these techniques as "building blocks" to create more complex visual effects.

The code samples are primarily for fun. You can experiment with them to create other interesting effects by modifying additional CSS properties dynamically.

ACCELEROMETER VALUES WITH JQUERY

In Chapter 5, you learned how to use jQuery in order to obtain accelerometer values, and the example in this section illustrates how you can use jQuery Mobile to obtain accelerometer values for a mobile device.

Listing 9.14 displays the contents of JQMAccelerometer1.html that illustrates how to display the accelerometer values of a mobile device whenever the device undergoes acceleration in any direction. Listing 9.15 displays the contents of the CSS stylesheet JQMAccelerometer1.css whose selectors are used to style elements in the HTML Web page.

Listing 9.14 JQMAccelerometer1.html

```
    <!DOCTYPE html>
<html lang="en">
<head>
  <meta charset="utf-8">
  <title>JQuery Mobile Accelerometer</title>

  <link rel="stylesheet" href="JQMAccelerometer1.css"/>

  <link rel="stylesheet"
   href="http://code.jquery.com/mobile/1.1.0
               /jquery.mobile-1.1.0.min.css"/>
  <script
     src="http://code.jquery.com/jquery-1.7.1.min.js">
  </script>
  <script src="http://code.jquery.com/mobile/1.1.0
                   /jquery.mobile-1.1.0.min.js">
  </script>
```

```
<script>
  var colorX = "", colorY = "", colorZ = "";
  var intx = 0, inty = 0, intz = 0;
  var colors = ['#f00', '#ff0', '#00f'];

  $(window).bind("devicemotion", function(e){
      var accelEvent = e.originalEvent,
          acceler = accelEvent.accelerationIncludingGravity,
          x = acceler.x, y = acceler.y, z = acceler.z;

      if(x < 0)        { intx = 0; }
      else if(x < 1)   { intx = 1; }
      else             { intx = 2; }

      if(y < 0)        { inty = 0; }
      else if(y < 1)   { inty = 1; }
      else             { inty = 2; }

      if(z < 0)        { intz = 0; }
      else if(z < 1)   { intz = 1; }
      else             { intz = 2; }

      colorX = colors[intx];
      colorY = colors[inty];
      colorZ = colors[intz];

      $("#valueX").css("backgroundColor", colorX);
      $("#valueY").css("backgroundColor", colorY);
      $("#valueZ").css("backgroundColor", colorZ);

      $("#valueX").html("<p>Acceleration x: <b>" + x + "</b></
p>");
      $("#valueY").html("<p>Acceleration y: <b>" + x + "</b></
p>");
      $("#valueZ").html("<p>Acceleration z: <b>" + x + "</b></
p>");

      $("#values").html(
          "Acceleration x: <b>" + x + "</b><br/>" +
          "Acceleration y: <b>" + y + "</b><br/>" +
          "Acceleration z: <b>" + z + "</b>"
      );
  });
</script>
</head>
```

```
<body>
  <div data-role="page" id="page1">
    <div data-role="header"><h3>JQuery Mobile Accelerometer</div>
    <div data-role="content" id="content">
      <h2>JQuery Mobile and Accelerometer Values</h2>
      <div id="outer">
        <div id="valueX"></div> <div id="radial1"></div>
        <div id="valueY"></div> <div id="radial2"></div>
        <div id="valueZ"></div> <div id="radial3"></div>
      </div>
    </div>
    <div data-role="footer"><h3>Footer</h3></div>
  </div>

  <script>
    $("#page1").live('pageinit', (function(event){}));
  </script>
</body>
</html>
```

Listing 9.14 contains jQuery Mobile code that renders three HTML5 <div> elements (one for each axis of the acceleration) whose color depends on the acceleration of the mobile device. The acceleration in each direction is adjusted to provide an index into an array of colors, which is then used to display the appropriate color, as shown here for the x axis:

```
var accelEvent = e.originalEvent,
    acceler = accelEvent.accelerationIncludingGravity,
    x = acceler.x, y = acceler.y, z = acceler.z;

if(x < 0)       { intx = 0; }
else if(x < 1) { intx = 1; }
else            { intx = 2; }

colorX = colors[intx];
$("#valueX").css("backgroundColor", colorX);
$("#valueX").html("<p>Acceleration x: <b>" + x + "</b></p>");
```

Similar code is used for rendering the color for the acceleration along the y axis and the z axis for the mobile device.

Listing 9.15 JQMAccelerometer1.css

```
#outer {
width:   650px;
```

```
height: 350px;
position: relative; top: 10px; left: 10px;
}

p { font-size: 16px; }

#valueX {
width:   350px;
height: 100px;
position: absolute; top: 0px; left: 0px;
background-color: white;
}

#valueY {
width:   350px;
height: 100px;
position: absolute; top: 100px; left: 0px;
background-color: white;
}

#valueZ {
width:   350px;
height: 100px;
position: absolute; top: 200px; left: 0px;
background-color: white;
}

#radial1 {
width:   200px;
height: 100px;
position: absolute; top: 0px; left: 350px;
background: -webkit-gradient(
  radial, 500 40%, 0, 301 25%, 360, from(red),
  color-stop(0.05, orange), color-stop(0.4, yellow),
  color-stop(0.6, green), color-stop(0.8, blue),
  to(#fff)
 );
-webkit-background-size: 50% 33%;
-webkit-border-radius: 100%;
}

#radial2 {
width:   200px;
height: 100px;
position: absolute; top: 100px; left: 350px;
```

```
background: -webkit-gradient(
  radial, 500 40%, 0, 301 25%, 360, from(yellow),
  color-stop(0.05, orange), color-stop(0.4, yellow),
  color-stop(0.6, green), color-stop(0.8, blue),
  to(#fff)
 );
-webkit-background-size: 50% 33%;
-webkit-border-radius: 100%;
}

#radial3 {
width:  200px;
height: 100px;
position: absolute; top: 200px; left: 350px;

background: -webkit-gradient(
  radial, 500 40%, 0, 301 25%, 360, from(blue),
  color-stop(0.05, orange), color-stop(0.4, yellow),
  color-stop(0.6, green), color-stop(0.8, blue),
  to(#fff)
 );
-webkit-background-size: 50% 33%;
-webkit-box-shadow:  0px 0px 8px #000;
-webkit-border-radius: 100%;
}
```

Listing 9.15 contains familiar CSS3 selectors, and you can find the entire code listing on the accompanying DVD.

Figure 9.14 displays JQMAccelerometer1.html in Listing 9.15 in land-scape mode on an Asus Prime tablet with Android ICS.

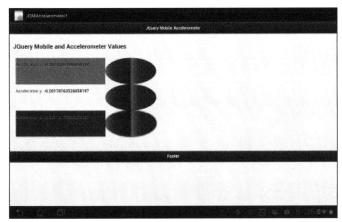

FIGURE 9.14 jQuery Mobile accelerometer on an Asus Prime tablet with Android ICS.

SUMMARY

This chapter introduced you to animation effects in jQuery Mobile, and you saw code samples that illustrated how to perform various effects. You learned how to do the following in jQuery Mobile:

- Handle page transition Events
- Positioning the header and footer
- Page hide and show events
- Portrait mode versus landscape mode
- Creating animation effects with jQuery methods
- Animation with fade-related methods
- Animation with slide-related methods
- CSS3 2D animation effects
- CSS3 3D animation effects
- CSS3 3D animation with tap events
- jQuery Mobile with bouncing balls and cubes
- jQuery Mobile and accelerometer

The next chapter provides an overview of several HTML5-related technologies and the availability of jQuery and jQuery Mobile plugins for those technologies.

OTHER HTML5 TECHNOLOGIES

This chapter provides an overview of several HTML5-related technologies and code samples for many of these technologies. Keep in mind that new jQuery plugins are continually being written, so it's worth comparing the latest jQuery plugins with the plugins that are covered in this chapter. Then you can decide which ones are best suited for your specific requirements.

The HTML5 technologies in this chapter are presented according to their W3C status: W3C Recommendation (REC), Candidate Recommendation (CR), Last Call (LC), Working Draft (WD), and experimental APIs. They are presented alphabetically by section. This approach enables you to quickly determine the status of each HTML5 technology, which is the main advantage over using a pure alphabetical listing of HTML5 technologies.

The first part of this chapter briefly describes the stages of the W3C process, after which you will discover that the only two HTML5 technologies in the REC status are SVG (covered in a previous chapter) and MathML (which is not covered in this book).

The second part of this chapter contains the HTML5 technologies with a W3C CR status, which includes the Battery API, Geolocation, WebSockets, the Vibration API, and XHR2. The XHR2 section contains three Ajax-related examples, starting with a generic Ajax code sample, followed by a jQuery-based Ajax code sample. You will then learn about CORS, after which the code sample that uses Ajax with XHR2 (`XmlHTTPRequest2`) will make sense.

Next, you will see a jQuery-based code sample that illustrates drag and drop for JPG files (which is simpler than "pure" HTML5 Drag and Drop APIs), an example of invoking some of the HTML5 file APIs in jQuery, and finally a jQuery plugin for obtaining geolocation information about users. You will also learn about the jQuery plugins jStorage and jStore that provide a layer of abstraction on top of the HTML5 storage APIs.

The third part of this chapter presents HTML5 technologies whose W3C status is LC, which includes HTML5 Contacts, Drag and Drop (DnD), Web Messaging, and Sever-Sent Events (SSE).

The fourth part of this chapter provides an overview of HTML5 technologies whose W3C status is WD, which includes Audio Processing, HTML5 File APIs, Web Intents, Microdata, Web Notifications, WAI ARIA, Web Workers, History APIs, and Offline Web Applications. The final portion of this chapter covers the experimental HTML5 technologies, which includes Firefox OS (formerly B2G) and Voice Recognition (TTS).

This chapter also contains information about jQuery plugins that are available for various HTML5 technologies because it's often easier to use jQuery plugins than the underlying HTML5 APIs, which are presented in broad brushstrokes. However, if you do decide to use jQuery plugins, you also need to consider the tradeoffs that are involved, such as greater file size overhead, performance differences, and memory footprint for smaller devices that may affect your decision to use jQuery, jQuery Mobile, or other toolkits in your Web applications. Moreover, loading extra files might also load more code than you actually need, and there is also the maintenance aspect (such as keeping up with version changes) for your code.

If you have the choice (and perhaps the "luxury"), you probably prefer ease of coding instead of getting bogged down in long and tedious code samples when there are simpler alternatives available. For example, the code sample that uses jQuery for HTML5 Drag and Drop is much more straightforward than a code sample that directly invokes the existing HTML5 DnD APIs.

The other advantage of simpler code samples is that they will quickly introduce you to a number of HTML5 technologies, after which you will be in a better position to explore the nuances of those HTML5 technologies. Another scenario is to combine jQuery Mobile with other toolkits, such as PhoneGap (discussed in Chapter 13) or appMobi (which is not discussed in this book). Toolkits such as PhoneGap provide support for hardware functionality, and you can also combine PhoneGap with jQuery Mobile. Your application requirements and constraints will determine your choice of toolkits (if any) for your mobile Web applications.

In general, jQuery and jQuery Mobile will work with other toolkits, but you ought to check online forums for any issues that might affect your Web applications. Finally, if you prefer not to use jQuery plugins, you can perform an Internet search to find online tutorials that illustrate to create HTML5 Web pages using pure HTML5 APIs for all the HTML5 technologies that are covered in this book.

THE STAGES IN THE W3C REVIEW PROCESS

If you are unfamiliar with the various stages of the W3C process, a brief description (from earliest stage to final stage) is provided below.

A WD (Working Draft) document is the first form of a standard that is publicly available. Comments are widely accepted (but not guaranteed to be incorporated), and this document could differ significantly from its final form.

A LC (Last Call) status involves the creation of a public record of the responses of a working group to all comments about a specification. This stage also handles bug reports about a specification. Incidentally, HTML5 reached the LC status in the W3C in May of 2011.

A CR (Candidate Recommendation) status is firm than the WD document (major features have been finalized). The goal is to elicit assistance from the development community regarding the extent to which the standard can be implemented.

A PR (Proposed Recommendation) status means that the standard has passed two previous stages, and at this point the document is submitted to the W3C for final approval.

A REC (Recommendation) status is the final stage of a ratification process, comparable to a published technical standard in many other industries. The criterion for the specification becoming a W3C Recommendation is "two 100% complete and fully interoperable implementations."

Recall that Chapter 1 describes some of the groups that create specifications, with detailed information about APIs for the technologies that are discussed in this chapter.

HTML5 APIS IN W3C RECOMMENDATION STATUS (REC)

This section of the chapter contains a set of HTML5 APIs that have Recommendation status. You might be surprised to discover that SVG and MathML are the only two technologies with REC status. Both of these technologies are mature and included under the HTML5 umbrella. You read about SVG in Chapter 4 (and additional material is in an Appendix), whereas MathML 3.0 is not covered in this book.

HTML5 APIS IN W3C CANDIDATE RECOMMENDATION STATUS (CR)

This section of the chapter contains a set of HTML5 APIs that have Candidate Recommendation status. Although the HTML5 technologies Navigation Timing, RDFa, and Selectors have CR status, they are not discussed in this book.

Battery API (DAP)

The Battery API (maintained by the DAP working group) provides information about the battery status of the hosting device. The following simple code snippet writes the battery level to the console each time the level changes:

```
navigator.battery.onlevelchange = function () {
   console.log(navigator.battery.level);
};
```

Listing 10.1 displays the contents of the HTML Web page `Battery.html` that illustrates how to use the Battery API in a Web page.

Listing 10.1 `Battery.html`

```
<!DOCTYPE html>
<html>
<head>
 <meta charset="utf-8"/>
 <title>Battery Status API Example</title>
 <script>
  var battery = navigator.battery;

  if(battery != null) {
      battery.onchargingchange = function () {
         document.querySelector('#charging').textContent =
            battery.charging ? 'charging' : 'not charging';
      };

      battery.onlevelchange = function () {
         document.querySelector('#level').textContent =
                                          battery.level;
      };

      battery.ondischargingtimechange = function () {
        document.querySelector('#dischargingTime').textContent =
                                  battery.dischargingTime / 60;
      };
```

```
    } else {
        console.log("Battery not Supported in this Browser");
    }
  </script>
</head>

<body>
  <div id="charging">(charging state unknown)</div>
  <div id="level">(battery level unknown)</div>
  <div id="dischargingTime">(discharging time unknown)</div>
</body>
</html>
```

Listing 10.1 contains JavaScript code that first ensures that `navigator.battery` is non-null, and then defines three straightforward JavaScript functions that handle change-related battery events: `onchargingchange`, `onlevelchange`, and `ondischargingtimechange`. The JavaScript functions simply update the contents of an associated `<div>` element that is located in the `<body>` element of Listing 10.1.

You can find additional information about the Battery API in the W3C specification:

http://www.w3.org/TR/battery-status

HTML5 GEOLOCATION

Geolocation allows users to share their current location. Location may be determined by the following methods:

- Cell tower
- GPS hardware on the device
- IP address
- Wireless network connection

The actual method that is used depends on the browser and the capabilities of the device. The browser then determines the location and passes it back to the Geolocation API. Note that the W3C Geolocation specification mentions that there is no guarantee that the Geolocation API returns the device's actual location.

The `geolocation` object is a child object of `window.navigator`. You can check if your browser supports `geolocation` with the following type of code block:

```
if(window.navigator.geolocation) {
  // geolocation supported
} else {
  // geolocation not supported
}
```

The W3C Geolocation API enables you to obtain geolocation information in a browser session that is running on a device. The `geolocation` object is available in the global `window.navigator` object, accessed via `window.navigator.geolocation`.

Note that the Geolocation API requires users to allow a Web application to access location information.

The Geolocation object contains the following three methods:

- `getCurrentPosition(successCallback, errorCallback, options)`
- `watchPosition(successCallback, errorCallback, options)`
- `clearWatch(watchId)`

The method `getCurrentPosition()` tries to get geolocation information, and then calls the first method if it's successful; otherwise, it calls the second method in its argument list.

The method `watchPosition()` obtains the geolocation at regular intervals; success and failure are handled through the two JavaScript methods in its list of arguments.

Finally, the method `clearWatch(watchId)` stops the watch process based on the value of `watchId`.

The major difference between the two methods is that the `watchPosition()` method will return a value immediately upon being called which uniquely identifies that watch operation.

A table that displays support for geolocation on desktop and mobile browsers is here:

http://caniuse.com/geolocation

Obtain a User's Position with getCurrentPosition()

The `PositionOptions` object is an optional parameter that can be passed to the `getCurrentPosition()` method, which is also an optional parameter to the `watchPosition()` method. All of the properties in the `PositionOp-`

`tions` object are optional as well.

For example, you can define an instance of a `PositionOptions` object by means of the following JavaScript code block:

```
var options = {
  enableHighAccuracy: true,
  maximumAge: 60000,
  timeout: 45000
};
```

Next, we can invoke the `getCurrentPosition()` method by specifying a JavaScript success function, a JavaScript error function, and the previously defined `options` variable, as shown here:

```
navigator.geolocation.getCurrentPosition(successCallback,
                                          errorCallback,
                                          options);
```

Track a User's Position with watchPosition()

This method is useful when an application requires an updated position each time that a device changes location. The watch operation is an asynchronous operation that is invoked as shown here:

```
var watcher = null;
var options = { enableHighAccuracy: true, timeout: 30000 };

if (window.navigator.geolocation) {
    watcher = navigator.geolocation.watchPosition(
                successCallback,errorCallback, options);
} else {
    alert('Your browser does not support geolocation.');
}

function successCallback(position) {
    console.log("Success obtaining the device location");
}

// Error obtaining the location
function errorCallback(error) {
    console.log("Error obtaining the device location");
    }
```

If your browser supports Geolocation, the JavaScript variable `watcher` is initialized via an invocation of the `watchPosition()` method of the `geolocation` object. Notice that the JavaScript functions `successCallback()` and `errorCallback()` for handling success or failure, respectively (in our case these functions simply display a message in you browser's console).

The W3C Geolocation API provides a method for clearing a watch operation by passing a `watchId` to the `clearWatch()` method, as shown here:

```
navigator.geolocation.clearWatch(watcher);
```

After creating a new watch operation you can remove that watch after successfully retrieving the position of a device, as shown here:

```
var watcher = null;
var options = {enableHighAccuracy: true,timeout: 45000 };

if (window.navigator.geolocation) {
watcher = navigator.geolocation.watchPosition(successCallback,
            errorCallback, options);
} else {
alert('Your browser does not support geolocation.');
}

function successCallback(position) {
  navigator.geolocation.clearWatch(watcher);
  // Do something with a location here
    }
```

As you can see, the JavaScript `successCallback()` function does nothing more than "clearing" the Javascript variable `watcher`; the key point is that you will continue receiving information until you clear this variable.

The DVD contains the HTML Web page `JQGeolocation1.html` that shows you how to use Geolocation with `geoPlugin` (which is not a jQuery plugin):

http://www.geoplugin.com

However, if you prefer to use a jQuery plugin for Geolocation, there are several available, including this one:

http://mobile.tutsplus.com/tutorials/mobile-web-apps/html5-geolocation/

HTML5 WEBSOCKETS

The purpose of WebSockets is to provide a bi-directional channel over a single TCP socket. WebSockets is designed for Web browsers and Web servers, but it can actually be used by other client or server applications.

A clarification is in order regarding two technologies for channel-based communication. Server-Sent Events (SSE) is another HTML5 technology that is used for communication (and also covered later in this chapter), but there's a major difference between SSE and WebSockets: both of these are capable of pushing data to browsers, but SSE connections can only *push* data to the browser, whereas WebSockets connections can both send data to the browser and receive data from the browser. Applications that send online stock quotes or update a Twitter timeline can benefit from SSE; on the other hand, a chat application can benefit from WebSockets.

Although SSE and WebSockets are not competing technologies, the functionality of SSE is a subset of the functionality that is available in WebSockets. Keep in mind that browser support for WebSockets appears to be greater than the corresponding support for SSE.

You can programmatically test for WebSockets support in any browser by including the following code block in an HTML5 Web page:

```
if(window.WebSocket) {
  alert("WebSockets is supported.");
} else {
  alert("WebSockets is supported.");
}
```

These links will report WebSockets support in your browser:

http://jsconsole.com/?WebSocket
http://websockets.org/

In addition, you can check the *www.caniuse.com* Web site for browser support for WebSockets.

Listing 10.2 displays the contents of `WebSockets2.html` that illustrates how to make a Web request from an HTML5 Web page to a WebSocket server.

Listing 10.2 WebSockets2.html

```
<!DOCTYPE HTML>
<html lang="en">
<head>
```

```
<meta charset="utf-8"/>
<title>HTML5 Web Sockets </title>

<script>
function WebSocketTest() {
  if ("WebSocket" in window) {
     alert("WebSocket is supported by your Browser");

     // Open a web socket...
     var ws = new WebSocket("ws://localhost:9998/echo");

     ws.onopen = function() {
        // send data using send()
        ws.send("Message to send");
        alert("Message is sent...");
     };

     ws.onmessage = function (evt) {
        var received_msg = evt.data;
        alert("Received message: "+received_msg);
     };

     ws.onclose = function() {
        // websocket is closed
        alert("Connection is closed...");
     };

     ws.onerror = function(evt) {
        console.log("Error occurred: "+evt.data);
     };
  } else {
     // The browser doesn't support WebSocket
     alert("WebSocket not supported by your Browser");
  }
}
</script>
</head>

<body>
<div id="sse">
   <a href="javascript:WebSocketTest()">Run WebSocket</a>
</div>
</body>
</html>
```

Listing 10.2 contains the JavaScript function `WebSocketTest()` that defines all of the WebSockets code, starting with conditional logic that checks for WebSockets support in your browser. If WebSockets are supported, then one line of code initializes the JavaScript variable `ws`, which references a WebSocket at a specific port number, as shown here:

```
var ws = new WebSocket("ws://localhost:9998/echo");
```

The remaining code defines handlers for `open` (which makes a request to the server), `message` (which handles messages received from the server), `close` (which closes the connection), and `error` (which reports error messages).

The next section shows you a simple example of using WebSockets to update the contents of an HMTL5 Web page.

A Simple WebSockets Web Page

Listing 10.3 displays the contents of `WSTestSupport2.html` that illustrates how to make a WebSocket invocation at *ws://echo.websocket.org*, which is a well-known endpoint that specifies the `ws` protocol instead of the `http` protocol.

Listing 10.3 WSTestSupport2.html

```
<!doctype html>
<html lang="en">
<head>
 <meta charset="utf-8"/>
 <title>Client-Side WebSocket Invocation</title>

 <script>
   // http://websocket.org/echo.html
   var wsUri = "ws://echo.websocket.org/";
   var websocket;

   function init() {
     testWebSocket();
   }

   function testWebSocket() {
     websocket = new WebSocket(wsUri);

     websocket.onopen    = onOpen;
     websocket.onclose   = onClose;
     websocket.onmessage = onMessage;
     websocket.onerror   = onError;
   }

   function onOpen(evt) {
```

```
    var msg = "Hello from Web Sockets Client";

    console.log("CONNECTED");
    websocket.send(msg);
    console.log("SENT: "+mmsg);
  }

  function onClose(evt) {
    console.log("DISCONNECTED");  }
    function onMessage(evt) {
    console.log("RESPONSE: "+evt.data);
    websocket.close();
  }

  function onError(evt) {
    console.log("ERROR: "+evt.data);
  }

  window.onload("init()");

 </script>
 </head>

<body>
  <h2>WebSocket Test</h2>
 </body>
</html>
```

Listing 10.3 contains HTML markup and the JavaScript function `init()` that is executed after the Web page is loaded into a browser. The `init()` function first finds the HTML `<div>` element whose `id` attribute has value `output`, and then it defines a set of event handlers for multiple socket-related callbacks, as shown here:

```
function testWebSocket() {
    websocket = new WebSocket(wsUri);
    websocket.onopen = function(evt) { onOpen(evt) };
    websocket.onclose = function(evt) { onClose(evt) };
    websocket.onmessage = function(evt) { onMessage(evt) };
    websocket.onerror = function(evt) { onError(evt) };
}
```

As you can see, the JavaScript functions in the preceding code block are defined in Listing 10.3, and each function reports its results by appending an HTML `<p>` element to the Web page with the following JavaScript function:

```
function writeToScreen(message) {
    var pre = document.createElement("p");
    pre.style.wordWrap = "break-word";
    pre.innerHTML = message;
    output.appendChild(pre);
}
```

You can find additional information about WebSockets in the W3C specification:

http://dev.w3.org/html5/websockets/

You can download a free copy (PDF) of the DZone Reference Card for WebSockets here:

http://refcardz.dzone.com/refcardz/html5-websocket

SPDY AND HTML5 WEBSOCKETS

SPDY (pronounced "speedy") is an experimental protocol developed by Google. It is intended to enhance HTTP to make synchronous HTTP requests faster, as described in the SPDY Whitepaper:

http://www.chromium.org/spdy/spdy-whitepaper

Although SPDY is not an official part of HTML, it's included in this chapter because it could become important and useful for your Web applications (and if this turns out not to be the case, it's still useful information for you).

SPDY adds a layer between HTTP and SSL that allows for multiple concurrent streams over a single TCP connection. SPDY Push is a technique that sends multiple files (such as JavaScript, CSS, and images in a Web page) in a single request, which can reduce the round trip time. Thus, SPDY does not replace HTTP; its purpose is to modify the way HTTP requests and responses are sent "over the wire."

SIDEBAR

By contrast, WebSockets is an alternative to HTTP that supports bidirectional real time communication; in fact, WebSockets and SPDY are complementary protocols. WebSockets makes its initial handshake with servers over

HTTP to determine whether or not the `ws://` protocol is supported, whereas SPDY's primary methods of optimization is compressing and caching HTTP request headers.

At this point, the performance gains through SPDY depend on various factors (discussed in the link by Guy Podjamy below). On one hand, the SPDY white paper asserts that performance gains can be significant:

"Header compression resulted in an ~88% reduction in the size of request headers and an ~85% reduction in the size of response headers... We found a reduction of 45 – 1142 ms in page load time simply due to header compression."

On the other hand, Guy Podjamy of Akamai performed a set of tests on "real-world" Web sites and he concluded that SPDY did not offer significant performance improvements, which he has documented here:

http://www.guypo.com/technical/not-as-spdy-as-you-thought/

Both Chrome and Firefox support SPDY, and Twitter now supports SPDY on its servers.

MIGRATING TO HTML5 WEBSOCKETS

Every application maintains state in some form, and in server-side web applications, the server has to do extra work to maintain state since 1.) HTTP is stateless, intended as a fire-and-forget way to retrieve documents; and 2.) browsers were optimized as rendering platforms, not as uniform application platforms.

Richard Clark points out that although state can be stored in the client or on the server, keep in mind the existence of XSS exploits, which suggests that server-side state might be a weaker solution. The question of which side maintains state (client or server) is more a question of trust: if the data has to be managed securely, it's held on the server side (inside the trust boundary.) However, something like a shopping cart can be safely held on either side; in fact, you want to keep as much of the state on the client as possible to improve responsiveness and post updates to the server asynchronously. See the following link for more details:

http://alexmaccaw.com/posts/async_ui

An interesting white paper on the topic ("Building Living Web Applications") is here:

http://kaazingcorp.cachefly.net/com/file/Kaazing-WP-Living-Web-Architecture-Mar-2012.pdf

Richard Clark also suggests that people will not migrate simply for the sake of migration; rather, they will build a next-generation application using WebSockets when there is sufficient pain involved in using the old application. For instance, there are customers who use applications that involve shopping carts, placing orders over an unreliable network connection (dial-up is in more common use than you would think), and their Web systems force the user to start over each time. Solutions that involve WebSockets are available that can handle this type of situation gracefully.

Given the benefits of WebSockets, you might be wondering if there are ways to speed up current systems to emulate some of the benefits of Web-Sockets.

For example, suppose someone sets up a Unix/Linux machine to handle 50K connections, installs Apache, and sets the "keep-alive" header. This configuration is akin to a "poor man's SPDY server," because the difference between WebSockets and HTTP is beyond "keep-alive."

A comparison between highly optimized Comet and stock WebSockets (note the 50K case on both sides) is here:

http://webtide.intalio.com/2011/09/cometd-2-4-0-websocket-benchmarks/

Incidentally, cookies are still valid for storing tiny bits of data that need to be sent back to the server with every request. Specifically, they can also be sent when establishing a WebSockets connection, which also helps maintain interoperability with systems that expect cookies on a request (such as legacy single sign-on systems).

OTHER PROJECTS WITH HTML5 WEBSOCKETS

This section briefly mentions some of the other initiatives involving Web-Sockets and how you can use them with mobile devices.

Atmosphere is a framework that enables you to use WebSockets in order to send data to mobile applications (specifically, an Android mobile application):

https://github.com/Atmosphere/atmosphere

The GitHub Web site states that Atmosphere is "The only Portable Web-Sockets/Comet framework supporting Scala, Groovy, and Java."

A description of how to use Atmosphere with mobile devices is here:

http://www.slideshare.net/misterdom/html5-websockets-the-mobile-web
http://www.webofthings.org/2011/10/24/websockets-push-to-mobile/

XSockets.NET is a WebSockets server for Microsoft .NET:

http://xsockets.net/xsockets-news

A project that uses XSockets.NET, KnockoutJS, and jQuery Mobile is here:

http://dathor.blogspot.com/2011/12/knockoutauction-knockoutjsjquery-mobile.html

This Web site contains the code, videos, and a detailed description of how to use jQuery Mobile with WebSockets.

Another interesting tool is Easy WebSocket, which provides WebSockets broadcasting capability:

http://easywebsocket.org/

An example of using the Device API to access to the camera on a device and communicate with WebSockets is here:

https://www.youtube.com/watch?v=jqXo-AEVhK4&feature=related

The preceding demo captures video from the camera on a mobile device and then sends a snapshot to a remote client through WebSockets.

AVAILABLE WEBSOCKET SERVERS

There are many WebSocket servers available, written in languages such as Java, JavaScript, Ruby, Python, and C++. Some of the popular ones include NodeJS, Kaazing, and mod_pyWebSocket (which is used in a code sample in Chapter 12), but there are many others.

The following link lists the support for WebSockets in modern browsers (desktop and also mobile):

http://caniuse.com/#search=websocket

A list of WebSocket servers is here:

http://www.slideshare.net/fullscreen/peterlubbers/html5-realtime-and-connectivity/55

A tabularized display that itemizes the feature support for multiple Web-Socket servers is here (but be sure to read the caveats at the top of the page):

http://en.wikipedia.org/wiki/Comparison_of_WebSocket_implementations

Another important point to keep in mind is that the WS standard went through multiple iterations and developers often implemented one of the interim versions before settling on the final protocol. Thus, the WS implementation that you select may need to support an older protocol as well as the latest until the majority of devices catch up.

VIBRATION API (DAP)

The Vibration API (maintained by the DAP working group) defines an API that provides access to the vibration mechanism of a hosting device. The Vibration API consists of a single method `vibrate()` whose implementation must run the algorithm for processing vibration patterns (see link below for details).

In the following example the device vibrates for one second:

```
// vibrate for 1 second
navigator.vibrate(1000);
```

Using the following code snippet to cause a device to vibrate for one second, stop vibration for 0.5 seconds, and vibrate again for two seconds:

```
navigator.vibrate([1000, 500, 2000]);
```

Cancel any existing vibrations:

```
navigator.vibrate(0);
```

A second way to cancel any existing vibrations:

```
navigator.vibrate([]);
```

For additional information, navigate to the W3C Vibration API (currently a working draft):

http://www.w3.org/TR/vibration/

XMLHTTPREQUEST LEVEL 2 (XHR2)

The `XMLHttpRequest` Level 2 specification supports the following new features:

- Handling byte streams such as File, Blob, and FormData objects for upload and download
- Showing progress events during upload and download
- Making cross-origin requests
- Making anonymous requests (not HTTP referer)
- Setting a timeout for the request

Before we look at an XHR2 code sample, we'll start with a code sample that shows you how to make a simple Ajax request, followed by an Ajax request that uses jQuery. Next you will learn about CORS, and the final portion of this section discusses XHR2.

Making Ajax Calls without jQuery

The code sample in this section shows you how to make a "traditional" Ajax call, after which we will look at how to accomplish the same task using jQuery. The purpose of this example is to illustrate the fact that jQuery (once again) enables you to write simpler code that is easier to maintain, debug, and enhance with additional functionality (which you already know from the code samples you have seen throughout this book).

Listing 10.4 BasicAjax1.html

```
<!DOCTYPE html>
<html>
<head>
 <meta charset=utf-8/>
 <title>Basic Ajax</title>

 <script>
   var xmlHTTP, myFile = "http://localhost:8080/sample.xml";

   function loadXML(url, callback) {
     if (window.XMLHttpRequest) {
       // Chrome, Firefox, IE7+, Opera, and Safari
       xmlHTTP = new XMLHttpRequest();
     } else {
       // IE5 and IE6
```

```
        xmlHTTP = new ActiveXObject("Microsoft.XMLHTTP");
      }

      xmlHTTP.onreadystatechange = callback;
      xmlHTTP.open("GET", url, true);
      xmlHTTP.send();
    }

    function init() {
      loadXML(myFile, function() {
        if(xmlHTTP.readyState==4 && xmlHTTP.status==200) {
          document.getElementById("myDiv").innerHTML =
                                        xmlHTTP.responseText;
        }
      });
    }
  </script>
</head>

<body onload="init()">
  <div id="myDiv"></div>
</body>
</html>
```

Listing 10.4 contains a JavaScript function `init()` that is executed when the Web page is loaded into a browser. The `init()` function invokes the `loadXML()` function with the name of an XML document, along with a JavaScript function that is executed when the Ajax request is completed.

The `loadXML()` function contains conditional logic that determines how to initialize the JavaScript variable `xmlhttp`, followed by a code block that sets the name of the callback function, specifies a GET method and a URL in the `url` variable (not shown in this code sample), and then makes the actual Ajax request, as shown here:

```
xmlHTTP.onreadystatechange = callback;
xmlHTTP.open("GET", url, true);
xmlHTTP.send();
```

When the Ajax request is completed, the HTML `<div>` element in Listing 10.4 is updated with the data that is returned by the Ajax request. In this code sample, the XML document `sample.xml` is the same file that you saw in Chapter 8, so we will not reproduce its contents here. Refer back to Chapter 8, and you will see that `sample.xml` is an SVG document that contains three SVG-based rectangles, and these rectangles are rendered inside the HTML `<div>` element whose `id` attribute is `myDiv`.

If you are new to Ajax, then this code might seem convoluted (and perhaps confusing as well). Fortunately, jQuery simplifies the process of making Ajax requests by shielding you from the lower-level details, as you will see in the next section.

Making Ajax Calls with jQuery

This example is the modified version of Listing 10.4, which adds jQuery functionality to the code. There are several jQuery methods that provide Ajax-based functionality, including `jQuery.load()`, `jQuery.get()`, `jQuery.post()`, and `jQuery.ajax()`.

Listing 10.5 displays the contents of `JQueryAjax1.html` that illustrates how to use the first of these jQuery Ajax methods in an HTML Web page in order to produce the same result as Listing 10.4.

Listing 10.5 JQueryAjax1.html

```
</script>
<!DOCTYPE html>
<html>
<head>
 <meta charset="utf-8"/>
 <title>JQuery Ajax</title>

 <script src="http://ajax.googleapis.com/ajax/libs/jquery/1.7.1/
jquery.min.js">
 </script>

 <script>
  var url = "http://localhost:8080/sample.xml";

  $(document).ready(function() {
    $("#myDiv").load(url, function() {});
  });
 </script>
</head>

<body>
  <div id="myDiv"></div>
</body>
</html>
```

Listing 10.5 contains a mere one line of code that performs an Ajax request via the jQuery `load()` method, as shown here:
```
$("#myDiv").load(url, function() {});
```

The result of executing the code in Listing 10.5 is the same as the result of executing the code in Listing 10.4: the contents of the HTML `<div>` element whose `id` attribute is `myDiv` is replaced with the contents of `sample.xml` and three SVG-based rectangles are rendered.

Alternatively, you can use the `jQuery.ajax()` method as shown here:

```
$.ajax({
    url:   url,
    type: "get",
    success: GotData,
    dataType: 'xml'
});
```

In the preceding code block, you also need to define a JavaScript function called `GotData()` where you would process the result of the Ajax invocation.

As you would expect, jQuery provides much more Ajax functionality. Specifically, jQuery provides support for the following callback hooks:

```
beforeSend()
fail()
dataFilter()
done()
always()
```

The functions `beforeSend()`, `error()`, and `done()` are intuitively named and behave as expected. The `dataFilter()` callback is the first callback to receive data; after it performs its processing, the `done()` callback is invoked. Finally, the `always()` callback is invoked, regardless of whether the result of the Ajax invocation was successful or in error.

A concise example of jQuery code that makes an Ajax request using method chaining with several of the preceding APIs is here:

```
// Assign handlers immediately after making the request,
// and get a reference to the jqxhr object for this request
var jqxhr = $.ajax( "example.php" )
    .done(function() { alert("success"); })
    .fail(function() { alert("error"); })
    .always(function() { alert("complete"); });

// perform other work here ...

// Set another completion function for the request above
```

```
jqxhr.always(function() { alert("second complete"); });
```

If you want to explore more Ajax-related features in jQuery, a complete list of jQuery Ajax methods is here:

http://api.jquery.com/category/ajax/
http://api.jquery.com/ajaxComplete/

This chapter contains one more Ajax-based code sample that users XHR2, but first we need to discuss Cross-Origin Resource Sharing and some of the features that it provides in HTML5.

HTML5 Cross-Origin Resource Sharing (CORS)

In brief, the "same origin policy" allows scripts that originate from the same site to execute, and they can access each other's methods and properties with without restriction. On the other hand, Cross-Origin Resource Sharing (CORS) specifies the ways in which a web server can allow its resources to be accessed by web pages from different domains. Although CORS is more flexible than "same origin policy," it does not allow access to resources by any and all requests.

In simplified terms, the CORS specification provides support for cross-domain communication by means of a simple header exchange between a client and a server.

Some of the new HTTP headers for the CORS specification are OPTIONS, ORIGIN, and Access-Control-Allow-Origin. When the appropriate CORS headers are provided, CORS makes it possible to make asynchronous HTTP requests to other domains.

The CORS API uses the XMLHttpRequest object as a "container" for sending and receiving the requisite headers for CORS, and also the withCredentials property that can be used for determining programmatically whether or not an XMLHttpRequest object supports CORS.

For a more detailed description of CORS, perform an Internet search. You will find many free articles with such information.

Ajax Requests Using XMLHttpRequest Level 2 (XHR2)

Listing 10.6 displays AjaxForm.html, which illustrates how to create an HTML5 Web page that uses the new FormData object XHR2.

Listing 10.6 AjaxForm.html

```
<!doctype html>
<html lang="en">
```

```
<head>
 <meta charset="utf-8"/>
 <title>Ajax Form</title>

 <script>
  function sendForm(form) {
    var formData = new FormData(form);

    var xhr = new XMLHttpRequest();
    xhr.open('POST', form.action, true);
    xhr.onload = function(e) {
      // do something here
    };

    xhr.send(formData);

    // Prevent page submission
    return false;
  }
 </script>
</head>

<body>
<form id="myform" name="myform" action="xhr2.php">
  <input type="text"   name="uname" value="asmith">
  <input type="number" name="id"    value="33333">
  <input type="submit" onclick="return sendForm(this.form);">
</form>
</body>
</html>
```

Listing 10.6 is straightforward. The `<body>` element contains a HTML `<form>` element with several input fields. Next, the form data is submitted via the JavaScript function `sendForm()` that creates a `FormData` object and then submits the user-provided data via XHR2, as shown in this code block:

```
var xhr = new XMLHttpRequest();
xhr.open('POST', form.action, true);
xhr.onload = function(e) {
    // do something here
};
xhr.send(formData);
```

Two more points to know is that the `XMLHttpRequest` Level 2 specification supports the transfer of binary data and also tracking the upload progress through the `XMLHttpRequestUpload` object; consequently, XHR2 can be used for binary file transfers via the File APIs and the `FormData` object.

If you need to use XHR2 in your HTML Web pages, there is an XHR2 library here:

https://github.com/p-m-p/xhr2-lib

More tutorials and information regarding XHR2 are here:

http://www.html5rocks.com/en/tutorials/file/xhr2/
http://www.matiasmancini.com.ar/jquery-plugin-ajax-form-validation-html5.html

HTML5 APIS IN W3C LAST CALL STATUS (LC)

This section contains a set of HTML5 APIs that have Last Call status. The following HTML5 APIs also have LC status as well, and they are discussed in the following chapters:

- Audio and Video (Chapter 1)
- Canvas 2D APIs (Chapters 11 and 12)
- HTML Markup (Chapter 1)
- Web Storage (introduced in Chapter 1)

HTML5 CONTACTS

The HTML5 Contacts API enables you to access information about your contacts. A contact record is an instance of the Contacts interface, which contains various attributes and contact interface subtypes such as `ContactName`, `ContactAddress`, and so forth.

The following (somewhat lengthy) code block shows you how to retrieve three attributes of a user's contacts by invoking the `find()` method of the `contacts` object. Notice that the `find()` method specifies an error callback function and a success callback function, and that the latter is where the actual processing of the contacts list is performed:

```
function findMyContacts() {
```

```
  // is the Contacts API available?
  if (navigator.contacts) {
    // set the array of fields to retrieve
    var fieldList = ['displayName', 'phoneNumbers', 'emails'];

    // invoke the find method on the contacts object
    navigator.contacts.find(fieldList,
                            contactsSuccess,
                            contactsError);
  } else {
    alert("This Browser does not support the Contacts API");
  }
}

// Success callback function for finding contacts
function contactsSuccess(contactList) {
  // locate the 'div' for displaying the results
  var myContacts = document.getElementById('myContacts');

  for(var c in contactList) {
   if(contactList.hasOwnProperty(c)) {

     // find phone numbers for each contact:
     for(var p in contactList[c].phoneNumbers) {
      if(contactList[c].phoneNumbers.hasOwnProperty(p)) {

        contactDetails = contactList[c].displayName + ': ' +
                         contactList[c].phoneNumbers[p].value;

       if (contactList[c].phoneNumbers[p].type === 'mobile') {
          contactDetails += " (mobile) ";
        }

        // Display the contact name and phone number
        myContacts.innerHTML += contactDetails;
       }
     }

     // find email addresses for each contact:
     for(var e in contactList[c].emails) {
  if(contactList[c].emails.hasOwnProperty(e)) {
```

```
            contactDetails = contactList[c].displayName + ': ' +
                             contactList[c].emails[e].value;

            // Display the contact name and email address
            myContacts.innerHTML += contactDetails;
        }
      }
    }
  }
}


// Error callback function for finding contacts
function contactsError(error) {
    alert(error.code);
}
```

As this book goes to print, the latest editor's draft of the Contacts API uses a Web intent (discussed later in this chapter) instead of the `find()` method. You can find more information in the W3C draft of the Contacts API:

www.w3.org/TR/contacts-api

HTML5 DRAG AND DROP (DND)

HTML5 Drag and Drop enables you to rearrange the layout of HTML elements in an HTML Web page. HTML4 does not have built-in support for DnD, and creating such support requires considerably more JavaScript code than a toolkit such as jQuery.

On the other hand, HTML5 provides Drag and Drop APIs that support Drag and Drop in HTML5 Web pages. HTML5 Drag and Drop supports the following events:

```
drag
dragend
dragenter
dragleave
dragover
dragstart
drop
```

In addition, the HTML5 DnD provides a source element, the data content, and the target, which represent the drag "start" element, the data that is being dragged, and the "target" element, respectively.

In your HTML5 Web page, you attach event listeners to elements, as shown here:

```
myElement.addEventListener('dragenter', handleDragEnter, false);
myElement.addEventListener('dragleave', handleDragLeave, false);
myElement.addEventListener('dragover',  handleDragOver,  false);
myElement.addEventListener('dragstart', handleDragStart, false);
```

Next, you define custom code in each of the JavaScript event handlers that will be executed whenever the associated event occurs.

However, keep in mind that HTML5 Web pages with DnD functionality still require browser-specific code, which means that you need to maintain the code in multiple HTML5 Web pages if you want to support multiple browsers.

HTML5 Drag and Drop is probably one of the most tedious of the HTML5 APIs. Peter Paul Koch of "QuirksMode" fame expresses his thoughts regarding DnD in one of his blog posts (please note that there is strong language here):

http://www.quirksmode.org/blog/archives/2009/09/the_html5_drag.html

Eric Bidelman has written an extensive and detailed blog entry that shows you how to write an HTML5 Web page with Drag and Drop functionality:

http://www.html5rocks.com/en/tutorials/dnd/basics/

We will skip examples of "native" HTML5 DnD and proceed to an example of using jQuery with HTML5 DnD, which is covered in the next section.

JQUERY AND HTML5 DRAG AND DROP

Drag and Drop is exceptionally simple in jQuery: only one line of code is required for an HTML element.

Listing 10.7 displays the contents of the HTML5 Web page `JQDragAnd-Drop1.html`, which illustrates how easy it is to create an HTML5 Web page with Drag and Drop using jQuery.

Listing 10.7 JQDragAndDrop1.html

```html
<!doctype html>
<html lang="en">
<head>
 <meta charset="utf-8"/>
 <title>JQuery DnD</title>

<style>
 div[id^="draggable"] {
   position:relative; width: 100px; height: 100px;
 }

 #draggable1 { background: red; }
 #draggable2 { background: yellow; }
 #draggable3 { background: blue; }
</style>

<script      src="http://ajax.googleapis.com/ajax/libs/jque-
ry/1.7.1/jquery.min.js">
</script>

<script
src="http://ajax.googleapis.com/ajax/libs/jqueryui/1.8.9/jquery-
ui.min.js">
</script>

<script
  $(document).ready(function() {
    $('#draggable1').draggable();
    $('#draggable2').draggable();
    $('#draggable3').draggable();
  });
</script>
</head>

<body>
  <div id="content" style="height: 400px;">
    <div id="draggable1">
        <img src="Laurie1.jpeg" width="100" height="100"/>
    </div>
    <div id="draggable2">
        <img src="Laurie2.jpeg" width="100" height="100"/>
    </div>
    <div id="draggable3">
        <img src="Laurie3.jpeg" width="100" height="100"/>
    </div>
```

```
    </div>
</body>
</html>
```

Listing 10.7 contains a block of jQuery code that makes three HTML `<div>` elements (which are defined in the `<body>` element) draggable using this type of code snippet:

```
$('#draggable2').draggable();
```

The `<body>` element contains three `<div>` elements, each of which contains a JPEG image that you can drag around the screen.

Figure 10.1 displays the result of rendering Listing 10.7 in a Chrome browser on a Macbook.

FIGURE 10.1 Three images in a Chrome browser on a Macbook.

Figure 10.2 shows an example of dragging the images in Listing 10.7 to different positions in a Chrome browser on a Macbook.

FIGURE 10.2 Three dragged images in a Chrome browser on a Macbook.

More information about jQuery Drag and Drop (including the list of available options) is available here:

http://jqueryui.com/demos/draggable/

- There are several jQuery plugins for drag and drop functionality that are listed here:

http://plugins.jquery.com/projects/plugins?type=45

- You can also use jQuery Mobile with HTML5 DnD, and although we will not discuss an example, you can perform an Internet search to find tutorials and code examples, or you can start with the details in this link:

http://www.jsplugins.com/Scripts/Plugins/View/Jquery-Mobile-Drag-And-Drop/

JQUERY AND HTML5 LOCALSTORAGE

Chapter 1 discusses HTML5 localStorage, and this section introduces you to jQuery plugins that provide a layer of abstraction over localStorage and sessionStorage.

The jQuery plugin `jStorage` is a cross-browser plugin that enables you to use jQuery syntax in order to manage data in localStorage, and its homepage is here:

http://www.jstorage.info/

The JStorage APIs enable you to get, set, and delete data in storage; you can also check if storage is available, as well as the size of the stored data (in bytes). The intuitively named JStorage APIs are listed here for your convenience:

```
$.jStorage.set(key, value)
     $.jStorage.get(key)
     $.jStorage.deleteKey(key)
$.jStorage.flush()
$.jStorage.index()
$.jStorage.storageSize()
$.jStorage.currentBackend()
$.jStorage.reInit()
$.jStorage.storageAvailable()
```

Listing 10.8 displays the contents of `JQJStorage1.html` that illustrates how to use JStorage in order to save data in the storage area of your browser.

Listing 10.8 JQJStorage1.html

```
<!DOCTYPE html>
<html lang="en">
  <head>
   <title>JStorage Example</title>
   <meta charset=utf-8/>

   <link rel="stylesheet"
   href="http://code.jquery.com/mobile/1.1.0/jquery.mobile-
1.1.0.min.css"/>

   <script
       src="http://code.jquery.com/jquery-1.7.1.min.js">
   </script>
   <script src="http://code.jquery.com/mobile/1.1.0
                   /jquery.mobile-1.1.0.min.js">
   <script src="jstorage.js"></script>
```

```
<script>
  $(document).ready(function() {
    // Check if "key" exists in the storage
    var value = $.jStorage.get("key");

    if(!value){
      // if not - load the data from the server
      value = load_data_from_server()

      // save the value
      $.jStorage.set("key",value);
    }
  });
</script>
</head>

<body>
  <div> </div>
</body>
</html>
```

The core functionality in Listing 10.8 takes place in a short JavaScript code block with conditional logic that checks for the existence of a data item in localStorage with the value key. If this value does not exist, then the `load_data_from_server()` JavaScript function (which is not shown) is invoked, and then the return value is stored in localStorage.

You can also use the jQuery plugin `jStore` for HTML5 storage, which is a cross-browser plugin that enables you to use jQuery syntax in order to manage data in localStorage, and its homepage is here:

http://code.google.com/p/jquery-jstore/source/browse/trunk/src/engines/jStore.Html5.js?r=6

LIBRARIES FOR HTML5 LOCALSTORAGE

A number of JavaScript toolkits are available for localStorage, some of which use jQuery. This short section briefly describes some of the available toolkits.

`lscache` emulates `memcache` functions using HTML5 localStorage for caching data in a client browser, along with an expiration time for each data item.

The `lscache` homepage is here:

https://github.com/pamelafox/lscache

If the localStorage limit (approximately 5MB) is exceeded, items that are closest to their expiration date are removed. If localStorage is unavailable, `lscache` does not cache anything (and all cache requests return null).

The `lscache` methods are `set()`, `get()`, `remove()`, and `flush()`. A jQuery `lscache` plugin is available here:

https://github.com/mckamey

`YQL LocalCache` is a wrapper for YQL to support localStorage, and its homepage is here:

https://github.com/phunkei/autoStorage

A sample invocation with `YQL LocalCache` with self-explanatory parameters is here:

```
yqlcache.get({
  yql: 'select * from flickr.photos.search where text="warsaw"',
  id: 'myphotos',
  cacheage: ( 60*60*1000 ),
  callback: function(data) {
    console.log(data);
  }
});
```

The returned data in the callback is an object with two properties: `data` (the YQL data) and `type` ("cached" for cached data or "freshcache"). You can get additional code samples here:

https://github.com/codepo8/yql-localcache

Savify is a jQuery plugin for automatically recording a user's progress in a form while it is being completed, and its homepage is here:

https://github.com/blackcoat/Savify

HTML5 WEB MESSAGING

Web Messaging enables documents to share information without exposing their underlying DOM structure, which reduces the risk from malicious cross-origin scripts. Web messaging actually involves **cross-document messaging** and **channel messaging**. Cross-document messaging uses the `window.postMessage()` function, and channel messaging is also known as `MessageChannel`.

Keep in mind that the Web Messaging API is different from the Messaging API (WD status) that defines a high-level interface to messaging functionality, including SMS, MMS, and e-mail.

Web Messaging, SSE, and WebSockets are the three primary communication interfaces that are available in HTML5, and all three technologies involve `message` events. The structure of a `message` is specified by the `MessageEvent` interface (which inherits from the DOM `Event` interface) that contains five read-only attributes: `data` (a string sent from the originating script), `origin` (such as *http://www.acme.com*:12345), `lastEventId` (a string that uniquely identifies the current message event), `ports` (an array of `MessagePort` objects that are sent with a message), and `source` (which references the window of the originating document).

One point to keep in mind is that message events do not have a default action, do not "bubble," and they are not cancelable.

As a simple example, suppose that you want to send a message from the parent document to a document contained in an IFRAME that is hosted on another server. Web Messaging makes this type of communication possible by passing data as a `message` event, where the "send" code from the parent to the IFRAME would look something like the following:

```
var iframe = document.querySelector('iframe');
var button = document.querySelector('button');
var clickHandler = function() {
// iframe.contentWindow refers to the iframe's window object
iframe.contentWindow.postMessage('The message to send.',
                                 'http://dev.opera.com');}
button.addEventListener('click',clickHandler,false);
```

The "receive" code that handles the message sent from the IFRAME back to the parent would look like this:

```
var messageEventHandler = function(event) {
    // check that the origin is correct:
    if(event.origin == 'http://dev.opera.com'){
      alert(event.data);
    }
}
```

```
window.addEventListener('message', messageEventHandler,false);
```

For more information, navigate to the W3C Web Messaging specification here:

http://www.w3.org/TR/webmessaging/

USING HTML5 SERVER-SENT EVENTS (SSE)

Server-Sent Events (SSE) is an HTML5 technology for sending data from a server to a client after the initial client connection has been established. This one-way communication from a server to a client is useful in cases where you need to send message updates or data streams.

Keep in mind that SSE is a "push" from the server to the client, which is the opposite of a client "pull" from a server. Second, you might be thinking that SSE is "half" of WebSockets in the sense that there is no communication from the client to the server.

The SSE specification requires message IDs and reconnection on the server side, whereas the client-side API is essentially identical to WebSockets.

SSE uses the JavaScript EventSource API, which clients use in order to request a URL and then receive a series of events, as shown in Listing 10.9.

Listing 10.9 EventSource1.html

```html
<html>
  <head>
    <meta charset="utf-8"/>
    <title>SSE Event Source </title>

    <script>
        var source = new EventSource('Events');
        source.onmessage = function (event) {
            ev = document.getElementById('events');
            ev.innerHTML += "<br>[in] " + event.data;
        };
    </script>
  </head>
  <body>
    <div id="events"></div>
```

```
    </body>
  </html>
```

Listing 10.9 contains HTML markup and some JavaScript code that starts by instantiating a JavaScript variable source that is a reference to an Event-Source object, followed by a block of code for the callback function that processes the data that is received from the server, as shown here:

```
source.onmessage = function (event) {
   ev = document.getElementById('events');
   ev.innerHTML += "<br>[in] " + event.data;
};
```

The preceding code block simply appends the latest information from the server, which is available in event.data, to the HTML <div> element whose id attribute has the value events.

Prior to HTML5 SSE "server push" technologies were employed to provide the functionality that is available in HTML5 SSE. In particular, Comet is a popular model that can be implemented by "long polling," whereby a server maintains an HTTP request from a client in order to periodically send data to the client.

However, the original Comet document did not specify an implementation, which means that in practice you don't know whether a given Comet implementation uses polling, long polling, or HTTP streaming (or perhaps something else). Each of these approaches places different demands on the infrastructure, whereas SSE is standardized on HTTP streaming, which provides consistency.

Incidentally, other terms for Comet include "Ajax Push," "Reverse Ajax," and "HTTP server push." More information about Comet is here:

http://en.wikipedia.org/wiki/Push_technology
http://en.wikipedia.org/wiki/Comet_(programming)

Listing 10.10 displays the contents of the HTML5 Web page HTML5SSE1. html that illustrates how to use HTML5 SSE.

Listing 10.10 HTML5SSE1.html

```
<!DOCTYPE html>
<html>
<head>
 <meta charset="utf-8"/>
 <title>Server Sent Events (SSE)</title>
```

```
<script>
  function SetupSSE() {
    //check for browser support
    if(typeof(EventSource) !== "undefined") {
console.log("Browser supports EventSource");

      // create an EventSource object with the name
      // and the location of the server-side script
      var eSource = new EventSource("echo");
//console.log("eSource: "+eSource);

      // receive server-side messages
      eSource.onmessage = function(event) {
console.log("Processing data from server...");
        // display the data from the server
        document.getElementById("serverData").innerHTML = event.
data;
      };
    }
    else {
console.log("Browser does not support EventSource");
      document.getElementById("serverData").innerHTML =
                            "No support for server-sent events.";
    }
  }
 </script>
</head>

<body onload="SetupSSE();">
  <div id="serverData"> </div>
</body>
</html>
```

Listing 10.10 invokes the JavaScript function `SetupSSE()` after the Web page is loaded into a browser. After confirming that the `EventSource` object is non-null, this function instantiates the JavaScript variable `eSource` to communicate with the server-side program called "`echo`," as shown here:

```
var eSource = new EventSource("echo");
```

Next, the `SetupSSE()` function defines a function for the `onmessage` event that updates an HTML `<div>` element in the client with data that is received from the server, as shown here:

```
eSource.onmessage = function(event) {
  // display the data from the server
```

```
document.getElementById("serverData").innerHTML = event.data;
};
```

As an example, in Python 2.x you can start a Python-based HTTP server by typing the following command (you can replace [portnumber] with a port number other than the default port 8000):

```
python -m SimpleHTTPServer [portnumber]
```

In Python 3, you can use the following command:

```
python -m http.server [portnumber]
```

After a few moments you will see the following message:

```
Serving HTTP on 0.0.0.0 port 8000 ...
```

In Listing 10.8, you also need a program on the server called `echo` that periodically sends data to the browser that has established a connection with the server.

Additional information about HTML5 Server-Sent Events is available in the W3C specification:

http://dev.w3.org/html5/eventsource/

A Comparison of Ajax and SSE

In the previous section, we briefly contrasted SSE with WebSockets, and you might also be wondering about Ajax versus SSE. Some of the advantages of SSE are here:

- One long-lived HTTP connection is required
- Well-supported in modern browsers
- Simpler and "cleaner" client-side implementation
- Designed "from the ground up" to be efficient

Since one persistent connection is required for each client, a large number of clients will result in many open connections on the server, so your server obviously needs to be able to handle such a volume. On the other hand, Ajax polling adds a lot of HTTP overhead due to the process of establishing and then "tearing down" HTTP connections.

Keep in mind that a "bullet list" of features will only provide you with guidelines for helping you select the most suitable technology for the task that you are trying to solve. It's a good idea to get feedback regarding proposed solutions from someone who has the requisite experience.

Incidentally, if you use an IE browser, you can perform an Internet search to find a jQuery plugin that will provide SSE support in your browser. In addition, since SSE uses an established technique (HTTP streaming), implementers could create a compatible library using older APIs.

HTML5 APIS IN W3C WORKING DRAFT STATUS (WD)

The HTML5 technologies in this section currently have a "Working Draft" status. IndexedDB has WD status and is discussed in Chapter 1, so we will not repeat that content here. In addition, the following HTML5 technologies also have WD status but are not discussed in this chapter:

- Media Capture
- RDFa
- Touch Events

AUDIO PROCESSING

The W3C Audio Processing API introduces two APIs: Google's Web Audio API specification and Mozilla's MediaStream Processing API specification. The code sample in this section illustrates how to use the audio APIs for Mozilla, which means that you need to launch the HTML Web page in Firefox.

In Chapter 1, you saw an example of the HTML5 <audio> element, and in this section you will see a code sample that uses the Web Audio APIs, which enable you to access low-level data. The code sample shows you how to play an audio file and then render a set of rectangles that are rendered along a sine wave that represents the amplitude of the sounds in the audio file.

The code sample in this section works in Firefox and Safari 6, and undoubtedly will be available in Chrome in the future. This code sample in Listing 10.11 is one of the few code samples in this book that are not Web-Kit-based code samples because the visual effects are interesting and worth including in this book.

Listing 10.11 displays the contents of the HTML Web page WebAudio1. html that illustrates how to use the Web Audio API in an HTML Web page.

Listing 10.11 WebAudio1.html

```html
<!DOCTYPE html>
<html lang="en">
<head>
 <meta charset="utf-8"/>
  <title>HTML5 Audio Visualization</title>
 </head>

 <body>
   <h2>Audio Sampling Example</h2>
   <audio tabloop="0" src="HelloWorld.ogg" controls="controls">
   </audio>

   <div>
     <canvas width="512" height="200"
                         style="background-color:yellow;">
     </canvas>

     <canvas width="512" height="200"
                         style="background-color:yellow;">
     </canvas>

     <canvas width="512" height="200"
                         style="background-color:yellow;">
     </canvas>

     <canvas width="512" height="200"
                         style="background-color:yellow;">
     </canvas>
   </div>

   <script>
     var sampleCount = 512, rectWidth=sampleCount,
                                          rectHeight=200;
    var barWidth = 10, barHeight = 0, deltaX1 = 2, deltaX4 = 5;
     var x1, y1, x2, y2, x3, y3, x4, y4, index, loop = 0;
     var fillColors = ["#f00", "#ff0", "#00f", "#0ff", "#804"];
     var smallWidth = 10, smallHeight = 40, fbLength, channels;

     var audio   = document.getElementsByTagName("audio")[0];
     var canvas1 = document.getElementsByTagName("canvas")[0];
     var canvas2 = document.getElementsByTagName("canvas")[1];
     var canvas3 = document.getElementsByTagName("canvas")[2];
     var canvas4 = document.getElementsByTagName("canvas")[3];

     var context1 = canvas1.getContext('2d');
     var context2 = canvas2.getContext('2d');
```

```
var context3 = canvas3.getContext('2d');
var context4 = canvas4.getContext('2d');

context1.lineWidth = 2; context1.strokeStyle = "#FFFFFF";
context2.lineWidth = 4; context2.strokeStyle = "#FFFFFF";
context3.lineWidth = 6; context3.strokeStyle = "#FFFFFF";
context4.lineWidth = 1; context4.strokeStyle = "#FFFFFF";

audio.addEventListener("MozAudioAvailable", writeSamples,
                                                     false);
audio.addEventListener("loadedmetadata", getMetadata,
                                                     false);

function getMetadata() {
  channels = audio.mozChannels;
  fbLength = audio.mozFrameBufferLength;
}

// Render the waveforms
function writeSamples (event) {
  var data = event.frameBuffer;
  var step = (fbLength / channels) / sampleCount;

  if(loop % 4 == 0) {
    // clear the canvas:
    context1.fillRect(0, 0, rectWidth, rectHeight);

    context1.beginPath();
    for(var x=1; x<sampleCount; x+= deltaX1){
      barHeight = 2*data[x*step]*rectHeight/2;
      context1.fillStyle = fillColors[x % fillColors.
                                                  length];
      context1.fillRect(x, rectHeight/2-barHeight,
                        barWidth, barHeight);
    }
  } else if(loop % 4 == 1) {
    context2.strokeStyle = fillColors[loop % fillColors.
                                                  length];

    context2.beginPath();
   context2.moveTo(0, rectHeight/2-data[0]*rectHeight/2);

    for(var x=1; x<sampleCount; x++){
context2.lineTo(x, rectHeight/2-data[x*step]*rectHeight/2);
    }
    context2.stroke();
  } else if(loop % 4 == 2) {
```

```
        index = Math.floor(Math.random()*5);

        x1 = (8*loop) % sampleCount;
        y1 = rectHeight  - (loop % rectHeight);
        x2 = sampleCount - (loop % sampleCount);
        y2 = rectHeight/2-
                   data[step*(sampleCount-1)]*rectHeight/2;
        x3 = sampleCount/2;
        y3 = rectHeight/2-data[step*sampleCount/2]*rectHeig
                                                       ht/2;

      context3.strokeStyle = fillColors[index % fillColors.
                                                     length];
      context3.fillStyle = fillColors[(index+1)%fillColors.
                                                     length];
        context3.moveTo(x1, y1);
        context3.quadraticCurveTo(x2, y2, x3, y3);

        context3.fill();
        context3.stroke();
      } else {
        context4.strokeStyle = fillColors[loop % fillColors.
                                                     length];

        context4.beginPath();
      context4.moveTo(0, rectHeight/2-data[0]*rectHeight/2);

        for(var x=1; x<sampleCount; x+=deltaX4){
          context4.strokeRect(
                   x, rectHeight/2-data[x*step]*rectHeight/2,
                      smallWidth, smallHeight);
        }
        context4.stroke();
      }

      ++loop;
    }
  </script>
 </body>
<html>
```

The graphics effects in Listing 10.11 involve a sine-based bar chart, squiggly lines, a set of Bezier curves, and then another set of "fuzzy" random squiggly lines.

Listing 10.11 contains four HTML5 <canvas> elements that are used for rendering graphics that are based on the amplitude of the sounds in the audio file. The JavaScript function `writeSamples()` uses the value of the expression `loop%4` to select one of the four HTML5 `<canvas>` element and then render some graphics in that element. Although this rendering is done in a "round robin" fashion, the speed of code execution creates the illusion that the rendering effects is performed simultaneously in all four `<canvas>` elements.

The first part of the code initializes a `channels` variable (which is an object) and the variable `fbLength` (which is the length of the frame buffer of the audio), so that we capture the amplitude of the audio signal that we are sampling, as shown here:

```
function getMetadata() {
  channels = audio.mozChannels;
  fbLength = audio.mozFrameBufferLength;
}
```

The actual graphics images are easy to render, as you can see from the following block of code that computes the height of bar elements based on the values of the audio that are contained in the `data` array (which is pre-populated for us), and then renders a sine-based bar chart:

```
for(var x=1; x<sampleCount; x+= deltaX1){
  barHeight = 2*data[x*step]*rectHeight/2;
  context1.fillStyle = fillColors[x % fillColors.length];
  context1.fillRect(x, rectHeight/2-barHeight,
                    barWidth, barHeight);
}
```

Figure 10.3 displays the result of rendering Listing 10.11 in a Chrome browser on a Macbook.

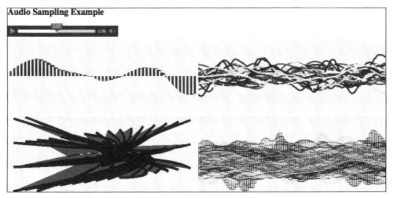

FIGURE 10.3 Converting audio waves into graphics on a Macbook.

Note that the code in Listing 10.11 is based on a code sample from this Web site:

http://html5videoguide.net/chapter8.html

Chris Wilson created a Web site that enables you to drag and drop components onto a Web page in order to apply various effects to audio files:

https://webaudioplayground.appspot.com/

Chris Wilson is also a co-editor of the W3C Web MIDI API specification:

https://dvcs.w3.org/hg/audio/raw-file/tip/midi/specification.html

Other interesting Web Audio code samples are here:

http://updates.html5rocks.com/2012/02/HTML5-audio-and-the-Web-Audio-API-are-BFFs
http://www.html5audio.org/2012/05/new-google-doodle-uses-web-audio-api.html
http://www.html5rocks.com/en/tutorials/webaudio/positional_audio/
http://chromium.googlecode.com/svn/trunk/samples/audio/index.html
http://jeromeetienne.github.com/slides/webaudioapi/#1
https://bleedinghtml5.appspot.com/#1

JQUERY AND HTML5 FILE APIS

The HTML5 File APIs enable you to create, read, and write files on the file system. The first step is to obtain access to the HTML5 FileSystem, after which you can perform file-related operations. You can read about these APIs and also see code examples here:

- *http://aquantum-demo.appspot.com/file-upload*
- *http://www.htmlgoodies.com/html5/other/responding-to-html5-filereader-events.html*
- The DVD contains the HTML Web page `JQFileInfo1.html` that illustrates how to use jQuery in order to display the attributes of a file that is selected by users. A more interesting (and more useful) example is `JQ-FileUpload2.html` in Listing 10.12 that illustrates how to use jQuery and XHR2 to upload files.

Listing 10.12 JQFileUpload2.html

```html
<!DOCTYPE HTML>
<html lang="en">
 <head>
   <meta charset="utf-8"/>
   <title>JQuery File Upload</title>

   <title>File Upload with XHR2</title>
   <script src="http://ajax.googleapis.com/ajax/libs/jquery/1.7.1/
jquery.min.js">
   </script>
 </head>

 <body>
  <script>
   $(document).ready(function () {
      $("body").on("change", '#fileUploader', function() {
         // Prepare post data
         var data = new FormData();
         data.append('uploadfile', this.files[0]);

         // invoke the jQuery .ajax method:
         $.ajax({
           type: 'POST',
           url: url,
           data: data,
           success:  function(data) {
                        // do something here
                     },
           dataType: 'text'
         });
      });
    });
  </script>

  <div>
    <input id="fileUploader" type="file" multiple/>
  </div>
 </body>
</html>
```

Listing 10.12 contains an HTML `<input>` field that enables uses to select a file from the file system. After a file is selected, the jQuery "change" event is triggered, and an XHR2 `FormData` object (discussed earlier in this chapter) is created and populated, as shown here:

```
var data = new FormData();
data.append('uploadfile', this.files[0]);
```

The selected file is uploaded via the jQuery `.ajax()` method, which contains a "success" function that is invoked after the Ajax request has been completed successfully.

If you want to use a jQuery plugin for uploading files in HTML5 Web pages, there are several available, such as the cross-browser jQuery plugin `jquery-filedrop`:

https://github.com/weixiyen/jquery-filedrop

HTML5 WEB INTENTS

Web Intents is an upcoming framework that provides Web-based communication between applications and service discovery. Web Intents provides a discovery mechanism and a lightweight RPC mechanism, modeled after the Intents system in Android.

One of the advantages of Web Intents is that it enables Web applications to communicate with each other, without requiring them to know each other's identity. Google Chrome 18+ natively supports Web Intents, and there is a JavaScript shim with support for IE 8+ (and other browsers).

The proposed method of intent registration is via the Intent tag, as shown here:

```
<intent
  action="http://webintents.org/share"
  type="image/*"
  href="share.html"
  disposition="window|inline"
/>
```

An invocation of an Intent is shown here:

```
var intent = new Intent("http://webintents.org/share",
                        "text/uri-list",
                        "http://news.bbc.co.uk");


window.navigator.startActivity(intent);
```

Additional information about Web Intents is here:
http://webintents.org/

http://dvcs.w3.org/hg/web-intents/raw-file/tip/spec/Overview.html
A video demo of Web Intents by Robin Berjon is here:

*https://docs.google.com/file/d/0B-2pb_m94nPxRGV5LTRvM0pLaUU/
edit?pli=1*

USING HTML5 MICRODATA

Unlike the other HTML5 technologies in this chapter, HTML5 Microdata does not provide JavaScript APIs. Even if this technology is not important to you now, it's worth skimming through the material in this section so that you are aware of its purpose in case you need to use this technology at some point in the future. Keep in mind that HTML5 Microdata is markup only, and unlike other HTML5 technologies, there are no APIs available.

There are many specialized types of microformats that provide information about different types of entities. Some of the more common microformats include Breadcrumbs (displays the location of a given page relative to the structure of a Web site), Businesses and Organizations (for corporate structure and related contact information), Events (provides Calendar data), Product Information (provides product catalog data), People (information about people, such as contact information).

Microdata provides a standardized way to include additional semantics in HTML5 Web pages. Microdata defines five HTML attributes that can be applied to any HTML5 tag, where each attribute is essentially a name/value pair. The most commonly used tags are `itemscope`, `itemtype`, and `itemprop`, whereas `itemref` and `itemid` are not needed by most common formats.

Microdata also supports customized elements and allows you to embed custom properties in HTML5 Web pages. Each group is called an item, and each name-value pair is a property. Items and properties are represented by regular elements. You can create an item using the `itemscope` attribute and you add a property to an item using the `itemprop` attribute on one of the item's descendants.

As a simple example, the following code block contains two items, each of which has the property "name:"

```
<div itemscope>
<p>My name is <span itemprop="name">Zara</span>.</p>
</div>

<div itemscope>
```

```
<p>My name is <span itemprop="name">Nuha</span>.</p>
</div>
```

For additional information, navigate to the W3C Microdata specification (currently a work-in-progress):

http://dev.w3.org/html5/md/

You can also find Google's currently supported Microdata formats here:

http://www.google.com/support/webmasters/bin/topic.py?topic=21997

If you want to write HTML5 Web pages with Microdata functionality using jQuery, you can find a jQuery plugin for Microdata here:

http://www.vanseodesign.com/web-design/html5-microdata/

HTML5 WEB NOTIFICATIONS

The Notifications API allows you to display notifications to users for given events. You can display notifications in various ways, including e-mails messages, tweets, or calendar events.

You can easily check for notifications support in your browser with this code block, whose conditional logic checks for the presence of `window.notifications` and `window.webKitNotifications` (which you can expand to include prefixes):

```
if(window.webkitNotifications ||
   window.notifications) {
   console.log("Notifications are supported.");
}
else {
   console.log("Notifications are not supported.");
}
```

Notification objects dispatch events during their lifecycle, which you can use to generate desired behavior. For example, the `show` event occurs whenever a notification is shown to users, and the following code snippet illustrates how to display a notification for 15 seconds:

```
new Notification("New Email Received",
                 { iconUrl: "mail.png",
                   onshow: function(){
                             setTimeout(notification.close(),
15000);
```

```
                                    }
                            });
```

The `close` event occurs when users dismiss a notification, and the following code snippet shows you how to ensure that additional reminders are suppressed:

```
new Notification("Meeting about to begin",
                    { iconUrl: "calendar.gif",
                      body: "Room 101",
                      onclose: function() { cancelReminders(event); }
                    });
```

For more information, navigate to the W3C Web Notifications draft specification here:

http://www.w3.org/TR/notifications/

You can find working code samples that illustrate how to grant permissions to a Web site to display notifications here:

http://www.html5rocks.com/en/tutorials/notifications/quick/

The preceding Web site contains a code sample that shows you the ease with which new Twitter tweets can be displayed in a Web page.

HTML5 WAI-ARIA

WAI-ARIA (Web Accessibility Initiative: Accessible Rich Internet Applications) is a W3C specification that specifies how to increase the accessibility of Web pages (including dynamic content) and user interface components developed with Ajax, HTML, JavaScript, and related technologies.

Although WAI-ARIA predates HTML5, the HTML5 WAI ARIA specification defines support for accessible Web applications, which involves markup extensions that are often attributes of HTML5 elements. Web developers can use these markup extensions to obtain more information about screen readers and other assistive technologies.

As a simple example, consider the following code snippet of an enhanced HTML `<li>` element from the ARIA specification illustrates the use of the `role` and `aria-checked` attributes:

```
<li role="menuitemcheckbox" aria-checked="true">
  <img src="checked.gif" role="presentation" alt="">
```

```
<!-- note: additional scripts required to toggle image
                                                source -->
Sort by Last Modified
</li>
```

The two new attributes in the preceding code snippet have no impact on the manner in which browsers render the `<li>` element. Browsers that support ARIA will add OS-specific accessibility information to the rendered `<li>` element, and enable screen readers to read information aloud in a contextual manner.

If you are planning to use jQuery and also to support ARIA, there is a jQuery plugin that provides ARIA support here:

http://webcloud.se/code/jQuery-Collapse/

You can get more information about the WAI-AIA specification here:

http://www.w3.org/TR/wai-aria/

HTML5 WEB WORKERS

JavaScript runs in a single-threaded environment, which means that events will not interrupt running code; instead, event delivery is deferred until the browser is idle. The key benefit of supporting threads in the browser is the ability to handle events in the main thread (the UI thread) and also the ability delegate long-running code to different threads.

In simplified terms, HTML5 Web Workers provides support for threads that can perform heavy computational tasks, where those threads are separate from the UI thread, thereby improving browser responsiveness.

There are restrictions for Web Workers: they cannot access the window object of a Web page, which means that they cannot access the DOM of a Web page. However, Web Workers are background scripts that you need to use in a judicious manner because they can consume resources to the point where a system becomes noticeably less responsive.

A Web Worker is initialized with the following line of code, where `worker1.js` contains the code that is to be executed for a Web Worker:

```
var worker1 = new Worker("worker1.js");
```

In the preceding code snippet, your browser session will spawn a new worker thread that downloads the file asynchronously and executes the code in the JavaScript file (which in this case is called `worker1.js`).

If the JavaScript file does not exist, you can register for an error event from the worker. The JS Event model ensures that event will be queued until the browser goes idle, so you can define the handler right after creating the worker and still receive the event.

You can use the `importScripts` statement in order to reference JavaScript files that contain code for your Web Workers, as shown here:

```
importScripts("helper1.js", "helper2.js", "helper3.js");
```

The `postMessage()` method enables the main Web page to communicate to a Web Worker; depending on your browser and the specific version, you can specify a string or a JSON string as the lone argument for this method. On the other hand, Web Workers use the `onmessage()` method in order to communicate with the main Web page.

As powerful as Web Workers are, there are also certain things they cannot do. For example, when a script is executing inside a Web Worker it cannot access the Web page's window object (`window.document`), which means that Web Workers don't have direct access to the web page and the DOM API. Although Web Workers cannot block the browser UI, they can still consume CPU cycles and make the system less responsive.

The majority of the modern Web browsers support Web Workers. Check the Web site *http://caniuse.com* (search for Web Workers) for the most up-to-date support matrix. Although there are "polyfill" (emulation) libraries available for most other APIs (such as `excanvas.js` and `flashcanvas.js` for HTML5 Canvas that provide an emulation of the Canvas APIs, where the latter uses Flash under the covers), an emulation library for Web Workers does not seem worthwhile. You can either invoke your worker code as a worker, or run the same code inline in your page, which blocks the UI thread. The improved responsiveness of the worker-based page may induce people to upgrade to a more modern browser.

Meanwhile, code samples that use Web Workers frequently to do things such as finding prime numbers (which are somewhat contrived), or something similar that involves partitioning a problem domain into multiple disjoint subsets. Since you can find those code samples online, there is no need to reproduce them here. If you are interested in using jQuery Mobile with Web Workers, an example is here:

http://www.davetech.com/blog/web_workers_jquery

HTML5 HISTORY APIS

Prior to HTML5, the browser support for history-related APIs provided limited functionality. You could find the number of items in the browser history, move forward and backward, and several links backward, as shown here:

```
console.log(history.length);
console.log(history.forward());
console.log(history.back());
console.log(history.go(-2));
```

Several new APIs are available, as shown here:

```
history.pushState(data, title, url);
history.replaceState(data, title, url);
```

The parameters in the `history.pushState()` method are as follows:

- `data` is some type of structured data, assigned to the history item
- `title` is the name of the item in the history drop-down that is displayed by the browser's back and forward buttons
- `url` is the (optional) URL that is displayed in the address bar

The parameters in the `history.replaceState()` method are the same as the `history.pushState()` method, except that the former updates information that is already in the browser's history.

In addition, there is the new `popstate` event, which occurs when users view their browser history, and you can use it in the following manner:

```
window.addEventListener("popstate", function(event) {
    // do something here
});
```

Keep in mind that different browsers implement HTML5 browser history in different ways, so the following JavaScript toolkit is useful:

https://github.com/balupton/History.js/

The `History.js` toolkit supports jQuery, MooTools and Prototype, and in HTML5 browsers you can modify the URL directly without resorting to hashes.

HTML5 OFFLINE WEB APPLICATIONS

The purpose of Offline Web Applications is simple: users can work on an application even when they are disconnected from the Internet. When users do have access to the Internet, their data changes are synchronized so that everything is in a consistent state.

A Web site that contains demos, additional links, and tutorial-like information is here:

http://appcachefacts.info/

The HTML5 specification requires a so-called "manifest file" (with a "appcache" as the suggested suffix) that contains the following three sections:

- CACHE (the list of files that are going to be cached)
- NETWORK (the files that can only be accessed online)
- FALLBACK (specifies the resource to display when users try to access non-cached resources)

As a simple example, Listing 10.13 displays the contents of a sample manifest file called MyApp.appcache.

Listing 10.13 MyApp.appcache

```
CACHE MANIFEST
# Verson 1.0.0
CACHE:
Index.html
Cachedstuff.html
Mystyle.css
Myimage.jpg

NETWORK:
*
FALLBACK:
/ noncached.html
```

You must ensure that the manifest file is served with the following MIME type:

```
text/cache-manifest
```

Second, every Web page that uses offline functionality must reference the manifest file at the top of the Web page:

```
<html lang="en" manifest="mymanifest.manifest">
```

If you have a Web page that is hosted by a provider, you can verify that the Web page contains the correct MIME type by issuing the following type of command:

```
curl -I http://www.myprovider.com/mymanifest.manifest
```

DETECTING ONLINE AND OFFLINE STATUS

The simplest way to determine whether or not an application is offline in an HTML5 Web page is with the following code snippet:

```
if(navigator.onLine) {
   // application is online
} else {
   // application is offline
}
```

For mobile applications that uses jQuery Mobile, you can use the following type of code block:

```
$(document).bind("offline", function() {
   // application is offline
}
```

Binding the offline event as shown in the preceding code block is useful for handling situations whereby an application goes offline while users are actively viewing an application.

In addition, you would send data to a server only when you are online, and store data locally via HTML5 localStorage when you are offline.

The jQuery plugin `jquery-offline` is a cross-browser plugin that enables you to use jQuery syntax for offline applications, and its homepage is here:

https://github.com/wycats/jquery-offline

HTML5 APIS IN EXPERIMENTAL STATUS

This section covers HTML5 APIs in the early stage of the W3C process, so they are covered lightly.

The CSS Compositing specification is an "Editor's Note" and work-in-progress, and it has recently appeared in the WebKit "nightlies," which means that as this book goes to print, the code will probably be part of the mainline for `WebKit`. Compositing pertains to combining shapes of different elements into a single image. Previous versions of SVG used Simple Alpha Compositing, and the latest specification defines a new compositing model that expands upon the Simple Alpha Compositing model. Full details are here:

http://dvcs.w3.org/hg/FXTF/raw-file/tip/compositing/index.html

Mozilla *Firefox OS* (previously called B2G (Boot to Gecko) is intended to be a new open mobile ecosystem based on HTML5. Mobile devices that run Firefox OS will support HTML5 Web pages that can access all the capabilities of mobile devices. The operating system (which uses Firefox) will enable developers to access the capabilities of these mobile devices as part of HTML5 applications. More details are here:

https://blog.mozilla.org/blog/2012/07/02/firefox-mobile-os/

The Voice Recognition (TTS) specification involves converting text to speech, which involves CSS properties for declaratively controlling the rendering of documents via speech synthesis, along with optional audio cues. Full details are here:

http://www.w3.org/TR/css3-speech

OTHER UPCOMING HTML5 FEATURES

There are several sets of APIs that are under development and discussion at the W3C, some of which are listed here:

- Web Components
- The Shadow DOM
- The Pointer Lock API (game-oriented)
- The Gamepad API (game-oriented)

Details about Web Components are here:

http://www.w3.org/TR/components-intro/

The Shadow DOM specification is here:

http://www.w3.org/TR/shadow-dom

The specification for the Pointer Lock API (WebApps Working Group) is here:

http://dvcs.w3.org/hg/pointerlock/raw-file/tip/index.html

You can get information about the GamePad API here:

https://dvcs.w3.org/hg/gamepad/raw-file/default/gamepad.html

Some experimental GamePad code (Firefox only) is here:

https://developer.mozilla.org/en/API/Gamepad/Using_Gamepad_API

SUMMARY

This chapter provided an overview of various HTML5 technologies and grouped them according to their current W3C status. For your convenience, these HTML5 technologies are listed alphabetically below:

- Ajax (XHR2)
- Drag and Drop
- File APIs
- Forms
- Geolocation
- Offline applications
- Server-Sent Events
- WebSockets
- Web Workers

In this chapter, you saw how to test browsers for WebSocket support, and how to make a WebSocket invocation. In addition, you learned how to use jQuery in conjunction with various HTML5-related technologies.

The next chapter provides an overview of HTML5 Canvas, which is a technology that enables you to write graphics programs that draw directly to a part of a Web page.

CHAPTER 11

INTRODUCTION TO HTML5 CANVAS

This chapter provides an overview of HTML5 Canvas, which is a technology that enables you to write graphics programs that draw directly to a part of a Web page. HTML5 Canvas supports various APIs for rendering 2D shapes with an assortment of graphics effects. Although there are many online Canvas-related and CSS3-related tutorials available, few of them provide code examples of using both HTML5 Canvas and CSS3 graphics effects.

As you will see, various code samples in this chapter contain (sometimes striking) combinations of HTML5 Canvas, CSS3 graphics, and CSS3 2D/3D animation effects that you are unlikely to find in any online resources or topic-related books. These code samples provide a starting point for you to create your own visually compelling graphics effects.

In addition, most of the sections in this chapter start with the syntax of the APIs that are used in the associated code listings, partly because the code samples contain a lot of details and also illustrate multiple concepts. So, even though this is an "introductory" chapter about HTML5 Canvas, you will learn considerably more than you would expect from a basic overview that you might find in other books.

The first part of this chapter shows you how to render line segments, rectangles, and circles in HTML5 Canvas, and also how to combine HTML5 Canvas with CSS3 stylesheets.

The second part introduces you to linear and radial gradients in HTML5 Canvas, with examples of how to apply them to Bezier curves and JPG files. The third part of this chapter discusses jCanvas, which is a jQuery plugin for HTML5 Canvas, and also an example of combining Canvas-based graphics with jQuery Mobile.

The concepts and code samples in this chapter will help you understand the HTML5 Canvas-based charts and graphs in Chapter 12, all of which are based on 2D shapes. Moreover, if you want to explore additional HTML5 Canvas graphics after you have finished reading this chapter, an extensive set of code samples is available here:

http://code.google.com/p/html5-canvas-graphics

This chapter provides techniques for creating various visual effects that you can use in your custom charts and graphs. At the same time, it's also important for you to assess the trade-off (time, effort, and cost) between writing low-level Canvas-based graphics code, such as the code samples in this chapter, versus the availability of open source projects and commercial products.

WHAT IS HTML5 CANVAS?

Several years ago Canvas began in OS/X as a widget toolkit, and after Canvas had already been available in the Safari browser, it became a specification for the Web, and now it's commonly referred to as HTML5 Canvas.

HTML5 Canvas and SVG both allow you to programmatically render graphics in a browser via JavaScript. However, HTML5 Canvas uses "immediate mode," which is a write-and-forget approach to rendering graphics. Thus, if you want to write a sketching program in HTML5 Canvas and you also want to provide an "undo" feature, then you must programmatically keep track of everything that users have drawn on the screen. On the other hand, SVG uses a "retained mode," which involves a DOM (Document Object Model) structure that keeps track of the rendered objects and their relationship to one another.

If you are going to write HTML Web pages that make extensive use of graphics effects, you'll probably need to understand the differences between HTML5 Canvas and SVG in terms of performance. You have the freedom to use one technology exclusively, but you can also create HTML Web pages that contain a mixture of HTML5 Canvas, SVG, and CSS3, and performance-related information can help you decide how you are going to code your HTML Web pages.

Although this chapter does not delve into the preceding points in any more detail, you can find a good overview of some features/advantages of HTML5 Canvas here:

http://thinkvitamin.com/code/how-to-draw-with-html-5-canvas/

Incidentally, if you need HTML5 Canvas support in Internet Explorer 8, you can use ExplorerCanvas, which is an open source project that is available here:

http://code.google.com/p/explorercanvas/

You can use the preceding code project simply by including the following code snippet in your HTML Web pages:

```
<!-- [if IE]><script src="excanvas.js"></script><![endif]-->
```

HTML5 CANVAS VERSUS SVG

One point to consider is when it's advantageous to use HTML5 Canvas instead of a technology such as SVG. The following short list contains some features to consider when you are making this type of analysis:

- Native versus plugin browser support
- Level of SVG support in different browsers
- Animation support
- Support for filters (SVG only)
- Built-in support for HTML-like widgets
- Third-party support

Most modern browsers provide varying degrees of built-in support for SVG, and Adobe's SVG viewer can be used with Microsoft's Internet Explorer. If you need filter-based visual effects, then SVG provides a very rich (perhaps even the best) functionality. If you need built-in support for HTML controls, then frameworks such as Wijmo might be a good solution for your needs. Another point to consider is that Adobe no longer supports its SVG viewer. This is a significant decision, because Adobe's SVG viewer had been the de facto standard for SVG viewers for many years. Although Firefox and Opera have made significant progress in terms of their support for SVG, and both are enhancing their support for SVG, they still lag the feature support of Adobe's SVG viewer. Thus, you need to weigh the most important factors in order to make the decision that will meet your project-related needs.

A very good article containing examples and diagrams that compares the use of HTML5 Canvas and SVG is here:

http://blogs.msdn.com/b/ie/archive/2011/04/22/thoughts-on-when-to-use-canvas-and-svg.aspx

The HTML5 Canvas Coordinate System

Think back to your days in high school, where you learned that the Cartesian coordinate system identifies any point in the Euclidean plane by means of a pair of numbers, often written as (x,y). The first number represents the horizontal value and the second number represents the vertical value. The horizontal axis is labeled the x-axis, and positive values on the x-axis are to the right of the vertical axis (i.e., toward the right). The vertical axis is labeled the y-axis, and positive values on the y-axis are above the horizontal axis. The origin is the intersection point of the x-axis and the y-axis.

The situation is almost the same in the HTML5 Canvas coordinate system. The x-axis is horizontal and the positive direction is toward the right. The y-axis is vertical, but the positive direction is downward, which is the opposite direction of most graphs in a typical mathematics textbook. In the HTML5 Canvas coordinate system, the origin is the upper-left corner of the screen (not the lower-left corner), the unit of measurement is the pixel, and until recently the largest visible display was 1024x728. However, Apple recently introduced a new Apple laptop that has a 2880x1800 display.

As a simple illustration, Figure 11.1 displays four points in an HTML5 <canvas> element.

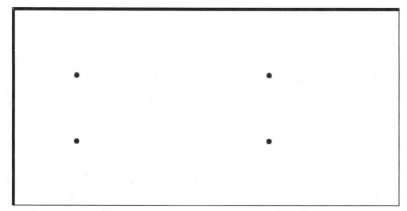

FIGURE 11.1 Four points rendered in HTML5 Canvas.

If you start from the origin (the upper-left corner of the screen) and move 50 pixels to the right, followed by 50 pixels downward, you will reach the upper-left point in Figure 11.1. Next, if you start from the origin and move 200 pixels to the right and 50 pixels downward, you will reach the upper-right point in Listing 11.1. In a similar fashion, the two points in the second "row" have coordinates (50,100) and (200,100). Notice that the two points in the first row have the same value for the y-coordinate, which makes sense because they are the same distance away from the top of the Web page; the same is true for the two points in the second row. Similarly, the two points in the left "column" have the same x-coordinate because they are both the same distance from the left side of the Web page.

Now that you have an understanding of the HTML5 Canvas coordinate system, let's take a look at the contents of Listing 11.1, which displays a minimal HTML5 Web page that is ready for rendering HTML5 Canvas-based graphics. Every Canvas-based code sample in this book uses the code (or some variant) that is displayed in Listing 11.1. Note that if you launch this code in a browser session, you will only see a blank screen.

Listing 11.1 Canvas1.html

```
<!DOCTYPE html>
  <html lang="en">
   <head>
    <meta charset="utf-8">
    <title>Canvas Drawing Rectangles</title>

    <script><!--
      window.addEventListener('load', function () {
        // Get the canvas element
        var elem = document.getElementById('myCanvas');
        if (!elem || !elem.getContext) {
          return;
        }

        // Get the canvas 2d context
        var context = elem.getContext('2d');
        if (!context) {
          return;
        }

        // Insert your custom Canvas graphics code here
      }, false);
      // --></script>
   </head>

   <body>
    <p>
     <canvas id="myCanvas" width="300" height="300">No support for
   Canvas.
     </canvas>
     </p>
```

```
    </body>
</html>
```

Listing 11.1 contains an HTML `<head>` element that checks for the existence of an HTML `<canvas>` element inside the HTML `<body>` element of the Web page, and then gets the 2D context from the HTML `<canvas>` element. If you skip over the various conditional statements in Listing 11.1, there are two lines of code that enable us to get a reference to the variable `context`, which represents a drawable surface:

```
var elem = document.getElementById('myCanvas');
var context = elem.getContext('2d');
```

If you launch Listing 11.1 in a browser that does not support HTML5 Canvas, the text message "No support for Canvas." is displayed.

The following code snippet is executed whenever you launch the Web page because of an anonymous JavaScript function that is executed during the `load` event:

```
<script><!--
window.addEventListener('load', function () {
  // do something here
}, false);
// --></script>
```

Now that you understand the underlying code for rendering Canvas-based 2D shapes, you can focus on the code that actually draws some 2D shapes, starting with the example in the next section.

LINE SEGMENTS, RECTANGLES, CIRCLES, AND SHADOW EFFECTS

This section contains an assortment of code samples that illustrate how to render 2D shapes in HTML5 Canvas. There are many concepts introduced in this section, so before delving into the code sample, let's look at some of the HTML5 Canvas APIs that are used in this section. Chapter 2 contains a section that describes various ways for specifying colors, and the material in that section is relevant for the code sample in this chapter.

HTML5 Canvas provides the `fillRect()` method for rendering a rectangle, which requires four parameters: the upper-left vertex (defined by its x-coordinate and its y-coordinate) of the rectangle, the width of the rectangle, and the height of the desired rectangle. The Canvas `fillRect()` API looks like this:

```
context.fillRect(x, y, width, height);
```

HTML5 Canvas allows you to render line segments by specifying the (x,y) coordinates of the two endpoints of a line segment. The two new APIs that are used in the code sample in this section are moveTo() and lineTo(), and they look like this:

```
context.moveTo(x1, y1);
context.lineTo(x2, y2);
```

The preceding code snippet represents the line segment whose two endpoints are specified by the points (x1, y1) and (x2, y2). Note that you can also render the same line segment with the following code snippet:

```
context.moveTo(x2, y2);
context.lineTo(x1, y1);
```

Shadow effects provide a richer visual experience that is an improvement over the use of non-shadow effects. You create a shadow effect by assigning values to three shadow-related attributes that control the size of the underlying shadow and also the extent of the "fuzziness" of the shadow, as shown here:

```
context.shadowOffsetX = shadowX;
context.shadowOffsetY = shadowY;
context.shadowBlur    = 4;
```

You can also assign (R,G,B) or (R,G,B,A) values to shadowColor (which is an attribute of the drawing context) as shown here:

```
context.shadowColor   = "rgba(0,0,64,1.0)";
```

The HTML5 Web page RandRectanglesShadow.html in Listing 11.2 uses this technique in order to render a set of randomly generated rectangles with a shadow effect.

Listing 11.2 RandRectanglesShadow.html

```
<!DOCTYPE html>
<html lang="en">
<head>
  <meta charset="utf-8">
  <title>Canvas Random Rectangles With Shadow Effects</title>
  <link href="CSS3Background2.css"
        rel="stylesheet" type="text/css">

  <style>
```

```
  input {
    width:300px;
    font-size:24px;
    background-color:#f00;
  }
</style>

<script><!--
  window.addEventListener('load', function() {
    var clickCount = 0;

    // Get the canvas element
    var elem = document.getElementById('myCanvas');
    if (!elem || !elem.getContext) {
      return;
    }

    // Get the canvas 2d context
    var context = elem.getContext('2d');
    if (!context) {
      return;
    }

    var basePointX = 10;
    var basePointY = 10;
    var canWidth   = 800;
    var canHeight  = 450;
    var shadowX    = 10;
    var shadowY    = 10;
    var rectCount  = 100;
    var rectWidth  = 100;
    var rectHeight = 100;
    var colorIndex = 0;
    var fillStyles = ['#f00', '#ff0', '#0f0', '#00f'];

    redrawCanvas = function() {
        // clear the canvas before drawing new set of rectangles
        context.clearRect(0, 0, elem.width, elem.height);

        for(var r=0; r<rectCount; r++) {
           basePointX = canWidth*Math.random();
           basePointY = canHeight*Math.random();

           // Alternate shadow effect based on an even/odd
           // click count with different (R,G,B,A) values
           if(clickCount % 2 == 0) {
```

```
            context.shadowColor    = "rgba(0,0,64,1.0)";
        } else {
            context.shadowColor    = "rgba(64,0,0,1.0)";
        }

        // code that specifies the size and also the
        // "fuzziness" of the underlying shadow effect
        context.shadowOffsetX = shadowX;
        context.shadowOffsetY = shadowY;
        context.shadowBlur    = 4;
        context.lineWidth     = 1;

        // render a colored rectangle
        colorIndex = Math.floor(basePointX)%fillStyles.length;
        context.fillStyle = fillStyles[colorIndex];

        context.fillRect(basePointX, basePointY,
                         rectWidth, rectHeight);

        ++clickCount;
        }
    }

    // render a set of random rectangles
    redrawCanvas();
   }, false);
   // --></script>
</head>

<body>
 <div>
  <canvas id="myCanvas" width="800" height="450">No support for
Canvas
  </canvas>
 </div>

 <div>
  <input type="button" onclick="redrawCanvas();return false"
         value="Redraw the Rectangles"/>
 </div>
 </body>
</html>
```

The HTML5 code in Listing 11.2 starts by initializing some JavaScript variables and then defining the JavaScript function redrawCanvas() that contains a loop for rendering the rectangles on the screen. The loop calculates the coordinates of the upper-left vertex of each rectangle, as shown here:

```
basePointX = canWidth*Math.random();
basePointY = canHeight*Math.random();
```

The next part of the loop assigns the background color (which alternates between a dark blue and dark red shadow), and then sets up the shadow effect by specifying values for the attributes shadowOffsetX, shadowOffsetY, and shadowBlur, as shown here:

```
context.shadowOffsetX = shadowX;
context.shadowOffsetY = shadowY;
context.shadowBlur    = 4;
```

The actual rendering of each rectangle is performed by the following code:

```
context.fillRect(basePointX, basePointY,
                 rectWidth, rectHeight);
```

Notice that the clickCount variable is incremented each time users click inside the HTML5 <canvas> element, and its value determines which shadow color is applied to the randomly generated rectangles.

Although shadow effects create a pleasing effect, they also have an impact on performance. If you need shadow-like effects but performance becomes an issue, one alternative is to render a background shape in black (or some other dark color), and then render the same shape (with a small offset) using a different color.

For example, you can create a shadow effect for rectangles by first rendering a black rectangle and then rendering a red rectangle on top of the black rectangle, as shown here:

```
// render a black rectangle
context.fillStyle = '#000';
context.fillRect(50+shadowX, 50+shadowY, 200, 100);

// render a red rectangle
context.fillStyle = '#f00';
context.fillRect(50, 50, 200, 100);
```

The values for shadowX and shadowY determine the size of the background "shadow," and the choice of positive versus negative values for shadowX and shadowY will determine the relative position of the black rectangle with respect to the red rectangle.

Listing 11.3 CSS3Background2.css

```
#myCanvas {
position: relative; top: 0px; left: 0px;
```

```
background-color:white;
background-image:
  -webkit-radial-gradient(red 4px, transparent 18px),
  -webkit-repeating-radial-gradient(red 0px,  green 4px, yellow
8px,
                                    blue 12px, transparent 28px,
                                    green 20px,  red 24px,
                                    transparent 28px,
                                    transparent 32px),
  -webkit-repeating-radial-gradient(red 0px,  green 4px, yellow
8px,
                                    blue 12px, transparent 28px,
                                    green 20px,  red 24px,
                                    transparent 28px,
                                    transparent 32px);
background-size: 50px 60px,  70px 80px;
background-position: 0 0;
-webkit-box-shadow:  30px 30px 30px #000;

resize:both;
overflow:auto;
}

#myCanvas:hover {
position: relative; top: 0px; left: 0px;

background-color:white;
background-image:
  -webkit-radial-gradient(red 4px, transparent 48px),
  -webkit-repeating-radial-gradient(red 2px,  green 4px, yellow
8px,
                                    blue 12px, transparent 16px,
                                    red 20px, blue 24px,
                                    transparent 28px,
                                    transparent 32px),
  -webkit-radial-gradient(blue 8px,  transparent 68px);

background-size: 120px 120px,  4px 4px;
background-position: 0 0;
}
```

Listing 11.3 contains two similar CSS3 selectors for rendering the HTML5 <canvas> element defined in Listing 11.3, as well as a hover-based selector that changes the background of the HTML5 <canvas> element whenever users hover over this element with their mouse. The #myCanvas selector defines a radial gradient, followed by two repeating radial gradients that specify various combinations of red, green, yellow, and blue at different pixel locations. A key point involves the use of `transparent`, which changes the gap between consecutive colors that are rendered.

As you can see in the definition of the `#myCanvas` selector, there are many possible combinations available for the colors, the gradients (and their types), and the colors for the gradients, along with the values for the background-size attribute. There is no "right" way to define these patterns; feel free to experiment with different combinations, and you might create unexpectedly pleasing results.

Figure 11.2 displays a set of randomly generated rectangles with a shadow effect based on `RandRectanglesShadow.html` in Listing 11.2, rendered in landscape mode on an Asus Prime tablet with Android ICS.

FIGURE 11.2 Canvas random rectangles on an Asus Prime tablet with Android ICS.

HTML5 CANVAS LINEAR GRADIENTS

HTML5 Canvas provides two primary types of color gradients (similar to SVG and CSS3): linear gradients and radial gradients.

Linear color gradients can be further sub-divided into three types: horizontal linear gradients, vertical linear gradients, and diagonal linear gradients. Thus, HTML5 Canvas provides color gradients that enable you to create pleasing visual effects.

A linear gradient is defined in terms of `addColorStop` elements, each of which contains a decimal (between 0 and 1) and a hexadecimal value that represents a color. For example, if you define a linear gradient with an initial color of `#FF0000` (the hexadecimal value for `red`) and a final color of `#000000` (the hexadecimal value for black), then the resultant color gradient will range (in a linear fashion) from red to black. Linear gradients enable you to create vivid and interesting color combinations, and they are available in three varieties: horizontal, vertical, and diagonal. Note that "linear gradient" and "linear color gradient" are used interchangeably in this book.

Horizontal, Vertical, and Diagonal Linear Gradients

As you learned in the introduction of this chapter, HTML5 Canvas supports the method `createLinearGradient()` that you can use to programmatically create linear gradients, and its syntax looks like this:

```
context.createLinearGradient(startX, startY, endX, endY);
```

The HTML5 page `LGradRectangles1.html` in Listing 11.4 demonstrates how to render a set of rectangles with horizontal, vertical, and diagonal linear gradients. Listing 11.4 references the CSS3 stylesheet `HoverAnimation1.css` that applies CSS3 `keyframes`-based 2D animation to the first HTML5 `<canvas>` element whenever users hover over this `<canvas>` element with their mouse. Listing 11.4 also references the CSS3 stylesheet `HoverAnimation2.css`, which acts in a similar fashion; however, this stylesheet applies CSS3 3D animation effects to the second HTML5 `<canvas>` element in Listing 11.4. Since the animation techniques in these CSS stylesheets are discussed in Chapter 2, we will omit them from this chapter, but the entire source code is available on the DVD.

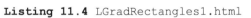

ON THE DVD

Listing 11.4 `LGradRectangles1.html`

```html
<!DOCTYPE html>
<html lang="en">
 <head>
  <meta charset="utf-8">
  <title>Canvas Linear Gradient Rectangles</title>
  <link href="HoverAnimation1.css"
        rel="stylesheet" type="text/css">
  <link href="HoverAnimation2.css"
        rel="stylesheet" type="text/css">

  <style>
```

```
  input {
    width:350px;
    font-size:24px;
    background-color:#f00;
  }
</style>

<script><!--
  window.addEventListener('load', function () {
    var elem = document.getElementById('myCanvas');
    if (!elem || !elem.getContext) {
      return;
    }

    var context = elem.getContext('2d');
    if (!context) {
      return;
    }

    var elem2 = document.getElementById('myCanvas2');
    if (!elem2 || !elem2.getContext) {
      return;
    }

    var context2 = elem2.getContext('2d');
    if (!context2) {
      return;
    }

    var basePointX = 0;
    var basePointY = 0;
    var currentX   = 0;
    var currentY   = 0;
    var rectWidth  = 200;
    var rectHeight = 200;
    var clickCount = 0;
    var gradient1;

    redrawCanvas = function() {
       // clear the canvas before drawing new set of rectangles
       //context.clearRect(0, 0, elem.width, elem.height);
       //context2.clearRect(0, 0, elem.width, elem.height);

       // upper left rectangle: horizontal linear gradient
       currentX = basePointX;
       currentY = basePointY;
```

```
gradient1 = context.createLinearGradient(
                        currentX,
                        currentY,
                        currentX+rectWidth,
                        currentY+0*rectHeight);

gradient1.addColorStop(0, '#f00');
gradient1.addColorStop(1, '#00f');
context.fillStyle = gradient1;
context.fillRect(currentX, currentY,
                rectWidth, rectHeight);

// upper right rectangle: vertical linear gradient
currentX = basePointX+rectWidth;
currentY = basePointY;

gradient1 = context.createLinearGradient(
                        currentX,
                        currentY,
                        currentX+0*rectWidth,
                        currentY+rectHeight);

gradient1.addColorStop(0, '#ff0');
gradient1.addColorStop(1, '#00f');
context.fillStyle = gradient1;
context.fillRect(currentX, currentY,
                rectWidth, rectHeight);

// render the lower rectangles in the second <canvas> el-
ement
// lower left rectangle: diagonal linear gradient
currentX = basePointX;
currentY = basePointY;
//currentY = basePointY+rectHeight;

gradient1 = context2.createLinearGradient(
                        currentX,
                        currentY,
                        currentX+rectWidth,
                        currentY+rectHeight);

gradient1.addColorStop(0,  '#f00');
gradient1.addColorStop(0.5,'#0f0');
gradient1.addColorStop(1,  '#00f');
context2.fillStyle = gradient1;
context2.fillRect(currentX, currentY,
```

```
                              rectWidth, rectHeight);

        // lower right rectangle: diagonal linear gradient
        currentX = basePointX+rectWidth;
        currentY = basePointY;
      //currentY = basePointY+rectHeight;

        gradient1 = context2.createLinearGradient(
                                    currentX+rectWidth,
                                    currentY,
                                    currentX+0*rectWidth,
                                    currentY+rectHeight);

        gradient1.addColorStop(0,  '#fff');
        gradient1.addColorStop(0.3,'#000');
        gradient1.addColorStop(0.6,'#ff0');
        gradient1.addColorStop(1,  '#f00');
        context2.fillStyle = gradient1;
        context2.fillRect(currentX, currentY,
                          rectWidth, rectHeight);

        ++clickCount;
        basePointX += 4;
        basePointY += 2;
      }

    // render linear gradient rectangles
    redrawCanvas();
  }, false);
  // --></script>
 </head>

<body>
   <div>
    <canvas id="myCanvas" width="600" height="250">No support for
Canvas
           alt="Rendering linear gradient rectangles.">
    </canvas>
    </div>

   <div>
    <canvas id="myCanvas2" width="600" height="250">No support for
                                                            Canvas
           alt="Rendering linear gradient rectangles.">
    </canvas>
    </div>
```

```
    <div>
     <input type="button" onclick="redrawCanvas();return false"
            value="Redraw the Rectangles"/>
    </div>
  </body>
</html>
```

Listing 11.4 renders four rectangles with linear gradient shading. The linear gradients have two, three, or four invocations of the `addColorStop()` method, using various combinations of colors (expressed in hexadecimal form) so that you can see some of the gradient effects that are possible.

Experiment with different values for the color stop definitions to see how their values change the appearance of the rendered rectangles.

Figure 11.3 displays a set of randomly generated rectangles with a shadow effect based on `LGradRectangles1.html` in Listing 11.4, in landscape mode on a Nexus 7 tablet with Android Jelly Bean.

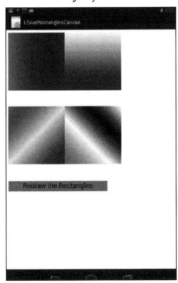

FIGURE 11.3 Linear gradient rectangles on a Nexus 7 tablet with Android Jelly Bean.

RADIAL COLOR GRADIENTS

A radial color gradient is the second type of HTML5 Canvas-based color gradient. You can define a radial color gradient via the `createRadialGradient()` method, using the `addColorStop()` method to add color values, and its syntax (without the `addColorStop()` method) looks like this:

```
context.createRadialGradient(startCenterX, startCenterY,
                startRadius, endsCenterX, endCenterY, endRadius);
```

A radial color gradient can be compared to the ripple effect that is created when you drop a stone in a pond, where each "ripple" has a color that changes in a gradient fashion. Each ripple corresponds to a color stop element. For example, if you define a radial gradient with a start color of #FF0000 (which is red) and an end color of #000000 (which is black), then the resultant color gradient will range—in a radial fashion—from red to black. Radial gradients can also contain multiple start/stop color combinations. The point to keep in mind is that radial gradients change colors in a linear fashion, but the rendered colors are drawn in an expanding radial fashion. Note that "radial gradient" and "radial color gradient" are used interchangeably in this book.

Listing 11.5 displays the contents of the HTML5 page RGradRectangles1.html that renders line segments, rectangles, and circles in an HTML5 <canvas> element using linear and radial gradients.

Listing 11.5 RGradRectangles1.html

```
<!DOCTYPE html>
<html lang="en">
 <head>
  <meta charset="utf-8">
  <title>Canvas Radial Gradient Rectangles</title>
  <link href="HoverAnimation1.css" rel="stylesheet" type="text/
css">

  <style>
    input {
      width:300px;
      font-size:24px;
      background-color:#f00;
    }
  </style>

  <script><!--
    window.addEventListener('load', function () {
      var elem = document.getElementById('myCanvas');
      if (!elem || !elem.getContext) {
        return;
      }
```

```
var context = elem.getContext('2d');
if (!context) {
  return;
}

var basePointX = 10;
var basePointY = 10;
var currentX   = 0;
var currentY   = 0;
var rectWidth  = 200;
var rectHeight = 200;
var clickCount = 0;
var gradient1;

redrawCanvas = function() {
    // clear the canvas before drawing new set of rectangles
    //context.clearRect(0, 0, elem.width, elem.height);

    // upper left rectangle
    currentX = basePointX;
    currentY = basePointY;

    gradient1 = context.createRadialGradient(
                                   currentX,
                                   currentY,
                                   0,
                                   currentX+rectWidth,
                                   currentY+rectHeight,
                                   rectWidth);

    gradient1.addColorStop(0, '#f00');
    gradient1.addColorStop(1, '#00f');
    context.fillStyle = gradient1;
    context.fillRect(currentX, currentY,
                  rectWidth, rectHeight);

    // upper right rectangle
    currentX = basePointX+rectWidth;
    currentY = basePointY;

    gradient1 = context.createRadialGradient(
                                   currentX,
                                   currentY,
                                   0,
                                   currentX+rectWidth,
```

```
                                        currentY+rectHeight,
                                        rectWidth);

      gradient1.addColorStop(0, '#ff0');
      gradient1.addColorStop(1, '#00f');
      context.fillStyle = gradient1;
      context.fillRect(currentX, currentY,
                       rectWidth, rectHeight);

      // lower left rectangle
      currentX = basePointX;
      currentY = basePointY+rectHeight;

      gradient1 = context.createRadialGradient(
                                  currentX,
                                  currentY,
                                  0,
                                  currentX+rectWidth,
                                  currentY+rectHeight,
                                  rectWidth);

      gradient1.addColorStop(0,  '#f00');
      gradient1.addColorStop(0.5,'#0f0');

      gradient1.addColorStop(1,  '#00f');
      context.fillStyle = gradient1;
      context.fillRect(currentX, currentY,
                       rectWidth, rectHeight);

      // lower right rectangle
      currentX = basePointX+rectWidth;
      currentY = basePointY+rectHeight;

      gradient1 = context.createRadialGradient
                                  (currentX,
                                  currentY,
                                  0,
                                  currentX+rectWidth,
                                  currentY+rectHeight,
                                  rectWidth);

      gradient1.addColorStop(0,  '#fff');
      gradient1.addColorStop(0.3,'#000');
      gradient1.addColorStop(0.6,'#ff0');
      gradient1.addColorStop(1,  '#f00');
      context.fillStyle = gradient1;
```

```
      context.fillRect(currentX, currentY,
                        rectWidth, rectHeight);

      ++clickCount;
      basePointX += 2;
      basePointY += 2;
    }

    // render a set of rectangles
    redrawCanvas();
  }, false);
  // --></script>
</head>

<body>
  <div>
    <canvas id="myCanvas" width="600" height="500">No support for
Canvas
            alt="Rendering radial gradient rectangles.">
    </canvas>
  </div>

  <div>
    <input type="button" onclick="redrawCanvas();return false"
           value="Redraw the Rectangles"/>
  </div>
</body>
</html>
```

Listing 11.5 is similar to Listing 11.4, except for the use of a radial gradient (instead of a linear gradient) that ranges in a radial fashion from `blue` to `red`. The method `addColorStop()` is invoked four times in order to add four "color stop values" to the radial gradient. Listing 11.5 also references `HoverAnimation1.css`; that entire source code is available on the DVD.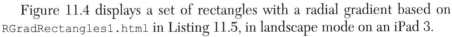

Figure 11.4 displays a set of rectangles with a radial gradient based on `RGradRectangles1.html` in Listing 11.5, in landscape mode on an iPad 3.

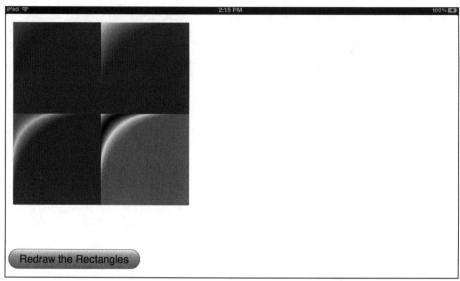

FIGURE 11.4 Radial gradient rectangles on an iPad 3.

BEZIER CURVES

HTML5 Canvas provides support for both quadratic Bezier curves and cubic Bezier curves. The code samples in this section show you how to generate interesting combinations of Bezier curves, using various types of gradient shading. Later in this book you will see how to use ECMAScript in order to programmatically change the values of attributes.

Bezier curves are named after Pierre Bezier, who promoted them during the 1970s. Bezier curves can represent many non-linear shapes, they can be found in interesting applications, including PostScript for the representation of fonts. An Internet search will yield many Web pages with interesting demonstrations (some of which also require additional plug-ins). You'll find computer programs written in C and Java, some of which are interactive, that demonstrate Bezier curves.

Cubic Bezier curves have two end points and two control points, whereas quadratic Bezier curves have two end points and a single control point. The x-coordinate and y-coordinate of a cubic Bezier curve can be represented as a parameterized cubic equation whose coefficients are derived from the control points and the end points. The beauty of HTML5 Canvas is that it allows you to define both quadratic and cubic Bezier curves via the `<path>` element without having to delve into the mathematical underpinnings of Bezier curves. If you're interested in learning the specific details, you can browse the web, where you'll find books and plenty of articles that cover this interesting topic.

BEZIER CURVES WITH LINEAR AND RADIAL GRADIENTS

HTML5 `Canvas` provides the `quadraticCurveTo()` method for creating quadratic Bezier curves, which requires one control point and an end point. HTML5 `Canvas` also provides the `bezierCurveTo()` method for creating cubic Bezier curves, which requires you to specify two control points and an end point. The context point (which is the location of the most recently rendered point) is used as the start point for quadratic Bezier curves and cubic Bezier curves.

The syntax for the HTML5 Canvas `quadraticCurveTo()` method looks like this:

```
quadraticCurveTo(controlX, controlY, endX, endY);
```

The syntax for the HTML5 Canvas `bezierCurveTo()` method looks like this:

```
bezierCurveTo(controlX1,controlY1,controlX2,controlY2,endX,
                                                         endY);
```

The HTML5 page `LRGradQCBezier1.html` in Listing 11.6 demonstrates how to render a quadratic Bezier curve with linear gradient shading and a cubic Bezier curve with radial gradient shading.

The source code for `CSS3Background4.css` and `HoverAnimation1.css` that are referenced in Listing 11.6 are available on the DVD.

Listing 11.6 LRGradQCBezier1.html

```
<!DOCTYPE html>
<html lang="en">
 <head>
  <meta charset="utf-8">
  <title>Canvas Quadratic and Cubic Bezier Curves</title>
  <link href="CSS3Background6.css"
        rel="stylesheet" type="text/css">
  <link href="HoverAnimation1.css"
        rel="stylesheet" type="text/css">
```

```
<style>
  input {
    width:300px;
    font-size:24px;
    background-color:#f00;
  }
</style>

<script><!--
  window.addEventListener('load', function () {
    var elem = document.getElementById('myCanvas');
    if (!elem || !elem.getContext) {
      return;
    }

    var context = elem.getContext('2d');
    if (!context) {
      return;
    }

    var basePointX  = 0;
    var basePointY  = 250;
    var currentX    = basePointX;
    var currentY    = basePointY;
    var currentX2   = currentX;
    var currentY2   = currentY;
    var lineWidth   = 8;
    var rectWidth   = 50;
    var rectHeight  = 40;
    var clickCount  = 0;
    var multiplier  = 5;
    var gradient1;

    redrawCanvas = function() {
        // clear the canvas before drawing new set of rectangles
        //context.clearRect(0, 0, elem.width, elem.height);

        // DRAW THE CUBIC BEZIER CURVE
        currentX = currentX2/2;
        currentY = currentY2/2;

        gradient1 = context.createRadialGradient(
                                  currentX,
                                  currentY,
                                  0,
```

```
currentX+multiplier*rectWidth,

currentY+multiplier*rectHeight,
                                  3*rectWidth);

        gradient1.addColorStop(0,   '#f00');
        gradient1.addColorStop(0.2,'#ff0');
        gradient1.addColorStop(0.4,'#fff');
        gradient1.addColorStop(0.6,'#f00');
        gradient1.addColorStop(0.8,'#00f');
        gradient1.addColorStop(1,   '#f00');

        context.fillStyle = gradient1;
        context.fill();

        context.beginPath();
        context.lineWidth = lineWidth;
        context.moveTo(currentX, currentY);

        context.bezierCurveTo(
          currentX+3*multiplier*rectWidth,
          currentY+2*multiplier*rectHeight,
          currentX+2*multiplier*rectWidth,
          currentY-multiplier*rectHeight,
          currentX+100, currentY+300);
        context.fill();


        // DRAW THE QUADRATIC BEZIER CURVE
        currentX = currentX2/2;
        currentY = currentY2/2;

        gradient1 = context.createLinearGradient(
                     currentX,
                     currentY,
                     currentX+multiplier/2*rectWidth,
                     currentY+multiplier/2*rectHeight);

        gradient1.addColorStop(0,   '#f00');
        gradient1.addColorStop(0.3,'#ff0');
        gradient1.addColorStop(0.6,'#00f');
        gradient1.addColorStop(0.9,'#0f0');
        gradient1.addColorStop(1,   '#f00');

        context.fillStyle = gradient1;
```

```
            context.beginPath();
            context.lineWidth = lineWidth;
            context.moveTo(currentX, currentY);
            context.quadraticCurveTo(
               currentX+3*multiplier*rectWidth,
               currentY+1*multiplier*rectHeight,
               currentX+2*multiplier*rectWidth,
               currentY-multiplier*rectHeight);

            context.fill();

            ++clickCount;
            currentX2 += 10;
            ++currentY2;
         }

      // render bezier curves
      redrawCanvas();
    }, false);
    // --></script>
  </head>

  <body>
    <div>
    <canvas id="myCanvas" width="800" height="500">No support for
Canvas
            alt="Rendering Bezier Curves.">
    </canvas>
    </div>

    <div>
    <input type="button" onclick="redrawCanvas();return false"
            value="Redraw Bezier Curves"/>
    </div>
  </body>
</html>
```

Listing 11.6 initializes some JavaScript variables and then defines the JavaScript function.

redrawCanvas() that contains code for creating linear gradients that you have seen in previous code samples, so we will omit their details. Notice that the HTML5 Canvas moveTo() method is invoked before rendering both quadratic Bezier curves, and that point serves as the initial or "context" point for both curves.

The cubic Bezier curve in Listing 11.6 is rendered with a radial gradient using six color stops, based on several calculated points, as shown here:

```
context.bezierCurveTo(
    currentX+3*multiplier*rectWidth,
    currentY+2*multiplier*rectHeight,
    currentX+2*multiplier*rectWidth,
    currentY-multiplier*rectHeight,
    currentX+100, currentY+300);
```

Experiment with different values for the points in a Bezier curve and you might find other ways to create pleasing visual effects. The next portion of Listing 11.6 renders a quadratic Bezier curve using a linear gradient with five color stops.

Note that whenever users click on the "redraw" button, another cubic and quadratic Bezier curve are drawn, based on the value of the variable `click-Count` that is incremented each time that users click on the "redraw" button. The new curves are superimposed on the previous curves, thereby creating a nice visual effect. However, if you want to refresh the HTML5 `<canvas>` element prior to rendering another pair of Bezier curves, simply uncomment the second line in the following code snippet:

```
// clear the canvas before drawing new set of rectangles
//context.clearRect(0, 0, elem.width, elem.height);
```

Figure 11.5 renders the quadratic and cubic Bezier curves that are defined in `LRGradQCBezier1.html` in Listing 11.6, in landscape mode on an iPad 3.

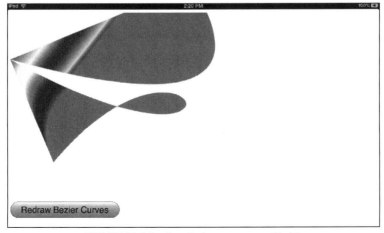

FIGURE 11.5 Gradient Bezier curves on an iPad 3.

RENDERING IMAGES ON CANVAS WITH CSS3 SELECTORS

HTML5 Canvas supports the rendering of JPG files, and you can also apply CSS selectors to the HTML5 <canvas> element. Listing 11.7 displays the contents of Image1.html and Listing 11.8 displays the contents of Image1.css whose selectors are applied to the HTML5 <canvas> element in Listing 11.7.

Listing 11.7 Image1.html

```
<!DOCTYPE html>
<html lang="en">
<head>
  <meta charset="utf-8"/>
  <title>Rendering JPG Files in HTML5 Canvas</title>

  <link href="Image1.css" rel="stylesheet" type="text/css">
  <link href="HoverAnimation1.css" rel="stylesheet" type="text/
css">

  <script>
    function renderJPG() {
       // Get the canvas element
       var elem = document.getElementById('myCanvas');
       if (!elem || !elem.getContext) {
         return;
       }

       // Get the canvas 2d context
       var context = elem.getContext('2d');
       if (!context) {
         return;
       }

       var basePointX  = 30;
       var basePointY  = 30;
       var rectWidth   = 150;
       var rectHeight  = 200;
       var borderX     = rectWidth/2;
       var borderY     = rectHeight/2;
       var offsetX     = 20;
       var offsetY     = 20;
       var gradientR   = 60;

       // Create a radial gradient:
       var rGradient = context.createRadialGradient(
                                   basePointX+rectWidth/2,
```

```
                                basePointY+rectWidth/2,
                                gradientR,
                                basePointX+rectWidth/2,
                                basePointY+rectWidth/2,
                                3*gradientR);

      rGradient.addColorStop(0,    '#FF0000');
      rGradient.addColorStop(0.5, '#FFFF00');
      rGradient.addColorStop(1,    '#000044');

      // rectangular background with radial gradient:
      context.fillStyle = rGradient;
      context.fillRect(basePointX-offsetX,
                       basePointY-offsetY,
                       rectWidth+borderX+2*offsetX,
                       rectHeight+borderY+2*offsetY);

      // Load the JPG
      var myImage = new Image();
      myImage.onload = function() {
         context.drawImage(myImage,
                            basePointX,
                            basePointY,
                            rectWidth,
                            rectHeight);
      }

      myImage.src = "Laurie1.jpeg";
    }
  </script>

  <style type="text/css">
    canvas {
      border: 0px solid #888;
      background: #FFF;
    }
  </style>
</head>

<body onload="renderJPG();">
  <header>
    <h1>Hover Over the Image</h1>
  </header>

  <div>
   <canvas id="myCanvas" width="500" height="300">No support for
                                                   Canvas
```

```
   </canvas>
  </div>
 </body>
</html>
```

Listing 11.7 contains JavaScript code that creates a radial gradient rGradient with three color stops. Next, a rectangle is rendered with using the radial gradient that is referenced by the variable rGradient, followed by a section of code that renders the JPG file Lauriel.jpeg. The inline CSS code in the <style> element renders a white background with a zero-width border (so it's invisible), but you can modify this CSS code to produce additional effects. The <body> element contains the onload attribute whose value is renderJPG(), which is a JavaScript function that renders the JPG file inside the HTML5 <canvas> element.

Listing 11.8 Image1.css

```
    #myCanvas:hover {
    width:   500px;
    height: 300px;
    position: relative; top: 0px; left: 0px;

    background-color:white;
    background-image:
      -webkit-radial-gradient(red 4px, transparent 24px),
      -webkit-repeating-radial-gradient(red 1px,   green 4px, yel-
low 8px,
                                    blue 12px, transparent 16px,
                                    red 20px, blue 24px,
                                    transparent 28px,
                                    transparent 32px);
    background-size: 30px 30px,  40px 40px;
    background-position: 0 0;
    }

    #myCanvas {
    width:   500px;
    height: 300px;
    position: relative; top: 0px; left: 0px;

    background-color:white;
```

```
background-image:
    -webkit-radial-gradient(black 4px, transparent 20px),
     -webkit-repeating-radial-gradient(blue 1px,    yellow 4px,
blue 8px,
                                    red 12px, transparent 16px,
                                    red 20px, blue 24px,
                                    transparent 28px,
                                    transparent 32px);
    background-size: 30px 30px, 40px 40px;
    background-position: 0 0;
    }
```

The first selector in Listing 11.8 displays another pattern (based on a different radial gradient) whenever users hover with their mouse over the HTML5 `<canvas>` element. The second selector in Listing 11.8 renders a colorful pattern (also based on a radial gradient) as a background rectangle for the HTML5 `<canvas>` element.

Incidentally, HTML5 Canvas also supports a `clip()` method that enables you to "clip" JPG files in various ways. Moreover, you can perform compositing effects, and you can even manipulate the individual pixels of a JPG file. Search the Internet for articles that describe the technical details of these effects.

Figure 11.6 displays a JPG file with two radial gradient background effects, in landscape mode taken on a Nexus 7 tablet with Android Jelly Bean.

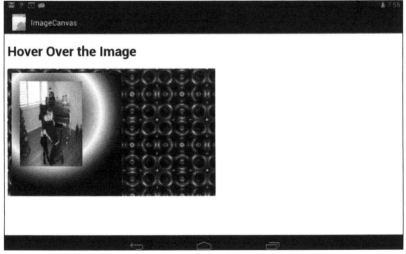

FIGURE 11.6 Canvas radial JPG on a Nexus 7 tablet with Android Jelly Bean.

REPEATING AN IMAGE ON CANVAS WITH PATTERNS

HTML5 Canvas provides the method `createPattern(image, type)` that enables you to render a set of images according to a `pattern` type, whose values can be `repeat`, `repeat-x`, `repeat-y`, and `no-repeat`. An example of the syntax (and also how to use it) looks like this:

```
var pattern = canvas.createPattern(img,"repeat");
canvas.fillStyle = pattern;
canvas.fillRect(0,0,500,300);
```

Listing 11.8 displays the contents of `RepeatingImage1.html` that illustrates how to repeat a JPG image on an HTML5 `<canvas>` element.

Listing 11.8 RepeatingImage1.html

```
<!DOCTYPE html>
<html lang="en">
<head>
  <meta charset="utf-8"/>
  <title>Repeating Images in HTML5 Canvas</title>

  <script>
    var elem, canvas, filename = "BlueBall1.png";

    function init() {
      elem = document.getElementById("myCanvas");
      canvas = elem.getContext('2d');

      var img = new Image();
      img.src = filename;
      img.addEventListener("load", modImage, false);
    }

    function modImage(e) {
      img = e.target;
      var pattern = canvas.createPattern(img,"repeat");

      canvas.fillStyle = pattern;
      canvas.fillRect(0,0,500,300);
    }

    window.addEventListener("load", init, false);
  </script>
</head>

<body>
```

```
<div>
  <canvas id="myCanvas" width="500" height="300">No support for
Canvas
  </canvas>
  </div>
</body>
</html>
```

Listing 11.8 contains the following line of code that invokes the JavaScript `init()` method when this Web page is loaded into a browser:

```
window.addEventListener("load", init, false);
```

The `init()` method finds an HTML5 `<canvas>` element in the Web page, and for simplicity, no error checking is performed (which can be handled by using code from previous examples).

The `init()` method also initializes a JavaScript variable `img` that references a JPG file, and then adds an event listener that executes the JavaScript function `modImage()`, as shown here:

```
var img = new Image();
img.src = filename;
img.addEventListener("load", modImage, false);
```

Finally, the `modImage()` method invokes the Canvas method `createPattern()` with the parameter repeat in order to create a rectangular grid of images that is based on one PNG file (which is `BlueBall1.png` in this example), as shown here:

```
var pattern = canvas.createPattern(img,"repeat");
canvas.fillStyle = pattern;
canvas.fillRect(0,0,500,300);
```

Figure 11.7 displays `RepeatingImage1.html` in Listing 11.8 in landscape mode on a Chrome browser on a Macbook.

FIGURE 11.7 Repeating JPG on a Chrome browser on a Macbook.

HTML5 CANVAS TRANSFORMS AND SAVING STATE

HTML5 Canvas enables you to rotate, scale, shear, or translate (which shifts horizontally and/or vertically) 2D shapes and text strings with the following methods:

```
rotate(x,y)
scale(x,y)
transform(x1,y1,x2,y2,x3,y3)
translate(x,y)
```

One thing to keep in mind is that you specify the transforms that you want to apply (along with setting attributes values) before actually rendering a graphics shape in your HTML5 Web pages.

The following code snippets illustrate sample values that you can use in the preceding Canvas methods, where context is a JavaScript variable that references the context of an HTML5 <canvas> element:

```
context.rotate(30*Math.PI/180);
context.scale(0.8, 0.4);
context.translate(100, 200);
context.transform(1, 0, 0.5, 1, 0, 0);
```

The rotate() method in the preceding code block references the JavaScript constant Math.PI whose value equals PI radians. In case you have forgotten, PI radians equal 180 degrees, so 2*PI radians is 360 degrees, and PI/2 radians is 90 degrees. Hence, Math.PI/6 radians (or 30*Math.PI/180) is the same as 30 degrees. You won't need to know anything more about radians, but feel free to perform an Internet search if you want to read some tutorials that provide additional examples.

Two additional APIs in HTML5 Canvas are save() and restore(), which enable you to save the current state of a Canvas, make some changes, and then restore the original state of the Canvas. You can save (and later restore) a Canvas state after having applied any of the transformations listed in this section, and also after having specified values for shadow-related attributes (among others). You can invoke the save() and restore() methods multiple times on a Canvas state, which makes these two methods very useful for game-related Web pages. We will not use these two methods in any code samples in this chapter, but you can perform an Internet search to read tutorials and also find code samples.

Listing 11.9 displays the contents of JQMCanvasTransforms1.html that illustrates how to apply four HTML5 Canvas transforms to a text string.

Listing 11.9 JQMCanvasTransforms1.html

```
<!DOCTYPE html>
<html lang="en">
 <head>
  <meta charset="utf-8">
  <title>Canvas Transforms on Text Strings</title>

  <style>
    input {
      width:300px;
      font-size:24px;
      background-color:#f00;
    }
  </style>

  <script><!--
    window.addEventListener('load', function () {
      var elem = document.getElementById('myCanvas');

      if (!elem || !elem.getContext) {
        return;
      }

      var context = elem.getContext('2d');
      if (!context) {
        return;
      }

      context.shadowColor   = "rgba(0,0,128,0.5)";
      context.shadowOffsetX = 5;
      context.shadowOffsetY = 5;
      context.shadowBlur    = 10;
      context.lineWidth     = 2;
      context.font          = "Bold 60pt Helvetica";

      redrawCanvas = function() {
        // render text...
        context.fillStyle   = "#f00";
        context.strokeStyle = "#00f"
        context.fillText("Hello World", 40, 150);
        context.fill();

        // render scaled text...
        context.scale(0.3, 0.3);
```

```
            context.fillStyle    = "#ff0";
            context.fillText("Hello World", 40, 100);
            context.fill();

            // render skewed text...
            context.transform(1, 10*Math.PI/180, 20*Math.PI/180,
1,0,0);
            context.fillStyle    = "#0f0";
            context.fillText("Hello World", 0, 700);
            context.fill();

            // render rotated text...
            context.transform(1, -10*Math.PI/180, -20*Math.PI/180,
1,0,0);
            context.rotate(-Math.PI/8);
            context.scale(3, 1);

            context.fillStyle    = "#00f";
            context.fillText("Hello World", 0, 1400);
            context.fill();
        }

        redrawCanvas();
      }, false);
      // --></script>
  </head>

<body>
    <div>
      <canvas id="myCanvas" width="800" height="450">No support for
Canvas
               alt="Rendering transformed objects">
      </canvas>
    </div>
  </body>
</html>
```

Listing 11.9 contains the usual initialization code that you've seen in the other examples in this chapter, and the attributes for rendering the text strings are set in this code block:

```
context.shadowColor    = "rgba(0,0,128,0.5)";
context.shadowOffsetX = 5;
context.shadowOffsetY = 5;
context.shadowBlur    = 10;
context.lineWidth     = 2;
context.font           = "Bold 60pt Helvetica";
```

You have already seen examples of the first five attributes, and as you would expect, the `font` attribute enables you to set the font family and the font size.

The `redraw()` JavaScript function renders the string "Hello World," and then repeats it three more times after applying a transform to this text string.

Figure 11.8 displays the result of rendering `JQMCanvasTransforms1.html` in Listing 11.8, which displays four text strings in a landscape-mode screenshot on an iPad 3.

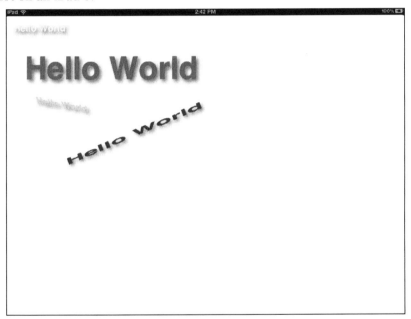

FIGURE 11.8 Rendering text with transforms on an iPad 3.

Experiment with the transformations in this section by applying them to 2D shapes from earlier code samples in this chapter.

JCANVAS: A JQUERY PLUGIN FOR HTML5 CANVAS

The `jCanvas` jQuery plugin enables you to use jQuery syntax in order to specify 2D shapes that are rendered in an HTML5 `<canvas>` element, and its homepage is here:

http://calebevans.me/projects/jcanvas/

Listing 11.10 displays the contents of JCanvasSamples1.html that illustrates how to render several 2D shapes using jCanvas.

Listing 11.10 JCanvasSamples1.html

```
<!DOCTYPE html>
<html lang="en">
  <head>
    <meta charset="utf-8"/>
    <title>JCanvas Graphics</title>

    <link rel="stylesheet"
     href="http://code.jquery.com/mobile/1.1.0/jquery.mobile-
1.1.0.min.css"/>
    <script
       src="http://code.jquery.com/jquery-1.7.1.min.js">
    </script>
    <script src="jcanvas.js"></script>

    <style>
      #canvas { width:100%; height:90%; }
    </style>

    <script>
      $(document).ready(function() {
        $("canvas").drawEllipse({
          fillStyle: "#f00",
          x: 100, y: 50,
          width: 160, height: 60,
          fromCenter: true
        })

        $("canvas").drawRect({
          strokeStyle: "#f00",
          fillStyle: "#f08",
          strokeWidth: 3,
          x: 100, y: 120,
          width: 150,
          height: 50,
          cornerRadius: 10
        })

        $("canvas").drawPolygon({
          fillStyle: "#00f",
          x: 220, y: 80,
          radius: 50,
          sides: 5,
```

```
        angle: 25
    })

    $("canvas").drawQuad({
        strokeStyle: "#ff0",
        strokeWidth: 3,
        x1: 20, y1: 20,
        cx1: 200, cy1: 50,
        x2: 200, y2: 300
    })

    $("canvas").drawBezier({
        strokeStyle: "#404",
        strokeWidth: 8,
        x1: 50, y1: 50,
        cx1: 200, cy1: 50,
        cx2: 50, cy2: 150,
        x2: 200, y2: 150,
        cx3: 300, cy3: 150,
        cx4: 150, cy4: 1,
        x3: 320, y3: 50
    })
  });
  </script>
</head>

<body>
  <div id="CanvasParent" name="CanvasParent">
    <canvas name="canvas" id="canvas">
    </canvas>
  </div>
</body>
</html>
```

The code in Listing 11.10 is straightforward and intuitive, so we'll simply summarize its contents. The code for rendering an ellipse and a rectangle maps almost directly to the corresponding HTML5 Canvas code that you saw in previous examples in this chapter. The code block for rendering a polygon is concise and intuitive, and definitely less effort than the set of lineTo() methods that are required in order to render a polygon in HTML5 Canvas. Finally, the code for rendering a quadratic or a cubic Bezier curve uses a notation that distinguishes endpoints from control points, and it is comparable to the corresponding code in HTML5 Canvas.

Figure 11.9 displays the result of rendering `JCanvasSamples1.html` Listing 11.10 in landscape mode on an iPad 3.

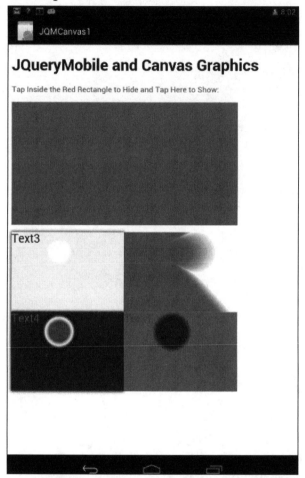

FIGURE 11.9 A jQuery Canvas plugin on an iPad 3.

You can also use jQuery Mobile with HTML5 Canvas, as shown in the code sample in the next section.

HTML5 CANVAS WITH CSS3 AND JQUERY MOBILE

Now that you understand how to render 2D shapes in HTML5 Canvas, this section contains a code sample that shows you how to combine jQuery Mobile, HTML5 Canvas, and the dynamic creation of HTML <div> elements whenever users tap inside the HTML5 <canvas> element in this Web page.

Keep in mind that although the graphics effects are not necessarily relevant to your requirements, this code sample does illustrate how to handle dynamic creation of elements and also tap events in jQuery Mobile, which are handled differently from tap events in jQuery.

Listing 11.11 displays the contents of the HTML5 Web page JQMCanvas1.html, followed by Listing 11.12 that displays the contents of the CSS stylesheet JQMCanvas1.css whose CSS3 selectors are applied to elements in the HTML5 Web page JQMCanvas1.html.

Listing 11.11 JQMCanvas1.html

```
<!DOCTYPE html>
<html lang="en">
  <head>
    <meta charset="utf-8"/>
    <title>JQueryMobile and Canvas Graphics</title>

    <link rel="stylesheet" href="JQMCanvas1.css"/>

    <link rel="stylesheet"
     href="http://code.jquery.com/mobile/1.1.0
                   /jquery.mobile-1.1.0.min.css"/>
    <script
        src="http://code.jquery.com/jquery-1.7.1.min.js">
    </script>
    <script src="http://code.jquery.com/mobile/1.1.0
                        /jquery.mobile-1.1.0.min.js">
    </script>

    <script>
      var tapCount = 0;
      var xCoord = 0, yCoord = 0;
      var rectWidth = 20, rectHeight = 20;
      var rectColors = new Array('#ff0', '#0f0', '#00f');
      var elem, context;

      var gradient1 = '-webkit-gradient(radial, 5 25%, 5, 10 50%,
20, from(red), color-stop(0.05, orange), color-stop(0.4, yellow),
color-stop(0.6, red), color-stop(0.9, blue), to(#fff))';

      var gradient2 = '-webkit-gradient(radial, 5 25%, 5, 10 50%,
20, from(blue), color-stop(0.05, orange), color-stop(0.4, red),
```

```
color-stop(0.6, black), color-stop(0.9, blue), to(#f00))';

    var gradient3 = '-webkit-gradient(radial, 5 25%, 5, 10 50%,
20, from(blue), color-stop(0.05, yellow), color-stop(0.4, green),
color-stop(0.6, red), color-stop(0.9, blue), to(#fff))';

    var gradient4 = '-webkit-gradient(radial, 5 25%, 5, 10 50%,
20, from(blue), color-stop(0.05, yellow), color-stop(0.2, green),
color-stop(0.6, blue), color-stop(0.8, red), to(#fff))';

   var currentBG;

   $("#page1").live('pageinit', (function(event){
     // Get the canvas element
     elem = document.getElementById('MyCanvas');
     if (!elem || !elem.getContext) {
       return;
     }

     // Get the canvas 2d context
     context = elem.getContext('2d');
     if (!context) {
       return;
     }

     // user tapped MyCanvas...
     $("#MyCanvas").live('vmousedown',function(event) {
       xCoord = 0.40*(event.clientX)*window.devicePixelRatio;
       yCoord = 0.40*(event.clientY)*window.devicePixelRatio;

       context.fillStyle = rectColors[++tapCount%rectColors.
length];
       context.fillRect(xCoord, yCoord, rectWidth, rectHeight);

       $("#MyCanvas").hide("slow");
     });

     // this makes MyCanvas visible again
     $("#tapInside").live('tap',function(event) {
       $("#MyCanvas").show("slow");
     });

     $("#CanvasParent").live('vmousedown',function(event) {
       if(tapCount % 4 == 0) {
         currentBG  = gradient1;
       } else if(tapCount % 4 == 1) {
```

```
          currentBG   = gradient2;
        } else if(tapCount % 4 == 2) {
          currentBG   = gradient3;
        } else {
          currentBG   = gradient4;
        }

        newNode = $('<div>').css({'position':'absolute',
                                  'background': currentBG,
                                  'width':rectWidth+'px',
                                  'height':rectHeight+'px',
                                  top: event.clientY,
                                  left: event.clientX
                                 });

        //append the new rectangle to CanvasParent
        $("#CanvasParent").append(newNode);
      })
     })
    );
  </script>

  <style>
    #tapInside { color: #f00; }
    #MyCanvas  { width: 80%; height: 30%; }
  </style>
</head>

<body>
  <div data-role="page" id="page1"
       data-role="page" data-theme="b">
    <div data-role="header">
       <h2>JQuery Mobile and Canvas Graphics</h2>
    </div>

    <div data-role="content">
      <div id="tapInside">
        <p>Tap Inside the Red Rectangle to Hide and Tap Here to
Show:</p>
      </div>

      <div id="CanvasParent" name="CanvasParent">
        <canvas name="MyCanvas" id="MyCanvas"
                style="background:#f00;width=80%;height=200px">
        </canvas>
```

```
<div id="outer">
  <div id="radial3">Text3</div>
  <div id="radial2">Text2</div>
  <div id="radial4">Text4</div>
  <div id="radial1">Text1</div>
</div>

<!-- jQuery toggle-handling code -->
<script>
  $(document).ready(function() {
    $("#outer").toggle(function(){
      $("#radial1").show("slow");
      $("#radial2").hide("slow");
      $("#radial3").hide("slow");
      $("#radial4").show("slow");
    },function(){
      $("#radial1").hide("slow");
      $("#radial2").show("slow");
      $("#radial3").show("slow");
      $("#radial4").hide("slow");
    });
  });
</script>
</div>

<div data-role="footer">
  <h3>JQuery Mobile and Canvas Graphics</h3>
</div>
</div>
</body>
</html>
```

Listing 11.11 is an HTML5 Web page that contains a single jQuery Mobile page view. After initializing some JavaScript variables, Listing 11.11 contains the definition of the JavaScript variables gradient1, gradient2, gradient3, and gradient4, each of which contains the definition of a WebKit-based radial gradient.

When users tap on the <canvas> element whose id has value MyCanvas, the code adds a new rectangle at the location of the tap event, and then the <canvas> element slowly disappears, as shown here:

```
$("#MyCanvas").live('vmousedown',function(event) {
  xCoord = 0.40*(event.clientX)*window.devicePixelRatio;
  yCoord = 0.40*(event.clientY)*window.devicePixelRatio;

  context.fillStyle = rectColors[++tapCount%rectColors.length];
```

```
context.fillRect(xCoord, yCoord, rectWidth, rectHeight);

$("#MyCanvas").hide("slow");
});
```

Keep in mind that you must use the vmousedown event because a tap event in jQuery Mobile does not provide you with the coordinates of the location of the tap event. You also need to use the value of window.devicePixelRatio in the calculations for the location of the tap event.

When users tap on the <canvas> element whose id has value tapInside, the hidden <canvas> element is displayed again, along with any rectangles that were previously rendered via the fillRect() method.

When users tap on the <canvas> element whose id value is CanvasParent, the code first uses conditional logic to determine which radial gradient to select and assign to the JavaScript variable currentBG.

Next, a new HTML <div> element is dynamically created at the location of the tap event and then appended to the CanvasParent element, as shown here:

```
newNode = $('<div>').css({'position':'absolute',
                          'background': currentBG,
                          'width':'35px',
                          'height':'35px',
                          top: event.pageY,
                          left: event.pageX
                          });

//append the new rectangle to CanvasParent
$("#CanvasParent").append(newNode);
```

Notice that the position property is set to absolute in the preceding code block, which means that this dynamically created <div> element will remain visible whenever the MyCanvas element slowly fades from view, but all the rectangles that are rendered using the fillRect() method will also slowly disappear.

Finally, whenever users click on any of the bottom four <div> elements that are rendered with radial gradients, the code will cause them to disappear "out of sequence," and the remaining visible elements will be shifted accordingly.

Listing 11.12 JQMCanvas1.css

```
#outer {
position: relative; top: 10px; left: 0px;
}
```

```
#radial1 {
color: red;
font-size: 24px;
height: 100px;
width:  300px;
position: relative; top: 0px; left: 0px;

background: -webkit-gradient(
  radial, 100 25%, 20, 100 25%, 40, from(blue), to(#fff)
 );
}

#radial2 {
color: red;
font-size: 24px;
width:  300px;
height: 100px;
position: absolute; top: 0px; left: 300px;

background: -webkit-gradient(
  radial, 100 25%, 20, 150 25%, 40, from(red), to(#fff)
 );
}

#radial3 {
color: blue;
font-size: 24px;
width:  300px;
height: 100px;
position: relative; top: 0px; left: 0px;
background: -webkit-gradient(
  radial, 100 25%, 30, 100 25%, 20, from(yellow), to(#fff)
 );
-webkit-box-shadow:  0px 0px 8px #000;
}

#radial4 {
color: red;
font-size: 24px;
width:  300px;
height: 100px;
position: absolute; top: 100px; left: 300px;

background: -webkit-gradient(
  radial, 100 25%, 20, 100 25%, 40, from(green),
```

```
color-stop(0.2, orange), color-stop(0.4, yellow),
color-stop(0.6, green), color-stop(0.8, blue),
to(#fff)
);
}
```

Listing 11.11 contains four selectors that correspond to the HTML <div> elements with id values radial1, radial2, radial3, and radial4 in JQM-Canvas1.html. Since each of these selectors defines WebKit-based radial gradients that you have already seen in earlier examples in this book, we won't discuss the details of those gradients.

Figure 11.10 displays the result of rendering JQMCanvas1.html in Listing 11.11 in landscape mode on a Nexus 7 tablet with Android Jelly Bean.

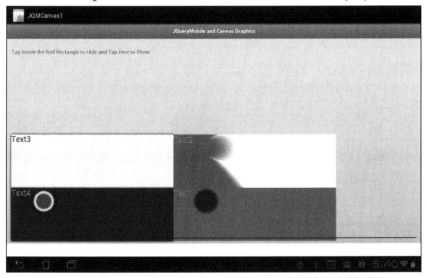

FIGURE 11.10 A jQuery Mobile application on a Nexus 7 tablet with Android Jelly Bean.

OTHER HTML5 CANVAS TOPICS

There are other interesting things that you can do with HTML5 Canvas, and some of the toolkits are briefly described here.

The K3D toolkit (created by Kevin Roast) enables you to create 3D Effects in HTML5 Canvas with JavaScript. This toolkit does not require WebGL, and you can download it here:

https://launchpad.net/canvask3d/+download

Some interesting demos are shown here:

http://kevs3d.co.uk/dev/canvask3d/k3d_test.html

Canvas3D is another toolkit for rendering 3D shapes in HTML5 Canvas, and its homepage is here:

http://www.cs.cornell.edu/zeno/projects/Canvas3D/

Appendix D discusses the JavaScript toolkit `Three.js` that provides a layer of abstraction over WebGL. Since `Three.js` provides support for three renderers, one of which is a Canvas renderer, it's relevant for this chapter as well:

https://github.com/mrdoob/three.js/

You can find more 3D effects with downloadable code here:

http://msdn.microsoft.com/en-us/library/hh535759(v=vs.85).aspx

You can convert audio files to HTML5 Canvas graphics, and the code samples on the following Web site (which only work in Firefox) create some interesting graphics effects based on various audio files:

http://js.do/

A good tutorial for HTML5 Canvas Drag and Drop (and other effects) is here:

http://www.html5canvastutorials.com/labs/html5-canvas-drag-and-drop-resize-and-invert-images/

An example of creating thumbnails with HTML5 Canvas is here:

https://hacks.mozilla.org/2012/02/creating-thumbnails-with-drag-and-drop-and-html5-canvas/

If you are interested in animating sprites in HTML Canvas, a nice article is here:

http://www.codeproject.com/Articles/271509/HTML5-Gaming-How-to-Animate-Sprites-in-Canvas-with

OTHER HTML5 CANVAS TOOLKITS

There are several very good JavaScript toolkits available that provide a later of abstraction on top of HTML5 Canvas. Appendix C on the DVD discusses some of these JavaScript toolkits, including `Easel.js`, `Fabric.js`, and `Paper.js`.

In addition to the code samples that are available on the respective home pages of these toolkits, you might enjoy the contents of following open source project that uses `Easel.js` to create graphics code samples:

http://code.google.com/p/easeljs-graphics

SUMMARY

This chapter introduced you to HTML5 Canvas and showed you examples of creating 2D shapes with the HTML5 `<canvas>` element. You also learned how to combine HTML5 Canvas with jQuery custom code so that you can manipulate HTML5 Web pages with Canvas-based 2D shapes. In particular, you learned how to do the following in HTML5 Canvas:

- Render line segments, rectangles, and circles
- Create linear and radial gradients
- Create Bezier curves
- Display JPG files
- Use `jCanvas` (a jQuery plugin for Canvas)
- Combine HMTL5 Canvas with CSS3
- Combine HTML5 Canvas with jQuery Mobile

Now that you understand how to use various HTML5 Canvas APIs, you are ready for the next chapter, which uses many of the concepts from this chapter to render various charts and graphs using HTML5 Canvas.

CHARTS AND GRAPHS IN HTML5 CANVAS

HTML5 Canvas enables you to create charts and graphs using some of the Canvas APIs that you saw in Chapter 11, including Canvas-based linear and radial gradients and CSS3 stylesheets with gradient effects. The code samples in this chapter illustrate how to write custom code for charts and graphs, and they rely heavily on the concepts introduced in Chapter 11, so you can refer to that chapter when you encounter HTML5 Canvas APIs that are unfamiliar to you.

This chapter starts with an example of rendering a bar chart in HTML5 Canvas using gradient effects, followed by an example of an HTML5 Web page with a mouse-enabled bar chart. In the second half of this chapter, you will learn how to render line graphs, area graphs, pie charts, and a three-dimensional bar chart. The final example in this chapter shows you an HTML5 Web page that receives data that is sent periodically from a WebSockets server, which is used to update and then render a 2D bar chart. Note that this example requires a basic understanding of WebSockets, which is covered in Chapter 10.

There are several useful points to keep in mind as you read the code samples. First, the samples in this chapter vary between two and four pages, but the level of complexity is very similar in all of them. Second, the code samples usually contain one block of code to render the bar chart or line graph (or pie chart), a second block of code that renders horizontal and vertical axes, and a third block of code that renders text or handles mouse-related events. Third, the code block that performs the rendering of the chart or graph is almost always the shortest section of a code sample; in addition, this is the section of code that typically changes the most between different code listings. As a simple suggestion: you can always "comment out" the code that renders axes and labels so that you can concentrate on the code that renders the chart or graph (but obviously doing so makes the visual effect less appealing).

Although it's conceptually easy to understand charts and graphs, the code for rendering them can be lengthy and somewhat tedious ("the devil is in the details"). Consequently, you might decide to use open source projects instead of creating your own custom charts and graphs. However, after you finish reading this chapter you will be in a better position to understand third party toolkits, you might also be equipped to modify external code samples in order to fit your specific requirements.

As a final point, you might be surprised to discover that you only need three HTML5 Canvas APIs for this chapter: the `fillRect()` method renders rectangles for the bar charts; the `lineTo()` method renders line segments in the line graphs as well as trapezoids in the area graphs; and the `arc()` method renders each wedge in the pie charts. In addition, approximately half of the code samples use CSS3 stylesheets whose selectors are similar to the code samples that are discussed in Chapters 2 and 3.

RENDERING GRADIENT BAR CHARTS

You can render a bar chart in HTML5 Canvas with a gradient effect by adding a linear gradient or a radial gradient (whose syntax you learned in Chapter 11), which can create a much richer visual effect than using standard colors for the bar chart.

The HTML page `BarChart2LG1.html` in Listing 12.1 illustrates how to render a bar chart with linear gradient shading. The complete source code for the CSS3 stylesheet `CSS32Background2.css` that is referenced in Listing 12.1 is available on the DVD.

Listing 12.1 BarChart2LG1.html

```
<!DOCTYPE html>
<html lang="en">
<head>
  <meta charset="utf-8"/>
  <title>HTML5 Canvas Bar Chart Linear Gradient</title>

  <link href="CSS32Background1.css" rel="stylesheet" type="text/
                                                              css">
```

```
<script>
    var currentX     = 0;
    var currentY     = 0;
    var barCount     = 12;
    var barWidth     = 40;
    var barHeight    = 0;
    var maxHeight    = 280;
    var xAxisWidth   = (2*barCount+1)*barWidth/2;
    var yAxisHeight  = maxHeight;
    var labelY       = 0;
    var indentY      = 5;
    var shadowX      = 2;
    var shadowY      = 2;
    var axisFontSize = 12;
    var fontSize     = 16;
    var leftBorder   = 30;
    var topBorder    = 15;
    var arrowWidth   = 10;
    var arrowHeight  = 6;
    var barHeights   = new Array(barCount);
    var elem, context, gradient1;

    function drawGraph() {
      // Get the canvas element
      elem = document.getElementById('myCanvas');
      if (!elem || !elem.getContext) {
        return;
      }

      // Get the canvas 2d context
      context = elem.getContext('2d');
      if (!context) {
        return;
      }

      drawGraph2();
    }

    function drawAndLabelAxes() {
        // draw vertical axis...
      context.beginPath();
      context.fillStyle = "rgb(0,0,0)";
      context.lineWidth = 2;
      context.moveTo(leftBorder, topBorder);
      context.lineTo(leftBorder, yAxisHeight);
      context.stroke();
```

```
// draw top arrow...
context.beginPath();
context.moveTo(leftBorder-arrowHeight/2, topBorder);
context.lineTo(leftBorder+arrowHeight/2, topBorder);
context.lineTo(leftBorder, topBorder-arrowWidth);
context.lineTo(leftBorder-arrowHeight/2, topBorder);
context.fill();

// draw horizontal axis...
context.beginPath();
context.moveTo(leftBorder, yAxisHeight);
context.lineTo(xAxisWidth, yAxisHeight);
context.stroke();

// draw right arrow...
context.beginPath();
context.moveTo(xAxisWidth, yAxisHeight-arrowHeight/2);
context.lineTo(xAxisWidth+arrowWidth, yAxisHeight);
context.lineTo(xAxisWidth, yAxisHeight+arrowHeight/2);
context.lineTo(xAxisWidth, yAxisHeight);
context.fill();

// label the horizontal axis
context.font = "bold "+axisFontSize+"pt New Times Roman";
context.lineWidth   = 2;
context.strokeStyle = "#000";

for(var i=0; i<barCount; i++) {
   context.beginPath();
   currentX = leftBorder+i*barWidth;
   currentY = maxHeight+axisFontSize;
//context.fillStyle = fillColors[i%4];
   context.fillStyle = "#000";

  // Outline a text string
  context.strokeText(""+currentX,
                     currentX+shadowX,
                     currentY+shadowY);

  // Fill a text string
  context.fillStyle = "#FF0";
  context.fillText(""+currentX,
                   currentX,
                   currentY);
}

// label the vertical axis
```

```
    context.font = "bold "+axisFontSize+"pt New Times Roman";
    context.lineWidth   = 2;
    context.strokeStyle = "#000";

    for(var i=0; i<barCount; i++) {
       context.beginPath();
       currentX = 0;
       currentY = Math.floor(maxHeight-i*maxHeight/barCount);
       labelY   = Math.floor(i*maxHeight/barCount);

     //context.fillStyle = fillColors[i%4];
       context.fillStyle = "#000";

       // Outline a text string
       context.strokeText(""+labelY,
                          currentX+shadowX,
                          currentY+shadowY);

       // Fill a text string
       context.fillStyle = "#FF0";
       context.fillText(""+labelY,
                        currentX,
                        currentY);
    }
}

function randomBarValues() {
  for(var i=0; i<barCount; i++) {
     barHeight = (maxHeight-indentY)*Math.random();
     barHeights[i] = barHeight;
  }
}

function drawGraph2() {
  // clear the canvas before drawing new set of rectangles
  context.clearRect(0, 0, elem.width, elem.height);

  drawAndLabelAxes();
  randomBarValues();
  drawElements();
}

function drawElements() {
  for(var i=0; i<barCount; i++) {
    currentX = leftBorder+i*barWidth;
    currentY = maxHeight-barHeights[i],
```

```
    gradient1 = context.createLinearGradient(
                            currentX,
                            currentY,
                            currentX+barWidth,
                            currentY+barHeights[i]);

    gradient1.addColorStop(0,  '#f00');
    gradient1.addColorStop(0.3,'#000');
    gradient1.addColorStop(0.6,'#ff0');
    gradient1.addColorStop(1,  '#00f');

    context.fillStyle = gradient1;

    context.shadowColor   = "rgba(100,100,100,.5)";
    context.shadowOffsetX = 3;
    context.shadowOffsetY = 3;
    context.shadowBlur    = 5;

    context.fillRect(leftBorder+i*barWidth,
                     maxHeight-barHeights[i],
                     barWidth,
                     barHeights[i]);
  }

  drawBarText();
}

function drawBarText() {
  // Define some drawing attributes
  context.font = "bold "+fontSize+"pt New Times Roman";
  context.lineWidth   = 2;
  context.strokeStyle = "#000";

  for(var i=0; i<barCount; i++) {
     context.beginPath();
     currentX = leftBorder+i*barWidth;
     currentY = maxHeight-barHeights[i]+fontSize/4;
   //context.fillStyle = fillColors[i%4];
     context.fillStyle = "#000";

     barHeight = Math.floor(barHeights[i]);

     // Outline a text string
     context.strokeText(""+barHeight,
                        currentX+shadowX,
                        currentY+shadowY);
```

```
         // Fill a text string
         context.fillStyle = "#F00";
         context.fillText(""+barHeight,
                           currentX,
                           currentY);
      }
   }
 </script>
</head>

<body onload="drawGraph();">
  <header>
    <h1>Linear Gradient Bar Chart</h1>
  </header>

  <div>
   <canvas id="myCanvas" width="500" height="300">No support for
Canvas</canvas>
   </div>

  <input type="button" onclick="drawGraph();return false"
        value="Update Graph Values"/>
</body>
</html>
```

Listing 12.1 contains one loop for initializing the randomly generated heights of the bar chart elements, followed by another loop that renders those bar chart elements with a linear gradient consisting of four color stops.

The variable barHeight is used for the height of each rectangle, and it is assigned an integer-based value of a randomly generated number. A simple conditional ensures that the bar height is always at least equal to a minimum value. The x-coordinate of the upper-left vertex for the current bar element is assigned to the variable currentX and the variable currentY is assigned a value that will be used in the computation of the y-coordinate of this same vertex.

The width and height of each rectangle are assigned the values of bar-Width and barHeight, respectively, and each rectangle is rendered with a linear gradient. Since the bar heights are based on randomly generated numbers, the chart will change each time that you refresh the display. You can use the code in this example as a starting point from which you can add more details, such as labels for the horizontal and vertical axes.

Figure 12.1 renders a bar chart with linear gradient shading, in a landscape-mode screenshot taken on an Asus Prime tablet with Android ICS.

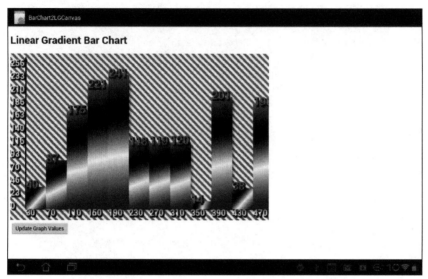

FIGURE 12.1 HTML5 Canvas bar chart on an Asus Prime tablet with Android ICS.

MOUSE-ENABLED BAR CHART

HTML5 Canvas supports all the mouse-related events that have worked with in earlier versions of HTML, and those mouse events can be processed in JavaScript functions.

Listing 12.2 displays the contents of the HTML page `MouseBarChart2LG1. html` that illustrates how to handle mouse click events in an HTML5 `<canvas>` element.

Listing 12.2 MouseBarChart2LG1.html

```
<!DOCTYPE html>
<html lang="en">
<head>
  <meta charset="utf-8"/>
  <title>HTML5 Canvas Bar Chart With Mouse Events</title>

  <style type="text/css">
    canvas {
        border: 5px solid #888;
        background: #CCC;
    }
  </style>
```

```
<script>
  var basePointX    = 20;
  var basePointY    = 0;
  var currentX      = basePointX;
  var currentY      = basePointY;
  var barCount      = 12;
  var barWidth      = 40;
  var barHeight     = 0;
  var shadowX       = 2;
  var shadowY       = 2;
  var axisFontSize  = 12;
  var fontSize      = 16;
  var lineWidth     = 2;
  var currentBar    = 0;
  var maxHeight     = 330;
  var xAxisWidth    = (2*barCount+1)*barWidth/2;
  var yAxisHeight   = maxHeight;
  var labelY        = 0;
  var indentY       = 5;
  var leftBorder    = 30;
  var topBorder     = 15;
  var arrowWidth    = 10;
  var arrowHeight   = 6;
  var barHeights    = new Array(barCount);
  var gradient1;
  var elem, context, gradient1;

  function drawGraph() {
     elem = document.getElementById('myCanvas');
     if (!elem || !elem.getContext) {
       return;
     }

     // Get the canvas 2d context
     context = elem.getContext('2d');
     if (!context) {
       return;
     }

     drawGraph2();
  }

  function drawAndLabelAxes() {
     // code omitted for brevity
  }
```

```
function randomBarValues() {
    for(var i=0; i<barCount; i++) {
        barHeight = (maxHeight-indentY)*Math.random();
        barHeights[i] = barHeight;
    }
}

function drawGraph2() {
    // clear the canvas...
    context.fillStyle = "#ccc";

    context.fillRect(0, 0, 600, 350);
    context.fill();

    drawAndLabelAxes();
    randomBarValues();
    drawElements();
}

function drawElements() {
    for(var i=0; i<barCount; i++) {
        currentX = leftBorder+i*barWidth;
        currentY = maxHeight-barHeights[i],

        gradient1 = context.createLinearGradient(
                                currentX,
                                currentY,
                                currentX+barWidth,
                                currentY+barHeights[i]);

        gradient1.addColorStop(0,   '#f00');
        gradient1.addColorStop(0.3,'#000');
        gradient1.addColorStop(0.6,'#ff0');
        gradient1.addColorStop(1,   '#00f');

        context.fillStyle = gradient1;

        context.shadowColor   = "rgba(100,100,100,.5)";
        context.shadowOffsetX = 3;
        context.shadowOffsetY = 3;
        context.shadowBlur    = 5;

        context.fillRect(leftBorder+i*barWidth,
                        maxHeight-barHeights[i],
                        barWidth,
                        barHeights[i]);
    }
```

```
      }

      function drawBarText(e) {
        var event = window.event || e;
        var currX = event.clientX;

        currentBar = Math.floor((currX-basePointX)/barWidth);

        if((currentBar >= 0) && (currentBar < barCount)) {
           barHeight = Math.floor(barHeights[currentBar]);

           currentX  = leftBorder+currentBar*barWidth;
           currentY  = maxHeight-barHeight;

           // Define some drawing attributes
           context.font = "bold "+fontSize+"pt New Times Roman";
           context.lineWidth   = 2;
           context.strokeStyle = "#000";

           // Outline a text string
           context.strokeText(""+barHeight,
                              currentX+shadowX,
                              currentY+shadowY);

           // Fill a text string
           context.fillStyle = "#F00";
           context.fillText(""+barHeight,
                           currentX,
                           currentY);
        }
      }
    </script>
</head>

<body onload="drawGraph();">
  <header>
    <h1>HTML5 Canvas Bar Chart Linear Gradient</h1>
  </header>

  <div style="margin-left:0px;">
    <canvas id="myCanvas" width="600" height="350"
            style="border: 5px blue solid"
            onmousemove="drawBarText()"
            onclick="drawBarChart()">
    </canvas>
  <div>
```

```
<input type="button" onclick="drawGraph();return false"
       value="Update Graph Values"/>
</body>
</html>
```

Listing 12.2 renders a bar chart with code that is similar to earlier examples in this chapter. The key difference in this code sample involves the additional attributes in the HTML5 <canvas> element, as shown here:

```
<canvas id="myCanvas" width="600" height="350"
        style="border: 5px blue solid"
        onmousemove="drawBarText()"
        onclick="drawBarChart()">
</canvas>
```

Whenever users click inside the HTML5 <canvas> element, the JavaScript function drawBarChart() is invoked, which refreshes the bar chart. Whenever users move their mouse, the drawBarText() method is invoked, which checks whether or not users have clicked inside the bar chart by means of the following code fragment:

```
var currX = event.clientX;
currentBar = Math.floor((currX-basePointX)/barWidth);
if((currentBar >= 0) && (currentBar < barCount)) {
     barHeight = Math.floor(barHeights[currentBar]);
     // the omitted code displays a text string that
     // contains the height of the current rectangle
}
```

Note that the preceding code only checks if the x-coordinate of a mouse click is inside one of the bar elements of the bar chart; if you want ensure that the y-coordinate is also inside a bar chart, you need additional conditional logic in the code.

Figure 12.2 displays a bar chart that displays bar-related information as users move their mouse around the screen, in a landscape-mode screenshot taken from an Android application running on an Asus Prime Android ICS 10" tablet.

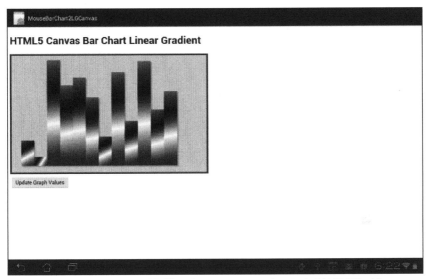

FIGURE 12.2 Mouse-enabled bar chart on an Asus Prime Android ICS 10" tablet.

RENDERING 3D BAR CHARTS

In Chapter 4, you saw how to render a cube in HTML5 Canvas by rendering the top face (a parallelogram), the front face (a rectangle), and the right face (a parallelogram) of the cube. The same technique is used in this section in order to render each "bar element" in the bar chart.

The HTML page `BarChart13D1Mouse.html` in Listing 12.3 illustrates how to render a mouse-enabled bar chart with a three-dimensional effect.

Listing 12.3 BarChart13D1Mouse1.html

```
<!DOCTYPE html>
<html lang="en">
<head>
  <meta charset="utf-8"/>
  <title>HTML5 Canvas 3D Bar Chart Linear Gradient</title>

  <script>
    var currentX    = 0;
    var currentY    = 0;
    var barCount    = 12;
    var barWidth    = 40;
    var barHeight   = 0;
```

```
var maxHeight     = 330;
var slantX        = barWidth/3;
var slantY        = barWidth/3;
var shadowX       = 2;
var shadowY       = 2;
var axisFontSize  = 12;
var fontSize      = 16;
var labelY        = 0;
var indentY       = 10;
var leftBorder    = 30;
var topBorder     = 15;
var arrowWidth    = 10;
var arrowHeight   = 6;
var topShading    = "#888";
var rightShading  = "#444";
var xAxisWidth    = (barCount+1)*barWidth;
var yAxisHeight   = maxHeight;
var barHeights    = new Array(barCount);
var elem, context, gradient1;

function drawGraph() {
   elem = document.getElementById('myCanvas');
   if (!elem || !elem.getContext) {
     return;
   }

   // Get the canvas 2d context.
   context = elem.getContext('2d');
   if (!context) {
     return;
   }

   drawBarChart();
}

function drawAndLabelAxes() {
   // code omitted for brevity
}

function randomBarValues() {
   for(var i=0; i<barCount; i++) {
      barHeight = (maxHeight-indentY)*Math.random();
      barHeights[i] = barHeight;
   }
}
```

```
function drawBarChart() {
   // clear the canvas before drawing new set of rectangles
   context.clearRect(0, 0, elem.width, elem.height);

   drawAndLabelAxes();
   randomBarValues();
   drawElements();
}

function drawElements() {
   for(var i=0; i<barCount; i++) {
      currentX = leftBorder+i*barWidth;
      currentY = maxHeight-barHeights[i];

      // front face (rectangle)
      gradient1 = context.createLinearGradient(
                              currentX,
                              currentY,
                              currentX+barWidth,
                              currentY+barHeights[i]);

      gradient1.addColorStop(0,  '#f00');
      gradient1.addColorStop(0.3,'#000');
      gradient1.addColorStop(0.6,'#ff0');
      gradient1.addColorStop(1,  '#00f');

      context.fillStyle = gradient1;

      context.shadowColor   = "rgba(100,100,100,.5)";
      context.shadowOffsetX = 3;
      context.shadowOffsetY = 3;
      context.shadowBlur    = 5;

      context.fillRect(currentX,
                       currentY,
                       barWidth,
                       barHeights[i]);

      // top face (parallelogram)
      // CCW from lower-left vertex
      context.beginPath();
      context.fillStyle = topShading;
      context.shadowColor   = "rgba(100,100,100,.5)";
      context.shadowOffsetX = 3;
      context.shadowOffsetY = 3;
      context.shadowBlur    = 5;
```

```
      context.moveTo(currentX, currentY);
      context.lineTo(currentX+barWidth, currentY);
      context.lineTo(currentX+barWidth+slantX,
                      currentY-slantY);
      context.lineTo(currentX+slantX,
                      currentY-slantY);
      context.closePath();
      context.fill();

      // right face (parallelogram)
      // CW from upper-left vertex
      context.beginPath();
      context.fillStyle = rightShading;

      context.shadowColor   = "rgba(100,100,100,.5)";
      context.shadowOffsetX = 3;
      context.shadowOffsetY = 3;
      context.shadowBlur    = 5;

      context.moveTo(currentX+barWidth, currentY);
      context.lineTo(currentX+barWidth+slantX,
                      currentY-slantY);
      context.lineTo(currentX+barWidth+slantX,
                      currentY+barHeights[i]-slantY);
      context.lineTo(currentX+barWidth,
                      currentY+barHeights[i]);
      context.closePath();
      context.fill();
   }

   drawBarText();
}

function drawBarText() {
   // Define some drawing attributes
   context.font = "bold "+fontSize+"pt New Times Roman";
   context.lineWidth   = 2;
   context.strokeStyle = "#000";

   for(var i=0; i<barCount; i++) {
      context.beginPath();
      currentX = leftBorder+i*barWidth;
      currentY = maxHeight-barHeights[i]+fontSize/4;
    //context.fillStyle = fillColors[i%4];
      context.fillStyle = "#000";
```

```
        barHeight = Math.floor(barHeights[i]);

        // Outline a text string
        context.strokeText(""+barHeight,
                           currentX+shadowX,
                           currentY+shadowY);

        // Fill a text string
        context.fillStyle = "#F00";
        context.fillText(""+barHeight,
                         currentX,
                         currentY);
      }
    }
  </script>

  <style type="text/css">
    canvas {
      border: 5px solid #888;
      background: #CCC;
    }
  </style>
</head>

<body onload="drawGraph();">
  <header>
    <h1>HTML5 Canvas 3D Bar Chart</h1>
  </header>

  <figure>
    <canvas id="myCanvas" width="600" height="350">No support for
Canvas</canvas>
  </figure>

  <input type="button" onclick="drawGraph();return false"
         value="Update Graph Values"/>
</body>
</html>
```

Listing 12.3 extends the functionality of the code in Listing 12.2 by adding two parallelograms to each bar element of the bar chart: one is above the bar element (which is a rectangle) and one is to the right of the bar element, thereby creating a three-dimensional effect. Listing 12.3 contains code for creating the front "face" of the bar elements and for rendering the horizontal and vertical axes, which is the same as the code in Listing 12.2.

The main loop in Listing 12.3 creates a linear gradient (with four stop colors) that is used for rendering the top, front, and right face of each bar element in the bar chart.

Figure 12.3 displays a three-dimensional bar chart in which the height of individual bar elements is highlighted when users move their mouse over the bar elements, in a landscape-mode screenshot on a Nexus 7 tablet with Android Jelly Bean.

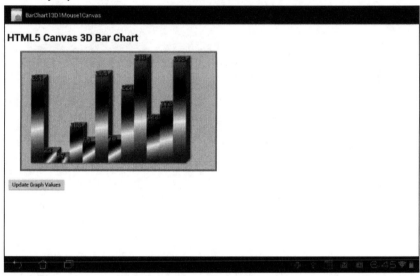

FIGURE 12.3 Mouse-enabled 3D bar chart on a Nexus 7 tablet with Android Jelly Bean.

RENDERING MULTIPLE LINE GRAPHS

In the previous section, you learned how to render a simple line graph, and in this section you will see how to render multiple line graphs in the same HTML page.

Listing 12.4 displays the contents of the HTML page MultiLineGraphs2. html that illustrates how to render a set of line graphs.

Listing 12.4 MultiLineGraphs2.html

```
<!DOCTYPE html>
<html lang="en">
<head>
  <meta charset="utf-8"/>
```

```
<title>HTML5 Canvas Line Graphs</title>

<style type="text/css">
  canvas {
      border: 5px solid #888;
      background: #CCC;
  }
</style>

<script>
  var currentX     = 0;
  var currentY     = 0;
  var barCount     = 12;
  var barWidth     = 40;
  var barHeight    = 0;
  var maxHeight    = 280;
  var xAxisWidth   = barCount*barWidth;
  var yAxisHeight  = maxHeight;
  var shadowX      = 2;
  var shadowY      = 2;
  var axisFontSize = 12;
  var fontSize     = 16;
  var labelY       = 0;
  var indentY      = 5;
  var leftBorder   = 30;
  var topBorder    = 15;
  var arrowWidth   = 10;
  var arrowHeight  = 6;
  var dotRadius    = 6;
  var lineCount    = 3;
  var barHeights   = new Array(barCount);
  var barHeights2  = new Array(barCount);
  var barHeights3  = new Array(barCount);
  var currHeights  = new Array(barCount);
  var multiLines   = new Array(lineCount);
  var fillColors   = new Array("#F00", "#FF0", "#0F0", "#00F");
  var elem, context, gradient1;

  function drawGraph() {
    // Get the canvas element
    elem = document.getElementById('myCanvas');
    if (!elem || !elem.getContext) {
      return;
    }

    // Get the canvas 2d context
    context = elem.getContext('2d');
```

```
    if (!context) {
      return;
    }

    drawGraph2();
}

function drawAndLabelAxes() {
   // code omitted for brevity
}

function randomBarValues() {
    for(var i=0; i<barCount; i++) {
       barHeight = maxHeight*Math.random();
       barHeights[i] = barHeight;

       barHeight = maxHeight*Math.random();
       barHeights2[i] = barHeight;

       barHeight = maxHeight*Math.random();
       barHeights3[i] = barHeight;
    }

    multiLines[0] = barHeights;
    multiLines[1] = barHeights2;
    multiLines[2] = barHeights3;
}

function drawGraph2() {
   // clear the canvas before drawing new set of rectangles
   context.clearRect(0, 0, elem.width, elem.height);

   randomBarValues();
   drawAndLabelAxes();
   drawElements();
}

function drawElements() {
   for(var h=0; h<multiLines.length; h++) {
      currHeights = multiLines[h];

      currentX = leftBorder;
    //currentY = maxHeight-barHeights[0];
      currentY = maxHeight-currHeights[0];

      // draw line segments...
```

```
        for(var i=0; i<barCount; i++) {
           context.beginPath();
           context.moveTo(currentX, currentY);
           currentX = leftBorder+i*barWidth;
         //currentY = maxHeight-barHeights[i];
           currentY = maxHeight-currHeights[i];

           context.shadowColor   = "rgba(100,100,100,.5)";
           context.shadowOffsetX = 3;
           context.shadowOffsetY = 3;
           context.shadowBlur    = 5;

           context.lineWidth   = 4;
           context.strokeStyle = fillColors[i%4];
           context.lineCap     = "miter"; // "round";

           context.lineTo(currentX, currentY);
           context.stroke();
        }

        // draw the dots...
        for(var i=0; i<barCount; i++) {
           context.beginPath();
           currentX = leftBorder+i*barWidth;
         //currentY = maxHeight-barHeights[i];
           currentY = maxHeight-currHeights[i];
           context.fillStyle = fillColors[i%4];

           context.arc(currentX,
                       currentY,
                       dotRadius, 0, Math.PI*2, 0);
           context.fill();
        }
     }

   drawBarText();
}

function drawBarText() {
   // Define some drawing attributes
   context.font = "bold "+fontSize+"pt New Times Roman";
   context.lineWidth   = 2;
   context.strokeStyle = "#000";

   for(var i=0; i<barCount; i++) {
      context.beginPath();
      currentX = leftBorder+i*barWidth;
```

```
              currentY = maxHeight-barHeights[i]+fontSize/4;
          //context.fillStyle = fillColors[i%4];
            context.fillStyle = "#000";

          barHeight = Math.floor(barHeights[i]);

          // Outline a text string
          context.strokeText(""+barHeight,
                             currentX+shadowX,
                             currentY+shadowY);

          // Fill a text string
          context.fillStyle = "#F00";
          context.fillText(""+barHeight,
                           currentX,
                           currentY);
       }
    }
  </script>
</head>

<body onload="drawGraph();">
  <header>
    <h1>HTML5 Canvas Line Graphs</h1>
  </header>

  <div>
   <canvas id="myCanvas" width="500" height="300">No support for
Canvas
   </canvas>
  </div>

  <input type="button" onclick="drawGraph();return false"
         value="Update Graph Values"/>
</body>
</html>
```

The JavaScript function drawGraph() in Listing 12.4 is invoked when the HTML5 Web page is loaded, and this function consists of three distinct loops. The first loop calculates the vertices for three distinct line graphs and stores the calculated values in the arrays barHeights, barHeights2, and bar-Heights3, respectively.

Next, a new array is created that references the vertices of the three line graphs using the following code:

```
multiLines[0] = barHeights;
```

```
multiLines[1] = barHeights2;
multiLines[2] = barHeights3;
```

Now that the line graph arrays have been initialized, we can proceed with rendering the three line graphs. This is accomplished by nested loop, where the outer loop iterates through the elements of the array `multiLines`, and the inner loop renders one line graph, as shown here in high-level form:

```
for(var h=0; h<multiLines.length; h++) {
    currHeights = multiLines[h];
    // code omitted

    // draw line segments...
    for(var i=0; i<barCount; i++) {
      // code omitted
    }

    // render the dots
    for(var i=0; i<barCount; i++) {
      // code omitted
    }
}
```

Figure 12.4 renders a set of line graphs based on the code and data values in Listing 12.5, in a landscape-mode screenshot on a Nexus 7 tablet with Android Jelly Bean.

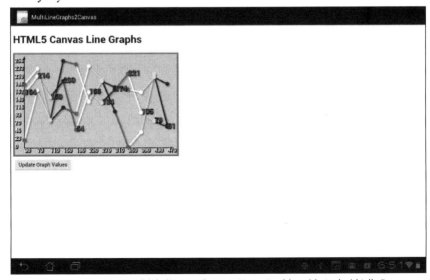

FIGURE 12.4 Canvas multiple line graphs on a Nexus 7 tablet with Android Jelly Bean.

RENDERING AREA GRAPHS

A bar chart consists of contiguous rectangles, whereas an area graph consists of a set of contiguous trapezoids that "sit" on the same horizontal line segment (which is often the horizontal axis for the graph). Since rectangles have two pairs of parallel sides whereas trapezoids have only one pair of parallel sides, bar charts and area graphs are programmatically similar. However, we will render an area graph by rendering line segments via the `moveTo()` method.

The HTML page `AreaGraph2.html` contains four pages of code that is similar to code that you saw in the HTML5 page `MultiLineGraphs2.html`. Consequently, Listing 12.5 displays only the function `drawElements()` that contains a new section of code. You can find the entire code listing on the DVD.

Listing 12.5 AreaGraph2.html

```
<!DOCTYPE html>
<html lang="en">
<head>
  <meta charset="utf-8"/>
  <title>HTML5 Canvas Area Graph</title>

  <style type="text/css">
    canvas {
        border: 5px solid #888;
        background: #CCC;
    }
  </style>

  <script>
  // code omitted for brevity

    function drawElements() {
        for(var i=0; i<barCount-1; i++) {
            currentX1 = leftBorder+i*barWidth;
            currentY1 = maxHeight-barHeights[i];
            currentX2 = leftBorder+(i+1)*barWidth;
            currentY2 = maxHeight-barHeights[i+1];

            gradient1 = context.createLinearGradient(
                              currentX1,
                              currentY1,
                              currentX1+barWidth,
```

```
                                    currentY1+barHeights[i]);

        gradient1.addColorStop(0,   '#f00');
        gradient1.addColorStop(0.3,'#000');
        gradient1.addColorStop(0.6,'#ff0');
        gradient1.addColorStop(1,   '#00f');

        context.beginPath();
      //context.fillStyle = fillColors[i%4];
        context.fillStyle = gradient1;

        context.shadowColor    = "rgba(100,100,100,.5)";
        context.shadowOffsetX = 3;
        context.shadowOffsetY = 3;
        context.shadowBlur    = 5;

        // this code renders the current trapezoid
        context.moveTo(currentX1, currentY1);
        context.lineTo(currentX2, currentY2);
        context.lineTo(currentX2, maxHeight);
        context.lineTo(currentX1, maxHeight);

        context.fill();
      }

      drawTheDots();
      drawBarText();
    }

</head>

<body onload="drawGraph();">
  <header>
    <h1>HTML5 Canvas Area Graph</h1>
  </header>

  <div>
    <canvas id="myCanvas" width="500" height="300">No support for
Canvas
    </canvas>
  </div>
  <input type="button" onclick="drawGraph();return false"
         value="Update Graph Values"/>
 </body>
</html>
```

The JavaScript function `drawGraph()` in Listing 12.5 is invoked when the HTML5 page is loaded, and this function consists of three distinct loops (which is similar to previous examples in this chapter). The first loop calculates the vertices of the line segments that represent the "top" of the contiguous trapezoids. The second loop uses the values of the vertices in order to construct each trapezoid. The final loop renders a set of circles on the end points of the line segments.

Figure 12.5 renders an area graph based on the code and data values in Listing 12.5, in a landscape-mode screenshot on a Nexus 7 tablet with Android Jelly Bean.

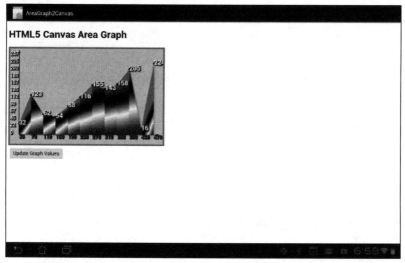

FIGURE 12.5 Canvas area graph on a Nexus 7 tablet with Android Jelly Bean.

RENDERING PIE CHARTS

Pie charts are very popular for representing data in a graphical manner, and you often see presentations rendering a set of data in a pie chart as well as a bar chart.

The HTML5 page `PieChart1.html` in Listing 12.6 contains the code that renders a pie chart.

Listing 12.6 PieChart1.html

```
<!DOCTYPE html>
<html lang="en">
```

```
<head>
  <meta charset="utf-8"/>
  <title>HTML5 Canvas Pie Chart</title>

  <style type="text/css">
    canvas {
        border: 5px solid #888;
        background: #CCC;
    }
  </style>

  <script>
    var basePointX   = 200;
    var basePointY   = 150;
    var sumAngles    = 0;
    var endAngle     = 0;
    var startAngle   = 0;
    var fontSize     = 16;
    var shadowX      = 1;
    var shadowY      = 1;
    var currentX     = 0;
    var currentY     = 0;
    var pieAngle     = 0;
    var piePercent   = 0;
    var legendWidth  = fontSize;
    var legendHeight = fontSize;
    var wedgeRadius  = 140;
    var wedgeCount   = 6;

    var maxAngle     = 360/wedgeCount;
    var minAngle     = 3*maxAngle/4;
    var pieAngles    = new Array(wedgeCount);
    var wedgeAngles  = new Array(wedgeCount);
    var fillColors   = new Array("#F00", "#FF0", "#0F0", "#00F",
                                 "#F0F", "#0BB", "#B44", "#44B",
                                 "#484", "#888", "#0FF", "#BB0");

    var elem, context, gradient1;

    function drawGraph() {
        elem = document.getElementById('myCanvas');
        if (!elem || !elem.getContext) {
          return;
        }

        context = elem.getContext('2d');
```

```
    if (!context) {
      return;
    }

    drawGraph2();
}

function randomPieValues() {
    sumAngles     = 0;
    totalPieCount = 0;

    for(var i=0; i<wedgeCount; i++) {
        pieAngle = maxAngle*Math.random();

        if(pieAngle < minAngle) {
            pieAngle = minAngle;
        }

        pieAngles[i] = pieAngle;
        totalPieCount += pieAngle;
    }

    wedgeAngles[0] = 0;

    for(var i=1; i<wedgeCount; i++) {
        wedgeAngle = Math.floor(pieAngles[i]*360/totalPieCount);
        wedgeAngles[i] = wedgeAngles[i-1]+wedgeAngle;
    }
}

function drawGraph2() {
    // clear the canvas before drawing new pie chart
    context.clearRect(0, 0, elem.width, elem.height);

    randomPieValues();
    drawElements();
    drawPieText();
    drawLegend();
}

function drawElements() {
    for(var i=0; i<wedgeCount; i++) {
        startAngle = wedgeAngles[i]*Math.PI/180;

        if(i==wedgeCount-1) {
            endAngle = 360*Math.PI/180;
```

```
      } else {
         endAngle = wedgeAngles[i+1]*Math.PI/180;
      }

      context.fillStyle = fillColors[i%fillColors.length];
      context.shadowColor   = "rgba(64,64,64,.5)";
      context.shadowOffsetX = 3;
      context.shadowOffsetY = 3;
      context.shadowBlur    = 5;

      context.beginPath();

      context.moveTo(basePointX, basePointY);
      context.arc(basePointX,
                  basePointY,
                  wedgeRadius,
                  startAngle, endAngle, 0);

      context.closePath();
      context.fill();
   }
}

function drawPieText() {
   // Define some drawing attributes
   context.font = "bold "+fontSize+"pt New Times Roman";
   context.lineWidth    = 2;
   context.strokeStyle = "#000";

   for(var i=1; i<wedgeCount; i++) {
      context.fillStyle = "#000";

      pieAngle = (wedgeAngles[i]-wedgeAngles[i-1]);

      currentX = basePointX+(wedgeRadius-20)*
                             Math.cos(wedgeAngles[i]*Math.
PI/180);

      currentY = basePointY+(wedgeRadius-20)*
                             Math.sin(wedgeAngles[i]*Math.
PI/180);

      context.moveTo(currentX, currentY);

      piePercent = Math.floor(100*pieAngle/360);
```

```
            // Outline a text string
            context.strokeText(""+piePercent,
                               currentX+shadowX,
                               currentY+shadowY);

            // Fill a text string
            context.fillStyle = "#F00";
            context.fillText(""+piePercent,
                             currentX,
                             currentY);
         }

      }

   function drawLegend() {
      // Define some drawing attributes
      context.font = "bold "+fontSize+"pt New Times Roman";
      context.lineWidth   = 2;
      context.strokeStyle = "#000";

      for(var i=0; i<wedgeCount; i++) {
         currentX = basePointX+11*wedgeRadius/10;
         currentY = basePointY-wedgeRadius/2+i*(fontSize+4);

         context.fillStyle = fillColors[i%fillColors.length];

         context.fillRect(currentX,
                          currentY,
                          legendWidth,
                          legendHeight);

         context.fillText("Company "+(i+1),
                          currentX+2*legendWidth,
                          currentY+legendHeight);
      }
   }
  </script>
 </head>

<body onload="drawGraph();">
 <header>
   <h1>Canvas Pie Chart</h1>
 </header>

 <div>
  <canvas id="myCanvas" width="500" height="300">No support for
                                                  Canvas
```

```
  </canvas>
  </div>

  <input type="button" onclick="drawGraph();return false"
         value="Update Graph Values"/>
 </body>
</html>
```

The JavaScript function `drawGraph()` in Listing 12.6 is executed when this HTML5 Web page is loaded in a browser. This function uses the `random()` function in order to initialize the array `wedgeAngles` with values for a set of angles (measured in degrees).

The second loop uses the HTML5 Canvas `arc()` method with the values in the `wedgeAngles` array in order to render the pie chart. Note that the angle span of the "wedges" changes in a random fashion whenever users reload this HTML Web page. The second loop uses the loop variable as an index into the array `fillColors` to select a standard color for rendering each wedge of the pie chart.

In addition, each wedge is rendered with a shadow effect with the following code block:

```
context.shadowColor   = "rgba(100,100,100,.5)";
context.shadowOffsetX = 3;
context.shadowOffsetY = 3;
context.shadowBlur    = 5;
```

Figure 12.6 displays a pie chart based on the code and the data values in Listing 12.6, in a landscape-mode screenshot on an Asus Prime tablet with Android ICS.

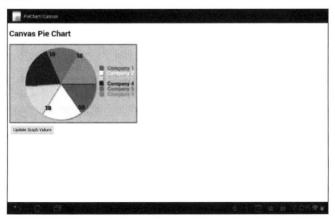

FIGURE 12.6 Canvas pie chart on an Asus Prime tablet with Android ICS.

RENDERING MULTIPLE CHARTS AND GRAPHS

Now that you have completed this chapter, you know techniques that can be used to create many types of charts and graphs, and also how to add custom modifications. The example in this section is based on the code for a bar chart, line graph, and pie chart that you have seen in previous examples. Since the code is virtually the same it is not covered, but you can find the entire listing on the DVD.

Figure 12.7 displays a bar chart, a line graph, and a pie chart based on the code in the HTML5 page `BarChart2LG1Line1Pie1.html` and the CSS3 stylesheet `BarChart2LG1Line1Pie1.css` (both of which are on the DVD), in a landscape-mode screenshot taken from an Android application running on an Asus Prime tablet with Android ICS.

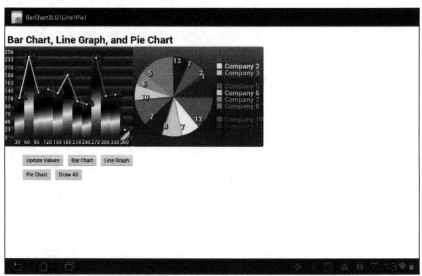

FIGURE 12.7 Canvas bar, line, pie chart on an Asus Prime tablet with Android ICS.

BAR CHARTS WITH HTML5 CANVAS AND JQUERY MOBILE

The previous example showed you how to render a bar chart, line graph, and a pie chart using HTML5 Canvas, and this section shows you how to render a bar chart using jQuery Mobile.

Listing 12.7 displays the contents of the HTML5 page `JQMBarChart1.html`, and the CSS stylesheet `JQMCanvas1.css` is available on the DVD.

Listing 12.7 JQMBarChart1.html

```
<!DOCTYPE html>
<html lang="en">
<head>
 <meta charset="utf-8"/>
  <title>A Bar Chart with Random Data and jQuery Mobile</title>

  <link rel="stylesheet"
   href="http://code.jquery.com/mobile/1.1.0/jquery.mobile-
1.1.0.min.css"/>
   <script
       src="http://code.jquery.com/jquery-1.7.1.min.js">
   </script>
   <script src="http://code.jquery.com/mobile/1.1.0
                     /jquery.mobile-1.1.0.min.js">
   </script>

  <script>
      var tapCount = 0, touchX = 0, touchY = 0;
      var bar = 0, barCount = 15;
      var barWidth = 30, barHeight = 0, maxBarHeight = 200;
      var leftBorder = 20, topBorder = 50;
      var xPos = 0, yPos = 0, radius = barWidth/8;
      var circleColor = "rgb(255, 255, 255)";
      var barHeights = new Array(barCount);
      var barXSlots = new Array(barCount);

      var rectColors = new Array('#f00', '#ff0', '#0f0', '#00f');
      var elem, canvas, ctx, cWidth, cHeight, canvasString;

      $(function() {
         resizeCanvas();
         $(window).resize(function() { resizeCanvas() });

         function resizeCanvas() {
            cWidth  = window.innerWidth / 1.2;
            cHeight = window.innerHeight / 2.0;

            canvasString = '<canvas id="mainCanvas" width="' +
                                                        cWidth +
                       '" height="' + cHeight +
                       '">Canvas is not supported</canvas>';

            $('#chartholder').empty();
            $(canvasString).appendTo('#chartholder');
            ctx = $('#mainCanvas').get(0).getContext('2d');
            canvas = document.getElementById("mainCanvas");
```

```
$('#mainCanvas').bind('tap', function(event){
   touchX = event.pageX;
   touchY = event.pageY;

   ctx.clearRect(0, 0, canvas.width, canvas.height);
   for(bar=0; bar<barCount; bar++) {
      barHeights[bar] = maxBarHeight*Math.random();
      barXSlots[bar] = leftBorder+bar*barWidth;

      xPos = barXSlots[bar];
      yPos = topBorder+(maxBarHeight-barHeights[bar]);

      ctx.fillStyle = rectColors[bar%rectColors.
                                              length];
      ctx.fillRect(xPos, yPos, barWidth,
                                   barHeights[bar]);
   }

   ctx.moveTo(barXSlots[0]+barWidth/2,
              topBorder+(maxBarHeight-barHeights[0]));

   for(bar=0; bar<barCount; bar++) {
      xPos = barXSlots[bar]+barWidth/2;
      yPos = topBorder+(maxBarHeight-barHeights[bar]);

      ctx.lineTo(xPos, yPos);
      ctx.stroke();
   }

   for(bar=0; bar<barCount; bar++) {
      xPos = barXSlots[bar]+barWidth/2;
      yPos = topBorder+(maxBarHeight-barHeights[bar]);

      ctx.beginPath();
      ctx.fillStyle = circleColor;
      ctx.arc(xPos, yPos, radius, 0, 2*Math.PI, true);
      ctx.closePath();
      ctx.fill();
   }
});
   }
 });
</script>

<style>
```

```
    #mainCanvas {
      background-color: #888;
      border: solid 3px #FF0;
    }

    #chartholder {
      width: 90%;
      height: 50%;
      margin: 0 auto;
      text-align: center;
    }
  </style>
</head>

<body>
  <div data-role="page" data-theme="a">
    <div data-role="header">
      <h2>Tap Inside to Render a New Bar Chart</h2>
    </div>
    <div data-role="content">
      <div id="chartholder"></div>
    </div>
    <div data-role="footer">
      <h2>Each Tap Renders a Different Bar Chart</h2>
    </div>
  </div>
</body>
</html>
```

Almost all the code in Listing 12.7 is already familiar to you: the code for the bar chart is almost identical to a code sample in Chapter 11, and the jQuery Mobile code consists of a single page view that contains "header," "content," and "footer" <div> elements.

The bar chart is rendered in an HTML <div> element (whose parent is the jQuery Mobile "content" <div> element) whose id value is chartholder.

An HTML5 <canvas> element with an id value of mainCanvas is created by dynamically constructing a string that specifies an HTML5 <canvas> element with its id value, width, and height, as shown here:

```
canvasString = '<canvas id="mainCanvas" width="' + cWidth +
               '" height="' + cHeight +
               '">Canvas is not supported</canvas>';
```

The HTML5 <canvas> element is then appended to the chartholder element with this code snippet:

```
$('#chartholder').empty();
```

```
$(canvasString).appendTo('#chartholder');
ctx = $('#mainCanvas').get(0).getContext('2d');
canvas = document.getElementById("mainCanvas");
```

When users resize their browser, the `chartholder` element is resized by invoking the `resizeCanvas()` during the `resize` event, as shown here:

```
$(window).resize(function() { resizeCanvas() });
```

The new width and height of the resized `<canvas>` element are calculated as follows:

```
cWidth  = window.innerWidth / 1.2;
cHeight = window.innerHeight / 2.0;
```

Now you can combine jQuery Mobile with the other charts and graphs that you saw in Chapter 11 in order to create chart-based jQuery Mobile applications. A good example of an "exploding" pie chart (with downloadable code) that uses jQuery is here:

http://www.elated.com/articles/snazzy-animated-pie-chart-html5-jquery/

Figure 12.8 displays a bar chart with jQuery Mobile in landscape mode on an Asus Prime tablet with Android ICS.

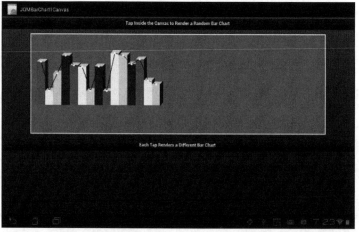

FIGURE 12.8 JQuery Mobile bar chart on an Asus Prime tablet with Android ICS.

UPDATING HTML5 CANVAS BAR CHARTS WITH A WEBSOCKET SERVER

Chapter 11 showed you how to create various chart and graphs, and the previous section showed you how to use jQuery Mobile so that you can display a bar chart on a mobile device. In this section, you will learn how to dynamically update and render a bar chart on a client browser with data that is periodically "pushed" from a WebSockets server. Recall that Chapter 10 contains a section regarding WebSockets, and you can review the information in that section to help you understand the code in this section.

The code sample in this section consists of three files: the HTML5 Web page JQWSBarChart1.html, for rendering the bar chart; the Python script echo_wsh.py (using Python 2.7.1) that sends data to the client browser; and the shell script run.sh that launches the WebSockets server.

Listing 12.8 displays a portion of the contents of JQWSBarChart1.html that illustrates how to receive data from a WebSockets server and refresh a bar chart with that data in HTML5 Canvas. Note that the code for the bar chart has been omitted for brevity, but the complete listing is available on the DVD.

Listing 12.8 JQWSBarChart1.html

```
<!DOCTYPE HTML>
<html lang="en">
<head>
  <meta charset="utf-8"/>
  <title>WebSockets and Bar Chart</title>
  <link href="CSS32Background1.css" rel="stylesheet" type="text/
css">
  <script
        src="http://code.jquery.com/jquery-1.7.1.min.js">
</script>

  <script>
    var currentX     = 0;
    var currentY     = 0;
    var barCount     = 10;
    var barWidth     = 40;
    var barHeight    = 0;
    var maxHeight    = 300;
    var xAxisWidth   = (2*barCount+1)*barWidth/2;
    var yAxisHeight  = maxHeight;
    var labelY       = 0;
    var indentY      = 5;
    var shadowX      = 2;
    var shadowY      = 2;
    var axisFontSize = 12;
```

```
var fontSize      = 16;
var leftBorder    = 50;
var topBorder     = 50;
var arrowWidth    = 10;
var arrowHeight   = 6;
var barHeights    = new Array(barCount);
var fillColors    = ['#f00', '#0f0', '#ff0', '#00f'];
var elem, context, gradient1;

var WSData = "", sendMsg = "Client-side Message", receiveMsg =
                                                            "";
var theTimeout, pollingDelay = 2000;

function initialGraph() {
   var foundCanvas = setup();

   if(foundCanvas == true) {
      getWebSocketData();
   }
}

function setup() {
  // Get the canvas element
  elem = document.getElementById('myCanvas');
  if(!elem || !elem.getContext) {
     return false;
  }

  // Get the canvas 2d context
  context = elem.getContext('2d');
  if(!context) {
     return false;
  }

  return true;
}

///// bar chart code omitted for brevity

function getWebSocketData() {
  if ("WebSocket" in window) {
     console.log("Your Browser supports WebSockets");

     // Open a web socket
     var ws = new WebSocket("ws://localhost:9998/echo");
```

```
        // specify handlers for open/close/message/error
        ws.onopen = function() {
            // Web Socket is connected, send data using send()
            ws.send(sendMsg);
            console.log("Sending Message to server: "+sendMsg);
        };

        ws.onmessage = function (evt) {
            var receivedMsg = evt.data;
            console.log("Message from server: "+receivedMsg);
            setupBarChart(receivedMsg);
        };

        ws.onclose = function() {
            // websocket is closed.
            console.log("Connection is closed...");
        };

        ws.onerror = function(evt) {
            console.log("Error occurred: "+evt.data);
        };
    } else {
        // The browser doesn't support WebSocket
        console.log("WebSocket NOT supported by your Browser!");
    }
  }

  function setupBarChart(dataStr) {
      // populate the barHeights array
      barHeights = dataStr.split(" ");

      barCount   = barHeights.length;

      drawGraph2();
  }
 </script>
</head>

<body onload="initialGraph();">
  <script>
    $(document).ready(function() {
      $("#StartClientPoll").click(function() {
         getWebSocketData();
         theTimeout = setInterval("getWebSocketData()",
                                                pollingDelay);
      })
```

```
      $("#StopClientPoll").click(function() {
         clearInterval(theTimeout);
         theTimeout = null;
      })

      $("#StartWSPull").click(function() {
         getWebSocketData();
         theTimeout = setInterval("getWebSocketData()",
                                              pollingDelay);
      })

      $("#StopWSPull").click(function() {
         clearInterval(theTimeout);
         theTimeout = null;
      })
    });
  </script>

  <div id="conn"></div>

  <div>
   <canvas id="myCanvas" width="800" height="400">No support for
                                              Canvas
          alt="Example rendering of a bar chart">
   </canvas>
  </div>

  <div id="WSDataDiv">
    <input type="button" id="StartClientPoll"
          value="Start Client Polling"/>
    <input type="button" id="StopClientPoll"
          value="Stop Client Polling"/>
    <input type="button" id="StartWSPull"
          value="Start Server"/>
    <input type="button" id="StopWSPull"
          value="Stop Server"/>
  </div>
</body>
</html>
```

One point to keep in mind is that some other browsers may implement older versions of the WebSockets protocol. In this example, Chrome 19 implements the current WebSockets protocol that is available in late 2012.

The <body> element in Listing 12.8 invokes the function initialGraph() that performs some initialization and then invokes the function getWebSocketData() to get the bar chart data (if the HTML5 <canvas> element exists in the Web page), as shown here:

```
function initialGraph() {
    var foundCanvas = setup();

    if(foundCanvas == true) {
        getWebSocketData();
    }
}
```

Next, the function getWebSocketData() implements the standard callback functions in JavaScript, including the onmessage function, which gets the data from the WebSockets server and passes the data to the setupBarChart() function for rendering the bar chart, as shown here:

```
    function getWebSocketData() {
if ("WebSocket" in window) {
// Open a web socket
var ws = new WebSocket("ws://localhost:9998/echo");

    // code omitted for brevity
ws.onmessage = function (evt) {
        var receivedMsg = evt.data;
        console.log("Message from server: "+receivedMsg);
        setupBarChart(receivedMsg);
    };
}
```

As you know, the code samples in this book render correctly in WebKit-based browsers, and in some cases the code samples work in other browsers. One exception is the code snippet shown in bold in the previous code block, which will not work in most versions of Firefox; however, it's possible that future versions of Firefox will support this code.

The setupBarChart() JavaScript function accepts a string parameter that consists of a space-delimited set of values for the bar heights of the bar chart, which is used to populate a JavaScript array with those bar heights, as shown here:

```
function setupBarChart(dataStr) {
        // populate the barHeights array
        barHeights = dataStr.split(" ");
```

```
      barCount     = barHeights.length;

      drawGraph2();
   }
```

The rendering of the bar chart is handled by the JavaScript function `draw-Graph2()`, which is not shown in Listing 12.8.

The other part to consider is the code on the WebSockets server that returns the data values for the bar chart. The data is retrieved with the following code snippet that is contained in the `getWebSocketData()` function, as shown here:

```
// Open a web socket
var ws = new WebSocket("ws://localhost:9998/echo");
```

Now let's turn our attention to the server-side code. Before delving into the details of the code, you need to download `pywebsocket`, which is here:

https://code.google.com/p/pywebsocket/

Now let's examine the relevant portion of the Python script `echo_wsh.py` that sends data from the WebSockets server to the client (via port `9998`), whose contents are displayed in Listing 12.9.

Listing 12.9 echo_wsh.py

```
# Copyright 2011, Google Inc.
# All rights reserved.
#
# Redistribution and use in source and binary forms, with or with-
out
# modification, are permitted provided that the following condi-
tions are
# met:
#
#     * Redistributions of source code must retain the above copy-
right
# notice, this list of conditions and the following disclaimer.
#     * Redistributions in binary form must reproduce the above
# copyright notice, this list of conditions and the following dis-
claimer
# in the documentation and/or other materials provided with the
# distribution.
#     * Neither the name of Google Inc. nor the names of its
# contributors may be used to endorse or promote products derived
```

```
from
# this software without specific prior written permission.
#
# THIS SOFTWARE IS PROVIDED BY THE COPYRIGHT HOLDERS AND CONTRIBU-
TORS
# "AS IS" AND ANY EXPRESS OR IMPLIED WARRANTIES, INCLUDING, BUT
NOT
# LIMITED TO, THE IMPLIED WARRANTIES OF MERCHANTABILITY AND FIT-
NESS FOR
# A PARTICULAR PURPOSE ARE DISCLAIMED. IN NO EVENT SHALL THE COPY-
RIGHT
# OWNER OR CONTRIBUTORS BE LIABLE FOR ANY DIRECT, INDIRECT, INCI-
DENTAL,
# SPECIAL, EXEMPLARY, OR CONSEQUENTIAL DAMAGES (INCLUDING, BUT NOT
# LIMITED TO, PROCUREMENT OF SUBSTITUTE GOODS OR SERVICES; LOSS OF
USE,
# DATA, OR PROFITS; OR BUSINESS INTERRUPTION) HOWEVER CAUSED AND
ON ANY
# THEORY OF LIABILITY, WHETHER IN CONTRACT, STRICT LIABILITY, OR
TORT
# (INCLUDING NEGLIGENCE OR OTHERWISE) ARISING IN ANY WAY OUT OF
THE USE
# OF THIS SOFTWARE, EVEN IF ADVISED OF THE POSSIBILITY OF SUCH
DAMAGE.

_GOODBYE_MESSAGE = u'Goodbye'

from random import randint

def web_socket_do_extra_handshake(request):
    pass  # Always accept.

def web_socket_transfer_data(request):
    while True:
        line = request.ws_stream.receive_message()
        if line is None:
            return
        if isinstance(line, unicode):
            barCount = 10;
            randomValues = ""

            for x in range(1, barCount):
                randomValues = randomValues + str(randint(50,
                                                  300))+" "
```

```
      print 'randomValues2: %s' % randomValues
      request.ws_stream.send_message(randomValues,
                                       binary=False)

   if line == _GOODBYE_MESSAGE:
       return
else:
   print 'Sending2: %s' % line
   request.ws_stream.send_message(line, binary=True)
```

The code shown in bold in Listing 12.14 is the code that creates a string containing a randomly generated set of integers that represent the ten bar heights of a bar chart:

```
barCount = 10;
randomValues = ""

for x in range(1, barCount):
   randomValues = randomValues + str(randint(50, 300))+" "

   print 'randomValues2: %s' % randomValues
```

After the string of concatenated bar heights has been created, it is sent to the client with the following code snippet:

request.ws_stream.send_message(randomValues, binary=False)

The third file that we need is a simple Bourne shell script run.sh that launches the WebSockets server on port 9998.

Listing 12.10 run.sh

```
CURRDIR=`pwd`
PYTHONPATH=$CURRDIR
python ./mod_pywebsocket/standalone.py -p 9998 -d $CURRDIR/example
```

Listing 12.10 is straightforward: it sets two shell script variables and then launches the Python script standalone.py located in the mod_pywebsocket subdirectory, specifying port 9998 and also the example subdirectory of $CURRDIR, which is the parent directory of the Python script echo_wsh.py in Listing 12.9.

Open a command shell, navigate to the subdirectory pywebsocket/src, and launch the shell script in Listing 12.10 as follows:

./run.sh

Listing 12.9 contains a copyright notice that is required for displaying the contents of this Python script. The new section of code (displayed in bold in Listing 12.14) is shown here:

```
barCount = 10;
randomValues = ""

for x in range(1, barCount):
  randomValues = randomValues + str(randint(50, 300))+" "

request.ws_stream.send_message(randomValues, binary=False)
```

Figure 12.9 displays a very colorful bar chart and also the data that is returned from a server, which specifies the height of each bar element in the graph.

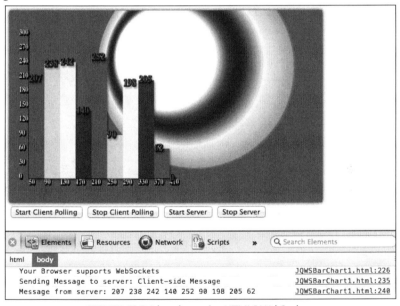

FIGURE 12.9 A bar chart using HTML5 WebSockets.

If you prefer using open source toolkits for handling the various WebSockets details for multiple browsers, there are also jQuery plugins available that use jQuery as a layer of abstraction on top of WebSockets (and provide support for multiple browsers, such as the one that is here):

https://code.google.com/p/jquery-graceful-websocket/

This jQuery plugin provides fallback support for Ajax if WebSockets is unavailable, along with options to override the default options.

AN INTEGRATED EXAMPLE WITH HTML5 CANVAS, CSS3, AND SVG

Now that you have seen how to create charts and graphs, how to create CSS3 graphics effects (Chapters 2, 3, and 4), and how to use SVG (Chapter 4), you are ready to read the code in this section. Since the code for the line graph, the bar chart, and the pie chart is very similar to previous code samples, that code will not be repeated here, but the complete code listings are available on the DVD.

The code sample in this section is comprised of the following files:

```
MouseCSS3SVGCanvas1.html
```

```
MouseCSS3SVGCanvas1.css
```

```
MouseCSS3SVGCanvas1.svg
```

```
MouseCSS3EllipticPieChart1.svg
```

```
CSS3Background1.css
```

Listing 12.11 displays a portion of the code in `MouseCSS3SVGCanvas1.html` that shows you how to send data to the associated SVG document in Listing 12.12.

Listing 12.11 MouseCSS3SVGCanvas1.html

```
//-------------------------------------------------
// call JS function in MouseCSS3EllipticPieChart1.svg
   var svgDoc = null, svgWin = null;

   function renderSVGPieChartInit() {
      var embed = document.getElementById('embed1');
      svgDoc = embed.getSVGDocument();

      if (svgDoc) {
        svgWin = svgDoc.defaultView;
      } else {
        alert("The embedded SVG document is null");
      }
   }

   function renderSVGPieChartMain() {
     svgWin.renderSVGEllipticPieChart();
   }

   // pass the pieAngles array
   function renderSVGPieChartAngles() {
     svgWin.renderSVGEllipticPieChartAngles(pieAngles);
```

```
        }
//-------------------------------------------------
```

Listing 12.11 contains the JavaScript function `renderSVGPieChartInit()` that obtains a reference to the SVG document in Listing 12.11 so that data can be sent to the appropriate JavaScript function in order to update the values for the "slices" in its pie chart. The data for the pie chart slices is contained in the JavaScript array `pieAngles` whose values are calculated in the JavaScript function `randomPieValues()` that is located elsewhere in the code.

The rendering of the bar chart and the pie chart is performed using code that you have already seen in previous code samples, so that code is omitted.

Listing 12.12 MouseCSS3EllipticPieChartSVG1.svg

```
function init(evt) {
        svgDocument = evt.target.ownerDocument;
        gcNode = svgDocument.getElementById("gc");

        initializeChart();
        drawChart();
}

//-------------------------------------------------
// JS function called from MouseCSS3SVGCanvas1.html
    function renderSVGEllipticPieChart(evt) {
        // reset to original vertex count (to be safe)
        vertexCount = vertexCountOri;
        angles = new Array(vertexCount);

        initializeChart();
        drawChart();
    }

    function renderSVGEllipticPieChartAngles(pieAngles) {
        newPieAngles = pieAngles;

        updateLocalPieAngles();
        drawChart();
    }

    function updateLocalPieAngles() {
        var localCount = newPieAngles.length;

        if(localCount > angles.length) {
            localCount = angles.length;
        }
```

```
        // vertexCount of the shorter array
        vertexCount = localCount;
        angles = new Array(vertexCount);

        for(var v=0; v<vertexCount; v++) {
          angles[v] = newPieAngles[v];
        }
      }
    }
//-------------------------------------------------
```

Listing 12.12 shows you the code that obtains a reference to the element whose id attribute has value gc, which is where the graphics is rendered. Because the JavaScript code is essentially the same as a previous example in this chapter, that code is omitted.

Listing 12.13 MouseCSS3SVGCanvas1.svg

```
<?xml version="1.0" encoding="iso-8859-1"?>
<!DOCTYPE svg PUBLIC "-//W3C//DTD SVG 20001102//EN"
 "http://www.w3.org/TR/2000/CR-SVG-20001102/DTD/svg-20001102.dtd">

<svg xmlns="http://www.w3.org/2000/svg"
     xmlns:xlink="http://www.w3.org/1999/xlink"
     width="100%" height="100%">
  <defs>
    <linearGradient id="pattern1">
      <stop offset="0%"   stop-color="yellow"/>
      <stop offset="40%"  stop-color="red"/>
      <stop offset="80%"  stop-color="blue"/>
    </linearGradient>

    // gradients omitted for brevity
  </defs>

  <g id="chart1" transform="translate(0,0) scale(1,1)">
    <rect width="30" height="235" x="15"  y="15"  fill="black"/>
    <rect width="30" height="240" x="10"  y="10"
          fill="url(#pattern1)"/>

    // bar elements omitted for brevity

    <rect width="30" height="175" x="225" y="75"  fill="black"/>
    <rect width="30" height="180" x="220" y="70"
          fill="url(#pattern3)"/>
  </g>

  <g id="chart2" transform="translate(250,125) scale(1,0.5)"
```

```
                  width="100%" height="100%">
   <use xlink:href="#chart1"/>
  </g>
</svg>
```

Listing 12.13 contains an SVG document with "static" data, in the sense that the same bar chart is rendered whenever users render the HTML Web page. As you can see, Listing 12.13 does not contain any JavaScript code, and this functionality is included so that you know how to render read-only data that is specified in an SVG document.

Listing 12.14 CSS3Background1.css

```
#myCanvas {
  opacity: 0.8;
  position: relative; top: 0px; left: 0px;
  background-image: -webkit-gradient(linear, 0% 50%, 100% 50%,
                                     from(#f00),
                                     color-stop(0.4, yellow),
                                     to(#00f));
  -webkit-border-radius: 4px;
  border-radius: 4px;
  -webkit-box-shadow:  30px 30px 30px #000;
}

#myCanvas:hover {
  background-image:
   -webkit-radial-gradient(red 4px, transparent 48px),
   -webkit-repeating-linear-gradient(0deg, red 5px,  green 4px,
                                     yellow 8px, blue 12px,
                                     transparent 16px, red 20px,
                                     blue 24px, transparent 28px,
                                     transparent 32px),
   -webkit-radial-gradient(blue 8px, transparent 68px);

  background-size: 120px 120px, 24px 24px;
  background-position: 0 0;
}
```

Listing 12.14 contains some straightforward definitions of CSS selectors that you have seen in earlier examples and in the CSS3-related chapters of this book.

Listing 12.15 MouseCSS3SVGCanvas1.css

```
#columns {
-webkit-column-count : 4;
-webkit-column-gap : 40px;
-webkit-column-rule : 1px solid rgb(255,255,255);
column-count : 3;
column-gap : 40px;
```

```
column-rule : 1px solid rgb(255,255,255);
}


#ellipticPieChart1 {
opacity: 0.5;
color: red;
width: 550px;
height: 300px;
position: absolute; top: 50px; left: 420px;
font-size: 20px;
-webkit-border-radius: 4px;
border-radius: 4px;
-webkit-background: url(MouseCSS3EllipticPieChart1.svg) top right;
background: url(MouseCSS3EllipticPieChart1.svg) top right;
}


#ellipticPieChart1:hover {
opacity: 0.5;
color: red;
width: 550px;
height: 300px;
position: absolute; top: 60px; left: 430px;
font-size: 20px;
background-image: -webkit-gradient(linear, 0% 50%, 100% 50%,
                                   from(#f00),
                                   color-stop(0.4, yellow),
                                   to(#00f));
-webkit-border-radius: 4px;
border-radius: 4px;
}
```

Listing 12.15 contains familiar CSS3 selectors that enable you to render text in three columns. This CSS code is useful when you want to create column-based styling to an HTML document that contains primarily (or exclusively) text.

Don't forget that you can also add CSS3 Media Queries to Listing 12.15 in order to change the number of columns based on the dimensions of the screen, or whether a mobile device is in portrait mode or landscape mode.

Figure 12.10 displays a bar chart, a line graph, and a pie chart that are rendered when you launch Listing 12.11 in a Safari browser.

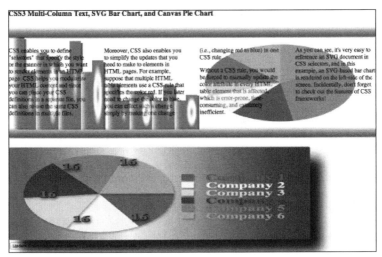

FIGURE 12.10 Charts using HTML5 Canvas, CSS3, and SVG.

THIRD PARTY CHART LIBRARIES

If you prefer not to create custom charts and graphs, you can use existing libraries for rendering charts and graphs as an alternative to creating your own charts and graphs. One advantage of using existing libraries is the fact that you do not need to be responsible for bug fixes, and you can avail yourself of upgrades containing new features or enhancements to those libraries.

You can also find third party chart libraries that use jQuery, and several are discussed here:

http://www.1stwebdesigner.com/css/top-jquery-chart-libraries-interactive-charts/

You might also be interested in using the `jqPlot` chart library, which is a jQuery plugin whose homepage is here:

http://www.jqplot.com/

jqPlot provides "hooks" for adding your own custom event handlers and for creating new plot types. Moreover, jqPlot has been tested on Safari, Firefox, IE, and Opera, and you can even use jqPlot on tablets. Some live jqPlot samples are available online here:

http://www.jqplot.com/tests/

If you prefer to use SVG instead of HTML5 Canvas, another toolkit is the SVG Google Charts API. You can see some code samples that use this toolkit here:

http://www.netmagazine.com/tutorials/create-beautiful-data-visualisations-svg-google-charts-api

The jQuery Visualize plugin uses Progressive Enhancement (and also provides support for ARIA) to render charts and graphs. A set of detailed code samples and download information are available here:

http://www.filamentgroup.com/lab/update_to_jquery_visualize_accessible_charts_with_html5_from_designing_with/

Finally, you can also perform an Internet search to find various open source packages as well as commercial products that provide charts and graphs. The decision will depend on your budget and the functionality that you need for your Web pages.

SUMMARY

This chapter showed you how to create charts and graphs with linear gradients defined in HTML5 Canvas and also linear gradients defined in CSS3 selectors. You learned how to render the following:

- Bar charts with gradient shading
- 3D mouse-enabled bar charts
- Simple line graphs and multi-line graphs
- Area graphs
- Pie charts

The next chapter shows you how to create Android hybrid mobile applications that render HTML5 Web pages. If you are unfamiliar with Android, an Appendix on the DVD contains an overview of various aspects of writing Android applications.

13

HTML5 MOBILE APPS ON ANDROID, IOS, AND TIZEN

This chapter shows you how to create HTML5-based hybrid mobile applications for Android, iOS, and Tizen. The code samples in this chapter contain HTML5 and various combinations of HTML5, CSS3, SVG, and jQuery or jQuery Mobile.

The first part of this chapter provides an overview of how to develop hybrid Android applications. The code samples in this section use the same code that you have seen in earlier chapters, and they show you how to create the hybrid Android mobile applications that will enable you to create the same screenshots. If you feel ambitious, you can create Android-based mobile applications for all the code samples in this book!

The second part of this chapter contains Android-based code samples that show you how to combine native Android applications with CSS3, SVG, HTML5 Canvas, and jQuery Mobile. This section contains an example of rendering a mouse-enabled multi-line graph whose values can be updated whenever users click on the button that is rendered underneath the line graph. Keep in mind that the discussion following the code samples moves quickly because the HTML Web pages contain simple markup, the CSS3 selectors contain code that you have seen in earlier chapters, and the SVG shapes are discussed in detail in Appendix A.

The third part of this chapter provides a quick overview of Apache Cordova, formerly known as PhoneGap, which is a popular cross-platform toolkit for developing mobile applications. In 2011, Adobe acquired Nitobi, the company that created PhoneGap, and shortly thereafter Adobe open sourced PhoneGap. This section explains what PhoneGap can do, and also some toolkits that you can use with PhoneGap. You will learn how to create a PhoneGap-based Android application that renders CSS3-based animation effects, and you can deploy this mobile application to Android-based mobile devices that support Android ICS or higher.

The final part of this chapter shows you some of the functionality of Xcode 4.3, and you will see the steps for creating a "Hello World" mobile application for iOS devices. You will also learn how to create hybrid iOS-based mobile applications using the PhoneGap plugin for Xcode.

As you will see in this chapter, PhoneGap allows you to create mobile applications using HTML, CSS, and JavaScript, and you can deploy those mobile applications to numerous platforms, including Android, iOS, BlackBerry and Windows Mobile. You can also create mobile applications that combine PhoneGap with Sencha Touch (another popular framework), but due to space limitations, Sencha Touch is not discussed in this chapter.

If you are unfamiliar with any of the mobile platforms in this chapter, you can still work through the examples because they consist of HTML5-based code, and the sequence of steps for creating HTML5-based mobile applications on a mobile platform is essentially independent of the actual code.

Incidentally, if you want to understand the Android-specific functionality, you can read or skim the contents of Appendix B that contains information about the structure of Android projects, Android `Activity`s, and Android `Intent`s. This Appendix also shows you how to create a "Hello World" Android application (using Android instead of HTML5) and then deploy the application to an Android device.

HTML5/CSS3 AND ANDROID APPLICATIONS

If you are unfamiliar with Android, you can read the Appendix for this book, which contains a concise overview of the Android-specific concepts in the code samples in this chapter. You can refer to the appropriate section whenever you encounter an Android concept that is not clear to you.

The code sample in this section shows you how to launch an HTML5 web page (which also references a CSS3 stylesheet) inside an Android application. The key idea consists of three steps:

1. Modify the Android `Activity` class to instantiate an Android `WebView` class, along with some JavaScript-related settings.
2. Reference an HTML5 Web page that is in the `assets/www` subdirectory of the Android project.

3. Copy the HTML5 Web page, CSS stylesheets, and JavaScript files into the `assets/www` subdirectory of the Android project.

In Step 3 above, you will probably create a hierarchical set of directories that contain files that are of the same type (HTML, CSS, or JavaScript), in much the same way that you organize your files in a Web application.

Now launch Eclipse and create an Android project called `AndroidCSS3`, making sure that you select Android version 3.1 or higher, which is necessary in order to render CSS3-based effects.

After you have created the project, let's take a look at four files that contain the custom code for this Android mobile application. Listing 13.1, 13.2, 13.3, and 13.4 display the contents of the project files `main.xml`, `AndroidCSS3.html`, `AndroidCSS3.css`, and `AndroidCSS3Activity.java`.

Listing 13.1   main.xml

```
<?xml version="1.0" encoding="utf-8"?>
<LinearLayout xmlns:android="http://schemas.android.com/apk/res/
android"
    android:orientation="vertical"
    android:layout_width="fill_parent"
    android:layout_height="fill_parent">
  <WebView android:id="@+id/webview"
          android:layout_width="fill_parent"
          android:layout_height="fill_parent">
  </WebView>
</LinearLayout>
```

Listing 13.1 specifies a `LinearLayout` that contains an Android `WebView` that will occupy the entire screen of the mobile device. This is the behavior that we want to see, because Android default browser is rendered inside the Android `WebView`.

Listing 13.2   AndroidCSS3.html

```
<!doctype html>
<head>
  <meta charset="utf-8"/>
  <title>CSS Radial Gradient Example</title>
  <link href="AndroidCSS3.css" rel="stylesheet">
</head>

<body>
 <div id="outer">
```

```
  <div id="radial1">Text1</div>
  <div id="radial2">Text2</div>
  <div id="radial3">Text3</div>
  <div id="radial4">Text4</div>
 </div>
</body>
</html>
```

Listing 13.2 is a straightforward HTML Web page that references a CSS stylesheet (displayed in Listing 13.3), along with an HTML <div> element (whose id attribute has value outer) that serves as a "container" for four more HTML <div> elements.

Listing 13.3 AndroidCSS3.css

```
    #outer {
    position: relative; top: 0px; left: 0px;
    }


    #radial1 {
    opacity: 0.8;
    font-size: 24px;
    width:    300px;
    height: 100px;
    position: absolute; top: 200px; left: 0px;


    background: -webkit-gradient(
      radial, 400 25%, 20, 100 25%, 40, from(red),
      color-stop(0.05, orange), color-stop(0.4, yellow),
      color-stop(0.6, red), color-stop(0.9, blue),
      to(#fff)
     );
    }


    #radial2 {
    opacity: 0.6;
    font-size: 24px;
    width:    200px;
    height: 100px;
    position: absolute; top: 50px; left: 50px;


    background: -webkit-gradient(
```

```
  radial, 200 50%, 20, 100 25%, 40, from(red),
  color-stop(0.05, orange), color-stop(0.4, yellow),
  color-stop(0.6, green), color-stop(0.9, blue),
  to(#fff)
 );
}

#radial3 {
opacity: 0.8;
font-size: 24px;
width:  600px;
height: 600px;
position: absolute; top: 0px; left: 0px;

background: -webkit-gradient(
  radial, 300 30%, 160, 250 25%, 80, from(red),
  color-stop(0.05, orange), color-stop(0.4, yellow),
  color-stop(0.6, green), color-stop(0.8, blue),
  to(#fff)
 );
-webkit-box-shadow:  0px 0px 8px #000;
}

#radial4 {
opacity: 0.4;
font-size: 24px;
width:  200px;
height: 200px;
position: absolute; top: 200px; left: 200px;

background: -webkit-gradient(
  radial, 300 50%, 20, 100 25%, 40, from(red),
  color-stop(0.05, orange), color-stop(0.4, yellow),
  color-stop(0.6, green), color-stop(0.9, blue),
  to(#fff)
 );

background-image: -webkit-gradient(linear, right top, left
```

```
                                                          bottom,
                          from(yellow),
                          color-stop(25%, yellow),
                          color-stop(25%, red),
                          color-stop(50%, red),
                          color-stop(50%, yellow),
                          color-stop(75%, yellow),
                          color-stop(75%, red),
                          to(red));
       -webkit-background-size: 20px;
    }
```

Listing 13.3 contains a CSS selector for styling the HTML <div> element whose id has value outer, followed by four CSS selectors radial1, radial2, radial3, and radial4 that are applied to the corresponding HTML <div> elements in Listing 13.2. The contents of these selectors ought to be very familiar (you can review the material for CSS3 gradients in an earlier chapter), so we will not cover their contents in this section.

Listing 13.4 AndroidCSS3Activity.java

```java
package com.iquarkt.css3;

import android.app.Activity;
import android.os.Bundle;

import android.webkit.WebChromeClient;
import android.webkit.WebSettings;
import android.webkit.WebView;
import android.webkit.WebViewClient;

public class AndroidCSS3Activity extends Activity
{
    /** Called when the activity is first created. */
    @Override
    public void onCreate(Bundle savedInstanceState)
    {
        super.onCreate(savedInstanceState);
        setContentView(R.layout.main);

        // Get a reference to the declared WebView holder
        WebView webview = (WebView) this.findViewById(R.
id.webview);

        // Get the settings
        WebSettings webSettings = webview.getSettings();
```

```
    // Enable Javascript for interaction
    webSettings.setJavaScriptEnabled(true);

    // Make the zoom controls visible
    webSettings.setBuiltInZoomControls(true);

    // Allow for touching selecting/deselecting data series
    webview.requestFocusFromTouch();

    // Set the client
    webview.setWebViewClient(new WebViewClient());
    webview.setWebChromeClient(new WebChromeClient());

    // Load the URL
    webview.loadUrl("file:///android_asset/AndroidCSS3.html");
  }
}
```

Listing 13.4 defines a Java class `AndroidCSS3Activity` that extends the standard Android `Activity` class. This class contains the `onCreate()` method that "points" to the XML document `main.xml` (displayed in Listing 13.2) so that we can get a reference to its `WebView` child element via `R.id.webview` (which is the reference to the `WebView` element in Listing 13.2), as shown here:

```
WebView webview = (WebView) this.findViewById(R.id.webview);
```

Next, the `webSettings` instance of the `WebSettings` class enables us to set various properties, as shown in the commented lines of code in Listing 13.4.

The final line of code loads the contents of the HTML Web page `AndroidCSS3.html` (which is in the `assets/www` subdirectory), as shown here:

```
webview.loadUrl("file:///android_asset/AndroidCSS3.html");
```

Figure 13.1 displays a CSS3-based Android application on an Asus Prime tablet with Android ICS.

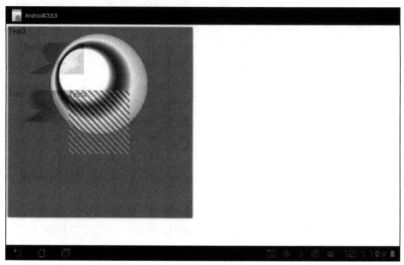

FIGURE 13.1 A CSS3-based 3D cube on an Asus Prime tablet with Android ICS.

SVG AND ANDROID APPLICATIONS

The example in this section shows you how to create an Android mobile application that renders SVG code that is embedded in an HTML5 Web page. Now launch Eclipse and create an Android project called `AndroidSVG1`, making sure that you select Android version 3.1 or higher, which is necessary in order to render SVG elements.

The example in the previous section contains four custom files, whereas the Android/SVG example in this section contains two files with custom code: the HTML5 Web page `AndroidSVG1.html` and the Java class `AndroidSVG1.java`, which are displayed in Listing 13.5 and Listing 13.6, respectively.

Listing 13.5 AndroidSVG1.html

```
<!DOCTYPE html>
<html>
  <body>
    <h1>HTML5/SVG Example</h1>
    <svg>
      <ellipse cx="300" cy="50" rx="80" ry="40"
               fill="#ff0" stroke-dasharray="8 4 8 1"
               style="stroke:red;stroke-width:4;"/>
```

```
    <line x1="100" y1="20" x2="300" y2="350"
          stroke-dasharray="8 4 8 1"
          style="stroke:red;stroke-width:8;"/>

    <g transform="translate(20,20)">
      <path
         d="M0,0 C200,150 400,300 20,250"
         fill="#f00"
         stroke-dasharray="4 4 4 4"
         style="stroke:blue;stroke-width:4;"/>
    </g>

    <g transform="translate(200,50)">
      <path
         d="M200,150 C0,0 400,300 20,250"
         fill="#00f"
         stroke-dasharray="12 12 12 12"
         style="stroke:blue;stroke-width:4;"/>
    </g>
   </svg>
  </body>
</html>
```

Listing 13.5 is an HTML Web page that contains an SVG document with the definitions for an ellipse, a line segment, and two cubic Bezier curves. Appendix A contains examples of these 2D shapes (among others), and you can review the appropriate material if you need to refresh your memory.

Listing 13.6 displays the contents of the Java class `AndroidSVG1Activity.java` that launches the HTML5 Web page `AndroidSVG1.html`.

Listing 13.6 AndroidSVG1Activity.java

```
package com.iquarkt.svg;

import android.app.Activity;
import android.os.Bundle;

import android.webkit.WebChromeClient;
import android.webkit.WebSettings;
import android.webkit.WebView;
import android.webkit.WebViewClient;

public class AndroidSVG1Activity extends Activity
{
   /** Called when the activity is first created. */
   @Override
   public void onCreate(Bundle savedInstanceState)
   {
```

```
    super.onCreate(savedInstanceState);
    setContentView(R.layout.main);

    // Get a reference to the declared WebView holder
    WebView webview = (WebView) this.findViewById(R.id.webview);

    // Get the settings
    WebSettings webSettings = webview.getSettings();

    // Enable Javascript for interaction
    webSettings.setJavaScriptEnabled(true);

    // Make the zoom controls visible
    webSettings.setBuiltInZoomControls(true);

    // Allow for touching selecting/deselecting data series
    webview.requestFocusFromTouch();

    // Set the client
    webview.setWebViewClient(new WebViewClient());
    webview.setWebChromeClient(new WebChromeClient());

    // Load the URL
    webview.loadUrl("file:///android_asset/AndroidSVG1.html");
  }
}
```

Listing 13.6 is almost the same as the contents of Listing 13.4 (the Java class name is different), and once again, the final line of code loads the contents of the HTML Web page `AndroidSVG1.html` (which is in the `assets/www` subdirectory), as shown here:

```
    webview.loadUrl("file:///android_asset/AndroidSVG1.html");
```

Figure 13.2 displays an SVG -based Android application on an Asus Prime tablet with Android ICS.

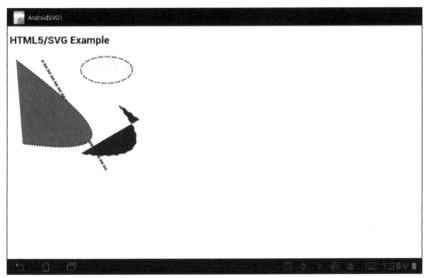

FIGURE 13.2 An SVG-based Android application on an Asus tablet with Android ICS.

HTML5 CANVAS AND ANDROID APPLICATIONS

In addition to rendering CSS3-based effects and SVG documents, you can also render Canvas-based 2D shapes in an Android application. Launch Eclipse and create an Android project called `AndroidCanvas1`, making sure that you select Android version 3.1 or higher, which is necessary in order to render SVG elements.

The example in this section contains one custom file called `AndroidCanvas1.html`, which is displayed in Listing 13.7.

Listing 13.7 AndroidCanvas1.html

```
<!DOCTYPE html>
<html lang="en">
<head>

<script>
  function draw() {
    var basePointX  = 10;
    var basePointY  = 80;
    var currentX    = 0;
    var currentY    = 0;
    var startAngle  = 0;
```

```
var endAngle       = 0;
var radius         = 120;
var lineLength     = 200;
var lineWidth      = 1;
var lineCount      = 200;
var lineColor      = "";

var hexArray       = new Array('0','1','2','3','4','5','6','7',
                               '8','9','a','b','c','d','e','f');

var can = document.getElementById('canvas1');
var ctx = can.getContext('2d');

// render a text string...
ctx.font = "bold 26px helvetica, arial, sans-serif";
ctx.shadowColor = "#333333";
ctx.shadowOffsetX = 2;
ctx.shadowOffsetY = 2;
ctx.shadowBlur = 2;
ctx.fillStyle = 'red';
ctx.fillText("HTML5 Canvas/Android", 0, 30);

for(var r=0; r<lineCount; r++) {
    currentX = basePointX+r;
    currentY = basePointY+r;
    startAngle = (360-r/2)*Math.PI/180;
    endAngle   = (360+r/2)*Math.PI/180;

    // render the first line segment...
    lineColor = '#' + hexArray[r%16] + '00';
    ctx.strokeStyle = lineColor;
    ctx.lineWidth    = lineWidth;

    ctx.beginPath();
    ctx.moveTo(currentX, currentY+2*r);
    ctx.lineTo(currentX+lineLength, currentY+2*r);
    ctx.closePath();
    ctx.stroke();
    ctx.fill();

    // render the second line segment...
    lineColor = '#' + '0' + hexArray[r%16] + '0';
    ctx.beginPath();
    ctx.moveTo(currentX, currentY);
    ctx.lineTo(currentX+lineLength, currentY);
    ctx.closePath();
```

```
        ctx.stroke();
        ctx.fill();

        // render the arc...
        lineColor = '#' + '00'+ hexArray[(2*r)%16];
        ctx.beginPath();
        ctx.fillStyle = lineColor;
        ctx.moveTo(currentX, currentY);
        ctx.arc(currentX, currentY, radius,
                startAngle, endAngle, false);
        ctx.closePath();
        ctx.stroke();
        ctx.fill();
    }
}
</script>

<body onload="draw()">
  <canvas id="canvas1" width="300px" height="200px"></canvas>
</body>
<html>
```

Listing 13.7 contains some boilerplate HTML markup and a JavaScript function draw() that is executed when the Web page is loaded into the Android browser. The draw() function contains JavaScript code that draws a set of line segments and arcs into the HTML5 <canvas> element whose id attribute has value canvas1. You can review the code samples in Chapter 11 that have similar functionality if you don't remember the details of the syntax of this JavaScript code.

Figure 13.3 displays a Canvas-based Android application on an Asus Prime tablet with Android ICS.

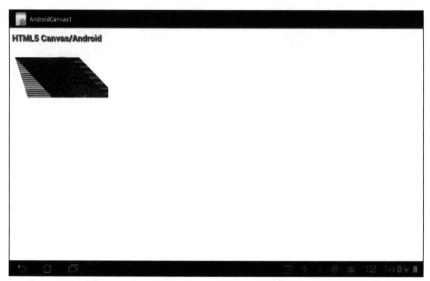

FIGURE 13.3 A Canvas-based Android application on an Asus tablet with Android ICS.

ANDROID AND HTML5 CANVAS MULTI-LINE GRAPHS

Although Android does not have built-in support for rendering charts and graphs, you can create them using Canvas-based code that is very similar to the code in the previous section.

Launch Eclipse and create an Android project called `AndroidCanvasMultiLine2`, making sure that you select Android version 3.1 or higher. Listing 13.8 displays the contents of the HTML5 Web page `AndroidCanvasMultiLine2.html` that contains JavaScript code for rendering multiple line graphs using HTML5 Canvas.

Listing 13.8 AndroidCanvasMultiLine2.html

```
<!DOCTYPE html>
<html lang="en">
 <head>
  <meta charset="utf-8"/>
  <title>HTML5 Canvas Line Graphs</title>

  <style type="text/css">
    canvas {
        border: 5px solid #888;
        background: #CCC;
```

```
    }
</style>

<script>
  var currentX      = 0;
  var currentY      = 0;
  var barCount      = 11; // 12;
  var barWidth      = 40;
  var barHeight     = 0;
  var maxHeight     = 280;
  var xAxisWidth    = barCount*barWidth;
  var yAxisHeight   = maxHeight;
  var shadowX       = 2;
  var shadowY       = 2;
  var axisFontSize  = 12;
  var fontSize      = 16;
  var labelY        = 0;
  var indentY       = 5;
  var leftBorder    = 30;
  var topBorder     = 15;
  var arrowWidth    = 10;
  var arrowHeight   = 6;
  var dotRadius     = 6;
  var lineCount     = 3;
  var barHeights    = new Array(barCount);
  var barHeights2   = new Array(barCount);
  var barHeights3   = new Array(barCount);
  var currHeights   = new Array(barCount);
  var multiLines    = new Array(lineCount);
  var fillColors    = new Array("#F00", "#FF0", "#0F0", "#00F");
  var elem, context, gradient1;

  function drawGraph() {
     // Get the canvas element
     elem = document.getElementById('myCanvas');
     if (!elem || !elem.getContext) {
       return;
     }

     // Get the canvas 2d context
     context = elem.getContext('2d');
     if (!context) {
       return;
     }

     drawGraph2();
```

```
}

function drawAndLabelAxes() {
   // draw vertical axis...
   context.beginPath();
   context.fillStyle = "rgb(0,0,0)";
   context.lineWidth = 2;
   context.moveTo(leftBorder, topBorder);
   context.lineTo(leftBorder, yAxisHeight);
   context.stroke();

   // draw top arrow...
   context.beginPath();
   context.moveTo(leftBorder-arrowHeight/2, topBorder);
   context.lineTo(leftBorder+arrowHeight/2, topBorder);
   context.lineTo(leftBorder, topBorder-arrowWidth);
   context.lineTo(leftBorder-arrowHeight/2, topBorder);
   context.fill();

   // draw horizontal axis...
   context.beginPath();
   context.moveTo(leftBorder, yAxisHeight);
   context.lineTo(xAxisWidth, yAxisHeight);
   context.stroke();

   // draw right arrow...
   context.beginPath();
   context.moveTo(xAxisWidth, yAxisHeight-arrowHeight/2);
   context.lineTo(xAxisWidth+arrowWidth, yAxisHeight);
   context.lineTo(xAxisWidth, yAxisHeight+arrowHeight/2);
   context.lineTo(xAxisWidth, yAxisHeight);
   context.fill();

   // label the horizontal axis
   context.font = "bold "+axisFontSize+"pt New Times Roman";
   context.lineWidth   = 2;
   context.strokeStyle = "#000";

   for(var i=0; i<barCount; i++) {
      context.beginPath();
      currentX = leftBorder+i*barWidth;
      currentY = maxHeight+axisFontSize;
    //context.fillStyle = fillColors[i%4];
      context.fillStyle = "#000";

      // Outline a text string
```

```
      context.strokeText(""+currentX,
                         currentX+shadowX,
                         currentY+shadowY);

   // Fill a text string
   context.fillStyle = "#FF0";
   context.fillText(""+currentX,
                      currentX,
                      currentY);
}

// label the vertical axis
context.font = "bold "+axisFontSize+"pt New Times Roman";
context.lineWidth   = 2;
context.strokeStyle = "#000";

for(var i=0; i<barCount; i++) {
   context.beginPath();
   currentX = 0;
   currentY = Math.floor(maxHeight-i*maxHeight/barCount);
   labelY   = Math.floor(i*maxHeight/barCount);

 //context.fillStyle = fillColors[i%4];
   context.fillStyle = "#000";

 // Outline 'a text string
 context.strokeText(""+labelY,
                      currentX+shadowX,
                      currentY+shadowY);

   // Fill a text string
   context.fillStyle = "#FF0";
   context.fillText(""+labelY,
                      currentX,
                      currentY);
   }
}

function randomBarValues() {
   for(var i=0; i<barCount; i++) {
      barHeight = maxHeight*Math.random();
      barHeights[i] = barHeight;

      barHeight = maxHeight*Math.random();
      barHeights2[i] = barHeight;
```

```
            barHeight = maxHeight*Math.random();
            barHeights3[i] = barHeight;
        }

     multiLines[0] = barHeights;
     multiLines[1] = barHeights2;
     multiLines[2] = barHeights3;
   }

   function drawGraph2() {
      // clear the canvas before drawing new set of rectangles
      context.clearRect(0, 0, elem.width, elem.height);

      randomBarValues();
      drawAndLabelAxes();
      drawElements();
   }

   function drawElements() {
      for(var h=0; h<multiLines.length; h++) {
         currHeights = multiLines[h];

         currentX = leftBorder;
       //currentY = maxHeight-barHeights[0];
         currentY = maxHeight-currHeights[0];

         // draw line segments...
         for(var i=0; i<barCount; i++) {
            context.beginPath();
            context.moveTo(currentX, currentY);
            currentX = leftBorder+i*barWidth;
          //currentY = maxHeight-barHeights[i];
            currentY = maxHeight-currHeights[i];

            context.shadowColor   = "rgba(100,100,100,.5)";
            context.shadowOffsetX = 3;
            context.shadowOffsetY = 3;
            context.shadowBlur    = 5;

            context.lineWidth   = 4;
            context.strokeStyle = fillColors[i%4];
            context.lineCap     = "miter"; // "round";

            context.lineTo(currentX, currentY);
            context.stroke();
         }
```

```
      // draw the dots...
      for(var i=0; i<barCount; i++) {
         context.beginPath();
         currentX = leftBorder+i*barWidth;
       //currentY = maxHeight-barHeights[i];
         currentY = maxHeight-currHeights[i];
         context.fillStyle = fillColors[i%4];

         context.arc(currentX,
                     currentY,
                     dotRadius, 0, Math.PI*2, 0);
         context.fill();
      }
   }

   drawBarText();
}

function drawBarText() {
   // Define some drawing attributes
   context.font = "bold "+fontSize+"pt New Times Roman";
   context.lineWidth   = 2;
   context.strokeStyle = "#000";

   for(var i=0; i<barCount; i++) {
      context.beginPath();
      currentX = leftBorder+i*barWidth;
      currentY = maxHeight-barHeights[i]+fontSize/4;
    //context.fillStyle = fillColors[i%4];
      context.fillStyle = "#000";

     barHeight = Math.floor(barHeights[i]);

     // Outline a text string
     context.strokeText(""+barHeight,
                        currentX+shadowX,
                        currentY+shadowY);

     // Fill a text string
     context.fillStyle = "#F00";
     context.fillText(""+barHeight,
                      currentX,
                      currentY);
   }
}
```

```
  </script>
 </head>

 <body onload="drawGraph();">
  <header>
    <h1>HTML5 Canvas Line Graphs</h1>
  </header>

  <div>
   <canvas id="myCanvas" width="500" height="300">No support for
Canvas
   </canvas>
  </div>

  <input type="button" onclick="drawGraph();return false"
         value="Update Graph Values"/>
 </body>
</html>
```

Since the code in Listing 13.8 is virtually identical to the multi-line graph in Chapter 12, we will not reproduce the same discussion regarding the code.

Figure 13.4 displays a Canvas-based multi-line graph Android application on a Nexus S 4G with Android ICS.

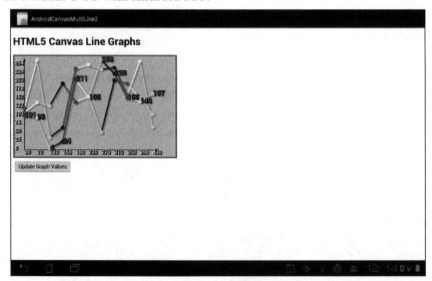

FIGURE 13.4 A Canvas-based multi-line graph on an Android smartphone.

ANDROID AND HTML5 CANVAS ANIMATION

This section shows you how to create an Android mobile application that renders a bouncing ball effect in HTML5 Canvas.

Launch Eclipse and create an Android project called `HTML5CanvasBBall2`, making sure that you select Android version 3.1 or higher. Listing 13.9 displays the contents of the HTML5 Web page `HTML5CanvasBBall2.html` that contains JavaScript code for creating a bouncing ball effect.

Listing 13.9 HTML5CanvasBBall2.html

```
<!DOCTYPE html>
<html lang="en">
<head>
<meta charset=utf-8"/>
<title>HTML5 Bouncing Ball</title>

 <script>
   var ballRadius = 20, cWidth = 300, cHeight = 300, context;
   var leftX = 0, rightX = 300, topY = 0, bottomY = 300;
   var dirX = 4, dirY = 4, currentX = ballRadius, currentY = 150;
   var tick = 0, shortPause = 20, stripWidth = 50, currStrip = 0;
   var fillStyle, fillColors = ["#ff0000", "#ffff00", "#0000ff"];

   function draw() {
      context = myCanvas.getContext('2d');
      context.clearRect(0, 0, cWidth, cHeight);
      context.strokeStyle = "#000000";
      context.strokeRect(0, 0, cWidth, cHeight);

      currStrip = ++tick / stripWidth;
      fillStyle = fillColors[currStrip % fillColors.length];

      context.beginPath();
      context.fillStyle = fillStyle;
      context.arc(currentX,currentY,ballRadius,0,Math.PI*2,true);
      context.closePath();
      context.fill();

      if( currentX < leftX+ballRadius || currentX > rightX-ballRa-
dius) {
          dirX *= -1;
      }

      if( currentY < topY+ballRadius || currentY > bottomY-ballRa-
dius) {
```

```
        dirY *= -1;
    }

    currentX += dirX;
    currentY += dirY;
  }

  setInterval(draw, shortPause);
 </script>
</head>

<body>
 <h1>HTML5 Bouncing Ball</h1>
 <div id="container">
   <canvas id="myCanvas" width="300" height="300"></canvas>
 </div>
</body>
</html>
```

Listing 13.9 contains boilerplate HTML markup and a JavaScript function `draw()` that is executed when the Web page is loaded into the Android browser. The `draw()` function contains JavaScript code that draws a bouncing ball inside the HTML5 `<canvas>` element whose `id` attribute has value `my-Canvas`. This function starts by getting a reference to the HTML5 `<canvas>` element and then clearing the screen, as shown in this code snippet:

```
context = myCanvas.getContext('2d');
context.clearRect(0, 0, cWidth, cHeight);
```

The next block of code sets some attributes for the current context, and the rendering of the bouncing ball is performed with this line of code:

```
context.arc(currentX,currentY,ballRadius,0,Math.PI*2,true);
```

The value of the JavaScript variables `currentX` and `currentY` represent the location of the ball; these values are updated each time the `draw()` method is executed.

The following code block ensures that the bouncing ball is always inside its bounding rectangle:

```
if(currentX < leftX+ballRadius || currentX > rightX-ballRadius) {
    dirX *= -1;
}
```

```
if(currentY < topY+ballRadius || currentY > bottomY-ballRadius) {
   dirY *= -1;
}
```

The position of the bouncing ball is updated with the following two lines of code:

```
currentX += dirX;
currentY += dirY;
```

Finally, the `draw()` method is executed repeatedly via this code snippet:

```
setInterval(draw, shortPause);
```

Figure 13.5 displays a Canvas-based animation effect with a bouncing ball in an Android application on an Asus Prime tablet with Android ICS.

FIGURE 13.5 A Canvas-based bouncing ball on an Android tablet.

ANDROID APPLICATIONS WITH JQUERY MOBILE

The example in this section shows you how to create an Android mobile application with jQuery Mobile using the HTML5 Web page `JQMTravelTabs1.html` that is discussed in Chapter 8.

In this section, we are going to use the identical HTML Web page, so we will avoid duplicating the listing of this Web page.

• jQuery, CSS3, and HTML5 for Mobile and Desktop Devices

Listing 13.10 displays the contents of `JQMTravel1Tabs1Activity.java` that launches the HTML5 Web page `JQMTravel1Tabs1.html`.

Listing 13.10 JQMTravel1Tabs1Activity1.java

```
package com.iquarkt.jqmandroid;

import android.app.Activity;
import android.os.Bundle;
import android.view.KeyEvent;
import android.webkit.WebView;
import android.webkit.WebViewClient;

public class JQMTravel1Tabs1Activity extends Activity
{
    WebView mWebView;

    public void onCreate(Bundle savedInstanceState) {
        super.onCreate(savedInstanceState);
        setContentView(R.layout.main);

        mWebView = (WebView) findViewById(R.id.webview);
        mWebView.setWebViewClient(new ChangeURLClient());
        mWebView.getSettings().setJavaScriptEnabled(true);
        mWebView.getSettings().setDomStorageEnabled(true);
        mWebView.loadUrl("file:///android_asset/www/JQMTravel1T-
abs1.html");
    }

    public boolean onKeyDown(int keyCode, KeyEvent event)
    {
        if ((keyCode == KeyEvent.KEYCODE_BACK) && mWebView.canGo-
Back())
        {
            mWebView.goBack();
            return true;
        }
        return super.onKeyDown(keyCode, event);
    }

    private class ChangeURLClient extends WebViewClient
    {
        public boolean shouldOverrideUrlLoading(WebView view,
String url)
        {
            System.out.println("Destination URL: " + url);
```

```
            view.loadUrl("javascript:changeLocation('" + url +
"')");
            return true;
        }
    }
}
```

Listing 13.10 ought to be very familiar to you. The only differences are the name of the Java class and the HTML Web page that is loaded into the Android browser, which is shown here:

```
    mWebView.loadUrl("file:///android_asset/www/JQMTravel1Tabs1.
html");
```

Figure 13.6 displays a jQuery Mobile application using HTML5 on an Asus Prime tablet with Android ICS.

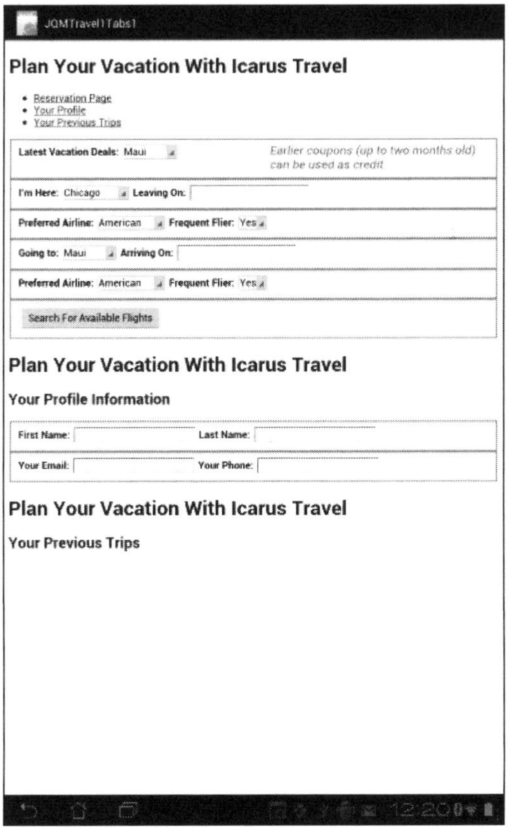

FIGURE 13.6 A jQuery Mobile application on an Asus Prime tablet with Android ICS.

This concludes our discussion of how to manually create Android applications with CSS3, SVG, and HTML5 Canvas. Hopefully you have gained an appreciation of the elegant simplicity with which you can create mobile applications with pleasing visual effects.

Fortunately, there are various jQuery plugins available for iOS and Android:

http://www.jquery4u.com/mobile/10-jquery-iphone-style-plugins/
http://www.jquery4u.com/mobile/10-android-style-jquery-plugins/

The two preceding Web sites contain links to jQuery plugins that enable you to create various effects with the look and feel of iOS as well as for Android. These jQuery plugins are helpful if you want the desired functionality without writing native iOS or Android code.

The next portion of this chapter delves into PhoneGap, which is a toolkit that automatically creates the lower level "scaffolding" that you performed manually in the previous part of this chapter. You will get instructions for installing the PhoneGap plugin for Eclipse to create Android mobile applications, and later in this chapter you will also learn how to install the PhoneGap plugin for Xcode in order to create HTML5-based mobile applications for iOS mobile devices.

WHAT IS PHONEGAP?

PhoneGap is an open source device-agnostic mobile application development tool that enables you to create cross-platform mobile applications using CSS, HTML, and JavaScript. Its homepage is here:

http://phonegap.com

The PhoneGap homepage provides documentation, code samples, and a download link for the PhoneGap distribution.

PhoneGap provides support for touch events, event listeners, rendering images, database access, different file formats (XML and JSON), and Web Services. PhoneGap enables you to create HTML-based mobile application for Android, BlackBerry, iPhone, Palm, Symbian, and Windows Mobile. Note that if you want to develop iPhone applications, you must have a Macbook or some other Mac-based machine, along with other dependencies that are discussed later in this chapter.

How Does PhoneGap Work?

PhoneGap mobile applications involve a Web view that is embedded in a native "shell," and your custom code runs in the Web view. In addition, PhoneGap provides a JavaScript API for accessing native features of a mobile device, and your code can use PhoneGap in order to access those native features. For example, PhoneGap contains JavaScript APIs for accessing Accelerometer, Camera, Compass, Contacts, Device information, Events, Geolocation, Media, Notification, and Storage.

Keep in mind that PhoneGap does not provide HTML UI elements, so if you need this functionality in your mobile applications, you can add other toolkits and frameworks, such as jQuery Mobile, Sencha Touch, or Appcelerator.

Now that you have a basic understanding of the capabilities of PhoneGap, install the PhoneGap 2.0 (which was released as this book goes to print) for XCode and Eclipse by following the instructions here:

http://outof.me/phonegap-2-0-getting-started/

Adobe DreamWeaver CS6 supports PhoneGap, and in addition, PhoneGap is the foundation for the SalesForce Mobile SDK:

https://wiki.developerforce.com/page/Developing_Hybrid_Apps_with_the_Salesforce_Mobile_SDK?d=70130000000sgHH&RRID=314250788

In case you prefer to compile your mobile applications in the "cloud," Adobe provides a Web site for this purpose:

https://build.phonegap.com/

Other Useful Links

There is a Google group devoted to answering questions about PhoneGap:

http://groups.google.com/group/phonegap

The PhoneGap FAQ is here:

http://wiki.phonegap.com/FAQ

You can also download the PhoneGap source code here:

http://github.com/sintaxi/phonegap

If you have completed the installation of the PhoneGap plugin for Eclipse, you are ready to create a PhoneGap application for Android, which is the topic of the next section.

CREATING ANDROID APPS WITH THE PHONEGAP PLUGIN

Create an Android project in Eclipse by clicking on the icon for the PhoneGap plugin and then (for the purposes of this example) specify PGJQM1 for the Project Name, check the checkbox for including the jQuery Mobile files, select the Android version that your Android device supports, and then enter com.iquarkt.phonegap as the package name.

Click the "Finish" button and after the project has been created, navigate to the assets/www subdirectory of the newly created Android project, and you will find the following files (version numbers might be different when this book goes to print):

```
index.html
phonegap-1.3.0.js
```

There is also a generated Java file PhoneGap1Activity.java, whose contents are displayed in Listing 13.11.

Listing 13.11   PhoneGap1Activity.java

```java
package com.iquarkt.phonegap;

import com.phonegap.*;
import android.os.Bundle;

public class PhoneGap1Activity extends Activity
{
    /** Called when the activity is first created. */
    @Override
    public void onCreate(Bundle savedInstanceState)
    {
        super.onCreate(savedInstanceState);
        super.loadUrl("file:///android_asset/www/index.html");
    }
}
```

Listing 13.11 contains an onCreate() method that launches the HTML page index.html, as shown here:
```
super.loadUrl("file:///android_asset/www/index.html");
```

The HTML page `index.html` is located in the `assets/www` subdirectory of the project, and its contents are displayed in Listing 13.12.

Listing 13.12   index.html

```
<!DOCTYPE HTML>
<html>
  <head>
    <meta name="viewport" content="width=320; user-scalable=no"/>
    <meta http-equiv="Content-type" content="text/html;
charset=utf-8">
    <title>PhoneGap</title>

    <link rel="stylesheet" href="master.css"
          type="text/css" media="screen"
          title="no title" charset="utf-8">
    <script src="phonegap-1.0.0.js"></script>
    <script src="main.js"></script>
  </head>

  <body onload="init();" id="stage" class="theme">
    <h1>Welcome to PhoneGap!</h1>
    <h2>this file is located at assets/www/index.html</h2>
    <div id="info">
        <h4>Platform: <span id="platform">  </span>, Version:
<span id="version"> </span></h4>
        <h4>UUID: <span id="uuid">  </span>, Name: <span
                                id="name"> </span></h4>
        <h4>Width: <span id="width">  </span>, Height:
                                <span id="height"> 
                </span>, Color Depth: <span id="colorDepth">
                                </span></h4>
     </div>

    <dl id="accel-data">
      <dt>X:</dt><dd id="x"> </dd>
      <dt>Y:</dt><dd id="y"> </dd>
      <dt>Z:</dt><dd id="z"> </dd>
    </dl>

    <a href="#" class="btn large" onclick="toggleAccel();">Toggle
                                Accelerometer</a>
    <a href="#" class="btn large" onclick="getLocation();">Get
                                Location</a>
    <a href="tel://411" class="btn large">Call 411</a>
    <a href="#" class="btn large" onclick="beep();">Beep</a>
    <a href="#" class="btn large" onclick="vibrate();">Vibrate</a>
```

```
    <a href="#" class="btn large" onclick="show_pic();">Get a
                                                      Picture</a>
    <a href="#" class="btn large" onclick="get_contacts();">Get
                                                Phone's Contacts</a>
    <a href="#" class="btn large" onclick="check_network();">Check
                                                      Network</a>

    <div id="viewport" class="viewport" style="display: none;">
      <img style="width:60px;height:60px" id="test_img" src=""/>
    </div>
  </body>
</html>
```

The first portion of Listing 13.12 contains a `<script>` element that includes the JavaScript file `phonegap.js`, which defines the functions that constitute the core functionality of PhoneGap.

The second portion of Listing 13.12 displays the anchor elements that enable you to test media-related features of your phone, including accelerometer, geolocation, making phone calls (from inside the Android application), beep effects, vibration effects, and taking pictures with the camera on your smartphone or tablet.

Listing 13.13 displays the contents of the Javascript file `main.js` that contains selected portions of the JavaScript code that supports the functionality in the HTML5 Web pages `index.html`.

Listing 13.13 main.js

```
var deviceInfo = function() {
    document.getElementById("platform").innerHTML = device.plat-
form;
    document.getElementById("version").innerHTML = device.version;
    document.getElementById("uuid").innerHTML = device.uuid;
    document.getElementById("name").innerHTML = device.name;
    document.getElementById("width").innerHTML = screen.width;
    document.getElementById("height").innerHTML = screen.height;
    document.getElementById("colorDepth").innerHTML =
                                                    screen.col-
orDepth;
};

// sections omitted for brevity
function dump_pic(data) {
    var viewport = document.getElementById('viewport');
    console.log(data);
    viewport.style.display = "";
    viewport.style.position = "absolute";
```

```
    viewport.style.top = "10px";
    viewport.style.left = "10px";
    document.getElementById("test_img").src =
                            "data:image/jpeg;base64," + data;
}

function fail(msg) {
    alert(msg);
}

function show_pic() {
    navigator.camera.getPicture(dump_pic, fail, {
        quality : 50
    });
}

// details omitted for brevity
```

The first part of Listing 13.13 contains the code for getting the data from the accelerometer of your Android device.

The second part of Listing 13.13 shows you the JavaScript code for taking a picture from this Android application.

Now navigate to Run > Android application in order to launch this Android project and on your Android device you will see something similar to Figure 13.8.

Figure 13.7 displays a set of menu items that enable you to access hardware-related functionality.

FIGURE 13.7 A PhoneGap-based Android mobile application.

PHONEGAP FORM INPUT EXAMPLE ON ANDROID

Create a PhoneGap project in Eclipse following the same sequence of steps that you used for creating previous PhoneGap-based applications for Android.

Listing 13.14 displays the contents of `PhoneGapForm1.html` (which will actually be named `index.html` in your Android project) that illustrates how to create a form for user inputs in PhoneGap.

Listing 13.14   PhoneGapForm1.html

```
<!DOCTYPE HTML>
<html>
 <head>
   <meta charset=utf-8"/>
   <title>PhoneGap</title>

   <meta name="viewport" content="width=320; user-scalable=no"/>
 <style>
  input {
    width: 180px;
    margin-bottom: 18px;
    margin-top: 4px;
    -webkit-border-radius: 5px;
    left:100px;
    position:absolute;
  }

  input.disabled {
    opacity: 0.5;
  }

  label {
    margin-bottom: 18px;
    line-height:36px;
  }
  </style>

  <script src="phonegap-1.3.0.js"></script>

  <script type="text/javascript" charset="utf-8">
    function onWinLoad() {
      document.addEventListener("deviceready",onDeviceReady,fal
se);
    }
```

```
      function onDeviceReady() { }
    </script>
  </head>

  <body id="stage" onload="onWinLoad()">
    <div>
      <span>Form Inputs</span>
    </div>

    <form action="/">
      <br/>
      <!-- display a standard keyboard -->
      <label for="tiText">Text:</label>
      <input type="text" id="tiText"/>
      <br/>

      <!-- display a telephone keypad -->
      <label for="tiTel">Telephone:</label>
      <input type="tel" id="tiTel"/>
      <br/>

      <!-- display a URL keyboard -->
      <label for="tiUrl">URL:</label>
      <input type="url" id="tiUrl"/>
      <br/>

      <!-- display an email keyboard -->
      <label for="tiEmail">Email:</label>
      <input type="email" id="tiEmail"/>
      <br/>

      <!-- display a numeric keyboard -->
      <label for="tiZip">Zip Code:</label>
      <input type="text" pattern="[0-9]*" id="tiZip"/>
      <br/>

      <label for="tiSearch">Search:</label>
      <input type="search" id="tiSearch" style="width:192px;"/>
      <br/>
    </form>
  </body>
</html>
```

Listing 13.14 supports different types of input, and types of the input fields are such that the following occurs when users navigate to this form:

- Text input displays a standard keyboard
- Telephone input displays a telephone keypad
- URL input displays a URL keyboard
- E-mail input displays an e-mail keyboard
- Zip code input displays a numeric keyboard

Figure 18.9 displays a `Form`-based PhoneGap Android application on an Asus Prime tablet with Android ICS.

FIGURE 13.8 A `Form`-based PhoneGap app on an Asus Prime tablet with Android ICS.

WORKING WITH HTML5, PHONEGAP, AND IOS

This section shows you how to create iOS mobile applications using PhoneGap, which is exactly the process that was used to create the iOS mobile applications in this book, whose screenshots on an iPad 3 are included in various chapters. Every iOS mobile application in this book was developed on a Macbook OS X 10.7.3 with Apple's Xcode 4.3.1 and PhoneGap.

Earlier in this chapter, you learned how to create Android applications in Eclipse, which is an IDE that runs on multiple OSes, but the situation is different for creating iOS applications (with or without PhoneGap).

First you need access to an Apple device (such as a Macbook, Mac Mini, or Mac Pro) with Apple's Xcode installed in order to create mobile applications for iOS mobile devices. If you register as a developer you can download for free, or for $4.99 in the Apple iStore. Although this section use Xcode 4.3.1 (which requires OS X 10.7.3), it's possible to install use a lower version of Xcode (such as 3.2) with a lower version of OS X.

Second, you need to install the PhoneGap plugin for Xcode 4 by following the detailed instructions here (which contain a link for installing PhoneGap on Xcode 3 as well):

http://wiki.phonegap.com/w/page/39991939/Getting%20Started%20 with%20PhoneGap%20iOS%20using%20Xcode%204

Third, you need to register as an Apple Developer (which costs $99 per year) if you want to deploy your iOS mobile applications to iOS devices. However, if you only plan to use the iOS Simulator, you can do so at no charge.

After you have set up a laptop with the required software, you will be ready to create an iOS mobile application with PhoneGap, which is the topic of the next section.

NOTE *PhoneGap applications always have the same filename* index.html, *so in order to provide multiple PhoneGap project files in the same directory on the DVD, the HTML Web page* index.html *for each PhoneGap project is saved in a Web page whose name is the same as the project. For example, the HTML Web page* ThreeDCube1.html *on the DVD is actually the same as the generated Web page* index. html *that is specific to the PhoneGap project in the next section.*

A CSS3 CUBE ON IOS USING PHONEGAP

Create an Xcode application called ThreeDCube1 by selecting the PhoneGap plugin (make sure that your filenames start with an alphabetic character or you will get errors when you attempt to compile and deploy your applications).

Note that if you are using Xcode 4.3.1, then you need to perform a manual copy of the generated www subdirectory into the project home directory of your current Xcode application. When you have performed this step correctly, you will no longer see an error message when you launch your mobile application in the Simulator or on your iOS device.

The CSS stylesheet ThreeDCube1.css is the same as the CSS file 3DCube1. css in Chapter 3, so we won't display its contents here. Listing 13.15 displays the contents of the HTML Web page index.html that is generated by the PhoneGap plugin in XCode.

Listing 13.15   index.html

```
<!DOCTYPE html>
<html>
  <head>
  <title>CSS 3D Cube Example</title>
  <link href="ThreeDCube1.css" rel="stylesheet" type="text/css">

  <meta name="viewport"
     content="width=device-width, initial-scale=1.0, maximum-
scale=1.0, user-scalable=no;"/>
  <meta charset="utf-8">

  <!-- iPad/iPhone specific css below, add after your main css >
  <link rel="stylesheet" media="only screen and (max-device-width:
1024px)" href="ipad.css" type="text/css"/>
  <link rel="stylesheet" media="only screen and (max-device-width:
480px)" href="iphone.css" type="text/css"/>
  -->

  <!-- If your application is targeting iOS BEFORE 4.0 you MUST
put json2.js from
        http://www.JSON.org/json2.js into your www directory and
include it here -->

  <script src="phonegap-1.3.0.js"></script>

  <script type="text/javascript">
  // If you want to prevent dragging, uncomment this section
  /*
  function preventBehavior(e)
  {
      e.preventDefault();
    };
  document.addEventListener("touchmove", preventBehavior, false);
  */

  function onBodyLoad()
  {
    document.addEventListener("deviceready", onDeviceReady,
false);
  }

  function onDeviceReady()
  {
    // do your thing!
  //navigator.notification.alert("PhoneGap is working")
```

```
    }
  </script>
  </head>

  <body onload="onBodyLoad()">
  <div id="outer">
   <div id="top">Text1</div>
   <div id="left">Text2</div>
   <div id="right">Text3</div>
  </div>
  </body>
</html>
```

Listing 13.15 is the result of combining the HTML Web page `3DCube1.html` from Chapter 3 (which is essentially a set of HTML `<div>` elements) with the HTML Web page `index.html` that is automatically generated by PhoneGap when you create a mobile application in Xcode using the PhoneGap plugin.

Now run this mobile application, either in the Xcode Simulator or on your mobile device, and you will see a graphics image that is similar to Figure 13.9.

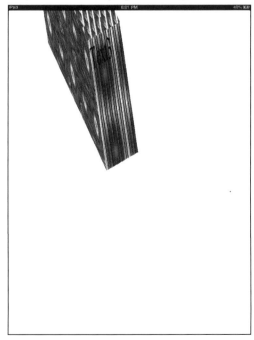

FIGURE 13.9 A CSS3 cube on an iPad 3.

The process for creating the other iOS-based mobile applications in this chapter is identical to the process for the preceding iOS mobile application, so there is no need to include additional examples. However, it's worth your while to spend some time creating additional iOS mobile applications, which will increase your comfort level, and perhaps also motivate you to learn about other features of Xcode.

TIZEN

Tizen is a new open source computing platform being developed specifically to support Web applications, including HTML5, JavaScript, and CSS. Tizen is intended to provide superior performance for Web apps over competitors, with architecture and features developed specifically for Web-based applications. Tizen 2.0 (expected toward the end of 2012) adds support for native Tizen applications and hybrid applications, which will take advantage of both Web and native capabilities.

The Tizen page includes links to download the Tizen SDK and source code, and links to community resources:

https://www.tizen.org

Tizen is under the umbrella of the Linux Foundation, and with the support of the Tizen Association, which is an industry consortium dedicated to providing in-market support and developing the industry presence of Tizen. Members of the Tizen foundation include:

- Huawei
- Intel
- NEC
- NTT DoCoMo
- Orange
- Panasonic
- Samsung
- SK telecom
- Sprint
- Telefonica
- Vodaphone

More information on the Tizen Association is available here:

http://www.tizenassociation.org

Tizen will support a wide range of device categories, including smartphones, tablets, netbooks, smart TVs, in-vehicle utilities and entertainment devices, and more.With HTML5's robust capabilities and cross-platform flexibility, it is gaining ground as a development environment for mobile apps and services. The Tizen SDK and API allow developers to use HTML5 and related Web technologies to write applications that run across multiple device segments. Tizen 2.0 will include support for native Tizen apps as well as hybrid apps that take advantage of both HTML5 and native Tizen components. Native Tizen applications will be developed in C++.

Benefits

Tizen will provide an environment ideal for HTML5 applications, including faster performance and support for more of HTML5's features. Since HTML5 applications are development platform-agnostic, they should be able to run on other platforms, like iOS and Android, without the need for porting or modification.

However, the performance of an HTML5 application currently varies widely depending on the browser and the platform on which it is being run. Currently HTML5 application performance is lackluster on desktop systems and poor on mobile devices. Tizen's objective is to provide a development platform specifically suited to support HTML5 applications, thereby offering superior performance for HTML5 applications.

Platform Overview

The Tizen platform provides a standards-based software platform for multiple device categories. The current platform software, described below, is targeted towards smartphones and tablet devices—additional device targets will be defined soon. The software platform supports Web applications.

Figure 13.10 illustrates the Tizen architecture for smartphone and tablet devices, which consists of three layers: application, core, and kernel.

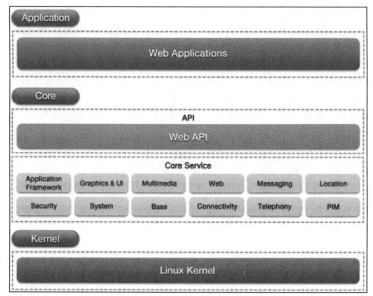

FIGURE 13.10 The Tizen architecture.

The Application Layer

Tizen supports Web applications. Tizen Web applications leverage the full power of the platform, just like native applications. The Core layer consists of Tizen API and Tizen Core Service.

Tizen API

Tizen Web applications can be developed using the Tizen Web API. The Tizen Web API is a collection of W3C (HTML5 and more), Khronos WebGL, and newly defined device APIs.

Tizen Core Service

The Tizen Core Service portion provides a number of services that are discussed in the following subsections.

Application Framework

The Application Framework provides application management, including launching other applications using the package name, URI, or MIME type. It also launches pre-defined services, such as the system dialer application.

The Application Framework also notifies applications of common events, such as low memory events, low battery, changes in screen orientation, and push notification.

Base

Base contains Linux-based essential system libraries that provide key features, such as database support, internationalization, and XML parsing.

Connectivity

Connectivity consists of all network- and connectivity-related functionalities, such as 3G, Wi-Fi, Bluetooth, HTTTP, and NFC (Near Field Communication).

Data network is based on ConnMan (Connection Manager), which provides 3G and Wi-Fi based network connection management.

Graphics and UI

Graphics and UI consist of the system graphic and UI stacks, which includes EFL (Enlightenment Foundation Libraries), an X11-based window management system, input methods, and OpenGL® ES.

The heart of the Graphics component, EFL, is a suite of libraries. It is for creating rich graphics with ease, for all UI resolutions. The libraries build UIs in layers, allowing for 3D transformations and more. EFL includes the Evas Canvas API library and the elementary widget library.

Location

Location provides location-based services (LBS), including position information, geocoding, satellite information, and GPS status. It is based on Geo-Clue, which delivers location information from various positioning sources such as GPS, WPS (Wi-Fi Positioning System), Cell ID, and sensors.

Messaging

Messaging consists of SMS, MMS, e-mail, and IM.

Multimedia

Multimedia is based on GStreamer. It provides support for media, including video, audio, imaging, and VoIP. It also provides media content management for managing media file metadata information.

PIM (Personal Information Management)

PIM enables managing user data on the device, including managing calendar, contacts, tasks, and retrieving data about the device context (such as device position, cable status).

Security

Security is responsible for security deployment across the system. It consists of platform security enablers, such as access control, certificate management, and secure application distribution.

System

System consists of system and device management features, including:

- Interfaces for accessing devices such as sensors, display, or vibrator.
- Power management, such as LCD display backlight dimming/off and application processor sleep.
- Monitoring devices and handling events, such as USB, MMC, charger, and ear-jack events.
- System upgrade.
- Mobile device management.

Telephony

Telephony consists of cellular functionalities communicating with the modem:

- Managing call-related and non-call-related information and services for UMTS and CDMA.
- Managing packet service and network status information for UMTS and CDMA.
- Managing SMS-related services for UMTS and CDMA.
- Managing SIM files, phone book, and security.
- Managing SIM Application Toolkit services for UMTS.

Web

Web provides a complete implementation of the Tizen Web API optimized for low power devices. It includes `WebKit`, which is a layout engine designed to allow Web browsers to render Web pages. It also provides Web runtimes for Web applications.

The Kernel Layer

Kernel layer includes Linux kernel and device drivers.

Development Tools

The Tizen 1.0 Web SDK enables you to create Web applications and widgets for mobile devices.

A Web application is a composition of HTML, JavaScript, and CSS combined as a package that is installed on the device. A widget package is self-contained, and it includes all the support files that are needed by the widget. Thus, a widget can become a complete standalone application that does not require any external resources and any access issues in running a widget can be avoided.

The HTML is based on standard HTML5. It supports a rich set of JavaScript with native extensions. These extensions support integration with the device in the form of e-mail, SMS, PIM (Personal Information Management), and device information. First-time developers can learn what a Web application is and how to use Web SDK to create one. Experienced developers can learn how to speed up the Web application development process.

Sample Web Applications

Sample Web applications can be found here:

https://developer.tizen.org/resources/sample-web-applications

Native and Hybrid Applications Support

Future versions of Tizen will include support for native Tizen applications as well as hybrid applications, which are a combination of Web applications and native Tizen code. Native Tizen applications will be developed in C++.

Links to More Information

You can find the latest information about Tizen by navigating to the following Web site:

https://tizen.org

Visit the following Web site to obtain documentation regarding Tizen and Tizen application development:

https://developer.tizen.org/documentation

ANDROID AND JQUERY MOBILE FOR ROBOT CONTROL

In simplified terms, you can think of robots as computers with motors and sensors, which means that they require software to interact with their environment. This software can run on the robot itself (also known as "native robot apps") or on external devices, such as smartphones, tablets, computers, or even from the cloud.

You might be surprised to discover that you can create HTML web pages with jQuery Mobile that can control the movements of a robot. In fact, you can create Android hybrid mobile applications that can control a robot in a geographically remote location, which in turn enables you to monitor various types of events. For example, you can develop a mobile application that can control robots to initiate tasks in your house while you are working in a remote location. You can also obtain real-time images from robots that are set up to monitor events in different parts of your home, which can be advantageous because robots are much more mobile than security cameras. There are many interesting possibilities, and you can use your imagination to create a variety of mobile applications.

The code sample in this section was developed in cooperation with the Robot App Store:

http://www.RobotAppStore.com

Using this Android mobile application you can drive your Roomba, race against other robots, and even make "beep" sounds. We will not cover the control and connectivity part of this Android mobile application; instead we will focus on the sleek user interface, and the interactivity the developers managed to create using jQuery Mobile.

Listing 13.16 displays the contents of JQMRobots.html that illustrates the type of jQuery Mobile code that can control a robot.

Listing 13.16 JQMRobots.html

```
<!DOCTYPE html>
<html lang="en">
<head>
 <meta charset=utf-8"/>
 <title>jQuery Mobile UI: Controlling Robots</title>

 <meta name="viewport" content="user-scalable=no,width=device-
                                                     width"/>
 <meta name="apple-mobile-web-app-capable" content="yes"/>
```

```
<link rel="stylesheet" href="http://code.jquery.com/mobile/1.1.0/
jquery.mobile-1.1.0.min.css"/>

<link rel="apple-touch-icon" href="http://www.google.com/im
gres?num=10&amp;hl=en&amp;biw=1366&amp;bih=689&amp;tbm=isch&
amp;tbnid=h7734DEtaTcpRM:&amp;imgrefurl=http://brickartist.
com/gallery/yellow/%3Ftag%3Dlego-art&amp;docid=_17mLzlqHy4-
NM&amp;imgurl=http://brickartist.com/img/gallery/yellow.jpg&amp;w=
600&amp;h=537&amp;ei=P43zT_HyA6nKmAWe3-yhBQ&amp;zoom=1&amp;iact=hc
&amp;vpx=921&amp;vpy=177&amp;dur=772&amp;hovh=212&amp;hovw=237&amp
;tx=125&amp;ty=123&amp;sig=109563213596407122448&amp;page=1&amp;tb
nh=140&amp;tbnw=158&amp;start=0&amp;ndsp=19&amp;ved=1t:429,r:4,s:0
,i:153"/>

<script src="http://code.jquery.com/jquery-1.6.4.min.js"></
script>
<script src="http://code.jquery.com/jquery.min.js"></script>
<script src="http://code.jquery.com/ui/1.8.21/jquery-ui.min.
js"></script>
<script src="http://code.jquery.com/mobile/1.1.0/jquery.mobile-
1.1.0.min.js">
</script>

<style>
  .centerDiv {
    height: 263px; width: 263px;
    background-image: url('Images/joystick_back.png');
    background-repeat: no-repeat;
  }
</style>
</head>

<body>
  <div data-role="page" id="page1">
    <div data-role="header">
      <h1>
        <a href="http://www.RobotAppStore.com"
           style="color:White;">http://www.RobotAppStore.com</a>
      </h1>
    </div>

    <div data-role="content" data-theme="a" >
      <center>
        <div class="centerDiv" id="container">
          <img src="Images/joystick.png"
               class="draggable" style="top: 45px"/>
        </div>
```

```
        </center>
      </div>

      <div data-role="footer">
        <h4>UI Code for the Roomba Driver Robot App</h4>
      </div>
    </div>

  <script>
    function touchHandler(event) {
        var touches = event.changedTouches,
        first = touches[0],
        type = "";

        switch(event.type) {
            case "touchstart": type = "mousedown"; break;
            case "touchmove":  type = "mousemove"; break;
            case "touchend":   type = "mouseup";   break;
            default: return;
        }

        var simulatedEvent = document.createEvent("MouseEvent");

        simulatedEvent.initMouseEvent(type, true, true, window, 1,
                          first.screenX, first.screenY,
                          first.clientX, first.clientY, false,
                          false, false, false, 0/*left*/, null);

        first.target.dispatchEvent(simulatedEvent);
        event.preventDefault();
    }

    function init() {
        document.addEventListener("touchstart", touchHandler,
                                                            true);
        document.addEventListener("touchmove", touchHandler, true);
        document.addEventListener("touchend",  touchHandler, true);
        document.addEventListener("touchcancel", touchHandler,
                                                            true);
    }

    $("#page1").live('pageinit', (function(event,ui){
        init();
        $('.draggable').draggable({ containment: '#container' });
    }));
  </script>
```

```
</body>
</html>
```

The first part of Listing 13.16 contains HTML markup and the familiar references to jQuery files, along with an HTML `<style>` element with a selector that is used for styling an HTML `<div>` element later in the code. Note the reference to jQuery UI (discussed in Chapter 7), which we need in order to "convert" a JPG into a draggable widget.

The second part of Listing 13.16 contains some standard jQuery Mobile code for a single page view HTML Web page, and also contains a link to the Robot App Store. The HTML `<img>` element (shown in bold) references a JPG file that will be made "draggable" by the code snippet at the end of Listing 13.16.

The third part of Listing 13.16 starts with the JavaScript function `touchHandler()` that handles touch-related and mouse-related events. The JavaScript function `init()` defines listeners for four touch-related events, all of which are handled by the `touchHandler()` function. The final code block in Listing 13.16 is jQuery code that makes the JPG (shown in bold) draggable. Note that in this code sample, the JPG is a joystick.

Figure 13.11 is a screenshot of a robot app that designed to control the well-known and very popular vacuum cleaner called the "Roomba." If you launch Listing 13.16 in a browser, you will see the image on the right side of Figure 13.11, which has been made draggable by the jQuery code.

UI Code for the Roomba Driver Robot App

FIGURE 13.11 A robot app rendered in a Chrome browser on a Macbook.

SUMMARY

This chapter showed you how to create hybrid Android mobile applications that contain HTML5, CSS3, SVG, and jQuery Mobile. You created such mobile applications manually, which involved creating Android projects in Eclipse, and then modifying the contents of the Android `Activity` class and populating an assets subdirectory with HTML-related files.

Next, you learned how to use the PhoneGap Eclipse plugin, which simplifies the process of creating an Android project. You also saw how the PhoneGap plugin creates a default page that allows you to use "live" features of your Android device.

The next chapter (and final) chapter of this book contains interviews with some well-known people in the IT industry. They share their thoughts regarding trends in the mobile space.

INTERVIEWS WITH INDUSTRY LEADERS

The previous chapters in this book concentrated on technical details of various technologies because there is so much to learn, and definitely more information than can fit in a single book. At the same time, it's important to obtain a broader view of the things to learn: the "why" is just as important as the "what" and the "how" in the previous chapters.

This chapter contains interviews with several well-known individuals who have made significant contributions and are continuing to make their presence felt in the IT industry.

The interviews (listed in alphabetical order by last name) are with Vincent Hardy, Brian Leroux, and Tony Parisi.

VINCENT HARDY

Vincent Hardy works on Web Standards with the CSS Working Group, the FX Task Force, and the SVG Working Group. Vincent is currently a Principal Scientist in the Web Standards and Innovation group at Adobe, where he works on CSS Shaders, CSS Regions, CSS Exclusions, and Scalable Vector Graphics (SVG). Prior to joining Adobe, Vincent worked at Oracle on graphical, interactive, and animated user interfaces in the field of business intelligence, helping make large sets of complex data visually understandable to help users navigate data sets more easily, detect trends, or find anomalies. Prior to Oracle, Vincent worked at Sun Microsystems, where he focused on graphical, animated, and interactive technologies, mainly the Java 2D API and the SVG format.

Vincent cofounded and led the Batik project at Apache, an open source Java toolkit for manipulating, viewing, or transcoding SVG content. Vincent contributed to the development of the SVG specification and its version for mobile devices, SVG Tiny. He chaired the Compound Documents Format

(CDF) effort in W3C. Vincent is the author of *Java 2D API Graphics* (SUN Microsystems Press, 1999) and has a passion for graphical design.

His previous companies include SUN, Kno, and Oracle Corporation. Vincent has multiple roles in various JCP and W3C initiatives:

- Co-editor of the SVG 1.1 specification
- Chair and co-editor of the JSR 290 specification
- Co-editor of the CSS Filter Effects specification
- Co-editor of the CSS Regions and CSS Exclusions specifications
- Chair of the Compound Document Format Working Group in W3C (now defunct)

Vincent has developed the following software and tools:

- Apache Batik (SVG toolkit)
- Mobile SVG Viewer
- Cross-platform JavaScript 2D graphics rendering and animation library
- SVG Authoring Tools
- Network Management Software for PBXs, Hubs, and Routers

What are you passionate about in technology?

I am passionate about making it as easy as possible to use technology. This is one of the things I love about the Web technologies, because among other things, they make it easier to do otherwise complex things. I think making things easy to use is the hard problem we need to solve. For example, in the area of graphics, we have known how to do complex Bezier curves and sophisticated fill style (such as gradients, meshes, or patterns) for a long time—several decades. But while authoring tools have been available (such as Adobe Illustrator), there have not been a lot of easy ways for developers to use graphical resources, manipulate these resources in scripts, deploy them to a wide audience, and so on. Two-dimensional graphics are just an example; this "ease of use" applies to other areas such as advanced text layout, typographic features, animation, or 3D transforms, too.

Which of your projects has given you the most satisfaction?

In the past, I have really enjoyed working on the Batik project at Apache, which was a Java toolkit for manipulating, rendering, and transforming Web graphics (in the Scalable Vector Graphics format). It was really fun to work on the implementation at Apache, with a great team, and participate to the

W3C activities at the same time, contributing tests and feedback to the SVG specification.

Currently, the projects I have a chance to work on at Adobe are even more exciting. For example, we work on CSS Regions and CSS Exclusions, which are bringing very advanced content layout to CSS (for example, you can flow text in a shape the form of a soda bottle or flow content from one area to another). We also work on CSS Filter Effects (in particular CSS Shaders) that enable cinematic effects to the Web. I really enjoy working on these new features that enhance the platform and let content creators deploy content that could not be created before.

What technologies are you most interested in learning about?

I am very interested in learning about how we could use more 3D effects in normal Web pages and user interfaces. CSS Shaders is an example of something I am really interested in. Shaders were originally designed for advanced 3D graphics effects in CAD tools or games, and we find they are extremely useful and adequate for regular Web user interface effects and content. There are other 3D functionalities such as particle effects that might help enhance the user experience as well. All those things that are both efficient (they are hardware-accelerated) and enhance the user experience are of high interest to me.

What is your preferred development environment (tools, editors, etc)?

For many years, I have used Emacs and loved it! But I have moved to using TextMate for most of my coding and I am now using Brackets for editing Web documents (HTML, CSS, and JavaScript). Brackets is a new tool that Adobe has been working on which is itself built using Web technologies.

Are there "too many" JavaScript toolkits for Web development?

It is true that there are a lot of them! I think it is the sign of an extremely active and creative Web developer community, which I consider a good thing. Also, there are different toolkits for different problems. For example, there are toolkits for UI components such as Twitter's Bootstrap or Michael Bostok's D3.js for data visualization. It is hard to say that one of them is superfluous: they address different problems and can be used in concert.

That said, it is true that it can be hard to select the appropriate framework for a given problem and it would be good to have some resources to help developers make their selection.

Is cloud-based mobile development going to become the de facto standard?

I think that we will see more and more services to help developers do their work, for mobile and desktop development alike. Simple services like Github are already the norm and this is a relatively new phenomenon.

I am hoping to see more services to help developers both get started more easily and deploy the result of their work more easily, and I believe these things will happen on the cloud.

What is the direction of CSS3?

The direction of CSS3 is defined collectively by the CSS working group in W3C which decides which specifications and areas to focus on. Adobe participates in that working group, along with other companies.

One of our focuses, as a contributor to that effort, has been to enhance the core features the Web Platform offers and that CSS3 exposes. For example, CSS Regions and CSS Exclusions aim at improved document layout abilities. Another example is CSS Compositing and Blending, that aims for improved core graphical features. I think that the core rendering and graphical abilities of the Web Platform are essential for regular content but also for games and applications, and this is one of our focuses.

The CSS working group is also making a long-lasting effort to modularize the language and while it is an intimidating task, I believe it is a worthy one that helps the Web be more reliable and interoperable in the long run.

When do you think that WebGL will become commonplace on devices such as tablets?

There has been a lot of work done in the WebGL Khronos working group to resolve the security issues which have held back a wider adoption so far. The work has been deep and wide, involving browser companies and hardware manufacturers. Now, it is hard to predict the time it will take for the new generation of hardware to be widely deployed and allow WebGL to be ubiquitous. But it is already available on the desktop (even though sometimes behind an "enabling" menu), in several browsers (Safari, Chrome, Firefox), and is starting to appear on Mobile (e.g., on some Nokia and BlackBerry phone or tablets).

What sort of immediate versus long-term impact will ECMA5 have on Web development?

Personally, I like the incremental approach that was used in ECMA's 5th edition. For example, the seal and freeze methods on Object are useful additions that deal with a fundamental issue when passing object references around in a program (prior to these methods, any part of a program or library could modify any object property). This improves encapsulation and security. Also, the useful additions to Array, String, and Function are great incremental improvements. All of them help reduce the code size (trimming libraries and/ or user scripts) and make the code more robust, sometimes easier to read. Some additional features on Object such as `Object.defineProperties` and `Object.getPrototypeOf` are providing more flexibility, but also introduce more complexity and I think should be used with care.

Although SVG is part of HTML5, do you think it will ever be used as widely as CSS3?

I think the vector graphics that SVG provides are a core need for the Web. Vector graphics are needed to support exchange with authoring environments (e.g., tools like Illustrator and InkScape) and they need to integrate well with the rest of the Web stack. I really like the current efforts to make applicable SVG features core to CSS in the joint efforts the CSS and SVG working groups lead (in the FX task force). For example, the effort to make SVG and CSS transforms consistent is key to a cohesive Web stack. Likewise, the desire to bring blend modes and compositing to both SVG and CSS in a consistent manner is important. Finally, there are many ways SVG and the rest of HTML5 are integrated. For example, it is possible to draw an SVG resource in an HTML5 2D Canvas context. It is also possible to use a 2D Canvas context and draw its content in an SVG image. Finally, it is possible to inline SVG in HTML, and this is very powerful.

Like other formats (such as PNG), it can take a lot longer than we would like for SVG to reach ubiquity. But I think SVG is getting there and in a world of widely varying screen resolutions (like Apple's retina displays), the need for a vector format (which renders crisply at all desired resolutions) is even more acute than ever.

That said, it is important to remember that CSS has a much broader scope than SVG and that even as we try to make some of the SVG features available in CSS, SVG is a great companion feature to CSS, but not a replacement or an overlapping technology.

What are the must-have skills for mobile developers right now?

I think first and foremost, mobile developers must have a clear understanding of responsive design and how their content can adapt to multiple screen sizes and resolutions. It is no longer the case that we have two or three sizes or form factors. With the explosion in the numbers and types of tablets and phones, it is important to design content with media queries and layouts that work for a range of sizes and resolutions, with "breaking points" where the content switches to a new design. Also, developers must be very careful to keep the high resolution displays in mind because it is very different to have a small, high resolution screen than having a larger, low resolution screen, while the two may have exactly the same number of pixels!

Then, I think that mobile developers should think about how to best deploy their applications. In some situations, it may be best to simply have a mobile-ready Web site. In some other situations (e.g., when more APIs than available on the browser are needed, such as camera capture), packaging the mobile HTML content as a PhoneGap/Cordova application is a great solution. It preserves the developers' investment in HTML/JS/CSS while providing a rich application environment and the ability to package and deploy the application on the most popular application stores.

Which new skills do you think Web developers need to acquire during the next several years?

I believe the Web is going to become more and more graphical, and we are just starting to see this happen with features such as rounded corners, gradients, opacity, and better support for backgrounds. The Canvas APIs are nice (and needed for particular use cases such as games), but I think the big wave is going to be declarative graphical features in CSS such as CSS Filter Effects, better SVG integration in HTML, and advanced things like CSS Shaders.

I also think that the distance between developers and graphic designers is closing and that many developers are becoming (and will need to become) more sensitive to graphic design and visual qualities while graphic artists are becoming more agile with programming and Web formats. The Web formats help a lot for this because it is now possible for graphic designers to author and share their compositions in the format that will be used for deployment. While there is still a lot to do around formats, features, and tooling, I think this is the direction we are heading towards.

What do you think the Next Big Thing will be in mobile development tools? Is it something that nobody has thought about yet, or are there already some people working on it?

Related to the previous question, I believe the next frontier for mobile development is to lower the bar for developers even more and make it as easy as possible to create, build, debug, and deploy mobile applications and mobile content. There are efforts such as PhoneGap build that are clearly going in that direction. Another example is Adobe Shadow, a utility that greatly simplifies the debugging and testing process for developers (they can display the same web content on multiple devices at the same time and debug it). I think we will see more and more of these tools that drastically simplify the process of creating, testing, and deploying content and applications for mobile.

BRIAN LEROUX

Brian LeRoux leads the open source PhoneGap project team at Adobe (currently undergoing incubation as Apache Cordova). He's been with the PhoneGap project from its very humble beginnings at Nitobi Software. In his own words, Brian is "a free/open source software developer at Adobe, formerly of Nitobi, working on PhoneGap, XUI, Lawnchair, and WTFJS. Love JS. Mostly mobile."

What are you passionate about in technology?

I feel we are only just beginning to see what impact free open source software has on the networked world. Nearly everyone is packing an Internet-enabled phone packed with sensors. We live in the amazing future envisioned by science fiction. I want to help ensure we don't screw that up.

Which of your projects has given you the most satisfaction?

I never really think about it. Obviously the whole PhoneGap thing has been a great project to be a part of but I'm not really attached to the work that much. I really try to enjoy whatever it is I'm doing at the moment. In this moment I'm writing, so that's cool.

What technologies are you most interested in learning about?

This might seem a little weird, but I collect out of print/old computer books. I love reading and discovering origins in technology and seeing how all the things evolved into what we see today. Sometimes I feel the bigger vendors, and other tech success stories, author a revised version of history and this can harm our perceptions of where we need to go.

What is your preferred development environment (tools, editors, etc)?

For my part, all I need is a Posix shell and modern Web browser. I use vim for editing text though I recently had my mind blown by an Emacs demo so I think I might try a switch for a little while. (check it out *http://emacsrocks. com.*) Given the power of the browser dev tools these days it's basically become a Web dev's IDE. Think about that: the delivery vehicle for content is basically the editor and runtime. Crazy world we live in.

Are there "too many" JavaScript toolkits for Web development?

No. Diversity is how technology evolves. We learn from each other and that's how we grow. A best practice is only a current understanding.

Do you think that mobile-only JavaScript toolkits will become prevalent?

I don't think we'll be making the distinction in a few years but they will all certainly be evolved for this use case. Touch event support comes to mind.

Is cloud-based mobile development going to become the de facto standard?

Depends on the situation but increasingly: yes. This creates a few problems because it really ties you to a vendor stack which may not be responsible choice, business strategy-wise. That said, if you hit the scale where you need the metal then you have a really good problem!

What is the direction of CSS3, and will it supplant other technologies?

I can honestly say I have no idea but I am grateful it is improving. We have a long way to go. Twitter Bootstrap, a baseline lib, weighs in at 5k LOC. That is a symptom of a bigger problem. This stuff isn't easy, and it's getting better, but requiring a megabyte of declarations to get a sane grid and nice looking buttons is incredibly lame.

When do you think that WebGL will become commonplace on devices such as tablets?

Already is on the BlackBerry Playbook. And of course there are tools that can emulate the context on Opengl (but no DOM). I don't think we're very far at all. The bigger issue is the tooling/stack/libs for WebGL. It's a verbose situation currently.

What sort of immediate versus long-term impact will ECMA5 have on Web development?

JS is about to evolve in a big way. The biggest and most crucial improvement from my perspective is first class modules. This is composed of two parts: module definition and module loading. This is sort of solved today with RequireJS but first class language constructs are going to really improve the client-side library and tooling ecosystem. I'm really excited for it. No more doc writing <script> tags or concatenation breakdancing.

Couple this w/ a decent offline story, WebGL, and Device APIs, and the Web platform becomes a whole lot more than URLs and documents. What does it become? I can honestly say I have no idea. James Pearce had a great quote/quip that ran along the lines, "The Web can't be broken; it's a self-healing system." I love that. And I hope he's right.

Do you think that using Node.js with HTML5 will become a major trend in mobile applications?

I don't know. NodeJS is certainly fun tech, moving fast, and proving to be a really viable stack for a whole ton of situations. It is rather well suited to speaking JSON and negotiating HTTP so it makes a nice proxy to the acres of XML left behind the SOAP era that aren't so mobile-friendly. There are always new toys to play with.

Which aspects of HTML5 are going to change significantly in the next five years?

It will all continue to evolve, and I think we'll be seeing more and more out of the Device API reality incorporated. Frankly I wish they'd fix App Cache as a priority.

What are the must-have skills for mobile developers right now?

Patience. Compassion. Mastery of the command line. Automation. Unit testing.

Which would you prefer for native development: Android or iOS?

Neither, but they both have strengths.

Some pundits claim that Android will stumble, and to what extent do you think that's true?

All technology deprecates to some degree with enough time. So, given this understanding, we know all tech stumbles at some point. The trick is being able to detach yourself from whatever stack you are passionate about enough so you can see when it's going to happen before it does and respond accordingly. The best way to defend your technology from deprecating is to be the one who does it.

It really bums me out when people hero worship a vendor platform. These organizations are amazing and push technology but they ultimately answer to shareholders and very often this is not to the benefit of society at large. Keep that in mind at all times. We're working with the largest accessible network in human history, the impacts of which are staggering. Let's not sell that out.

Which new skills do you think Web developers need to acquire during the next several years?

Patience. Compassion. Mastery of the command line. Automation. Unit testing.

What do you think the Next Big Thing will be in mobile development tools?

Well, almost every browser either has a remote debugger or one is being baked. (Opera Dragonfly, Chrome dev tools/Web Inspector, Firebug, and I suppose whatever they call the IE one.)

And while mastery of these new browser tools is crucial to being effective but I'd also like to stress this is not an excuse to drop unit testing!

Is it something that nobody has thought about yet, or are there already some people working on it?

When I see developers collaborating today I think the biggest issue is composing your stack appropriately. We tend to throw whatever open source thing that almost does what we need to solve the current problem we have. This is introducing big build time complexity. Virtual machines and/or firing those systems behind a Web API make life a little easier, but local dev environment crafting is tricky black magic.

I am not sure how we solve this just yet but I think more of our tools in the future will package themselves with their runtime environment, making distributed collaboration easier. Basically it goes back to the browser being more powerful.

Do you have any other comments or advice that you would like to share?

Always be good to yourself and others you work with. The Web is very large, and distributed written history. It is impossible to remove the record of your conduct so think about what sort of legacy you want to leave in every message you craft, every line of code you write.

TONY PARISI

Tony Parisi is an entrepreneur and career CTO/architect. He has developed international standards and protocols, created noteworthy software products, and started and sold technology companies. Tony's passion for innovating is exceeded only by his desire to bring coolness and fun to the broadest possible audience. Tony's first startup, Intervista Software (1995-1998), developed the first-ever real-time VRML plugin for Internet Explorer, which Microsoft bundled with millions of copies of their browser. His most recent company, Vivaty (2007-2010), created a novel end-to-end virtual world system fully integrated with the Web and serving up millions of virtual goods transactions. Tony is perhaps best known for his work as a pioneer of 3D standards for the Web. He is the co-creator of VRML and X3D, ISO standards for networked 3D graphics. Tony continues to build community around innovations in 3D as the co-chair of the WebGL Meetup (*www.meetup.com/ WebGL-Developers-Meetup*) and a founder of the Rest3D working group (*http://www.rest3d.org/*). Tony is also the author of the upcoming O'Reilly Media book, *WebGL Up and Running*. Tony is currently a partner in a stealth online gaming startup and has a consulting practice developing social games, virtual worlds, and location-based services for San Francisco Bay Area clients.

What are you passionate about in technology?

What excites me the most about technology is when I can build software products and graphically compelling user experiences that reach a big audience. I love new media technologies—3D rendering, animation, visualization, and social media. My ultimate goal is to bring those experiences to the Internet in a way that all consumers can enjoy them, and I have devoted the better part of my career to that end.

Which of your projects has given you the most satisfaction?

From a community standpoint, it would be hard to match the buzz that I got from creating VRML and X3D. While a lot of people groan at the notion of working with standards committees— the "sausage making" comparison comes to mind—that is just the flip side of the really rewarding community-building Mark Pesce and I fostered to get VRML out the door. Before the ISO committees and suits stepped in, it was a joy to create a new technology and work with a worldwide developer community to evolve it. These days I myself am gun shy about standards groups and prefer to work via collaborative open source efforts using tools like Github. But I am still a big believer in community efforts and would really love to relive that "old VRML feeling." My work with WebGL in terms of books and local Meetup groups is moving in that direction.

From a technical standpoint, the work I did at my old startup Vivaty was very rewarding. We built an end-to-end virtual world and social game system featuring fully immersive 3D. The entire product was built on Web standards and technologies, nothing proprietary. The 3D rendering was implemented using a plugin of our own creation—this was before WebGL so there was no other way to render true 3D in the browser—but it was all based on open standards such as X3D and XML. The back end was LAMP, and the communications were based on open protocols. To date, no one else has built such a full-featured immersive system on a fully open stack.

What technologies are you most interested in learning about?

I am fascinated by cloud computing. The combination of free and open application development technologies with inexpensive hosting promises to lower barriers for all kinds of innovation. I am spending a fair amount of time looking into cloud computing solutions such as Amazon Web Services to see how I can get the best value out of them and potentially use them as a backbone for new products and services I am looking to create.

Also, directly related to my gaming work in WebGL, I would like to see how other game-related technologies evolve in the browser. WebGL has the rendering and compositing covered, but there is so much more to game development. The JavaScript VMs need to get faster and do better with memory management. Google is leading the way there, and we are seeing great progress. Also, I would like stay on top of input technologies such as mouse lock and joystick support, and Web audio/video APIs as they standardize over the next few years.

What is your preferred development environment (tools, editors, etc)?

I am originally a C/C++ hack from the old days, but I have grown to love the JavaScript language. Of late I am enamored with Node.js, so that I can develop my server-side code in JavaScript too. Most days I write my code in Eclipse and debug in Chrome. I find that it has the best debugging built in.

For libraries, I am big fan of jQuery, not just for its brevity but for power. For my WebGL development I primarily use the Three.js toolkit, with a little bit of Tween.js thrown in; but I am also working on my own game engine, which is currently based on Three.js but someday may move to its own low-level rendering.

Are there "too many" JavaScript toolkits for Web development?

There are never too many. Different strokes for different folks.

Do you think that mobile-only JavaScript toolkits will become prevalent?

They may; that really depends on how quickly mobile platforms improve on their JavaScript performance. It's still pretty slow and there are memory issues. Remember, these are tiny devices with slower CPUs than desktop and less memory. But if they progress to the point where JavaScript becomes the de facto development language for mobile (I hope I live to see this), then I am sure we will see a proliferation of mobile-only tools.

Is cloud-based mobile development going to become the de facto standard?

If by cloud-based mobile development you mean, "rendering and game play in the cloud, just transmit video frames and send back clicks," a la the streaming services like Gakai, OnLive, and OTOY then I am very skeptical. I personally believe it's a flawed approach. Use the power of the device at hand. If the game is delivered on a desktop or laptop, take advantage of that computing power that is in front of the user. If the game is running on a mobile device, design the game for that platform and make the performance scream locally. Otherwise you're spending cycles and dollars in the cloud and not distributing the load.

On the other hand, if by cloud-based you mean that the game and transaction logic, and any multiplayer support, moves to the cloud, I would say we are already there.

When do you think that WebGL will become commonplace on devices such as tablets?

I am not a market researcher so I don't have the most current data readily available. With that caveat...WebGL seems to be making great strides on tablets: I have seen Samsung Android devices running it, RIM Playbook, the new ChromeBook netbooks, all gizmos that sell for around $500. That's awesome.

Do you think that using Node.js with HTML5 will become a major trend in mobile applications?

I think it's too early to tell. I certainly like the idea of just writing everything in JavaScript. However at this point in time the performance of HTML5 just isn't there on the mobile clients. Simple applications work well, but if you have a CPU or memory-intensive application (say, a twitch game), you will run into trouble. I have seen this happen with applications I worked on in the past year. In one case, we had a beautifully architected and totally portable HTML5-based game (only 2D canvas rendering, no WebGL) that we ultimately had to port to native iOS code because it was eating too much memory and would garbage-collect right in the middle of an animation transition.

As the mobile hardware platforms incorporate faster CPUs and more memory, and as the JavaScript virtual machines become further optimized and developers learn more tricks to manage their application memory, we will see this situation change and HTML5 fulfill its hoped-for potential as a mobile development platform.

Which aspects of HTML5 are going to change significantly in the next five years?

I have no crystal ball here, but I hope we see convergence on the audio and video APIs. From a selfish gamer-oriented standpoint I would also like to see more in the way of input support such as joysticks and mouse lock.

Another potentially interesting development is Google's new Dart language for programming structured Web applications. It's a Java and C#-like typed language designed for much better performance and reliability than JavaScript. Dart is more of a hardcore programming language and I wouldn't put it in front of today's average Web client developer; but serious engineers with computer science background will be able to take advantage of it for building industrial-strength Web apps. Right now Dart is only in development versions of Chromium; hopefully someday it will make it into production Chrome and all the other browsers.

For WebGL, I sure hope we see a standardized file format emerge. WebGL is just an API, which is a great strength but also an Achilles heel. Without a standard format for the content, the tools pipeline situation is really chaotic and interoperability will be really difficult. Of course, this may be my old VRML bias coming through.

What are the must-have skills for mobile developers right now?
Patience, flexibility, and a thick skin.

Which would you prefer for native development: Android or iOS?
I have only done production development for iOS so my purview is narrow. I'm not in love with Objective-C and Cocoa; on the other hand I don't hate them and I can be productive in that environment. One of these days I hope to dip a toe into Android development. The first step in that is to get over my irrational hesitance to write Java code. This is something that has been going on in my head for a decade…for no good reason.

Some pundits claim that Android will stumble, and to what extent do you think that's true?
I think Android will be hale and hearty for years to come. There is too much activity around Android, so many developers building for it, lots of manufacturer support, and Google solidly behind it. All that, and everyone is afraid enough of Apple that they want to make sure there is a viable alternative for some time to come.

Which new skills do you think Web developers need to acquire during the next several years?
First, multimedia programming. The unseating of Flash from its dominant position is going to rewrite the rules. The new world will be HTML5, CSS3, WebGL, Canvas. The fate of SVG is uncertain; perhaps it will have a resurgence. Animation isn't a first-class part of those standards, so we'll see toolkits

for developing animation and higher-level behaviors; programmers will first have to evaluate and explore the alternatives there, and perhaps some day a clear winner will emerge (the way jQuery did for document manipulation).

Second, asynchronous, event-driven server programming. `Node.js` is paving the way for a new kind of thinking. Everything is about events and listeners. This turns out to be great from a scalability perspective but fairly nightmarish for folks who are used to a more classic imperative approach like with PHP and Python. But an investment in learning this approach will yield benefits in scalability, performance, and modularity of server-side applications.

Finally, cloud services. It's clear that the days of the centralized data center are over for all but the giant companies.

This concludes the chapter interviews. Perhaps some of the answers in these interviews will provide you with valuable insight that can help you with your technical development and your choice of technologies.

In closing, these are exciting times in the Web arena, and the pace at which new toolkits and frameworks are created is both breathtaking and challenging for people who want to keep abreast of the latest cool technologies. Hopefully the information in this book will assist you in furthering your knowledge and also help you reach your technical goals.

APPENDICES A-E

Appendices A-E (titles listed below) are located on the companion DVD.

Appendix A: Overview of SVG
Appendix B: Introduction to Android
Appendix C: HTML 5 and JavaScript Toolkits
Appendix D: Programming the Roomba Robot
Appendix E: Introduction to SPA

INDEX